the Male

EXPERIENCE

third edition

james a. doyle

Roane State Community College

the Male

EXPERIENCE

WCB Brown & Benchmark
PUBLISHERS

Madison, Wisconsin · Dubuque, Iowa

Book Team

Executive Editor *Michael Lange*
Developmental Editor *Sheralee Connors*
Production Editor *Ann Fuerste*
Designer *Eric Engelby*
Art Editor *Joseph P. O'Connell*
Photo Editor *Laura Fuller*
Permissions Coordinator *LouAnn K. Wilson*
Visuals/Design Freelance Specialist *Mary L. Christianson*
Marketing Manager *Steven Yetter*
Advertising Manager *Mike Matera*
Production Manager *Beth Kundert*

WCB Brown & Benchmark

A Division of Wm. C. Brown Communications, Inc.

Executive Vice President/General Manager *Thomas E. Doran*
Vice President/Editor in Chief *Edgar J. Laube*
Vice President/Sales and Marketing *Eric Ziegler*
Director of Production *Vickie Putman Caughron*
Director of Custom and Electronic Publishing *Chris Rogers*

Wm. C. Brown Communications, Inc.

President and Chief Executive Officer *G. Franklin Lewis*
Senior Vice President, Operations *James H. Higby*
Corporate Senior Vice President and Chief Financial Officer *Robert Chesterman*
Corporate Senior Vice President and President of Manufacturing *Roger Meyer*

Cover design by Eric Engelby

Cover and part opener images © Bruce Ayres/Tony Stone Images

Copyedited by Emily Hughes

A Times Mirror Company

Library of Congress Catalog Card Number: 94–71373

ISBN 0–697–10458–3

Printed in the United States of America by Wm. C. Brown Communications, Inc., 2460 Kerper Boulevard, Dubuque, IA 52001

10 9 8 7 6 5 4 3 2 1

Credits

Pages 8, 9, 142–43: From W. Farrell "Beyond Masculinity: Liberating Men and Their Relationship With Women: in L. Duberman (Ed.), *Gender and Sex in Society,* page XXIII and pp. 71–72, 1975, Praeger Publishing, an imprint of Greenwood Publishing Group, Inc., Westport, CT. Reprinted with permission. **Pages 82–83, 86:** From J. Pleck, *The Myth of Masculinities,* 1981, The MIT Press, Cambridge, MA. Reprinted by permission. **Pages 106–108:** From S. Cahill, "Childhood Socialization as a Recruitment Process: in *Sociological Studies of Child Development,* pp. 163–186, Table 1, p. 181, 1986, JAI Press, Inc., Greenwich, CT. Reprinted by permission. **Pages 114, 115, 116:** From Margaret Mead, *Sex and Temperament in Three Primitive Societies,* © 1935, 1950, 1963 by Margaret Mead, pages 135, 189, and 245. William Morrow & Company, New York, NY. **Pages 146, 166, 194, 195, 196:** Reprinted by permission of Avon Books from *Men: A Book For Women,* by J. Wagenvoord and P. Bailey. Copyright © 1978 by Product Development International Holding n.v., as employer-for-hire of James Wagenvoord and Peyton Bailey. **Pages 178, 185, 187, 191:** From *Male Sexuality* by Bernie Zilbergeld. Copyright © 1978 by Bernie Zilbergeld. By permission of Little, Brown and Company. **Pages 199, 200, 201–202:** From Peter Stein and Steven Hoffman, "Sports and Male Role Strain" in *JSI,* Vol. 34, No. 1, 1978. The Society for the Psychological Study of Social Issues, Ann Arbor, MI. Reprinted by permission.

For   Nan

Contents

Preface   xi

Preface

Webster defines "change" as "to make different in some particular." The ancient Chinese thought little of change and in fact often offered it in the form of the curse "May you live in changing times." Apparently, anything that smacked of change undercut the stability and tradition so valued in the ancient Chinese culture, and as such was anathema.

In the west, however, change is viewed differently. As early as the fifth century B.C.E., the Greek philosopher, Heraclitus, speculated that change was all that really mattered by arguing that "Nothing endures but change." Ever since, we in the west have valued change by attaching positive meanings to it—the essence of creativity, making new from the old, pushing our boundaries, etc.

There is something to glean from these two approaches to change—one negative, the other positive—when it comes to the question of men. In the last several decades of the twentieth century, change is almost the only constant most men have experienced. How men act, what is expected of them, and how they define themselves—all these have been in flux. Should we view these changes as a curse undercutting the traditional values many men learned from their fathers and grandfathers, or as an inevitable and creative force pushing men toward new and more fulfilling ways of living?

Since the last edition of *The Male Experience* nearly six years ago, much has changed in society. The once fledgling men's movement has grown, bringing tens of thousands of men together to examine their lives. However, the once unified movement, coming as it did out of the spirit of the women's movement, has fractured into competing and often antagonistic camps. Now we find men positioning themselves in arguments over whether their concerns for the personal are based in the political, the personal, or somehow both. Should the men's movement find its legitimacy in addressing *only* issues of men's pain, their privileges and power, or both? Must a men's movement first focus *only* on women's oppression, men's oppression, or both? The camps of well-intentioned men have selected their causes and have set off on separate missions, spending considerable energy snipping at those who do not see men's issues in similar ways.

The divisiveness among those interested in men's issues has spilled over even to those involved with creating the new academic discipline referred to as men's studies. Many who once met in collegial community now bicker with each other, often making extreme and derogatory claims about the political correctness of those who view men's issues from different perspectives. This division, though, has spawned a healthy vitalization of the scholarly men's studies community. Men's studies scholars have been forced to examine their motives and paradigms, an act often avoided when everyone works in lockstep.

The study of men's lives is more vital now than ever before. Change—not for change sake of periodic refashioning—is the driving force in men's movements and in the scholarly analyses of men's lives. In this context change is not a curse but an opportunity; an opportunity for the growth of ideas, a chance for a vital inclusiveness that allows for dialogue and understanding.

This book, then, is offered with the hope (and not the curse!) that the changes we discover in men's lives might lead us away from the established path of sameness and exclusivity toward a new path of diversity and inclusivity in our work and study of men's lives.

Changes in the Third Edition

A number of changes can be found in this edition of *The Male Experience;* some quite significant while others less noticeable. In the former case, for instance, we find a substantive discussion of the discord within the men's movements (chapter 1), a defining description of the emergent men's studies field and its journals (chapter 1), a discussion of the controversial issue of the "battered husband" (chapter 9), and completely new chapters dealing with fatherhood (chapter 15) and men's health issues (chapter 16).

In the latter category, I have included an Important Terms section at the end of each chapter highlighting the significant terms found therein. Further, all references can be found in one section, making it easier for the reader to find a specific reference. Another change noticeable to only the most diligent is that the entire text has been thoroughly revised to improve its readability. I hope these changes make this edition much more helpful and involving for all.

Acknowledgments for the Third Edition

As with any scholarly venture, a number of people have been involved in bringing this new edition to press. Numerous reviewers made many valuable suggestions during the development/revision of the third edition of *The Male Experience,* and I am indebted to them for their contributions: Carol V. Apt, University of Texas, Health Science Center at San Antonio; Cynthia S. Burnley, East Tennessee State University; Michele D. Martin Charlton, Miami University; Susan Joel, Michigan State University; Robert Heasley, University of Alaska, Anchorage; Stephanie S. Rude, University of Texas, Austin; and Michael R. Stevenson, Ball State University.

The editorial and production team at Brown & Benchmark Publishers has been, as always, superb, and I am enormously grateful to these talented people for their hard work and commitment to quality. In particular, I want to mention my editors, Michael D. Lange and Sheralee Connors, for their unwavering confidence and support both of myself and for this project.

And last, I want to thank all the readers and reviewers of the previous editions who have taken the time to write me over the years with comments about the text. Their suggestions have proven extremely helpful and, I hope, they can see how their ideas found expression in this edition.

James A. Doyle
February, 1994

Chapter 1

Today's Uncertain Male

The criteria for manhood in this society are in a muddled state.
Carol Tavris (1977)

Too often, though, we treat men as if they had no gender.
Michael Kimmel and Michael Messner (1989)

Life is an epic journey that begins with birth and ends in death. . . . For men, this journey is treacherous.
Fredric Rabinowitz and Sam Cochran (1994)

"It's a boy!" reports the physician to the teenage mother exhausted from her marathon first labor.

"It's a boy!" shouts the wide-eyed cabby to the dazed woman pressed against his Checker's rear seat.

"It's a boy!" croons the midwife to the new mother resting in her bed at the rear of the farmhouse.

These dramas of new life differ in many respects but the significance of the words "It's a boy!" remains the same in each. The pronouncement "It's a boy!" immediately sets restrictions, grants privileges, and lays down expectations. What may appear as three rather simple and straightforward words defining a newborn's sex are probably the most important words spoken over a healthy newborn male.

All that lies ahead for these three males—and all males from their first day to their last—is what we shall call the **male experience.** Upon first glance, you might not think the male experience to be particularly troublesome or problematic. The words "It's a boy!" should set the stage for the unfolding of what some think of as the fundamental nature of manhood. But what is fundamental about being a male? What is the nature of manhood? What does being a man, a "real" man, that is, mean? Not that long ago, such questions would have seemed ridiculous. Today though, people are asking these and other related questions and their answers are challenging and changing how we view the male experience.

Scholars, therapists, and researchers have also begun to speculate about and study the processes involved in the male experience. Most have found it helpful to distinguish between two terms commonly used in any discussion of the male experience, **sex** and **gender.** Sex refers to the division of anatomical male and female forms based on observable biological differences. When we discuss the physical distinctions between men and women, for example the sex chromosomes X and Y, these are *sex* differences. Gender, on the other hand, relates to the meanings people attach to each sex. References to personality traits associated with men and women (e.g., rationality and emotionality) would be examples of *gender* differences. Thus, sex designates a biological characteristic while gender refers to a socially or culturally defined feature associated with men and women. In the following pages, our attention will primarily focus on gender in general, a male's gender in particular.

Although the male experience is unique for each male given his particular statuses (e.g., family background, race, class, sexual orientation), the male experience develops on two different but related levels, a public level and a private one. The public level contains all the expectations and norms, prescriptions and proscriptions, and sanctions and stereotypes placed on a male by his culture. Thus, the public level includes everything expected of one identified as male. What a particular society expects of its males is not, however, a static entity but rather, by definition, a set of socially constructed factors that have evolved over the centuries (see Chapter 2). Here we will call the totality of the public level of the male experience the male's **gender role.**

When it comes to the second level, the private one, we can only infer or at best speculate about it because it exists out-of-sight, within a male's mental or psychological processes. This part of the male experience is not present at birth but rather begins to develop when a young boy has attained a certain degree of cognitive or mental development wherein he can identify or label himself as male. Once this happens and he begins to differentiate and classify himself and others on the basis of a wide variety of gender cues (e.g., physical appearance, apparel, activities, etc.), he is said to develop a masculine **gender identity.** Accordingly, most boys begin to perceive, differentiate, and classify themselves as males and consequently begin to express and exhibit masculine gender-typed attitudes, behaviors, and interests sometime between their second and fourth birthdays (Etaugh, Grinnell & Etaugh, 1989; Katz, 1986; Money, 1987). Furthermore, once formed, little if anything can change one's gender identity (Money & Ehrhardt, 1972).

Both of these levels of the male experience are connected and it is easy to see how one can effect the other. If a society, for instance, expects its menfolk to be aggressive, then a man who is not particularly aggressive may come to think of himself as less than manly, less than fully masculine because of how others treat him.

Over the past several decades, especially in North America, much of what most adult men learned as youngsters about being "a man" has been challenged by several social movements or forces. Consequently, numbers of men have formed groups as they tried to make sense out of what it means to be a man today. Along with these men's groups, numerous scholars and researchers have also begun to develop courses and pursue research topics dealing with men's issues. In this chapter, we'll look at these three components of change in the male experience: several recent social forces that have challenged traditional definitions of the male gender role, the reactive men's movements that have arisen in response to these social forces, and, finally, the emergence of a new academic field that focuses its study on men's lives and issues. Let's turn our attention to the first of these issues, the forces challenging the traditional view of manhood.

Change is never easy and thus most people find change uncomfortable. Thus it should stand to reason that changing how a society views the male gender role is not accomplished without some difficulty. In fact, a society has a vested interest in maintaining, supporting, and even defending the established or traditional definitions and expectations associated with its male or female gender roles. When males and females comply with their society's gender roles, social and personal conflict are avoided. When change in either gender role occurs, however, confusion and anxiety may reign as people come to question what it means to be male or female.

"Nothing endures but change" the Greek philosopher Heraclitus noted some twenty-five hundred years ago. Thus even a society's gender roles change over time. Still, even minor changes are initially resisted by most people. Although it might not seem important today, not that many years ago the length of men's hair caused considerable conflict in America. Throughout most of this century, at least up until the early 1960s, barbers cut boy's and men's hair short, above the ears. However, in the late 1960s prompted by a growing antiestablishment fervor and the popularity of long-haired rock groups, many young men grew their hair shoulder-length, and longer. Consequently, hair length became a social issue as families erupted in intergenerational conflict and long hair became identified as un-American as well as

the rumblings of change

Today's Uncertain Male

un-manly in some quarters. American society it seemed, at least its more conservative elements, did not view long haired young men kindly. For many, long hair signified a challenge to the established social order as well as an affront to traditional views of what men were suppose to look like. Today, long hair has prevailed and few even take notice of men with shoulder-length hair.

Changes, like that of the accepted length of men's hair, occur in society's definition of the male gender mainly because of the combined effects of several social forces. Three specific social forces have challenged the traditional views of the male gender role, namely, technological advances, a recent and persistent distrust of established institutions, and the women's movement. Let's look at each of these social forces now and see how it impacted on men's lives.

Technology and the Male Gender

As most historians of the male gender see it, our society's move from an agricultural to an industrial nation during the nineteenth century drastically changed the way men defined their relationships, their status, and their abilities (Bernard, 1981; Pleck & Pleck, 1980; Rotundo, 1993). Over the centuries, males have been expected to prove their worth mainly by providing for the group by killing animals or raising grain. Males have also won praise and achieved status for their skillful abilities to produce artifacts by dint of their tools and talents. All that changed when the industrial revolution replaced the long-established male roles of strong provider and skilled artisan with that of keeper of the machines. Granted, the industrial revolution has provided mass-produced goods and an easier way of life, but it has also robbed most men of their sense of purpose and creativity.

During the twentieth century, the industrial revolution flowed into the age of technology. Although most modern-day technologies have made our lives easier, they have created some mind-numbing problems as well. Take the ever-present computers that have become a fixture of late twentieth-century life. Although touted as user-friendly, computers bode a sinister side if we give any credence to the possibility of one turning rogue and disregarding its human programmer's orders to shut down à la a "war games" scenario. For centuries, males have been taught they are the masters of their destinies. In the years ahead, could it be that computers, not humans, may take charge (Fjermedal, 1986)?

Thus beginning with the industrial revolution and accelerating with the dawn of computers, men have been driven farther and farther away from the long-cherished belief that they controlled their lives and their world. At one time, men reveled in their physical prowess as they applied their sinewy strength to whatever task required brute force. They were honored for their feats of courage in the face of untamed and uncharted frontiers. For those few who still continue to challenge the unknown and place their lives on the line, however, the adulation and esteem of millions await them as well as the singular honor that they are in possession of "the right stuff" (Wolfe, 1980).

Men have exulted in their wisdom and knowledge gained from years of experience and, consequently, gained pleasure in passing their knowledge to the next generation. Today, the abilities that allow a man to define his place in society as well as his worth as a man are quickly surpassed by machinery and computers.

Lost Confidences

If society's institutions (family, religion, politics, military, and so on) support the various traditional elements of the male gender, males, in turn, are expected to exhibit the behaviors that provide society's institutions with willing and able participants. In other words, a reciprocal relationship exists between society's institutions and the male gender.

For example, aggression is an important element of the traditional male gender (see Chapter 9). Consequently, boys are taught early to fight because as young men they may be expected to serve their country as soldier-fighters. (I purposely use the term "soldier-fighters" here rather than simply "soldiers" to make the point that soldiering is "fighting" not a sanitized stint between high school and whatever comes after the military.) Contrary to posters and recruiter speeches, the military requires young men to carry out its designated social function, namely, to aggress (kill first) or to defend (wait for the other to attack and then kill) against society's enemies. In return, as soldier-fighters young men have their masculinity validated. The reciprocal relationships between social institutions such as the military and the traditional male gender role require a mutual trust and confidence that both sides will live up to the social expectations imposed on them by society. If men refuse to become soldier-fighters or if the military does not honor (validate) its soldier-fighters, a problem can occur in one, the other, or both sides of the relationship. Such a problem occurred in the late 1960s and early 1970s and consequently challenged some elements of the traditional male gender (Fasteau, 1974; Gerzon, 1992).

The recent Vietnam era provides a prime example of a breakdown in the relationship between specific features in the male gender and two social institutions, the military and the government (Baritz, 1985). One of the causes for this breakdown was a major rupture in the public's confidence and trust in their leaders; that rupture led many who served in the Vietnam conflict to question certain features of their male gender, at the very least, or in far too many cases needlessly to suffer various debilitating post traumatic stress-related illnesses (Bachman & Jennings, 1975; Brooks, 1990; Gibson, 1994; Kaylor, King & King, 1987).

The Vietnam conflict began in the late 1950s and early 1960s as a purely advisory military operation. However, by the mid-1960s, the United States was involved in a full-scale war in Southeast Asia. Initially, most United States citizens supported the government's and the military's stated goals of supporting a besieged "democratic" Asian country and preventing the spread of communism into the Pacific basin. But as the 1960s drew to an end, the government's mishandling of dissenters—for example, the beating of demonstrators at the 1968 Democratic National Convention in Chicago and the killing of four students on the Kent State University campus in 1970—turned many against the government. Furthermore,

Today's Uncertain Male

with the publication of *The Pentagon Papers* (1971), the military as well as the government lost credibility in the eyes of many United States citizens. Consequently, the public's trust in its leaders was severely eroded by the early 1970s.

In a 1982 speech before a men's group, poet Robert Bly described how the Vietnam War contributed to an erosion of confidence among many middle-aged men. The Vietnam experience, unlike any previous conflict in United States history, found older men, our political and military leaders, purposely and consciously lying about the goals of the conflict, creating illusions of victory, and inventing benign euphemisms like "body count" or "Agent Orange." President Lyndon B. Johnson and General William Westmoreland, for instance, knowingly lied not only to the public but more importantly to the troops, the young soldier-fighters who were asked to put everything on the line. President Johnson and General Westmoreland lied about how just a few thousand more troops would turn the tide; how an inflated body count spelled an enemy's imminent defeat; and how our troops were never exposed to chemical defoliants. Seemingly, the whole of the Vietnam War was built on lies, lies told by older men to younger men.

"When men lose their confidence in older men," Bly (1987) asked his audience, "what happens then? When older men betray younger men, and lie to them, in government and in the field, what happens then to male values? What happens to a society in which the males do not trust each other?" (p. 67). For many men, especially those who served in Vietnam and returned home to find the extent of their elders' lies, the answer to Bly's questions is that they lost confidence—lost confidence not only in many of the institutions they grew up to respect and trust, but also lost confidence in how they felt about themselves as men, that part of their manhood that supposedly was validated by their being soldier-fighters.

The Women's Movement

Most people today agree that the women's movement has had a significant impact on our society during the last several decades. But what does a social movement whose goal is the elimination of the twin social evils of patriarchy and sexism have to do with the male gender? The English poet Alfred Tennyson may have provided an answer when he wrote, "The woman's cause is man's. They rise or fall together."

For the most part, the features of the male and female genders are interdependent and reciprocal. Men, for example, have been taught to behave in ways characterized as dominant, independent, and active. Women, on the other hand, have been expected to act in submissive, dependent, and passive ways. Thus any change in the characteristics of one gender sets off a chain-reaction in the characteristics of the other.

As more and more women come to question and then to change their traditional gender behaviors and attitudes, men are *forced* to look at their own gender behaviors and attitudes and deal with the very real possibility that they too will have to change their traditional ways. Consequently, the resocialization aimed at women and brought about by the women's liberation movement not only influences women's lives but men's as well.

There we have it, three separate social forces—an escalation of technology, a breakdown in confidence in established social institutions, and the women's liberation movement—all coming together during the latter 1960s and 1970s to challenge society's roles for women and men. People's reactions to these forces vary, but one thing is clear with respect to our focus here: traditional modes of men's behavior and attitudes changed drastically in a relatively short time. These challenges caused many men to experience varying degrees of uncertainty with their role. Consequently, many men formed support groups, organized workshops and men's retreats, and created organizations to redefine their male experience and to provide support for their tenuous male identities. The phenomenal growth of men's activities and the emergence of a fledgling "men's movement" is now what we turn our attention to.

More than thirty years ago, Betty Friedan (1963) described "the problem that has no name" in her book *The Feminine Mystique*. As Friedan explained it:

the men's movement(s)

> The problem lay buried, unspoken, for many years in the minds of American women. It was a strange stirring, a sense of dissatisfaction, a yearning that women suffered in the middle of the twentieth century in the United States. Each suburban wife struggled with it alone. As she made the beds, shopped for groceries, matched slipcover material, ate peanut butter sandwiches with her children, chauffeured Cub Scouts and Brownies, lay beside her husband at night—she was afraid to ask even herself the silent question—"Is this all?" (p. 11)

As women began to ask the heretofore unasked "Is this all," many became angry, confused, anxious, and, finally, motivated to do something about their situation. For many, the answer lay in joining with other women in kitchens, living rooms, dens, community centers, church basements, or anywhere women might gather to talk not about their husbands or lovers or kids, but about themselves, their feelings, their concerns. And so, a powerful social phenomenon called the **consciousness-raising group (C-R)** was born. Some women strengthened by their new found sisterhood organized into larger, more formal groups like the National Organization for Women. And the women's movement was born. Dedicated to changing social structures and public policies, the women's movement went on to affect millions of women's lives.

But what about men, especially young men? What were young men doing during these turbulent years (the mid-1960s to the mid-1970s) when society seemed to be coming apart. Many were experiencing firsthand the escalating Vietnam War while others attended college or entered the job market. One group on the home front, although small in number, witnessed firsthand the birth of the women's movement as they were here to witness the movement's founding. For many of these men, the women's movement was a cause of no little concern and anxiety. In response, a number of them formed their own C-R groups (Farrell, 1974), which provided a kind of refuge for those men facing changing times.

The Early Years

> Many of the early men's consciousness-raising (C-R) groups were organized by men whose relationships with women had been stressed as women became more dissatisfied with traditional heterosexual relationships. Joining men's groups was one response to relationship stress that often threatened to destabilize marriages and other primary relationships. Some joined seeking support during crises such as loss of child custody.

Today's Uncertain Male

Others were motivated to join after observing benefits obtained by women from women's movement groups that offered support and meaningful friendship not readily accessible to men. (Gross, Smith & Wallston, 1983, pp. 9–10)

Following a similar path like the one traveled by women, many men took their new found C-R group's insights and organized into larger, more formal groups. In the spring of 1975, the beginnings of a fledgling men's movement appeared when a group organized a weekend conference devoted to men's issues, the first national Men and Masculinity (M & M) Conference held at the University of Tennessee at Knoxville. Since then a national M & M conference has been convened nearly every year at some location around the United States attracting men and women from North America, Australia, and Europe.

For most of the early years (up to the mid-1980s), most involved with men's groups were bound together by a single guiding ideology, the eradication of **sexism,** or the belief that one sex is superior to the other. That the early men's movement espoused an ideology most associated with the women's movement should not surprise us for several reasons.

First, many of the "founding fathers" had strong ties to the women's movement. Warren Farrell, who served on the Board of Directors of the National Organization for Women in New York City, and whose book *The Liberated Man* (1974) was one of the first to call men to discard their outmoded gender roles, paid homage to the women's movement in his book's introduction.

> The women's movement meant a lot to me from the beginning. I had experienced my mother going into and out of depression as she went into and out of jobs. Yet she did not feel she should leave the children for a permanent job, although we were all in school. When I began seeing the pattern in neighbors and friends' parents I realized it was more than my mother's problem. *But it took the women's movement to get me to see the problem.* (p. xxiii; italics added)

And Gloria Steinem, herself one of the principle architects of the women's movement, endorsed another of the early men's movement books, Marc Feigen Fasteau's (1974), *The Male Machine,* calling it "a complement to the feminist revolution, yet . . . one no woman could write [as it represents] the revolution's other half" (p. xv).

Another reason these male activists embraced the women's movement was that it provided them with a vocabulary most had little understanding of or association with, but at some level of their identity knew they were in need of. On this point, Jonathan Rutherford (1992) writes:

> Like a sizable minority of other men who came into contact with it, the women's liberation movement held a great appeal [for me]. It had begun to speak a language of private life, making links between our affective relations and the public world of institutions and power. In some indefinable sense it offered us a key to understanding ourselves. It spoke of something that I wanted . . . a new sense of identity. In a time of radical questioning and the discarding of inherited attitudes and conventions, women's liberation was constituting new identities and a sense of belonging. (p. 8)

ten commandments of masculinity

1. Thou shall not cry or in other ways display fear, weakness, sympathy, empathy, or involvement before thy neighbor.
2. Thou shall not be vulnerable but shall honor and respect the "logical," "practical," or "intellectual"—as thou definest them.
3. Thou shall not listen for the sake of listening—it is a waste of time.
4. Thou shall not commit introspection.
5. Thou shall be condescending to women in every way.
6. Thou shall control thy wife's body and all its relations.
7. Thou shall have no other breadwinners before thee.
8. Thou shall not be responsible for housework or children.
9. Thou shall honor and obey the straight and narrow path to success: job specialization.
10. Thou shall have an answer to all problems at all times.

Warren Farrell (1975)

However, as with most social movements, the cement holding the proponents of the early men's movement together soon showed signs of cracking. During the mid-1980s, a few voices began to speak of sexism's other victim—men. Soon we began to hear of prejudice against male workers in child care facilities (Miller, 1987), or how many fathers were treated unfairly in child custody cases (Kruk, 1991; Stuart, 1990). The upshot of this was that men who had stood shoulder-to-shoulder in the early years found themselves on different sides of men's issues and the once unified men's movement began to fragment.

Discord within the Ranks

Initially, Martin Fiebert (1987) suggested that the rupture within the once solid men's movement produced a division—two opposing camps, the profeminists and the promasculinists—over the question of who was affected more by society's sexist practices—women or men. On the one side, the **profeminists,** those with strong ties to the academic community, argued that women were sexism's principle victims and that the vast majority of males experience considerable privilege due largely to living in a sexist society (Brod, 1987; Connell, 1987; Hearn, 1987).

The **promasculinists,** many of whom were therapists and counselors with a growing number of male clients, stressed men's considerable pain (primarily psychological in nature) and their need for personal growth, argued that the women's movement, or more precisely its more radical proponents, had only served to increase tensions and conflict between women and men (Baumli, 1985; Diamond, 1983; H. Goldberg, 1979). In a sense, the two sides differed in what issues needed to be emphasized in order to bring about positive change in men's lives, the profeminists argued against men's privileges while the promasculinists sought to heal men's pain.

However, Fiebert's analysis did not go far enough as the division proved even greater than he first proposed. In 1990, Kenneth Clatterbaugh outlined a fuller discussion of the breakup of the men's movement into several movements or, as he preferred to label them, perspectives. Using Clatterbaugh's analysis, it is a misnomer to speak of a *single* men's movement—a single ideologically-based social movement. Most now agree that several men's alliances have emerged over the last several decades each with its own focus on men's issues and favorite theories.

Clatterbaugh catalogued six perspectives: the profeminist; the mythopoetic or as he labeled it, the spiritual; the men's rights; the group-specific; the socialist; and the

Today's Uncertain Male

conservative. Here we will deal only with the first three—the profeminist, the mythopoetic, and the men's rights—as they have garnered the most attention in the media, attracted the greatest number of supporters, and appear to have sufficient claim to be social movements in their own right. Given that the conservative (i.e., biology shapes the male gender role, see S. Goldberg, 1974) and the socialist (i.e., class-economic structures shape traditional masculine identity, see Tolson, 1977) groups have attracted little support among those interested in men's issues, we will not deal with these two "minor" perspectives here. However, as we will focus on gay men and men of color in subsequent chapters (13 and 14, respectively), we will save our discussion of the group-specific perspective until then.

The profeminist group view the male role as a social construct defined, legitimated, and supported by society's institutions. This approach argues that both patriarchy and sexism serve a minority of males (those with power) by keeping most other males (those with little or no power) and all women in subordinate statuses. The profeminist perspective views **feminism,** the belief that patriarchal institutions oppress women, as the *only* acceptable ideology for an analysis of men's roles (Brod, 1987; Stoltenberg, 1989). As already noted, the profeminist approach grew out of the turbulent 1960s and has found considerable support among the academic and social research communities.

Carl Jung's (1933) depth psychology and Joseph Campbell's (1968, 1988) work on universal myths provide a basis for what is called the **mythopoetic** perspective. One of the first to take up this approach was Robert Bly (1982, 1990) who argues that contemporary men had become "soft," had lost touch with their fundamental or "deep masculine" core. Others have followed Bly's lead and have used myth, story, and ritual in their analyses of how men have been "wounded" over the last century or so in terms of the growing separation between generations (e.g., a breakdown in father-son relations) and women's growing influence over men's lives (e.g., Lee, 1991; Meade, 1993). High on the mythopoetic list of what modern Western society is guilty of is the lack of appropriate initiation rites to help young men gain a sense of their masculine spirit. The end result then is that today's young and middle-aged men have few ways to validate their manhood causing many to behave in extremely inappropriate ways harmful not only to themselves but to others as well (e.g., addictive behaviors, aggression).

Two concepts are of prime importance in the mythopoetic literature, namely, the "deep masculine," and the "Wild Man." Among the mythopoetic literati, the **deep masculine** is presented as a basic personality structure, an essential feature of maleness that has been corrupted by civilization but is still present only needing to be uncovered (Gurian, 1992; Kipnis, 1991; Meade, 1993; Moore & Gillette, 1991). Carl Jung's imprint is evident here as he theorized that at the very core of personality lies a strata of primordial images, what he called "archetypes." Most in the mythopoetic camp support the notion that men must work (via therapy, men's gatherings, etc.) through their shame (a powerful negative emotion that develops when their essential maleness is denied) and their wounds (psychic traumas caused by unhealthy relationships) to get at their essential mature masculine quality (e.g., Spielberg, 1993).

Bly's metaphor of the **Wild Man** stands for a basic "male energy," which men must tap into in order to be fulfilled as men. Accordingly, in "simpler" times, men were able to become men mainly through initiation rituals with older men. The wild man represents that essential manhood that has been lost in today's world. What we have in both of these concepts—the deep masculine and the Wild Man— are basic features that posit that men's very essence is biologically rooted and essentially different from women. The mythopoetic perspective accepts the essentialist (i.e., biological or nature over nurture) argument that gender roles developed out of the innate biological or psychological male and female "natures." In writing about the essentialist leitmotif running throughout Bly's (and consequently the whole mythopoetic) approach, Kenneth Clatterbaugh (1993) notes:

> Essentialism plays a central role in historical patriarchal ideology. Bad things are bound to happen if change is introduced that goes against essential natures. Women are women and men are men and what men and women traditionally have done reflects their real natures—unhappiness is the price of trying to alter gender roles. (p. 5)

The mythopoetic approach is not without its critics. Bly's writings and his appearances before men's gatherings have been especially targeted by the profeminist camp as expressing antiwomen sentiments and offering little if any challenge to patriarchal and sexist social structures (Clatterbaugh, 1993). Further, Bly's use of the imagery of the "Wild Man" has been interpreted as a lightly veiled attack on women. However, as Christopher Burant (1988) writes, Bly's "Wild Man" is no call for men to wreck havoc or unleash destructive frenzy on women but rather:

> [T]he Wild Man refers to a specific mythological being with a long and illustrious history, most elaborately defined during the Middle Ages. This Wild Man was a symbol of the conflict between civilized man and "natural" man. He was comparable to the unicorn or the phoenix; that is, an image with psychological potency for Medieval European society. The Wild Man was a mixture of projected and repressed qualities in the human personality; lost as cities and civilization developed. Often visualized as a hairy unclothed mute hulk, he lived in the forests and deserts surrounding cities. (p. 7)

As we noted above, the Wild Man imagery, according to Bly, represents a part of men (i.e., their basic male energy) that has been lost and must be found. Further, Bly argues that contemporary men have become "soft," overly influenced by women's definitions of masculinity (e.g., sensitive, caring, emotionally vulnerable), a caricature that sparks critics to see Bly as subtly arguing for a return to some macho, traditional past when John Wayne was every man's ideal.

Bly's popularity and his ability to draw large crowds and the mythopoetic movement in general has captured the attention of large numbers of men and the media as well. For whatever reason, Bly's message and that of other mythopoetic writers like Sam Keen (*Fire in the Belly,* 1991) have struck a resonant cord. Not surprisingly then, given all the publicity connected with best-selling books, well

Today's Uncertain Male

attended men's gatherings, successful PBS programs focusing on Robert Bly's work, the excessive media hype about "wild men's retreats," to many people's way of thinking, the mythopoetic approach is *the* men's movement.

According to the **men's rights** approach, men, not women, are the "real" victim of sexism in our society. Although outspoken in their attack on feminism, men's rights groups support the passage of the Equal Rights Amendment (Ault, 1992). With its passage they argue, men would no longer confront a variety of inherently sexist practices and discriminations perpetrated against them. For example, men's rights advocates point to the inequities many men face in divorce and child-custody proceedings. Why, they argue, should men be strapped not only with a restrictive gender role but one that also can be lethal (H. Goldberg, 1976; Jourard, 1974; see Chapter 16). Men's rights advocates argue that men are in relatively poorer health and have a shorter life expectancy than do women because they carry a disproportionate amount of the financial burden (the provider role) as dictated by society's view of what a man should do.

An interesting turn of events finds one of the founding fathers of the profeminist group, Warren Farrell, whose publication *The Liberated Man* (1974) was one of the first to expose readers to men's concerns from a feminist perspective, has over the years become one of the more outspoken and vocal champions of men's rights. His recent writings, *Why Men Are the Way They Are* (1986), and *The Myth of Male Power* (1993), address what he sees as the inequities that men face in our society, many of which he maintains are exacerbated by women. For instance, Farrell argues that while men are condemned for treating women as sex objects hardly a word is spoken about how women cast men as objects also, success objects. Farrell's point has some merit. When Simon Davis (1990) analyzed over 300 personal ads in a large metropolitan Canadian newspaper, "[t]he men were more likely than the women to specify some physical attribute. The women were considerably more likely to specify that the companion be employed, or have a profession, or be in good financial shape" (p. 48). Both women and men it seems, at least those who place personals, apparently want each other to live up to traditional gender roles. Why though, the men's rights groups ask, is it okay for society to give greater credence to women's claims of victimization and oppression while dismissing or even denying men's?

A Rapprochement of Sorts

Is there any hope for a rapprochement between the men's movements factions? Candidly, I think not. The acrimony between the various camps seems never ending. It appears to grow in intensity and furor each year. Apparently, it is the differences not the similarities that drive the engines pushing the various adherents of the men's movements. However, there are a few, very few, voices that speak of possible advantage for dialog rather than judgment. Recently, Michael Dash (1993) voiced a plea to end the internecine barbs and personal attacks and advocated that there may be some advantages to be gained by both the mythopoetic and profeminist camps if they would only see and appreciate that each has valuable insights on the male experience.

Having observed first hand and been active in both groups, Dash contends that the mythopoetic community provides a structure for developing a nurturing fellowship where men can gather together (e.g., wisdom councils, men's retreats) and gain support from each other as well providing rituals for personal growth and change. For its part, the profeminist perspective furnishes a broad-based social, historical, and political analysis of men's lives. The profeminist camp also provides the basis for social action, an analysis of the -isms that have poisoned our world—sexism, racism, heterosexism, classism, etc.

We often hear that the personal is political but we need also understand that the political is personal. People create new social movements and social movements create new people. The mythopoetic perspective may be guilty of being overly personal while the profeminist approach seemingly has no time for the individual, focusing instead only on the political. Arguing that women today have found spiritual (personal) sustenance from their sisterhood as well as strength from their feminist analysis, Dash argues (metaphorically) that men might be similarly served if they were to find their own wells of strength (intermingling the spiritual side of the mythopoetic and the analytical praxis of profeminism).

> . . . women have easy access both to a feminist political movement and to a feminist spirituality. Clearly, this is not the situation for men. It is as if mythopoetry is luxuriating in perfumed gardens and, understandably, many men are attracted to this. Meanwhile, pro-feminism is out in the desert, battling with evil and living on bread and water which doesn't appeal to many men. As a result, the pro-feminist movement is small and its numbers prone to burnout and isolation. We need access to both. (p. 51)

Men's Organizations Defining the Movement

Now that we have a sense of the major groups who claim to speak to the "real" concerns of men today, let's examine two national men's organizations who represent nearly totally different spectrums of men's issues—the **National Congress for Men and Children** (a men's rights group) and the **National Organization for Men Against Sexism** (a profeminist men's organization). Both have elected governing structures, national and regional meetings, regularly published newsletters (NCMC's *NetWORK* and NOMAS's *Brother*), and around 500 dues-paying members each. (The mythopoetic approach is not included here as no national organization has emerged to promote its message as yet. Rather the mythopoetic "message" is disseminated in its leaders' writings [e.g., Bly, Mead, Keen] and experienced in the countless seminars, men's councils, and weekend workshops convened across the country.) Let's begin then by looking at the National Congress for Men and Children.

Founded in 1981, the National Congress for Men and Children (NCMC) is a national organization devoted to "men's rights" issues, especially those that project a positive or promale image of fathers and the role of fatherhood. David Rose (1987), a former NCMC president, places "fatherhood" and working for fathers' rights as "central to the men's movement just as career opportunity is central to women." According to NCMC, fathers traditionally have been shortchanged in the media, being made to look like buffoons whose only contribution was to bring home a paycheck or hand out weekly allowances. Society views fathers, then, as simply the providers whereas mothers come out as the family's emotional center and wellspring. Consequently, NCMC claims these images influence judges who all too often automatically award child custody to mothers while fathers receive little more than infrequent visitation rights and child support duties. NCMC argues that such treatment is blatantly unfair and a form of legal discrimination against fathers. One of NCMC's major goals, is to rectify the inequities perpetrated on many divorced fathers in dealing with courts and other social agencies.

Although the National Organization for Men Against Sexism (NOMAS) was founded in 1982, it has gone through several name changes over the years—initially calling itself the National Organization for Men (NOM; 1982–1984), then the National Organization for Changing Men (NOCM; 1984–1990), and finally, after much debate within its membership, settling on NOMAS. A frequent criticism of NOMAS is that it is basically an "antimale" organization (mostly by men's rights groups, possibly getting back for being labeled "antifemale" by profeminists?). To combat this, NOMAS's governing document clearly states its support for "a male-positive" approach to men's issues along with being profeminist, and gay-affirmative (*Statement of Principles*, 1987).

In recent years though, some within NOMAS have distanced themselves from issues involving "men's pain" (loneliness, addictions, insecurities) focusing their attention more on the issue of "men's privileges." In a recent article on the popularity of "men's books," Michael Kimmel (quoted in Mehren, 1991), a NOMAS leader and profeminist activist, announced "[O]ne of the things we [speaking for NOMAS?] won't speak to is men's pain because I'm more interested in men's privilege than in men's pain."

It is safe to say that one of NOMAS's defining features is its complete commitment to total equality for all women—part of the rational for its last name change was to prevent the flight of some feminists from an organization for "changing men" (too ambiguous) and to garner feminist support for a men's organization openly "against sexism." Such concern over their image especially within the feminist community is totally compatible with NOMAS's allegiance to feminism as its defining ideology and stated purpose to eschew all forms of male dominance and patriarchy.

Another of NOMAS's guiding principles is its openly and unabashedly gay-affirmative stance. Most North American men harbor deep-seated anxieties and fears over being thought homosexual by others. For most men, **homophobia,** the belief system (prejudice) that sexual minorities are inferior and should be pitied and/or hated (Blumenfeld, 1992), is a powerful social force that supports traditional macho behaviors. Consequently, gay men have suffered extreme injustices, whereas, at the same time, heterosexual men have imposed needless restrictions on their own male-male relations to avoid being labeled homosexual. Overall then, NOMAS supports all men regardless of sexual orientation, works to end sexist institutions and practices, and supports life enhancing male characteristics.

As noted earlier, many within the early men's groups and some of the most visible leaders of the various men's factions have been scholars and researchers. Not surprising then, over the last decade, a new academic field has emerged that deals specifically with the many facets of men's lives. It is this new field called men's studies to which we now turn our attention.

One of the single most spectacular success stories coming out of the women's movement is the development of the academic field known as women's studies. Today, on college and university campuses across North America, over 750 women's studies programs and thousands of instructors and researchers provide a wealth of scholarship that gives voice to women's long-denied accomplishments and experiences. Although all scholarship has traditionally been presented as an objective, totally impartial endeavor, today most agree that our ways of understanding our world and the activities people use to acquire knowledge (e.g., reliance on authority, logical thought, science) are imbued with human values or biases. Furthermore, most of the Western world's accumulated knowledge is decidedly *androcentric* (*andro* = man, *centric* = centered) as the male has been judged the norm, the standard for human experience (see Brod, 1987; Spender, 1981). For its part, women's studies provided a much needed corrective to this one-sided view of human experience.

Beginning in the mid-1970s, a small number of graduate students and professors, prompted mainly by the kinds of questions asked by women, began looking at men's lives through a new kind of *gendered-consciousness* (Pleck & Sawyer, 1974). This new approach focused on the question of gender, the male gender, and how it was a creation of numerous social forces while dismissing the established androcentric view of accumulated knowledge. This new breed of scholar treated the study of men, their history, their lives, and their many experiences as simply representing half of the human equation. What emerged was a new academic field, **men's studies,** defined here as a collection of loosely-knit scholarly activities (e.g., teaching courses, theoretical and applied research) that share a common purpose: to understand more fully what is unique to males as males by using the tools afforded by various academic disciplines. Rather than merely an academic fad or a backlash against women's studies, men's studies has slowly gained stature and visibility within the academic community (August, 1993; Brod, 1990; Heller, 1993).

After surveying men's studies instructors across North America, Sam Femiano (1990) noted some common features running through most of their courses. These themes seemed to highlight a common heritage. He noted that:

> "Men's studies" describes a diversity of courses developed in colleges and universities throughout the United States and Canada over the past 15 years that have, as a common element, an exploration of notions of maleness and masculinity. The courses cover male psychological development, men's roles in society, and the evolution of the notion of masculinity in history and works of literature. In some respects, the term "men's studies" is a cognate of women's studies, and the influence of feminism and women's studies was important in the early growth of men's studies. Principally, however, the courses evolved out of the neonate men's movement, changes in society's notion of male roles, and the initiative of individual men themselves who, in response to these social changes, began to make changes in their personal lives. (p. 237)

How large is the field of men's studies? According to Femiano, "[I]n 1984, a national survey found about 40 courses in the United States. In the 6 years since that survey, however, the growth has been rapid and the current number of courses has risen to at least 200" (p. 237). For the moment then, somewhere around 200+ courses dealing with men's lives are taught on various campuses. Chances are, if you are reading this book, you are among a very select number of college students either taking a course on men's lives or dealing with men's issues within the context of another course.

As most men's studies scholars have been trained within other established disciplines (history, literature, psychiatry, psychology, sociology, theology), they have borrowed the methods of inquiry or tools specific to their own training to study men's lives. Someone trained in literary analysis, for example, may examine a type of literature to see how it portrays men's lives (e.g., how men interact within a turn-of-the-century Western novel like Owen Wister's *The Virginian;* see Miner, 1991, 1992; and Pettegrew, 1993). Men's studies comprises the work of those academically trained scholars and practitioners who bring to their study a heightened awareness of gender as a salient social construct and who use established methods of scholarship to understand men's lives.

The question of which theory, if any, should guide men's studies scholarship has already surfaced within the small men's studies community. On one side, we hear that feminism, with its emphasis on power and gender inequalities is the *only* acceptable theory to guide the development of men's studies. This decidedly exclusionary approach to men's studies is most often heard from those trained in the social sciences, especially sociology (e.g., Carrigan, Connell & Lee, 1985; Connell, 1987). Sociological analysis has a long-standing history of examining those social structures that perpetuated inequality among class, economic, and racial groups. Gender has now been added to this analysis to argue that the male gender is inherently privileged and that social institutions throughout history have supported males in power while oppressing (marginalizing) those with little power (e.g., women, men of color, non-heterosexuals).

Others argue for a more inclusive theoretical approach to men's studies. This side states that men's studies is advanced by any number of theories, *including* feminism, as long as the theories' value system or biases are clearly made known. Exemplifying this approach we find clinically-trained psychologists using neo-psychoanalytic concepts—Fromm, Erikson, and Sullivan—to understand male development (e.g., Diamond, 1992; Spielberg, 1993), Jungian-mythopoetic analysis elucidating aspects of men's "inner child" (Shor, 1993), or anthropological field research documenting diverse non-Western male gender roles (Gilmore, 1990; Kennedy, 1993). None of these specific examples rely on feminist principles to examine a part of the male experience. At the same time, most within this group would have no problem applauding feminism for what it has added to an understanding of men's lives. The debate over theoretical exclusion-inclusion has spilled over into other men's studies activities as well.

Men's Studies Organizations

Not surprisingly, as soon as a group of scholars identify a common interest, an organization to further their interests is bound to follow. In 1983, a number of academics holding membership within the profeminist National Organization for

Men (now the National Organization for Men Against Sexism—NOMAS) formed a task group (called an interest group by other organizations) to further their academic interests in men's issues. Beginning in 1984, the Men's Studies Task Group published a bi-annual newsletter (the *Men's Studies Newsletter)* that featured networking items and a comprehensive bibliography listing recent books of interest for group members. Over the next several years, the newsletter grew into a quarterly publication (the *Men's Studies Review*) and extended its range of materials to include articles and book reviews. The *Men's Studies Review* ceased publication in the fall of 1992.

In the late 1980s, the Men's Studies Task Group changed its name to the **Men's Studies Association (MSA)** reflecting its growing stature within the parent organization (i.e., NOMAS). In 1990, at the national Men & Masculinity Conference (Atlanta, Georgia), the MSA leadership and a number of its members discussed the feasibility of incorporating as an independent organization with its own board of directors and holding its conference separate from the M & M conference. The intent behind the plan for separation was to allow MSA to exercise greater control over its organizational needs and greater flexibility in scheduling future men's studies conferences (i.e., making them more accessible to its primarily academic membership). However, the MSA leadership was committed to staying "loosely affiliated" with NOMAS owing to the historical ties and extensive interpersonal network between NOMAS and MSA. Again at the 1991 Men & Masculinity Conference (Tucson, Arizona), the process toward independence was discussed in the MSA business meeting. The overall sense from those in attendance was that the separation process would begin during the following year. However, that fall, NOMAS withheld its support of this separation and moved to block any contact between the MSA leaders with their constituents (i.e., a legal maneuver prohibiting the MSA leaders from using the MSA members' mailing list). NOMAS also dismissed the MSA president and replaced him with a committee of four NOMAS leaders. Consequently, an organizational fracture occurred when the former MSA leaders proceeded with the original plans of separation. Thus we now have two men's studies organizations—the **American Men's Studies Association (AMSA,** an independent organization chartered in 1992 and led by the former MSA leadership) and the Men Studies Association of the National Organization for Men Against Sexism.

For the time being, with two organizations, men's studies scholars have two competing organizations and two annual men's studies conferences to chose between. While for some this presents a burden on time and finances, most see the division of the field as part of the natural growth process of any newly emergent academic field.

Although an organizational split can be very painful for those involved, no matter how bitter, some good can result. For instance, once the split became inevitable, the AMSA leadership were motivated to examine the goals and purposes for their group's very existence. Consequently, a major accomplishment came out of AMSA's first leadership meeting (Stony Point, NY, May, 1992) where a six-point "mission statement" detailing the rationale for another men's studies organization was

the american men's studies association mission statement

The American Men's Studies Association conceives men's studies to be concerned with the analyses of male experiences as social-historical-cultural constructions.

The Association is committed to serve as a multidisciplinary forum of men and women irrespective of class background, ethnic origin, religious background, sexual orientation, or physical abilities, whose purpose is to promote critical discussion of issues involving men and masculinities, and to disseminate knowledge about men's lives to a broad audience.

The Association is dedicated to supporting and encouraging scholars, teachers, and practitioners at all academic, educational, and professional levels. The Association invites into membership scholars, researchers, teachers, and practitioners who share its perspective and who subscribe to high standards of scholarship in research, teaching, and practice. The Association also intends to serve a mentoring function for young scholars in the field.

The major objectives of the Association are to encourage the refinement of the parameters of men's studies, to generate theory, and to develop methodologies of the study of masculinities, from an ethical perspective that eschews oppression in all forms (namely, sexism, racism, homophobia, antisemitism, classism, et al.).

Given the pluralistic nature of men's studies, it is the Association's intention to recognize and respect the many voices emerging from among those working with and/or studying men and masculinity. We are committed to provide a forum of open and inclusive dialogue that involves a spirit of mutual respect for our common humanity.

The Association values collegial relationships characterized by the kind of generativity and support that are mutually empowering, guiding, and affirming.

From The American Men's Studies Association, Northampton, MA. Reprinted by permission.

---

drafted and subsequently published (see AMSA's Mission Statement). A theme running throughout the meeting and the resultant document was that men's studies would be better served if the value of "inclusion" rather than "exclusion" was an explicit organizational goal. For the time being, no such statement has been drafted outlining the goals and purposes of the Men's Studies Association of the National Organization for Men Against Sexism.

To a considerable degree the future of men's studies rests on how the professional associations (at the present time AMSA and MSA) are able to put aside what for many of their leaders were bitter personal issues and focus on what they can do best—provide support for the teachers, students, researchers, and practitioners who make up men's studies. Only time will tell if this is to be.

Men's Studies Publications

Although there are numerous journals, magazines, and newsletters devoted to the many political voices of the men's movements (Clatterbaugh, in press; see Resources at the end of this book), few solely academically oriented publications have appeared to present the emergent men's studies scholarship. I can only cite three publications who by definition have as their sole purpose to serve the men's studies community. Let's briefly discuss each of these publications here.

The National Council of African American Men (NCAAM) has sponsored a new bi-annual journal devoted to the thoughts and experiences of African American men entitled *The Journal of African American Male Studies*. The first issue appeared in the winter of 1993 under the capable editorship of sociologist Clyde Franklin whose work is known to most in the men's studies field (Franklin, II, 1984, 1988). However, given the press of other commitments, Franklin has turned the journal's editorial duties over to Courtland Lee of the University of Virginia.

The Men's Studies Association of the National Organization for Men Against Sexism has begun to publish, *Masculinities,* under the editorship of Michael Kimmel. After the *Men's Studies Review* ceased publication (fall 1992), *Masculinities* launched its premier issue (spring 1993) and has presented itself as the official voice of pro-feminist scholarship.

The Journal of Men's Studies, a new quarterly appeared in August, 1992. Believing there was a need of a scholarly journal open to the many voices (perspectives) within men's studies, the founding editor (J. Doyle) enlisted the support of over thirty distinguished men's studies scholars to serve on the journal's editorial board. In the premier issue's editorial, Doyle (1992) argued his case for an "inclusive" men's studies journal.

> Exploration, inclusiveness, sharing, and understanding—all within the framework of careful scholarship—will be the hallmarks of [the journal's] published material. Whereas each scholar must approach men's lives and their experiences from some sort of guiding principle, we must keep ever in mind that the tools used (models, perspectives, theories) for understanding men's lives are only that, tools that allow one to look at the phenomenon (men's lives) from a vantage point, not as inflexible doctrines that restrict or shut off dialogue. (p. 3)

What the future holds for these publications and, hopefully, other scholarly men's studies publications is of some concern. Given ever tightening library budgets and the residue of suspicion among the different factions within men's studies, each publication will have to work hard to win a place within the field.

a look ahead

Now that we have charted some of the social forces pushing for a change in the traditional ways the male role and masculinity has been defined, outlined the different men's movements, and described the emergent men's studies field, we are ready to move on to other issues that surround the male experience. In the next section then, we will outline what various academic disciplines (history, biology, psychology, sociology and social psychology, and anthropology) have added to our understanding of men's lives. From there we will detail five major elements or social features (anti-feminine, success, aggression, sexual, and self-reliance) that many researchers see as comprising the traditional view of masculinity in our society. And finally, we will look at several issues that have captured the attention not only of men's studies scholars but those interested in men's lives in general—namely, power and men's relationships, gay men, men of color, fatherhood, and men's health.

<table>
<tr><td>important
terms</td><td>

American Men's Studies Association (AMSA) *17*
Consciousness-raising group (C-R) *7*
Deep masculine *10*
Feminism *10*
Gender *2*
Gender role *2*
Gender identity *3*
Homophobia *14*
Male experience *2*
Men's rights *12*
Men's Studies Association (MSA) *17*

</td><td>

Men's studies *15*
Mythopoetic *10*
National Congress for Men and Children
(NCMC) *13*
National Organization for Men Against Sexism
(NOMAS) *13*
Profeminists *9*
Promasculinists *9*
Sex *2*
Sexism *8*
Wild man *11*

</td></tr>
</table>

suggested readings

Bly, R. (1990). *Iron John: A book about men.* Reading, MA: Addison-Wesley.

Brod, H. (Ed.). (1987). *The making of masculinities.* Boston: Allen & Unwin.

Clatterbaugh, K. (1990). *Contemporary perspectives on masculinity: Men, women, and politics in modern society.* Boulder, CO: Westview Press.

Farrell, W. (1993). *The myth of male power: Why men are the disposable sex—fated for war, programmed for work, divorced from emotion.* New York: Simon & Schuster.

Gerzon, M. (1992). *A choice of heroes: The changing faces of American manhood.* New York: Houghton Mifflin.

Gibson, J.W. (1994). *Warrior dreams: Paramilitary culture in post-Vietnam America.* New York: Hill and Wang.

Rabinowitz, F. E., and Cochran, S. V. (1994). *Man alive: A primer of men's issues.* Pacific Grove, CA: Brooks/Cole Publishing Company.

section one

Perspectives on the Male

In a far-off land, there was a remote village totally inhabited by blind people. One day nearby the village, a mighty king camped with his army and an enormous elephant.

The blind inhabitants had little experience with armies and even less experience with ponderous pachyderms. The unknown creature that shook the earth caused great fear among the villagers. To calm their fear, the village council decided to send out three scouts to discover the form of the thunderous beast. When the blind scouts returned, each spoke confidently of the elephant's form.

The first scout, who had felt the elephant's ear, reported to the village assembly that the elephant was like a large, rough fan that moved about creating great currents of air that almost knocked him off his feet.

The second scout, who had held the elephant's trunk, scoffed at the first scout's report and related how the elephant was like a long, bristly snake that had coiled and lifted her into the air.

The third scout, who had weaved amid the elephant's legs, dismissed the previous narratives as so much poppycock and proceeded to describe the elephant as four massive, moving pillars that could shake the ground, causing all nearby to tremble.

Clearly each scout thought he or she had experienced the elephant. The problem, however, was that each had focused on only a single portion of the animal's anatomy. Because the scouts reported conflicting versions of the colossal creature, the villagers remained confused and fearful of the king's elephant.

What connection do the exploits of three blind scouts and an elephant have with our discussion of the male experience? Well, in the next five chapters we are going to look at the male experience from five different perspectives: historical, biological, psychological, social, and anthropological. Each perspective presents a different version, so to speak, of the male experience. Each emphasizes certain features and downplays certain others. Analogously,

each perspective resembles one of the blind scouts. Each perspective deals with particular features of the male experience and thinks, all too often, that it has grasped the total picture. For the moment, let us briefly preview these perspectives and highlight one or two main issues in each.

How we define the male gender and how men experience their masculinity today are better understood in the context of how these features were defined a hundred, a thousand, or even ten thousand years ago. The *historical perspective* focuses on those stable and changeable features that have been a part of the male experience over the centuries. A knowledge of the past makes the present and future possibilities concerning the male experience more understandable.

Recent advances in microscopic enlargement and breakthroughs in genetics are extending the frontiers of our knowledge of human biology. At last, the information contained in the microscopic sex chromosomes is being decoded. Testosterone, dubbed by many the "male hormone," is now seen as responsible for much of the male's physiology as well as a possible basis for certain male behaviors. This is only one of the areas we will cover in the *biological perspective* of the male experience.

For well over half a century, psychologists have spent thousands of hours in research on how the sexes differ from each other. Elaborate theories of unconscious urges, external rewards, and mental images have been developed to explain how males come to perceive themselves as masculine, and females as feminine. However, some in the psychological community are beginning to challenge long-established views of masculinity; thus our discussion of the *psychological perspective* includes an examination of recent changes in the interpretation of the male gender and masculinity.

All of us from our very earliest days experience the impact of a miniaturized society, the family. The family group comprised of parents, siblings, and relatives interacts with the infant in ways that help the developing child define itself, first as a human and then as a male or a female. Groups large and small mold the infant in ways deemed acceptable by the larger society. In the *social roles perspective,* we will focus on the socialization process as well as other ways of describing how groups influence the development of the male gender.

For centuries people have asked questions about their existence, meaning, and purpose. These questions and the answers that people accepted became the ingredients for the most human of all creation: culture. In the broadest sense of the word, culture gives meaning to people's lives. Insight into and understanding of the richness and variation of the male experience can be gained from a knowledge of the ways, beliefs, and values of other peoples, both distant and near. The *anthropological perspective* views the male experience through eyes that at first appear exotic and unusual but through which we can gain a greater appreciation of the male experience.

Just as the three blind scouts perceived the elephant from three different vantage points, each perspective covered in the following chapters brings to the study of the male experience its own built-in assumptions about what features to look for, what questions to ask, how best to study it, and sometimes even what answers are most acceptable to the particular perspective. We must also keep in mind that each perspective is the work of humans, and the work of humans is often less than completely objective.

Therefore, we should not be put off by some contradictory stances among the perspectives (for example, the male experience is largely a product of biological factors versus the male experience is the end result of social forces). When we find opposing views, we should recall how physicists find it quite helpful sometimes to regard light as a continuous wave and sometimes as a series of particles. If physicists are comfortable with their seemingly contrary perspectives of what constitutes light, we need not be too perplexed about the differences among the various perspectives of the male experience.

Perspectives on the Male

Chapter 2

The Historical Perspective

A major task of a historical study of the male past is to find the roots of maleness and determine how profound they are.
Peter Stearns (1979)

The history of masculinity is a relatively new subject of inquiry with a small but growing literature.
Elizabeth and Joseph Pleck (1980)

Historians have heeded Gerda Lerner's call to fill in the "something missing" from the female past, but have not yet recognized that gender refers to two sexes. Something is also missing in men's own history. The time has come to fill in the blanks.
Peter Filene (1987)

Many define history as the written record of the cultural, social, economic, religious, and political dealings of the human race. If, however, we took the time to examine a number of history books published before the mid- to late-1970s, say, we would see that recorded history was rather one-sided in its recounting of the *human* story. Actually, our review would unmask more than a little favoritism toward male deeds while shunning for the most part female deeds. (For an excellent review of the long-standing bias against recounting the female presence in historical accounts, see Bullough, 1974.) Finding a pervasive male bias running throughout most historical treatises is only part, though, of what we would find in our review. Upon closer scrutiny, we would also find that most historians have been rather selective in their choice of which males to focus on. Most have been content to chronicle only the deeds of a few, namely, the kings, generals, presidents, dictators, bishops, and philosophers whose power and social positions made them stand out. Painfully absent are the stories of the multitudes of males who were merely soldiers, clerics, slaves, farmers, storekeepers, serfs, and workers whose lives unfolded in rather mundane and inauspicious ways. Consequently, we could argue that until very recently history has dealt almost exclusively with the lives of men, a few notable and powerful men, that is. Mention of women and powerless and nameless men was strikingly absent. But humanity's story is or at least should be more than a collection of dates, battles, intrigues, and reigns of great and near-great men. People's lives— male *and* female, the powerful *and* the powerless—are the fabric that makes up the rich tapestry of the human story.

Why, then, do we include a chapter on the history of the male gender and masculinity when so much has already been written about men? First of all, as we have already stated, historians have generally written only about a few men and in so doing have concentrated on their "public" lives, the visible and, hence, the side where these few lived out what their society and culture expected of them. Consequently, historians have paid little heed to what historian Peter Filene (1987) refers to as the "secret" side, the nearly invisible side of the male gender. Thus one of our concerns in this chapter is to note what ordinary men's lives have been like as well as to document some of the missing parts in males' long-standing story.

Furthermore, to give some continuity to this chapter, we will trace the development of one of the key historical elements of the male gender, namely, **patriarchy.** Originally, patriarchy meant the supremacy of a father over his family members. However, as most people use it today, patriarchy means rule of men in general. We trace patriarchy back to those ancient societies in which males began to exert more influence and power over females than vice versa. Next we move through the centuries and see the power invested in the male gender grow more prominent, especially during the Greco-Roman period. Then we discover the almost total power that is placed in a father's hands during the Middle Ages. Finally, we discuss patriarchy and the male gender in North American history. But first let's take a small detour into the recent past and note how several social movements have brought about a reinterpretation of history's content.

During the late 1920s, several French historians set out to correct what they believed was an incomplete portrayal of human history. Two historians in particular, Marc Bloch and Lucien Febvre, were instrumental in developing a school of historical investigation that has since become known as the *Annales*. The purpose of the Annales school was to move away from the traditional historical analysis of the notable and the powerful throughout history and to focus rather on the lives of ordinary people and everyday events. This particular approach to historical analysis became known as "social history" (Marwick, 1970). Accordingly, social historians argued that social customs, traditions, marriage patterns, fertility rates, death records, and other facets of common people's lives provided a wealth of historical material that gave a whole new dimension to human history.

Until recently, most students in North American history courses read little or were exposed to few of the contributions of groups such as African-Americans, Mexican-Americans, and women. During the late 1960s and 1970s, several groups called attention to these glaring omissions. Furthermore, feminists like Elizabeth Gould Davis (1972) charged that the prevalent view of world history was decidedly male biased and that historians had for centuries, consciously or unconsciously, left out the significant role women had played in the development of the human race. Consequently, scholars—mostly females—have moved to correct this one-sided, male-dominant historical perspective with several excellent scholarly works and numerous courses on the role of women in both past and recent human history (Eisler, 1988; Lerner, 1979; Miles, 1990).

On a hot June night in 1969, an incident in New York City sparked the birth of the gay liberation movement. A group of police raided the Stonewall, a popular gay bar, and many of the clients fought back after being harassed by the police. Since what has been dubbed the Stonewall Rebellion, large numbers of gays have come out openly to defend their life-style and to demand an end to the discrimination that has plagued them almost continuously. Not only has the gay movement of the 1970s permitted countless gays to take pride in themselves as human beings, but it has also caused an awakening of interest in an accurate account of gays in history (Cruikshank, 1992; D'Emilio, 1983; Katz, 1983, 1985; Plant, 1986).

The concerns and questions generated by the women's movement and the gay liberation movement also spawned an interest among some historians in the male gender and conceptions of masculinity. One area of investigation that grew out of this new interest was that of the historical roots of the male gender, how it took shape throughout history, as well as the "secrets" of men's experiences (Bell, 1981; Dubbert, 1979; Filene, 1985, 1986, 1987; Griffen & Carnes, 1988; Kirshner, 1977; Mangan & Walvin, 1987; Pugh, 1983). And this is the subject of our chapter. Because it would be impossible to cover every aspect of the traditional male gender, we shall concentrate on the historical development of *patriarchy* and then only on how it evolved in Western civilization. The reason for this "selectivity" is simple: patriarchy is a defining concept of Western civilization and thus has influenced the lives of nearly every male and female in Western society for the last several thousand years (Lerner, 1986). Let's begin our discussion, then, by looking back almost three thousand years to a time when the male gender role as we presently know it was being shaped in Greece.

table 2.1   Five Historical Male Role Ideals

Ideal	Source(s)	Major Features
Epic Male	Epic sagas of Greece and Rome (800–100 B.C.E.)	Action, physical strength, courage, loyalty, and beginning of patriarchy.
Spiritual Male	Teachings of Jesus Christ, early church fathers, and monastic tradition (400–1000 C.E.)	Self-renunciation, restrained sexual activity, antifeminine and antihomosexual attitudes, and strong patriarchal system.
Chivalric Male	Feudalism and chivalric code of honor (twelfth-century social system)	Self-sacrifice, courage, physical strength, honor and service to the lady, and primogeniture.
Renaissance Male	Sixteenth-century social system	Rationality, intellectual endeavors, and self-exploration.
Bourgeois Male	Eighteenth-century social system	Success in business, status, and worldly manners.

It is hard to say exactly how long there has been a distinct set of expectations and demands for each sex. The basis for different gender roles as we understand them today appears to have been established long ago in an attempt by early humans to divide essential labor between those individuals who could best accomplish specific tasks (Kelly, 1981). It seems certain, however, that throughout most of *recorded* history the male's power and influence within the group has been greater than the female's (Lerner, 1986). This feature of male dominance within the group we interpret here as the basis of patriarchy. Some feminists, however, contend that prior to recorded history some evidence in myth and legend suggests an earlier period in human history when woman-rule, or *gynecocracy,* was the norm (Cantarella, 1987). Furthermore, some archaeological evidence suggests women's prominent and strong presence in many early societies, especially in terms of the influence of female goddesses in the everyday lives of common folk (Baring & Cashford, 1993; Berger, 1985; Eisler, 1988). Rather than extend our discussion of the history of the male gender back into these more shadowy periods of human history, we will confine our discussion here to that of recorded time, beginning with Greece in the eighth century B.C.E. (B.C.E. [Before the Common Era] and C.E. [Common Era] are the alternative designations used in scholarly literature to correspond to B.C. and A.D.).

According to the analysis presented here, during roughly the last three thousand years, there have been at least five distinct male models, or ideals, that Western men were expected to imitate. As with all ideals, each of the five is a larger-than-life exaggeration impossible for any one man to achieve in its entirety. Even so, most of the males who lived during each of these periods knew of the ideal's distinctive features and were influenced by them in their daily lives. One feature, however, permeated all five ideals; the support of a patriarchal social order in which the male, especially the father, was seen as the dominant force in all male-female relations.

We have given the following names to the five male models, or ideals: the epic male, the spiritual male, the chivalric male, the Renaissance male, and the bourgeois male (see Table 2.1).

the patriarchal tradition

The Historical Perspective

The male ideal depicted in the ancient Greek and Roman periods comes down to us primarily through the epic sagas written by men like Homer and Virgil. In these sagas, we enter a decidedly masculine world, a world inhabited by soldiers, adventurers, warriors, kings, and gods (Keuls, 1985). Men were the "doers," the conquerors and rulers, of a threatening and barbaric world. Women were peripheral to the action and were accorded importance only to the degree that they served men's needs (Cantarella, 1987).

The **epic male** was first and foremost a fighter and a leader. The essential characteristics of this period's male gender were prowess and skill in battle, physical strength and courage, and loyalty—first to leader and king, then to male comrades, and finally to clan and family. Essentially, the epic male role embodied the features of the warrior-ruler.

The female figure of epic times was honored more for her physical beauty, charms, and dedication to men than for any endeavor based on talent or ability (Cantarella, 1987). The female was viewed as a passive object of men's desire. Most people, for example, know of Helen of Troy not because of any achievement or special talent but rather because her exquisite and compelling beauty drove men to wage the Trojan War. When we do read of powerful women in the epics, they are usually goddesses who derive much of their power from a male figure. A case in point is the goddess Athena—born out of the head of the god Zeus—who stands more for patriarchal values than for matriarchal concerns. Recall it was Athena who defended Orestes for killing his mother Clytemnestra. Clytemnestra had killed her husband-king, Agamemnon, after his return from the Trojan War. Out of revenge for his father's murder, Orestes killed his mother. To the Greeks, killing a husband-father was more serious than killing a wife-mother. According to the medical knowledge of the day, the father was seen as the creative source of a child, whereas the mother was viewed as a mere incubator. In Athena's defense and Orestes' acquittal, we see the foundation of patriarchy well established in fifth-century B.C.E. Greek society.

The same epic proportions are carried over to the classical Roman period. In Virgil's *Aeneid,* we read of the masculine world of Aeneas and his journey from Troy to Italy and the founding of Rome. Once again, the male is an adventurer and doer of great deeds. Likewise, the female of the Roman epic is portrayed as a bystander to men's actions or a helpless victim of men's relentless pursuits (Gardner, 1986).

Before leaving the epic period, we must mention one last feature of the male gender, a feature that has drawn considerable attention and subsequent condemnation for centuries. Both the Greek and the Roman societies showed wide acceptance of homosexual and pederast (man-boy) sexual relationships. From the fifth century B.C.E. onward, we see in various works of art and common practices the degree to which homosexual relationships were an acceptable and even a noble social practice among a majority of men (Keuls, 1985; Tannahill, 1982). The Greek philosopher Plato, speaking in the *Phaedrus,* calls the love between men "nobler and more spiritual than the love between men and women." We see here evidence of the belief that the male is thought superior to the female. Even in sex, many males preferred homosexual to heterosexual activity.

The dawn of Christianity brought about a radical change in basic human values that influenced the course and development of Western civilization. The Christian faith and its teachings added new features to and changed some features of the classical epic ideal of the male gender. The life and teachings of Jesus Christ provided the basic tenets of Christianity, but it was the early church fathers who largely influenced the male gender ideal.

The image Christ gave to humanity was one of nonviolence (Matthew 26:52) and service to others (John 13:12–16). The poverty, purported celibacy, and self-renunciation of Jesus' life provided a new role model for men that radically differed from anything witnessed in classical times or even in the teachings of the Hebrew Bible (what Christians refer to as the Old Testament). However, the ideal male gender under Christianity did not take complete form as we have come to know it until several centuries after Christ's death. Although Jesus' teachings supported and valued the Jewish tradition of the female's family role, his message did undermine certain aspects of patriarchy within Jewish society (Moltmann-Wendel, 1990; Torjesen, 1993; Witherington, III, 1984). As one historian has noted, "Jesus neither feared women, nor treated them as a sub-species. It would appear that he was prepared to defy convention in this regard and to befriend women in a time and place when the sexes were not supposed to mix on socially equal terms" (Wilson, 1993, p. 151).

Much of what we refer to today as the Christian view of the male and the female genders came from the writings of the early church fathers and the monastic tradition of the fourth and fifth centuries (Buckley, 1986; Pagels, 1988; Ruether, 1987). In fact, contrary to the indivisible human ideal contained in Christ's original message, the early church fathers followed the classical view of the separation of the sexes and reinforced the traditional version of two distinct genders, one for each sex (Ruether, 1987). Underlying these two roles was the church fathers' belief in the causal link between sexuality and sin (Prusak, 1974). The ideal Christian man, especially one called to the clergy, was expected to renounce the flesh, in other words, to avoid all sexuality. Thus the **spiritual male** ideal endorsed celibacy, or at least infrequent sexual experiences, and a turning away from earthly pursuits. In the Christian ethos developed out of the rulings of the early church synods, the ideal male was one in whom the spiritual was preeminent over the worldly (Laeuchli, 1972).

Patriarchy found itself a highly favorable niche in the Christian church. The male, portrayed as the image of God the Father, was seen as the ultimate authority in all matters, both spiritual and secular (see Boyd, 1990, 1993). Women were to subjugate themselves to all males' rulings, their priest's, father's, husband's. To support this strict patriarchal world view, the church fathers were quick to quote from Paul's letter to the Corinthians:

> For a man indeed ought not to cover his head, forasmuch as he is the image and glory of God: but the woman is the glory of man. For the man is not of the woman; but the woman of the man. Neither was the man created for the woman; but the woman for the man (1 Cor. 11:7–9).

Not only did Christianity portray men as women's ultimate authority, men were also expected to disdain the female (Ruether, 1974). Under Christianity, women especially suffered from the link between sexuality and evil (Mortley, 1981). By virtue of their presumed insatiable sexual nature, women were cast as the embodiment of all that was evil. Following the earlier traditions of viewing women as the source of all evil (for example, the Hebrew's conception of Eve and the Greek's view of Pandora), the early church fathers portrayed women as the reason for men's and humanity's downfall and subsequent sinfulness. Pope Clement, an early church father, captured the antifeminine sentiment by pronouncing, "Every woman should be overwhelmed with shame at the very thought that she is a woman" (quoted in Davis, 1972, p. 231).

One other feature relating to the spiritual male ideal was the stance the church fathers took against homosexuality (Tannahill, 1982). They viewed the widespread acceptance and practice of homosexuality among the Greeks and Romans as further evidence of the moral degeneracy of those pagan societies. To be a man, a spiritual man, a male was expected to renounce his sexual desires and activities. But for those men too weak to follow the celibate life, the only acceptable sexual outlet was to be found in heterosexual activity. To have sex with another man was a degradation of human nature and an abhorrence before God. Thus the antihomosexual sentiment that has been so prominent a historic feature of Christian societies owes its legacy to the preachings and exhortations of the early church fathers (Boswell, 1980; Ide, 1985).

The Chivalric Male

Beginning in twelfth-century Europe, a new social order called *feudalism* developed and ushered in a new stability for the people of Western Europe. During the previous six centuries, the Roman church stood almost alone as the unifying authority in Western Europe. However, with the rise of feudalism, authority spread out from the church to include a cultured aristocracy and a military class. Feudalism spawned the growth of towns, expanded trade, and developed a money economy and the cult of the Virgin Mary. The rise of the soldier, or knightly, class provided a new ideal for the male gender, one that transformed the asexual spiritual male into a sensual **chivalric male.**

The male gender during the feudal period focused on the model of a fighter, a soldier, although not just a common soldier but a very special soldier—the knight-errant. No longer did the male ideal include the spiritual male's sense of asexual self-renunciation and nonviolence; rather, the chivalric male ideal emphasized physical strength, prowess in combat, loyalty to the king or liege lord, and devotion to a lady. We see in the chivalric ideal a return to many of the same qualities of the epic male figure of classical times. But there were also some differences between them. The most apparent difference lay in the chivalric's fantasized sensual relationship between a knight and his lady.

The view of womanhood in the guise of the lady is a significant feature of the feudal period (Gold, 1985). Recall that in the centuries that followed the Christianization of Europe, women were singularly portrayed as the source of temptation and evil because they were the daughters of Eve. Even the purity and sinless nature of the Virgin Mary, the mother of Jesus, was played down in the early church.

Although the cult of Mary did flourish for a short time among some early Christian communities, the church fathers squashed this veneration of Mary because of the similarity between Mary's veneration and certain pagan practices of worshiping a mother goddess (Berger, 1986; Pagels, 1976). But under feudalism a new view of womanhood developed, one that included a dualistic version of woman's nature. Women were seen as either pedestaled virgins or lusty temptresses and prostitutes (Dillenberger, 1985; Shahar, 1983).

The lady of the feudal period was a secularized version of the Virgin Mary. She existed more in men's fantasy than in reality. The knight devoted his strength and skills to her service. The love between a knight and his lady, although sensual, was not usually consummated. To consummate such a relationship usually brought about tragedy for both parties as we see in the Arthurian legend of Lancelot and Guinevere. In the other view, women were portrayed as insatiable creatures who pleased men with their lusty sexuality. Feudalism's dualistic view of womanhood has come down through the ages and contributed to the present-day conception of woman's nature.

Patriarchy continued to grow in importance under feudalism. A prime example of this can be seen in the practice of **primogeniture,** which became well established during this period. The right of primogeniture assured the wealth and property that made up a father's estate passed directly to his eldest male heir. Thus the power of the eldest male over his siblings and his mother was guaranteed under this patriarchal arrangement.

England of the sixteenth century witnessed the rise of the **Renaissance male** ideal. Feudalism with its two social extremes, the rich aristocracy and their subjects the serfs, made room for a growing middle class. The knight riding his horse in quest of glory and his lady's approval changed into a man searching for knowledge. The once powerful Roman church lost much of its authority over what people could believe and think. The Renaissance rekindled the virtues of knowledge that were prominent during the late classical period. No longer was authority vested in a few church leaders or kings. Consequently, men and some few women began to think for themselves about the wonders of the world and its mysteries.

The Renaissance Male

The Renaissance male ideal stressed the rational and intellectual abilities of men. Men were still expected to be doers, active and in control, but the goals of their activity had changed. Classical, or epic, man sought physical perfection, spiritual man was motivated toward an afterlife, but Renaissance man sought intellectual goals that would free him from the restraints of a dogmatic church authority. An archetypal example of Renaissance man was Michelangelo, whose intellectual achievements in both the arts and sciences could not have been accomplished under the restrictions of the powerful Roman church two or three hundred years earlier.

There was yet another side to Renaissance man, a dark, forbidding, and even tragic side. He discovered many secrets of nature long thought to be only the domain of gods and goddesses. He also explored the secrets of his personality, and these secrets sometimes led to personal anguish and internal conflict. The great English playwright William Shakespeare captured the essential tragedy in men's hidden secrets through characters like Hamlet, Macbeth, and Lear (see Dews, 1994).

The Historical Perspective

Patriarchy during the Renaissance continued to be the norm for Western society. The power of men over women's lives continued along the established paths of the preceding periods (Maclean, 1980). The "established path," according to Renaissance historian Patricia Labalme (1980), steered women toward either one of two lives, marriage or the convent. Some few women, though, such as Elizabeth I, Eleonora of Aragon, Marguerite de Navarre, and Catherine of Sienna detoured and became powerful persons in their own right; but in their political, social, and religious involvements, we still find a male presence in the background (Gies & Gies, 1980; Gundersheimer, 1980). Some earlier women such as Hildagard of Bingen and Herrad of Landsberg were even widely respected for their scholarly and scientific learning and writings, an achievement long thought proper only for males (Ferrante, 1980; Flanagan, 1989; Grant, 1980).

The Bourgeois Male

By the eighteenth century a strong and powerful middle class had become well established in England. The previous aristocratic goals and manly pursuits of territorial conquest, spiritual fulfillment, and acquisition of knowledge were replaced by the middle class's more mundane goals of money, status, and prestige. The middle class of urbanized Europe and England helped create the new **bourgeois male** ideal.

The middle-class man of the eighteenth century was driven to achieve what he saw as the ultimate symbol of power: money. This bourgeois man was seeking status and prestige, and the way to gain these was through success in business dealings. The entrepreneur, or business adventurer, was his model. To risk and then to succeed in business was the final proof of a man's worth.

The female role in the eighteenth century continued to be one of subjugation to man. The ideal of the young virgin as a reward for the hard-working and successful male played a dominant role in eighteenth-century literature.

Summarizing the Western Roots of the Male Gender

We now come to the end of our brief survey of the male gender ideals that have existed during the history of Western civilization. Obviously, many of the expectations typically linked to the contemporary male gender have their roots in earlier historical periods. For example, the emphasis on man as a doer and the expectations of physical strength, courage, and loyalty owe their heritage to the epic male of classical Greek and Roman times. The view of man as the priestly link to God, his assumed authority in religious matters, and the rejection of the behaviors associated with females and homosexuals extend back to early Christianity. The conception of man as the champion of women and protector of the weak owes its legacy to the chivalric male ideal of the feudal period. The belief in man's superior rational and intellectual abilities owes much to the Renaissance male model. The expectation of success in the competitive world of business is a more recent male characterization that reaches back only two or three hundred years to the bourgeois period. By combining these elements, we have a fair composite of the complete man as most know him in the twentieth century.

The one consistent theme that runs through all of these distinctive periods is patriarchy. We saw how father-rule was already fairly well established during the epic period, although the classical societies did allow for a definite female presence in their religions. But the early Christian church fathers' belief in the causal links among sex, evil, and women removed most vestiges of female influence from religion and substituted a singularly stern and unforgiving father figure. Consequently, a total patriarchal system flowered during the early Christian era. Even though the cult of the Virgin Mary allowed for a certain feminization of the social order during the feudal period, patriarchy became stronger with the advent of primogeniture, the passage of wealth from father to eldest son. Patriarchy continued unabated during the subsequent Renaissance and bourgeois periods. In fact, patriarchy went unchallenged until the middle of the nineteenth century, when certain social movements began their assault on the established male-dominated social order in England and North America. We will have more to say about the erosion of male dominance in North America in the next section.

After just spanning a period of more than twenty-five hundred years (from 800 B.C.E. to 1800 C.E.), we might think that North America's relatively short history would provide little change in the male gender ideal. Nothing could be further from the truth. In just three and a half centuries, North America has provided a rich social climate for several male gender transitions. But how shall we divide the North American historical scene and its perspectives on the male role? Elizabeth and Joseph Pleck (1980, p. 6) write that the history of gender in North America is best conceived and divided into specific "periods that correspond to much broader and far-reaching changes in American politics and warfare and to new directions in economic, religious, and family life." Consequently, the Plecks divided the history of the male gender role and masculinity in North America into four periods: agrarian patriarchy (1630–1820), the commercial age (1820–1860), the strenuous life (1861–1919), and companionate providing (1920–1965).

the north american versions of the male gender role

Recently, historian E. Anthony Rotundo (1993) devised yet another historical classification outlining how North American manhood has evolved over the past three and a half centuries. Spanning the colonial period (roughly late 1600s to early 1800s), Rotundo marshalled evidence suggesting that a man's gender identity was chiefly shaped by his "duties," his service to his community. Further, a man's worth or value—both to himself and to his community—was, for the most part, set at birth and based on his family of origin. Highlighting the influence of one's community in shaping a man's view of his manhood, Rotundo labeled this period **communal manhood.**

With the nineteenth century and the drive for Westward expansion, manhood was no longer defined in terms of one's family of origin or community service. Rather a man's identity was to a large part created in terms of his effort or achievements, resulting in what Rotundo called a period of **self-made manhood.** Consequently, a man's gender identity could change given the nearly unlimited business and commercial opportunities available in an expanding country in need of men willing to risk.

Finally, the twentieth century found most of the frontiers conquered with only one area still relatively uncharted, a man's internal life—his passions. A period of **passionate manhood** arose where men's identities became wrapped around their ambitions and their competitiveness. No longer expected to deny or hold themselves in check, men now were simply expected to channel their basic drives and to live life more fully.

The Historical Perspective

table 2.2   The North American Male Role Ideals

Ideal	Historical Period	Source(s)	Major Features
Aristocrat	1630–1820	Late seventeenth- and early eighteenth-century English aristocratic values	Self-confidence, intellectualism, strong patriarchal tradition, individualism.
Common Man	1820–1860	The values of the new Republic	Common sense, success in business, personal ingenuity, heightened sexual interests and activity.
He-Man	1861–1919	Westward expansion and the rise of feminism	Strenuous activity, involvement in sports, two-fisted preparedness.
Partner	1920–1965	Loosening of nineteenth-century Victorian values	Good provider, hard worker, concerned about family matters.

Although Rotundo's analysis is quite fascinating, in the following discussion, we will opt for and develop more fully the historical outline devised by the Plecks as it provides us with a slightly more detailed analysis—providing four categories rather than three. We will pay particular attention to the economic, legal, and social changes that influenced women during these periods because as we noted earlier changes in the female's status directly influenced the male's gender. And we will continue to focus on the influence of patriarchy over both men's and women's lives (see Table 2.2).

The Aristocrat and His Family (1630–1820)

According to history, the Puritans left England for the New World to escape persecution and to express their particular brand of stern religious beliefs. Being a contentious minority, the Puritans saw themselves as vastly superior to the liberal majority of seventeenth-century England because of their strict moral code and belief in a rigid patriarchy. The Puritans especially disdained the "feminization" of English society that had come down from the earlier chivalric period. Central to Puritan belief was the view that God intended men to be superior to women, who were to defer and subjugate themselves to the male in all matters. Thus, with the Puritans, a strict patriarchal tradition was planted early and deep in the New England colonies.

As the New World's wilderness was settled, the colonists became less preoccupied with mere survival and turned their energies to establishing a new way of life, a life based on English patriarchal standards. In the colonies of the late seventeenth century, for example, English common law played a significant role in the colonists' daily lives. Under common law, the father as head of the household was the only one permitted to enter into contracts, buy or sell land, and represent the family in civil matters. Consequently, women had few legal rights in the early colonies (Frey & Morton, 1986; Salmon, 1986).

Land or rather its ownership became a significant feature in colonial men's lives. A landowner was thought to have greater power, influence, and status than a man without land. Over time, New World landowners formed a nucleus of what can be considered an "aristocracy." The **aristocrat** soon became the model by which early colonial men measured their masculinity. Furthermore, certain features became associated with the landed aristocrat, features such as independence, self-confidence, intelligence, and a spirit of individualism.

During this period, the role of the father in most family matters was that of an unquestioned authority figure. The father controlled his sons' education, choice of careers, and future economic status by passing down his land and wealth through the long-established practice of primogeniture. Daughters were equally under their father's control, even to his choice of their future husbands. And, by virtue of the law, the wife was totally dependent on her husband's goodwill.

As this period drew to a close with the Colonial Revolution and the formation of the new Republic, the woman's role began to change. The mother took a more active and influential role in the rearing of her children (Stewart, Winter, & Jones, 1975). The family model took on a quasi-democratic appearance with the husband and wife splitting responsibilities; the father became even more involved in the worldly matters of business, and the mother assumed family responsibilities such as the education of her children (Butterfield, Friedlander, & Kline, 1975; Kerber, 1974). The beginning of the nineteenth century brought about a decline in the aristocratic ideal for men and a turn toward specific social concerns for women.

The Common Man and the Suffragette (1820–1860)

During the early colonial years, the male was the center of the social order and the ultimate authority in most matters. The female was almost a nonentity, a passive figure in the background whose mission was to bear children in silence and keep to herself in loyal submission—first to her father and later, as an adult, to her husband (Basch, 1982). But the first half of the nineteenth century witnessed a new social order, a new pattern of living for each sex, commonly referred to as the "doctrine of the separate spheres" (Cott, 1977).

In the fervor and upheaval of the new Republic, we find the ingredients for a social revolution wherein two separate but theoretically equal spheres or cultures became evident; one sphere for males and the other for females. The two were divided according to presumed gender differences. The male, who was viewed as more aggressive and competitive by nature, was thought more fit for the masculine pursuits of politics and economic ventures. The ideal of the colonial period's male aristocrat gave way to the ideal of the **common man.** The model of the common man not only looked the part of the opportunistic hard worker but he was expected to possess common sense and an eye for practical matters that made him especially well suited for the give and take of hard bargaining in the business world (Gordon, 1980). Some few men even abandoned the emergent common man-worker rule and ventured out for what one historian called "anarchic freedom" found in the uncivilized, or "savage," Western frontier (Smith, 1980). The female, on the other hand, by virtue of her presumed genteel and emotional nature, was thought best suited for "womanly" activities involving home and religion (Jensen, 1986; Welter,

The Historical Perspective

1974). The ideal wife was pictured as possessing a high degree of domestic ability and was expected to create an inviting shelter to which her husband could return after a hard day of business dealings in the unfriendly male world (Welter, 1966).

A dramatic turnabout occurred in the commercial period with respect to the sexual element of the male gender. Recall that ever since the early Christian period women, not men, were thought to be oversexed. For centuries women were portrayed as the source of passion and sensuality. Of course, men were sexual creatures also, but it was women's nature that was given to carnal desires and, as the Christian church taught, was the cause of the male's downfall. However, during the early nineteenth century, men were portrayed as having a stronger sexual bent than women, who were viewed as being above sex, or at least put off by it. For this reason, men were encouraged to exert themselves in their work, to become successful in their business ventures because through work a man could expend a large portion of his sexual energies on tasks more worthwhile than mere sexual release. After a hard day's work, the passionate husband had little energy or spirit left for baser things, which was perfectly all right with his "cool" wife.

Although the woman's role during this period revolved around the home, she also became involved in the most pressing issue of the day, slavery. Large numbers of Northern and Southern women became advocates of the growing abolition movement. Furthermore, concern over the plight and oppression of the slave caused a growing number of women to focus on their own sex's inequality (Hole & Levine, 1984). The legal subjugation of the wife to her husband was finally rescinded by a series of laws collectively known as the Married Women's Property Acts. (The first such law was passed in Mississippi in 1839.) Under these laws, women gained the rights to enter into contracts, to sue or be sued in their own name, to control the property they brought into their marriages, and to take on paid employment without their husband's consent (Warbasse, 1987).

As the Republic grew more stable, women in growing numbers reacted against their second-class citizenship. The Declaration of Independence had proclaimed the lofty ideal that "all *men* are created equal," and women found themselves left out, with few rights or privileges other than those granted them by their husbands. Furor over the patriarchal social system and women's oppressed status caused some women to band together to fight for their rights as equal citizens under the law (Taylor, 1983). The energy and indignation these women felt came together at the first feminist convention in Seneca Falls, New York, in 1848. Even though the convention focused on women's oppression and their lack of the vote, a third of the signers of the Seneca Falls' Declaration of Principles were men (Pleck & Pleck, 1980).

Although this period lasted only forty or so years, it left an indelible imprint on both sexes. Men were thought highly sexed, and in order to control their lusty passions, they were exhorted to turn their energies to work. The patriarchal tradition was under attack, and men found their esteemed privileges slowly eroding. Women, on the other hand, ruled the house and were encouraged by a reformist religion to fight for equal rights and justice for blacks and women alike. The commercial period found men and women living in two almost completely separate worlds, and the sexes were not to come together again for another half century. (For a discussion on marriages and the roles of husbands and wives, see Hersh, 1980.) On a larger scale, the Republic was about to divide over the issue of states' rights. With all of these forces, the stage was set for the third period in the history of the male gender, a period in which men turned to physical exertion and battle to bolster their sagging sense of masculinity.

The Plecks refer to the years between 1860 and 1919 as the period of the "strenuous life." This period began with a war in which brother fought brother and ended with World War I, which was heralded as the war to end all wars. Sandwiched between these bloody conflicts, men struggled with changing times that provided them few opportunities to bolster their masculinity. With the erosion of patriarchy and the Victorian attack on men's sexuality, men answered the challenges to their manhood by turning to all-male activities in which they could play at being rough and tough. Teddy Roosevelt set the tenor of this period in an address before a men's group in Chicago:

The He-Man and His Compatriots (1861–1919)

> I wish to preach, not the doctrine of ignoble ease, but the doctrine of the strenuous life, the life of toil and effort, of labor and strife; to preach that highest form of success which comes, not to the man who desires mere easy peace, but to the man who does not shrink from danger, from hardship, or from bitter toil, and who out of these wins the splendid ultimate triumph. (Filene, 1986, p. 71)

The decades directly preceding the twentieth century found large numbers of men migrating from farms to cities. The United States was fast becoming an industrial giant, and the factories needed strong backs to stoke the furnaces of progress. Opportunities for individual male enterprise and success were becoming scarce, and men needed other ways to validate their flagging sense of masculinity (Kimmel, 1987). To counter the depersonalized regimentation and routine drudgery of factory work, the working male organized team sports such as football and baseball (Kimmel, 1990; Pettegrew, 1993; Walvin, 1987). Where else could men pit their strength, release their pent-up aggressiveness, and once again feel the masculine stirrings prompted by a hard-fought victory as well as on the football field? The popularity of organized sports spilled over to include large numbers of male spectators who could vicariously live through some aspect of their manhood with the mock battle of one team against another. Along with team sports, men frequented all-male saloons and clubs to find a shelter from the female presence and to revel in masculine comraderie. We can appreciate the strength of men's need to be with other men when we note that membership in fraternal lodges in the United States grew to an estimated 5.5 million members by 1901 (Carnes, 1989; Clawson, 1989; Pleck & Pleck, 1980) as well as the phenomenal popularity of "masculine" fictional literature (Miner, 1992; Pettegrew, 1993). Thus large numbers of working-class and middle-class men turned to other men for companionship on the playing fields, in saloons, and in fraternal clubs for reassurance that they were still, in fact, real men (Clawson, 1986; Gorn, 1986; Kingsdale, 1980).

Few formal organizations captured the spirit of the strenuous life and men's attempt to validate their masculinity by physical means better than the Boy Scouts of America (Hantover, 1980; Macleod, 1983; for an overview of Boy Scouts in British

The Historical Perspective

society, see Warren, 1987). In 1910 Ernest Thompson Seton, one of the founders of the Boy Scout movement in the United States, noted how scouting with its emphasis on the outdoors and strenuous physical activities was a desirable way to achieve manhood. To make his point, Seton emphasized the physical aspects of manhood over most others (for example, the intellectual) in the introduction to his book *Boy Scouts of America:*

> Realizing that *manhood,* not *scholarship,* is the first aim of education, we have sought out those pursuits which develop the finest character, the finest physique, and which may be followed out of doors, which, in a word, *make for manhood.* (Filene, 1986, p. 95)

The scouting movement was only one in a long line of social movements that attempted to give disenchanted males another chance at being real, muscular men. Where the scouting movement succeeded, others failed. One of the most ambitious and costly ventures in promoting the strenuous life occurred in East Tennessee. During the 1870s, the English author Sir Thomas Hughes felt compelled to assist the latter-born sons of England's aristocracy to develop their physical stamina and proper manly character. The "Will Wimbles," as Hughes dubbed them, were not entitled to their fathers' estates or titles because of primogeniture. Many of these men squandered their lives on frivolous activity and were a blight to many families. Hughes, a believer in a creed known as "muscular Christianity," thought honest labor and fresh air were the only salvation for the Will Wimbles. With a group of Boston capitalists, Hughes purchased some 40,000 acres in the East Tennessee wilderness and founded the village of Rugby. The transplanted Will Wimbles began a new life based on hard work and the principles of Christianity. Not surprisingly, the social experiment failed after only a few years, perhaps because the land was ill fit for farming but more probably because the Will Wimbles were ill fit for the strenuous life they found in the mountains of East Tennessee (Crowley & Crowley, 1963; Hughes, 1881/1973).

Men were not alone in the search for appropriate ways to express their roles during this period. Women also were moving into new areas and trying new roles (Peiss, 1986). Women who had been prevented from taking paid employment outside of the home during the early years of the nineteenth century were, by the middle of the century, a visible part of the work force. For example, between the years 1850 and 1870, the number of female factory workers jumped from 225,992 to 323,370 (Flexner, 1959). Besides factory work, women were moving into previously all-male occupations such as teaching, clerical work, and librarianship in increasing numbers (Garrison, 1974; Widdowson, 1984). The feminist movement that began at Seneca Falls continued to grow as women from different backgrounds became more vocal in their demands for an end to the separate and unequal spheres (Degler, 1980; Taylor, 1983).

Some few progressive men also joined forces with feminist women to struggle for women's rights. William Lloyd Garrison, Frederick Douglass, Robert Owen, Martin Delany, Parker Pillsbury, James Mott, and Thomas Wentworth, to name only a few, championed a profeminist stand in the latter decades of the nineteenth-century's battle against historic sexism (Kimmel & Mosmiller, 1992). Until very recently, these and other men's courageous stand went nearly unnoticed even among feminist historians (Strauss, 1982). Men's history will be added to immeasurably when their lives and contributions to nineteenth-century feminism are better known. Such study has recently caught the attention of a few dedicated historians and scholars (Doyle, 1987; Mosmiller, 1987; Strauss, 1982; Wagner, 1984, 1986).

The period of the he-man's strenuous life finally ended with men validating their masculinity in the ageless way of warfare and bloodshed. For almost sixty years, men had turned to sports, exclusive male enclaves, the glories of the Wild West, and even a few short-lived battle campaigns, all in an attempt to bolster their feelings of manliness. During these years, more and more women continued to fight for their basic right as citizens of this country—the right to vote. Most men feared the defiant suffragette movement because they knew that with this change in women's status, other more significant changes in the gender roles were sure to follow (Barker-Benfield, 1976; Donegan, 1985; Douglas, 1977). Almost as if providence had stepped in, World War I began and once more men were called upon to fulfill their manly destiny, that of warrior-soldier, and all was well in the separate spheres, at least for a few more years (Mrozek, 1987).

With the end of World War I, the separate worlds of the sexes turned topsy-turvy. The passage of the Nineteenth Amendment to the Constitution gave women the right to vote, and the war years showed that they could take over in a man's world when the doughboys had gone "over there." During the early 1920s, social customs and traditions changed drastically with the advent of the flapper, the

Moving toward Partnership (1920–1965)

The Historical Perspective

speakeasy, the Charleston, and sexual dalliances in the backseats of mass-produced Fords. The old props of the male role quickly became cultural dinosaurs. The modern era of gender roles, or the period of what the Plecks called "companionate providing," was ushered in.

The separate cultural spheres began to crumble as men and women spent more time in each other's company. For companionship, men turned to women rather than to other men, who now were seen as competitors and not as companions. With technology and specialization, men no longer validated their manliness in purely physical activities but turned to providing for their families as evidence of their manhood. The role of breadwinner, or good provider, became the primary element in the definition of masculinity.

During the 1920s, as the discharged soldiers traded in their rifles and shoulder patches for steady jobs and bimonthly paychecks, an economic disaster of monstrous proportions loomed on the horizon. In 1929 the stock market crash that set off the Great Depression struck affecting countless men, women, and children (Watkins, 1993). The male role of breadwinner became an anachronism almost overnight. A man without a job not only lost status in his own eyes but also in the eyes of his family (Komarovsky, 1940). Even though the ordinary jobless man had little to do with the causes of the depression, "[t]he suddenly-idle hands," wrote Studs Terkel (1970, p. 19), "blamed themselves, rather than society. . . . No matter that others suffered the same fate, the inner voice whispered, 'I'm a failure.'" Men once again found themselves caught in the dilemma of not being able to live up to the social expectation that counted, that of being a breadwinner. Rather than laying the blame for their emasculation on the rightful social sources, in this case the male gender itself and the economy, these angry men blamed themselves and felt the stinging self-indictment of being failures.

Either by chance or some sinister international plot, the United States economy and the male's damaged manhood were revitalized by yet another war. The age-old masculine attributes of courage, endurance, toughness, and "guts" were once again unfurled, and men found themselves playing at being real men, this time by dint of the combat role (Holmes, 1986; Stouffer, Suchman, DeVinney, Starr, & Williams, 1949). Men's lives weren't the only ones changed by the world wars. Untold numbers of women exchanged their aprons and kitchen utensils for coveralls and riveting guns during both global wars, an experience that helped shatter the stereotype of the "weaker sex" (Braybon, 1989; Honey, 1984; Milkman, 1987; Summerfield, 1989). After World War II, hundreds of thousands of men returned to take up the role of breadwinner in earnest, and women were forced to abdicate their wartime jobs and return to their kitchens and nurseries (Kesselman, 1990).

During the 1950s and early 1960s, North American men reasserted their superior role over women. Being a man meant raising career aspirations and accumulating status symbols as proof of masculinity (Whyte, 1957). Being a woman meant shuffling the kids to school and supporting your husband's driving ambition to make it to the top. Many women found themselves trapped in a monotonous life-style that some years later Betty Friedan would call the "feminine mystique." The "normalcy" of this period ended abruptly with the chaotic social movements of the late 1960s. The decade of the 1970s brought an end to cheap energy, and women joined the work force in unprecedented numbers (Bergman, 1986). Once again men faced new challenges to their superior male role and were finding fewer opportunities to prove themselves real men. Finally, some men began to ask themselves questions such as, "What does it really mean to be a man today?" or "What do other men and women expect of me simply because I have a penis between my legs?" Questions like these do not lend themselves to easy answers.

What value does a historical perspective of the male gender provide? We could answer this question in a general way by paraphrasing the words of the philosopher George Santayana and stating that ignorance of history dooms one to repeat the same mistakes over and over. One mistake that we can avoid as the result of a greater understanding of the history of the male gender is the erroneous belief that what society expects of males today has *always* been expected. For example, many males today believe they must appear to be strongly sexed and completely competent in sexual relationships in order to prove to themselves and to other men and women that they are, in fact, truly masculine. But we know from history that the expectation that men be more highly sexed than women is a relatively recent addition to the male gender. Likewise, many men today feel that aggressiveness is an essential and long-standing feature of the male gender. Again, however, we know that during the Christian era the ideal male was nonviolent. The practice of "turning one's cheek" rather than striking back in anger was expected of the spiritual man. Thus one of the significant values of a knowledge of the historical perspective is that we can see the contemporary male gender for what it really is—*a changing social phenomenon.*

Are there any features to today's male gender that do extend back to the beginnings of recorded history? The answer to this question is a straightforward "yes." The patriarchal social system in which the male in the role of father or husband dominates the female does appear throughout recorded Western history. Of course, there exists the possibility that in some prehistoric period the relationship between the sexes was more egalitarian or possibly even gynocratic. However, since the Greek and Roman eras, the prevalence of father-rule appears to be a consistent phenomenon in Western civilization.

Certainly other questions can be raised by our discussion of the history of the male gender and masculinity, but we will end our discussion of the historical perspective here and move on to an examination of the male experience from the biological perspective.

Aristrocrat 35	Passionate manhood 33	**important**
Bourgeois male 32	Patriarchy 25	**terms**
Chivalric male 30	Primogeniture 31	
Common man 35	Renaissance male 31	
Communal manhood 33	Self-made manhood 33	
Epic male 28	Spiritual male 29	

The Historical Perspective

suggested readings

Carnes, M. C., & Griffen, C. (Eds.). (1990). *Meanings for manhood: Constructions of masculinity in Victorian America*. Chicago: University of Chicago Press.

Filene, P. G. (1986). *Him/her/self* (2nd ed.). Baltimore: Johns Hopkins University Press.

Lerner, G. (1986). *The creation of patriarchy*. New York: Oxford University Press.

Mangan, J., & Walvin, J. (Eds.). (1987). *Manliness and morality: Middle-class masculinity in Britain and America, 1800–1940*. New York: St. Martin's Press.

Pleck, E., & Pleck, J. (Eds.). (1980). *The American man*. Englewood Cliffs, NJ: Prentice-Hall.

Rotundo, E. A. (1993). *American manhood: Transformations in masculinity from the Revolution to the modern era*. New York: Basic Books.

Chapter 3

The Biological Perspective

. . . the biological disadvantages accruing to the male are not so much due to what is in the Y chromosome as to what is not in it.
Ashley Montagu (1974)

When it comes down to the biological imperatives that are laid down for all men and women, there are only four: Only a man can impregnate; only a woman can menstruate, gestate, and lactate.
John Money and Patricia Tucker (1975)

To consider masculinity as dependent on innate biologic factors is to misunderstand the basis of genetics. But to consider masculinity as a purely social construct with no physiologic basis is scientifically dangerous.
Perry Treadwell (1987)

Ignorance of biological processes may doom efforts at social change to failure because we misidentify what the targets for change should be, and hence what our means should be to attain the change we desire.
Alice Rossi (1984)

At one time or another, we have all admired a curvaceous female or a muscular male. Clearly, we can all see that the sexes *are* different. But some people have gone beyond the obvious physical differences and concluded that the sexes differ in other less notable ways as well. For instance, some scientists theorize that male and female genders and traditional gender-typed characteristics such as male aggressiveness and female nurturance are largely the result of genetic differences (Wilson, 1978). Even the controversial double standard of sexual conduct that condones male promiscuity and restricts female sexual activity is thought to be programmed by genetic material (Symons, 1979; Wilson, 1982). However, others find little or no research evidence for the idea that biology is the *sole* cause of either gender-related roles or gender-typed behaviors or characteristics (Bleier, 1984; Pleck, 1981; Schifellite, 1987; Smoll & Schutz, 1990).

Although the "nature (biology) versus nurture (environment)" controversy is not new to scholarly circles, the tedious arguments over which one predominates in the shaping of human social behavior have once again, in the past decade or so, grabbed center stage. Surely, one reason for this encore performance is attributable to the rise in popularity of a new "hybrid" science called "sociobiology." Edward Wilson (1978, p. 16), the Harvard scientist primarily responsible for outlining sociobiology's basic tenets, defines it as "the systematic study of the biological basis of all forms of social behavior." While sociobiologists argue that gender-related roles, for instance, are by and large programmed by genes, sociobiology's opponents marshal contradictory evidence suggestive that genes alone are inadequate to explain the complexities of such social behaviors (Lewontin, Rose & Kamin, 1984).

Setting aside the merits, or the lack thereof, for sociobiology's position, we still find many social scientists who automatically turn a deaf ear, or worse, upon hearing the term *biology*. Why should the mere mention of biology cause so many to see red, so to speak? Surely, one reason for biology's "bad press" stems from how biology has been used in the last century or so. The unconscionable fact is that many have found biology a convenient means to oppress many minority groups or to bolster the status quo that favors the few over the many (Fausto-Sterling, 1985; Gould, 1981; Sapiro, 1985; Sayers, 1982). Given the historic misuses of biology, then, it is little wonder that many socially and politically conscious social scientists today find the mere mention of biology a stimulus that elicits more than a little anger and hostility.

A case in point may help illustrate the depth of animosity that biology engenders among many learned social scientists. Some years ago, Alice Rossi (1977) published a seminal paper on the interactive influences of biological and social forces on parenting behavior. Therein Rossi noted that a biosocial perspective—a meld of social, cultural, and biological factors—could provide new insights into some of the differences commonly found between women and men in their treatment and care of infants and children. However, the publication of this article soon became a *cause célèbre* among many social scientists who took Rossi to task for her views branding her along the way as a biological determinist and an advocate of the maternal instinct, one who didn't understand the political ramifications of her thinking, and stopping just short of suggesting that Rossi might even be a closet sociobiologist simply masquerading as a scholarly, feminist-oriented sociologist (Gross et al., 1979). All this because Rossi suggested that social scientists could benefit from taking an informed look at the chemicals circulating through women's and men's bodies when it comes to discussing parenting behavior! No one, a social scientist or otherwise, doubts for a minute that prenatal exposure to exogenous (i.e., external) chemicals like alcohol alters subsequent postnatal behavior (e.g., *Fetal Alcohol Syndrome*) or the use of synthetic steroids by athletes influences their performance (Barr, Streissguth, Darby, & Sampson, 1990; Taylor, 1985a, 1985b). Why, then, the big fuss over discussing some possible effects stemming from the many endogenous (i.e., internal) chemicals circulating through one's body?

Rossi defended herself by noting that in her opinion many in the social sciences either are limited to little more than a knee-jerk response or suffer a blind spot when it comes to an understanding of basic biological principles or of the many new advances in behavioral endocrinology (Crews, 1987). In other words, traditionally social scientists have little training or course work in the natural sciences during their professional schooling. For the most part, cultural anthropologists, psychologists, and sociologists are more comfortable theorizing about the socialization practices or the principles of reinforcement found in tribal societies rather than speculating about the subtle effects of the many interactive and circulating hormones found in the human body. Possibly, then, some of the antagonism found among social scientists toward biology today could be defused, at least in the future, if social science students would take more than a cursory look at both biology or chemistry during their college careers.

One fact must be kept in mind as we begin this chapter: Humans *are* biological creatures. Rather than present traditional gender-related roles and gender-typed behaviors as the inevitable outcomes of some biological imperative, however, we will present the biological perspective as one component—albeit an important component—in the male experience. Our overriding hope here is to help defuse some of the ignorance and/or antagonism toward taking a biological look at the male experience.

In this chapter we will first outline biological events that shape the physical development of the male fetus. Here we will concentrate on the functions that the Y chromosome and certain hormones play during crucial prenatal periods. Then we will examine the influence that testosterone, a powerful hormone, has on adult characteristics. Specifically, we will discuss testosterone's role in certain physical and behavioral areas.

prenatal events

To help us understand how our biology influences our development, we need to review some of the basic biological principles that pertain to genetic development.

Every human body contains billions of cells that we can think of as the building blocks of the body. Most cells in the human body contain twenty-three *pairs* of chromosomes, which under a powerful microscope look like tiny, threadlike strands of colored beads. Packed with their genetic materials, the chromosomes are chiefly responsible for either physical features such as height, hair texture, eye color, and skin pigmentation or the genetic sex of the body.

During pregnancy, cell bodies grow at a phenomenal rate. But how does cell growth occur? When we speak of cell growth, we usually mean the division of a cell's chromosome materials. When a cell divides, its twenty-three pairs of

The Biological Perspective

chromosomes first double to forty-six pairs, and then the cell divides into two separate cells, each again containing twenty-three pairs of chromosomes. Thus the original fertilized cell becomes two cells, then four cells, then eight cells, and so on. Within a matter of weeks, there are literally millions of cells.

We said that most cells contain twenty-three *pairs* of chromosomes. The sex cells, however, contain *only* twenty-three chromosomes. These sex cells are the unfertilized egg, or ovum, produced in a woman's ovaries and the sperm produced in a man's testes. Sex cells are an exception to the rule of division. The division of an unfertilized egg or sperm takes place without first doubling its chromosome materials; consequently, both egg and sperm have only half of the necessary chromosome materials for a complete human being. In fact, the only way an egg cell can survive is to be fertilized by a sperm cell. If unfertilized, the egg dies in a matter of days.

Now that we have briefly noted some of the biological principles relating to cells, chromosomes, and the division of cells, let's look more closely at how the male experience begins with a special sperm cell.

The Role of the X and the Y Chromosomes

For this discussion of biological sex development, we will divide the prenatal period into five stages (see Table 3.1). We will discuss the first two stages in this section, and the last three in the next section.

Conception occurs when a male's sperm penetrates a female's unfertilized egg. Of the twenty-three chromosomes in each, twenty-two govern the physical characteristics, and the twenty-third is a sex-determining chromosome, which is labeled either X or Y. A female's egg always contains an X chromosome, whereas a male's sperm can have either an X or a Y chromosome. With an **XX** combination, the genetic sex is female, and with an **XY** combination, the genetic sex is male. Therefore, a father's sperm determines the genetic sex of the embryo. Geneticists have determined in the last several years that a very small portion of the Y chromosome determines maleness, what they call the **testis-determining factor** or **TDF** for short (Angier, 1990; Page et al., 1987; Sinclair et al., 1990).

The sex-determining characteristics of male sperm are only one of the interesting features coming to light in various laboratories across the country. For example, all sperm are not equal. Sperm bearing a Y chromosome are what scientists call **androsperm,** and they are different in size and structure from sperm carrying an X chromosome, or **gynosperm.** Androsperm have a sharp, spearlike head, while gynosperm have a rounder, more blunted head (see Figure 3.1). The androsperm's longer, more energetic whiplike tail allows it to move faster than a gynosperm. Furthermore, the androsperm appear to move better in an alkaline environment, whereas the gynosperm better tolerate an acidic environment.

The fact that the androsperm are faster than the gynosperm raises an interesting point. Androsperm impregnate more eggs than do gynosperm, accounting for what scientists believe to be a ratio of somewhere between 145 and 160 male conceptions for every 100 female conceptions (Money & Tucker, 1975). Of course, this male-biased imbalance does not last for long. Given the male embryo's greater chance of spontaneous abortion, some nine months later, the male-female ratio has dropped to

table 3.1	The Five Stages of Male and Female Development
Stage I.	Chromosome Sex: XY = genetic male, XX = genetic female.
	During the first weeks of the embryo's growth, the same internal and external sex tissue, or anlagen, develop in both genetic sexes.
	A. Internal anlagen
	1. Sex gland
	2. Wolffian duct
	3. Müllerian duct
	B. External anlagen
	1. Genital tubercle
	2. Urethral fold
	3. Labioscrotal swelling
Stage II.	Gonadal Sex: testes = male, ovaries = female.
	After the eighth week of gestation, the sex gland develops as either testes or ovaries. The factor responsible for this difference is a genetic message contained in the Y chromosome.
Stage III.	Hormonal Sex: In males, testosterone and the Müllerian-inhibiting substance are produced by the testes.
	A. Testosterone causes the Wolffian duct to develop as
	1. Vas deferens
	2. Seminal vesicles
	3. Prostate gland
	B. The Müllerian-inhibiting substance prevents the Müllerian duct from developing into the female structures:
	1. Fallopian tubes
	2. Uterus
	3. Upper part of the vagina
Stage IV.	External Sex: In males, testosterone causes the external sex anlagen (Stage IB) to develop into the male form rather than the female form.
	A. The genital tubercle becomes the penis rather than the clitoris.
	B. The urethral fold becomes the shaft of the penis rather than the labia minor.
	C. The labioscrotal swelling becomes the scrotum rather than the labia major.
Stage V.	Assigned Sex: At birth, the announcement, "It's a boy!"

approximately 105 male live births for every 100 female. The androsperm's greater speed in the race for the egg appears to be a biological "hedge" against their susceptibility to abort.

Moreover, the X chromosome contains considerably more genetic material and is about 5 times larger than the Y chromosome prompting some to suggest the Y chromosome is rather "puny" compared to the X chromosome. The difference in

The Biological Perspective

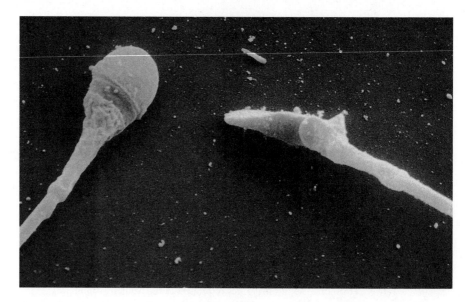

an X's and a Y's genetic materials becomes crucial in sex-linked diseases. A **sex-linked disease** is one that is directly attributable to a defect in a particular gene. As males have less genetic material in their Y chromosome they are prone to a greater number of sex-linked conditions than are females. In *The Natural Superiority of Women,* Ashley Montagu (1974) lists over sixty specific sex-linked conditions that primarily afflict males (e.g., hemophilia, retinitis pigmentosa, and juvenile glaucoma). Let's turn our attention to one such sex-linked disease and see how the Y chromosome's lack of genetic material causes harmful, if not lethal, consequences for a male.

Hemophilia, or the bleeder's disease, is an inherited illness caused by a defective recessive gene located in a mother's X-bearing sex chromosome. If a father's contribution is a *normal* X-bearing sex chromosome—causing an XX genetic female—his X chromosome will suppress the effects of the mother's defective gene. However, such is not the case for an XY genetic male. In this case, the Y-bearing sex chromosome contributed by the father does not contain the necessary genetic material to suppress or override the mother's defective gene. Thus the Y chromosome's lack of genetic material accounts to a great degree for most of the inherited sex-linked conditions noted by Montagu.

However, not all problems associated with a male's genetic endowment relate to the Y chromosome's smallness or sparsity of genetic material. In some rare instances, the problem is just the reverse: a surplus of sex chromosomes. Recall that normally a male has two sex chromosomes, an X and a Y. Sometimes, however, a male has an additional X chromosome, or an XXY genetic pattern **(Klinefelter's syndrome),** or an extra Y chromosome, or an XYY pattern (the **"supermale" syndrome).** The Klinefelter male has an unusually small penis, sterile testes, and usually some sign of mental retardation. As for the supermale, when a group of researchers found a higher than expected number of XYY genetic patterns among prison inmates, speculation grew that the additional Y sex chromosome predisposed these men to a life of crime. However, subsequent research found that the su-permale is not prone to crime, although he is thought more likely to lose his control and "fly off the handle," thus coming to the attention of authorities more often than the normal XY genetic male (Money & Ehrhardt, 1972; Schifellite, 1987).

Now that we've discussed some of the problems that can occur to a biological male, let's turn our attention to the majority of cases in which conception produces a normal XY genetic male and follow his course during the remainder of the prenatal period.

During the first several weeks after conception, the XY embryo goes through an explosive growth period in which the original fertilized egg divides and redivides into millions of cells. Throughout this period, both internal and external sex structures begin to take shape. One point that is frequently overlooked is that for the first six to eight weeks after conception the embryo is *ambisexual,* meaning it has specialized internal and external sex tissues, or **anlagen,** for both sexes (see Table 3.1, Stage IA and B). For example, the embryo has a general, all-purpose sex gland that could develop into either testes or ovaries. Although scientists do not as yet fully understand what makes an XY embryo's sex gland develop into testes rather than ovaries, growing evidence suggests that a specialized chemical substance called *H-Y antigen* located in the Y chromosome causes the sex gland to develop into testes and not ovaries (Jones et al., 1979). However, one thing is clear; sometime during the third month, a male embryo's sex gland develops into testes (see Table 3.1, Stage II). This development causes the powerful hormone testosterone to begin its crucial work on the remaining internal and external sex structures. In the next section we will focus on testosterone's contribution to the development of a normal male.

A male embryo's newly formed testes produce **testosterone,** one of a group of hormones commonly referred to as *androgens*. Strictly speaking, testosterone's major role is to masculinize the already formed genetic male embryo. It may sound strange that a hormone is needed to accomplish the work already begun by the Y chromosome. However, the fact remains that without sufficient amounts of testosterone—or if the male embryo's sex tissues (that is, anlagen) are somehow immune to testosterone's masculinizing effects—the male embryo will develop as a female, albeit a sterile female (Hines, 1982; Money, 1974, 1987; Svare & Kinsley, 1987).

Testosterone's Contribution to Prenatal Development

The Internal Sex Structures. As noted in Table 3.1 (Stage III), sometime during the third or fourth month, a male embryo's testes begin to produce testosterone, which subsequently directs the developmental course of the Wolffian duct. The **Wolffian duct** is an important part of a male embryo's sex structures for it will, with the help of testosterone, develop into three separate sex-related structures: the vas deferens, the seminal vesicles, and the prostate gland (see Figure 3.2). We will describe the workings of these three structures in detail in a later section of this chapter. For the moment, we should note that the sole purpose of these structures is to move the sperm produced in a mature male's testes outward, all the way to the end of the penis. Working together, these three structures form a type of transportation system that allows mature sperm to fulfill their primary purpose, impregnation.

The Biological Perspective

figure 3.2

The prenatal development sequence of the male and female internal sex structures. From John Money, *Sex Errors of the Body: Dilemmas, Education, Counseling,* figs. 3 and 4, 1968. Reprinted by permission of Johns Hopkins University Press, Baltimore, MD.

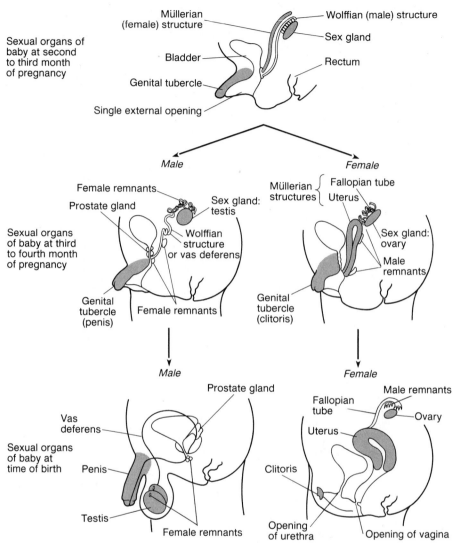

The testosterone-induced Wolffian duct's evolution into separate male sex structures leaves a fetus with one other internal sex tissue, the **Müllerian duct.** The Müllerian duct is also programmed to develop into three structures: the female's fallopian tubes, uterus, and upper part of the vagina. If by some quirk of nature the Müllerian duct were to develop in a male fetus along with the post-Wolffian structures, the male would have both male and female internal sex structures and be classified as a *hermaphrodite* (for a fascinating discussion of the social construction of hermaphroditism, see: Epstein, 1990). But most often, nature's way is to prevent this from happening. To accomplish this, the testes produce a chemical substance that prevents the

Male and Female Identical

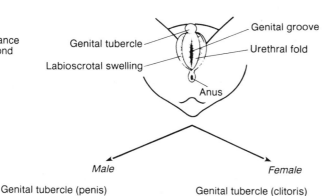

Sexual appearance of baby at second to third month of pregnancy

Genital tubercle
Labioscrotal swelling
Genital groove
Urethral fold
Anus

figure 3.3
The prenatal developmental sequence of the male and female external sex structures. From John Money, *Sex Errors of the Body: Dilemmas, Education, Counseling,* figs. 3 and 4, 1968. Reprinted by permission of Johns Hopkins University Press, Baltimore, MD.

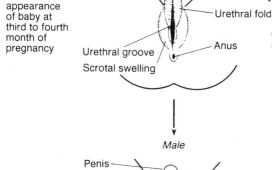

Male

Female

Sexual appearance of baby at third to fourth month of pregnancy

Genital tubercle (penis)
Urethral fold
Urethral groove
Scrotal swelling
Anus

Genital tubercle (clitoris)
Vulval groove
Inner labial fold
Outer labial swelling
Anus

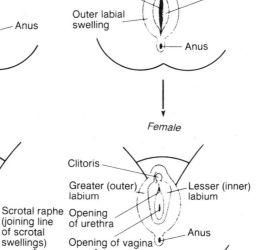

Male

Female

Sexual appearance of baby at time of birth

Penis
Urethral raphe (joining line of urethral fold)
Scrotum
Scrotal raphe (joining line of scrotal swellings)
Anus

Clitoris
Greater (outer) labium
Lesser (inner) labium
Opening of urethra
Opening of vagina
Anus

Müllerian duct's development and subsequently causes the duct to shrivel up. The exact chemical ingredient responsible for this is not known. For obvious reasons, scientists call this inferred chemical the **Müllerian-inhibiting substance.**

The External Sex Structures. When most people speak of external sex organs, they normally mean a male's penis and scrotum and a female's clitoris. Many people are unaware that a male's penis and a female's clitoris both develop out of an identical, or ambisexual, sex tissue known as a **genital tubercle** (see Figure 3.3). During the first six to eight weeks after conception, both genetic male and female fetuses have three identical, or ambisexual, sex organs, namely, a genital tubercle, a **urethral fold,** and a **labioscrotal swelling** (see Table 3.1, Stage IB). Once again, the

The Biological Perspective

development of a penis instead of a clitoris is dependent on the presence or absence of testosterone. If testosterone is present during the third or fourth month, as we would expect in a genetic male fetus with normal testes, then the genital tubercle will develop as a penis. If, on the other hand, a genetic male's testes do not produce enough testosterone, then the genital tubercle will develop as a clitoris or as an immature and poorly developed penis. Clearly, testosterone plays the significant role in the development of a male's external sex organs. With testosterone, each of the original ambisexual sex tissues develops as a specific male sex organ: The genital tubercle becomes a penis, the urethral fold develops as the shaft of the penis, and the labioscrotal swelling forms the scrotal sack that holds a male's testes.

Thus far we have seen how testosterone causes the original ambisexual internal and external sex tissues to develop into their respective male sex structures or organs. But testosterone's effects on a developing fetus are not limited only to sex structures; certain portions of the brain are also affected.

Testosterone and the Brain. Most people recognize a very basic sex difference in the fact that women menstruate and men do not. A woman's menstrual cycle is controlled by certain hormones secreted by the pituitary gland. For a woman, certain glands located in the brain secrete specialized hormones that cause menstruation if she is not pregnant and lactation if she is pregnant. For a man, however, there are no clear-cut external signs of an interaction between certain glands located in the brain and his sex organs. But scientists are now convinced that testosterone causes the male's brain or more specifically certain glands in the male's brain to secrete specific hormones that influence his sex organs and their functions (Changeux, 1985; De Vries et al., 1984; Snyder, 1985; Wundram, 1984). Let's see how this happens.

As already noted, testosterone is chiefly responsible for the masculinization of the internal and external sex tissues. However, some testosterone finds its way through the blood system to the hypothalamus located deep in the brain causing some regions in a male's brain to develop differently than in a female's brain (Allen et al., 1989). Under the influence of the hypothalamus, the pituitary gland secretes a second hormone called the **interstitial cell stimulating hormone** (ICSH) back to the testes. Within the testes, ICSH stimulates the Leydig cells to produce more testosterone and the entire cycle starts over (see Figure 3.4). In a mature male, the pituitary gland secretes a second hormone called the **follicle stimulating hormone** (FSH). The major function of FSH is to produce sperm in the testes. Testosterone is therefore essential during certain critical periods of fetal development to establish an important link to parts of the brain, which then secrete other hormones thought to be necessary for male development (Levine, 1966).

Testosterone is the crucial ingredient that assures a genetic male will develop normally. Because of testosterone, the words, "It's a boy!" are spoken at birth (Table 3.1, Stage V).

For the first three to four months after birth, the testosterone level remains high, after which it drops off the next ten to twelve years. Testosterone production dramatically increases with the onset of puberty, and once again several physical changes occur in a male's body.

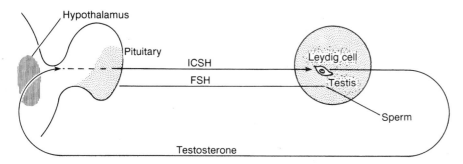

figure 3.4
Testosterone's effects on the hypothalamic–pituitary glands and the resultant hormones. Adapted from *"Sex Differences in the Brain,"* by Seymour Levine. Copyright © 1966 by *Scientific American, Inc.* All rights reserved.

During adolescence, the period between childhood and early adulthood, family ties weaken and an adolescent male begins to move toward a more diverse and extended network of friends and acquaintances. Consequently, he is often beset with new social demands as he tries to fit in with his peer group. As if the social aspects were not unnerving enough, his body also begins to play strange tricks on him. For years, a young boy took his body for granted, but no longer.

In this section we will focus first on the physical changes brought on by a resurgence of testosterone in the body. Next we will discuss some of the research that deals with sexual arousal, emotions, and mood changes that appear to be related to testosterone levels. Finally we will examine the evidence linking hormones with male aggression and nurturing behaviors.

postnatal events

Adolescence begins with the onset of puberty. Puberty is normally considered as that period when a male's and a female's internal sex organs (testes and ovaries) are capable of producing the means for reproduction (sperm and eggs). For a female, puberty is ushered in rather dramatically with the beginning of a regular monthly menstrual cycle. For a male, however, puberty sneaks up; no single sign tells him when his sperm are viable, or capable, of reproduction. Puberty for a young adolescent male is marked, rather, by a series of physical changes known as **secondary sex characteristics,** which develop slowly (Katchadourian, 1987). What follows are some of the major physical changes that mark a boy's passage into puberty.

During the early teen years, a biological mechanism somehow programs the hypothalamus and the pituitary glands to begin producing quantities of FSH and ICSH to stimulate the testes to produce viable sperm and large amounts of testosterone, respectively. As the production of testosterone increases, the testes become larger and the scrotal sack takes on a wrinkled look. The shaft of the penis becomes larger, and sprouts of coarse pubic hair appear at the base of the shaft. Besides the appearance of pubic hair, other parts of the body begin to show alterations in hair distribution, for example, the armpits, the chest, the upper lip, and the hairline around the temples. The larynx, or voice box, grows larger and causes the voice to deepen. The skin coarsens and becomes oily, causing skin problems such as acne. A male's overall physique changes as his shoulders broaden, his musculature increases, and he gets taller and heavier. A male's physical strength dramatically increases as his bones harden and his muscle tone increases. So, as this quick review shows, within a matter

The Changing Male Body

The Biological Perspective

of a few years, an adolescent male's body goes through some remarkable changes all because of that wondrous hormone—testosterone. If these changes weren't enough, adolescence also finds a young male's attention turning more and more toward matters of sex. Testosterone seems to play a role here as well.

Testosterone and Male Sexual Arousal

As just noted, adolescence is a time when a young male's thoughts often turn to sex. His first sexual stirrings may come unexpectedly in nocturnal emissions (commonly called "wet dreams") or possibly in the first serious conscious exploration of sexual feelings, thoughts, and experiences through masturbation. No matter though, for while an adolescent male's interest in sexual matters is rising, so too is his testosterone level. The obvious question then becomes what role, if any, does a male's testosterone level play in his sexual arousal and interests?

For some time now researchers have studied testosterone and the role it plays in adolescent male growth and sexual development (e.g., Buckley et al., 1988; Richman & Kirsch, 1988). However, many of the early studies produced more confusion than clarity. Much of the confusion was a product of poorly designed studies that all too often confounded the effects of hormones with those of certain psychosocial factors like early socialization and peer group pressures on a young male's sexual arousal and activity. More recent studies have attended to correcting methodological issues and have begun to shed insight into testosterone's effect on males' sexual interest and behavior. In this section, we'll focus on testosterone's effect on a male's sexual behavior by concentrating on studies dealing with castration, androgen-blocking drugs, and reduced gonadal functioning.

For centuries, **castration** (i.e., the removal of the testes) was a common enough procedure sometimes having nothing to do with reproductive sexuality per se. For instance, during the middle ages, prepubertal choir boys whose voices soared into the soprano and contralto ranges were often castrated (called *castrati*) to preserve their "angelic" voices. However, in most instances, castration was generally performed to eliminate a man's sexual interest or prevent sexual activity. Abundant documentation exists of the common practice of castrating men so that they could watch asexually over their female charges (eunuchs) or of those castrated because a civil or religious authority judged their sexual behavior too aberrant or perverted for customary social standards (D'Emilio & Freedman, 1988; Katz, 1985; Tannahill, 1982). And more recently, castration has been indicated as therapy for men suffering from advanced testis cancer, a treatment likely to produce physical, emotional, and psychological side effects (Reiker, Edbril, & Garnick, 1985). Given all the history then, can we say emphatically that castration supports a case for testosterone's influence on a man's sexual interest or activity? Well, not necessarily so.

While some studies find castration leads to a marked reduction in a man's sexual interest and behavior (Heim, 1981), others report little or no lessening of a man's sexual activity after castration (Ford & Beach, 1951). Still others report that the most important variable in judging the effect of castration on a man's sexual interest and activity is the timing of the procedure itself. Specifically, males castrated *before* puberty show little subsequent sexual interest as adults whereas males castrated *after* puberty show few signs of reduced sexual motivation and activity (Feder, 1984). Thus studies of castration's effects do not provide a clear answer about the relationship between male hormones and sexual arousal and behavior.

One reason why such studies may not be the best way to study testosterone's effect on male sexuality is that for most men castration is the ultimate act of emasculation. The fact that most men define their manhood, at least a significant part of it, in terms of an intact genitalia prevents one from finding a large enough sample of men for whom castration would not have significant emotional and psychological consequences. Thus if sexual interest subsides after a man is castrated, we could not unequivocally say whether such a condition resulted either from his absented testosterone or his anxiety over "being less of a man." For the moment then, castration studies are not the best way to approach the issue of testosterone and sexual arousal.

Through the marvels of chemistry a number of synthetic drugs have recently been introduced in both European and North American markets that markedly reduce the levels of male testosterone without genital mutilation. One of the more widely marketed "chemical-castrators," known best by its trade name **Depo-Provera,** has been used primarily with sex offenders as a way to stop their unacceptable sexual behavior. Although Depo-Provera drastically reduces male androgens, evidence that it also reduces sexual motivation is not clear (Bain, 1987; Brown, 1987; Cooper, 1986). However, "for some patients," write sex researchers John Money and Richard Bennett (1981, p. 132), "[Depo-Provera] proved to be the only form of treatment that induced a long-term remission of symptoms and kept them off a treadmill of imprisonment." Thus studies of Depo-Provera and other antiandrogenic drugs lend credibility to the argument that testosterone influences a man's sexual arousal.

A man's androgen production can also be reduced by a number of diseases leading to a condition called **hypogonadism.** If such a condition occurs before puberty, a male's yet-to-be developed primary and secondary sex characteristics will be severely blunted as will his subsequent sexual arousal. However, if the condition occurs after puberty, there is far less disruption in male development and sexual interests, a finding much like that reported in castrated post-pubertal males. Thus, based on numerous studies, most sex researchers today accept that testosterone production appears essential for "normal" male sexual development (Bancroft, 1984).

Not surprisingly, hypogonadal males are often treated with androgen-replacement therapy. Although these males can experience erections if stimulated with erotic films, for example, their flagging sexual interests often require the introduction of androgens to rehabilitate their nearly nonexistent sexual arousal (Drucker, 1984; Findlay, Place, & Snyder, 1989). Interestingly, numerous studies have found women's sexual interests and activity similarly related to their androgen levels—a woman's ovaries and adrenal glands produce androgens (Sherwin, Gelfand, & Brender 1985).

In conclusion then, testosterone's role in male sexual interest and behavior seems quite substantial. However, after reviewing the recent literature on androgen's effects on male sexual arousal, Robert Crooks and Karla Baur (1990, p. 178) still

The Biological Perspective

sound a cautionary note, "we must continue to be aware that human sexual behavior is so tremendously individual that it is difficult to specify the precise effects of hormones on erotic arousal and expression."

Testosterone and Emotions

Many people believe that women are susceptible to bouts of elation, happiness, or plain good feelings on one day and sullen, morose, or even depressed a week later. One of the more prevalent stereotypes of women is the extreme changes in their emotionality. Ask almost anyone the cause for a woman's changeable emotional state and he or she will probably answer: because of her menstrual period (McFarlane, Martin & Williams, 1988). Translated, that simply means a woman's emotional life is supposedly controlled by the cyclic nature of her hormones. For centuries, people have believed a woman's menstrual cycle and the flow of menstrual blood were chiefly responsible for all sorts of negative female characteristics, ranging from volatile personality to being thought unclean and therefore to be avoided (Delaney, Lupton & Toth, 1988).

When asked about men's emotionality though, people are likely to recite another popular stereotype that men are not particularly emotional. Furthermore, most people believe that men are not influenced by their hormones, at least not to the extent that women are. Because men do not have an obvious sign of a regular cyclic event like menstruation, most people doubt that men are as likely to be influenced emotionally by their hormones. But we have already noted how testosterone affects a male's body and his sexual interests. Can it be that testosterone also affects a male's emotionality? Similarly, does testosterone in men's bodies go through periodic rising and falling cycles as the hormones estrogen and progesterone do in women's bodies? The answers to these questions have only recently been sought by researchers, and the initial studies are quite enlightening.

During the early 1970s, a few researchers reported that males have fluctuations or large cyclical intervals in their hormonal levels (Kihlstrom, 1971; Ramey, 1972). Since then, a small number of studies about the various lengths of men's hormone cycles have been published. For example, C. A. Fox (et al., 1972) took daily blood samples from one male for a period of eighty-six days and found large fluctuations in his testosterone levels. Interestingly, Fox reported that high levels of testosterone were not associated with this man's desire for sex. Fox's research would suggest, then, that high levels of testosterone are not the cause of an adolescent male's interest in sex.

Although Fox found large daily fluctuations in testosterone, he found them only in one man. Some may argue though we cannot infer the same fluctuations for all men. Furthermore, Fox did not report any fluctuating cycles of more than a day. What about the possibility that testosterone may fluctuate in increasing and decreasing cycles from week to week or even longer, much like a female's normal twenty-eight-day menstrual cycle? An extensive study conducted by Charles Doering may shed light on these questions.

Doering and several colleagues (1978) studied the testosterone levels of twenty men for sixty days. They found a majority had identifiable testosterone cycles ranging from three to thirty days, with several of the cycles clustering around twenty-one to twenty-three days. Based on the research reported thus far, testosterone levels definitely fluctuate daily and also reveal longer cycles from several days to several weeks in length. But is there a relationship between a man's testosterone level and his emotional state?

Once again, Doering's research has provided some interesting findings. Every other day, when the men had their blood samples taken, they also completed a psychological test called the *Multiple Affect Adjective Checklist* (MAACL). The MAACL measures several different emotional states, including anxiety, hostility, and depression. Doering found testosterone levels did not relate to either hostility or anxiety measures. Surprisingly, however, testosterone levels did relate in a significant way to reported feelings of depression. As the males' levels of testosterone *increased,* they were more likely to report feeling depressed. Generalizing from Doering's research, we might infer that a male's feeling sad or mildly depressed *may* be linked to an increase in his testosterone. In another study Mary Brown Parlee (1978) found evidence of regular cycles in men's emotional states. Parlee did not measure the testosterone levels of her fifteen males, however. Nevertheless, men, like women, seem to have regular fluctuating hormone cycles, and there is some slight evidence that a male's testosterone level affects his emotional state, at least with respect to depression.

One of the most persistent beliefs about males is that they are predisposed toward aggression. *Aggression* is defined here as the *intentional* inflicting of physical or psychological pain on another. In looking to the animal kingdom, we find evidence that the males of most species are more aggressive than the females (Svare & Kinsley, 1987), although there are several exceptions to this sex difference; for example, among hamsters and gibbons where the females display more aggressivity than the males (Moyer, 1978). Not surprisingly then, with the weight of countless animal studies, many social scientists have looked to biology for a clue to understand human aggression. After reviewing over fifty studies of human aggression, psychologists Eleanor Maccoby and Carol Jacklin (1974, p. 243) concluded, "Aggression is related to levels of sex hormones, and can be changed by experimental administration of these hormones." But before we too quickly close the book on male aggression and testosterone, let's review some of the studies.

Testosterone and Aggression

As already noted, testosterone levels increase during adolescence, a period often noted also for increases in physical aggression (Sands, 1954). But can we then assume that testosterone and physical aggression are causally linked? During the 1970s, a spate of studies appeared giving a rather mixed set of answers to this question.

One of the first to put the issue to a test was Harold Persky and several of his colleagues (1971) who studied two groups of normal men; a group of eighteen college students whose ages ranged between seventeen and twenty-eight and another group of fifteen whose ages ranged between thirty-three and sixty-six. Persky measured their testosterone levels as well as their scores on a variety of psychological tests one of which was the *Buss-Durkee Hostility Inventory,* a paper-and-pencil test purported to measure the likelihood that a respondent would get into a fight or lose his temper, for instance. Persky did find a significant relationship between testosterone levels and the scores on the *Buss-Durkee* but only among the younger group.

The Biological Perspective

Soon afterwards, Leo Kreuz and Robert Rose (1972) studied the testosterone levels of a very different set of men—prison inmates who were classified as either fighters or nonfighters on the basis of the number of times they had been put into solitary confinement for fighting. Both groups were also given the *Buss-Durkee* test—the same one used by Persky. Kreuz and Rose found no relationship between the prisoners' testosterone levels and their incidents of fighting nor on their hostility scores. Other researchers followed suit and, in the main, tended to find little or no relationship between testosterone levels and various measures of aggression (Doering et al., 1975, 1978; Ehrenkranz, Bliss & Sheard, 1974; Meyer-Bahlburg et al., 1974).

What can be said of testosterone levels and male aggression then? Do increased levels of testosterone stimulate male aggression as some think (Bahr, 1976)? Or could it be the other way around: Aggressive acts lead to an increase in testosterone levels? Or could it be that some other variable such as stress may affect both aggression and androgen levels (Hoyenga & Hoyenga, 1979)? A majority of researchers tend to discount a causal link between testosterone levels and physical aggression (Fausto-Sterling, 1992; Pleck, 1981; Tieger, 1980). One thing seems certain, though, male aggression and its causes will remain a serious issue for further research. If we are going to continue studying the connections between hormonal influences and aggression, though, we need more accurate and valid methods for measuring both variables (Fausto-Sterling, 1992; Rose, 1975).

Let's now move to yet another area of adult behavior where researchers have looked for possible hormonal influences.

Testosterone and Nurturant Behaviors

In many people's minds, men are not cut out to take care of infants. After being asked to hold their baby or to change its diaper, more than a few have responded, "That's woman's work! Anyway, women know how to do it better." Apparently, many men believe that something in women—possibly an instinct or their hormones—naturally predisposes them to bathe, powder, diaper, and feed little ones better than men can. But the facts do not support such thinking.

In many animal species, males perform a number of care-taking behaviors such as nest building, incubating the eggs, and later on protecting the young while the mother is off in search of food. Among primates, there is considerable evidence of strong childrearing behaviors among males (Lamb, 1986; Mitchell, 1969). Therefore, we cannot say that males in all species do not take an active and responsible role in raising the young. But what of the research evidence among humans?

In a study conducted by Anke Ehrhardt and Susan Baker (1978), seventeen young females who had been prenatally exposed to high levels of androgen were found to exhibit few socially prescribed "maternal" behaviors. For example, these young girls showed little interest in playing with dolls and taking care of infants, and in general, they did not prefer to play the role of mother in fantasies or games. However, we cannot generalize from this study that normal males with their exposure to prenatal androgens are predisposed against acting in nurturant ways. In Ehrhardt and Baker's study, ten young males who were prenatally exposed to excessive amounts of androgens were actually *more* interested in taking care of infants than were their normal brothers. After reviewing this study, Joseph Pleck (1981, p. 173) concludes that "the presence of male sex hormones during prenatal development appears to suppress nurturant interest in females but not in males." In fact, the only barriers preventing males from behaving in nurturant ways seem to be the long-standing prejudices on the part of society and many men's reluctance to share in the daily activities of raising their children.

We have covered several topics in our discussion of testosterone's influence on a male after birth. First we saw how testosterone sets off a series of physical changes in the adolescent male. Next we found that testosterone is linked to a male's sexuality. Then we reviewed some evidence that suggests that high levels of testosterone may play a role in depression among males. Lastly we could find little conclusive evidence that testosterone either causes aggression or limits nurturant activity among males.

Most people would agree that a powerful hallucinogenic drug like lysergic acid diethylamide (LSD) can cause a person to act in unusual ways. Even so, few people would condemn the study of drugs and their effects on people's behaviors. However, whenever the effects of hormones are discussed, many feminists immediately react negatively, often labeling the discussion reactionary or politically motivated. Hormones are neither political nor biased in favor of traditional, egalitarian, or ultrafeminist definitions of male and female behaviors. The fact is hormones produce and control certain biological functions. Testosterone causes a penis rather than a clitoris to develop in a fetus. How the penis is used or what symbolic significance is attached to it has nothing to do with the workings of the hormone on the basic sex tissue. Likewise, testosterone causes a young male to develop broad shoulders and large muscles. How a young male uses his strength depends on the environment in which he finds himself, not on the amount of testosterone circulating in his bloodstream. It is hoped that we can move beyond the rhetoric that condemns the biological perspective as being the enemy of change in outdated and culturally determined gender-related roles and begin to appreciate and understand more fully the mysteries locked in puny chromosomes and powerful hormones.

---

important terms

Androsperm *46*
Anlagen *49*
Castration *54*
Depo-Provera *55*
Follicle stimulating hormone (FSH) *52*
Genital tubercle *51*
Gynosperm *46*
Hemophilia *48*
Hypogonadism *55*
Interstitial cell stimulating hormone (ICSH) *52*
Klinefelter's syndrome (XXY) *48*
Labioscrotal swelling *51*
Müllerian duct *50*
Müllerian-inhibiting substance *51*
Secondary sex characteristics *53*
Sex-linked disease *48*
Supermale syndrome (XYY) *48*
Testosterone *49*
Testis-determining factor (TDF) *46*
Urethral fold *51*
Wolffian duct *49*
XX *46*
XY *46*

The Biological Perspective

suggested readings

Bleier, R. (1984). *Science and gender: A critique of biology and its theories on women*. New York: Pergamon Press.

Fausto-Sterling, A. (1985). *Myths of gender: Biological theories about women and men*. New York: Basic Books.

Gould, S. (1981). *The mismeasure of man*. New York: Norton.

Julty, S. (1979). *Men's bodies, men's selves*. New York: Delta.

Money, J., & Tucker, P. (1975). *Sexual signatures*. Boston: Little, Brown.

Schifellite, C. (1987). Beyond Tarzan and Jane genes: Toward a critique of biological determinism. In M. Kaufman (Ed.), *Beyond patriarchy: Essays by men on pleasure, power, and change* (pp. 45–63). New York: Oxford University Press.

Treadwell, P. (1987). Biologic influences on masculinity. In H. Brod (Ed.), *The making of masculinities: The new men's studies* (pp. 259–285). Boston: Allen & Unwin.

Chapter 4

The Psychological Perspective

The great enemy of the truth is very often not the lie—deliberate, contrived and dishonest—but the myth—persistent, persuasive and unrealistic. Too often we hold fast to the clichés of our forebears. We subject all facts to a prefabricated set of interpretations. We enjoy the comfort of opinion without the discomfort of thought.

John F. Kennedy (1962)

The story of psychologists' attempts to understand and to measure femininity and masculinity is a chronicle of failure. For 60 years psychologists have tried to quantify "MF," but without success.* They failed, I believe, not because methodology for studying personality traits was in the early stages of its development—although it was—but because adequate conceptions of femininity and masculinity were lacking. The failure was fundamentally conceptual, not technical.

Miriam Lewin (1984a)

*In this context, *MF* refers to the predominantly psychological measures of a person's gender-typed attitudes, interests, and traits considered as indications of a person's sense of masculinity or femininity.

Now that we've had a chance to examine some of the historical roots and biological underpinnings of the male experience, we begin yet another perspective, the psychological one. For the most part, psychologists focus their study on the individual, on those unique and personal characteristics that distinguish one person from another. To begin, we will look briefly at what most people believe typifies or distinguishes males from females; in other words, we will look at the common gender stereotypes as well as noting some of the problems and pitfalls in the research dealing with gender differences. Next we will deal with the many presumed intellectual and social differences attributed to each gender. After this, we will turn our attention to a developmental overview of the important features found in a male's life span. Lastly we will highlight a mainstay in the psychological perspective, namely, one's gender identity, and concentrate on two very different approaches to this construct.

Although psychology borrows heavily from other disciplines such as sociology and anthropology, we will save our discussion of their contributions for the two chapters that follow. Now let's consider some presumed gender differences and see what psychologists have learned about male-female similarities and differences in over fifty years of research.

gender differences

Obviously, males and females differ in their genital and secondary sex characteristics. But do they differ in the ways they think and act as well? If we accept how people typically describe males and females, the answer is a resounding yes. In fact, for decades now, people have typically portrayed females and males as possessing relatively antithetical, or opposite, traits and/or personality characteristics. For instance, males are usually cast as aggressive, decisive, independent, and unemotional, whereas females are viewed as submissive, dependent, flighty, and emotional (Broverman, Vogel, Broverman, Clarkson & Rosenkrantz, 1972; Fernberger, 1948; Williams & Bennett, 1975; see Table 4.1). Although we might think such generalizations or **gender stereotypes** are a thing of the past, researchers continue to uncover that people still believe that males and females differ in relatively stereotypical ways (Bales, 1988; Freeman, 1987; Rajecki, DeGraaf-Kaser, & Rasmussen, 1992; Smith & Midlarsky, 1985; Walczak, 1988; Werner & LaRussa, 1985; Williams, De La Cruz, & Hintze, 1989; Zammuner, 1987). (For an excellent review of the gender stereotype literature, see Ashmore, Del Boca & Wohlers, 1986; Spence, 1993.) As noted recently, "Even though women perform competently in many traditionally male roles—as astronauts, lawyers, chief of police, or state governors, for example—the stereotypes of men and women have changed very little in the last twenty years," (Cross & Markus, 1993, pp. 57–58).

Psychologists have often been portrayed as preoccupied with measurement. Some years ago, Anne Constantinople (1973) suggested as much when she noted that the axiom "Everything that exists, exists in some quantity, and if it exists in some quantity, it can be measured" seems a likely guiding principle for many psychologists. Such a view seems justified given the amount of research devoted to the development and refinement of psychological measures going back to the late 1920s and extending to the present (Craik, 1986). For much of this time, psychologists such as Joseph Jastrow,

table 4.1 Common Gender Role Stereotypes

Males	Females
Aggressive	Submissive
Ambitious	Modest
Cold	Warm
Decisive	Indecisive
Independent	Dependent
Rational	Flighty
Strong	Weak
Unemotional	Emotional
Unexpressive	Expressive
Worldlywise	Homecentered

Lewis Terman, Catherine Cox Miles, J. P. and Ruth Guilford, Kate Frank, Sandra Bem, and others have pioneered the development of psychological measures that tap supposedly basic differences in male and female identities, namely, **masculinity** and **femininity,** respectively. (For a thorough review of the masculinity-femininity literatures, see Lewin 1984a, 1984b; Morawski, 1985, 1987; Pleck, 1984; Windle, 1987.) Although the study of **gender differences** has produced some rather interesting notions, it is not without its problems.

One problem found in many of the gender difference studies surfaces when we generalize too far afield from a study's results referred to as the **fallacy of the average.** To illustrate this, let's measure a common enough sex difference, the difference in men's and women's height.

The average height of the North American male is about five feet, nine inches, whereas the average height of the North American female is about five feet, four inches. Consequently, we can say "on average" North American men are significantly taller than North American women. However, we cannot say that *all* North American men are taller than *all* North American women. Why not? Simple; about half of all North American women are taller than five feet, four inches, whereas half of all North American men are shorter than five feet, nine inches. In fact, if we were to plot a large number of men's and women's heights, we would find them normally distributed with a sizable portion of women being taller than the average man, with many of the men being shorter than the average woman (see Figure 4.1). If, however, we focused only on the difference in average heights, we might declare that "men are taller than women." The problem with such a generalization, based on the averages alone, is that it doesn't take into account the many exceptions. Relying on averages alone, even those that are statistically significantly different, in other words, can be misleading.

Furthermore, just because a statistically significant sex/gender difference is found along some dimension, it does not necessarily mean that much. After reviewing a number of gender difference studies, Carol Jacklin (1979) argued that regardless of the significant differences found most were merely trivial in nature. In other

The Psychological Perspective

figure 4.1

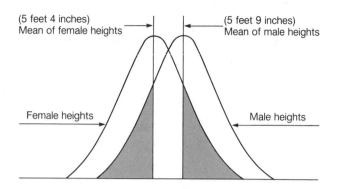

Normal distribution of adult male and female heights. Note the shaded areas: a sizable portion of females exceed the male mean score (shaded area on the right) while a sizable number of males fall below the female mean (shaded area on the left).

words, all too often much is made of the statistically significant differences found *between* males and females while overlooking the far greater differences existent *among* males and females.

Another frequent problem encountered in the gender difference literature is the number of studies that, for various reasons, report conflicting results. For instance, take the issue of male aggressiveness. For years researchers reported that generally males were both more physically and verbally aggressive than females (Terman & Tyler, 1954). The evidence for such a difference seemed strong enough for Eleanor Maccoby and Carol Jacklin (1974) to assert that greater male aggressiveness was "well established." However, some years later Timothy Tieger (1980) suggested they were mistaken and that the cumulative evidence did not support their claims. Later, Maccoby and Jacklin (1980) countered Tieger's claims by extending their research, and once again they argued that the data supported their claim of greater male aggressivity. What is the public to think when all we seem to read in the literature is one reviewer refuting another or claiming that the area is so fraught with inconsistencies and poorly controlled studies that the only answer is further study (Hyde, 1986a). Can we never disentangle the Gordian knot that seems to snarl any meaningful analysis of male-female differences?

Before we throw up our hands in exasperation over the continual conflicting results, we may take heart in a new statistical method that synthesizes the results of many separate studies, namely, meta-analysis (Glass, McGaw & Smith 1981; Rosenthal, 1984). In somewhat simplified terms, meta-analysis is a mathematical procedure that combines large sets of data taken from a number of separate studies regardless of their results and arrives at an overall and, hopefully, more parsimonious and integrated summary of the combined results (Oliver, 1987).

Recently, researchers have used meta-analysis to combine and reanalyze large numbers of gender studies; the results have been quite illuminating (Eagly, 1987a; Feingold, 1988; Hyde & Linn, 1986). Thus to help us separate the real from the fictional gender differences, we will borrow from these meta-analytic studies quite frequently in the material that follows.

To make our discussion of gender differences a bit more manageable, we will separately treat two general areas, namely, intellectual differences and social differences. Each contains a large store of assumed gender differences and a fair number of unwarranted generalizations. As we will see in the ensuing discussion, many of the purported gender differences suffer from a lack of substantiating evidence. Although finding the genders more similar than dissimilar may not seem particularly exciting, the idea that the genders are more alike than many may think is an important notion to ponder (Eagly, 1987b).

Throughout the ages, males tended to be identified with large numbers of highly valued skills, talents, and abilities. In hunting societies, for instance, brute strength was essential, and men epitomized the brute. With the dawn of domesticated animals and cultivated crops, men became the par excellence herdsmen and farmers; no matter that women probably invented the digging stick and trained the first wild canines. Following industrialization, men found themselves better suited for the machine by dint of their inherent mechanical talent, whereas women supposedly marveled from afar over the complexity of the pulleys and levers. Finally in the technological age, men found themselves naturals at interfacing with computers; women seemed only suited to operate a keypunch. One could say that whatever skill a society values men have such a talent in spades. Even when the female is found able, someone is apt to argue for certain restrictions. Take the German philosopher Arthur Schopenhauer who wrote, "Women have great talent but no genius, for they always remain subjective" (Morgan, 1970, p. 36).

Intellectual Differences

While we might wonder why and on what grounds, many a male has been known to gloat over the self-flattering belief that they are smarter than women. One argument for such male puffery goes something like: "Look back through history; who were the leaders, inventors, philosophers, and scientists? Why, men of course!" However, such a historical analysis may rest on the questionable foundation that any mark of women's intellectual abilities was either overlooked or possibly dismissed by scientists and historians with selective attention. For many reasons—not the least of which is their questionable impartiality—let's set aside the historical lists of the mainly male luminaries and focus on the question, Are males smarter than females? However, let's use a more psychological-sounding term and rephrase our question, Who is more "intelligent," males or females? Before we can answer this, we need first to decide on what is meant by "intelligent."

Although a totally acceptable and complete definition of intelligence is beyond the scope of this work, we will fall back on a somewhat well-known if not somewhat slightly facetious definition of intelligence offered some years ago by Edwin Boring, a noted historian of psychology. "Intelligence," quipped Boring, "is whatever the intelligence test measures." As most contemporary "intelligence tests" measure various aspects of a person's verbal, mathematical, and visual-performance skills, we might conclude that differences in these areas would answer which gender is the more intelligent, that is, more skilled in verbal, mathematical, or visual abilities. Although controversy exists over whether such tests can ever be "culture free" and thus of questionable value in measuring a person's inherent intellectual abilities, we will use the approach that we can know something about a person's intelligence by noting how well they do on different kinds of abilities' tests. (For a recent discussion of gender bias in intelligence tests, see Roznowski, 1987.)

The Psychological Perspective

As previously noted psychologists have long been noted for their test-making abilities, and constructing "intelligence tests" has been one of the more controversial "accomplishments" bedeviling psychology this century. Interestingly, some of the early pioneers in intelligence testing such as G. Stanley Hall and Joseph Jastrow were captivated by the nineteenth-century biological notion dubbed the **variability hypothesis.** The variability hypothesis argued that a female's mental abilities were much more narrowly limited than a male's, leading many of the early champions of intelligence testing to claim that males were more intelligent than females (Shields, 1982). As fate would have it though, on many of the early intelligence tests, females actually scored higher than their male counterparts (Morawski, 1985). But can we definitely say that an IQ score is a good way to determine whether males or females are more intelligent? The answer is a definite no!

As historians of intelligence tests tell us, intelligence test makers purposely constructed their scales in such a way as to eliminate any possible gender difference in their scoring (Anastasi, 1988). Essentially then, when a test item was found to favor one or the other gender, it was simply thrown out or paired with another that favored the other gender (Halpern, 1986). Thus we will not find an answer of who is more intelligent by use of standardized intelligence tests. If IQ scores won't work, what other options are available that may give us a hint about the overall mental abilities of males and females?

In her review of cognitive differences, Diane Halpern (1986) noted two other areas that some might use to determine whether males are more intelligent than females, or vice versa, namely, occupational status and school achievement. If, for instance, we take a quick glance at who holds those jobs thought to require above normal intelligence (e.g., physicians, lawyers, judges, architects, physicists), we would find that a majority of these are occupied by males. For illustration sake, we find that nearly 94 percent of all attorney judgeships are held by males (Cook, 1987). Could it be that females don't possess the needed intelligence to sit on the bench and deliver juridical decisions? Absolutely not! More than likely the reason behind the severe lack of females in the high-intelligence-as-a-requisite professions has more to do with prohibitive social factors and a lack of opportunities rather than a lack of intellectual ability.

What about school achievement? Who gets better grades? When everything is taken into account, females, on the average, get better grades than males at nearly every level. Can we say then that girls are more intelligent? Again, no! The research suggests that social factors play a significant role in fostering greater female achievement (Halpern, 1986). It seems, then, that if IQ scores, occupational status, and academic achievements are not good indicators of which gender is smarter, what is left to conclude?

After an exhaustive review of the literature on gender differences in mental abilities, researchers have concluded that there is *no* difference in overall general intelligence between males and females (Halpern, 1986; Maccoby & Jacklin, 1974). However, several areas linked to intelligence are susceptible to gender differences and to these we now turn our attention.

Verbal Ability. Women have long been thought to excel at talking. Comedians have made women's verbal output part of their stock material, and audiences have laughingly approved of the sexist image. (For a discussion on sexist humor, see Moore, Griffiths & Payne, 1987.) Notwithstanding this unflattering portrait, a majority of studies have shown that females are slightly superior to males in a number of **verbal abilities** such as vocabulary size, spelling, sentence complexity, grammar, creative writing, and many other elements of general verbal fluency (Edwards, Honeycutt, & Zagacki, 1989; Halpern 1986; Pearson, Turner, & Todd-Mancillas, 1991). Although some early studies found young girls exhibiting greater verbal skills much earlier than comparably aged boys (Moore, 1967), more recent reviews caution that girls' verbal superiority actually begins around the time of early adolescence and continues onward into early adulthood (Feingold, 1988; Halpern, 1986). However, in a recent meta-analysis of some 165 studies on gender differences in verbal ability, Janet Shibley Hyde and Marcia Linn (1988) found sufficient evidence to suggest that the purported gender differences in verbal ability favoring females "no longer exist."

As for which gender talks more, contrary to the popular stereotype, from preschool onward males talk more (Cook, Fritz, McCornack, & Visperas, 1985; Pearson, Turner, & Todd-Mancillas 1991). In fact, males who act more traditional in terms of exhibiting what most would call masculine behaviors are more likely to "hog" the conversation with others rather than take turns in a dialogue with another (Drass, 1986). An interesting twist to the issue of who is better in their verbal skills is found in the fact that males show more language problems such as stuttering and evidence more language impairment following brain surgery or strokes (Corballis & Beale, 1983; Springer & Deutsch, 1985). Given the possible slight advantage females have in verbal skills and the number of problems males have with their verbal performances, one wonders how men have been able to overcome their verbal deficits and to end up as the world's greatest orators! One reason for a male's greater oratory skills may be accounted for by his penchant to dominate conversations, a skill learned early by any good orator (Austin, Salehi & Leffler, 1987).

Visual-Spatial Ability. When it comes to what psychologists call **visual-spatial abilities,** males excel over females (Baenninger & Newcombe, 1989). Visual-spatial abilities are those that allow one to pick out and make sense of objects in one's field of vision. For example, a bird-watcher who spots a scarlet tanager on a distant tree limb is said to have a keen visual-spatial ability. To spot the tanager, a bird-watcher has had to ignore a large amount of irrelevant visual material, such as moving tree limbs and different shaped leaves, and to pick out the silhouette of the beautiful tanager against the backdrop of the forest mural.

Psychologists in their quest to measure visual-spatial abilities have moved into darkened rooms rather than out into forest and field. Herman Witkin and several colleagues (1954, 1962) have compiled a great deal of information about visual-spatial abilities based on their use of a device called the *rod-and-frame test,* or RFT. In the RFT, a person typically sits in a dark room facing an illuminated rectangular frame that encloses a rod (see Figure 4.2). The frame and rod are both adjustable, and the viewer's

figure 4.2
Various positions for the rod-
and-frame test.

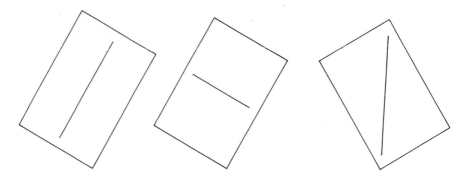

task is to tell when the rod appears in a true vertical position. The difficulty comes from the frame's position, which can confuse the viewer's judgment of the rod's verticality. To align the rod in a true vertical position, the viewer must ignore the frame. Generally speaking, researchers using the RFT have found that beginning in adolescence and continuing into adulthood males have a keener visual-spatial ability than do females (Linn & Petersen, 1986; McGee, 1979; Sanders, Soares & D'Aquila, 1982).

In his research Witkin speculated that males' ability to ignore the frame and concentrate on the rod in judging its verticality was linked to a specific thinking process called an **analytical cognitive style.** According to Witkin, the possession of such an analytical style predisposes males to ignore and avoid the irrelevant aspects of a task and any impulse that may lead to an incorrect solution. Put more simply, Witkin reasoned that males with their purported analytical ability were better able to focus on the task at hand and to come up with a correct solution regardless of other competing demands. Because females use the frame to assist them in their judgment of the rod's verticality, Witkin argued they possessed a **global cognitive style.** Consequently, females purportedly have difficulty disregarding extraneous material and are quick to rely on impulse and are possibly prone to make more mistakes. In Witkin's thinking, then, the bottom line on analytical and global cognitive styles is that men think differently than women. Following this line of reasoning, then, men would seem better suited for some jobs than women. For example, men with their analytical ability should make better organizers, whereas women with their global style should make better followers than leaders.

However, women and men do not differ on all tests that require a person to ignore the extraneous or irrelevant. Consider the *Stroop color-word test* where a person is given a set of color names (e.g., red, blue, yellow) printed in a color of ink that is different than the color name. The object of the test is for a person to name the color of the ink while ignoring the printed word. For instance, if the word *red* is printed in blue, a person would say "blue" rather than read "red." On this test, researchers can find no difference between how well females and males do (Maccoby & Jacklin, 1974, p. 99). Thus if having an analytical ability means disregarding some material in favor of others, males tend to exhibit this quality when it comes to purely visual-spatial tests (e.g., RFT) but not when the test involves something besides visual-spatial ability (e.g., *Stroop color-word test*). Although some might believe that men and women think differently, Maccoby and Jacklin could find no substantive evidence for such an alleged gender difference in thinking styles.

Quantitative Ability. History and tradition would have us believe that men are superior to women in mathematical ability. Research into **quantitative abilities** does indicate that beginning in adolescence males show *slightly* superior quantitative aptitude (Feingold, 1988; Halpern, 1986; Hyde, 1981). All too often, when a study finds such a difference, the media "run wild" (Jacobs & Eccles, 1985). However, the evidence for male "superiority" begs more caution because of the many confounding variables that may influence why males as a group do better in math than females. The blanket statement that "boys score higher than girls" in math is one where the underlying reasons for such a difference have not been determined to everyone's satisfaction (Hogrebe, 1987; McLoughlin, 1988).

In the minds of most people, the belief that males are superior in math carries over to include the idea that males are similarly gifted in science, especially in the natural sciences. Visit almost any university or industrial research facility, or check the names of the winners of the Nobel prizes in physics, chemistry, physiology, or medicine, and you will come away with the impression that the natural sciences are an almost exclusively male preserve. But numbers alone should not lead us to the conclusion that males are somehow predisposed toward the natural sciences. Maccoby and Jacklin argue that although males seem drawn to science, it may not be on account of their superior mathematical ability but rather some other ability, for example, their visual-spatial aptitude.

> During adolescence, boys' superiority in math tends to be accompanied by better mastery of scientific subject matter and greater interest in science. The two disciplines are of course closely linked in that science relies heavily upon math in formulating its problems and finding their solutions. One may ask whether male superiority in science is a derivative of greater math abilities or whether both are a function of a third factor. In this connection, some findings of the Harvard Project Physics are interesting. Physics achievement tests were given to a large sample of high school students. On the portion of the test calling for visual-spatial skills, the male physics students did better; on verbal test items, female physics students obtained higher scores. It would appear that verbal and spatial factors account for some of the variance in science achievement. (pp. 89, 91)

Creativity. Creativity is both an elusive and a desired ability. One who can discover a unique solution or produce a novel work of art or machinery or whatever is usually thought to be creative and finds public attention turned his or her way. (For an analysis of the creative process, see Abra, 1988; Weisberg, 1986.) Because the majority of well-known creative people were and are male, the assumption is that males somehow are predisposed to creative acts. Probably because of the lack of female names in the annals of creativity, females are thought to be less prone to creative insights. Research on the proprietors of creative abilities portrays a somewhat different image though. In their summary of some thirty studies of both verbal and nonverbal creativity, Maccoby and Jacklin concluded,

> . . . on verbal tests of creative ability no sex differences are found in the preschool and the earliest school years, but from about the age of 7 girls show an advantage in a majority of studies. On nonverbal measures, no clear trend toward superiority of either

The Psychological Perspective

sex can be discerned. In general, then, it may be said that tests of creativity reflect the already documented difference between the sexes in verbal skills; clearly, girls and women are at least as able as boys and men to generate a variety of hypotheses and produce unusual ideas. Thus the underrepresentation of women in the ranks of the outstanding creative figures of earlier and present times would not appear to arise from any general deficiency in "the production of associative content that is abundant and unique." (pp. 113–114)

We have reviewed several abilities, most of which are presumed to be found more readily in males or females. But more often than not, researchers find no evidence for a supposed gender difference, or the difference unexpectedly favors the gender stereotypically thought deficient. For example, research finds no difference between males and females in their general intelligence, styles of thinking, or nonverbal creative abilities. For reasons yet unknown, beginning in early adolescence, boys excel in visual-spatial abilities and girls excel in verbal abilities. Although boys seem to have a slight advantage in math, their presumed edge in science may be related to factors other than mathematical ability. Girls, on the other hand, outperform boys in creative tasks that involve words. Overall, the genders do not seem radically different in their abilities, at least not in the ones that count when one considers the ingredients for a productive life (Baker, 1987; Feingold, 1994).

Social Differences
Gender differences in social behaviors are especially noteworthy to our discussion of the male experience. The common gender stereotypes portray males, for example, as much more likely to act more aggressively, coldly, reservedly, and self-assuredly toward others than are females. Before we discuss the evidence relating to several commonly assumed gender differences in social behaviors, we should keep in mind one important fact. In those instances where gender differences are shown, they are more likely the result of society's pressures than some innate biological sex difference.

Self-Disclosure. If we find ourselves in the company of friends, most of us will open up and talk about ourselves. Talking about ourselves makes us, more often than not, feel good. "To get something off one's chest" supposedly is a helpful and practical aid for one's mental health. Social scientists refer to this kind of personal or intimate self-revelation as **self-disclosure.**
The late Sidney Jourard not only identified but also conducted much of the early research on self-disclosure. Much of Jourard and others' research pointed to a gender difference in self-disclosure, namely, most males reported they not only disclosed less about themselves to others but also when they did disclose they did so to far fewer people than females did (Jourard, 1964; Komarovsky, 1967, 1976; Snell et al., 1989). While some few studies have found no gender difference in self-disclosure, far fewer have reported males disclosing more than females (Derlega & Winstead, 1986; Pearson, Turner, & Todd-Mancillas 1991).
Given these patterns of self-disclosure, then, we should not conclude that males never self-disclose. However, when males do self-disclose, they usually do so with women and not other men. Furthermore, the females to whom males choose to self-disclose are usually close relatives or friends (mothers, girlfriends, or wives). In fact,

males generally look upon other males who are self-disclosers with some skepticism, if not outright disdain. Why most males keep their personal feelings from others, especially other males, is a matter of speculation. Although we will speculate about this matter at length in chapter 7, suffice it to say here that one possible reason for males keeping their feelings to themselves is because they are taught very early in life to hide their feelings from others, especially other males (see Reid & Fine, 1992).

Dependency. Napoleon Bonaparte is credited with saying, "Nature intended women to be our slaves . . . they are our property; we are not theirs. They belong to us, just as a tree that bears fruit belongs to a gardener." Many people still believe this today, and their belief is portrayed in the common stereotype of the dependent and clinging woman (see Henderson & Cunningham, 1993).

As we will see in the next chapter, much of a young boy's socialization revolves around efforts to make him independent. Dependency-independency is a multifaceted dimension and thus somewhat difficult to define. In the following paragraphs we will look at three facets of **dependency:** proximity; susceptibility to others' pressure, or conformity; and a special form of dependency, namely, using others to help define one's gender.

When a child clings to or stays close by a parent or an adult caregiver, he or she is exhibiting what psychologists call *proximal behaviors.* Observing proximal behaviors in young children is both a common method and a valid behavioral measure for defining dependency. In one early study, the researchers found thirteen-month-old females showed more proximal behaviors than did thirteen-month-old males (Goldberg & Lewis, 1969). Furthermore, these researchers found the higher incidence of proximal behaviors among females was linked to how their mothers treated them earlier on. Therefore, do males and females differ in proximal behaviors naturally, or are they a product of differential treatment by parents or other adult caregivers? As of the moment, we do not have a definite answer. However, after reviewing more than twenty-five studies dealing with touching and proximal behaviors, Maccoby and Jacklin (1974, p. 196) concluded that ". . . the number of studies finding no difference in proximity outnumber the 'girls higher' studies by more than three to one, and hence the picture as a whole is quite clearly one of sex similarity rather than sex difference."

As children grow older, they begin to turn more toward peers for acceptance and approval. The kinds of peer groups females form are quite different from those formed by males. Girls are more likely to form "chumships," which are exclusive two-person or three-person groups. Boys, on the other hand, tend to congregate in larger groups, which by their very size come to exert considerable pressure on their members (Berger, 1988). In their respective same-sex groups, there is no evidence that either males or females are more or less susceptible to peer pressure (Billy & Udry, 1985; Ward, Seccomb, Bendel & Carter, 1985). (For a review of peer group influence and gendered behavior, see Carter, 1987; Lueptow, 1984.)

During the 1950s, a spate of research focused on the many variables affecting a person's susceptibility to others' persuasion or influence. One variable that continually cropped up in the research was gender; much of the research found that females

The Psychological Perspective

tended to conform more than males in a variety of conditions (Asch, 1956; Hovland, Janis & Kelley, 1953; Janis & Field, 1959; Tuddenham, 1958). By the 1960s, finding females more persuasible and conforming became almost a social-psychological given. During the 1970s, however, the tide turned when researchers began pointing out that much of the earlier research contained mitigating or biasing factors (e.g., male-biased content, a preponderance of male researchers) that made the commonly accepted gender difference somewhat questionable (e.g., Eagly, 1978; Eagly & Carli, 1981; Maccoby & Jacklin, 1974; Sistrunk & McDavid, 1971). As fate would have it, though, the tide turned again with the dawn of meta-analysis. By combining large numbers of studies, researchers have found that males do appear more resistant to others' influence, especially in group situations (Becker, 1986; Cooper, 1979; Eagly, 1987a, 1987b).

Alice Eagly (1987a, p. 100) explains the gender difference with respect to others' influence and persuasion with reference to what she calls her "social-role analysis." She writes, "the presence of an audience should ordinarily heighten self-presentational concerns and encourage gender-role consistent behavior, which for women tends to be agreeing with other people and for men tends to be remaining independent in the face of social pressure." We should note, though, that the obtained gender difference appears strongest in group situations, and thus the generalized statement that females are more conforming, persuasible, or dependent on others in all situations is not warranted.

We come now to a third type of dependency, which some people may argue is not really dependency in the traditional sense of the word. Recently, Joseph Pleck (1980, p. 421) outlined a unique male-female situation in which some men depend on women to validate certain features of their masculinity (see Cohen, 1992). Pleck writes that "In traditional masculinity, to experience oneself as masculine requires that women play their prescribed role of doing the things that make men feel masculine." For example, a clinging woman makes some men feel very masculine in the sense of being protective and powerful in the relationship. Furthermore, Pleck describes how men who act traditionally need women to act as an emotional outlet. Thus some men experience emotions such as compassion, joy, and ecstasy only through their relationships with women. These men are almost fearful, it seems, to feel these emotions for themselves. In a sense they experience their emotions vicariously through women. This leads us to suggest that men who define their masculinity in the traditional manner are dependent on women not only to act as a support for their masculinity but to be a bridge for some emotional experiences they may think of as too feminine to express.

Nurturance. Women have traditionally been thought to possess a certain predisposition for providing aid to others. Their supposed natural concern and ready willingness to help others have made them candidates for nursing, teaching, and social work careers, as well as a career as wife and mother. Men, on the other hand, are thought more prone to withhold assistance from others and to show what may be called indifference in the face of other people's adversity. Maccoby and Jacklin's review of some twenty studies reveals little evidence of gender differences in **nurturant**

behaviors. Recently though, Judith Owen Blakemore (1990) found young females (ages 4–7 years) showed more nurturant behaviors toward a younger sibling (under 1 year) as compared to young males.

However, one program of research is worth noting because of its counter-stereotypic conclusions regarding adult men and nurturant behaviors. Douglas Sawin and Ross Parke (1979) observed parents' interactions with their newborn infants with an eye especially on the number of nurturant behaviors (holding, rocking, looking, fondling, and smiling) engaged in by each parent. When both parents were together, fathers engaged in *more* nurturant behaviors (with the exception of smiling) than mothers did. When the fathers were alone with their babies, they engaged in as many or more nurturant behaviors as did mothers when they were alone with their babies. Interestingly, Sawin and Parke's sample of fathers consisted of two significantly different groups of men. The first group was mainly well educated and interested in natural childbirth. (Several from this group had been in the delivery room during the birth of their baby.) The second group was primarily working-class, and no members of this group were in the delivery room during the birth of their baby. Even with two such different groups of men, finding that fathers can and do provide as much nurturance as mothers do should put to rest the notion that men are incapable of nurturant behavior. In recent years, attention has been forthcoming on the very real nurturant qualities that males can and do show not only in their relations with their children but with others as well (Blakemore, Baumgardner & Keniston, 1988; Doyle, 1986; Pruett, 1987).

If permitted to broaden the scope and definition of nurturant behavior to include the more generalized pattern called helping behavior, or altruistic behavior, we find considerable evidence that males are quite helpful. Although females have long been thought more helpful than males, again with the advent of meta-analysis, we find a surprising wrinkle in this belief. In general, recent work finds males more helpful than females, at least with strangers, whereas females appear more helpful than males toward those in close or long-term relationships (Eagly & Crowley, 1986). The reason such a gender difference has gone virtually undetected for some years, according to Alice Eagly, is that social psychologists have not focused enough attention on the type of relationship that existed between a helper and a helpee (e.g., stranger versus close relation). A possible reason why males may be more helpful to a stranger than females could simply be that given their "on average" greater physical strength, males feel less threatened and less likely to be attacked than a female encountering a stranger supposedly in need of help.

Aggressiveness. The picture of the male as aggressor and the female as pacifier is a stereotype ingrained in many people's minds. As noted in the previous chapter, the question of whether or not male aggressivity is rooted in biological or social factors is a matter of some dispute. However, in this section we will only note the research bearing on the issue of a purported gender difference in aggression, not its underlying cause(s).

A majority of both the narrative and quantitative literature reviews dealing with a gender difference in **aggression** finds strong evidence for arguing that males, in

The Psychological Perspective

Calvin and Hobbes

by Bill Watterson

general, are more aggressive than females (Hyde, 1984, 1986b; Maccoby & Jacklin, 1974; Thompson, 1990). However, much of the research noted in these reviews dealt almost entirely with children and young adults. Thus we can say that beginning in early childhood and moving into adolescence, males appear more aggressive than females. When it comes to adulthood, however, the picture changes somewhat, and an added distinction between physical and psychological aggression must be added to the equation.

As defined here, physical aggression occurs when one inflicts or intends to inflict physical injury or harm on another. Psychological aggression, on the other hand, covers a whole range of hurtful or abusive activities either of a verbal type (e.g., yelling, screaming, and swearing) or of a nonverbal type (e.g., glaring, frowning, and making obscene gestures).

In an extensive review of adult studies on aggression, Eagly (1987a, p. 91) noted that the single "strongest predictor" of a gender difference in aggression was "whether aggression caused physical or psychological harm to its target." Basically, Eagly found a gender difference favoring male aggression when "the situation provided an opportunity for physical rather than psychological harm." In other words, males are more physically aggressive than females, although there are few appreciable differences between the sexes when it comes to psychological aggression. In sum then, the stereotype of the male aggressor holds up during childhood and adolescence and in adulthood primarily when it comes to acts involving physical aggression. (For a review of the many problems encountered in social psychological research on gender differences and aggression, see Macauley, 1985.)

We have examined a number of common stereotypic gender differences in social behaviors. Surprisingly, researchers have found little evidence to support many of these commonly accepted stereotypes. Granted, most males seem to be less willing than most females to disclose their intimate feelings to others, with the possible exceptions of a few close females. Males are more physically aggressive than are females, but little can be found to suggest a gender difference in other forms of aggressiveness. Depending on how we define them, the stereotypic portrayals of females as dependent, conforming, and nurturant are grossly unfounded. Thus with respect to gender differences regarding the social behaviors and intellectual abilities that we have examined, males and females appear more similar than the common gender stereotypes would have us believe.

Although few significant differences can be established in how males and females think and behave in social situations, a majority of social scientists contend that at least one important difference can be substantiated. Specifically, beginning very early in life and continuing throughout the life span, males and females learn to define and, consequently, come to experience themselves and their worlds differently. That such is the case should not surprise us. From the moment the words, "It's a boy" or "It's a girl" are pronounced, multiple social forces and, yes, some few biological influences, direct most newborn males and females down very different paths leading to two different experiential worlds. (For two very good analyses of the separate female world, see Bernard, 1981; Brehm, 1988.) For some years now, social scientists from various disciplines (e.g., personality development, social psychology, anthropology, and sociology) have theorized and studied a psychosocial construct called gender identity that embodies this most important developmental feature in males' and females' lives (Herdt, 1987; Shaver & Hendrick, 1987; Stewart & Lykes, 1985).

> **a developmental perspective on the male gender identity**

In this section we will describe the developmental progress of the male gender identity and chart its many changes throughout the life course. To accomplish this we will borrow from Phyllis Katz's (1986) insightful essay on gender identity. Following Katz's lead (1979, 1986), we will divide the development of male gender identity into three periods: an infant and early childhood period with its emphasis on *learning* society's gender norms, an adolescent period with its focus on *preparing* for the adult world of marriage and work, and, lastly, the adult period with its accent on *enacting* the many adult gender norms.

> *What Is Gender Identity, Anyway?*

Before we describe the developmental path a male's gender identity takes, we need to understand just what we mean by gender identity. To do this, let's pose a scenario of sorts. Suppose that tomorrow morning you wake up, notice some strange bodily sensations, throw back the covers, and discover that somehow during the night, your body changed into the opposite sex. What would your first reactions be? Total disbelief, a full-blown state of apoplexy, or would you think it all a dream, and a bad one at that. More than likely, when faced with this very unlikely occurrence, most would, to put it mildly, freak out. Why such a drastic reaction, though? Simply, most of us take our being male or female for granted. We might question our sanity, our intelligence, or even our feelings for others, but never (for most of us, that is) do we question our being male or female. The fact that one is a male or a female is so ingrained in one's thinking, one's very being as a person, that the idea of changing into the other sex overnight is something most reject outright. Now you have a sense of just what is meant by gender identity.

Most experts agree that gender identity is a central or an essential ingredient (e.g., a basic "image" or essential "personal experience") related to a person's basic definition of himself or herself as a male or female person. For our purposes here,

The Psychological Perspective

let's define **gender identity** as a person's total experience of being male or female structured along the lines defined by their society. Let's now discuss the developmental path of the male gender identity beginning with infancy.

Infancy and Childhood: The Formative Years

During the first two to two and one-half years of a male's life, a variety of people (i.e., parents, siblings, grandparents, and other adults) begin to shape the young infant into a "little man." Researchers have found that as early as the first days after his birth, parents, for instance, see their newborn child in rather stereotypical ways (Rubin, Provenzano & Luria, 1974). In the days and months that follow not only those involved with the infant but aspects of his environment converge to create a different experiential world for the male (e.g., different nursery environments and different toys). (We will detail these and other social factors that contribute to the differential socialization of a young male in the next chapter.)

Near the end of these first years, an essential ingredient in a male's gender identity shows itself, namely, as a young boy's verbalization of himself (i.e., self-labeling) as "boy." Prior to this event, during the preverbal stage (i.e., the first eighteen months or so), it seems unlikely that an infant experiences himself, or herself in terms of a gendered category (i.e., male or female). For the time being, we have no way of assessing what kind of personal experience a preverbal infant has.

If we think of the infant during his or her first two years as being primarily a recipient of others' actions, the early childhood years (three to six years of age) finds a child becoming a more active participant in his relations with others. Active participation with his expanding social world is due mainly to a growing mastery of both locomotive and verbal skills. During these active years, boys and girls display ample evidence that they not only differentiate between the genders but also exhibit different social behaviors (e.g., boys are more physically active than girls and both genders tend to segregate into same-sex play groups; Katz, 1986; Maccoby, 1990; Maccoby & Jacklin, 1974; Wynn & Fletcher, 1987). In describing this period's heightened awareness of gender differences, Katz (1986, p. 38) writes:

> There is probably no other area in a child's life (with the possible exception of language) that is as overlearned as gender. There may well be 5-year-olds who do not know the alphabet or color names, but there probably is not one who does not recognize the separate play worlds of boys and girls and which objects belong to each.

Theoretically, it is the emergent gender identity during these childhood years that is the most likely factor accountable for each sex's experience of different and separate worlds. But how does gender identity develop? This question has stimulated much speculation and research. We will, however, put off a discussion of the primary explanations of how gender identity develops until the next chapter.

We now move into the latter stage of the formative years, that of the early grade-school years. Arguably, a child's gender identity is firmly established by the time he or she enters the first grade. Although the physical setting found in the primary grades shows little in the way of supporting a differential experiential setting for boys and girls—unlike those preschool classrooms with their partially sex-segregated "kitchen corner" and "workshop area," many gender differences show up during these years (Block, 1978). For instance, same-sex friendships peak during these years; very different interests both in and out of school can be found in males and females. Furthermore, boys seem to have more problems in school than girls, leading some to assert that the school environment is more suited to females than males with its pressure to sit quietly and pay attention, both of which seem somewhat more problematic for males than females.

During the few years just prior to when one's biological nature goes into overdrive, most boys and girls have become quite comfortable with who they are and what it means to be a male or female. In other words, before Tom, Bill, Gary, and all their male cohorts move into their teen years, their sense of what it means to be a male is remarkably stable. However, the calm of the last childhood years is about to end as boys (and girls) enter the next developmental period—adolescence.

Early pioneers in developmental psychology such as G. Stanley Hall (1904) saw adolescence, or the period sandwiched between childhood and adulthood, as a time filled with stress, confusion, and turbulence. However, a more contemporary view sees adolescence as a period filled with significant physical and psychosocial changes but *not* necessarily one filled with strife and anxiety (Adelson, 1979; Eccles, 1987; Lerner & Foch, 1987; Petersen, 1987). But what is this adolescence anyway? When does it occur, and what are some of the more important biological, psychological, and social changes and their influences on one's gender identity?

First, let's be clear on what adolescence is and what it is not. Adolescence is a transitional period falling between childhood and adulthood beginning anywhere between eleven to thirteen years of age and ending anywhere—arbitrarily defined by one's society—between the ages of seventeen to the early twenties. The beginning of adolescence is much easier to define because most point to the onset of puberty or the start of reproductive maturity as its telltale indicator. Rather than conceptualize adolescence as a single period, though, we will split it into two periods—the first period where one must confront and adapt to the many biological changes confronting one's body and a second one where one must deal with the establishment of more lasting intimate relations as well as come to grips with one's future career options and life-style. Although here we will deal with adolescence's two periods, keep in mind that overall it is a time of trying out new roles and dealing with an ever-widening circle of individuals and that such experiences form the basis for one's later adult roles and experiences.

Early Adolescence. Early adolescence (eleven to fifteen years of age) begins with the onset of puberty. Developmental psychologists generally point to a period of significant growth, or the growth spurt, as an indication of when a young boy's or girl's pubertal changes are occurring. During this time, young boys and girls will grow several inches (some boys add three or four inches to their height in under a year), put on several pounds (as much as twenty to twenty-five pounds), develop pubic hair, and worry about their frequent bouts with acne. Some changes during this time are more sex-specific such as a young girl's breast development and onset of menstruation or a boy's voice deepening and his face sprouting its first facial hair. (For a complete review of the many biological changes associated with boys and girls, see Katchadourian, 1977). Obviously, puberty does not arrive at the same time for all youngsters. Some mature early, and others later leading to different effects for each sex.

Being an early (say, during the sixth grade) or a late (during the eighth grade) maturer affects a youngster's body image and satisfaction with one's body appearance. Boys who mature early appear more satisfied with their bodies and exhibit more positive moods than late-maturing boys. We might attribute this positive state to our society's linking size with signs of virility or masculinity and thus a "strapping" young boy is more likely viewed more favorably by his peers than those (late maturers) who are smaller.

During early adolescence the school scene also generally shifts bringing new opportunities but also its share of disruptions. A child's primary grades (i.e., grades one through five) normally provide a sense of continuity and a stable environment—one room and usually one teacher. However, in our society a majority of students normally transfer to a middle school or junior high school, which brings changing classrooms and teachers. Consequently, one's earlier close-knit friendships are often disrupted as one encounters a wider group of peers.

During early adolescence, boys and girls often deal with problems very differently. Anne Petersen (1987) has studied several hundred young adolescents and found that when boys have problems such as adjusting to changes in school, not finding adequate peer acceptance and support, or facing family problems (e.g., divorce) they are more likely to act out their frustrations and fears by becoming rebellious and disobedient. On the other hand, girls with similar problems are more likely to keep their problems in, oftentimes leading to changes in their moods (e.g., becoming more depressed). Interestingly, we find this same gender difference in many adults as well.

Overall then, we can say that the early adolescent period brings about significant changes in a youngster's biology and his or her social world. Generally speaking, being an early maturer has more positive benefits for boys than for girls. The school environment presents a wider social network that comes with a cost—a breakdown of one's earlier and more child-centered peer group thrusting one into a wider social network with its individuals with very different values and life-styles. In summing up her research on this period, Petersen (1987, p. 34) noted that "[t]he adolescent's journey toward adulthood is inherently marked by change and upheaval but need not be fraught with chaos or deep pain."

Late Adolescence. Late adolescence (sixteen to nineteen years of age) finds a young person less troubled with a changeable body. Now, however, they must contend with two additional issues: intimate relations and future career options.

Exploring intimate relationships becomes more important in these years, especially among sixteen- and seventeen-year-olds. During these years, many young girls become overly concerned with their appearance and their acceptance by males. Such concerns can lead to some rather serious problems centering around a girl's attempting to change her body image (e.g., bulimia and anorexia nervosa). Although boys are not immune from concerns related to being seen as acceptable to girls during this period, boys seem especially concerned about proving their masculinity.

Athletics, for many, is a perfect arena to prove one's manhood. For those gifted with talent and skill, athletics serves them well. For those less talented, finding other proofs of manhood is especially difficult. The fact is that being the brainiest guy isn't as manly as being the team's quarterback.

Besides proving one's masculinity by being accepted by girls and playing sports, a boy must also begin to think more seriously during the later adolescent years about his future career. Near the end of high school, many a young male begins to think much more seriously about his grades and about what he'll do after graduation: the military, a full-time job, or college. No matter what choice he makes, the young man is preparing to enter the adult world.

Most adolescents can't wait until they can go out on their own and establish themselves as adults in a world where adults seem to have it all. For sometime developmental psychologists paid little attention to the adult years, thinking of them as little more than the forty or so years that separate the growth of childhood and adolescence from the decline of old age. In the past several decades, however, developmental psychologists have "done a one-eighty." One of the first to address adulthood as an important time for personal development and change was Erik Erikson, a brilliant theorist who took Freud to task for not going far enough in his theory of personality development. Unlike Freud, Erikson believed that a person faced several significant "development crises" after childhood. Specifically, Erikson (1968) saw several crises and their resolutions as the basis of adult development: one's adolescence as centering around "finding one's self," one's early adult years as forming "meaningful and intimate relationships," and one's middle years as being either stagnant or generative. Although we can conceptualize the primary concerns or "crises" of the adult years under many headings (e.g., affiliation and achievement, intimacy and generativity), Sigmund Freud (1935/1960) captured much the same flavor several years earlier with his insistence that adulthood was that time when a person must deal with love and work.

Adulthood: The Payoff

In recent years, adulthood has begun to receive the kind of attention it deserves from developmental psychologists (Bromley, 1974; Gould, 1978; Havighurst, 1972; Vaillant, 1977). Rather than try to cover every model of the many changes occurring in adulthood, we will concentrate here on only one—Daniel Levinson's (Levinson, Darrow, Klein, Levinson & McKee, 1978) stage theory of adulthood. Arguably, Levinson's work has been criticized because it dealt only with men's adult years. However, for the interested reader who wishes to address this deficit, one can find few better sources than Jessie Bernard's (1981) excellent treatise, *The Female World* (also see Helson & Moane, 1987).

Levinson's model is based on an extensive longitudinal study of forty men. After hours of interviews with these men, Levinson conceptualized men's adult years as comprised of several age-related stages each with its own particular problems and concerns. Levinson's stage theory is outlined in Figure 4.3.

Levinson saw the years between the ages of seventeen to twenty-two as comprising an *early adult transition* period. Leaving high school brings new challenges and options (e.g., college, full-time job, military). Obviously, a young man who takes a full-time job and a wife soon after high school will lead a very different life than one

The Psychological Perspective

figure 4.3

Levinson's stage theory of adult male development. From *The Seasons of a Man's Life,* by Daniel J. Levinson, et al. Copyright © 1978 by Daniel J. Levinson. Reprinted by permission of Alfred A. Knopf, Inc.

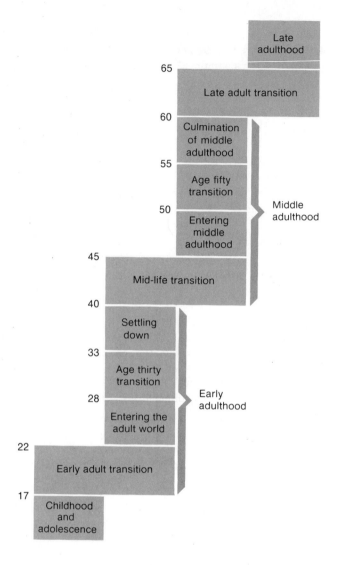

who opts for college and no wife. A job, a wife, and possibly a child can push a young man into the adult world much faster than one who goes off to the state university or opts for a stint in today's career-oriented military. Usually, college affords a higher lifelong earnings potential for a young man. Whatever the choices, though, young men in this transitional period are no longer kids, and the adult world looms just over the horizon.

By their early twenties, most males have settled into the adult world. Levinson sees the years between ages twenty-two to twenty-eight as an initial adult period where most have married, started a family, and begun in earnest to establish a career. Furthermore, most men begin to establish those values they believe important in life. Interestingly, many of the values a young male rebelled against in his teen years now become more reasonable, especially if he is married and a father. Generally, these years are not ones where men question their masculinity. Having a healthy body, a happy marriage, possibly a child or two, and a keen mind seem proof enough of one's manhood.

The years between the ages of twenty-eight to thirty-three, according to Levinson, bring yet another transitional period. By this time, a man's career is probably taking off and his family settling into a routine. The children are in school, the wife is either going back to school or working in an office, and he is putting in more time at work. There may be some stress showing up, however, in his marriage during these years for any number of reasons, not the least of which are his longer hours at work and the somewhat conflicting demands of juggling work and home responsibilities.

Levinson calls the years between ages thirty-three to forty a period of *settling down*. Generally, by this time a man has found his niche at work and has usually established a reputation among his colleagues. His children demand less of his time now that their interests lie more with their friends than with being with him. For many men, these years are some of the most productive and a time when one's work can be quite satisfying.

Moving into the forties, we have yet another transitional period, one where the calm of the previous period can be shaken, if not totally destroyed. The *mid-life transition* years often find a man questioning everything, his relations with his wife and family, his accomplishments at work, his values, and for some, his sense of masculinity. For many men, this is an especially difficult time when their marriages end in divorce, careers are changed, and friends abandoned. This period of upheaval has led some to think that more than a few men go through a kind of **mid-life crisis** where they act totally out of character (Hallberg, 1978).

As late middle-aged men begin to accept the inevitability of their pending retirement, many of their personal values change. Levinson found many of his men restructuring their lives along new values based on facing the fact that retirement is no longer something others must deal with. Concern over financial security and one's health are also beginning to become more prominent in many men's minds. Another issue more than a few men must deal with as they enter *middle adulthood* is the realization that many of their earlier goals have not and, more than likely, will not be accomplished. For instance, many a twenty-five-year-old man who planned on being in upper management by the time forty-five rolled around finds himself pushing fifty and his earlier career goals still unmet.

During his early fifties, a man encounters yet another transitional period wherein he again addresses many of his values and comes to grips with his advancing age. This transitional period is followed by a period culminating his middle years—the later fifties—where a man prepares to make his break with the work world. The early sixties find most men leaving the workplace and beginning a new life where retirement with its new life-style and greater freedom presents some new challenges. For some men, this transition from work to retirement is extremely difficult because they have few interests outside their work. On the other hand, for

The Psychological Perspective

those men who have nurtured other interests besides their work, their retirement years can be quite satisfying as they now have more time for hobbies and other interests (Anson et al., 1989).

As should be obvious, Levinson's stages are only a rough outline, and an arbitrary one at that, of the changes affecting men during their adult years. Although some may question his calculations for when and what stages and transitional periods supposedly appear, the real value in Levinson's and others' work on men's adult years is that finally some are taking an interest in detailing just what occurs to men during the many decades that have for so long been neglected.

Rather than seeing Levinson's work as the last word on men's lives, we should see it as a first draft with many other drafts to follow. (For a closer look at men's gender role changes, work involvement, relations with others, and retirement, see Farr, 1988; Ochberg, 1987, 1988; O'Neil et al., 1993; Osherson, 1986, 1992; Parnes, 1981.) One thing is clear from all the recent attention directed toward men's adult years: The forty or fifty years between adolescence and old age are years filled with many changes that are finally being looked at more seriously.

psychology looks at gender identity and gender role

Although many psychologists for the past several decades have focused their research on measuring how males and females differ in a variety of areas (e.g., Gill, Stockard, Johnson & Williams, 1987), others have focused their attention on the psychological processes underlying a person's perception of being male or female. One who has contributed much to this latter venture is Joseph Pleck, whose research and writings over the past two decades and a half have immeasurably enriched the field of gender studies. Although we could focus on any number of seminal workers in this area, we will concentrate on Pleck's work here because his theoretical and research analyses have particular bearing on the male's gender identity and gender role.

The Male Gender Identity Paradigm

In 1981 Pleck published *The Myth of Masculinity* wherein he presented an overview of how most psychologists have traditionally viewed the concept of masculinity, its development, and associated problems. Pleck called this "established" view of masculinity the **male gender identity paradigm,** or more simply, the "identity" paradigm. (A paradigm is a set of ideas or assumptions that researchers use to understand their subject matter better.) According to Pleck (pp. 4–5), the basic assumptions underlying the identity paradigm are:

1. Gender role identity is operationally defined by measures of psychological gender typing, conceptualized in terms of psychological masculinity and/or femininity dimensions.
2. Gender role identity derives from identification-modeling and, to a lesser extent, reinforcement and cognitive learning of gender typed traits, especially among males.
3. The development of appropriate gender role identity is a risky, failure-prone process, especially for males.
4. Homosexuality reflects a disturbance of gender role identity.
5. Appropriate gender role identity is necessary for good psychological adjustment because of an inner psychological need for it.
6. Hypermasculinity in males (exaggerated masculinity, often with negative social consequences) indicates insecurity in their gender role identities.

7. Problems of gender role identity account for men's negative attitudes and behaviors toward women.
8. Problems of gender role identity account for boys' difficulties in school performance and adjustment.
9. African American males are particularly vulnerable to gender role identity problems.
10. Male adolescent initiation rites are a response to problems of gender role identity.
11. Historical changes in the character of work and the organization of the family have made it more difficult for men to develop and maintain their gender role identities.

To get a better sense of the identity paradigm, let's describe in more detail some of these assumptions. First of all, for sometime scientists interested in studying masculinity or femininity accepted that both developed out of an innate psychological need, not as a consequence of something a person learned or acquired from social agents. Further, the more a male's behavior fit his society's stereotypes of masculine behavior (see Table 4.1 on page 63), the more psychologically healthy he was thought to be. Conversely, the more distant a male's behaviors were from the male gender stereotypes, the less psychologically healthy he was.

The identity model also posits any number of things can go wrong, and often do, during one's early developmental years, especially for males. For example, if a boy's mother is domineering and strong willed and his father is weak and passive, a boy's sense of masculinity may become disturbed, leading possibly to his becoming homosexual. Or if a boy has an insecure and poorly developed sense of masculinity, he may try to overcompensate for this condition by exaggerating certain features of the male gender such as acting more aggressively against others, especially women.

Furthermore, because one's masculinity or femininity is supposedly an *innate* feature of a male's or a female's personality, respectively, traditional ways of defining masculinity and femininity should not be tampered with. The idea here is that any change in society's conceptions of male or female gender roles and specific gender-typed behaviors can only lead to harmful consequences for both society and the individual.

How the identity paradigm developed and what psychological theories of masculinity and femininity account for it provide a revealing analysis of the trends of psychological research over the past forty years. Pleck outlined three specific research trends that underlie the present-day identity model of masculinity: the bipolar, the multilevel, and the androgynous theories of masculinity. Let's examine each in turn.

The Bipolar Perspective on Masculinity. Beginning in the 1930s and lasting well into the 1950s, psychologists devised all kinds of psychological measures of masculinity and femininity. Basically, masculinity and femininity were viewed as mutually exclusive categories of gender-appropriate traits, interests, and attitudes. For example, if a man stated he liked to play football, work on a car, and read sports magazines—all traditionally defined gender-typed masculine activities—it was assumed that he would not like to play croquet, do needlework, and read romance stories—all traditionally defined gender-typed feminine activities. In terms of this approach, masculinity was defined simply as a score earned on any number of masculinity-femininity (m-f) tests.

The Psychological Perspective

Let's illustrate this bipolar approach to m-f testing by referring to what one author calls the "world's second most widely used personality measure" (Lewin, 1984b, p. 183), Harrison Gough's (1952) *California Personality Inventory* (CPI) that contains a masculinity-femininity scale within it. The goal for devising what Gough called his femininity (Fe) scale was "to develop an instrument which is brief, easy to administer, relatively subtle and unthreatening in content, and which will, at the same time, differentiate men from women" (p. 427). To get a sense of what kinds of items appear on a scale such as Gough's femininity scale, let's list several of its items here. The feminine response—that which is the opposite of masculine—follows each item and is noted by T (true) or F (false).

- I think I would like the work of a building contractor. (F)
- I prefer a shower to a bathtub. (F)
- Sometimes I feel that I am about to go to pieces. (T)
- I get excited very easily. (T)
- In school I was sometimes sent to the principal for cutting up. (F)
- I like mechanics magazines. (F)

As we can see with these items, Gough conceived of psychological masculinity-femininity as measurable by the responses a person gave to statements describing any number of emotional reactions, preferred activities, and occupational preferences. The more items a male answered in the male direction (e.g., the opposite true-false response of those items in the above list), the more masculine he was thought to be. However, a male who answered in the feminine direction and thus obtained a high femininity score was thought to have a poorly developed or inadequate masculine identity. The important features of this perspective were that masculinity was thought an inherent part of personality, was considered the opposite of femininity, and could be measured, that is, defined, by various psychological tests.

The Multilevel Perspective on Masculinity. During the 1950s and 1960s, a second theoretical perspective emerged: this one incorporated Sigmund Freud's psychoanalytic views on the dual nature of consciousness and unconsciousness and the bipolar perspective on masculinity and femininity. Freud had theorized that personality contains both conscious and unconscious levels, and thus several psychologists speculated that masculinity must also have both unconscious and conscious levels. According to this view, then, gender identity could be cast in terms of having two distinct levels, either of which could be masculine or feminine in its makeup. Theoretically, a male's gender identity could take on one of four possible combinations: (1) unconscious and conscious masculinity, (2) unconscious and conscious femininity, (3) unconscious femininity and conscious masculinity, and (4) unconscious masculinity and conscious femininity. As psychologists grew more skillful in constructing ambiguous tests (i.e., projective tests), attention focused on those tests that purportedly measured the deeper, more unconscious features of masculinity (Franck & Rosen, 1949). Although the psychoanalytically oriented approach to gender identity is not as popular as it once was, some still examine the male gender from its perspective (Fogel, Lane & Liebert, 1986).

The Androgynous Perspective on Masculinity. The third and most recent theoretical perspective of the identity model is referred to as *androgynous.* Although psychological research into the construct of androgyny and the differences between an androgynous person and others is little more than a decade old, an air of controversy already swirls about its meanings and measurements. Here we will only trace some of the high points in this fascinating area.

What is **androgyny,** and what does it mean to call a person androgynous? Alexandra Kaplan and Mary Anne Sedney (1980, p. 6) define androgyny as "the combined presence of socially valued, stereotypic, feminine and masculine characteristics." In other words, in most people's minds androgyny refers to a combination, or a blend, of socially acceptable masculine and feminine stereotypical traits. As for an androgynous person, he or she is one who possesses and exhibits through his or her behaviors a combination of socially valued masculine *and* feminine traits. Such a person might describe himself or herself as competitive and assertive (both positively valued masculine traits) *as well as* warm and supportive (both positively valued feminine traits). Although androgyny may be relatively new to the social sciences, it has a long history in literature (C. Heilbrun, 1973).

During the mid-1970s, two different measurement scales were published comprised of sets of socially desirable, self-descriptive adjectives designed to measure masculinity and femininity as independent or unrelated constructs rather than as negatively related bipolar constructs. Sandra Bem's (1974; the *Bem Sex Role Inventory,* or BSRI) and Janet Spence's (Spence, Helmreich & Stapp, 1974; *Personal Attributes Questionnaire,* or PAQ) scales soon became the measures of choice for those interested in androgyny and gender research. (For a review of these and other androgyny measures, see Ballard-Reisch & Elton, 1992; Cook, 1985; Kelley & Worrell, 1977; Lenney, 1991.) Not only were these measures easy to administer to groups and easy to score but the resulting research seemed to buttress a growing acceptance that a person's mental health and social adjustment were related to his or her being androgynous.

Using these measures, a person could fall into one of four categories, each with their own gender-typed characteristics: a masculine type (i.e., high masculine-low feminine), a feminine type (i.e., low masculine-high feminine), an androgynous type (i.e., high masculine-high feminine), and lastly, an undifferentiated type (i.e., low masculine-low feminine). Soon after the arrival of the BSRI and PAQ scales, a virtual plethora of research appeared looking at androgyny and its many relationships with other constructs such as self-esteem and personal or social adjustment (Cook, 1985; Marsh & Myers, 1986; Payne, 1987).

However, after the initial positive acclaim for the androgyny scales, critical voices could be heard noting some of the psychometric problems inherent in them (e.g., Taylor & Hall, 1982). For example, some criticized the BSRI and PAQ for only containing socially desirable traits leading to what researchers call a method effect (Baumrind, 1983). In other words, a person's response to two sets of socially desirable items (i.e., the masculine and the feminine items) may mask the real, or true, relationship between one's masculine and feminine traits, which include some negative masculine and feminine traits as well.

The Psychological Perspective

Another problem with these scales was their masculine items seemed to play a larger role in the relationship to other variables (e.g., self-esteem) rather than both the masculine and feminine items contributing jointly to this relationship (Antill & Cunningham, 1980; Lau, 1989). It seemed androgyny, then, was more advantageous for females than for males (Heilbrun, 1984; Heilbrun & Mulqueen, 1987). Some even began to question the independence of masculine and feminine traits, an assumption underlying the androgyny construct (Heilbrun & Bailey, 1986). Even Janet Spence (1984), herself an author of one of the original androgyny scales, argued that the concepts of masculinity and femininity should be relabeled (i.e., instrumentality and expressiveness). Furthermore, she contended that androgyny scales, her own and others, should not be used to measure gender-related constructs.

While the construct of androgyny has captured the interest of many in the gender area, it has also spawned more than a few methodological and theoretical problems in its wake. What the future of androgyny holds is anyone's guess for the time being. Already some have moved to abolish any mention of gender-specific notions seeing the wave of the future in terms of a transcendence of gender, a period when people will no longer be seen in terms of masculine, feminine, or androgynous traits. What a transcendent world would be like is difficult to imagine given the centuries of gender-based categorization we would have to dismiss to accomplish a gender-free world. However, some science fiction authors like Ursuala LeGuin (1969) have created worlds where gender differences are totally nonexistent.

Even though these perspectives vary in how they describe the dimensions of masculinity and femininity, they share some common elements, including the beliefs that personality traits (for example, toughness, warmth, aggressiveness) can be described as either masculine or feminine gender-typed characteristics and that can be tapped or measured by psychological tests. These commonalities suggest that the bipolar, multilevel, and androgynous perspectives are more similar than might first be apparent.

The Male Gender Role Strain Paradigm

Although psychologists have been enamored with the propositions and tenets of the identity paradigm for several decades now, recent research findings have forced many to question its validity. As a critique of the identity paradigm, Pleck has proposed a new gender paradigm, the **gender role strain paradigm,** which he outlined in the following ten propositions:

1. Gender roles are operationally defined by gender role stereotypes and norms.
2. Gender roles are contradictory and inconsistent.
3. The proportion of individuals who violate gender roles is high.
4. Violating gender roles leads to social condemnation.
5. Violating gender roles leads to negative psychological consequences.
6. Actual or imagined violation of gender roles leads individuals to overconform to them.
7. Violating gender roles has more serious consequences for males than females.
8. Certain characteristics prescribed by gender roles are psychologically dysfunctional.
9. Males and females both experience gender role strain in their work and family roles.
10. Historical changes cause gender role strain.

If we compare these ten propositions with the eleven contained in the identity paradigm (see pages 82–83), we can discern a definite shift or change in the basic assumptions underlying how one can best understand the male gender and masculinity.

First of all, recall the identity paradigm insists that psychological masculinity or femininity is an innate feature of personality that can be measured by certain psychological tests. However, in the strain paradigm one's gender, or what some call masculinity or femininity, is viewed as a complex set of widely shared beliefs about gender-typed traits that are typical (i.e., gender-related stereotypes) and desirable (i.e., gender-related norms) for males and females (Proposition 1). In other words, the strain model argues that what people commonly refer to as psychological masculinity is not an innate feature of a male's personality but rather a compilation of gender-typed behaviors learned by a male in order to adapt to situational demands and social pressures. The identity paradigm sees masculinity as a basic and an innate psychological feature of a male's personality, whereas in the strain paradigm, masculinity is a set of behaviors thought useful to adapt to various social demands and pressures. Here then is a crucial difference in how each paradigm looks at and defines masculinity.

Second, the identity paradigm posits that one's identity is a risky and failure-prone feature of personality development, especially for males. In other words, many things can go wrong in a male's developing gender identity and often do; by and large, the end result of a poorly developed or inadequate masculine gender identity is the cause of many other psychological problems experienced by the male. However, the strain model states that because of the built-in inconsistencies and contradictions among various elements of the male gender role, many males think of themselves as inadequate and feel a sense of insecurity; they experience personal role strain as a result of not living up to society's expectations for them (Propositions 2–7). For example, when a male feels he is not as aggressive, successful, or tough as he thinks other males are, he may feel it is his fault rather than sensing that the problem lies not in himself but in the contradictory social expectations placed on him by the male gender. Basically, then, the identity paradigm places full blame for many of the male's problems on his supposedly underdeveloped or inadequate masculine gender identity, whereas the strain paradigm indicts society for its support of contradictory gender role expectations that make many males feel less masculine than they think other males are.

More recently, Pleck along with his research colleagues (1993, in press) have built upon this notion and underscored the negative consequences associated with males' enactment of certain behaviors, especially among adolescent males, in their discussion of the **masculinity ideology,** a construct which refers to people's attitudes or beliefs about the importance of men adhering to culturally defined standards for male behavior.

A third component of the strain paradigm points out that in their attempt to live up to the male gender role many males actually develop unhealthy or dysfunctional behaviors (Proposition 8). For example, a male who believes he must be aggressive or emotionally constricted in order to be masculine may find himself

The Psychological Perspective

behaving in an unhealthy fashion. Such a male may develop serious psychological problems or behave in antisocial ways simply by trying to live up to unrealistic and, more often than we might think, overly risky gender role expectations.

A fourth feature of the strain paradigm notes that many men feel personal conflict when they cannot realistically accomplish all of the demands placed on them by virtue of their family and work roles (Proposition 9). Because a man is expected to be successful in the competitive world of work and also a dutiful and sensitive husband and father, many men literally feel inadequate in their masculinity because they are not able to accomplish all of their goals and objectives in these roles.

Fifth, the strain paradigm suggests that because society is changing so rapidly and available opportunities to prove oneself to be a real he-man seem to be shrinking, many males feel less masculine than men apparently did in previous generations (Proposition 10). Granted, society is changing, and many of today's men simply do not feel they can prove themselves and their masculinity in the ways that, for example, the adventurous frontiersmen did. The question the strain model asks is, how can a man feel like John Wayne, Sylvester Stallone, or even Tom Cruise when there are so few physically demanding frontiers to conquer or so few ways to be a "top gun"?

Pleck's gender role strain paradigm and the masculinity ideology construct present a new perspective on a number of troubling issues facing many men nowadays. Many psychologists and psychiatrists would have men look inside and examine their masculine gender identity for the root of their problem. Pleck's approach, on the other hand, would have men look at society's standards and expectations for males and question and challenge their reasonableness. As Pleck sees it (and others as well), the problems facing many men today rest not inside a purportedly fragile masculine identity but rather in a man's society with its overly restrictive and often contradictory definitions of what it means to be a man today.

As we might expect, Pleck's views have begun to stimulate research looking with particular interest at many of their underlying assumptions. To a considerable extent, researchers are finding it a fertile field of study and one where the onus of many men's problems seems more related to society's expectations for men rather than to something residing within today's men (Eisler & Skidmore, 1987; O'Neil, Helms, Gable, David & Wrightman, 1986; Ravinder, 1987; Snell, Jr., Belk & Hawkins II, 1986; Thompson, 1990; Thompson, Pleck & Ferrara, 1992).

As more and more contemporary women and men begin to question and challenge their respective gender roles, psychology can best assist them by systematically debunking those persistent myths that have grown up and supported the unrealistic, contradictory, and oftentimes, debilitating aspects of gender roles (Benderly, 1987; Del Boca & Ashmore, 1986). Rather than helping people adjust to or fit into outmoded gender expectations, clinical psychologists, counselors, and psychiatrists would do better to assist people in their strivings for *self-actualization* (i.e., helping people develop their full capabilities and potentialities regardless of their gender). Once we all learn to see ourselves and others as basically capable, competent, and growing individuals with considerable potential rather than as people trying to cope with restrictive gender norms and gender stereotypes, we might find the world a better place to live in.

important terms

Ashmore, R., Del Boca, F., & Wohlers, A. (1986). Gender stereotypes. In R. Ashmore & F. Del Boca (Eds.), *The social psychology of female-male relations: A critical analysis of central concepts* (pp. 69–119). Orlando, FL: Academic Press.

Baker, M. (Ed.). (1987). *Sex difference in human performance*. New York: Wiley.

Beall, A. E., & Sternberg, R. J. (Eds.). (1993). *The psychology of gender*. New York: Guilford Press.

Benderly, B. (1987). *The myth of two minds: What gender means and doesn't mean*. New York: Doubleday.

Carter, D. (Ed.). (1987). *Current conceptions of sex roles and sex typing: Theory and research*. New York: Praeger Publishers.

Eagly, A. (1987). *Sex difference in social behavior: A social-role interpretation*. Hillsdale, NJ: Erlbaum.

Hare-Mustin, R., & Marecek, J. (1988). The meaning of difference: Gender theory, postmodernism, and psychology. *American Psychologist, 43,* 455–464.

Hyde, J., & Linn, M. (Eds.). (1986). *The psychology of gender: Advances through meta-analysis*. Baltimore: Johns Hopkins University Press.

Katz, P. (1986). Gender identity: Development and consequences. In R. Ashmore & F. Del Boca (Eds.), *The social psychology of female-male relations: A critical analysis of central concepts* (pp. 21–67). Orlando, FL: Academic Press.

Levant, R. F., & Pollack, W. S. (Eds.). (1995). *Toward a new psychology of men*. New York: Basic Books.

Pleck, J. (1981). *The myth of masculinity*. Cambridge: The MIT Press.

suggested readings

The Psychological Perspective

Chapter 5

The Social Roles Perspective

All the world's a stage, and all the men and women merely players. They have their exits and entrances; and one man in his time plays many parts.

William Shakespeare

As described in the last chapter, the psychological perspective focuses on the individual or, more specifically, a person's abilities, traits, and behaviors. In this chapter though we move our focus back from the solitary person to include the interactions between people, or more precisely the social situations wherein a person *interacts* with others. As we will see, gender plays a large role in these social interactions. The fact is a person's *perceived* gender—whether others think of one as a male or female—influences how they treat the person. People interact according to how they perceive the other's gender and on the basis of what they then think is appropriate for each gender. For this reason, sociologists and social psychologists have turned their attention and research to explaining how gender influences interactions and, in turn, how interactions influence gendered behaviors (Hearn & Morgan, 1990; Kimmel, 1987; Oskamp & Costanzo, 1993; Shaver & Hendrick, 1987). In this chapter then we will examine the work of both disciplines—sociology and social psychology—and speak of their combined contributions as the **social roles perspective.**

To exemplify the social roles perspective on gender, especially the male gender, we will examine first the socialization process and the several socializing agents that shape a person's gender development: parents, media, education, and peers. We will then discuss several theories that explain how a person acquires his or her gender identity.

At the moment of birth a human infant is a totally dependent and helpless creature. Born with a few reflexes such as sucking and orienting its head, a newborn could not survive for more than a few hours without the assistance of other people. In contrast, the young of most animal species are born with innate and complex behavior patterns called *instincts* that allow the animal to adjust quickly to its environment. Humans, on the other hand, are born ignorant of the ways of their environment. The primary means that a helpless and dependent human infant has to acquire the necessary skills and talents to adapt effectively to its environment is socialization (Handel, 1988). **Socialization** is the process by which humans, beginning in infancy and extending throughout life, learn the ways of their group.

Every society has their own distinctive features, including certain behaviors, traditions, values, and beliefs. By means of the socialization process, these features are passed from one generation to another (Kohn, 1977; Stopes-Roe & Cochrane, 1990). In our society, children learn to eat with forks, knives, and spoons; in Japan, children learn to eat with chopsticks. We are not only taught what utensils to eat with but also other, more complex behaviors such as how we should interact with others. For instance, in social interactions, Arabs stand much closer together in conversation, touch more often, and lean toward each other more than North Americans do (Hall, 1959, 1966). Socialization even accounts for the values a particular society espouses. For example, children in the United States are taught to share primarily with members of their immediate family; children living on an Israeli kibbutz learn to share with many other people outside the immediate family. Socialization thus accounts for a variety of behaviors and values that distinguish one society from another.

the socialization process and gender

The Social Roles Perspective

Let's now discuss some specific ways society inculcates its young in the ways of their gender. To do this, we will take a look at some of the more important socializing agents that most sociologists and social psychologists consider as primary shapers of gender-related behavior.

**the
socializing
agents**

Let's begin by examining the ways in which the socialization process molds a young male into what his society deems essential for manhood. We will focus on what sociologists call **socializing agents,** or those "significant individuals, groups, or institutions that provide structured situations in which socialization takes place" (Robertson, 1987, p. 128; see also Jacklin & Reynolds, 1993). Here, then, we will concentrate on four important socializing agents that shape a boy's gender development: his parents, the media, the educational system, and his peers (Handel, 1988).

Parents

The study of the family is undergoing a reexamination of its past, present, and future. Topics such as the feminist movement, varying sexual patterns, new family structures, changing social expectations, and inherent role conflicts (e.g., juggling the often conflicting demands of the workplace against those of the family) within the traditional family unit are being examined in countless courses around the country. In this section we will examine how parental expectations and treatments affect both genders, especially the male.

Even before a child is born, society's values influence couples who plan on having children. In countless ways, males are more valued in our society than are females. For example, for well over fifty years, researchers have documented that a majority of couples want their firstborn child to be a male (Doyle & Paludi, 1995; Winston, 1932). Historically, having males rather than females may have provided parents with an economic hedge against their old age. But today, preferring a male over a female seems at least an anachronism if not a foreboding of possible future problems. Several years ago Amitai Etzioni (1968), a highly respected social scientist at Columbia University, pointed to this problem when he noted that with the expanding field of prenatal technology the day is fast approaching when parents will be able to select their child's gender, and if males are still preferred, we will run the risk of males outnumbering females. One can hope that before the day of "select-a-sex," society will have progressed beyond its biased favoritism of one gender over the other (Leo, 1989; Warren, 1985).

In general, parents have different expectations for each gender (Eccles et al., 1993; Forisha, 1978), many of which can be seen even before birth. For example, many a pregnant woman has remarked that she must be carrying a boy because of her fetus's excessive movements. Why a boy and not a girl? These women are simply expressing what is commonly accepted by many adults: Boys are more active and energetic, and girls more gentle and sedentary, even *in utero*.

Aside from the expectant parents' frequent references to the probable gender of their growing fetus, the socialization process begins in earnest at birth. Others besides the parents are quick to differentiate between the genders. After a quick check of the genitals, the attending doctor and nurses often describe a male newborn as robust and strapping and a female as petite and adorable. Even in the delivery room, society views each gender in very different ways. It is not surprising, then, that parents follow suit and view their newborn infant as robust or adorable.

In a classical study conducted by Jeffrey Rubin (1974) and his associates, parents described their newborn infant on the day of its birth. Rubin interviewed the fathers after each had observed his infant in the nursery and the mothers later on the same day after each had handled and fed her infant. Furthermore, the parents rated their infant on an eighteen-item bipolar scale containing items such as *active* versus *passive, strong* versus *weak,* and *noisy* versus *quiet*. Parents of male infants described their sons as "firmer, larger, better coordinated, more alert, stronger, and hardier." Parents of females, on the other hand, described their daughters as softer, smaller, prettier, and more delicate. Fathers, more so than mothers, described their infants of either gender in more extreme ways. Surprisingly in light of the different physical descriptions given by these parents, the infants of both genders were not appreciably different in their average heights, weights, and Apgar scores, which are ratings of color, muscle tonicity, reflex irritability, and heart and respiratory rates assigned by the attending physician within ten minutes of birth.

The Social Roles Perspective

Obviously, parents do more than just attribute one set of characteristics to one gender and another to the other. Parents also encourage gender-typed activities. For example, when Jerrie Will and her associates (1976) told a group of mothers they were playing with a nine-month-old male, they offered "him" a toy train to play with. When a different group of mothers played with the same infant, this time identified as female, these mothers offered "her" a doll. In the minds of these mothers, it seems, little boys should enjoy trains more than dolls. What gender label a child is assigned does, then, seem to influence the ways adults act toward a child (Delk, Madden, Livingston & Ryan, 1986; Sidorowicz & Lunney, 1980). However, recently Michele Paludi and Dominic Gullo (1987) found some evidence that an infant's gender label *alone* may not affect people's perceptions of how an infant should act. Furthermore, when numerous gender-labeling studies are taken together, knowledge of an infant's sex is not found to be a powerful determinant of adults' reactions (Stern & Karracker, 1989).

It is clear that if little boys are to grow up to be "real men," they need more than toy trains to play with. Little boys need to learn certain male-appropriate behaviors. But how do parents teach their sons to act differently from girls? At least part of the answer is provided by the findings of a longitudinal study conducted by Susan Goldberg and Michael Lewis (1969) who observed thirty-two males and thirty-two females and their mothers in free-play activities and in a frustration-producing situation. At thirteen months of age, the girls were more dependent on their mothers, clung to them more, showed less exploratory behaviors, and displayed a quieter play style. The boys, on the other hand, showed considerable independence of their mothers, were more vigorous and exploratory, and displayed frequent gross motor activities such as jumping, banging on objects, and running around the playroom. To produce frustration in the children, the researchers placed a barrier between a child and his or her mother. In this situation, girls generally stood at the barrier and cried for their mothers, whereas most of the boys tried to get around the barrier. (For different reactions from young children, see Brooks & Lewis, 1974; Jacklin, Maccoby & Dick, 1973.) In both the play and the frustration settings, then, the children showed striking gender differences in their behaviors (Wasserman & Lewis, 1985).

When Goldberg and Lewis examined these gender differences, they found a link between the behaviors of the thirteen-month-old children with different mother-child interactions when the children were six months old. In general, the mothers of females touched, talked with, and handled their daughters significantly more than the mothers of the males did. Therefore, Goldberg and Lewis concluded that the early differential interaction accounted for a part of the children's later behaviors.

Parents also create different environments for each gender. In a study of preschoolers' bedrooms, Rheingold and Cook (1975) found obvious differences in the decor and the toys provided for males and females. Boys' rooms were more likely to be furnished in a "masculine" motif with sports equipment, trucks, and military paraphernalia. Girls' bedrooms showed a preference for a "feminine" decor with dolls and domestic materials very much in evidence. A more recent study also found gender-stereotypic decors in children's bedrooms (Pomerleau et al., 1990). Further, Cythinia Miller (1987) found that adults can easily differentiate children's toys as "boy toys" and "girl toys" and that children as young as 18 months showed a decidedly gender-stereotyped preference for them (see Caldera et al., 1989; Idle, Wood & Desmarais, 1993). It seems then that people have little trouble segregating "boy toys" from "girl toys."

In the research cited thus far, we see that parents generally attribute different characteristics, present different gender-typed activities, interact differently, and create different environments for each gender. What do parents wish to accomplish with these different parenting practices? They obviously want their sons to become men and their daughters to become women. But is there a single feature that parents expect more of in their male children and less of in their female children? Apparently, yes; the much sought-after feature appears to be independence. A young boy must be taught to be independent or self-reliant if he is to become a real man in our society. Of course, parents want both their sons *and* daughters to be independent, but independence in the male is considered more important, a *primary* requisite for manhood. Some of the research in differential parenting practices points out that parents strive to push their sons toward independence more than they do their daughters (Aries & Olver, 1985).

Recall that in Goldberg and Lewis' research, thirteen-month-old boys clung less to their mothers and explored more (both early examples of independence) than similarly aged girls did. This gender difference was found to relate to the boys' mothers' withholding contact or touch at an earlier age. In another study, a group of mothers was asked at what age they would allow their child to use a pair of scissors unsupervised and when their child could play away from home without them (Hoffman, 1975). Mothers of boys gave much earlier ages for both activities than did mothers of girls. Furthermore, in a study conducted in Canada some years ago, parents of boys reported that they would be less likely to offer comfort to their son if he complained of a minor injury than they would if their daughter so complained (Lambert, Yackley & Hein, 1971). While some parents say they are more likely to leave a boy alone (Fagot, 1978), other parents intervene more quickly when boys engage in risky behaviors (Kronsberg, Schmaling & Fagot, 1985). Overall, we can say boys' activities tend to be more exploratory (Block, 1983) and less structured by adults than girls' (Carpenter, 1983; Huston & Carpenter, 1984).

Granted, withholding contact and comfort and allowing a child to play unattended encourage a type of independence; another powerful determinant of independence appears to be the type of punishment used to teach desired behaviors in a child's early years (Fagot, 1985; Felson & Russo, 1988; Herzberger & Tennen, 1985). One can punish a child in a variety of ways. Here, again, parents use different types of punishment for each gender. Lenore Weitzman (1984, p. 173) points out that

> Boys are subjected to more physical punishment, whereas psychological punishments, such as the threat of withdrawal of love, are more frequently used for girls. *Children trained with physical punishment have been shown typically to be more self-reliant and independent.* The other method of childtraining—the love-oriented or psychological method—usually produces children who are more obedient and dependent. As girls are most often trained with psychological methods they are exposed to more affection and less punishment than boys. (Italics added.)

The Social Roles Perspective

If, as Weitzman suggests, physical punishment is more likely to create a sense of independence—a "desired" goal for a young male—it seems only reasonable to ask if physical punishment may produce some undesirable traits as well. In an early analysis of the male gender, Ruth Hartley (1974, pp. 7–8) suggested that boys are generally subjected to more physical punishment than are girls and added that physical punishment brings on some negative consequences. In particular, she noted that:

> . . . more stringent demands are made on boys than on girls and at an early age, when they are least able to understand either the reasons for or the nature of the demands. Moreover, these demands are frequently enforced harshly, impressing the small boy with the danger of deviation from them, while he does not quite understand what they are. To make matters more difficult, the desired behavior is rarely defined positively as something the child *should* do, but rather, undesirable behavior is indicated negatively as something he should *not* do or be—anything, that is, that the parent or other people regard as "sissy." Thus, very early in life the boy must either stumble on the right path or bear repeated punishment without warning when he accidently enters into the wrong ones. This situation gives us practically a perfect combination for inducing anxiety—the demand that the child do something which is not clearly defined to him, based on reasons he cannot possibly appreciate, and enforced with threats, punishments, and anger by those who are close to him.

While much of the research discussed up to this point makes a case that parents treat their male and female children differently, we need to voice a caveat here. Recently, Lytton and Romney (1991) conducted a meta-analysis of 127 studies dealing with parental treatment of children. Overall, while their large-scale analysis found that parents do treat their children differently in terms of encouraging gender-typed activities (e.g., apparel), they also found that parents do *not* interact with the male and female children differently in certain other areas (e.g., type and kinds of verbal interaction, encouragement toward achievement). Further, in a recent review of the parent-child interaction literature, Jacklin and Baker (1993) argued that parents probably do not socialize their children along gender lines as much as other non-parent adults do (relatives, teachers, peers). Thus, although parents play a significant role in shaping their offsprings' understanding of gender, we need to look more carefully at some of the other socializing agents that may be more influential in shaping the young along gendered-lines.

The Media

A few years ago, the saying, "You are what you eat," made the rounds among dieting circles. Of course, eating is important, but food isn't everything. We could just as well substitute the idea, "You are what you see and read." Europeans and Americans are a visual people who take in their world, by and large, through documentaries and sitcoms and articles and books. The values, beliefs, and gender-appropriate behaviors of a majority of young people are shaped by the various media (Dorr, 1986; Liebert & Sprafkin, 1988; Remafedi, 1990; Signorielli, 1990). Let's begin our discussion of the media and their socializing impact on the young with a look at television.

Television Programming. Several years ago, Newton Minnow, then chairperson of the Federal Communications Commission, indicted television as being a "vast wasteland." Possibly following Minnow's lead, many people today take pleasure in vilifying television. However, television still remains a popular entertainment form and a powerful educational source, as well as a primary means that young people have for defining their respective genders (Dorr, 1986; Signorielli & Lears, 1992).

For preschool children, television, or the "flickering blue parent" as some disparagingly call it, is a primary socializing agent and one that attracts different pre-school audiences as well as presents different messages to these audiences. For instance, in a recent 2-year longitudinal study of children from 3- to 5-years-old, Aletha Huston (et al., 1990) found that boys watched more cartoons and action-adventure programs than girls did. Overall such television fare portrays males and females in very gender-stereotypical ways (Signorielli, 1989).

Besides showing traditional gender patterns, children's television shows portray the genders in a biased and somewhat unrealistic fashion. The males are usually presented as aggressive, dominant, and engaged in exciting activities from which they receive rewards from others for their "masculine" accomplishments. Females, on the other hand, are often presented in auxiliary roles; they are usually deferential to boys and men and receive little reward or feedback for their activities (Sternglanz & Serbin, 1974). Thus many social scientists believe that children's television programming has a decided male bias in the fare that it serves its young preschool audience.

Obviously, children do not limit their viewing only to "children's" programs. Young children watch prime-time shows as well. The television industry allegedly exhibits sensitivity to the young viewer's presence during the late afternoon and early evening by presenting situation comedy and family-oriented shows. Adult fare with its flair for violence and sex is reserved for later hours when children are supposedly in bed. But the demarcation between family and adult hours is something of a prefabrication on the part of television programmers. Some experts estimate that approximately three-quarters of a million young children are in the television audience between midnight and 2 A.M. (*U.S. News & World Reports,* 1981). Thus it is legitimate to ask how the genders are portrayed during prime time.

Michele Long and Rita Simon (1974) in a study of twenty-two family programs found women generally portrayed as dependent on men and men generally portrayed as independent of women and in control of the situation. In another study, male characters were shown in ambitious, adventuresome, strong, and dominant roles, whereas females were cast in dependent, submissive, and weak roles (Busby, 1974). Overall, television depicts men as either heroes or villains and women as either adulators or victims (Tedesco, 1974). The conclusion drawn from these and other more recent studies is that men are expected, at least in the minds of the producers, to act independently and aggressively and to be in charge, whereas women are the bystanders in life's drama (Greenberg, 1982; McCauley, Thangavelu & Rozin, 1988; *Media & Values,* 1989; Signorielli, 1989).

Although we've concentrated on children's and prime-time shows here, recently, a whole new video genre has come on the screen—one that may have a

The Social Roles Perspective

greater impact on how the young see their respective genders—namely, music videos. In a study of their content, Jane D. Brown and Kenneth Campbell (1986) found that music videos present the genders in rather stereotypic ways. For instance, most males are not shown doing domestic work, and most females are not shown doing professional work. In the world of MTV, then, it seems that men's and women's work are still worlds apart (Sommers-Flanagan et al., 1993).

Television Commercials. Television commercials have also been studied for their prevailing messages about the genders. Thirty- or sixty-second advertising spots contain potent messages not only about a product but about life as well. Frequently, a product is wrapped in social values, a particular life-style, or some other ploy, such as sex, to capture a viewer's interest. Children learn much about their gender from commercials.

Commercials are usually aimed at women—the primary purchasers at grocery and retail counters. Keenly aware of the traditional female roles of housewife and mother or the multi-role woman as wife-mother-job holder, Madison Avenue generally shows women alarmed over the waxy buildup on the floor, recoiling from unpleasant odors emanating from toilet bowls, reeling from a head-thumping migraine, or vexed over the softness of toilet tissue. In general, women are often portrayed as concerned only with household problems. Interestingly, the voice-over in a majority of these "for women only" commercials is male—authoritative and always ready to ease a woman's burden with a cure-all product (Bretl & Cantor, 1988; Marecek et al., 1978).

However, Madison Avenue presents a completely different picture of men in commercials. Men are shown as involved with cars and tools and as sharing the natural reward after a trying day at office or plant—a beer (Postman et al., 1987). In television commercials, males are aggressive, competitive, independent—always macho. The only time men are portrayed as less than "real men" is when they are trapped in the house. Several years ago Bardwick & Schumann (1967) took note of this feature in television commercials:

> The image of the American man in TV commercials as muscular, knowledgeable, dominating, independent, sexy, cosmopolitan, athletic, authoritative and aggressive exists only when he is seen away from his family. In embarrassing contrast the American father and husband is portrayed as passive, stupid, infantile and emasculated. . . . But outside the house trouble is what he's looking for. Swift as a panther, stealthy as a cougar, free as a mustang he speeds to his rendezvous with status, independence and violence.

Research on the relationship between various products and the portrayal of the genders supports the assertion that commercials present both genders in rather stereotypic ways (Kolbe & Langefeld, 1993; Stein, 1993). For example, women—young, attractive, and seductive—appear in cosmetic commercials; men—strong, decisive, and virile—appear in car and beer commercials (Courtney & Whipple, 1974; Lovdal, 1989). The underlying message is that women are concerned only with their physical attributes, preservation of their beauty, and delay of the aging process, and men are interested only in power, status, and achievement (Chappell, 1983; Harris & Stobart, 1986; Livingstone & Green, 1986).

Children, whether we like it or not, do learn from commercials. They not only pester parents for a specific cereal touted by a favorite cartoon character, they also see women on their knees in a kitchen or perplexed over which brand of laundry soap to use, whereas men are flying planes, playing baseball, and drinking beer.

Children's Books. Children's books are another source for socializing young children into society's image of appropriate gender-typed behaviors. Again Lenore Weitzman (1979, p. 7) writes,

> Through books, children learn about the world outside their immediate environment: they learn what other boys and girls do, say, and feel, and they learn what is expected of children their age. Picture books are especially important to the preschool child because they are often looked at over and over again at a time when children are in the process of developing their own sex role identities. In addition, they are read to children before other socialization influences (such as school, teachers, and peers) become important in their lives.

In the past decade or so, several studies have been conducted on the content of children's picture books especially with an eye to the representation of and activities engaged in by male and female characters, as well as how gender-neutral storybook characters are labeled by adults (Collins, Ingoldsby & Dellman, 1984; DeLoache, Cassidy & Carpenter, 1987). Several years ago Weitzman studied just how children's books presented gender. Weitzman et al. (1972) analyzed those children's books that had been awarded the prized Caldecott Medal for excellence in children's literature. The analysis was revealing about how these books portrayed the genders and what social expectations were placed on each. A majority of these books presented males and their adventures; whereas for the most part, females were remarkably absent. Furthermore, male characters were involved in a variety of challenging roles that required skill, competence, and independent action; female characters were presented in passive or auxiliary roles. The message contained in most of these first readers is quite clear: Boys and men lead exciting lives in which they are expected to overcome difficult obstacles and eventually achieve the sought-after goal; girls and women—when they are shown—are presented as secondary to the plot and usually performing monotonous and less demanding tasks.

Although in recent years authors of children's books have attempted to rectify many of the gender stereotypes so prevalent in years past, change is slow and not as significant as many want (Crabb & Bielawski, 1994; Davis, 1984; Kolbe & LaVoie, 1981; Kortenhaus & Demarest, 1993; Purcell & Stewart, 1990). In a recent study of children's creative writing, Mary Trepanier and Jane Romatowski (1985) found elementary children continue to see males and females in very different and relatively gender-stereotypic ways. Though we might want to think the past several decades have seen significant changes in how people, especially the young, view men's and women's lives in various print media, this may be more hope than reality (see Luebke, 1989).

Beginning in their most impressionable years, boys learn from various media what it means to be a real man. The message presented serves males in only limited ways. Given the one-dimensional, stereotypic view of the male gender, Newton Minnow could have broadened his disparaging remark to include more than just television (Klumas & Marchant, 1994).

The Social Roles Perspective

table 5.1 Numbers and Percentages of Women in Various Professional Occupations in 1978 and 1988★

| | **Scientists** | | | **Engineers** | |
	1978	*1988*		*1978*	*1988*
Computer specialists	40,200	218,700	*Chemical*	2,500	12,500
	23%	31%		3%	8%
Biological	30,000	89,200	*Aeronautical*	600	5,300
	18%	30%		1%	4%
Mathematical	13,100	44,900	*Electrical*	3,500	23,800
	24%	27%		1%	4%
Physical	18,500	46,500	*Civil*	3,300	9,300
	9%	15%		2%	3%
Environmental	7,200	12,300	*Mechanical*	4,100	16,900
	10%	11%		1%	3%

★Source: National Science Foundation

The Educational System

Generally speaking, the educational system is responsible for preparing the young for adulthood. In earlier times, the young learned all they needed to know from their family. Formal education was a privilege reserved primarily for the wealthy. Nowadays, the young must acquire many skills in order to fit into our specialized world; consequently, no single family can provide all of the necessary education. Many young people enter school at around three or four years of age and continue through college and beyond. Given the importance of education in today's world, one would like to think that the educational system approaches each child with a minimum of bias and preconceived expectations. Nothing could be further from the truth.

Academic, Career-Orientation, and Athletic Programs. We should be somewhat skeptical of the platitudes dispensed by the educational system about the weights given a student's intellectual potential, socioemotional development, or even a student's own preference for one career or another. Statistics on different careers—a major by-product of the educational system—suggest that a student's gender determines in large part what careers await him or her (Blau & Ferber, 1985; Shakeshaft, 1987). Although the numbers of women holding various scientific and engineering positions have increased over the past decade, they still are quite low when compared to men in these positions. For instance, when we look at the numbers and percentages of women in Table 5.1, we realize that these high paying positions have a very definite male bias about their compositions.

How can one account for the wide disparity in career options between the genders? One answer appears to be the educational system's "tracking program." Students are counseled into programs that lead to specific careers on the basis of test results, student preferences, and more often than most would openly admit, the student's gender. Females—considered deft with their fingers and temperamentally suited to routine and monotonous tasks—make ideal "girl Fridays." Males—judged to excel in math and science—are "natural" candidates for professional careers (Jacobs, 1985; Stanworth, 1983).

Varied academic and career-oriented programs are not the only areas in education where males have been granted more favored status. Historically, athletic programs, especially team sports, have been a male preserve at all educational levels. In the minds of many, team sports are seen as an adolescent male's *rite de passage* through which boys become men. From grade school through college, team sports are considered the crucible in which boys learn the values of competition and cooperation that will serve them later on in the business world (see Messner & Sabo, 1990). However, there is a downside to sports participation finding it linked, for instance, to negative attitudes toward women among some male athletes (Houseworth et al., 1989). With the passage of Title IX of the Education Amendment of 1972, the more obvious forms of sex discrimination in school athletic programs were outlawed. In a report published in 1978 by the Department of Health, Education, and Welfare on the implementation of Title IX, the authors noted that the ". . . rules and policies that perpetuate unequal treatment of males and females—which are now clearly illegal—are still going uncorrected in the nation's schools." However, although today's college female athletes have more athletic resources, better coaching techniques, and greater visibility (Coakley, 1986), they still experience problems in gaining sufficient financial support and a modicum of role conflict between the expectations found in the athletic and female norms (Desertrain & Weiss, 1988).

We should not jump to the conclusion, however, that the educational system is completely enamored of the male from his first day in preschool until the final cap-and-gown ceremony many years later. For example, frequently in classrooms, boys are more apt to be distracted and distracting, evidencing behaviours referred to as "off-track." Such behaviors lead most to agree that boys present more discipline problems than girls (Kedar-Voivodas, 1983; Stockard et al., 1985). However, after studying elementary teachers' reactions toward pupils, one group of researchers noted "boys' frequent discipline problems do not seem to affect the overall picture of their achievement, perhaps because these are classified under normal 'naughty' conduct of boys" (Ben Tsvi-Mayer et al., 1989, p. 242).

Teachers. Until now we have focused on the educational system's tracking programs, the preferential treatment given males in athletic programs, and the charge that boys present more problems than girls. But what of day-to-day student-teacher interactions? Do teachers treat their students differently on the basis of gender? According to the literature, the latter question can be answered with a resounding yes (American Association of University Women, 1992; Gold, Crombie & Noble, 1987; Villimez, Eisenberg & Carroll, 1986). Let's focus on one study, although conducted over twenty years ago, still revealing to the degree to which teachers treat the genders differently and the behavioral consequences of this treatment on shaping boys' and girls' behaviors.

Psychologist Lisa Serbin (et al., 1973) observed fifteen preschool teachers in their classrooms. Serbin was interested in how these teachers handled problem behaviors among their students, especially aggressive and dependent behaviors. Overall, boys

The Social Roles Perspective

displayed more aggression and girls more dependence in the classroom. Serbin found this difference linked to how the teachers treated the genders and not to some innate gender difference.

In the classroom the teachers responded to each gender with a definite pattern. Simply put, the teachers responded to the boys' aggression but not to the girls'. In fact, the teachers reprimanded the boys more than three times more frequently for their aggressiveness than they did the girls for their aggressiveness. Common sense would suggest that aggressiveness that leads to reprimands should have caused the boys' aggression to decrease. If this were so, the boys should have been less aggressive than the girls. But common sense fails us in this matter. Paying attention, even a negative kind of attention such as a reprimand, does not decrease aggression but rather *increases* it. Aggression that is ignored, as it was with the girls, is less likely to continue. Boys' more frequent aggressiveness may therefore be the result of the teacher's attention to it rather than to some natural inclination among boys to act aggressively.

In regard to dependency, remember Serbin found girls were more dependent on their teachers than boys. Again Serbin found teachers' actions influencing this gender difference. When a boy asked for help with some task, his teacher gave aid no matter where he was in the room. On the other hand, when a girl requested help, her teacher complied only when she was nearby. The message is clear. Boys may venture away from authority and still receive help from an adult, but girls must stay nearby if they are to learn from an adult (an early form of dependency on others). Thus preschool teachers may unwittingly foster stereotypic behaviors in their students and add still more pressure to the socialization of young children into traditional gender-related behaviors.

Textbooks. Textbooks also have a definite socializing influence on young students. The materials presented in textbooks can and often do encourage traditional gender-typed attitudes and behaviors (Stanworth, 1983). Quite often the picture of the genders given in textbooks does not mirror the reality as experienced by students. For example, in an early study of the content of textbooks, Marjorie U'Ren (1971) found women in only 15 percent of the illustrations. U'Ren remarked that "The significance of this imbalance is obvious. We tend to forget the simple fact that the female sex is half the species, that women are not merely a ladies' auxiliary to the human race." (For a review of gender bias in college-level psychology and anatomy textbooks, see Denmark, 1983; Giacomini, Rozee-Koker & Pepitone-Arreola-Rockwell, 1986.)

Thus the educational system in general and teachers and textbooks in particular direct male and female students into traditionally prescribed gender categories. Boys are "tracked" into programs leading to jobs and careers that will enable them to become good providers for their future wives and children. The same socializing agents "track" girls into programs that will enable them to become good wives and mothers (Bybee et al., 1990).

The Peer Group

As children grow older they begin to spend more time with one very special group made up of other people about their own age and background—the peer group (Mueller & Cooper, 1985). School-aged children spend considerably more time with their peers than they do with their family. Children learn from one another, and what they learn from other socializing agents (parents, television, books, teachers) they often practice with other children (Billy & Udry, 1985; Davies & Kandel, 1981; Duveen, Lloyd & Smith, 1988; Lueptow, 1984; Thorne, 1993). The peer group provides a unique social situation in which children can rehearse new behaviors and a variety of roles with relative impunity from adult authority figures. As children become more independent of their parents, they grow more dependent on their peers. Peer acceptance and approval become highly valued personal needs that motivate most young people. Beginning in a child's preschool years and continuing well into adolescence, peer pressure is a powerful socializing agent for shaping one's gender-related behaviors (Fine, 1979, 1987; Mandell, 1986).

As suggested earlier, peer influence plays an important role in teaching and maintaining gender-typed behaviors. In fact, peer influence can override the influence of significant adults. For example, several years ago Beverly Fagot and Gerald Patterson (1969) observed boys in a preschool nursery playing with trucks, cars, and building materials, whereas girls played with dolls and artwork. When the teachers encouraged the boys to join in some "feminine" activities, the boys resisted. According to Fagot and Patterson, the boys appeared to ignore the attention and reinforcement from their teachers and preferred the company and approval of other boys. The fact that the boys resisted their teachers' influence points up an interesting feature of peer influence. It seems that boys try to influence others' behaviors more than girls do (Whiting & Edwards, 1973). Boys not only try to control others but they are probably more likely themselves to be controlled by other boys. We might therefore suggest that peer pressure is a more powerful influence in a young boy's life than in a young girl's.

Peer groups tend to be gender segregated throughout the childhood years. The interests and activities of these gender-segregated groups are clearly defined, at least in the minds of most young children (Paley, 1984). Interestingly, when Hartley and Hardesty (1964) asked a group of eight- to eleven-year-old boys and girls what activities they believed were appropriate for boys and girls, both groups showed a high degree of agreement. For example, both boys and girls believed playing with dolls and toy dishes was more appropriate for girls and playing with trucks and toy soldiers more appropriate for boys.

When we examine the activities that boys and girls attribute to each other, there is a continuity of sorts between girls' activities and the traditional adult female homemaker activities (for example domestic chores and child care), whereas there is an apparent lack of continuity between boys' activities and traditional adult male worker activities. Girls, it seems, have a more accurate view of the traditional female roles, whereas boys show an "ignorance" of traditional adult male roles. Gregory Stone noted this feature of children's play in the following anecdote.

> . . . a colleague noticed a boy and girl playing house in the front yard. The little girl was very busy sweeping up the play area, rearranging furniture, moving dishes about, and caring for baby dolls. The boy, on the other hand, would leave the play area on his bicycle, disappear to the back of the (real) house, remain for a brief while, reappear in the play area, and lie down in a feigned sleep. The little girl had a rather extensive knowledge of the mother role, but for the boy, a father was one who disappeared, reappeared, and slept, *ad infinitum*. (Stoll, 1979, p. 88)

Probably at no other time in a male's life are the demands to conform to peer group pressures greater than during adolescence. Philip Costanzo and Marvin Shaw (1966) found young people between eleven and seventeen years of age more likely to conform to peer pressures than at any other age. In many ways, a young male's acceptance and approval by his peer group is contingent on his acting out traditional features of the male gender in exaggerated ways. For example, proving oneself a man through acts of aggression and toughness is a necessary part of peer acceptance among many adolescent male groups (Chaze, 1981). The male who acts like a "chicken" or a "sissy" quickly finds himself spurned by his male peers. Overall, the adolescent male finds himself confronting numerous demands from his peers. He discards certain roles and activities associated with childhood and tries on newer ones related to his newly acquired status as a young male adult (Eder & Sanford, 1986).

learning one's gender identity

As noted in the last chapter, before we could discuss how a young child acquires his gender identity as male or female, we needed to describe the major socializing agents that affect or shape a person's gender identity. Now that we've covered the primary socializing agents (i.e., parents, media, school, and peers), we can speculate on how a person acquires specifically his or her gender identity. To do this we will describe several prominent theories that have addressed this issue. The first three theories take a decidedly psychological bent in explaining gender identity development, whereas the last one is more sociologically oriented in its analysis.

Theories of Gender Identity Development

For most of this century, one school of thought has dominated the field of psychology—behaviorism. Behaviorism argues that for psychology to be a legitimate scientific discipline it must focus solely on the observable when explaining people's behavior. But how does a behavioral model deal with gendered behavior? Quite simply: One *learns* to exhibit appropriate gender-related behaviors much like one learns any number of other behaviors. For several decades now, behaviorally oriented psychologists have argued that one's environment and its many socializing agents are the main determinants for teaching a child what and how to express appropriate gender-related behaviors. A concrete example of this perspective may prove helpful.

As noted earlier, many parents see their male and female children somewhat differently, as if they were looking through "gender-colored" glasses. Consequently, many parents treat their boys and girls somewhat differently (for example, rewarding their boys for playing ball and rewarding their girls for playing with dolls). The result of such differential treatment, according to one behaviorally oriented perspective, namely, Walter Mischel's (1966) **social-learning model** of gender identity acquisition, has a young boy or girl learning through others' rewards and reinforcements to act in certain gender-typical ways and, consequently, to experience their selves in different ways. Furthermore, this approach contends that a child learns gender-appropriate behaviors not only through others' reinforcements but also by first observing and then imitating significant and gender-similar models (i.e., young boys observe and imitate fathers, older brothers, important male peers, and respected male adults). In sum then, according to the social-learning model, gender identity is the end product of a years-long learning process where young boys or girls acquire gender-appropriate behaviors, attitudes, and beliefs through various learning principles (i.e., reinforcements, observation, and imitation).

A second perspective takes a more cognitive approach in describing just how gender identity unfolds. The central architect for this model, Lawrence Kohlberg (1966), argued that with the dawn of a young child's ability at self-labeling (i.e., "I am a boy" or "I am a girl") the first rays of a gender identity shine through. Following the establishment of this **self-labeling ability,** Kohlberg noted that a young boy or girl is more apt to begin imitating the behaviors of those others with a similar gender label (e.g., his father, brother, grandfather).

The final linchpin of a boy's gender identity comes with the development of what Kohlberg calls **gender constancy,** which is well established sometime between the fourth to sixth year. A youngster exhibits gender constancy when he or she becomes aware that his or her gender category ("boy" or "girl") and its many accompanying traits (e.g., "Boys are tough" or "Girls are polite") are a relatively fixed and stable part of his or her self-identity. In other words, when a child can reason as seen in his or her verbalizations that what makes him (or her) a boy (or a girl) and some of the basically socially prescribed differences cannot be changed by simply altering outside appearances or by age, one is displaying a sense of gender constancy. Once a child exhibits gender constancy, Kohlberg reasons that one's gender identity is firmly in place.

Another explanation for a boy's and girl's gender identity comes from the writings of Sigmund Freud and his ideas on **attachment-identification.** During the first two to three years, Freud stressed a child's growing attachment to its mother. Somewhere around three or four years, however, a male child develops even stronger feelings toward his mother and concomitant negative feelings for his father. The combination of these antithetical feelings and the resulting anxiety and fears they arouse within the young boy prompts him to relinquish his attachment to his mother and to identify strongly with his father. Once this process is complete by about the sixth year, Freud theorized a boy's gender identity was firmly established. Although Freud's work has provided considerable grist for many novelists, playwrights, and other artistic types, most in the scientific community think his work on gender identity development falls far short of giving a credible portrayal of how children develop a sense of who they are. Furthermore, Freud's ideas on female development seem especially off the mark and as such could not have helped, as some believe, but to bias his views of male development as well (Lerner, 1986).

For our fourth model of gender identity development, we turn to Spencer Cahill's (1983, 1986a & 1986b) proposal of a "distinctively sociological theory of gender identity acquisition." Rather than seeing a person's gender identity as simply the end product of various outside social forces (e.g., differential parental treatment, media's stereotypic images), Cahill envisions gender identity arising from a series of categorization practices that grow out of a young child's concern over being seen as

The Social Roles Perspective

a socially competent person. To analyze gender acquisition, Cahill divides the process into five stages each with their own characteristic social activities. Let's examine each to understand better what Cahill means by the **recruitment process** for gender acquisition.

Acquiescent Participation Stage. As should be abundantly clear by now, soon after birth and based on the presence of unambiguous external genitalia, a child is placed in one of two categories: male or female. Over the next few weeks and months, it matters little how a young child acts; others will see pretty much what they want to see. If an adult "sees" a young male (i.e., associates the label "male" with a particular child), the little youngster in the crib or on one's lap will in all probability be described as a "strapping and robust" little fellow regardless of his actions. Researchers have found that adults do treat little ones according to the gender label assigned them (Delk et al., 1986). According to well-established learning theory then, when a person is treated in a certain way, such treatment will eventually lead to certain future behaviors. Cahill (1986b, p. 170) notes as much:

> Because others tend to respond to male and female infants differently, it is likely that a male infant's and a female infant's performance of identical behavior will be followed by different consequences. If, as seems likely, the so-called "Thorndike principle," which states that the consequences which follow a behavior affect the probability of its future performance, has any empirical validity, then others' sex differentiated responses to infants will eventually result in perceptible sex differences in infants' behavior.

Unwitting Participation Stage. Beginning early in the second year, we find some subtle and some not so subtle gender differences in boys' and girls' behaviors. Earlier we noted that thirteen-month-old boys and girls respond quite differently to frustrating situations—boys acted in appropriately autonomous male fashion, whereas girls acted in socially prescribed female dependent ways (Goldberg & Lewis, 1969). Granted, other researchers have not found such easily categorized gender differences when they placed young male and female children in frustrating situations (Brooks & Lewis, 1974; Jacklin et al., 1973). However, some few gender differences are nevertheless noticeable by the second year.

According to Cahill, during this second year a child produces the first recognizable words that provide him or her with a basic vocabulary for social identification (e.g., "mama" and "dada"). Taking a lead from those who have made language a central consideration in how people learn to deal with their social world (Constantinople, 1979; Foote, 1951; Mead, 1934), Cahill sees language acquisition as essential if one is to take the role of the other in order to see how others see them. By "seeing" ourselves as others see us (i.e., Mead's role-taking behavior), we begin to develop a certain amount of self-regulation over our actions. Furthermore, by learning language, we begin to establish the basis for constructing a social identity.

Exploratory Participation Stage. As a child begins to acquire his or her native language, he or she also learns how to differentiate between various other symbols and their meanings. For instance, young children quickly learn how to play "dress up," wherein they put on various kinds of clothes in order to play at being a "mommy" or a "daddy," for instance. From such play activity then, youngsters not only learn what kinds of behaviors go along with different labels, they also learn how they should interact with others.

Speaking of this stage, Cahill notes that children learn that there are only two social categories, or identities, available to them: "baby" a demeaning or discrediting identity or, depending on their external genitalia, either "big boy" or "big girl" both of which convey others' approval.

> When, for example, children engage in disapproved behavior, they are often told "You're being a baby" or "Only babies do that." In contrast, they are often encouraged to perform approved behaviors with statements such as "You're a big girl" or "Be a big boy." In effect, these typical verbal responses to young children's behavior convey to them that they must behaviorally choose between the discrediting identity of "baby" and their anatomically determined sex identity. Because . . . children continually seek recognition as "bona-fide persons," they appropriate the identity which aids them in gaining recognition as such persons, their anatomically determined sex identity. (1986b, p. 175)

Generally speaking then, the exploratory stage finds the three- or four-year-old child actively constructing his or her behavior to fit what he or she has learned through role-taking activities to be socially approved and appropriate for his or her assigned gender. To be accepted and seen by others as socially competent, a child takes on the identity (i.e., "big boy" or "big girl") he or she has discovered from their role-taking activity as constituting what is acceptable. While involved in a preschool program, Cahill reported the following brief interchange between a teacher (T) and a four and one-half-year-old boy (B) who was trying to unlock the clasp on a necklace.

T: Do you want to put that on?
B: No. It's for girls.
T: You don't have to be a girl to wear things around your neck. Kings wear things around their necks. You could pretend you're a king.
B: I'm not a king. I'm a boy.

Although a king would be an appropriate identity for a young boy to construct, obviously this young boy's understanding of the symbolic meaning associated with a necklace—associated with girls—prevented him from even considering the possibility that boys could wear a necklace.

The Social Roles Perspective

Apprentice Participation Stage. During the preadolescent period, youngsters begin to spend more time with their peer groups. Cahill (1986b, p. 177) sees these years as especially important ones when youngsters "acquire practical skill in the interactional negotiation of shared meanings." These years' nearly closed social worlds of same-sex peers becomes the social world where young people can explore and learn the meanings of various interpersonal actions with less concern over how adults will evaluate their performances. The world of the preadolescent becomes, then, a kind of refuge wherein youngsters acquire and refine in relative security the interactional skills they need later on. Recently, Gary Fine (1979, 1987, 1988) and Janet Lever (1978, 1988) have begun to cast a light on the interactional rules and activities found in preadolescent subcultures finding that what goes on is often quite different than what adults see.

During this period, a preadolescent must achieve a certain facility with what Cahill calls "heterosocial skill." In other words, a youngster must show that he or she is able to behaviorally exhibit appropriate masculine or feminine behaviors and at the same time interact in appropriate ways with opposite-gendered people. Basically, boys should have an understanding and a facility to interact with girls in appropriate and acceptable ways, and vice versa, if they are to move to a last stage of gender acquisition, that of evidencing a bona fide or deep-seated grasp of what it means to express one's own essential gender nature.

Although Cahill's theory of gender acquisition is still relatively new, the assumption that a child acquires a gender identity primarily to be seen as a socially competent person is especially intriguing. Although role theory and the socialization model continue to have many proponents, a more person-social environment interactive and reflexive theory such as Cahill's is bound to make many a social scientist rethink her or his views on gender identity development.

Generally speaking, the social roles perspective presents the male experience as the end product of the socialization process fitting them, as it were, into certain gender role prescriptions. Some may argue the traditional gender roles (e.g., males work outside, whereas females tend to the chores inside) are the inevitable outcomes of centuries-long male-female roles (e.g., males ventured away from the group on the hunt, females tended to the close-at-hand needs of the children). We no longer live in an environment, though, where a man's worth is determined by the meat brought back from a hunt, or a woman's by how many children she successfully bears. If we are to survive into the twenty-first century, perhaps we should give serious consideration on how best to raise (i.e., shape, reinforce, guide) our children as free as possible from the restrictions of outmoded gender roles.

Cahill, S. (1986). Language practices and self-definition: The case of gender identity acquisition. *The Sociological Quarterly, 27,* 295–311.

Carrigan, T., Connell, B., & Lee, J. (1987). Toward a new sociology of masculinity. In H. Brod (Ed.), *The making of masculinities: The new men's studies* (pp. 63–100). Boston: Allen & Unwin.

Fine, G. (1987). *With the boys: Little League baseball and preadolescent culture.* Chicago: University of Chicago Press.

Kessler, S., & McKenna, W. (1978). *Gender: An ethnomethodological approach.* Chicago: University of Chicago Press.

Klumas, A., & Marchant, T. (1994). Images of men in popular sitcoms. *The Journal of Men's Studies, 2,* 269–285.

West, C., & Zimmerman, D. (1987). Doing gender. *Gender & Society, 1,* 125–151.

Chapter 6

The Anthropological Perspective

The one regularity that concerns me here is the often dramatic ways in which cultures construct an appropriate manhood—the presentation or "imaging" of the male role. In particular, there is a constantly recurring notion that real manhood is different from simple anatomical maleness, that it is not a natural condition that comes about spontaneously through biological maturation but rather is a precarious or artificial state that boys must win against powerful odds. This recurrent notion that manhood is problematic, a critical threshold that boys must pass through testing, is found at all levels of sociocultural development regardless of what other alternative roles are recognized.

David Gilmore (1990)

When asked why they brutalize women Baruya men reply, "They merit it!" This attitude is not untypical in the New Guinea highlands. Coupled with this brutalization is a series of beliefs and practices that isolate men from women, but in the New Guinea context, also reinforces their economic and political dominance. These include ritualized homosexuality, the symbolic identification of males with certain aspects of female physiology, the existence of men's houses (barred to women), and strong notions of female pollution (particularly by means of menstrual blood).

Alexander Alland, Jr. (1988)

Thus far we have covered several perspectives—the historical, the biological, the psychological, and the social roles—and noted how each has added to our understanding of the male experience. In our discussions we have moved across an analytical continuum of sorts—a continuum where we've adjusted the depth of our analysis, or how close we allowed ourselves to get to our subject. At one end of this continuum, the biological end, we examined the male experience close up, as if we were looking through a microscope to see how incredibly small features such as chromosomes and hormones lay a foundation for the male experience. We then moved to a psychological analysis and, consequently, moved back a bit so we could examine individual traits and abilities and a psychological construct called gender identity. Next our analysis forced us to look at the male experience from a perspective that focused on the social dynamics of small group interactions. And finally, with this chapter, we come to the other end of the continuum. Here we must move still further back until we have a larger, more macroview of the male experience.

In this chapter we will review the impact of culture on people's lives and behaviors. **Culture** is defined here as a particular group's systematic knowledge and behaviors that are passed from one generation to the next. We will begin our discussion of culture and the anthropological perspective by first examining the wide variations among groups in what is defined as appropriate behaviors for the genders. Next we will discuss the nearly universal phenomenon of male dominance and several of the theories that have been proposed to explain it. Finally we will describe several North American Indian societies in which there are more than two gender categories.

For centuries, philosophers and scientists alike have tried to unravel the mysteries surrounding human nature. What are the basic elements of human nature? How do humans differ from other animals? Are humans more a product of their biology or their culture? These are only a few of the questions people ask when they try to understand what it means to be a human being.

cultural variations in gender behaviors

The prevailing view of human nature was drastically changed when Charles Darwin (1859/1967) published his *On the Origin of Species*. Therein Darwin theorized that all living species evolved from a common ancestry over countless millions of years. Before Darwin, scholars held the view that all species had been created in their final form by a Divine Creator. Since Darwin, scientists have searched for evidence that would show a gradual evolution of the human species—homo sapiens—from other earlier hominoid and hominid species (Johanson & Edey, 1981; Lewin, 1984, 1987).

Physical scientists speculate that the early hominids' upright posture, bipedal (two-footed) walking ability, and exceptionally large brains were significant features in the evolution of the human species. These features, along with opposable thumbs, permitted early hominid groups to become highly adaptive and creative creatures in a changing environment. Thus one basic feature of human nature is its adaptability to a wide range of environmental situations.

The Anthropological Perspective

Among most Western societies, human nature is often defined as selfish, self-centered, competitive, and aggressive. The problem with such a definition is that not all human groups evinced such "Western" behaviors. The fact of the matter is that in many non-Western societies cooperation and harmony among group members were the major features, not selfishness and competition. For example, the Arapesh of New Guinea, the Ituri Pygmies of Central Africa, and the Shoshone Indians of the western United States all exhibited a strong predisposition toward group harmony and cooperation (O'Kelly & Carney, 1986, chap. 2; Turnbull, 1982). Thus the belief that human nature is basically self-centered, competitive, and violent seems more characteristic of Western societies' values than of the values of the entire human race. What we can say with certainty as we look at various human groups down through the ages is that human beings are a highly adaptive species with an almost limitless capacity to create.

Early Nonindustrial Human Groups

Too often people base their views of human nature on the types of behavior they see around them. If we were to generalize about the human race while focusing only on the human behaviors found in large, overly crowded, technologically oriented metropolises such as New York City, London, Paris, and Moscow, we could easily conclude that human beings are indifferent to other people's sufferings, are given to violence, and are highly competitive for their society's scarce goods (Baum & Paulus, 1987; Saegert, 1978). But if we are to get a more accurate picture of basic human nature, we must also look at nonindustrial groups. In this section we will focus on the interactions and behaviors of such human groups.

In addition to bipedalism, a large brain, and opposable thumbs, two other biological features also played significant roles in the evolution of the human group, namely, year-round mating and a long period of childhood dependency. Mating among most animal species occurs during biologically defined periods when a female is in heat. Even among the great apes such as the chimpanzee and the gorilla, mating takes place only when a female is biologically receptive (see Fedigan & Fedigan, 1989 for a review of how the study of primates has influenced our understanding of gender). Among humans, however, sexual mating can occur at any time. This year-round mating was probably responsible for the greater stability found in early human male-female relations.

Along with year-round mating, humans have a significantly long period of childhood dependency. Because a mature human brain cannot pass through a mother's birth canal, humans are born with a prematurely developed brain that continues to develop during the first several years after birth. Consequently, a human infant remains dependent on adult care for a much longer period than do most other animal species. This dependency and the necessity for the mother to remain nearby to nurse the infant curtailed the mobility of early women (Zihlman, 1989).

These two features taken together promoted a stable social organization commonly thought of as a family and fostered what has come to be known as the basis for a **division of labor.** Throughout most of history, humans have formed into small social groups based on family or kinship ties. Within these groups, adult males were chiefly responsible for hunting; adult females were obligated to childrearing duties and to foraging for fruits and vegetables close to the campsite (De Rios, 1978; Friedl, 1978; Gough, 1986). The basic hunter-and-gatherer social organization has existed for the greater part of human history; even today, it can be found among the Aranda aborigines of Australia (Nanda, 1987). For some time anthropologists have noted a generalized division of labor along gender lines in hunter-gatherer societies, namely, men hunt, women gather and tend to the young (Brace, 1979; Dahlberg, 1981; Hayden, 1981). Most argue this arrangement is based to a considerable degree on the female's reproductive capabilities and subsequent responsibilities or restrictions (e.g., pregnancy, breastfeeding, etc.) that supposedly limit her participation in the physically demanding and far-ranging hunting expeditions. This view has been challenged in the past several years, however (Martin & Voorhies, 1975). Recently, for instance, anthropologists Madeleine Goodman, Agnes Estioko-Griffin, and several colleagues (Estioko & Griffin, 1981; Estioko-Griffin & Griffin, 1985; Goodman, Griffin, Estioko-Griffin & Grove, 1985) studied the Agta Negrito people of northern Luzon (Philippines) and found that women did, in fact, engage in hunting activities. However, before we dismiss the division found among most foraging groups between hunters and gatherers, we should note that in Agta territory hunting activity is carried out within a twenty- to thirty-minute walk from camp. When hunting requires greater travel from a group's campsite, though, females are less likely to engage in hunting activity.

Despite this evidence of a basic division of labor between the sexes, there is actually great diversity in the kinds of work that males and females are expected to perform in the vast majority of preindustrial societies (see Table 6.1). The predominant Western view that biology plays a prominent role in the activities expected of males and females receives little support in a cross-cultural analysis of the divisions of labor in these societies. If biology were the sole determinant of male and female activities, we would then expect much less variation among the groups. But such is not the case.

When we examine male and female roles in various preindustrial societies, what is expected from each differs from what is expected from each in Western society. Probably few studies point out the extreme variations in male and female activities more graphically than the field work conducted by anthropologist Margaret Mead. Between 1931 and 1933, Mead conducted an anthropological and sociological study of three tribal groups living in northeastern New Guinea. After her field work, Mead (1935/1963) wrote the classic *Sex and Temperament*. Therein we read of the gentle Arapesh, the cannibalistic Mundugumor, and the head-hunting Tchambuli.

The mountain-dwelling **Arapesh** lived in an area bounded by the sea to the north and extending back into the coastal mountains and grassy plains to the south. Mead characterized the Arapesh life as "organized . . . in a common adventure that is primarily maternal, cherishing, and oriented away from the self toward the needs of the next generation." As Mead saw them, Arapesh men and women were best described as cooperative, unassertive, and gentle. Whether caring for their crops or

Field Studies and Gender Behaviors

The Anthropological Perspective

table 6.1   Division of Labor in 224 Societies by Sex

Activity	Number of societies in which activity is performed by				
	Males always	*Males usually*	*Either sex equally*	*Females usually*	*Females always*
Pursuing sea mammals	34	1	0	0	0
Hunting	166	13	0	0	0
Trapping small animals	128	13	4	1	2
Herding	38	8	4	0	5
Fishing	98	34	19	3	4
Clearing land for agriculture	73	22	17	5	13
Dairy operations	17	4	3	1	13
Preparing and planting soil	31	23	33	20	37
Erecting and dismantling shelter	14	2	5	6	22
Tending fowl and small animals	21	4	8	1	39
Tending and harvesting crops	10	15	35	39	44
Gathering shellfish	9	4	8	7	35
Making and tending fires	18	6	25	22	62
Bearing burdens	12	6	35	20	57
Preparing drinks and narcotics	20	1	13	8	57
Gathering fruits, berries, nuts	12	3	15	13	63
Gathering fuel	22	1	10	19	89
Preserving meat and fish	8	2	10	14	74
Gathering herbs, roots, and seeds	8	1	11	7	74
Cooking	5	1	9	28	158
Carrying water	7	0	5	7	119
Grinding grain	2	4	5	13	114

Reprinted from *Social Forces* 15 (May) 1937. "Comparative Data on the Division of Labor by Sex," by George Murdock. Copyright © The University of North Carolina Press.

their children, both genders worked cooperatively for the good of all. Aggressive behaviors and seductive sexual advances were prohibited in Arapesh society. An Arapesh male who displayed aggressive behavior was ostracized from the group or at least shunned for any such display of "deviant" behavior. Competition in any form brought shame and disgust for the participants. In Arapesh society, status and prestige came to those who shared and cooperated within their group. Mead best explained the Arapesh in terms that we in the West associate with the feminine role:

> To the Arapesh, the world is a garden that must be tilled, not for one's self, not in pride and boasting, not for hoarding and usury, but that the yams and the dogs and the pigs and most of all the children may grow. From this whole attitude flow many of the other Arapesh traits, the lack of conflict between old and young, the lack of any expectation of

jealousy or envy, the emphasis upon cooperation. Cooperation is easy when all are whole-heartedly committed to a common project from which no one of the participators will himself benefit. Their dominant conception of men and women may be said to be that of regarding men, even as we regard women, as gently, carefully parental in their aims. (p. 135)

Thus Mead concluded that the traits expected of Arapesh men showed them to be caring, cooperative, gentle, kind, loving, nurturant, sharing, and concerned not with self-interest but rather with others' interests. The ideal Arapesh male appeared diametrically opposite the ideal we set for males here in the West. Mead's observations of the Arapesh people permit a glimpse of a society built on mutual trust and cooperation. For a people who come closer to our culture's ideal male, we must travel further inland to meet the Mundugumor.

Traveling up the Sepik river, Mead encountered the **Mundugumor** people, who were known especially for their cannabilistic practices and their fondness for warfare. For the Mundugumor male, life was a constant battle:

The Mundugumor man-child is born into a hostile world, a world in which most of the members of his own sex will be his enemies, in which his major equipment for success must be a capacity for violence, for seeing and avenging insult, for holding his own safety very lightly and the lives of others even more lightly. From his birth, the stage is set to produce in him this kind of behavior. (p. 189)

Because the Mundugumor mother saw her maternal responsibilities as burdensome, a child quickly learned to fend for itself within the village. The early experiences of neglect and rejection fostered a degree of self-reliance that led to a child's development of the prized traits of competition and aggression. Mundugumor society was filled with prohibitions against any show of tenderness, kindness, or other gentle emotional expressions. The submissive and reticent Mundugumor native was deemed a misfit and shunned by others. Life among the Mundugumors was a trial, and only those most fit—the aggressive and unyielding ones—were viewed with honor and respect.

Mead found in both the Arapesh and the Mundugumor societies a fundamental similarity: Males *and* females were both molded toward identical trait patterns. The Mundugumor's emphasis was on a harsh self-centeredness, and the Arapesh's pattern was toward a gentle other-centeredness. Basic gender differences in the personality traits were not encouraged in either group. To find a society in which basic gender differences were clearly defined and encouraged, Mead traveled west of the Mundugumor to a people called the Tchambuli.

Living around Lake Aibom, the **Tchambuli** were a head-hunting society in which the usual gender-typical behaviors as we know them in Western society were reversed. Tchambuli *women* were responsible for the business of the village. They earned the money used by the family to purchase goods. They were responsible for the farming, fishing, and manufacturing required by the village. When it came to important events such as marriage, the women's approval was necessary. Temperamentally, the Tchambuli women were easygoing and reliable. Generally, an air of affability existed among the women of the village. Tchambuli men were another matter. Men were considered the weaker sex. They seemed interested only in their own adornment and self-aggrandizing pursuits. Their days were spent in other men's company, where they compared costumes and other body adornments. The men were especially adept at artistic skills. Their relationships among themselves could only be described as catty and suspicious. Around women, Tchambuli men were timid, and they appeared in awe of them:

> . . . the Tchambuli [man] may be said to live principally for art. Every man is an artist and most men are skilled not in some one art alone, but in many: in dancing, carving, plaiting, and so on. Each man is chiefly concerned with his role upon the stage of his society, with the elaboration of his costume, the beauty of the masks he owns, the skill of his own flute-playing, the finish and *elan* of his ceremonies, and upon other people's recognition and valuation of his performance. (p. 245)

Although Mead's interpretations of the Arapesh's basic "feminine" gender, the Mundugumor's "masculine" gender, and the Tchambuli's "reversed" genders have been criticized as too subjective, we cannot doubt that her field research shows that gender-typical behaviors vary greatly among cultures. Other anthropologists have found additional preindustrial societies in which particular features of gender behaviors vary in extreme ways. For example, anthropologist Mervyn Meggitt (1964) studied the Mae Enga and Kuma peoples, two New Guinea highland cultures, and found extreme cultural differences in their attitudes and behaviors toward sexuality. Meggitt found that Mae Enga men, for instance, shun almost all contact with women, going to such lengths as constructing separate sleeping huts for each sex. Among Mae Enga men menstrual blood is thought of as a pollutant that causes those males who come in contact with it to become gravely sick. Furthermore, sexual intercourse is considered harmful for a male, who afterwards must retire to a smoke-filled hut to purify himself and to regain his strength. Not surprisingly, among Mae Enga people, all sexual activity is prohibited between unmarried people.

On the other hand, Meggitt found the Kuma's sexual attitudes and practices almost the complete opposite of the Mae Enga. Kuma males and females regularly sleep together with no concern over menstrual blood. Kuma males gain honor and status with other males by bragging about sexual conquests and prowess. Young Kuma females frequently attend festivals where they choose sexual partners from among the married and unmarried males.

Recently, Gilbert Herdt (1981, 1987) spent several years among the Sambia of New Guinea. What is particularly fascinating to read about the Sambia males who pride themselves for their aggressive and warlike exploits against their enemies is that all young Sambia males are initiated into manhood through a secret society that practices male homosexuality as a ritual way of becoming more manly. The fact is that Sambian culture requires its young boys to leave their mothers and move into a communal house where older boys initiate them into the practices of homosexuality as an essential part of becoming a fierce warrior. After their passage into Sambian adulthood, though, the young men marry women and lead a virtual heterosexual life-style. So much for the belief that early homosexual practices necessarily lead to a homosexual life-style.

Mead's, Meggitt's, and Herdt's anthropological studies all point to one incontrovertible fact: what are considered appropriate gender behaviors by Western society are extremely varied in many non-Western cultures. (For other examples of diverse non-Western gender patterns, see Basow, 1985; Randolph, Schneider & Diaz, 1988; Rao & Rao, 1985; Ward, 1985; Williams & Best, 1982, 1990.)

male dominance

In general, the unique roles that males and females play vary from one social group to another. However, whether one is looking at the gender-typical behaviors of Western society or at those of some preindustrial tribe in New Guinea, males appear to play a controlling role over females in many social spheres (Godelier, 1985; Strathern, 1987). Ernestine Friedl (1978, p. 70) sees **male dominance** as a nearly universal culture feature of the male experience suggesting that "Male dominance is so widespread that it is virtually a human universal; societies in which women are consistently dominant do not exist and have never existed." Assuming that Friedl's assumption is correct, what is it that causes males to dominate females, and what about the current thinking among some that females once dominated men in prehistoric times (Lee & Daly, 1987; Schifellite, 1987)? Let's begin our discussion of male dominance with the latter question, that of the purported period in human history when females dominated males.

Matriarchal Rule: Fact or Fiction?

Some years ago, a rather interesting twist on long-standing male-female relations was argued by describing a mythical period when women ruled during a **golden age of matriarchy** (Davis, 1972; Stone, 1976). According to this historical rendition, approximately 8,000 to 10,000 years ago women ruled over a highly advanced civilization. During this age, women ruled with justice, love, and sensitivity. Women controlled their fertility through natural methods. Religion centered on the worship of the Great Mother Goddess, and her priestesses glorified the inherent beauties and sensual nature of the female sex. The civilized world was a peaceful and serene place for all inhabitants, females and males alike (Baring & Cashford, 1993).

Somehow, for reasons never really explained, the harmony of the matriarchal world was disrupted by a small group of discontented and rebellious men who seized power and set out to destroy all evidence of matriarchy. First of all, men prevented women from using contraception and thus forced women into an oppression brought on by continuous pregnancy. The religion of the Great Mother Goddess was replaced by the worship of a stern and unforgiving father figure who allowed only males to worship in the temples. No longer were love, peace, and harmony dominant themes in human relations but rather warfare, conflict, and aggression. Down through the ages, historians—another role males usurped for themselves—purposely rewrote the historical records to exclude any mention of that time when women ruled the civilized world. The only vestige of this peaceful period in human history can be found in certain mythical legends.

The Anthropological Perspective

Although most anthropologists discount the evidence of a golden age of matriarchy based solely on legend and a few artifacts of female religious figures found in certain ancient ruins (Binford, 1979), Ruby Rohrlich-Leavitt (1977) suggests that Minoan Crete "women participated at least equally with men in political decision making, while in religion and social life they were supreme." However, we should be skeptical of Rohrlich-Leavitt's claim about Minoan Crete's matriarchal social structures because her evidence can be interpreted to mean that Minoan Crete society was an egalitarian society at best, if not basically a patriarchal society (Billigimeier & Turner, 1981). In the words of anthropologists Michelle Rosaldo and Louise Lamphere (1974, p. 3),

> Whereas some anthropologists argue that there are, or have been, truly egalitarian societies . . . and all agree that there are societies in which women have achieved considerable social recognition and power, none has observed a society in which women have publicly recognized power and authority surpassing that of men.

Part of the problem concerning the questionable existence of a matriarchal society lies in the confusion between several terms, namely, matriarchy, matrilineality, and matrilocality. **Matrilineality** refers to the descent system based on the ancestral line's being reckoned through the female's side of the family rather than through the male's, whereas **matriarchy** refers to a society ruled by females. Several North American Indian nations were matrilineal but not necessarily matriarchal, the most notable being the Choctaw, Creek, Iroquois, and Hopi. **Matrilocality** refers to a married couple residing with the wife's family or kin group. For example, a Hopi male typically moved in with his wife's family. The older woman and her husband, her daughters and their husbands, and the unmarried sons made up the average Hopi family unit. The Hopi had an interesting way of settling a family dispute. If for some reason a Hopi woman became disenchanted with her husband, all she needed to do was put his belongings outside of the dwelling and the marriage was dissolved. The same privilege did not extend to the husband. In Hopi society, then, the female had a great deal of power within the *domestic* sphere, but in the ceremonial, religious, and political spheres, the Hopi male retained control.

Although much is made of those societies where a person's descent is reckoned through one's mother or her kin group (i.e., a matrilineal society), we should note that in most such societies a mother's brother or one's maternal uncle plays a significant role in teaching boys what is expected of them (Radcliffe-Brown, 1965, chap. 1). Among the Hopi, for instance, young boys learn the ways of manhood not from their biological fathers whose influence over their sons is minimal but rather from their mother's brother (Dozier, 1966; Miller, 1987). Such a relationship is known as **avuncular** and shows that even in those societies where females have considerable power, males—in this case a mother's brother—are responsible for teaching young boys what it means to be a man.

The Iroquois is one Indian nation often mentioned as a society in which the female had considerable political power over the male. And in some ways the Iroquois women were exceptional when compared to most other women in terms of their social and political status. The basis of Iroquois women's power centered on their being able to elect the men who served on the nation's governing council. By influencing the election, the women indirectly had a voice in the decisions of tribal importance. However, the women themselves were not permitted to sit on the council, and once elected, the men could dismiss much of their female backers' advice. Thus the Iroquois nation was definitely not a matriarchal society (Brown, 1975).

Recently, men's studies historian Sally Roesch Wagner (1988) argued convincingly that the six nations making up the Iroquois confederacy—Seneca, Onondaga, Cayuga, Oneida, Mohawk, and Tuscarora—supported an egalitarian social structure. She noted that "[T]he decision to place women in the highest position of governmental authority was thoughtfully made by the founding mothers and fathers of the Iroquois confederacy years before Columbus 'discovered' America" (p. 33).

At the present time then, there is no conclusive anthropological evidence to show that a matriarchy once existed in the Western world.

Explanations for Male Dominance

Over the past several years, anthropologists have focused much of their attention on the issue of male dominance. Why have males for so long and in virtually every society dominated the political and economic spheres, for the most part leaving women to dominate the domestic sphere? There are several explanations for this state of affairs, four of which we will consider in this section. The first is the Judeo-Christian explanation of divine origin, one given little credence by social scientists but one that holds considerable sway in many people's minds. The other three explanations for male dominance are the center of much controversy among different scientific perspectives; these include the genetic (biological), the socioeconomic, and the social psychological.

Judeo-Christian Explanation for Male Dominance. The first book of the Hebrew Bible, Genesis, describes how human creation took place. Accordingly, Yahweh, the God of Moses and the Jewish people, formed the first man (called Adam) from the earth's slime. In time, God saw that Adam was lonely. God then created Eve out of Adam's rib to be his companion. They were childlike in their pastoral Eden until one fateful day when Eve, the more gullible of the two, believed a serpentine promise of supernatural knowledge if she would eat of the forbidden fruit. Eve lured Adam into sharing the fruit with her. Later, God saw the shame of sin on each of his creations and cast them out into the world's travail. To impress woman of the depth of her luring sinfulness, God sealed woman's subordinate fate with these words: "You shall bear children in intense pain and suffering; yet even so, you shall welcome your husband's affections, and *he shall be your master*" (Gen. 3:16, italics added).

For those for whom a literal reading of the Bible is the basis for "the way things are," this biblical command is sufficient explanation for male dominance. For many males and females alike, especially in the current resurgence of fundamentalism, male domination has been God's way ever since that day when Eve led Adam into a land of toil and tears. (For a thoughtful discussion of how the "Adam and Eve story" has influenced Western culture, see Pagels, 1988.)

In many male-dominant societies in the Middle East when women leave their homes they must wear the *chador,* the head-to-toe garment. Within conservative Islamic societies, wearing such garments is seen as a way to protect women's honor and chastity, a view held by women and men alike. (Mandelbaum, 1988; Rapoport et al., 1989.) © Sam Waagenaar/Photo Researchers, Inc.

The Biological Explanation for Male Dominance. During the 1960s, a number of books promulgated the idea of a biological basis for various human behaviors. For example, in *On Aggression,* Nobel-prize laureate Konrad Lorenz wrote that aggressive behavior was a positive "life-preserving" feature rather than a "diabolical" or "destructive" human activity. Zoologist Desmond Morris wrote in *The Naked Ape* of how contemporary human relations could be explained in terms of our evolutionary link with the great hairy apes. In *The Territorial Imperative,* playwright-turned-historian Robert Ardrey compared the human inclination to defend property and possession to that of a dog's tenacious defense of a meat-clad bone. Each of these authors stirred controversy with his particular brand of biologically based explanation of human behavior. But none caused the furor that anthropologist Lionel Tiger (1970) created with his book *Men in Groups.*

In *Men in Groups,* Tiger dealt with two issues. First, he hypothesized that certain cultural and social features are more simply explained in biological terms. Second, he was convinced of a biological predisposition among human groups to establish exclusive all-male groups. Tiger speculated that the inclination to form all-male groups, a feature he called **male bonding,** has "underlying biological . . . roots in human evolutionary history." According to Tiger, male bonding led inevitably to an inequality between genders and the eventual exclusion of women from the sources of power within the group:

> Males dominate females in occupational and political spheres. This is a species-specific pattern and is associated with my other proposition: that males bond in a variety of situations involving power, force, crucial or dangerous work, and relations with their gods. They consciously and emotionally exclude females from these bonds. The significant notion here is that those various different expressions of male dominance and male bonding in different communities are what one would expect from a species highly adaptable to its physical and social environments. . . . (pp. 143–144)

Tiger's idea of a male bond has been criticized on several counts, not the least of which was Tiger's tendency to report on only those societies with highly visible male organizations, while excluding others with well-established female groups. Tiger's secondary task of demonstrating the biological basis for a male bond proved overly ambitious for the available ethnographic data. Even so, Tiger's primary task of grounding specific social and cultural behaviors within a biological framework has become the basis for the new hybrid science of sociobiology. Let's move from the questionable male bond principle to the sociobiologists' belief in a genetic foundation for male dominance.

Sociobiology rests on the basic belief that biological principles can be applied advantageously to the social sciences and their subject matter. Just how the sociobiologist accomplishes this goal is quite simple. He or she first identifies a cultural pattern found in most societies (for example, male dominance) and then examines this social feature with an eye to how it enhances human survival. If the feature appears to enhance the odds of the species' survival, then the sociobiologist hypothesizes a genetic basis for it and develops ways to test the hypothesis.

Incest provides a good example of how the sociobiologist sets out to prove a link between a cultural pattern and a biological element such as the genes. *Incest* (that is, sexual intercourse between close family members such as father and daughter, mother and son, or brother and sister) is prohibited in most societies. The survival-enhancing feature of this cultural prohibition is well known. Specifically, children born of incestuous relationships are more likely to carry defective or mutant genes that predispose them to various forms of mental retardation, physical afflictions, and even premature death. Consequently, such children are less likely to develop normally and later on to mate successfully, thus preventing their genes from being passed on to the next generation. On the other hand, children born of a non-incestuous relationship are more likely to succeed in passing along their genes because of fewer mental and physical problems. Hence sociobiologists argue that people with a genetic predisposition *against* incest are more likely to pass their genes to subsequent generations.

To test the hypothesized predisposition against incestuous relationships, sociobiologists point to the marital arrangements found in an Israeli kibbutz. Beginning in the late 1940s and 1950s, the kibbutz was a social experiment in collective living

The Anthropological Perspective

where all of the inhabitants would be free of traditional gender-typical behaviors found in most other social groups (O'Kelly & Carney, 1986, chap. 9). The children in a kibbutz are raised in extremely close-knit, mixed-sexed groups. What can only be called a strong family spirit pervades each children's group. When the children grow up, marriage between a twosome from the same kibbutz is unheard of even though no social prohibition exists against such a marriage. The sociobiologist argues from such naturally acquired data that people must have a built-in aversion to mating with someone with whom they have a close familylike relationship.

Moving from incest to male dominance, Edward Wilson, a proponent of the sociobiological perspective, argues that male dominance can be explained as an extreme social pattern that developed out of the basic division of labor found among primitive hunter-gatherer societies. First of all, early groups who divided the work of subsistence between males who ranged far from the camp for game and females who stayed close to camp to gather vegetation and care for the young provided an optimal social arrangement for the group's survival. Over time, these early genetically based social patterns became even more rigidly fixed by tradition and custom. As groups grew larger and more elaborate in their political, economic, and social patterns, the male's preeminence in external affairs (away from the camp) transferred to other areas, including those relating to women's lives. In Wilson's (1978, pp. 91–92) words,

> When societies grow still larger and more complex, women tend to be reduced in influence outside the home, and to be more constrained by custom, ritual, and formal law. As hypertrophy [extreme development of a preexisting social structure; in this case, male domination over external affairs] proceeds further, they can be turned literally into chattel, to be sold and traded, fought over, and ruled under a double morality. History has seen a few striking local reversals, but the great majority of societies have evolved toward sexual domination as though sliding along a ratchet.

The Socioeconomic Explanation for Male Dominance. Some anthropologists believe that male dominance is an outcome of certain social and/or economic forces rather than a survival-enhancing, genetic arrangement. For example, Marvin Harris (1977a, 1977b) argues that warfare and infanticide have occurred throughout human history because people are driven toward these actions by social pressures and/or economic scarcity. Specifically, Harris links male dominance, or what he calls male supremacy, with the institution of warfare; he believes that warfare has been the major social institution that societies have used down through the ages to control population and preserve natural resources:

> The practice of warfare is responsible for a widespread complex of male supremacist institutions among band and village societies. The existence of this complex is a source of embarrassment and confusion to advocates of women's rights. Many women fear that if male supremacy has been in existence for so long, then perhaps it really is "natural" for men to dominate women. But this fear is groundless. Male supremacist institutions arose as a by-product of warfare, of the male monopoly over weapons, and of the use of sex for the nurturance of aggressive male personalities. And warfare, as I have already shown, is not the expression of human nature, but a response to reproductive and ecological pressures. Therefore, male supremacy is no more natural than warfare. (1977b, p. 57)

For Harris, then, male dominance developed as an early human response to certain life-threatening social and environmental conditions. Harris's view is more optimistic than those presented by the sociobiologists in that he allows for the possibility of an egalitarian relationship between the sexes given the absence of certain negative social and economic conditions.

Not all anthropologists who favor a socioeconomic explanation are willing to grant that male dominance stems from such a brutal history, though. Ernestine Friedl (1978), for instance, provides a more benign view of the causal basis of male dominance. She thinks the primitive male's physique and strength lent themselves to the role of roving hunter of large game and the female's maternal and nursing capabilities restricted her more or less to a fixed campsite. Beyond these basic physical sex differences, two specific socioeconomic features played a significant part in the male's influence and status in the early family group. First, on the far-ranging hunts, males made contact with other human groups. Over time, these chance encounters grew into formal meetings where bartering scarce items such as flint rocks could take place. Control over the traded goods and the intermediary function between the family and other groups provided the male with new power. Second, the hunter had control over the distribution of the meat brought back from the hunt. Meat was a desirable addition to a diet of nuts, berries, and other natural foods. The one who dispensed meat gained definite status in the early human groups. Friedl takes note of these two features of the early male role and suggests that they led to a social pattern of male dominance:

> Patriarchies are prevalent, and they appear to be strongest in societies in which men control significant goods that are exchanged with people outside the family. . . . The greater the male monopoly on the distribution of scarce items, the stronger their control of women seems to be. . . . The source of male power among hunter-gatherers lies in their control of a scarce, hard to acquire, but necessary nutrient—animal protein. (p. 70)

Studies of a number of preindustrial societies have shown that even though meat made up a little more than a quarter of the group's diet, the person who brought in and distributed meat from the hunt was cast in a superior role within the group (Hoffman, 1972). Other researchers have found a pattern of socialization among preindustrial societies that supports Friedl's thesis. In societies where a group's economy is based primarily on a male's superior strength and stamina, we are more likely to find large gender differences that in most cases foster greater male dominance over females (Barry, Bacon & Child, 1957).

Social Psychological Explanations for Male Dominance. Psychiatrists and social psychologists have long studied male dominance, and several have developed intriguing theories that suggest various psychological mechanisms to explain the basis for male dominance. We will focus here on three social psychological explanations, namely, envy of women's creative power, fear and dread of women, and avoidance of feminine identification.

Sigmund Freud, the founder of psychoanalysis, proposed that males were superior to women by virtue of having a penis. Furthermore, Freud (1925/1953) contended that the male personality was more fully developed and, consequently, that the male was the more creative of the two sexes. But not all who followed Freud believed in the natural superiority of males or in their inherent creative powers. For example, Karen Horney (1967), a psychoanalyst herself, rejected Freud's biological determinism and suggested that females were the more creative members of the species, especially when one takes into account the ultimate creative act of human birth:

> At this point I, as a woman, ask in amazement, and what about motherhood? And the blissful consciousness of bearing a new life within oneself? And the ineffable happiness of the increasing expectation of the appearance of this new being? And the joy when it finally makes its appearance and one holds it for the first time in one's arms? And the deep pleasurable feeling of satisfaction in suckling it and the happiness of the whole period when the infant needs her care? (p. 60)

But is there any evidence that males envy this naturally creative potential that women possess? Bruno Bettelheim (1962) thinks there is because of the existence of certain highly formalized male rituals in some preindustrial societies. Especially noteworthy are the practices of couvade and subincision. **Couvade** is a social ritual whereby a male whose wife is about to give birth is suddenly stricken with abdominal pains and is rushed to a specially prepared hut where a mock delivery occurs. After the mother's actual delivery, the newborn is taken to the father's hut where the baby becomes party to yet another birthing process, this time the ritualized one of the father. Bettelheim contends that couvade is a symbolic way for males to invest themselves with the creative power of the female (see Hall & Dawson, 1989). Another ritual that has feminine overtones is **subincision.** Generally, the practice of subincision is carried out in the context of puberty rites when a young man passes into adulthood. The practice involves slitting the underside of a male's penis, thus creating an opening similar to a vagina. The blood from the incision is treated as the symbolic equivalent of the first menstrual blood.

In other cultures, women are not envied for their "creative" abilities but rather portrayed as evil, sinister, and even a force to be dreaded (Altorki, 1986; Bennett, 1983; Hays, 1966). Some psychologists, Karen Horney among them, have suggested dread of women as a plausible explanation for male dominance. Yolanda and Robert Murphy (1985) studied the Mundurucú people and found some striking evidence supporting just such a contention.

The Mundurucú are a forest-dwelling people who live near the upper Tapajós region of north central Brazil. Mundurucú men and women live most of their lives apart from each other. Not only do the sexes work in separate groups, they live in separate houses. Women work together doing chores around the village, while men spend much of their time hunting. The extreme sex division is justified because men believe themselves superior to women. Blatant male supremacy is a ritualized part of Mundurucú society (Alland, Jr., 1988).

However, on the basis of their analysis of the folklore surrounding ancient Mundurucú male-female relations, the Murphys reported a mythlike quality about the Mundurucú practices of male supremacy. The folklore relates that the Mundurucú women once dominated the men. To account for this female domination, the women supposedly had acquired the men's magical, sacred flutes (possibly a lightly veiled symbol of the male penis), and this caused the men to subordinate themselves to the women. The men were subjected to a constant series of demeaning chores around the village, and they were made into sex objects for women's sexual gratification. The men's lives of drudgery, servitude, and sexual abuse lasted until the men stole back the sacred flutes and safely hid them in their segregated houses. The moral of this story is abundantly clear, at least to Mundurucú men: Unless women are kept subordinate, they may once again steal the sacred flutes and subjugate men. Thus the Mundurucú patriarchal social order, according to the Murphys' analysis, sits atop a precarious series of psychological defense mechanisms that help to allay the Mundurucú male's basic fear of women.

A third psychological explanation for male dominance is the avoidance of feminine identification. The theory states that because the mother is the primary model for the infant son in most cultures, he is likely to develop a feminine identity (that is, to perceive himself as a girl rather than as a boy) as he grows older unless he does something to counteract this feminine identity. What he does, according to this theory, is to subjugate and control those very people with whom he identified as a little boy—women. As Nancy Chodorow (1974) sees it,

> A boy, in his attempt to gain an elusive masculine identification, often comes to define his masculinity largely in negative terms, as that which is not feminine or involved with women. There is an internal and external aspect to this. Internally, the boy tries to reject his mother and deny his attachment to her and the strong dependency on her that he still feels. He also tries to deny the deep personal identification with her that has developed during his early years. He does this by repressing whatever he takes to be feminine inside himself, and, importantly, by denigrating whatever he considers to be feminine in the outside world. (p. 50)

The anthropological evidence for the avoidance of a feminine identity is slim but interesting. In those primitive societies where little boys' identification with their mothers is strongest and strong attachments are presumably formed between mothers and sons, severe and painful initiation rites involving genital operations are more common than in those societies where little mother-son identification takes place (Whiting, Kluckhohn & Albert, 1967). The idea here is that boys who identify with their mothers need some form of "shock treatment" in the guise of a painful pubertal rite to counteract their unconscious feminine identity. In these societies, male dominance is an additional way in which males can support their "fragile" masculine identity.

Putting Male Dominance in Perspective. Several interesting features run through the foregoing social psychological explanations for male dominance. Women, in the final analysis, are to blame for their own domination. If women were not so creative, fear provoking, dreadful, or easy to identify with, men would not have a need to dominate them. In a sense, the social psychological perspectives are little better than the divine-origin explanation that squarely lays the blame for male domination on Eve's shoulders. We should also question the notion of a need for male dominance. The assumption of an unseen or unconscious psychological need is in many ways similar to suggesting that male dominance originally was a biological feature that allowed all humans to better adapt or survive in a hostile environment. Thus the social psychological explanations for male dominance suffer from many of the same flaws that undercut the divine-origin and the biological explanations.

The socioeconomic view appears to offer a much better explanation of male dominance in that it suggests that male power developed out of social and economic conditions (Sanday, 1981). Once the advantages and privileges of power became known, men continued to ritualize their dominant status in other cultural ways. Few would deny that having power over others feels good. Perhaps the best explanation for the practices of male dominance is simply this: Long ago men discovered that dominating women won them all kinds of privileges that were too good to give up.

are there more than two gender categories?

Throughout this chapter, we have noted the variety of gender-typical activities that females and males have played in various preindustrial cultures. Not surprisingly, these activities have fallen into one of two categories normally built around the different activities expected and prescribed for each gender. The fact is that in the majority of societies we find only two gender categories, two formalized patterns of behavior that males or females supposedly fit by virtue of talent, temperament, and sex. But what about the possibility of more than two genders? Might there be other socially prescribed categories that a person could adopt? There are a few societies that allow a person to live her or his life in a way that is considerably different from the ways in which the majority of females and males live (Kennedy, 1993). Before we discuss these societies, we want to describe two situations that emphasize the changeable quality of gender categories as some see them. Unlike most groups in Western society, some non-Western societies view a person's gender as something that can be changed if the situation warrants it.

Imagine a couple growing old with several daughters and no sons. Because of his age and limited strength and stamina, the father is having great difficulty feeding his family with the little he brings back from the hunt. The daughters stay home to learn the ways of women and to wait for the young men who will take them in marriage. The couple's future appears bleak with no son to help them in their declining years. Then the couple decides to take drastic action. Their youngest daughter, a mere child, is dressed like a boy. The father teaches "him" how to make arrowheads and how to shoot a bow. The "boy" accompanies the father on the hunt and learns the ways of the forest. The "boy" is given a pouch that contains the dried ovaries of a bear. This is considered powerful medicine that will prevent the "boy" from becoming pregnant. The couple is happy now for they have a strong son who will provide for them in the future, and the village has another fine male hunter.

Imagine yet another village in which a couple worries about their youngest son. The boy acts differently from the other boys his age. He does not play the games that other boys play. The boy spends most of his days in the company of the village's young girls. His parents are gravely concerned about what kind of man their son will grow up to be. To settle their minds, they decide to test their son. They build an enclosure and one day place their son in it. In the enclosure they also place a bow and an arrow and some weaving materials in a wooden box. Next they set fire to the enclosure. Nervously, they await their son's escape; they are especially curious about what he may be clutching as he runs from the flames. After several anxious moments, their son bolts out of the fiery pen holding the weaving materials. Now the parents understand and accept the way their son is to be. He is to become another woman of the village.

These accounts are not fanciful stories but prescribed ways in which some North American Indian tribes dealt with what they considered a changeable aspect of human life (Kessler & McKenna, 1978). For several Indian tribes, a person's gender was not a biological given but rather a creation of sociocultural conditions and thus subject to change over time. Therefore, it was not uncommon among some North American Indian tribes for a young person of one sex, usually a male, to take on the gender thought more appropriate for the opposite sex. Some other tribes had additional gender categories that were neither male nor female. The berdache is the best example of such a special gender category.

The Crow Indians looked upon the **berdache** as a special human being in that he was viewed as neither a male nor a female. The Crow Indians, as well as certain other native American groups, did not cast a person's gender as necessarily fitting into one of two mutually exclusive categories. The berdache was a biological male who simply chose not to follow the ideal Crow role of warrior. The berdache suffered neither shame nor scorn for his role (Garbarino, 1976). We should likewise not confuse the berdache with a homosexual as did many early non-Indian writers (Mihalik, 1989; Roscoe, 1987; Williams, 1986). Some berdaches chose to live with men, but others did not. A Crow warrior who took a berdache for a wife suffered neither scorn nor ridicule from other males of the tribe.

The Berdache

One of the most colorful portrayals of a berdache is presented in Thomas Berger's (1964) novel *Little Big Man.* Berger gives a graphic description of a berdache called *Little Horse,* who comfortably interacted with both males and females of the tribe. Choosing not to be a warrior and to live up to the warrior ideal, Little Horse took on the attire and many of the mannerisms of a female, but even so he was not considered a female.

Anthropologist Michael Olien (1978) reported on two other Native American Indian tribes, the Navajo and the Mohave, that allowed for other gender categories. When a Navajo infant was born with ambiguous genitals, the child was assigned the role of a **nadle.** In addition to those assigned this role at birth, the Navajos allowed others to assume the role later on. A nadle was treated with extreme deference. When engaged in women's work, a nadle dressed as a woman; when involved with men, a nadle appeared as a man. The only activities denied a nadle were hunting and warfare. A nadle was allowed to intervene in delicate tribal problems such as marital disputes and to choose either a male or female sexual partner.

The Nadle

The Anthropological Perspective

A Crow Indian berdache. Courtesy of the Museum of the American Indian Smithsonian Institution, #34256.

The Alyha and the Hwame

The Mohave Indians of the Far West recognized four distinct gender categories: the traditional male and female gender categories and the alyha and the hwame. A male who chose to live as a woman was called an **alyha.** The male-turned-female underwent a special initiating ceremony that conferred the alyha status. From that time onward, such an individual was treated as a woman. An alyha dressed as a woman, worked with women, and even mimicked a woman's menstrual flow by cutting the upper thigh. When the alyha married a man (and again this carried no shame), the alyha performed all of the duties expected of a wife. After a suitable period, the alyha would get pregnant and prepare for the birth of a child. Near the end of the pregnancy, the alyha would drink a strong potion that would cause cramps associated with the beginnings of the birth process. The baby born to an alyha was always stillborn and would have to be buried immediately by the mother as was customary among the Mohave people. In this way, the alyha mother saved face with her husband and the tribe. After the burial and a suitable period of grief, the alyha resumed her normal wifely duties.

It was also possible for a Mohave female to become a male. As with the Mohave male-turned-alyha, the female who wished to become a male was ceremoniously ushered into a special role known as a **hwame.** The hwame dressed and acted in every way expected of a man. The hwame was prevented from only two activities, going into battle and assuming a leadership role within the tribal structure. As for marriage, the hwame married a female and set up residence much like other Mohave males.

It is important to emphasize that the hwame, the alyha, the nadle, and the berdache were not considered deviant or abnormal by their own tribe's standards. Each had chosen a role that was different from that of the majority, but was not stigmatized for assuming that role.

What can we learn from the anthropological perspective on the male experience? One striking feature that should be apparent is that the male gender as defined in Western society in the latter part of the twentieth century is unique to our own society and its history. Other non-Western societies define the male gender in quite different ways. To say that ours is the ultimate or best way would be foolish. For the thousands and thousands of years that humans have lived in groups, the male and female gender categories have changed because social situations and pressures warranted change. In our contemporary society, where brute strength has been superseded by machines and where meat does not come from a dangerous hunt but from the local supermarket, it is ridiculous to hang onto the view that the male gender must emphasize certain biological features that have little meaning other than to keep the genders separate. The anthropological perspective presents us with the valuable insight that the contemporary Western male gender category is not universal and that change is an inevitable part of cultural features (Shapiro, 1988).

suggested readings

Gilmore, D. D. (1990). *Manhood in the making: Cultural concepts of masculinity.* New Haven: Yale University Press.

Herdt, G. (1987). *The Sambia: Ritual and gender in New Guinea.* New York: Holt, Rinehart and Winston.

Lee, R., & Daly, R. (1987). Man's domination and woman's oppression: The question of origins. In M. Kaufman (Ed.), *Beyond patriarchy: Essays by men on pleasure, power, and change* (pp. 30–44). Toronto: Oxford University Press.

Mandelbaum, D. (1988). *Women's seclusion and men's honor: Sex roles in North India, Bangladesh, and Pakistan.* Tucson, AZ: University of Arizona Press.

O'Kelly, C., & Carney, L. (1986). *Women and men in society* (2nd ed.). Belmont, CA: Wadsworth.

Randolph, R., Schneider, D., & Diaz, M. (Eds.). (1988). *Dialectics and gender: Anthropological approaches.* Boulder, CO: Westview Press.

Sanday, P. (1981). *Female power and male dominance: On the origins of sexual inequality.* Cambridge: Cambridge University Press.

Williams, W. (1986). *The spirit and the flesh: Sexual diversity in American Indian culture.* Boston: Beacon Press.

section two

Elements of the Male Role

What are little boys made of?
Snips and snails, and puppy dogs' tails;
That's what little boys are made of.
ANONYMOUS

What makes for a really light chocolate soufflé or a really hearty loaf of yeast bread? Why the ingredients, of course, and the cook's skill in mixing and baking them so the finished product tastes like we expect it to taste.

Well, what makes a biological male into a complete psychosocial man? A male is a man to the degree he follows the prescribed norms or social expectations laid down by his society. In other words, a male is a man when he displays the gender-appropriate role traits and behaviors expected of males in a particular group or society at large.

In the next five chapters we are going to discuss several elements that we think encompass the "male role." As in all delicate creations, the recipes for what constitutes a real man may vary somewhat. Not everyone agrees with the specific elements, their proportions, or for that matter, whether all of the ingredients are necessary for the finished product. Let's take a brief look at what some other social scientists believe to be the essential elements of the male role.

After reviewing several studies in which people noted the stereotypic traits of the "typical male," psychologists Michael Cicone and Diane Ruble (1978) found that certain traits occurred more often than others. Traits such as ambition, unemotionality, strength, interest in sex, courage, and aggressiveness were frequently associated with the designation of "typical male." The researchers then discovered that these traits fit into three general descriptive categories, which they outlined as follows:

1. How a man handles his life (*active* and *achievement-oriented*). This group includes the qualities adventurous, ambitious, independent, courageous, competitive, leader, and active. The common denominator is a kind of go-getting, dynamic attitude toward life in general, with the possibility of worldly accomplishment and success.

2. How a man handles others (*dominant*). This group includes aggressive, powerful, dominant, assertive, boastful. It is the putting of the self over and against other people which characterizes these traits.

3. How a man handles his psyche (*level-headed*). Here we put logical, realistic, stable, unemotional, and self-control. The "typical man" is seen as cool and self-contained. (p. 11)

Another "blueprint" for what constitutes the male role was elaborated by Robert Brannon. Brannon (1976) drafted his version of the male role in terms of four major themes, to which he gave the following headings:

1. No Sissy Stuff: The stigma of all stereotyped feminine characteristics and qualities, including openness and vulnerability.

2. The Big Wheel: Success, status, and the need to be looked up to.

3. The Sturdy Oak: A manly air of toughness, confidence, and self-reliance.

4. Give 'Em Hell!: The aura of aggression, violence, and daring. (p. 12)

In both these descriptions, the elements of the male role are quite similar. In the following chapters we will borrow heavily from both analyses, especially from Brannon's. Before we begin, however, a quick preview of each element seems in order.

One of the first lessons little boys learn is to avoid anything that may make them appear feminine or sissified; under no circumstances do they want to be caught acting like a girl. The lessons can be cruel and even terrifying. A little boy found playing quietly with one of his sister's dolls may hear his father yell as he yanks the doll away, "Damn it, no son of mine is going to play with dolls like a girl!" If his father's outburst causes the boy to cry, the father may try to soothe his son by saying, "Now, now, son, stop your crying, only girls cry, and for damn sure you don't want to act like a girl, now do you?" Of course, the question is only rhetorical. The little boy is expected to want to be anything but a girl. The first element in the male role, then, is designated

Elements of the Male Role

here as the *antifeminine element* because after awhile boys learn not only to avoid anything identified as feminine, but as they grow older, they actually begin to dislike everything even vaguely connected with what society calls "feminine."

The second element is called the *success element*. Early in a boy's life, he is taught to get out there and be a winner, a champ, numero uno, in other words, a success. The introductory lessons usually revolve around competitive sports and may even include his achievements in school. As a boy grows up, the initial lessons translate into other expectations normally related to his first job and later on into his long-term aspirations for a career. Success in work usually allows a young man to prove himself successful in terms of another expectation: the role of breadwinner for his family. Failure at any of these expectations may bring some of the harshest criticisms directed at a man. The bottom line reads that a man who is not successful at what he does is thought unmanly.

The third element in our discussion is the *aggressive element*. Today most men do not see themselves or wish others to see them as quarrelsome bullies. The time when a man was frequently expected "to step outside and prove himself a man" is pretty much limited to television's portrayal of the Wild West. Even so, most young men are expected to stand up and fight, especially if someone else starts it. This male lesson is simple and straightforward: If goaded or bullied by another, a man must fight. To run away or to avoid a fight casts a male in a cowardly and unmanly light or possibly causes him to become fearful of others (Gilmartin, 1987).

Men are commonly thought insatiable when it comes to sex, and this view brings us to the fourth element, the *sexual element*. Many a woman has been told by her concerned mother never to trust men because they are out for only one thing—sex. Further, more than a few middle-aged men can remember their father's jocular quip, "Don't do anything I wouldn't do." The end result of these early messages and many others is that most people believe that men are virtual satyrs in their relations with women. Whether men are driven by their biology, by social pressures, or by a combination of both, most men believe that sex and an interest in sexual matters are essential features of their role.

The final element in our discussion is the *self-reliant element*. Of all the manly expectations, the self-reliant element is probably the most difficult one to analyze. One of the problems here is that a man does not show others how self-reliant he is just by what he says or by what he does. No, being self-reliant is a matter of style, a particular personal bearing in the way a man talks and behaves. A second problem is that this element encompasses many additional attributes that a man is expected to exhibit. For example, under the heading of self-reliance, we also find references to toughness, courage, confidence, independence, determination, and coolness.

There we have the five elements that appear central to the North American conception of the male role. It should be obvious that no man can exhibit all five elements at one time. There is simply no way a man can be antifeminine, successful, aggressive, sexual, and self-reliant on any one given occasion. However, even though a man need not display all elements simultaneously, he must be able to exhibit each of them when the situation warrants it if he is to be considered a "real man."

It should be equally obvious that various groups place different weights or values on each of the five elements. Not every group a man identifies with requires that he act out each of these elements in order to be seen as manly. For example, among academics, achieving success through publications is an important way a male college professor can substantiate his masculinity. For a gang member, though, a young man may be expected to mug a pedestrian or shoot a rival gang member in order to prove his masculinity. A college professor is not usually seen as an aggressive or violent type of person, and so the aggressive element would undoubtedly play a lesser role in his overall male role than it would in a gang member's.

Thus we must be cautious in our generalizations of the five elements of the male role. Each and every man cannot exhibit all of them in every facet of his life, neither do all of the elements carry equal weight in regard to every man's life.

Chapter 7

The Antifeminine Element

A fundamental guide for men's behavior may be a negative touchstone—anything feminine. This conclusion may first appear as a simple tautology that males endorsing the traditional male role are "antifeminine." While . . . the data do not suggest that males endorsing the male role are singularly anxious about being perceived as feminine, nor are they necessarily endorsing misogyny. . . . Instead, the conclusion is that the antifeminine norm within the traditional male role is more pervasive and salient than other norms. Thus, we would expect that men endorsing the traditional male role are likely to always be guided by the antifemininity norm in conjunction with other situationally specific norms.

Edward Thompson, Jr., Christopher Grisanti, and Joseph Pleck (1985)

The first and possibly the strongest element in the entire fabric of the male role is a negative or prohibitive injunction that states in its most basic form, "Boys, whatever you do, don't be like or do anything like a girl." Even before boys learn the other major lessons of their role, they are taught to avoid anything that even vaguely smacks of femininity.

If the first lesson on the male role contained a simple statement to the effect that boys are different from girls by virtue that boys cannot do some things that girls can do (for example, "Johnny, when you grow up you can't have a baby; only girls like Mommy and your sisters can have babies") that would be all right. But this first lesson does not end with a simple explanation of basic biological differences and some elementary sex education. No, it goes on to demean females. The first lesson of "don't be like a girl" is followed by several **misogynist** (hatred of women) postscripts. The complete first lesson goes something like this: "Don't be like a girl because . . . well, girls are bad, stupid, inferior, subordinate, and . . . well, girls are just plain icky!"

Along with the prohibition of "don't be like a girl because . . ." the first lesson contains other messages that add still other negative dimensions. For example, boys are taught never to express, at least not publicly, certain emotions that might be seen as signs of weakness and vulnerability. Emotions such as joy, love, compassion, tenderness, and fear are, if not avoided, at least played down by boys. The message to boys is once again quite clear: Only girls show these emotions, and boys would appear unmanly if they were to show them. And, of course, boys should never express their gentle or affectionate feelings toward other boys. Girls can express affection for other girls because that's what girls do anyway. But the lesson is straightforward with respect to boys: Boys should beware of other boys who are overly expressive of their tender feelings. You know, they may not be real men!

In this chapter we will analyze the blatant misogyny or sexism that is an outgrowth of a boy's first lesson of "don't be like a girl because. . . ." We also will discuss the lengths to which boys and men go in order to avoid certain "troublesome" emotions and the consequences of such emotional constriction. Finally, we will take a look at certain prohibitions surrounding male-male relationships.

avoid the feminine

Males and females are different. For most people, the obvious anatomical differences are the icing on the cake and cause for the exclamation of *vive la différence!* But there is one experience both male and female children share equally. In most instances, both sexes are raised by women. Even if the woman is not the biological mother but rather a female relative or some other maternal surrogate, it would be a woman in almost nine out of ten cases. Thus both girls and boys spend considerably more time during their first impressionable years in close proximity to a woman and not a man. Having an adult female for her primary caretaker allows a young female ample opportunity to learn from another same-sex person the ways of womanhood in a realistic fashion. For many a young male, though, he spends relatively little time in the company of his father or other same-sex adults, and thus he must rely on other means (for example, television and male peers) to learn the ways of manhood. The inherent problem facing most young boys who learn their male role from television and peers is that these sources tend to exaggerate and separate the activities of each gender into strictly stereotypic gender categories. The way that television and peers present the male role has a definite air of unreality about it. Take for example television. Television portrays the genders in rigid and unrealistic ways (Oskamp, 1987). Men are shown as dominant, forceful, and in control of themselves and others (that is, females), and women are portrayed as support systems for males. According to most television programs, males do only stereotypic manly things, females do only stereotypic feminine things, and never the twain shall meet. A little boy sitting on the floor in the living room absorbs the intended message all too well: Don't be like a girl. Whatever girls do, boys don't. If girls play with dolls, boys don't; if girls help around the house, boys don't; if girls cry when they fall and skin their knees, boys don't. (For a thorough discussion of television's impact on gender development, see Durkin, 1985a, 1985b, 1985c; Jeffery & Durkin, 1989).

If all that young boys learned was "you're not like girls in certain ways," that would be one thing. But a rider is attached to the lesson. The additional message is that girls (women) and all that is associated with females are not only different but they are also unequal to whatever is associated with males. The notion of different is quickly translated in many young males' minds to mean bad and inferior. Thus the total first lesson in the male role for many males is "don't be like girls (women) because they are unequal, bad, and inferior." The outcome of such training is that "one half of the human race regards the other at best with condescension and suspicion, at worst with hatred and fear" (Hays, 1966, p. 1). (For a thorough presentation on the effects of an undercurrent of "fear of the feminine" on men's lives, see O'Donovan, 1988a, 1988b; O'Neil, 1981, 1982; O'Neil, Helms, Gable, David & Wrightsman, 1986.) For those who think we overstate the case, a small sampling of some notable quotables may testify to the depths of some men's (that is grown-up boys') misogynous or sexist beliefs.

- I thank thee, O Lord, that thou has not created me a woman.
  Daily Orthodox Jewish Prayer (for a male)
- When a woman thinks . . . she thinks evil.
  Seneca
- How can he be clean that is born of a woman?
  Job 4:4
- Let the women learn in silence with all subjection . . . . I suffer not a woman to usurp authority over men, but to be in silence.
  St. Paul
- God created Adam Lord of all living creatures, but Eve spoiled it all.
  Martin Luther
- Regard the society of women as a necessary unpleasantness of social life, and avoid it as much as possible.
  Count Leo Tolstoy
- And a woman is only a woman but a good cigar is a smoke.
  Rudyard Kipling
- The only position for women in SNCC is prone.
  Stokely Carmichael, 1966

The Antifeminine Element

- It would be preposterously naive to suggest that a B.A. can be made as attractive to girls as a marriage license.

    Dr. Grayson Kirk (former President, Columbia University)
- The only alliance I would make with the Women's Liberation Movement is in bed.

    Abbie Hoffman
- Women? I guess they ought to exercise Pussy Power.

    Eldridge Cleaver, 1968 (quoted in Morgan, 1970)

These are not the insignificant ramblings of a few inconsequential men but rather definite value statements from several notable men whose ideas have influenced millions of people. If we are to understand fully the male role, we must face the ignoble fact that sexism and misogyny are definite parts of the first crucial lessons many a boy learns about what it means to be a man. No less an authority on male-female relations than Jessie Bernard (1981) sums up the issue of men's feelings toward women in this statement:

> . . . there is clear evidence that although individual men may love individual women with great depth and devotion, the male world as a whole does not. Terms like "hatred" or "hostility" may be too strong to describe this response, so the term "misogyny" has been invented. As long as women know their place and keep in it, misogyny need not rear its ugly head. Women are "dears" and "lovelies." But when they intrude on the male world, they become "damfool women." (p. 11)

To get a better appreciation of the depth and magnitude of sexism as an integrated feature of the first lessons in the male role, let's briefly review the roots and historical traditions of sexism and misogyny and the pervasiveness of sexism in present-day society.

Much of the antifeminine perspective, or sexism, owes its heritage to the institution of patriarchy (Hearn, 1987). **Patriarchy,** or the rule of the father, with its own distinct system of values, beliefs, laws, religions, and economics can be traced back to the beginnings of the Greco-Roman civilizations. The religious traditions of the Judeo-Christian perspective likewise initiated a strict patriarchal cosmology and world view and instituted the belief that women were "the source of all male difficulties" (Bullough, 1974). Down through the ages, patriarchy became the norm for all "civilized" societies (Howell, 1986). When in the seventeenth century the Puritans fled England to the New World with its promise of religious freedom, the basic human freedoms were withheld from women, who worked alongside their men in building a new nation. When the colonists struck out on a rebellious road, the constitutional document that outlined the sought-after freedoms for its independent citizenry stated that "all *men* are created equal." Women and blacks were intentionally left out of the document's protection. Since that time, the United States has come a long way in granting freedoms and rights to those who were at first disenfranchised. Even so, with the defeat of the Equal Rights Amendment (ERA), women still do not have a constitutional guarantee of their full and equal rights under the law (Mansbridge, 1986).

But that's all history, all in our past, some will insist. Surely, women are not discriminated against now, not in these enlightened times. The problem is, however, that sexism is alive and well in these final years of the twentieth century. Even in prominent institutions of higher learning, young men confess that although they espouse egalitarian attitudes in public, down deep they feel threatened by and somewhat hostile toward women of equal or superior intelligence (Komarovsky, 1976). Negative attitudes toward women are also found at less prestigious colleges as well and among some groups of college males more so than others (Doyle & Shahade, 1977). College males' attitudes toward women's roles may have improved (become more accepting of women's roles and rights) relative to previous generations of college males, but the prevalence of negative stereotypic attitudes toward women is as entrenched in the male role today as it ever was (Doyle, 1976; Helmreich et al., 1982; McKinney, 1987; Spence & Helmreich, 1978). The sad truth is that most men talk a good line about gender equality, but when push comes to shove, they think women should stay in their place and not make "damn fools" of themselves.

Nowhere is the virus of sexism more obvious and more debilitating to women than in the workplace. Differential pay scales, common myths and fallacies about women's abilities and potentialities, and men's attitudes toward women's managerial capabilities are just a few of the seemingly insurmountable obstacles women face.

Historically, a woman's work has been valued less than a man's. No matter what it was that a woman produced, compared to what a man produced, her product was of less merit. Especially in terms of pay, women's work is much less valued than a man's (Marini, 1989). Author and human relations expert Stan Kossen (1987) elaborated on the problem of unequal pay for women's work in the following passage.

If you were an "average" full-time female worker, you would discover that the gap between men's earnings and your own was the same in 1986 as it was in 1955. In 1955, you earned slightly less than 64 percent as much as men. After skidding to 59 percent in 1980, you gained a few points and once again earned 64 percent of men's earnings in 1986. (p. 373)

Could it be that women's average pay is less than men's not because of sexism but rather because women choose low-paying and less responsible jobs such as waitressing? Hardly. No matter what type of work women perform, they are usually paid less than men who do the same work (England & McCreary, 1987). Even those few

The Antifeminine Element

table 7.1   Comparison of Median Weekly Salaries in Selected High Paying Occupations for Men and Women (1988)

	Men	Women	% Ratio Women/Men
Lawyer	$930	$774	83
Physician	$815	$553	68
College Professor	$752	$555	74
Personnel and Labor-Relations Manager	$785	$563	72
Mathematical and Computer Specialist	$733	$575	78
Education Administrator	$757	$499	66
Engineer	$734★	$639★★	87

★Reported as lowest salaried engineer (i.e., civil) within male workforce
★★Reported as highest salaried engineer (i.e., not designated) within female workforce
Source: U.S. Department of Labor

women in prestigious positions are likely to be paid less than men in comparable positions (Simeone, 1987; see Table 7.1). Although equal pay for equal work continues to be an issue in the 1980s and the 1990s, the Supreme Court decision that ruled in favor of equal pay for work of "comparable worth" has only fired the contest between those in favor of and those opposed to women's rights (Remick, 1984).

There is no shortage of myths and half-truths about women's inherent abilities or the lack thereof for the competitive workplace. For the most part, the stereotypic notions about women act as a deterrent keeping them from gaining a meaningful foothold in the business world (Bose, 1987). Several years ago Paul Samuelson (1976, p. 790), one of this country's leading economists, detailed some of the more common myths about women:

> Women are built by nature to tend babies in the home. They are emotional. They have monthly ups and downs. They cannot carry heavy weights. They lack self-confidence. Men will not work under a woman. Man-to-man talk will be inhibited by the presence of women. Even women prefer a male physician to a female one. Women lack imagination and creativity. If you mix men and women on the job, they will carry on to the detriment of efficiency and good morals. By the time you have trained a woman, she'll get married and leave you; or have a baby; or alternatively, you won't be able ever to get rid of a woman once you've hired her. If a woman does turn out to be a superlative economic performer, she's not feminine, she's harsh and aggressive with a chip on her shoulder against men and the world (and she's killing her chances of getting married). Women workers, seeking pin money, take bread from the mouths of family breadwinners.

The myths of women act as a kind of catch-22. First, we are told, women won't stay in a job because of the lure of wedding bells or the purported urges of the maternal instinct. Then if she does stay, she can't be gotten rid of, we are told. If

how to tell a businessman from a businesswoman

A businessman is aggressive; a businesswoman is pushy.

A businessman is good with details; a businesswoman is picky.

He loses his temper because he's so involved in his job; she's a bitch.

When he's depressed or hungover, everyone tiptoes past his office. If she's moody, it must be her time of the month.

He follows through; she doesn't know when to quit.

He's confident; she's conceited.

He stands firm; she's hard.

His judgments are her prejudices.

He is a man of the world; she's been around.

If he drinks it's because of job pressure; she's a lush.

He's never afraid to say what he thinks; she's always shooting off her mouth.

He exercises authority diligently; she's power mad.

He's close-mouthed; she's secretive.

He's a stern taskmaster; she's hard to work for.

He climbed the ladder of success; she slept her way to the top.

she does her job too well, it must be because she is not really a woman. Women, it seems, are in a no-win situation; no matter what they do, it is interpreted negatively (see "How to Tell a Businessman from a Businesswoman").

Many women have learned there is no place for them on most companies' management teams. Somehow, management is seen as an exclusively male activity, and the sign in the personnel office might as well read, "Women need not apply." The problem in many companies is that a substantial minority of males hold sexist attitudes about women's abilities in general and especially with respect to a woman's being able to handle managerial responsibilities (Kossen, 1987). This point was borne out several years ago in the research of industrial psychologist Virginia Schein.

Schein (1973) asked 300 middle-level *male* managers to describe the requisite personality characteristics, attitudes, and temperaments needed to fulfill the responsibilities of a middle-level managerial position. Furthermore, she asked these managers to describe the characteristics of men in general as well as of women in general. Not surprisingly, the managers described almost identical personality profiles for successful managers and men in general. On the other hand, they saw women as *not* having the requisite personality characteristics or temperament for management. Schein concluded that men in managerial positions see the male, but not the female, as having the necessary personal characteristics for the demands of a management position. Although we might expect male managers and male management students' attitudes to have changed over the past decade or so given all the publicity over women in the workforce, more recent research continues to find most still espouse gender-stereotypical attitudes toward management characteristics in general and women in particular (Heilman et al., 1989; Maier, 1993; Schein et al., 1989). A few years later, Schein (1975) again asked yet another group of managers to select those characteristics typical of a manager, of males, and of females. Again, she found this second sample also grouped managers and males together separate from females. Although this second study seems a simple replication of her first, her sample this time was made up of *female* managers. However, in a more recent study, Schein (et al., 1989) found female managers *less* likely to cast management characteristics in a male mold.

Why, though, do so many males think that males make better managers? Are male and female managers really that different in performing their managerial duties?

The Antifeminine Element

Some researchers say yes (Dobbins, 1986; Statham, 1987; Winther & Green, 1987), while others say no (Donnell & Hall, 1980; Steinberg & Shapiro, 1982). Could it be that people are just plain prejudiced against females in the business world (Sanders & Schmidt, 1980)? Is prejudice the answer, or are there other factors that prevent women from being represented in the managerial world in proportion to their numbers in the work force or in terms of their numbers coming out of business schools?

Another reason beyond simple prejudice why many just don't think of women as managers has something to do with how people explain others' behaviors—what social scientists call the attribution process (Wittig, 1985). All too often when people hear of a man's success in the business world, people assume his success is attributable to or caused by his ability or talents—what attribution theorists call an internal or dispositional cause. For instance, a man who has just received a promotion or a raise is seen by many to have earned these important rewards by dint of his past skillful performances. However, when people hear of a female's success in the corporate world, more than a few will attribute her success not to her talent but rather to luck or to some other factor such as getting ahead because of her being a female, and a token female at that (Kanter, 1984; Stevens & DeNisi, 1980; Yoder & Sinnett, 1985). And if seeing female success as attributable to something outside of her control weren't enough, more than a few women in the business world handicap themselves by setting lower expectations for their careers than many of their male colleagues (Major & Konar, 1984).

Although no one can deny that many women suffer from prejudice in the workplace, recent evidence suggests that some change for the better is taking place. For instance, in one study, Lawrence Peters (1984) and several of his colleagues found that contrary to popular thought, female managers actually received higher performance ratings—a key factor in determining a person's promotions and merit raises—than comparable male managers. Although we shouldn't believe that everything is A-OK with women in the workplace based on this one study, women have made some very impressive gains in the workplace's managerial sector in the last few years (Will & Lydenberg, 1987). However, there is considerable room for more change and advancement.

a v o i d e m o t i o n s

If we were to ask a group of people, say, a group of college students whether they would describe males as emotional or unemotional, most of the students would probably answer unemotional. The perception of men as stereotypically unemotional is a fairly consistent finding in many social psychological studies dealing with gender stereotypes (King & Emmons, 1990). But the fact of the matter is that men are emotional. Men do express their feelings or emotions, ones that appear harsh, raw, and often harmful to themselves and others. Emotions such as anger, disgust, hostility, contempt, and cynicism are just a few of the emotions that men express quite openly in public. However, the reason so many people consider men unemotional is that the word "emotion," to many people's way of thinking, is linked with the notion of femininity. Of course, women, too, show their emotions of anger and hostility, but the emotions women are most often associated with are the more gentle emotions such as love, joy, compassion, ecstasy, and fear. Thus when people are asked about emotions, they often think of the "feelings of the heart"—of women swooning with love—and not of men pounding their fists on a table and yelling obscenities at their neighbor (Shields, 1987). To think of a man swooning or expressing concern over a lost puppy is almost unthinkable for many people and especially for many men. Overall, males tend to think that the fewer female gender-typed traits they possess—and this especially holds true of emotionality—the more masculine they are. Remember the male's first lesson: "Don't be like a girl." Girls are emotional and so boys must not be.

Some men go to all kinds of lengths to hide or rid themselves of what they consider "troublesome emotions." These are emotions that leave a person open and vulnerable to others. For example, when one expresses one's love for another person, there is no way of knowing whether or not the other person will return that love. If Jim tells Jack that he fears something, Jack may ridicule Jim and say what a fool he is for fearing something that Jack himself does not fear. Love, fear, and compassion are just a few of the more troublesome emotions that many men try to rid themselves of. Now and then, we even find a man such as convicted Watergate conspirator and prototypical macho man, G. Gordon Liddy (1980), who considers any emotion whatsoever (even anger and disgust) that competes with "reason and will" to be troublesome. For Liddy, a real man should be cold, calculating, unemotional, inscrutable, and totally in control of all his faculties. More than a few men agree with Liddy's analysis of masculinity, believing that the more they control or hide their emotions, the more inscrutable and cool and manly they appear to others (Henley, 1977).

In this section we will discuss some of the consequences men face when they repress their troublesome emotions and why men diligently defend themselves from their own emotional experiences.

Warren Farrell, author of *The Liberated Man* (1974), writes of the debilitating outcomes many men experience when they avoid or try to rid themselves of their troublesome emotions. First, Farrell describes a condition he calls **emotional incompetency.** The emotionally incompetent man in Farrell's analysis is one who is unable to handle, or deal with, other people's emotions. For example, many men find themselves extremely uncomfortable around other people who are expressing their emotions freely and openly. It is as if these men do not know how to act, how to respond to other people's emotional expressions. Many women who have expressed their feelings of, say, sadness or hurt with tears have heard their husband or lover say, "Please, honey, stop crying; you know how that makes me feel." Yes, most women know all too well how men feel around a woman who is crying—either insensitive or awkward! These men are really saying, "I can't deal with these emotions, so stop it!" The other side of the coin turns up when a man complains to one of his male friends, "You know any time my wife wants something from me, all she has to do is open the old floodgates, and—wham—she gets it." Here a man is saying that he distrusts a woman's emotions. In his eyes, emotions are a form of blackmail. The fact is many men just do not permit themselves the human luxury of shutting up long

The Antifeminine Element

enough to let another person have an emotional release; they cannot seem to resist opening their big mouths and showing just how very little they know about the emotional experience. Many men are truly emotionally incompetent.

The second condition men face with their troublesome emotions is what Farrell calls **emotional constipation,** a man's inability to express his own troublesome emotions. Although males do feel love, pain, tenderness, sadness, sorrow, compassion, joy, and so forth, by the age of five or six, they learn not to show these emotions, at least not in public. The rule among many males is simple: Don't show any emotion that may make you appear weak, vulnerable, or feminine. Many a father has chastised his son for crying: "Now stop it! No son of mine is going to be a crybaby and act like a sissy. Get up to your room, and don't come down till you can act like a man!" (Choti, Marston & Holston, 1987; Ross & Mirowsky, 1984; Williams, 1982.) There we have it again, the concern among men for not being thought unmanly. A classic example of the consequences men suffer when they show their troublesome emotions in public happened in the 1972 presidential race. After a newspaper editor printed slanderous remarks about his wife, presidential candidate Edmund Muskie broke down and cried in public while defending his wife's name. After the news services ran a picture of Muskie weeping, standing out in the cold New England weather, his chances for election were about as good as the proverbial snowball's chance in hell. Defending his wife's honor is perfectly all right for a man to do, but to break down and cry—no real man would do that! Muskie had committed an unpardonable sin in the minds of many people. He showed his troublesome emotions, and for many males and females alike, the question of his manhood and masculinity were in doubt from that moment on. It seems that many people do not want their leaders to show any sign of weakness. Farrell relates an incident wherein one of his friends paid dearly because he allowed himself to express some "unmanly" emotions in the office:

A friend explained to me that he broke down and cried in front of a colleague at the office after some personal tragedies and office frustrations. He explained, "The news of my crying was all over the office in an hour. At first no one said anything. They just sort of looked. They couldn't handle the situation by talking about it. Before this only girls had cried. One of the guys did joke, 'Hear you and Sally been crying lately, eh?' I guess that was a jibe at my masculinity, but the 'knowing' silence of the others indicated the same doubts. What really hurt was that two years later, when I was doing very well and being considered for a promotion, it was brought up again. My manager was looking over my evaluations, read a paragraph to himself and said, 'What do you think about that crying incident?' You can bet that was the last time I let myself cry." (pp. 71–72)

Some emotions are more troublesome for men to deal with than others. One emotion many men deny even to the point of its being harmful to their personal relations is fear. Fear is something women are assumed to be given to, and that is enough to make it something men should not even admit to. When men fear, say, the possibility of losing their job, they often will not even admit their fear to their wife: "No sense in bothering the little woman with things she can't do anything about anyway." Keeping fears hidden from others, especially those who care a great deal, is one way in which many men keep others at a distance (Rawlins, 1983).

The late psychologist Sidney Jourard referred to the condition of a person's openly sharing his or her personal, or intimate, thoughts and feelings with another person as **self-disclosure.** Men tend to self-disclose less than women, regardless of age, education, or economic status. Jourard suggested men suffer a sort of psychological isolation because of their self-imposed restriction against self-disclosing to others. He leveled one of his harshest indictments against men when he noted that

> [If] a man is reluctant to make himself known to another person, even to his spouse—because it is not manly thus to be psychologically naked—then it follows that *men will be difficult to love.* That is, it will be difficult for a woman or another man to know the immediate present state of the man's self, and his needs will thereby go unmet. Some men are so skilled at dissembling, at "seeming," that even their wives will not know when they are lonely, bored, anxious, in pain, thwarted, hungering for affection, etc. And the men, blocked by pride, dare not disclose their despair, or need. (1974, p. 26)

Charging that "men will be difficult to love" is a strong statement. And yet with so many men working so hard to guard their emotions and feelings for fear they will appear weak, vulnerable, feminine, or less than a real man, no wonder so many men live lives of desperate isolation. When a man refuses to admit his love or fears or anxieties or joys, the other people in his life may well interpret his reserve as a signal that all is well when in fact it may not be so (May, 1990; Moore, 1990).

We have noted the deep antipathy many men feel about women in general and about their own troublesome emotions. We now want to discuss one last prohibition that men live with in order to live up to their male role, a prohibition that restricts the kinds of relationships men have together. Again, the antifemale bias lurks in the shadows wherever and whenever men congregate.

Men have always seemed to enjoy one another's company. Historically, men were expected to enjoy one another's company more than the company of women. In the distant past, men ventured into the bush or onto the savannah after large game in all-male groups. Hunting parties, drinking bouts in all-male saloons, athletic

avoid unmanly men

The Antifeminine Element

clubs, fraternities, service clubs, and the proverbial "boys' night out" are just a few of the social rituals attesting to men's attachments to one another. The prevalence of all-male groups over the ages and in many disparate cultures led one anthropologist, Lionel Tiger (1969), to hypothesize a genetic "male bond." Although the evidence for a male bond is highly questionable, the phenomenon of men spending more time in women's company than with men is a relatively recent social expectation (see "Moving Toward Partnership" in Chapter 2). Even with the recent addition of male-female social relationships, there is no lack of activities wherein men can be with other men.

One would think that with all of the time men spend together—at work, at the neighborhood bar, at the ballpark, at the bowling alley, around the barbecue pit, or under the hood of a car—the resultant relationships would be deep, sharing, and emotionally open. Who better to turn to than to another man, another man who knows firsthand the pressures, anxieties, fears, and, yes, the joys of what it means to be a man. One might think that there are just some things another man would understand better than a woman would (Michaels, 1981). Women have these types of relationships with each other. What about men? Many male-male relationships are anything but emotionally satisfying and personally gratifying though (Griffin & Sparks, 1990). Again, a major stumbling block is the difficulty men have with their emotions, especially in expressing the caring emotions (Doyle, 1986). There is also another impediment to male-male relations. Constantly lurking in the shadows of men's minds is the fear, and for some men the horror, that other men may think them less than a real man (Miller, 1983, 1985).

As we suggested earlier, men have trouble expressing their own or dealing with others' more gentle emotions. Women, on the other hand, often are able to share these emotions with other women. Women, in fact, are allowed and encouraged to comfort one another, to show concern and love for one another, to share one another's sadnesses and joys. But these emotional experiences are almost never encouraged among men. Boys are taught to hold back, to close off, to negate their positive feelings toward other boys. If, for instance, a boy slips and shows concern or compassion for another boy's pain, he must be taught a lesson so that he will not do so in the future. Marc Feigen Fasteau (1974, p. 14) relates just such an incident that happened to him when he was eight years old:

> What is particularly difficult for men is seeking or accepting help from friends. I, for one, learned early that dependence was unacceptable. When I was eight, I went to a summer camp I disliked. My parents visited me in the middle of the summer and, when it was time for them to leave, I wanted to go with them. They refused, and I yelled and screamed and was miserably unhappy for the rest of the day. That evening an older camper comforted me, sitting by my bed as I cried, patting me on the back soothingly and saying whatever it is that one says at times like that. He was in some way clumsy or funny-looking, and a few days later I joined a group of kids in cruelly making fun of him, an act which upset me, when I thought about it, for years. I can only explain it in terms of my feeling, as early as the age of eight, that by needing and accepting his help and comfort I had compromised myself, and took it out on him.

The older male camper had transgressed, had broken a provision in the lesson of the male role. He had shown concern for another male's plight. Fasteau, as the young camper, likewise broke a male role expectation—he had shown himself weak and in need of comfort. That also is forbidden to men. Why are caring behaviors so powerfully prohibited to males? Well, again, remember the first lesson in the male role: Don't be like a girl. If girls show compassion one for the other and openly express their hurts in each other's company, then boys must not do the same. But there is also another dimension to this prohibition against boys and men showing other boys and men their positive and caring feelings one for another. An extra taboo overshadows male relations, a veritable sword of Damocles hangs over them, the constant specter of homosexuality.

Few words strike as much horror or fear in a man's mind as does the word "homosexuality." Parents fear it, clergy denounce it, politicians campaign against it, and men in general control each other with the threat of it (DeCecco, 1985). Gregory Lehne (1976) in an article about **homophobia,** or the irrational fear of homosexuality, states that the major function of homophobia is to act as "a device of social control, directed specifically against men to maintain male behavior appropriate to the social situation." To see what Lehne means, watch almost any group of boys or men in almost any situation. If one of the group members acts in a way that makes the other males uncomfortable in their male role, the others will usually make some disparaging remarks about the one male's masculinity. When men make remarks about another male's masculinity, even in jest, the message is clear: "You'd better shape up, conform to what is expected, or else we might think you're one of those . . . one of those queers." Quickly, then, most men fall in line to the drumbeat of the male role (Blumenfeld, 1992; Ficarrotto, 1990; Neisen, 1990).

One of the consequences of the fear of homosexuality and the constant concern over what other men think about one's masculinity is that men have very few close male friends. Men have plenty of buddies with whom they drink and talk over politics, sports, work, and sex. But other men with whom they can share their fears and

The Antifeminine Element

anxieties as well as their pleasures and joys is another matter (Bell, 1981; Rubin, 1985; Sherrod, 1987). Quite often the fact that a man has no real male friends becomes painfully clear only when he needs someone to lean on:

> After my divorce I realized that I had allowed all of my friendships to drop, and I had no one to talk to. It was pretty lonely, I began sleeping around a lot just to be with someone. And I started hanging around this one bar on nights I didn't have a date. I'd always be with people, but I never got what I wanted. It was like a sieve—the loneliness was a bottomless pit. (Wagenvoord & Bailey, 1978; pp. 269–270)

Listen to the painful loneliness of this man's cry for another human being. He found no one because like so many other males he had allowed his friendships to drop. Probably he had never allowed himself to have a real friendship with another man or perhaps with a woman either, not even his former wife. Men cannot allow themselves to get too close, to form deep and involved friendships with other men because they may have to deal with the gnawing fear of homosexuality. Even if a man begins to feel something positive for another man, he must, according to the male role, hold himself in check before something happens that may be misinterpreted by other men. Psychologist Robert Brannon (1976, pp. 18–19) points out this feature of male relationships most poignantly in an incident that happened to him in college:

> Like the majority of men (as I was greatly relieved to find out later!), I secretly feared at one time in my life that I was a "latent homosexual." In college the affection and caring I felt for my three roommates worried me, because I could sense that it wasn't really *all that* different from the affection I felt for the girlfriends I knew best and liked most. If the truth be known, I cared more genuinely for my male friends at this time than for any female I knew. What's worse, when we were sprawled out somewhere watching T.V. or reading, and our legs or arms would touch comfortably, it was . . . well, pleasant! Once one of my roommates and I were lying on our old sofa, talking and drinking beer. For some reason—as I recall there wasn't much room—he put his head in my lap with some wisecrack about getting comfortable. We continued talking. But I felt a closeness, a sort of emotional bond that hadn't been there before. And . . . after a while, I felt a very real desire to lightly stroke his hair, the way I would have done had he been a woman. Finally, I said something brilliant like "Get off me you lazy sonofabitch, you're gettin' heavy."

Two people at ease, comfortable, and sharing their thoughts of the moment; one feels the impulse to stroke the other's hair, a simple gesture of togetherness and human communication. And what happens? "Get off me you lazy sonofabitch!" Men can be so insensitive to each other because of a fear that one or the other may interpret an action as unmanly. Another missed opportunity to cement a relationship, to firm up a friendship. Men have many ways of subverting their own relationships. No wonder Jourard thought them difficult to love. Most men go out of their way to keep people, men and women alike, at an emotional arm's distance. This emotional distancing is one of the heaviest prices males pay for trying to live up to the first lesson in the male role.

Throughout this chapter we have avoided an in-depth analysis of misogyny. In early chapters we alluded to the connection between patriarchy and misogyny. Even so, why should physically powerful men feel it necessary to demean and degrade women, their emotions, and caring relationships among men? Men from earliest times could see that they were different from women. Why carry the obvious physical differences to such absurd lengths?

We could suggest some deep psychological basis, such as an unconscious feeling of inferiority that men feel toward women's creative ability (birth and natural feeding) and that men feel they must compensate for by putting down women and all that is thought of as feminine. Or we could note that because men are usually raised by women, men must go to extreme psychological lengths to rid themselves of an early feminine identification with their mothers, and so they attack women. Or perhaps misogyny had its roots in some earlier economic system and arose by virtue of who handed out the meat. Maybe misogyny is nothing more than the obscene outgrowth of one group's need to feel superior over another. When it comes to the human group, there are only two basic categories, females and males. Why men seem to have a penchant for prejudice and discrimination against women and not vice versa is a matter of speculation. But to argue for or against these or other possible causes of misogyny is beyond the scope of this book. What is obvious is that boys learn their first lesson in the male role very early and from several different sources: "Don't be like a girl."

This first lesson that boys must learn about what it means to be a real man is a negative one, with plenty of threats and accusations. In the next chapter we will turn our attention to a prescriptive rather than prohibitive lesson: "No matter what you do, be a success, make something of yourself, make us proud of you, son!"

---

important terms

Emotional constipation *142*	Misogynist *134*
Emotional incompetency *141*	Patriarchy *136*
Homophobia *145*	Self-disclosure *143*

---

suggested readings

Blumenfeld, W. J. (Ed.). (1992). *Homophobia*. Boston: Beacon Press.

Michaels, L. (1981). *The men's club*. New York: Farrar, Strauss & Giroux.

Miller, S. (1983). *Men and friendship*. Los Angeles: Tarcher.

Sherrod, D. (1987). The bonds of men: Problems and possibilities in close male relationships. In H. Brod (Ed.), *The making of masculinities: The new men's studies* (pp. 213–239). Boston: Allen & Unwin.

Townsend, R. (1985). The texture of men's lives. In A. Sargent (Ed.), *Beyond sex roles* (2nd ed., pp. 340–351). St. Paul, MN: West Publishing.

The Antifeminine Element

Chapter 8

The Success Element

. . . success and status are the bedrock elements of the male sex role, and no man in America escapes from the injunction to succeed.
Robert Brannon (1976)

A strange juggling of ethical perspectives takes place under the influence of a competitive standard. When a man competes, it seems winning becomes his primary objective; other concerns grow dim. As he struts toward pinnacles of success, too often he forgets the whole spectrum of rectitude and integrity which should, hopefully, line his avenue to the top.
Jack Nichols (1975)

The toughest thing about success is that you've got to keep on being a success.
Irving Berlin (1958)

Men validate their maleness in American society through achievement-oriented behavior such as winning in sports, winning in physical fighting, winning intellectually, winning financially, and winning in achieving power.
Fred Leafgren (1990)

Next to the negative injunction, "don't be like a girl," no other element is as important and universal for defining a male's role as the one that positively charges him to be a SUCCESS.

To begin our discussion of **success** then, we will first posit the idea that most North American males see the world or, better yet, social reality in a very different way than most North American females do. For many males, the world consists of a series of limited goods and rewards that must be competed for and won at any cost. Winning the goods and gaining the rewards become proofs of a man's success, which consequently bolsters his sense of being a real man. In contrast to competition, many North American males generally view cooperation as a stereotypically feminine trait, an unmanly approach to problem solving (Kohn, 1986).

In the second section we will examine what has been and still is for many men the single most definitive feature of the male role, the element of success. Since the beginning of the industrial revolution, men have focused much of their energy on fulfilling the bread*winner* role in the nuclear family. As the chief breadwinner, a man's success and ultimately his definition of masculinity has been primarily judged by himself and many others by how well he provides for his family's needs and wants. As we might suspect, severe consequences can befall a man who puts all of his proofs of masculinity, so to speak, in one basket, especially a basket so precariously woven with the strands of a changing and volatile economy.

No discussion of men and success would be complete without an obligatory "how-to" section. The "secrets" of success are big business, and men put considerable stock in what other supposedly successful men have to say about success. In the third section we will focus on one "expert's" prescription for success in the business world.

Finally, we will deal with what for a majority of men may come as a disquieting fact: Some men are turning their backs on the "success-at-all-costs" game. For a growing number of men, being a success no longer has the appeal it once did. The idea of "not making it" or settling for less rather than more is beginning to make inroads into the changing male role, and some men are proclaiming a variety of advantages in such a life-style.

An early American psychologist, famed Harvard professor William James, referred to men's obsession with success as a "bitch-goddess" plaguing their lives. (Why James thought it necessary to refer to success in this way may reveal more about James's nineteenth-century antifemale bias than about his insight concerning men and the element of success.) For most men, success is difficult to achieve and once achieved difficult to hold onto. However, many North American men still seem driven to worship success as if it were all that mattered in their lives. The sad truth is that for many men success *is* all that matters.

the male role and a competitive world view

Almost any man, no matter if he is a company president, a foreman on the second shift, or a janitor who picks up after others, shares with most others a common, burning passion "for the thrill of victory," for being the best at something. Being a winner is very masculine. Men recognize the qualities of a winner and spend vast amounts of time and energy trying to become winners in their own and in others' eyes. Vince Lombardi summed up the obsession when he said, "Winning isn't everything; it's the only thing."

The Success Element

Competition and winning are considered masculine characteristics in our society.
Source: © James L. Shaffer.

To become winners most men believe they must compete, and compete they do. Although a number of meanings have been applied to the term **competition** over the years (Deutsch, 1973; Harvey, Heath, Spencer, Temple & Wood, 1917; May & Doob, 1937; Ruben, 1981), here we will define competition as occurring when two or more people seek a reward that can only be achieved by one. Not too long after the diapers come off, boys learn that competition is an important feature of life. If they are ever going to amount to anything, if they are ever going to be real men, they quickly learn that they must beat out the other guy. In the early school grades, boys begin in earnest to grasp the competitive spirit; the school insists on ranking everyone's performance and hands out stars, favorable nods and smiles, and good grades for the few who come out on top. Competition is also fostered on the playground and the sandlot. Boys who might enjoy just throwing the ball around or hitting some balls just for the fun of it are quickly organized into a team, suited up in official uniforms with the local hardware store's name on the back, and coached into being part of the best team in town. Then on hot summer nights, their parents line the bleachers and scream at their sons to get out there and slam the ball over the fence. Boys see their parents agonize over a missed play or a strikeout and know deep down losers aren't loved (Fine, 1987; Messner, 1987; Millen & Hinds, 1976). So it goes that boys grow into manhood knowing that if they are to be loved, if they are to be winners, if they are to be real men, they had better play the game *to win* (Knight & Dubro, 1984; Knight & Kagan, 1981).

One of the major problems with the emphasis on competition is that males begin to see everything in their world solely in terms of competition. Too often, when males are given a choice between competing or cooperating with another person, they usually choose competition even if it costs them more in the long run

(Ahlgren & Johnson, 1979). For example, think of two seven-year-old boys meandering down a street on a summer day on their way to who knows where. Before long one or the other throws out the challenge, "Race ya to the corner!" And they're off. Moments later at the corner, the winner, somewhat out of breath, shrieks, "Yea, I beat ya!" The other boy shoots back between gasps, "Oh yeah, well you had a head start and you cut me off back there." The result is that one boy feels smug in the knowledge that he beat his friend in a "fair" race and the other boy tastes the agony of defeat at the hands of a male friend. Of course, they will continue to be friends, but now there is an unspoken element in their friendship. The winner knows that he beat his friend, and the loser wishes that just once he could beat his friend at something and let him sense how it feels to be a loser.

When competition becomes a major perspective, as it does for most males, it brings with it a distorted view of the world, a set of assumptions about what the world is really like. We will briefly examine several of these assumptions.

First, the competitive spirit forces men to think everything of value or worth in the world is *limited* or comes in *fixed quantities*. In other words, if something has value, it must be limited and can be measured. A man's valued masculinity can be measured as if it were a quantifiable element. Consequently, many males translate their sense of masculinity into how much money they earn, the size and number of windows in their office, the number of workers they have under them, the cost and horsepower rating of their new car, how far they live from the city, how many children they have, and the cost of their wife's new coat. If you can't win, buy, bargain, or steal it, it has no value in terms of a man's masculinity. That's the competitive way. Men begin to think in terms of quantifying even something like love. When at the breakfast table a wife mentions to her husband that he hasn't said "I love you" to her for over a year, he snaps, "What the hell are you talking about? Didn't I get you that new dishwasher that you've been wanting for over a year? What more do you want from me?" All she wants is to hear three words, and he gives her a cost analysis of his purchases for the home! The competitive spirit makes men think that all of life's values come in prepackaged and measured forms.

A second assumption grows out of the first. If "valued" things are limited, there are just so many of them to go around. This brings up a problem in male-male relationships. If there are just so many testaments to a man's success—a very valued

The Success Element

element in the male role—then every other man out there is a potential rival for the limited and available proofs of manly success. There are, for example, just so many large offices with windows, so many promotions, so many perks, or so many gold rings on the merry-go-round of life. If a man's friend gets a promotion at the office, all too often he may think that promotion could have been his if his friend hadn't brownnosed the boss so much. Men quickly learn ways to make their own track record look better than other men's. They produce more products, sell more products, write more reports, or complete the project sooner. The race for success is on, and every man soon learns the cardinal rule: "Don't trust the other guy, even your best friend, because he's after the same limited prizes you are."

A third assumption most men make is that competition is always good, not bad or neutral but always good. Fathers scream at their sons to get out there and beat the other boys no matter what the cost. On the playground or in the classroom, the important thing, the valued thing, the *good* thing is to be a competitor who wins. Competition is what made the United States great, and what's good for the United States is good for every man.

Thus competition forces many men to define part of their male role in terms of acquiring "limited" goods as proof of their masculinity, to view every other man as a potential rival for these goods, and to believe competition is always good for men.

An outgrowth of this preoccupation with competition and winning is that men come to view these features as exclusively male characteristics. Many men think that women do not have the same drive, ambition, or push to compete and win that men supposedly have. Boys and men compete, whereas girls and women cooperate. Granted, *all* women do not have the same desire for competition for competition's sake that many men have, but many women do value competition and winning

(Gill, 1986; Helmreich & Spence, 1977; Spence & Helmreich, 1983). Possibly, males think themselves more readily accepting of competition than women because of the popular belief that competition spurs action and achievement (Kohn, 1986; Rosenbaum, 1980). In the minds of these same men, action and achievement may be synonymous with masculinity. However, the belief that competition spurs action or achievement is questionable and not universally supported by research (Johnson & Johnson, 1983; Johnson, Maruyama, Johnson, Nelson & Skon, 1981). One problem we encounter with an assumed competitive-cooperative gender difference is that many men may feel any attempt on their part toward **cooperation** would make them appear unmanly, while many women may think competition robs them of their femininity. Consequently, some men denigrate cooperation as a viable way of solving problems or gaining valued goals.

The fact of the matter is that some tasks are better handled in a competitive way and others are more amenable to a cooperative problem-solving approach (Kohn, 1987). Tasks with definite rules and limits and unequivocal and measurable outcomes lend themselves to competition. For example, in a field and track meet, individual sporting events such as the 400-meter race or the pole vault fit nicely into a competitive format. Pitting one athlete against another or against the clock is one way to decide who covered the distance fastest or vaulted highest. However, there are many other tasks for which cooperation rather than competition works better. Specifically, in situations where there are few rules and regulations determining the limits of the problem, where the outcome is less certain or more equivocal, where there is a multitude of possible solutions for the task, or where the goal of harmonious personal relations is desired, a cooperative rather than a competitive approach may prove more beneficial (Sherif, Harvey, White, Hood & Sherif, 1961). Raising children, dealing with the problem of crime in the street, fighting inflation, rectifying the lowered productivity in United States industry are all problems that present ambiguous situations where the outcomes of separate approaches are not always predictable. With such problems, husbands and wives, politicians and citizens, and labor and management would accomplish more by cooperating with each other than by pulling against each other to see which side will win.

But that brings us back to the issue of the male's competitive world view and the "we" versus "they" approach. A husband and father often views his wife's or children's ideas about family concerns as an affront to his role as husband and father. Too often men approach family problems as yet another test of their patriarchal mandate. Consequently, there is little room for open discussion and mutual cooperation among all members of the family. Father is right and everyone else is wrong. The same competitive mentality can be found in many labor-management disputes. Each side (comprised mostly of males) sees the other side as competing for more than its rightful share of the scarce goods (wages, benefits, and so on). Instead of sitting down and communicating with each other, each side tries to outmaneuver the other and come away the victor. We find the same competitive spirit, the "we" versus "they" syndrome, in politics. No matter whether it is republicans, democrats, or independents, politicians look upon one another as the enemy who must be beaten in the next election. No matter what serious problems face our country, politicians

The Success Element

(again, mostly males) try to get as much political mileage as they can out of how their opponents are the ones to blame for all of the country's ills. Many politicians seem more concerned with fixing blame than with fixing problems and working for solutions.

Psychologist Judith Bardwick (1973, p. 12), in a study of businessmen, asked one man why he worked so hard; he replied,

> I don't know. I guess I enjoy it to a great extent. . . . I really hate to be a failure. I always wanted to be on top of whatever I was doing. It depends on the particular picture but I like to be on top, either chairman of the committee or president of an association or whatever.

This businessman's reply could as easily have been made by a politician. Success is the name of the game in politics as well as in business, and winning brings success, or so most males think.

If the truth be known, many of the problems men face daily are self-induced by virtue of men's competitive world view. We noted in the last chapter how lonely and isolated many men are by virtue of their not having many genuine male relationships. But given their deeply ingrained suspicious and competitive approach, how can men have such relationships? How can a man develop a genuine, open, and sharing friendship with another man when the other man is seen as being after the same promotion or after the same woman or the one to beat in a "friendly" game of tennis? Men cannot let up; they must constantly be on guard lest they be beaten and shown to be a loser. One never knows when the fellow next to them will yell, "Race ya to the corner!"

**nice guys
finish last**

Although former baseball coach Leo Durocher never wrote a book on success, he did win more than his share of games. He once uttered a phrase that has made him one of the "quotable notables" in success literature, "Nice guys finish last." If nice guys finish last, then what does it take to be a winner, a success in the world today? If we browse around in a bookstore, perhaps we will find the answer in the self-help section. There they are, so prominently displayed and with titles that almost jump off the shelves with the promise of revealing the real "secrets" of success. Here are just a few titles: *Winning Through Intimidation, Looking Out for Number One,* and *Power! How to Get It, How to Use It.* If we pick up any one and scan the table of contents, we soon get the feeling that being a success is no easy task. It's a jungle out there in the competitive world, and one has to be up to the biggest challenge of one's life. Let's select just one book and see how we, too, can become a success. This one was on the *New York Times* best-seller list—a sure sign of success in the book trade. It was written by Michael Korda and bears the not-so-subtle title *Success!*

Michael Korda can speak knowingly about success, he has already had a fair amount of it in his young life. Raised in a prominent family, Korda attended prestigious schools, authored several best-selling books, and is now senior editor for one of the larger publishing houses in New York. His book *Success!* (1978) maintains that one can achieve success by following certain basic principles. Here is a brief synopsis of some of Korda's major points. Instead of Korda's how-to-succeed prescriptions, some readers may prefer perusing Donald Trump's (Trump & Schwartz, 1988) or Lee Iacocca's (Iacocca & Novak, 1986) self-indulgent tributes to their own pathways to success.

Lesson #1: Let Your Energies Flow. Success comes to those who work for it. (Although the majority of anecdotes in the book are about successful men, Korda believes that women can also profit from his discussion.) Success and all its trappings (fame, money, status, promotions, perks, others' envy, and so on) are the pot of gold at the end of the rainbow for the hard worker. This first lesson fits neatly with the social expectations that men must do something or work at something, preferably something difficult, risky, or possibly even dangerous, to prove themselves real men.

Lesson #2: Controlled Paranoia. Korda's second lesson stresses that a man should be wary of others, and that means everybody, when it comes to reaching for success. The basic premise here is that no one really wants a man to be a success, at least not too much of a success. People love it when someone fails, and they are downright envious when someone succeeds. We see evidence of this in the public's insatiable appetite for gossip and tales of successful people's undoings. Even one's friends and loved ones are at least ambivalent if not unhappy when a man succeeds too well at something. For example, a wife may initially encourage her husband to go after a job promotion, but what happens after he gets it? She may become moody, withdrawn, and upset because he must travel more and work longer hours. Because many people prefer that others remain as they are, too much success may disrupt a relationship. Thus a man should learn to trust primarily only himself in his climb to success.

Lesson #3: Good Ole Machiavelli. More often than not, people must deceive others to get ahead in the cold world of business. As Korda sees it, if others in the business "jungle" are after the same promotion that you want, rest assured that they are not going to move aside or give way just because you are such a nice guy. All's fair in the business world. The quicker one learns how to manipulate and control others for one's own benefit, the better able that person will be to move ahead of the competition (Christie & Geis, 1970). To use other people's strengths and cash in on their weaknesses can only help in one's quest for success. Of course Korda does not suggest putting hemlock in a colleague's martini, but anyone seeking success should be aware that his colleague is after the same promotion or new client. In other words, get him before he gets you!

Lesson #4: Don't Fret. Fear of failing and fear of succeeding are the double-edged sword most men carry with them. On the one hand, a man is expected to be a winner in the everyday competition of life if he is to prove himself a real man. Failure is one of the worst catastrophes that could beset a man. On the other hand, men fear success as well. Since the late 1960s, much has been made in the psychological literature about women's supposed fear of success. But more recent psychological research suggests that men are likely to fear success as much as if not more than women do (Helmreich & Spence, 1977). When opportunities come along, many men undermine their chances of succeeding. Doubts and fears are more devastating to a man's success than any competition he may face from his colleagues. According to Korda, the hackneyed cliché, "Nothing ventured nothing gained," should be the motto each man subscribes to if he truly wants to be a success.

Of course, there is much more in Korda's book on how to become a success. What we have here may sound rather ruthless to some, but we should not forget that success in the competitive world is, for the most part, quite ruthless. Countless men are fired, passed over, transferred, or moved laterally into dead-end jobs every day by other men who want to dispose of the competition. Korda's presentation on how to get ahead is pretty tame when one hears some of the horror stories in almost any business enterprise. For all of the people who want to get ahead, to become a success, there are only so many slots. Whoever goes for big stakes has to play to win.

Is becoming a success worth it? Even though men are expected to relish success above all else as proof of their masculinity, success has its price. Addison Steele (1978), another book editor, puts the issue this way:

> Have you seriously considered the cost of getting ahead? The cost to your health? To your peace of mind? To your private life?
>
> Have you weighed the potential gains of such a sacrifice? Will the corporate advancement make you rich? Will it make you happy? Can such advancement be guaranteed to take place? Are there circumstances you can't control no matter how you comport yourself? Will the next rung be fulfilling or will it merely be a stepping-stone to the one after that? Is there an end to the treadmill? (p. 5)

These questions may be difficult for most men to answer. Some men may not wish even to think about them. But a few men are beginning to jump ship, to get off the treadmill of success so to speak, and are choosing a less success-oriented life-style by turning their back on the nine-to-five work cult.

dropping off the treadmill

In the nineteenth century, Washington Irving penned a classic tale about Rip Van Winkle, who stole away to a mountain and slept for twenty years. Irving's tale may be one of the first written accounts of a North American man who avoided the responsibilities of his provider role. Few men go to such lengths as Rip Van Winkle did to avoid work, but such avoidance was even a problem during the early years of the industrial revolution. It was not always easy to get men to make the transition from farmer to factory worker. During the nineteenth century, for instance,

> . . . mill owners and empire builders in the United States . . . complained that their straw bosses had to pull the workers out of the saloons every Monday—"Blue Monday"—to get them back on the job. There were too many holidays, too many feast days; at work, the spinners and tracklayers tended to daydream and chatter. It was increasingly difficult to get a full seventy hours of work out of them every week. (Lefkowitz, 1979, p. 38)

A plausible explanation for some of this early "mutinous" behavior is that males were not used to the regimentation that came with the new factory system. For centuries men had labored as farmers in concert with seasonal changes. Once a farmer became a factory worker, it mattered little what season of the year it was. Day after day, week after week, and month after endless month, the same job had to be done. Little wonder then that some men were prompted now and then to lay off and spend time in saloons in the company of other men. Where better could men who faced so many social changes feel more secure, more masculine than in the company of other men? After a few drinks and some ritual boasting, a man could always prove his masculinity in a "friendly" fight. Working in the factory took some getting used to (but get used to factory work men did).

By the end of the nineteenth century, the good provider role vis-á-vis the factory worker was an integral part of most male roles. To realize just how deeply men had identified with their work, we need only read of the personal devastation that befell a majority of men who were unemployed during the Great Depression. A man without a job lost more than a paycheck. He lost not only his family's but also his own respect for his manhood. As we noted earlier, the prosperous years that began with World War II found men once again aligning their masculinity with their work. During the early 1950s sociologists Nancy Morse and Robert Weiss (1955), both of the University of Michigan's Survey Research Center, found that over 80 percent of the working men they surveyed stated that they would continue to work even if they came into unexpected wealth. Work gave these men a powerful sense of worth, purpose, meaning, and possibly most important, a sense of manliness. Mere wealth alone could not substitute for all of this. However, North America was headed for a change by the early 1960s.

Stereotypes like myths take a long time to change and/or disappear. The stereotype of the working male leaving home every morning with either lunch pail or attaché case in hand is beginning to falter. A small but growing number of men are starting to challenge this masculine ideal by asking, "Do I want to work at the same job for the rest of my working years?" "Do I want to report to the same boss and push the same papers from one pile to the next forever?" or "Do I really want to climb higher up the work-success ladder?" The idea that men without work will crumble, will feel their masculinity shatter as many did during the depression era, is becoming a late-twentieth-century myth. Being without work, without a socially acceptable means to validate one's masculinity is no longer as devastating for some men as it once was. Professional and blue collar workers alike are finding that unemployment does not necessarily make a man less masculine (Lefkowitz, 1979).

How is it that something as ingrained in the North American value system as the work ethic has fallen on such hard times? Why is it that some men are beginning to question the value of climbing the ladder of success? The answer may be that more and more men define work in negative rather than positive ways. The climb for these men is considered dull, shallow, meaningless, and disspiriting rather than exciting, creative, and inspiriting. Work has lost many of its pleasure-giving features. Once again, Addison Steele puts his finger on a core problem of contemporary work as so many men feel it:

> How refreshing it would be if people could just take pleasure—keen, immediate
> pleasure—in the work they are presently involved with, instead of always being
> concerned with climbing, climbing, climbing. Climbing is so hard on the nervous
> system. I have known personally too many driving executives—mostly men in their late

The Success Element

thirties and early forties—who have had crippling and sometimes fatal heart attacks. I have had lunches with too many colleagues who were nursing an ulcer or a spastic colon. And I have seen too much needless fear, as evidenced by hands trembling in a meeting, backs that suddenly go into spasm at the sight of a closed door, and voices that either slide into the upper register or disappear completely when the boss leaves a note on the desk saying, "Please drop by my office right away." (p. 6)

For many men, work is no longer enjoyed for its own sake. Competitive work, which most think of as a means to success and achievement, has become perverted in some men's minds. On this point, S. A. Miller (1974) has suggested that both men and women need to redefine their notions of success and achievement if they are to cope more effectively with the social changes facing each gender in the near future. In proposing a new conception of success and achievement, Miller writes,

> While I am strongly of the mind that success drives should be banked and other humanitarian urges encouraged, I don't accept that all of the drive for success or achievement is pernicious or undesirable. This drive is exciting and can be fulfilling. It is a great danger to be avoided when it becomes all embracing or when it is a success without a content that is both personally and socially satisfying or beneficial.
>
> It should be made easier to do interesting and useful things, to feel a sense of accomplishment. As in military strategy, a "sufficing" level of achievement rather than a maximum level of security or position should be sought. Being "number one" should not be the goal; rather, high competence should be enough for both men and women. I have seen many talented people blighted in their work by number-oneism when they probably would have done outstanding and useful work by adopting a high-competence performance criterion.

important terms

Competition *150*
Cooperation *153*
Success *149*

suggested readings

Berglas, S. (1986). *The success syndrome: Hitting bottom when you reach the top.* New York: Plenum.
Kohn, A. (1986). *No contest: The case against competition.* Boston: Houghton Mifflin.
Korda, M. (1977). *Success!* New York: Ballantine.
Lefkowitz, B. (1979). *Breaktime: Living without work in a nine to five world.* New York: Hawthorne Books.
Messer, M. (1987). The meaning of success: The athletic experience and the development of male identity. In H. Brod (Ed.), *The making of masculinities: The new men's studies* (pp. 193–209). Boston: Allen & Unwin.
O'Neil, J. (1993). *The paradox of success.* New York: J. P. Tarcher.

Chapter 9

The Aggressive Element

The differences between boys and girls are defined in terms of violence. Boys are encouraged to rough-house; girls are taught to be gentle ("ladylike"). Boys are expected to get into fights, but admonished not to hit girls. (It is not "manly" to assault females—except, of course, sexually, but that comes later.) Boys who run away from fights are "sissies," with the implication that they are queer. As little boys become big boys, their education in violence continues. The leadership in this country today consists of such little boys who attained "manhood" in the approved and heroic violence of World War II. They returned to a society in which street and motorcycle gangs, fast cars, and fraternity hazing confirmed the lessons of war—one must be tough and ready to inflict pain in order to get ahead.
Lucy Komisar (1976)

Aggression for men is what aggression achieves socially: It imposes control over other people, and in doing so creates winners and losers. It publicly affirms the masculine hierarchy.
Anne Campbell (1993)

In the preceding chapter we discussed the significant place the achievement of success has in the male role. In the United States and Canada as in other postindustrial countries, success is often obtained by a competitive struggle among men who desire similar goals. Frequently, when competition gets out of hand and men go too far in their quest for success, some have been known to inflict pain, injury, and even worse on a competitor. That brings us to the third element in the male role—**aggression.**

With respect to the other four elements in the male role, aggression possesses a couple of unique features. First, the United States is one of the few postindustrial countries in which aggression is still seen as a desirable and "manly" characteristic. Many young boys in the United States are actively encouraged to get out there and aggressively show "what they're made of" against other boys. Consequently, in some groups, an aggressive boy is thought of as more masculine than one who shuns aggressive behaviors. (For a discussion of how people perceive aggressive and nonaggressive males, see Eron et al., 1987; Lockman, 1987; Roberts, 1988.) Second, most people think males rather than females are prone toward aggressive and violent behaviors. (For a different view see Fry & Gabriel, 1994.) In fact physical aggression is one of the few social behaviors in which a number of social scientists see a distinct gender difference (see Chapter 4).

In this chapter we will first analyze aggression and the part it plays in our culture, especially for men. Surprisingly, aggression is both denounced as a significant social problem and applauded as a masculine attribute. Then we will deal more specifically with men's aggression and violence against other men and against women. And last, we will discuss pornography and its relationship to violence.

the anomaly of aggression

Aggression and violence are unsettling social features of human behavior that on the one hand, excite and stimulate many North Americans and, on the other, repulse and horrify them. As proof of this cultural quandary, let's think about some examples of various aggressive and violent behaviors. Aggression fills the pages of United States history with military events that either stir people's patriotism (the exploits of the early freedom fighters at Bunker Hill and their twentieth-century descendants at Iwo Jima) or cause public consternation (the unconscionable tragedies at My Lai and Kent State). Witness the almost electrifying excitement among the crowds at boxing matches or hockey games as people scream for blood (Bredemeier & Shields, 1985; Horn, 1985). Later these same people decry violence on their city streets. A majority of American citizens report that they favor some form of control over handguns (Kellerman & Reay, 1986), and yet their elected officials refuse to legislate against handguns because of the "reprisals" from a small but powerful gun lobby. It is as if we cannot make up our minds about aggression. To most of the civilized world, the United States is a cultural paradox when it comes to their ambivalence over aggression.

Part of the problem lies in the fact that most people do not have a clear and unequivocal definition of the word "aggression." In the minds of most, the soldiers at Iwo Jima and My Lai clearly acted in decidedly aggressive and even violent ways against other human beings. Certainly, most people would agree that aggression occurred when John Hinckley reached out from a crowd and shot former President Rondald Reagan or when Lee Harvey Oswald killed former President John Kennedy. But what can we say of a dynamic salesperson who goes after a reluctant customer or a young suitor who persists in trying to get a date with an indisposed coed? Are these actions aggressive, or should they be labeled otherwise? Before we proceed then, we need to differentiate between *aggressive behavior* and *assertive behavior* (Krebs & Miller, 1985).

Most social scientists agree that the term *aggression* should be applied only to those behaviors where there is a clear *intention* to cause either physical or psychological harm, injury, or worse to another person. Accordingly, because the dynamic salesperson or determined suitor does *not* intend to inflict pain or harm on the perspective target of their behavior (i.e., the customer or the coed), we should label the respective behaviors assertive not aggressive. Both Oswald and Hinckley *did* intend to cause harm to another, however, and thus their behaviors can clearly be defined as aggressive.

How widespread is aggression in our culture? The fact is aggression and violence are nearing epidemic proportions in the United States. For instance, in a recent Federal Bureau of Investigation's *Uniform Crime Reports* (U.S. Department of Justice, 1992), an aggressive or violent crime is committed in the United States every seventeen seconds. This means that somewhere in this country *a human being is assaulted, robbed, raped, or murdered every seventeen seconds!* Other statistics further indicate that the United States is one of the most violent nations on earth. If we exclude many of the newly emergent and politically unstable Third World countries and some of the repressive Central and South American countries that seem constantly beset with bloody revolutions, we cannot find a more violent society than the United States. If we compare America with other countries with similar stable governments and sound economics, the United States stands out in the minds of many as a gigantic parody of the "shoot-'em-up Wild West." For example, United States citizens kill one another over ten times more frequently than do the citizens of Austria, Australia, Sweden, Poland, and France, and almost twenty times more frequently than do the citizens of Norway, Spain, Greece, and Denmark.

Why is the United States so violent? Once again we suggest that part of the problem is linked to its ambivalent feelings about aggression. On the one hand, United States citizens decry the breakdown of law and order and fear the upsurge of violent crimes in the streets. Yet they turn around and admire the unbridled aggressivity of the gunslingers on their television sets and flock to theaters to sit in voyeuristic darkness as directors strive for gruesome realism in depicting the various ways a body can be destroyed. Some of the most popular heroes on American television and movie screens have been aggressive and violent men. Take, for example, John Wayne's countless action movies in which the aggressive actions of red-blooded, two-fisted men were extolled or Sam Pechinpah's celluloid paeans to violence for violence sake in such movies as *The Wild Bunch* and *Straw Dogs* or the numerous Hollywood actors such as Clint Eastwood, Sylvester Stallone, Chuck Norris,

Arnold Schwarzenegger, and Charles Bronson who have made violence and aggression their trademark (Signorielli & Gerbner, 1988). "Our national icons," social commentator David Gelman (1993) noted:

> . . . tend to be men who excel at violence, from John Wayne to Clint Eastwood. When President Clinton ordered a retaliatory airstrike on Baghdad because of an alleged plot against George Bush, his popularity rating took a leap, just as Bush's had when, as president, he ordered up the Gulf War, in which an estimated 100,000 Iraqi civilians were killed by bombs and missiles. (p. 48)

Most United States citizens clearly have a love-hate relationship with aggression and violence. And yet there is another feature that encourages aggression in our country—the male role (Messerschmidt, 1993).

The fact is boys and men are expected to be aggressive toward others on supposedly *appropriate occasions* (Campbell, 1993). Most males, however, do not see themselves as violent or aggressive. Still, we find many parents of young boys encouraging their sons not to back down from a fight, especially if a bully starts it. In terms of the male role, a boy should always be ready to defend himself against others in a *masculine* way. The boy who runs away when someone else picks a fight is thought a sissy by many parents and peers alike. As boys grow older, many go out for team sports in school. In football, for example, the aggressive lessons continue when a coach spurs on his helmeted charges with peppery advice like, "Get out there and make the other team bleed" or "Don't be afraid to hurt the other guy; it's all part of the game!" At times it seems that the goal in some high school games is to inflict injury rather than to score points (Goldstein, 1983). For other young men, there is always a street gang in which aggression and violence form central values among gang members (Kantrowitz, 1993). A common practice among many street gangs is to have a new recruit perform a certain number of violent acts in order to win full membership in the gang and thus be seen as a real man (Chaze, 1981).

Initially, little boys are cautioned against hurting little girls. Girls—boys are told—are weak and soft and therefore should be cuddled not cudgeled. But somewhere along the path to adulthood, some males come to believe that "women like it when you're a little rough." Some men seem to think of aggression against women as part of the male's right to dominate and control women.

Another lesson in male aggression comes with the belief that a man has a right—some might insist a duty—to seek revenge in aggressive and violent ways if he or his have been violated. Even the Hebrew Bible allows for such aggressive behavior with its prescription of "an eye for an eye." Consequently, many men believe that a man wronged is a man who must retaliate in kind if he is to be considered a man again. The majority of men who sat through Charles Bronson's portrayal of a New York City architect-turned-midnight-vigilante in the movie *Death Wish* (and more recently *Death Wish II, III,* and *IV)* applauded the mayhem and destruction Bronson wrought on others. Somehow violence is seen as a cleansing experience for a man who has himself been victimized.

Given all of the lessons in the male role with respect to aggression, a real man is expected to act aggressively only on those occasions when another male starts a fight

"I'll have a nice day when I get damn good and ready." Drawing by Geo. Price; © 1987 The New Yorker Magazine, Inc.

or pushes him too far or when he wants to show his dominance over a woman. With the pressures to conform to the aggressive element of their role, men—and their exaggerated sense of rugged individualism and penchant for competition—make fertile ground for flowering aggressive behavior.

Thus far we have noted that because aggression is an important element in the male's role, boys and men are expected to inflict pain and injury on one another when the situation warrants it. But what kinds of situations call for the intentional harming of another person? Is it enough of an inducement when a neighborhood bully calls you a name, when someone carelessly bumps you in a crowded place,

men against men

The Aggressive Element

when someone cuts back too soon into your lane after passing you, or when someone intends to harm you? These situations and countless others are enough inducement for many North American men to fight or worse (Salholz, 1987). "Turning the other cheek" is something taught little boys and girls in Sunday school, but real men know down deep that such soppy counsel is really for girls and sissies.

Are North American males really as aggressive and violent as movies and television would have us believe? Setting aside the statistics on violent crimes noted earlier, is the average male likely to resort to aggression or even violence to "solve" a problem? Could it be that a few violent criminals give law-abiding North American males a bad name? The average North American male certainly would not inflict physical harm or injury on another intentionally unless in the *gravest* of circumstances. Or would he?

Several years ago, in the summer of 1969, a research team headed by Monica Blumenthal (1972) and associated with the University of Michigan's Institute for Social Research completed an in-depth survey of United States men's attitudes on the use of violence. A representative group of 1,374 men between the ages of sixteen and sixty-four made up the sample. The men were asked a series of questions, presented with numerous scenarios, and then asked how they thought each situation should best be handled. Here we will highlight only a few of the study's numerous findings, which form a fascinating glimpse into what United States men think and feel about the use of violence. Although some may question this study's "datedness," no more recent study contradicts Blumenthal's basic findings nor gives us pause to think that today's average young men are any less suppportive of using "controlled" aggression to quell certain situations.

To discover the men's attitudes toward the use of violence, the researchers developed a series of social situations, or scenarios, and then asked each male to indicate the amount of control the authorities, that is, the police, should take to remedy or contain the problem at hand. It was thought that the amount of control favored in each of several scenarios would accurately reflect in a general way the males' attitudes about violence and its use as a control mechanism.

For the first scenario, a researcher presented the following social situation.

> There have been times when gangs of hoodlums have gone into a town, terrified people, and caused a lot of property damage. How do you think the police should handle this situation?

After hearing the situation, each man was handed a card that listed several options that the police could use to control the public disturbance. Without any further assistance, each was requested to indicate his preference for each option (A, B, C, D, and E of Table 9.1).

In the "hoodlum" scenario, the respondents strongly believed in some form of police action. Eighty-one percent checked off the "never" category (option A) suggesting an attitude that the police should *never* let a disturbance blow over but step in and take some kind of action to quell it. When it comes to what kinds of actions the police should take, some interesting dilemmas presented themselves. When it

table 9.1

	Almost always	Some-times	Hardly ever	Never
A. The police should let it go, not do anything.	☐	☐	☐	☐
B. Police should make arrests without using clubs or guns.	☐	☐	☐	☐
C. Police should use clubs, but not guns.	☐	☐	☐	☐
D. The police should shoot, but not to kill.	☐	☐	☐	☐
E. The police should shoot to kill.	☐	☐	☐	☐

Reprinted with permission from the Institute for Social Research from: Monica D. Blumenthal, et al., *Justifying Violence: Attitudes of American Men* (Ann Arbor, Michigan, Institute for Social Research, The University of Michigan, 1972), page 26.

comes to the use of force (option C), 80 percent regarded the use of clubs as "almost always" or "sometimes" appropriate. Sixty-four percent saw no problem (combined total for "almost always" and "sometimes" categories, option D) with shooting "but not to kill." And finally, 32 percent felt that shooting "to kill" was acceptable (combined total for "almost always" and "sometimes" categories, option E)! This last figure is most unnerving given the fact that one out of every three men sampled believed that killing another human being was an acceptable way to deal with a disruptive social situation. Is it any wonder that so many public quarrels between men end in a shooting?

The men in the sample were also asked to indicate their feelings about various police actions in ghetto riots and campus disturbances. Recall that in the late 1960s, the United States went through a series of social spasms that rocked many of our social institutions. The civil rights movement was running into opposition, and African Americans were growing more and more agitated by the lack of any real progress in their quest for equal treatment. Adding still further to the volatile racial situation, a majority of African Americans were housed in poverty and humiliation in this country's inner cities. Across the United States the conditions were ripe, and the ghettos exploded with the crackle of gunfire and burning buildings. Furthermore, the Vietnam conflict continued to escalate, and opposition spilled onto many college campuses. Students protested with marches and sit-ins, and the National Guard and local police forces became strange additions to the academic scene.

Using the same "controlling" options that had been presented in the hoodlum scenario (Table 9.1), the sample of men indicated their attitudes toward how the police should deal with ghetto rioters and student protesters. The men in the sample

The Aggressive Element

felt much the same way about ghetto rioters as they did about marauding hoodlums. Once again, action is the key word in the minds of most of these men. The sample strongly supported stopping the rioters with minimal force (81 percent favored arrests without clubs or guns "almost always" or "sometimes"). The remaining categories (C, D, and E) showed the sample holding favorable attitudes toward stronger, even lethal, control options in about the same degree as expressed toward the hoodlums. How United States men can perceive hoodlums and rioting ghetto residents in similar ways is an interesting sociological question.

When it comes to campus disturbances, there is an apparent moderating trend in the sample's responses. In the first place, almost nine out of ten men, or 87 percent, felt that arrests should be made "without using clubs or guns." Furthermore, a substantial shift in attitudes comes in the categories D and E, where there is greater resistance to the use of lethal weapons. However, 48 percent of the sample believed that shooting "but not to kill" was appropriate at least some of the time. (The ironic feature of category D is many people's belief that a gun can be fired into a crowd and not kill!) What is undoubtedly the most chilling feature of the survey is that almost one out of every five men, or 19 percent, felt shooting to kill was an appropriate way to control student demonstrators at least some of the time. How prophetic that less than a year after this survey was concluded four students were killed and ten were wounded at Kent State University. When one of the respected townspeople was asked his opinion about the student killings, he remarked,

> We feel that the Guard did exactly what they are sent in to do: To keep law and order. Frankly, if I'd been faced with the same situation and had a submachine gun, there would not have been fourteen shot, there probably would have been 140 of them dead, and that's what they need. (Michener, 1971, p. 446)

Why did the men in this survey place such emphasis on doing something even if the action resulted in another's injury or even death? The answer, at least part of it, lies in the way men define their role. First and foremost, a man must do something to prove himself a man. Only women and fearful men would sit idly by and do nothing in a public disturbance, or at least that is what many men think. Perhaps North American boys and men have watched too many movies and television shows in which a man grabs for his gun when there's trouble. No self-respecting man would just wait for the trouble to blow over. No matter the sociological or psychological causes for the obsession for action, the results are usually the same— men aggress against each other in frightful ways.

men against women

Earlier we noted how parents often encourage their sons to be aggressive with other boys but warn them against hurting girls. However, as boys grow into manhood, something happens to the earlier lessons in appropriate masculine behavior and the prohibition against hurting females loses much of its force. All of a sudden, or so it seems, women who were once considered off-limits for male aggression now become a prime target of it (see *Some Frightening Facts*). Here we will discuss two types of aggression primarily directed against women: rape and domestic violence.

some frightening facts

Every hour 16 women confront rapists; a woman is raped every six minutes. Three to 4 million women are battered each year; every 18 seconds a woman is beaten.

Three out of 4 women will be victims of at least one violent crime during their lifetime. More than 1 million women seek medical assistance for injuries caused by battering each year.

The United States has a rape rate 13 times higher than Britain's, nearly 4 times higher than Germany's, and more than 20 times higher than Japan's.

Source: *Newsweek* (1990)

Rape is defined as the "carnal knowledge of a female (male) forcibly and against her (his) will." Although the vast majority of rape victims are female, we must note from the outset that males can be and are raped (Scacco, 1982). Studies emanating from rape crisis centers have revealed that men comprise anywhere from 6% to 20% of treated rape victims (Calderwood, 1987; Forman, 1982). Furthermore, the Federal Bureau of Investigation reported slightly less than 10,000 men were victims of rape or attempted rape in 1991 (U.S. Department of Justice, 1992).

Rape

According to recent statistics of *reported* rape cases compiled by the Federal Bureau of Investigation, in 1991, one rape occurred in the United States every 5 minutes (U.S. Department of Justice, 1992). Using the figure of one rape every 5 minutes, we can estimate that over 105,000 forcible rapes occurred that year. However, remember these statistics are based on reported cases. Most experts in crime statistics agree that rape is one of the *least* reported violent crimes and estimate that for every one reported rape case there are anywhere from three to ten *unreported* cases. Using the conservative estimate of three additional rapes (i.e., unreported) for every reported rape would mean that over 420,000 rapes occurred in the United States in 1991. (For reviews on some of the problems related to the lack of accurate information on the frequency of rape, see Koss, 1983, 1985; Russell & Howell, 1983; Soeken & Damrosch, 1986).

But the impersonal figures tabulated in neat columns tell little about the reality and depth of human suffering and degradation that accompany the rape victim for the rest of her life (Marhoefer-Dvorak, Resick, Hutter & Girelli, 1988). And what of the man, the rapist who forces a woman to have intercourse against her will? Why would a man rape? Some suggest men rape because they are driven by a powerful and natural sexual urge; because they are psychologically disturbed and consequently forced to rape by sheer strength of uncontrollable pathological impulses; because they feel a sense of insecurity or doubt about their masculinity; or because rape is an extreme extension of the aggressive element of the male role (Scully, 1988).

The notion that rape is a normal and natural consequence of men's powerful sexual urges is ridiculous. Little more than two hundred years ago, women were believed more prone to sexual passion and lust, and men were viewed as more disposed to reason and logic, not sexuality. Any explanation of rape based on such a recent historical flip-flop in what constitutes male and female sexuality certainly cannot now be expected to explain why men have raped for centuries.

The Aggressive Element

Many laypeople and some social scientists believe a rapist must be suffering from some form of psychological disturbance in order to commit such a serious crime against another person. In these people's minds, the rapist is acting out some pathological sexual impulse. The prevalence of what is called the *pathological perspective* of rape owes much to the work of a nineteenth-century physician, Richard von Krafft-Ebing. In 1886, Krafft-Ebing's major work *Psychopathia Sexualis* was published. Quickly, it became the standard text throughout Europe on sexual aberrations. Mirroring the widespread belief of his day, Krafft-Ebing viewed the rapist as a deranged imbecile, that is, a person with a very low intellectual capacity, who suffered from a serious lack of impulse control. In the following passage taken from *Psychopathia Sexualis,* Krafft-Ebing (1965/1886) emphasizes the psychological causes of the rapist's behaviors.

> The crime of rape presumes a temporary, powerful excitation of sexual desire induced by excess in alcohol or by some other condition. It is highly improbable that a man morally intact would commit this most brutal crime. Lombrosco considered the majority of men who commit rape to be degenerate, particularly when the crime is done on children or old women. He asserts that, in many such men, he has found actual signs of degeneracy.
>
> It is a fact that rape is very often the act of degenerate male imbeciles, who, under some circumstances, do not even respect the bond of blood. (pp. 544–545)

The scientific evidence is sorely lacking for this contention that rapists suffer some form of demented thought pattern or are generally of lower intelligence than other criminals convicted of serious violent crimes such as murder (Lang, Holden, Langevin, Pugh & Wu, 1987; Perdue & Lester, 1972). We can suggest, however, that rapists who brutalize, mutilate, or even kill their victims either before or after raping them, as in the cases of the Boston Strangler and Jack the Ripper, are probably psychologically disturbed in the most severe sense. In these extreme cases, rape is only one violation, although admittedly a most serious violation, in a sequence of bizarre and disturbed actions.

A third and very popular explanation of men's sexual violence against women is the suggestion that the rapist's violent behaviors stem from a poorly developed or insecure male gender role identity (Blanchard, 1959). Recall that many social scientists consider the development of a male's gender role identity to be an extremely risky and failure-prone psychological undertaking (see Chapter 4). Many things supposedly can go wrong in a young boy's life, especially in his relations with his mother, that may cause the boy, and later on the adult man, to feel confused over his masculine identity. Consequently, such a male may be driven to strike out against women in extreme and violent ways. In the final analysis, this perspective on rape blames women for men's violent sexual behaviors. If women as mothers would not cause so much confusion in their sons' minds about their male gender role identity there would be fewer rapists (Abrahamsen, 1960; Albin, 1977).

Rather than look for some clinical evidence of a compelling psychological syndrome or some deep-seated, basic insecurity in the rapist's gender role identity, we might better look more closely at the male role itself, especially the aggressive element. First of all, we must clearly understand that rape is not an act of sex or wanton lust. *Rape is an aggressive act perpetrated on another to show the dominance and power of the rapist* (Groth & Birnbaum, 1979; Groth, Burgess & Holmstrom, 1977). This fact becomes patently clear when we find that rape in prisons is generally viewed as one of the most brutal ways in which a male prisoner demonstrates his power and dominance over another male prisoner (Rideau & Sinclair, 1982; Wooden & Parker, 1982).

In a patriarchal society such as North America, males are taught certain values about how males and females should relate both sexually and nonsexually. A majority of North American males come to accept the notion that males are inherently superior to females. Pushing the view of male superiority even further, many men believe that women should submit to men's wills and be dominated by them. These basic beliefs in men's natural superiority and rightful dominance over women set the stage, so to speak, for rape (Costin & Schwarz, 1987; Hall, Howard & Boezio, 1986; Hanneke, Shields & McCall, 1986; Scott & Tetreault, 1987). Furthermore, certain myths or misconceptions about women's and men's sexuality and rape have grown in people's minds over time (Brinson, 1992; McKenzie and Zanna, 1990; Struckman-Johnson & Struckman-Johnson, 1992; see "Common Myths Associated with Rape"). Add to the ideology of male supremacy and certain myths about rape the social expectations that pressure men to act aggressively as proof of their masculinity, and we have a volatile atmosphere conducive to rape. From this perspective, rape occurs not because some males are driven by powerful sexual urges, mental illness, or an insecure masculine identity but rather, to a large degree, because of society's sexist views about women and the gender role expectations placed on men to be aggressively dominant over women (Cherry, 1983; Segel-Evans, 1987). On this point Diane Russell notes that:

Rape is not so much a deviant act as an over-conforming act. Rape may be understood as an extreme acting-out of qualities that are regarded as super masculine in this and many other societies: aggression, force, power, strength, toughness, dominance, competitiveness. To win, to be superior, to be successful, to conquer—all demonstrate masculinity to those who subscribe to common cultural notions of masculinity, i.e., the

The Aggressive Element

masculine mystique. And it would be surprising if these notions of masculinity did not find expression in men's sexual behavior. Indeed, sex may be the arena where these notions of masculinity are most intensely played out, particularly by men who feel powerless in the rest of their lives, and hence, whose masculinity is threatened by this sense of powerlessness. (quoted in Pleck, 1981, p. 146)

Although some might wish to think that a rape incident is more likely to occur between strangers, the fact is that all kinds of aggression—interpersonal violence and even rape—are common enough features between those people who are anything but strangers. Before we turn our attention to the violence that mars marital relations, we need to discuss the extent of rape commonly found among dating couples. (For a discussion of nonsexual aggression among dating couples, see Arias, Samios & O'Leary, 1987; Stets & Pirog-Good, 1987.)

In the last few years, Mary P. Koss along with several of her colleagues (Koss, Leonard, Beezley & Oros, 1985; Koss & Oros, 1982; Levine-MacCombie & Koss, 1986) have focused considerable attention on those rapes that occur on first or second dates or between those involved in a romantic relationship. Such rapes have been dubbed **date rape** or **acquaintance rape.** Such rapes are tragically all too common. To illustrate the magnitude of the problem, in a survey conducted by *Ms.* magazine one out of four college women reported being raped or the victim of an attempted rape by a date or an acquaintance (Warshaw, 1988). In another study, this one dealing with men, Koss (Koss et al., 1985) asked over 1,800 college males to fill out a survey that assessed their previous histories with respect to the degree of sexual coercion or aggression they had used on a date to gain sexual intercourse. Koss found some interesting psychological differences between those males who reported they had used either threats or physical force for sexual intercourse and those who did not use any aggressive means for sexual relations. Basically, those males whose previous dating behavior placed them in a sexually assaultive category viewed male-female relationships in an adversarial way, accepted traditional gender stereotypes, supported rape myths, thought rape prevention was a woman's responsibility, and tended to see sexuality and aggression as bound up together. Other researchers have also found that males tend to see certain circumstances as making date rape more justifiable, such as when a couple goes to a man's apartment for a date or when the man pays for the date rather than sharing the expenses (Muehlenhard, Friedman & Thomas, 1985).

Several experts argue that the psychological consequences of date rape are more serious than stranger rape (McCahill, Meyer & Fischman, 1979). Such a view predicates that a victim of date rape experiences extreme loss of trust—trust in her own ability to predict others' behavior and trust in those (i.e., future dates) who she consciously or unconsciously may feel are likely to place her in jeopardy once again. Lately, date rape has captured not only the public's attention (Brothers, 1987), but also the attention of various college fraternities. In fact, one college fraternity, the Pi Kappa Phi, has launched a national campaign to end date rape (Doyle, 1987; see Figure 9.1).

figure 9.1
Some college fraternities, like
Pi Kappa Phi, have begun a
national campaign to end date
rape. Posters like the one
pictured here can do much to
increase the public's
awareness of the problem.
Reprinted by permission of
Pi Kappa Phi Fraternity.

The Aggressive Element

When it comes to **domestic violence,** or marital violence, many people turn a blind eye and a deaf ear. It is as if there exists an unspoken rule that what goes on between a wife and a husband is nobody else's business (E. Pleck, 1987). But certainly this could not extend to marital violence, could it? Surely, if people saw a husband physically abuse his wife in public, most would step in and get involved, wouldn't they? In one study, a male and female staged an argument in a public restaurant that ended with the female being slapped (Straus, 1975). When during the course of the argument the female made it clear that she did not know the male who hit her, several witnesses came to her assistance. However, when the spectators were led to believe that the couple was married, most of the spectators refused to become involved. Furthermore, in a national survey, nearly 25 percent of the *women* questioned thought that marital violence was a normal and even a necessary part of marriage, and approximately 30 percent of the males sampled viewed marital violence as a good feature of marriage (Straus, 1977). Thus marital violence appears to be an almost acceptable cultural norm and probably much more common than most people would like to believe (Carmody & Williams, 1987; Finn, 1986; Gelles, 1987; Gelles & Cornell, 1985; Gelles & Straus, 1988; Hampton et al., 1993; Straus & Gelles, 1986).

Again we find the age-old legacies of patriarchy; this time serving as the foundation for much of the violence found in families. Even prior to Roman times, women have been considered the property of men. A daughter's life was completely in her father's hands as was a wife's. For centuries English Common Law recognized a husband's right to "domestic chastisement" of a wife who displeased him. Even though wife beating is no longer sanctioned by law, many men—at least nearly a third sampled in a national survey—believe that marital violence is an acceptable feature of marriage. (For a discussion of marital rape, see Finkelhor & Yllo, 1985; Russell, 1982.)

What causes a husband to batter his wife—to commit violence against a loved one? Although some might attribute such behavior to simple meanness or cruelty, researchers find a more complex and perplexing picture when trying to explain a male batterer's behavior. In fact, there may not be a single profile of the wife assaulter. "Wife assaulters are not all alike," Daniel Sonkin and Donald Dutton (1988, p. 4) write, "some are predatory conflict-generators, others resort to violence when they lose a 'war of words.' Some are hyperaggressive, others overcontrolled and unassertive." However, researchers are beginning to gain a better understanding of the various dynamics behind wife assault (Caesar, 1988; Dutton, 1988; Sonkin, 1988).

It seems that as long as women are seen as secondary citizens with little or no power, there will always be a number of men who feel it part of their male role to abuse sexually and physically the women they live with (Coleman & Straus, 1986). Rape and wife beating are two of the more sinister and disturbing features we find in male-female relations. Why men should find it necessary to commit such forms of human degradation and cruelty on women is a major concern among several segments of society (see Figure 9.2). Recently, attention has been directed at looking for ways to reduce wife beating by providing treatment programs for males who

figure 9.2
Social agencies across the country are making the elimination of domestic violence a top priority. Photography by Joshua Ets-Hokin.

have a history of such aggressive behavior (Finn, 1987; Hamberger & Hastings, 1986; Hotaling & Sugarman, 1986; Maiuro, Cahn & Vitaliano, 1986; Ryan, 1986; Sonkin, Martin & Walker, 1985).

the battered husband

Before we end our discussion of domestic violence, we need to raise one last issue, one that has been the stimulus for considerable debate over the last several years—the battered husband. For some years now, in the minds of most, the issue of domestic violence has been a women's issue—one closely associated with feminist ideology, institutional support, and political correctness. Any attempt to look at the other side of the domestic violence issue—physical aggression directed at husbands by wives—has been met with considerable suspicion and even some ridicule. The critics argue that a discussion of *men as victims* is fundamentally flawed. First, to allow that some men are battered (physically and/or psychologically) by some women implies that men and women are equally dangerous to one another—a notion that defies the common belief that males are more dangerous, more aggressive by virtue of their greater physical strength than females. Further, women's advocates point out that in those few cases when wives do aggress against their husbands, they must have good cause for such *atypical* behavior; she must be motivated by either her own defense or that of her children's. Regardless, most experts agree that both men *and* women commit violent acts in the home and, according to the best estimates, a significant minority of cases finds *only* the woman acted in an aggressive manner thereby eliminating the self-defense argument. Thus we need to look at this issue.

Richard Gelles's 1974 study of families was one of the first to present data that men also could be the victim in domestic violence. In 1977/1978, Suzanne Steinmetz published a small study dealing with family conflict wherein she found that wives aggressed against their husbands. She labeled the phenomenon the **battered husband syndrome.** Not surprisingly, Steinmetz's article (more likely her provocative title) drew considerable public attention and support from the men's community (see Farrell, 1986) as well as the anger of many within the women's movement. Consequently, a number of researchers attacked Steinmetz both on methodological grounds and for not emphasizing that, in those few cases where wives aggressed against their husbands, the vast majority occurred in self-defense (see Fields & Kirchner, 1978; Pagelow, 1985; E. Pleck et al., 1978). However, the debate continued as other studies reported evidence of aggression against husbands (Berk et al., 1983; Greenblatt, 1983; Straus, 1977–78; Straus, Gelles & Steinmetz, 1980; Steinmetz, 1980).

The next major firestorm occurred when Murray Straus and Richard Gelles (1986) published their findings based on two nationally representative surveys comparing the rates of domestic violence in a two year period—1975 and 1985. Straus and Gelles reported that violence against females had *decreased* while aggressive incidence against males had *increased* over the ten-year period. In a review article of numerous domestic violence studies, R. L. McNeely and Gloria Robinson-Simpson (1987) conclude that domestic violence is not essentially a masculine form of assaultive behavior while seriously questioning the notion that women are capable of aggressive behaviors only when motivated by self-defense.

Avoiding the political rhetoric and simply looking at the published studies over the last decade, what can we say about the issue of men-as-victim? Are there equal numbers of female victims and male victims found in domestic situations? No. Female victims significantly outnumber male victims in domestic situations. Are the actual numbers of assaults on men increasing? If we rely on Straus and Gelles's (1986) data we could argue yes. However, we must keep in mind that statistics on husband abuse are probably every bit as "soft" as the numbers of reported women-as-victim rape cases. Both are aggressive acts wherein the victim may be reluctant to come forward for any number of reasons, including shame. Are women capable of assaulting men for reasons other than self-defense? Yes. Some women do not fit the stereotype of the passive and frail female but rather are inclined to act aggressively and use violence against a male to get their way. Does it help the cause of female victims to hide the fact that some men are victims of spouse abuse? No. The evidence continues to grow that domestic violence occurs with numerous victims—wives, children, grandparents, and even husbands. Rather than cover up the issue of the battered husband we need to acknowledge it and explore its causes in an attempt to deal with it (see Straus, 1993).

Before we end this chapter, we must address a very important issue that all men should give serious thought to—one that has been a topic of serious debate among women's circles. The issue is **pornography,** or sexually explicit materials, and the question of what role they play in men's violence against women. The question of pornography's influence on males—unquestionably the largest audience for most pornographic materials—has recently stirred considerable interest among scholars in men's studies (Brod, 1984; Donnerstein & Linz, 1987; Moye, 1985).

Although graphic depictions of sexual anatomy and diverse sexual activities are as ancient as the "pornographic" drawings found on numerous walls in prehistoric caves (Byrne & Kelley, 1984), pornography and its effects have only recently captured the attention of politicians, feminists, religious fundamentalists, home video producers, and an assortment of social and behavioral scientists (*Attorney General's Commission on Pornography,* 1986; Donnerstein, Linz & Penrod, 1987; Linz, Donnerstein & Penrod, 1987; Malamuth & Donnerstein, 1984).

For our purposes here, we will focus on a single question: *Does exposure to sexually explicit material cause male viewers to harm others?* The issue of harm is at the heart of much of the current debate about pornography's effects, not only the harm allegedly affecting the consumer of pornography but the harm directed toward others by a person exposed to pornography. Although we could discuss the possible harm a male might experience from excessive exposure to pornographic material over the course of his life, we think the question of how pornography might stunt a male's development better left for others. Rather we will focus here on the harm directed at another following exposure to pornographic materials. As one might expect, the question of whether or not pornography influences one to harm another cannot be answered with a simple yes or no. Rather we must content ourselves with a somewhat more complicated answer.

the question of pornography and violence toward women

The Aggressive Element

First, we must express a truism that all but the most naive would accept—all sexually explicit materials are not the same. The fact is pornographic, or sexually explicit, materials are many and varied. Pornography comes in visual forms (e.g., still or moving, color or black and white, artistic or sleazy), written (i.e., prose or poetry), and verbal (e.g., obscene phone calls and "dirty" jokes), to name the more common forms. However, we will limit our categorization of pornography to only four types, the same ones outlined in the recent Attorney General's Commission on Pornography (1986), namely: (1) those containing sexually violent material; (2) those nonviolent materials that, however, depict some type of degradation, domination, subordination, or humiliation; (3) those nonviolent and nondegrading types; and (4) nudity.

Although some might wish to argue over religious or moralistic grounds, given all the available scientific research, there is no compelling evidence to suggest that exposure to nonviolent and nondegrading pornography (Type 3) and nudity (Type 4) have any serious long-term detrimental effects. However, Dolf Zillmann and Jennings Bryant (1988, p. 449) found "that repeated consumption of [nonviolent] pornography is capable of inducing dissatisfaction with numerous aspects of sexuality." More specifically, these researchers found that both male and female viewers of nonviolent pornography (i.e., x-rated movies) found their mates less physically appealing, their mates' sexual performance less gratifying, their mates' sexual curiosity and innovativeness wanting and their mates' affection lacking. These researchers suggest that most pornographic depictions of sexual activity (e.g., multiple partners and a variety of activities) may make an average person think his or her sex life somewhat boring in comparison to what they see on the screen.

Given these reservations then about viewing sexually explicit (i.e., nonviolent and nondegrading) materials and nudity, most researchers do not think such materials lead to or increase the chances of the viewer harming another. On the other hand, most researchers take an entirely different stance with respect to the first two categories of pornographic materials (i.e., sexually violent and degrading pornography).

Sexually explicit materials coupled with violence or degrading themes have been linked or related to a variety of negative effects on male viewers specifically. For instance, males exposed to explicit sexual material containing violence are apt to exhibit more callous or demeaning attitudes toward women in general and a greater acceptance of any number of rape myths (e.g., "Down deep women want to be treated roughly" or "No woman can be raped if she doesn't want to be").

However, can we say unequivocally that exposure to sexually explicit material containing violence and/or degrading material *cause* a male viewer to go out and harm another person? Anyone familiar with the basics of experimentation with its need for strict control and random assignment of research participants to a number of research conditions knows that a causal connection cannot be made on the basis of correlations or relationships. Furthermore, given the ethical restraints on human studies nowadays, we will probably never have a definitive experimental study that will provide an answer to this question. However, in the judgment of the very best minds on the question of pornography and men's violence toward others, there seems to be considerable consensus that "violent material, whether sexually explicit or not, has the *potential to promote violent behavior following exposure*" (Linz et al., 1987, p. 952, italics added; also see Koop, 1987; Malamuth et al., 1991; Wilcox, 1987).

Although we might lack the ultimate study to prove a causal link between men's exposure to violent and degrading pornography leading to their subsequently harming others, there seems no justifiable reason for any group to find pleasure in watching films or reading passages that portray degradation and heap abuse on another group. Would watching people marched into ovens or systematically brutalized be thought appropriate for a stag party? Why should it be any different if women are the victims?

North American society appears ambivalent toward aggression. In one breath, North Americans decry the mayhem brought on by aggression in the streets, and in another, North American parents encourage their sons to act aggressively in order to prove themselves manly. We noted also that many males believe that action is preferable to nonaction in the case of a public disturbance. A large percentage of males go so far as to condone aggressive action even to the point of killing others to restore public calm. We then enumerated the incalculable numbers of victims of violence in our country. We noted how men aggress against women by noting the frightening statistics involved in the various forms of rape and the extent of domestic violence. Turning our focus somewhat, we then raised the controversial issue and the disputed figures involving the battered husband. Finally, we explored the link between violent pornography and men's aggressive actions and demeaning attitudes toward women.

We cannot deny that our society encourages men to be aggressive. Furthermore, aggression and violence, it seems, is largely condoned in those societies where a large gulf or basic inequality exists between groups (e.g., the United States, South Africa). Overt aggression is one way a dominant group can control a less dominant group. If we are ever going to live up to our ideal that all people are equal, then we must begin to condemn all forms of aggression and violence no matter the victim.

---

important terms

---

suggested readings

Donnerstein, E., Linz, D., & Penrod, S. (1987). *The question of pornography: Research findings and policy implications*. New York: Free Press.
Gelles, R. (1987). *Family violence* (2nd ed.). Newbury, CA: Sage.
Gelles, R., & Straus, M. (1988). *Intimate violence*. New York: Simon and Schuster.
Kimmel, M. S. (Ed.). (1990). *Men confront pornography*. New York: Crown.
Russell, D. (1982). *Rape in marriage*. New York: Macmillan.
Segel-Evans, K. (1987). Rape prevention and masculinity. In F. Abbott (Ed.), *New men, new minds: Breaking male tradition* (pp. 117–121). Freedom, CA: The Crossing Press.
Warshaw, R. (1988). *I never called it rape: The* Ms. *report on recognizing, fighting and surviving date and acquaintance rape*. New York: Harper & Row.

The Aggressive Element

Chapter 10

The Sexual Element

A common myth in our culture deals with the supposed sexual differences between men and women. According to this bit of fantasy, female sexuality is complex, mysterious, and full of problems, while male sexuality is simple, straightforward, and problem-free.
Bernie Zilbergeld (1978)

While we may be mature in years, sexual maturity is a long, complicated process not systematically linked to physiological and chronological development. In fact, in modern societies, the individual's sexual self is the *least* and *last* explicitly developed dimension of self.
Jean Lipman-Blumen (1980)

Males are aroused differently than females. For example, it is probable, although not conclusively proven, that males are more dependent on visual stimuli than females, women being more dependent on haptic, or tactual, arousal. In an analysis of responses to a series of psychological tests it was noted that males differed from females in both direction and magnitude of their arousal response to a variety of erotic stimuli and that there was a stronger correspondence between subjective and physiological measures of sexual arousal for males than for females.
David A. Schulz (1988)

For most men, few other activities can be as exciting or anxiety provoking, as fulfilling or deflating, as stimulating or disturbing, as amusing or guilt producing as *sex* can be. Obviously, anytime we deal with a human feature as socially complex and as personally volatile as sex, we are bound to encounter all kinds of difficulties and problems. Several points need clarification before we begin our discussion.

In the first place, given the social expectations, demands, and prohibitions that surround sex in general and male sexuality in particular, we should not be surprised to find some social scientists have included sexuality in their discussion of the male role while others have not (see Brannon, 1976; Cicone & Ruble, 1973). Given the significance that sex plays in the adolescent's life and the preoccupation most adult men have with sex and their sexual performance in comparison to other men's, in our discussion here we consider male sexuality an element in the male role (Gould, 1982; Gross, 1978; Person, 1980).

Second, we must be clear about what we mean by the word "sex." *Sex* here means much more than what goes on between two people in bed. Sex includes everything that has an *erotic* component and takes place between people or with only one person. In other words, sex covers a wide range of behaviors, thoughts, and feelings. For example, the sexual element can be found in a loving glance between two people, a kiss on the cheek, an intimate fondling of one's own or another's body, or even an erotic fantasy about another person. **Male sexuality** designates all of the sexual features that involve men. Thus the sexual element in the male role is more than a collection of behaviors and techniques; it also includes a man's frame of mind, emotions, and expectations regarding all erotic situations.

This chapter covers a wide range of issues. We will begin by looking at the early psychosocial foundations of male sexuality—how parents treat their son, how they show affection toward him, and how he shows his feelings, especially love, toward others. These and many other basic interactions form a boy's early experiences in his developing sexuality. As a boy matures, he faces adolescence, that period in life when sexual urges, feelings, and social expectations for sexual expressions become increasingly focused on some form of genital expression. Later on, the male will likely settle into a pattern of sexual expression that may or may not be made more difficult by a series of sexual myths that burden a majority of males.

Next we will examine several clinical problems that many men face at some time or other. We will describe various male sexual dysfunctions and some of their underlying causes. We will also look at what is becoming a major problem affecting male sexuality today, a lack of interest in sexual expression.

Finally, we will examine what may seem to be an anomaly in our coverage of male sexuality: sexual abstinence. Sexual abstinence, or asexuality as some call this social phenomenon, is being touted by some men and women as an opportunity for self-examination. Some men claim sexual abstinence allows them a measure of freedom from the pressures and expectations of their intimate relationships.

Over the years male sexuality has received considerable press attention. Two notable examples of this genre are two classics: Gay Talese's (1980) *Thy Neighbor's Wife* and Nancy Friday's (1981) *Men in Love*. Talese gives his readers a rather intimate, inside

rites of passage

The Sexual Element

look at the extensive goings-on of a number of males engaged in a variety of sexual activities and exploits. To hear Talese tell it, sexual practices are no longer bounded by bedroom walls or strict prohibitions—if they ever were.

Nancy Friday provides the reader with a rare look into one of the most intriguing and least understood facets of male sexuality, the male sexual fantasy. To conjure up a mental image and to populate that cerebral picture with people and activity is a decidedly human ability that gives considerable pleasure (Schulz, 1988; chap. 12). In *Men in Love,* we read that a considerable portion of male sexuality resides in the mind, where a male can weave and spin images of his own glorious and fulfilling sexual exploits. In anecdotal form, Friday presents a large number of sexual fantasies gathered from over three thousand men. Two notions expressed in Friday's book are especially noteworthy for our present discussion. First, many men seemingly have a much more vivid and satisfying sexual life in their fantasies than they do in real life. Second, a male's present sexual fantasies can be used to cover up real or imagined past hurts or rejections. On this last point, Friday provides an interesting speculative note at the end of her book.

> Here at the end of these pages, I find that my years of research have confirmed something even the most uninstructed woman takes as given: Inside every male is a denied little boy.
>
> He loved his father, but was taught to show that love only through mindless imitation of his father's mindless imitation of *his* father's Victorian authoritarianism.
>
> He loved his mother, but feared her power.
>
> The male principle in society says he is expected to be tough and domineering with women, always in control, and sexually voracious. The female principle is the opposite; when he approaches women, he carries with him all his unconscious memories of mother's awesome powers of retaliation and rejection.
>
> How can he handle the fear and rage that sex means for a man under these conditions? He can't stop, doesn't want to stop, being a man. The frustration is blamed on women, *goddamn them!* Maybe the best thing to do is turn your back on them and forget the whole problem. In the end, it is the man's relentless desire for women that keeps him from his surrender. Fantasies are invented. At least for a sexual moment, magic is called in, reality altered, the perceived nature of women changed; the conflict healed.
>
> Fantasies are the triumph of love over rage. (p. 541)

Boys Need Loving Too   We have mentioned on several occasions that little boys are expected to be independent and self-sufficient. The ways of teaching these traits are numerous and varied, but research in childrearing generally suggests that little boys are treated more roughly, given more severe physical punishments, and encouraged more often to hold back their feelings of affection and caring than are little girls. On the average, little boys receive less hugging, holding, cuddling, kissing, caressing, and fondling than little girls do. The underlying message of most parenting practices for little boys seems to be, "You really don't need to be fussed over like little girls do. And anyway, we don't want you growing up to be a sissy."

But there is a problem with all of this "toughening up." The little boy is denied some of the warm, caring affection that only close, loving human contact can provide. In a sense, such a way of raising a boy creates the "denied little boy" of which

Friday speaks. Not only are denied little boys more apt to engage in human sexual fantasies rather than in genuine and fulfilling human sexuality, as Friday contends, but depriving boys of loving and affectional human contact early in life may have other, more serious consequences, not the least of which is poor sexual adjustment. To make a point on this matter, let's review the research on affectional deprivation among rhesus monkeys. Obvious ethical concerns prevent us from researching affectional deprivation among humans.

Some years ago, Harry (1958) and Margaret Harlow (1962) observed some intriguing behavioral problems brought on as a consequence of affectional deprivation among rhesus monkeys. Basically, monkeys raised in isolation in their laboratories acted in disturbed ways when they were later introduced to normally raised monkeys. One of the observed disturbances was related to sexual behaviors. When a male monkey raised in isolation was put with a sexually receptive (in heat), normally raised female monkey, the male did not mate and apparently could not be taught how to mate successfully. As strong a lure as a sexually receptive female monkey was, the male apparently could not overcome the earlier influences of social and emotional deprivations that he suffered in isolation.

We must be cautious when drawing any inference about human behaviors based on monkey behaviors, though. After all, human males are not monkeys. However, the Harlows' work provides us with some interesting avenues of speculation about the *possibility* of how depriving a little boy of emotional and loving treatment early in his life may cause him some difficulties in his sexual life later on (Maccoby, 1980). Even though we should not go too far in our comparison of such findings and human sexual difficulties, one thing is definite: All little boys need as much love, gentle and kind reassurance, and loving physical contact as little girls need. The problem is that most boys do not get this.

Boys, like girls, are curious creatures and seemingly have their hands in and on everything from a very early age onward. The first object of a boy's curiosity is his own body. This curiosity is a natural and beneficial feature in the early development of his sexuality. As a boy grows older, he soon learns that by stimulating his genitals he can cause an extremely pleasurable and satisfying sensation. Any self-stimulation that leads to erotic pleasure or arousal is called **masturbation** or **self-pleasuring** (Gordon & Snyder, 1989). In the words of James McCary (1979), a leading expert in human sexuality, masturbation is "a means of self-discovery and sensory awareness." Many parents, however, do not look upon their son's masturbatory behavior as one of the first natural steps in his developing sexuality. Some parents believe that masturbation is sinful, while some even think that masturbation can cause serious mental and physical deterioration. (There is absolutely *no* scientific evidence that masturbation causes blindness, hair growth on the palms, brain damage, or any other debilitating physical illness!) Because masturbatory behavior is prohibited in most American homes, young boys often learn to sneak their sexual pleasures behind a locked bathroom door or under the bedsheets in the dark of night. Consequently, their early sexual feelings and experiences become bound up with "shameful" thoughts and prohibited pleasures. A young boy soon learns that sex in general and his sexuality in particular are something to hide and be ashamed of.

Learning about Sex

The Sexual Element

masturbation: different views

Masturbation is an intrinsically and seriously disordered act.

Vatican Declaration on Sexual Ethics, 1975

Don't knock masturbation. It's having sex with someone I deeply love.

Woody Allen

It was at the end of my freshman year of high school—and freshman year of masturbating—that I discovered on the underside of my penis, just where the shaft meets the head, a little discolored dot that has since been diagnosed as a freckle. Cancer. I had given myself *cancer*. All that pulling and tugging at my own flesh, all that friction, had given me an incurable disease. And not yet fourteen! In bed at night the tears rolled from my eyes. "No!" I sobbed. "I don't want to die! Please—no!" But then, because I would very shortly be a corpse anyway, I went ahead and jerked off into my sock. I had taken to carrying the dirty socks into bed with me at night so as to be able to use one as a receptacle upon retiring, and the other upon awakening.

Philip Roth

Source: Reprinted in B. Strong, et al., *Human Sexuality,* 2d ed., 1981. West Publishing, St. Paul.

Nevertheless, by early adolescence, most young males have masturbated at least once. In one survey, over 60 percent of the males sampled reported that they had masturbated by the age of thirteen (Hunt, 1974). For the teenage male, then, masturbation plays a significant role in his growing awareness of his sexual self. This feature was noted in a recent book on human sexuality:

> Masturbation is the only sexual outlet for many adolescents. Because the accepted form of sexual behavior involves a partner of the opposite sex, masturbation may be viewed as a sign of sexual failure. This negative social value obscures the fact that self-masturbation is a means of erotic self-discovery and of erotic fulfillment, and that it is an important part of the psychosexual development of most adolescents. It teaches them how their bodies respond, providing a biologically healthy substitute for sexual intercourse during a period when young people are developing emotionally. (Strong et al., 1981, pp. 235–236)

Masturbation is only one feature of a young male's developing sexuality. As he ventures out from under the bedsheets, he soon encounters others for whom his sexual urges draw him into some kind of sexual relationship. The first intimate kiss and the faltering touch of another person's genitals are momentous events for most young males. However, before too many years, the earlier apprehensions and anxieties give way to various sexual activities such as heavy petting, oral-genital stimulation, and sexual intercourse. Depending on social influences such as family values and standards, religious training, amount of education, and peer pressures, by the time a young male reaches college age, he will have engaged in most of these intimate sexual activities (Sonenstein, Pleck & Ku, 1991). By the early twenties, most young males probably think of sex as one more element—albeit an important element—of their expanding role and self-identity.

Myths and Male Sexuality

By the time a young male reaches early adulthood, he probably thinks he knows just about everything there is to know about sex. Over the years, he has told or listened to almost every sex joke there is, he has seen almost every centerfold recently printed, and of course, he has done just about everything himself at least once. What more can a male learn about sex? Unfortunately, most young men fall prey to a whole series of half-truths, partial prefabrications and downright misconceptions about male sexuality. To set the record straight, we will now review some of the more persistent myths that cloud various features of male sexuality (Longwood, 1988).

Myth #1: The Other Guy's Is Better. Almost every male at one time or another thinks that other males' sexual experiences are better than his or at least that other males are having fewer problems in their sex lives than he is. Not surprisingly, the basis for such thinking stems from the lack of frank and open discussion about personal sexual matters among most males. Even though males talk a great deal about sex, they rarely if ever discuss their own sexuality with other people, especially other males. Most young men learn very early never to talk about their doubts, confusions, or ignorance of sexual matters, for to do so would make them appear less masculine in the eyes of others—or so they think. When a man has a problem or question about sexuality, he tends to see himself as the only one with such a concern.

Myth #2: Sex Is Just Like Falling Off a Log. As noted at the beginning of this chapter, psychologist Bernie Zilbergeld contends that most men view their sexuality as "simple, straightforward, and problem-free." Women and not men are supposed to be burdened with all kinds of sexual problems and hang-ups. Magazine articles and books abound telling women how to deal with this kind of sexual dysfunction or that kind of sexual disturbance. Female sexuality is no easy matter if we are to believe everything we read. As for male sexuality, little is written and even less said (at least among men) about the possibility that male sexuality may not be free of problems. One of the first holes punched in the myth of problem-free male sexuality came in 1976 when the popular magazine *Psychology Today* published the results of an extensive survey of its readership. More than 52,000 people participated in the survey. Surprisingly, more than half of the males, 55 percent to be exact, reported dissatisfaction with their sex lives (*Your Pursuit of Happiness*, 1976). Over 40 percent of the males surveyed reported various specific sexual problems such as premature ejaculation and trouble reaching orgasm. Thus the belief that male sexuality is free of problems is nothing more than a myth that most men carry around in their heads.

Myth #3: A Man Can't Get Enough Sex. Most men believe in the idea that there is no such thing as too much sex. To suggest otherwise, that a man—a real man—may want to say "no" or "that's enough," is just plain balderdash. Down deep most men revel in a story of some Don Juan with an insatiable sexual appetite. To refuse sex is something only a woman or a nerd would do. Psychologist Herb Goldberg (1976) believes that one of the reasons men are in such a present-day fix over their sexuality is their inability or unwillingness to say NO to sex. A man's sexuality is not like some machine that can be switched on at anytime and run for hours. A man's penis will not stand erect just because he barks "attention."

The Sexual Element

Myth #4: Men Run the Sex Show. Even in these days of supposed sexual liberation and equality, the average man would find something quite unsettling in the thought of a woman walking over to him, looking him straight in the eyes, and announcing, "Your place or mine?" Women may be in boardrooms and salesrooms, but there is still one room to which they are thought to follow a man's lead, to be subordinate to a man, and that is the bedroom. Most men believe themselves responsible for everything sexual: the initiation, the setting, the foreplay, and finally orgasm itself for both partners. (For a marvelous parody on this issue, read Gail Parent's novel *David Meyer Is a Mother,* 1977.)

Myth #5: Sex Is All That Counts. Probably the most insidious sexual myth of all is the belief that sex is all that really matters when it comes to a relationship with another person. All that business about wanting to be with someone just for the sake of being near, of sharing some tender moments, maybe just a simple touch or a loving caress is just so much hokum. A man wants one thing, and you spell it S-E-X. No wonder many women think that men are out for only one thing—many men are because they think they should be. The problem for a man who sees another only as a sex object, a piece, some tail, or whatever other demeaning phrase is used to describe women is that he misses the opportunity of knowing another person as a human being much like himself. Believing that sex is all that counts keeps men separated from full human contact (Shotland & Craig, 1988).

These sexual myths keep men from seeing sexuality as it really is. Men come to believe so many illusory notions about sex and their sexuality that many of them never really experience one of the most exquisite of human experiences. Many men were "denied little boys" who never really experienced the basic loving human contacts that make for healthy sexuality later on. Little boys who were shunned and toughened up never really learn to differentiate the sexual myths and fantasies from the reality of loving and caring human relationships. Consequently, many men end up experiencing any one of several sexual dysfunctions.

sexual dysfunctions

To hear some men tell it, the only problem they have with sex is not finding enough willing partners. The real truth, the sad and painful truth that is emerging more and more from sex therapy clinics, however, is that many men suffer from various sexual dysfunctions (Fracher & Kimmel, 1987; Swanson & Forrest, 1984; Zilbergeld, 1992). In this section we will discuss several clinical sexual dysfunctions (erectile insufficiency, premature ejaculation, and retarded ejaculation) and two other sexual problems that are receiving more attention of late (the Don Juan complex and lack of sexual interest). We will conclude the section with a consideration of some of the underlying causes for these male sexual problems.

Impotence

Few sexual problems are as devastating to a man as his inability to achieve or sustain an erection long enough for successful sexual intercourse. For many men the idea of not being able to "get it up" is a fate worse than death. The sexual dysfunction commonly known as **impotence,** or what clinicians now prefer to label as **erectile insufficiency,** can take any one of three forms: organic, functional, or psychological (Elliott, 1985; LoPiccolo, 1985).

Organic impotence occurs when a defect, injury, or disease affects the genital structures, the reproductive system, or the central nervous system itself, for example, as in cases of spinal-cord injuries. **Functional impotence** is the result of a failure in the musculature, blood circulation, or nerves related to the penis. Excessive use of alcohol or drugs, chronic kidney failure, or even surgery in the pelvic area that damages nerves or disrupts the blood supply can all cause this form of impotence (Heller & Gleich, 1988). The last form of impotence is psychological. **Psychological impotence** usually occurs when an emotional reaction such as fear, depression, or grief acts as an inhibitor to normal erectile functioning. Prolonged or even permanent impotence is often psychological in origin and usually requires some type of sex therapy for its relief (Arade, 1988; Bancroft, 1982; Barlow, 1986; Tiefer, 1987).

Premature ejaculation occurs when a man ejaculates before his partner has a satisfactory sexual experience. A basic problem with this sexual dysfunction—and one that causes many men much anxiety—is determining how long is long enough in withholding ejaculation. In Alfred Kinsey's (Kinsey, Pomeroy & Martin, 1948) pioneering work in male sexuality, which was completed in the late 1940s, 75 percent of the men interviewed reported that they ejaculated within two minutes of their beginning sexual intercourse. Is withholding ejaculation for two minutes premature or not (LoPiccolo, 1978; Spiess, Geer & O'Donohue, 1984)? Remember, the issue is not really one of time but rather of the partner's satisfactory sexual experience. Psychologist Bernie Zilbergeld (1978) makes this point when he recounts a client's purported problem of premature ejaculation.

Premature Ejaculation

> We'll never forget the man who called himself a premature ejaculator even though fairly regularly he lasted for forty-five minutes of vigorous thrusting. We know he lasted this long because his partner confirmed it. Actually, she had never been orgasmic in intercourse and had no desire to become so. She much preferred shorter intercourse because she sometimes became so sore through almost an hour of thrusting that she could barely sit down the next day. That had little influence on the thinking of our client, who was convinced that she would have orgasms if only he could last an hour. (p. 213)

Clearly, premature ejaculation is a problem that both parties should work out together.

It is also possible that a man may have sexual intercourse with a willing partner and not be able to ejaculate until very late or even at all. This is known as **retarded ejaculation,** or **ejaculatory incompetence.** We know about women who do not experience orgasm. But men? Such a problem runs contrary to all we know about, or at least think we know about, male sexuality. Because people hear so little about this condition many think that this sexual dysfunction is rare. As one group of researchers in abnormal psychology put it,

Retarded Ejaculation

> In fact, relatively few cases of ejaculatory retardation or incompetence are seen by sex therapists, but our own clinical experience suggests that the problem is much more widespread than this observation would seem to indicate. It appears that many men are too embarrassed by the problem even to contemplate therapy for it. (Carson, Butcher & Coleman, 1988, p. 415)

The Sexual Element

The next two sexual dysfunctions are opposite sides of the same coin. The first, the Don Juan complex, is not a problem of deficiency, or insufficiency, as are the sexual dysfunctions we have just discussed but rather a "hyperfunction" problem. The second, a problem reported by a growing number of men, is the lack of interest or desire in sexual matters.

The Don Juan Complex

Some men believe that to have sex with a different woman every night would be anything but a problem. To be a real-life Don Juan is a fantasy for many males. But there is a growing awareness that a man who looks upon women as just so many sexual conquests exhibits a type of sexual addiction or compulsion—one called the **Don Juan complex** (Carnes, 1983).

> The Don Juan . . . is a man who cannot make an emotional investment in his relationships with women. Overcompensation for insecurity, an obsessive need to prove masculinity, even hidden hostility toward women—any or all can drive a man from bed to bed without ever finding any real satisfaction. The he-man mask is in absolute control here; the only way a man can throw it off is to release his internal self. This is rarely easy. Dr. Rubin [author of *Compassion and Self-Hate*] writes: "It is particularly difficult to make even initial inroads in a man who is very immature and full of macho confusions. It must be remembered that an undeveloped infantile mentality is essentially a selfish one, which desires all kinds of feeding and knows little or nothing of sharing or giving."
> (Wagenvoord & Bailey, 1978, p. 189)

Lack of Sexual Interest

A recent survey conducted by *Redbook* magazine found that the most common sexual complaint for both men and women was a "lack of desire for sex" (Sarrel & Sarrel, 1981). This problem probably afflicts a majority of men at various times when the pressures of work, family, or some other demands squelch their normal interest in sex. Again, however, how long a time frame of "lacking interest" is sufficiently long enough for this to be a true sexual dysfunction? Probably, the best gauge is a personal one. When a man feels that his lack of sexual interest is troublesome either for himself or for his partner, then he is probably suffering from a sexual dysfunction (Leiblum & Rosen, 1988).

Causes of Sexual Dysfunctions

What can we say of the millions of men who suffer from sexual dysfunctions? Is there a common denominator, a common culprit, so to speak, lurking behind these varied sexual disturbances? Probably no more than 50 to 60 percent are caused by biological, physical, and chemical impairment. It seems likely that the other 40 to 50 percent or more of men's sexual dysfunctions are psychological in origin. Although some might argue that the numbers attributed to psychological factors are far too high, the current move to place the "blame" for most men's sexual dysfunctions on their biology seems little more than an attempt to shift responsibility away from themselves thus protecting their self-esteem (Tiefer, 1987). Even in those sexual dysfunctions where an organic basis seems likely, most experts agree that psychological factors play some role in the continuance of the dysfunction (Perelman, 1984; Schreiner-Engel, 1981). Take for example the case of a widowed man who reported that he was unable to sustain an erection.

A sixty-year-old man came over a thousand miles to see us. His wife of thirty-two years had died less than a year before and, while he had had a few erections by himself since then, he did not get one on the few occasions when he had gone out with a woman. He wanted to get married again but felt it would be impossible until he was capable of having erections with a partner. The man was clearly depressed and we asked who or what turned him on. He couldn't think of anyone or anything. Upon questioning, he admitted that he had not felt sexually aroused since his wife died. We tried some sexual fantasies with him and they failed to evoke any interest. The same was true of erotic literature and movies. Nothing elicited the slightest degree of sexual interest, and yet he was convinced he should be able to get an erection. Needless to say, his goal was somewhat unrealistic. Not until he finished mourning for his wife was he able to get aroused and erect again. (Zilbergeld, 1978, p. 62)

Why does a sixty-year-old man who has lost his wife and sexual partner of over thirty years think that he *should* be able to have an erection so soon after such a personal loss? Could it be that he and countless other men like him suffer various sexual dysfunctions because they are trying to live up to some set of inane expectations of masculinity, such as the notion that their penis is an instrument immune from the everyday problems, anxieties, and fears that besiege us all? Three common psychological conditions can lead to various sexual dysfunctions and are especially revealing of how deeply ingrained are men's erroneous views of their purported sexual capabilities. These conditions are sexual anxiety, performance anxiety, and an excessive need to please a partner.

Sexual Anxieties. As we have already noted, there are few fears that can upset a man as quickly as the fear of failure in the sexual realm. A man who fails in sex is by many men's standards an impotent, powerless, and an emasculated man. Even if there is sound reason for failure, many men will be consumed immediately with fear or anxiety over their future sexual adequacy and ability. For example, here a group of researchers explains how a one-time incident of impotence may lead to long-term impotence simply because of a man's excessive anxiety over sexual functioning.

If a man fails to experience an erection—because of drinking, drugs, fatigue, lack of interest, pressure from his partner or any number of reasons—anxiety and fear are a fairly common set of responses. Potency cuts to the very center of a man's identity; to be impotent is, in some sense, for most men, to be less a man. Many men can dismiss these episodes of non-erection for what they are: simply non-erection related to various factors. But if the man is particularly anxious about his sexuality or has repeated failures in responding with an erection, he may actually become impotent; a cycle of panic and resulting impotence begins, causing more panic and more failure. Some men respond to an occasional erectile failure with calm, knowing such failures are normal, while others react with panic, unaware that such failures are normal. (Strong et al., 1981, p. 260)

Performance Anxieties. Performance anxieties are similar in many respects to sexual anxieties. When fear of failure over *future* sexual activities underlies sexual anxieties, not being able to meet one's own or someone else's *current* sexual expectations forms the basis of performance anxieties. For example, a husband arrives home

The Sexual Element

from work to find his wife in an amorous mood. Although he is not sexually aroused himself, he believes the male sexual myth that a man *should* be able to have sex "at the drop of a hat." Consequently, in bed he experiences an erectile failure. Here is a man who believes it unmanly to say no to sex and suffers the consequences of an uncooperative penis. The outcome for this self-imposed expectation is a temporary sexual dysfunction. However, a larger problem may loom in the background, depending on how he handles this first erective failure. If he becomes upset and anxious over this experience, it could lead to a vicious and self-perpetuating cycle of future erective failures; in other words, the preceding inhibition of sexual anxieties could prohibit future satisfactory sexual experiences. If, on the other hand, the man can accept this onetime failure as a sign that he had better communicate his own arousal state to his wife and forget the myth of the ever-ready sex machine, the occasion may have a salutary effect on the sex life of both partners.

Excessive Need to Please a Partner. After sex, many women are greeted with innumerable questions about their just-completed sexual experience. "Did you have an orgasm?" "How many times did you come?" "Could you feel me inside you?" "Was it as good for you as the last time?" A man who expresses a genuine concern over his partner's sexual satisfaction is showing a mature and healthy aspect of his personality, but a man who acts like he is gathering data for a sexual survey on the modern woman is showing an immature obsession over failure. For such men, the notion of masculinity is somehow tied up with how well they accommodate a woman in bed. Sex techniques and orgasm counts become enmeshed in their definition of manhood. If, for some reason, a woman should mention that the sexual experience was not what it could have been, the eager beaver will feel like a failure. He may become depressed, fearful, and anxious over his performance, which could set him up for a future sexual dysfunction such as erectile failure. Women often sense this feature in a man's questions and begin to play the game of "let's not bruise his fragile ego." These women begin to say what they think the man wants to hear leading some women to pretend or fake their sexual experience, a condition one survey found among two-thirds of their female respondents (Darling & Davidson, 1986).

Other psychological factors can also adversely affect a man's sexuality (Lo Piccolo & Stock, 1986). A man's self-concept may be so poor and lacking in self-respect or self-esteem that he will not even try to engage in sexual relationships. Another negative factor that affects some men is discord, or trouble, in the relationship itself. For example, many married couples abstain from all sexuality because of a seething hostility or antipathy for each other.

The important point to keep in mind is that a man's expectations, attitudes, and emotions all directly relate to how well he functions as a sexual person (Freudenberger, 1987). The idea that successful and satisfying sex is 90 percent mental and only 10 percent physical is a truth many men never seem to grasp.

Up to this point, we have dealt with the developing aspects of male sexuality and some of the problems that can afflict men. Next we will discuss sexual abstinence, or celibacy, as it relates to a number of males.

pleasuring rather than conquering

The basic message is simple: Men who try to be sexual superstars often find themselves on a one-way trip to many of the sex problems that can turn lovemaking into a nightmare—coming too soon, inability to get it up, keep it hard or ejaculate, no-fun lovemaking, unwanted pregnancies, and unresponsive lovers who are prone to those proverbial late-night headaches. On the other hand, men who drop the idea of sexual domination and learn to appreciate sensuality, men who develop an ability to discuss their sexual tastes specifically, men who listen closely to what women have been saying recently about lovemaking—these men are considerably less likely to fall victim to men's common sex problems. In short, men who take women seriously—both in and out of bed—are more likely than tough-guy studs to become the accomplished lovers most men would like to be.

Michael Castleman (1980, p. 15)

The subject of **celibacy,** the conscious refraining from sexual activity for a specific time period, may seem out of place in this discussion of the sexual element of the male role. However, a brief discussion of celibacy, or sexual abstinence, seems pertinent because a few men have found sexual abstinence a part of their male experience. We are not talking here of the historic vow of celibacy required of Roman Catholic priests and nuns and other religious groups. We are talking about those men who have chosen sexual abstinence as a means of personal reflection or a temporary sexual halt for any number of reasons, such as an all-encompassing work project. But before we examine this modern version of celibacy, let's look back some two thousand years to its historical roots.

Our present-day views on sexuality, as we have noted in other chapters, owe much of their heritage to early Judeo-Christian traditions. Celibacy owes its legacy to one man, the Christian apostle Paul. Paul preached that a life of total sexual abstinence was a loftier and more spiritually accurate portrayal of the life to come. Even so, Paul conceded that for those Christians "too weak" to live a celibate life, marriage was the only alternative (it was "better to marry than to burn"). However, all sexual expression outside of marriage was strictly forbidden because it did not have a procreative end but rather a pleasure-seeking purpose. Paul's disparaging views on all sexuality became the cornerstone of the Christian ethos that developed over the ensuing two thousand years.

For approximately the first thousand years after Paul's pronouncements against sex, the Christian sexual prohibitions were applied equally to male and female Christians. Both sexes were expected to abstain from all sex unless they were married and then only to have sexual intercourse for the purposes of conceiving another soul for heaven. During the medieval period, however, the birth of the chivalric code brought about a transformation in gender roles. Women were viewed as pure, unblemished, earthly representatives of the Virgin Mary and placed on a pedestal. Men, on the other hand, were seen as more influenced by their nature to baser wants and needs, especially those of sexual gratification. Over the next several centuries, the double standard came to be an expected part of human sexual relationships. Women were expected to surrender to only one man, while men were expected to conquer as many women as possible. Women lost status after they lost their virginity, while men gained respect in the eyes of their male cohorts for their sexual achievements. As time passed, male celibacy, or long-term sexual abstinence, became associated with various harmful physical ailments, leading one nineteenth-century medical writer to note,

> Protracted celibacy is a violation of physical laws. Where the secretion of the semen is not discharged through the natural passages, it must be absorbed into the body in a decomposed state, to clog up the system, impart impurities in the blood, and derange the action of the lungs and the heart. (Wagenvoord & Bailey, 1978, p. 173)

Consequently, the double standard's exhortation that men are to have sex frequently and with many women (while women are expected to keep themselves for only one man) became an integral part of the male role. However, the double standard has shown signs of weakening in this century. (For a discussion of the present status of the double standard, see Mark & Miller, 1986; Sprecher, McKinney, & Orbuck, 1987.) The emphasis on the pleasurable aspects of sex and safer and more reliable forms of birth control have allowed women a greater measure of sexual freedom, yet many men seem to hold ambivalent views about sexuality, especially about premarital sex. On the one hand, a large majority of adult men think premarital sex is a violation of the moral code (Reiss, 1967). On the other hand, the masculine ideal calls for men to be sexually knowledgeable before marriage. In a study of college males conducted by sociologist Mirra Komarovsky, males who were virgins reported more "personal problems" and "hang-ups" than males who were not virgins. Komarovsky (1976) described the conflict for male virgins in this way:

> A [college] senior, who is still a virgin in the liberal subculture of our campus, has failed to live up to his own and his peers' ideal of masculinity. This relative failure to attain the norms of a given age-sex role may damage his self-esteem or lower his status among his peers. But, as conveyed by the phrase, "poverty is not a crime," this is not the kind of deviance that provokes moral outrage. (p. 126)

Virginity and sexual abstinence are not the norms in most male circles. Young men and older ones, too, as we have stated, are expected to be sexually active if they are to be considered real men. Fortunately for the virginal or abstinent male, these conditions do not show. A virginal college student can boast to his roommate about his sexual activities and the roommate may never be the wiser. More than a few males have done so!

Talk of virginity and sexual abstinence runs counter to the much touted sexual freedom of the last several decades. Many believe that we are in the midst of a sexual revolution. People—males and females, young and old—are more and more expected to put aside their sexual hang-ups and traditional moral precepts and encounter one another in the leveling arena of the bedroom. But with all of the talk of sexual involvements, why are some men and women opting for a period of sexual abstinence? What can come from such a period except maybe frustration and loneliness? Perhaps because sex is so open, so expected, so available in most social circles, some people are turning to abstinence as a way to reflect on what is going on within themselves. For some people, sexual abstinence may be the secular equivalent of a religious retreat where men or women can get to know themselves better and sort out some of their own priorities. One normal and healthy man who spent eight months in a celibate state described the experience in this way:

> It was generally a good time for me. I spent lots of time by myself, part of which was devoted to thinking about past relationships. I also spent time with friends, enjoying their company and sharing many of my feelings with them.
>
> The people who knew I wasn't having sex acted a bit strangely, continuously asking how I could do it. It was as if they thought I were performing some miraculous feat. Men were much more surprised than women. Actually, it wasn't very difficult. At times I was lonely, but it wasn't as difficult as I had anticipated. Sometimes I was aware of missing something, but it usually wasn't sex. What I missed most was sleeping next to someone and the cuddling and playing around in bed. I got lots of hugs from my friends, but nothing could replace the warm sense of snuggling with a lover in bed. And that was really the worst of it.
>
> Often I felt intense relief when alone. I didn't have to concern myself with anyone else's needs or feelings. Many times it felt very good to know that I didn't have to share my bed with someone. It was my bed and I could take it all up and do anything I wanted to there.
>
> To say I learned a lot is a cliché but nonetheless true. I learned about myself and relationships and, surprisingly, about myself and sex. I realized for the first time how often I had not gotten what I wanted in sex because I had been so busy trying to be nice and considerate. And I saw how the resentment I had accumulated during such occasions spilled over into other parts of my relationships. Another important thing I learned was that my need for solitude was much greater than I had ever imagined. I enjoyed my own company and needed some quiet time each day to be with me. This turned out to be quite useful in later relationships: I could get more of my alone time when I wanted it, thus making it easier for me to really be with my partner when I was with her. (Zilbergeld, 1978, pp. 153–154)

Whether celibacy will catch on is anyone's guess. Some argue that celibacy, or as the chic are calling it, *asexuality,* is found mainly among career-oriented males and females (Bell, 1978). One social scientist sees celibacy as a viable alternative for more and more people who want more out of their relationships than casual sex (Brown, 1978). It is possible that in the future more men will opt for celibate relationships before they make a long-term commitment. It sounds strangely familiar, like a repackaging of the old moral precept that sex must be reserved for people who are willing and able to accept more than a passing responsibility for their relationships.

Far too many men think of their sexuality almost solely in terms of a variety of physical activities "below the waist." In fact, a man's sexuality may be better understood in terms of specific mental activities "above the waist." Rather than his penis, a man's mind is his most erotic organ (Steinhart, 1982).

To a large degree many of the sexual problems that men face nowadays and their consequent concerns over their masculinity vis-á-vis sexuality can be better understood in relation to what a man thinks about, not what he does with his genitals. Many men undermine potentially satisfying and enjoyable sexual encounters because they allow negative thoughts to intrude into their consciousness: "What if I can't please my partner?" "What if I can't get an erection, or if I can and I come too quickly or not at all?" "What if my partner doesn't really care for me or is comparing me to someone else?" Such thoughts have caused more than a few men to develop a wide range of self-doubts.

Males and females are by nature sexual creatures. It should go without saying that sex can be one of the most pleasurable aspects of their makeup. However, far too many males, because of the sexual element of the male role, place unrealistic sexual demands on themselves, only to hamper the full range of their sexual potentialities. Most males would do better, sexually speaking, if they would stop trying to prove themselves more masculine through sex and learn to relax, that is, to turn off their negative and self-denigrating thoughts and expectations and learn to accept and enjoy their sexuality.

---

important terms

Celibacy *189*

Don Juan complex *186*

Ejaculatory incompetence *185*

Erectile insufficiency *184*

Functional impotence *185*

Impotence *184*

Male sexuality *179*

Masturbation *181*

Organic impotence *185*

Performance anxieties *187*

Premature ejaculation *185*

Psychological impotence *185*

Retarded ejaculation *185*

Self-pleasuring *181*

Sexual anxieties *187*

---

suggested readings

Beckstein, D. (1987). *1987 annotated guide to men's sexual & reproductive health resources.* Capitola, CA: Men's Reproductive Health.

Castleman, M. (1980). *Sexual solutions: An informative guide.* New York: Simon & Schuster.

Freedman, E., & D'Emilio, J. (1988). *Intimate matters: A history of sexuality in America.* New York: Harper & Row.

Friday, N. (1981). *Men in love.* New York: Dell.

Kelley, K. (Ed.). (1987). *Females, males, and sexuality: Theories and research.* Albany: State University of New York Press.

McCarthy, B. (1988). Male sexual awareness: Increasing sexual satisfaction. New York: Carroll & Graf Publishers.

Tiefer, L. (1987). In pursuit of the perfect penis: The medicalization of male sexuality. In M. Kimmel (Ed.), *Changing men: New directions in research on men and masculinity* (pp. 165–184). Newbury Park, CA: Sage.

Zilbergeld, B. (1992). *The new male sexuality.* NY: Benton Books.

Chapter 11

The Self-Reliant Element

If you can keep your head when all about you
Are losing theirs and blaming it on you,
If you can trust yourself when all men doubt you,
But make allowance for their doubting too;
If you can wait and not be tired by waiting,
Or being lied about, don't deal in lies,
Or being hated, don't give way to hating,
And yet don't look too good, nor talk too wise:

If you can dream—and not make dreams your master;
If you can think—and not make thoughts your aim;
If you can meet with Triumph and Disaster
And treat those two imposters just the same;
If you can bear to hear the truth you've spoken
Twisted by knaves to make a trap for fools,
Or watch the things you gave your life to, broken,
And stoop and build 'em up with the worn-out tools:

If you can make one heap of all your winnings
And risk it on one turn of pitch-and-toss,
And lose, and start again at your beginnings
And never breathe a word about your loss;
If you can force your heart and nerve and sinew
To serve your turn long after they are gone,
And so hold on when there is nothing in you
Except the Will which says to them: "Hold on!"

If you can talk with crowds and keep your virtue,
Or walk with Kings—nor lose the common touch,
If neither foes nor loving friends can hurt you,
If all men count with you, but none too much,
If you can fill the unforgiving minute
With sixty seconds worth of distance run,
Yours is the Earth and everything that's in it,
And—which is more—you'll be a Man, my son!

Rudyard Kipling (1976)

No man can rightly claim to be a man unless he is free and self-reliant.

Eugene Debs (Quoted in Filene, 1987)

We now come to the last element in our overview of the male role, self-reliance. Self-reliance implies a certain air or bearing that a man must learn to radiate in all of his activities. Self-reliance is supposedly revealed in how a man walks, talks, and dresses and in the countless ways that he deals with others. For instance, contemporary men's fashions stress the look of the ruggedly confident, outdoor type (Conant, 1988). Because this element lacks tangible and specific guidelines—unlike the other male role elements—it is difficult for a male to master. A young man who is told to act self-reliant on his first job interview wonders just what he should specifically do to accomplish this feat: "How should I act?" "What should I say?" "What should I wear?" In other words, how can he show the interviewer that he is cool, confident, tough-minded, and unflappable? These and many other traits make up the self-reliant element that males are expected to learn and to exhibit.

In this chapter we will first examine several of the characteristics considered to be essential features or building blocks of self-reliance. We will then move into the world of make-believe, into the celluloid fantasy created in motion pictures to focus on archetypal male heroes who epitomize the tough, self-reliant element. Finally we will examine some of the activities of athletes and soldiers suggesting these professions foster an image of self-reliance more strongly than most other professions do.

the precarious posture

Many people may be dismayed to learn that a vast number of men harbor a large number of fears, the kinds of fears that cause men's palms to sweat and stomachs to churn. Even though the male mystique downplays this purportedly unmanly emotion, the fact remains that men do fear. The most nagging fears that prick men's minds are generally related to the expectations that make up the male role. Many men, for example, fear that in some slight way or in some unconscious action they may reveal themselves as feminine and thus unmanly. As one man relates, even the way a man stands with arms akimbo can be a cause for fear of being seen as feminine by others.

> I was out by the mailboxes talking with my next door neighbor, a football coach, whom I respected enormously. We were standing there talking. I had my hands on my hips. He said jokingly that I was standing a woman's way, with my thumbs forward. I was 27 years old and I had never really thought about the best way to stand with my arms akimbo. But now, whenever I find myself standing with thumbs forward I feel an effeminate flash, even when I'm alone, and I quickly turn my hands around the other way. (Wagenvoord & Bailey, 1978, p. 44)

Besides their ever-present fear of lurking femininity, many men secretly fear that after all of the years they spend in the competitive struggle at work, they will receive only a pat on the back and an inflation-eroded pension as the final signs of their success. Some men spend countless hours and expend considerable energy worrying about the possible meanings of other people's behaviors. A man stews that his boss did not speak when they passed in the hallway, the head office is sending one of those college-trained know-it-all, knife-you-in-the-back management trainees to his office, or his secretary smirked at him after a gossip session at the water fountain. He constantly fears the worst, no matter how slight the signal.

Still other men fear the improbable occasion on which they will be found out as dyed-in-the-wool, leg-shaking, knee-knocking cowards. These men fear that some day they will find themselves in a crowded place where they unintentionally nudge some terrifying hulk who immediately asks for redress. Sensing a life-threatening experience, they envision themselves bolting for the nearest exit, leaving a room full of laughing and jeering onlookers. On the other hand, some men mask their fear of violence by imagining themselves meeting the same challenge by delivering a devastating blow that sends the hulk sniveling to his corner. No matter what the scenario, most men fear any occasion on which they might be called upon to fight.

And what of those men who fear that they will be found not to be as sexy as they pretend to be? In the minds of many men, the fear gnaws that someday after a particularly satisfying love-making experience a voice will whisper from the other pillow, "Is that the best you can do?" A woman can sense this fear in her partner when he questions how good he was in comparison to her former lovers. No man wants to think that his sexual performance pales in comparison to others. But a majority of men fear it all the same.

Men fear many other things ranging from aging, baldness, and excess weight to a loss of virility. Men not only fear, they are scared that others may discover their fear. Thus men learn to hide their fears behind a precarious posture, an air of cool confidence, a stance of toughness and self-reliance. The lessons in self-reliance begin early and last for most of a man's life.

Little boys are told from their early years onward that they are not supposed to fear, not supposed to be scared of things that they have little or no control over. As the years go by and the boys become men, the not-supposed-to-fear message is incessantly played over and over until a strange transformation takes place. The message that "men are not supposed to fear" becomes embedded in men's minds as "men do not fear." Thus most men come to believe that other men actually do not have fears. For those men who do have fears—the vast majority of men, that is—a cover is necessary; an image of self-reliance becomes a kind of ruse to hide behind.

The air of self-reliance and toughness is not something a boy learns quickly or easily. For the most part, the lessons begin in the home, where a boy learns the posture of self-reliance from his father or possibly other male figures. The first lessons deal with simple behaviors, the how-tos of acting like a man. By and large, these early lessons concentrate on what behaviors are expected of males. Behaviors as simple as how to sit or how to wear a towel in a locker room are part of the prescribed style of manly behavior. One man recounts such an early lesson:

> When I was a kid I was sitting on the sofa reading and my legs were crossed, right knee draped over left. My father said, "You're sitting like a girl!" and demonstrated the right way: He placed his left ankle on his right knee so that his thighs were separated at the immodest masculine angle. For a couple of years after that I thought men were supposed to cross legs left over right, while women crossed them right over left. Or was it the other way? I could never remember which. So rather than make a mistake and do it like a girl, I preferred not to cross my legs at all. (Wagenvoord & Bailey, 1978, p. 44)

The Self-Reliant Element

Still another man recalls an incident at the local YMCA:

> When I was eight I came out of a YMCA shower with my towel wrapped around my chest. The other boys laughed at me and said, "Hey, he's wearing his towel like a girl!" I had three older sisters at home and that's the way they wore bath towels. How the hell was I supposed to know? I thought everyone wore them that way. I didn't go back to the Y for weeks. But when I returned I wore the towel around my waist. (Wagenvoord & Bailey, 1978, p. 42)

Obviously, the air of self-reliance and toughness expected of men is more than just how a man sits or how he wears his towel in a locker room. The self-reliant element is more a matter of overall style than merely what a man does. A businessman attempts to create an aura of supreme confidence when he negotiates a contract that could spell life or death for his company. When eerie night sounds invade the campsite, a man musters up a stance of courage for others to take comfort in. A young boy rejects another's offer while he stands his post. Everything a man does he does to show others he is quietly confident of his abilities (Butler, Giordano, & Neren, 1985; Rosenthal, Gesten, & Shiffman, 1986). These and countless other situations demand that a male exhibit what psychologist Robert Brannon (1976, p. 25) refers to as "the cultivation of a stoic, imperturbable persona, just this side of catatonia" (Wilkinson, 1986).

Few men if any can bring together all of the features of self-reliance in a single situation. Because of the vastness and scope of this element, we need to turn to the world of make-believe, where life is often portrayed by men who are larger than life. Let's go to the movies where self-reliant and tough men abound and where the average man can sit in darkness and play out the self-reliant element in his mind if not in his life.

male heroes

Before television narcotized the North American public, countless millions of young males learned in neighborhood theaters what self-reliance and toughness were all about. For twenty-five or thirty-five cents, boys sat in darkened movie theaters every Saturday afternoon and watched as Randolph Scott acted out the archetypal Western good guy or as Errol Flynn portrayed a swashbuckling hero in his majesty's naval fleet. Today the large silver screen has been replaced for the most part by the nineteen-inch television screen. Not only have the screens shrunk but so have the male characters. We need to look back for a moment at some of the grand male heroes with whom generations of boys grew up, heroes who pointed the way toward the manly style of self-reliance and toughness.

Male movie heroes come in all shapes and sizes. Some are unshaven and crude and others are debonair and svelte. Even so, most of them are fiercely independent, coolly confident, tough, and self-reliant (Bingham, 1993; Cohan & Hark, 1993).

Of course, not every male star portrays these highly prized masculine attributes. Joan Mellen (1977) categorizes three types of male heroes. However, the type that is of particular interest to our discussion here is the one she labels as the "big bad wolves." These male heroes all portray a certain style of masculinity that men in the audience recognize as the mark of a "real man." According to Mellen,

> The indomitable male has populated our films since the last shot of *The Great Train Robbery,* made in 1903, when a sinister-looking gentleman with a fierce handlebar moustache pointed his gun and fired at the audience. To this tradition belong the male stars who are meant to fulfill our purported need for heroes: men who protect the weak, serve justice, defeat evil, and relieve us, men and women alike, of any need to take responsibility for doing those defiant things in our own lives. The Big Bad Wolves include all those "strong," dominant screen males such as William S. Hart, Tom Mix, Douglas Fairbanks, Sr., Gary Cooper, Errol Flynn, Henry Fonda, Alan Ladd, Marlon Brando, Kirk Douglas, Rock Hudson, Paul Newman, Charles Bronson, Steve McQueen, and Clint Eastwood. (pp. 4–5)

As we see in Mellen's list of "big bad wolves," Hollywood has created a veritable pack of male heroes who epitomize a particular masculine style. Take any one of the wolves and their movies and what do we usually find in their performance: a quiet strength, courage, independence, cool confidence, toughness, and self-reliance. More often than not, we find the heroes pitted against an enemy or fighting for a cause in which the odds are decidedly against them. For example, in the classic Western *High Noon,* a quiet and stoical marshal played by Gary Cooper is called upon to save his town from the ravages of three desperate gunslingers. The townspeople abandon the marshal and behave in cravenly and cowardly ways. (No heroes among that lot!) Mellen refers to *High Noon* as a classic paean to male strength and notes that even the movie's theme song reverberates the message of male courage and strength: "If I'm a man, I must be brave . . . else lie a coward in my grave."

Few movie heroes, however, have captured the element of toughness and self-reliance as did Humphrey Bogart. Bogart was not particularly handsome nor dashing like Clark Gable or Errol Flynn, but he conveyed a masculine style in a way few others could match. Mellen notes this quality in Bogart's film *Casablanca:*

> The hero who discovered his masculinity in the commitment to defeat fascism was most brilliantly and consistently played by Humphrey Bogart. And in no Bogart character are manliness and political commitment conjoined with more verve and flair than in his Rick of *Casablanca* (1942). . . .
>
> What grants this crude exercise in political propaganda its appeal is its association with Bogart's supreme style, *savoir-faire,* and romantic sophistication. His every gesture is cool and knowing, bespeaking an immense knowledge of the ways of the world. If Gable exuded a sense of unquenchable energy, Bogart expects the worst at any instant and lives for the moment. He is beyond being shocked: "I don't mind a parasite," he says in *Casablanca;* "I object to a cut-rate one." He is, paradoxically, a more powerful male than any of his predecessors because he is so cynical about his own or anybody else's capacity to create a world free of corruption and evil-doing. Tough and shrewd, he knows that life at any moment may trap him; if, despite this, we feel safe with him, it is because no event, however outrageous, seems to come as a surprise. (p. 141)

The Self-Reliant Element

Men in their late forties and fifties grew up with flickering images of Bogart, Flynn, and the other big bad wolves to show them the way in which a "real man" is supposed to act. During the late 1960s and 1970s, a new generation of male stars such as James Coburn, Robert Redford, Burt Reynolds, Jack Nicholson, and Charles Bronson had taken over the role of the male hero. Our appetite for male heroes has not diminished even into the last decades of the 20th century as attested to by the popularity, especially among young men, of Tom Cruise, Arnold Schwarzenegger, Nick Nolte, Michael Douglas, Wesley Snipes, and Mel Gibson. Although the names have changed, the message remains the same: Be cool, confident, independent, tough, and self-reliant.

However, one male superstar whom we could hardly call a big bad wolf is the bespectacled Woody Allen. Allen's characters portray the deep-seated anguish most men feel in the faltering attempts to be something they are not. Allen, the iconoclast on as well as off the screen, depicts the anxiety, pain, and frustration felt by millions of American men who do not quite meet the high standards set by Hollywood's big bad wolves. Allen's movies have become a kind of cinematic happening in which the average guy's strivings and failures at being a "real man" are shown in comic pathos. Even though most of Allen's characters fall short of the ideal, the dream is still the same: Be a big bad wolf. As Mellen points out,

> Woody Allen's comedies about the puny neurotic male in glasses attempting to be a man in a culture glorifying John Wayne and Humphrey Bogart have honest moments despite Allen's failure to transcend the values of Wayne. He is the small man who, protestations and irony aside, aspires to be six feet tall and strong. (p. 336)

Hollywood's version of the supermale is only one force that influences the strong and self-reliant element. Other cultural roles support this image and in some ways have a more insidious effect on young men's perceptions of what is expected of them. Let's turn our attention now to two very different aspects of American life.

the athlete and the soldier

Today, males have few opportunities to exhibit the full complement of attributes that go to make up the tough and self-reliant element. No longer can a man step out onto a sun-drenched, dusty street, as did Gary Cooper in *High Noon,* and display a manly sense of fierce determination and quiet courage in the face of potentially lethal odds. Neither can most men jet to some exotic spot and coolly liquidate some archetypal fiend all the while satisfying the sexual needs of a bevy of international beauties, as Sean Connery and Roger Moore did in the original James Bond movies. Such exploits exist only in the minds of movie producers and the millions of males who can only fantasize such "manly" roles. In fact, today there are few arenas in which a man can test his tough and self-reliant mettle in ways that will shore up his sense of masculinity. If contemporary males are finding it more and more difficult to prove themselves real men solely in terms of their physical strength as some social scientists claim (Gagnon, 1976), then where can men find the opportunity to exhibit and, probably more importantly, to practice being tough and self-reliant? We suggest that the roles of the athlete and the soldier still afford men opportunities to test their self-reliance.

"Sport in American society," write social scientists Peter Stein and Steven Hoffman (1978), "is a prominent masculine rite. Every boy has to wrestle with the all-pervasiveness of athletics. The development of athletic ability is an essential element in becoming a 'man'; sports is the training ground for 'the traditional male role.' "

Almost every adult male can remember the times out on the school playground when a group of boys huddled together to choose sides for a game of softball or football. Usually the two most athletically gifted boys acted as rival team captains who set about the serious task of choosing from the group of anxious players the members for the two opposing teams. As each captain picked his team, the waiting boys grew more solemn. The initial hollering and gleeful merriment quickly gave way to a type of deathwatch. Each boy silently prayed, "Please, God, let me be picked next." Finally, the last two or three unselected boys stood mute across from the two almost complete teams. The captains would begin haggling over who would take scrawny Joey or dumpy Peter. After what seemed an interminable wait, Joey and Peter were selected begrudgingly by each captain. The first-round choices made it because of their proven athletic skills. Joey and Peter were picked simply because they were there. Little will ever exceed the pain and anguish of being a Joey or a Peter. To be seen by one's peers as a bumbler, an athletic klutz, is an experience as unsettling and depressing as anything that can befall a young boy. Surprisingly, many a boy who didn't know the answer to one of the teacher's questions or who got a failing grade on a written assignment actually gained status in the young males' pecking order. But a boy who couldn't catch an infield fly or run for a gain on a football field was a nobody. Yes, sports and athletic prowess permeate all young boys' lives in some way (Fine, 1987).

Competitive sports such as baseball, basketball, hockey, and football are considered by many North Americans as activities that build character and give a young man a leg up on his climb toward manhood. Competitive sports emphasize the winning ethic as well as physical strength, endurance, toughness, independence, emotional insensitivity, and self-reliance. Everything a young man needs to learn about the real world can be learned in athletic competition, or so say most coaches and sports boosters (Messner, 1993; Sabo, 1986). Certainly, one advantage of athletic involvement is recognition and approval by one's peers, as James Coleman (1976) notes in his analysis of high school athletics. But we can still ask, are there trade-offs for this "manly" training, negative consequences that the athletic male accrues that may possibly be harmful to an adult man? According to sports sociologists Don Sabo and Michael Messner, the answer is a resounding yes (Messner, 1987; Messner & Sabo, 1990; Sabo, 1985, 1987; Sabo & Runfola, 1980). Several years ago, Peter Stein and Steven Hoffman (1978) studied a small group of athletic and nonathletic college males with an eye to the impact athletics have on young men's lives.

The primary focus of Stein and Hoffman's research was what is commonly referred to as *role strain* as it affects the male athlete in high school and in college. Stein and Hoffman borrowed heavily in their analysis of role strain from the research of sociologist Mirra Komarovsky (1976), who defined role strain as the "felt and latent difficulty in role performance and perceived paucity of rewards for role conformity." In other words, some males may experience personal anxiety and anguish because they do not measure up or have the necessary personality characteristics required to perform certain roles. For example, scrawny Joey and dumpy Peter may have experienced role strain because they did not have what it takes to "make it" as athletes in their peer group. Furthermore, both Joey and Peter may have felt less masculine because of their being seen by the other boys as not having the necessary attributes to perform the role of athlete. In their interviews with athletes, Stein and Hoffman found considerable evidence for role strain, if not at the high school level then most assuredly at the college level of athletic involvement. Here are the highlights of some of their more interesting findings.

First of all, several athletes mentioned the lack of rewards, the lack of recognition by others for their contribution to the team's achievements. Competitive sports such as baseball and football tend to reward the few superstars, the flashy players whom the media and the fans largely fawn over. But what of the average team player? What are his rewards for the hours of practice and his determination to give athletics his all? As Stein and Hoffman write,

> Our interviews suggest the importance of distinguishing between internal and external rewards. The available rewards operate in the dominant context of a star system which is based on high rewards for a few at the expense of the many. Superstars receive publicity, prestige, and glamour for performance, while teammates oftentimes feel devalued in their own performance. In . . . three sports, the average players reported that even though they performed well they felt overshadowed by the team's superstar. They sometimes felt contempt and envy toward the better-recognized players. The players reported feeling good about their performance when values predominating the team were such that every member gained recognition for his contribution. (p. 142)

Most dedicated high school athletes spend three to four hours a day in some form of practice. From August until late November, there is football practice; from December to March, there is basketball; and from March to May, there is baseball. Even so, the rewards and recognition from peers seem sufficient compensation for such arduous endeavors. Consequently, over the years, the young athlete absorbs certain role values such as unemotionality and toughness. However, once the athlete moves on to college, these values can cause role conflict in interpersonal relationships, for example, between male athletes and others, especially girlfriends. Again, Stein and Hoffman note this potentially negative consequence of the athletic role:

> With a shift to college, more of the athletes experienced conflict due to their dates' expectations of different personality traits. Women they dated expressed a preference for greater openness, a sharing of feelings, more verbal communication, more sensitivity to feelings, moods, and nonverbal gestures.
>
> The focus was on relating to each other and the men felt forced to reevaluate the characteristics stressed in their athletic role. They began to experience strain and conflict between these competing expectations. This role strain involved both interpersonal conflict with dates and some intrapsychic tension involving the surfacing of feelings about themselves and their athletic roles and heterosexual dating roles. (p. 144)

One other interesting feature of the role strain phenomenon that occurs among many college athletes is what Stein and Hoffman term the "overload of role obligations." As we just suggested, most high school athletes give themselves almost entirely to sports. However, in college a large number of other activities push in on the athlete's time. There are academic pressures if the athlete wishes to remain in college or to go on for advanced training in a professional or graduate school. Social obligations increase as the athlete probably begins to devote more spare time to one particular intimate relationship. These and other competing activities draw from the time, energy, and dedication the athlete once devoted to sports. Some of the athletes in Stein and Hoffman's study wished they had been less dedicated to sports earlier because of the relatively few payoffs that sports has for the male athlete who does not wish to make sports a life-long career.

Of course, athletes are not the only ones to experience role strain. The nonathletic sample in Stein and Hoffman's study also noted how sports and its values and expectations either directly or indirectly affected them:

> The role of nonathlete is rife with role strain. The child who is weaker and not well coordinated is chosen less and less often and begins to accept the definition of nonathlete. This development occurs through the early and middle grade-school years when his personality is being shaped. He experiences more and more role strain as his emerging personality does not fit the role of boy-athlete, terms which are closely linked in that age group. The men who did not play ball as children reported that the process of self-definition as a nonathlete was gradual but definite. There was an initial casting of roles (athletes and nonathletes) which became more rigidly defined with each sports contest. Less skillful boys became labelled as nonathletes by the other children. (p. 147)

Thus we see that sports, especially competitive team sports, extract a considerable toll on all boys, the athletes and nonathletes alike. Yet most North Americans see sports as a valued means whereby a young male gains in those virtues that will better prepare him for the competitive and tough adult world. As Stein and Hoffman's analysis points out, a majority of boys suffer at the very least some personal discomfort and at the most considerable anguish when the role expectations imposed by the sports ethic clash with those behaviors and values considered necessary for fitting in and getting along in the adult world. It is no longer enough for a young man to learn only how to block pain or how to shut off all emotion in order for him to live an interpersonally and intrapersonally satisfying life.

In order to avoid leaving the impression that all sports are somehow bad or evil, let's close this section with the conclusion that Stein and Hoffman drew after their insightful analysis.

> We do not mean to imply that positive experiences do not take place in sports. In fact athletes do learn, in varying degrees, to cooperate, compromise, and compete with peers. They learn strategic thinking, physical dexterity, and coordination. They learn competency and mastery of a skill. These functions can be very helpful to a person in leading a more productive adult life.

The Self-Reliant Element

Our research leads us to ask the question of how sports can be organized so as to allow all participants to benefit from its crucial developmental functions, while minimizing the role strain for both athletes and nonathletes. We can speculate that the optimum condition for successful modern male-role performance is related to some group of athletic experiences of a less competitive and more cooperative nature. The introduction of these values into male-male relationships through sports may result in their eventual introduction in other areas of social interaction. Cooperation, sharing, and compromising without suffering loss of self-esteem are hopeful aspects of change in the athletic role and in the male role. (p. 149)

You're in the Army Now

Most adult men who grew up in the late 1940s and 1950s can probably remember the childhood times when they and their buddies played war. The backyard, ragtag army gained a degree of credibility with the paraphernalia that the boys accumulated from various sources. One boy had a regulation army canteen and cartridge belt purchased from the local army-navy surplus store, while another sported a real, steel army helmet pirated from his dad's old trunk in the attic, and a third had an imitation, but genuine-looking M–1 rifle purchased at Woolworth's. The boys spent hours crawling belly fashion through bushes and locked in mortal combat with tenacious German or Japanese armies. On Saturday afternoons, boys could sit and learn new battle strategies from Hollywood's version of war games. The screens blazed into action as combat-toughened heroes such as John Wayne, Audie Murphy, and a cast of lesser known actor-soldiers defeated the United States' enemies. But boys grow up, and for millions of young men, the backyard war games and cinematic portrayal of the glory of war finally end when young men become real soldiers.

In the United States, the military is second only to athletics in being portrayed as a social institution that makes real men out of boys. Recruiting posters are a good example of the military's claim of such masculinizing effects—for instance, "Join the Marines and become a man." As with sports, the military stresses the physical side of a young man's development as the primary validation of his masculinity. At the heart of the military's view of masculinity is the role of the combat soldier. Not surprisingly, much of what is expected of the soldier, especially the combat soldier, is taken directly from what is expected of all "real" men, either civilian or military. Commenting on this core of masculine values and manly expectations, Samuel Stouffer (1976) and his associates write,

The codes according to which a combat unit judged the behavior of its members, and in terms of which conformity was enforced, differed in their generality. Perhaps the most general was one drawn largely from civilian culture but given its special interpretation in the combat situation: Be a man. Conceptions of masculinity vary among different groups, but there is a core which is common to most: courage, endurance, and toughness, lack of squeamishness when confronted with shocking or distasteful stimuli, avoidance of display of weakness in general, reticence about emotional or idealistic matters, and sexual competency. (p. 179)

As we can see in Stouffer's comment, the expectations for a young soldier are much the same as for his civilian counterpart and can be summed up with the same injunction: Be a man. But "be a man" takes on special significance for the soldier.

All of the elements in the male role of which we have spoken are exaggerated in the military. It is not enough just to avoid feminine behaviors; a soldier is taught total contempt for all women except his mother and possibly the one special girl back home. Women are to be used and abused for the soldier's pleasure. Success in the sense of being the best at whatever he does is ingrained in the soldier. Competition among individual soldiers, squads, platoons, and divisions is part of military training. Aggression not only means being ready to fight but also being ready to kill. (We tend to forget that the primary mission of a soldier is *to kill* the enemy.) A soldier also hears the not-so-subtle message that sex is one of the soldier's basic prerogatives. The notion of the soldier's use of his penis as a weapon comes through in the cadence learned by most recruits as they hold their rifle in one hand and their crotch in the other and yell,

> Sir: This is my rifle
> This is my gun
> This is for fighting
> This is for fun!

Likewise, the pressures to be tough, confident, and self-reliant are extreme for the soldier. Some argue that all of this is good for a young man, he gains a sense of personal security in knowing that he can do pretty much whatever he sets his mind to. The military builds character and the end product is a better, more competent man. Boys enter the military, but after a masculinizing hitch, they leave as men—or so many think.

Such a view, however, does not find support in one man's reminiscences of his military training.

> I went into the Army like a lot of people do—a young scared kid of 17 told he should join the Army to get off probation for minor crimes. At the time the Army sounded real fine: three meals, rent-free home, adventure and *you would come out a man.* (It's amazing how many parents put this trip on their kids.)
>
> In basic training I met the dregs of the Army. (Who else would be given such an unimportant job as training "dumb shit kids"?) These instructors were constantly making jokes such as "don't bend over in the shower" and encouraging the super-masculine image of "so horny he'll fuck anything." People talked about fucking sheep and cows and women with about the same respect for them all.
>
> Not many 17-year-olds could conform to such hard core experience. You're told the cooks were gay (pieces of ass for your benefit). The "hard core" sergeants with all these young "feminine" bodies (everyone appears very meek, i.e., feminine, when constantly humiliated, by having his head shaved and being harassed with no legitimate way of fighting back) were always dunghole talking ("your ass is grass and Jim's the lawnmower").
>
> These "leaders" are the *men;* that pretty much makes you the "pussies"—at the very most "boys." You have to conform to a hard core, tough image or you're a punk. And I began to believe it because of my insecure state of mind, which was so encouraged in training. I was real insecure, so I wanted to be a superman and went Airborne, which, unlike most of the Army, is more intense and worse than basic training. The pressures of assuming manhood are very heavy.

The Self-Reliant Element

Not only are you hard, you're Airborne hard—sharp, mean, ruthless. You have to be having an impressive sexual life or a quick tongue to talk one up. You've got to be ready to fight a lot because you're tough and don't take shit from anyone. All these fronts were very hard for me to keep up because they contradicted everything I felt. I didn't feel tougher than anyone. I was very insecure about my dick size and ability to satisfy women.

All I had was my male birthright ego. I stayed drunk to be able to struggle through the barroom tests of strength and the bedroom obstacle courses. The pressures became heavier and stronger, requiring more of a facade to cover up the greater insecurity. To prove I was tougher I went looking for fights and people to fuck over. To prove I was "cock strong" I fucked over more women and talked more about it. I began to do all the things I was most insecure about doing, hoping that doing them would make me that "real man."

Having survived the initial shock of such a culture I became very capable in such required role-playing as toughest, meanest, and most virile—the last meaning of a cold unreproachable lover (irresistible to women and unapproachable by other men). (Anonymous, 1974)

There is no reason to think that this man's experiences are unique. The military strips a young man of his previous identity and through a process of indoctrination creates a person who can follow orders and kill another human being if the situation warrants it. All the hoopla of making boys into men is more of a public-relations gimmick than a real concern of the military establishment. Rather than instilling character and ideals, the military seems more concerned with puffery and braggadocio.

However, since 1973, with the introduction of the All Volunteer Armed Forces (AVAF), the military has changed its public image somewhat. No longer are there as many recruiting posters picturing the soldier in battle gear challenging a young man to become a real man in the tradition of John Wayne taking enemy strongholds. Today the message is that the military is one of the few places where a young male or female can gain valuable and potentially marketable skills. As William Arkin and Lynne Dobrofsky (1978) point out in their analysis of contemporary military socialization,

> As a result of the AVAF, today we find becoming a man being defined in terms of learning an occupation or a skill, but basically the recruitment message of turning a boy into a man has only added the traditional work ethic dimension of masculinity, which equates masculinity with productivity, occupation, and breadwinning. This shift does not change one of the primary objectives of the military, that of turning boys into (fighting) men, but rather it attempts to widen the military appeal. As the result of the negative publicity that was spotlighted by Vietnam, this new appeal further represents a typical peacetime pattern where the masculine warrior appears superfluous to the population. (pp. 154-155)

One of the more pressing problems facing the modern military establishment is what to do with the female soldier. For many people—civilian and military alike—the presence of women in the military contradicts the idea of the military as one of the last all-male bastions. If women in the military can do everything that men can do with the exception of taking part in combat—a prohibition supported more by social convention than real evidence that women cannot perform effectively in combat—what particular masculinizing validation do men receive for their manhood by serving in the military? The military's validation of traditional masculinity has been further undermined by the numerous female soldiers who proved their combat skills and prowess during the Panama incursion and the Desert Storm campaign. Again, Arkin and Dobrofsky respond to this thorny issue:

> The influx of women in all traditional male occupations, with the exception of combat, can only serve to challenge the military socialization in masculinity since the military has yet to develop a female warrior model. Military women tend to represent a neutered or "little brother" role model. But whether a feminine or little brother model of socialization is used for women, it is questionable if the military model of masculinity can be preserved when shared. (p. 167)

The Self-Reliant Element

We can only speculate on how the growing presence of women will affect the long-held military traditions that support the masculinizing process. One thing seems certain: The military will change the women who enter the service in far greater ways than the women will change the military.

Men for so long have identified certain attributes as essential features of their masculinity and male role that most of them can think in no other terms. A man must always act in certain prescribed ways if he is to be judged a real man. If, for whatever reason, he should not play out the prescribed role, he is immediately condemned as being unmanly, as being less of a man. The pressures—self-imposed and otherwise—that come from such rigid role playing take their toll. Even so, most men continue in a never-ending quest to prove to themselves and to others that they are real men—tough and self-reliant to the core (Lederer & Botwin, 1982).

In this chapter we have suggested that most men act tough and self-reliant to cover up their gnawing fears that others may not think them real men unless they act in certain ways. Hollywood's male heroes or big bad wolves have played an integral part in educating males in those values, ideals, and behaviors that portray a certain masculine style. This style is particularly apparent in the roles of the athlete and the soldier.

suggested readings

Cohan, S., & Hark, I. R. (Eds.). (1993). *Screening the male: Exploring masculinities in Hollywood cinema.* New York: Routledge.

Fasteau, M. (1974). *The male machine.* New York: McGraw-Hill.

Komarovsky, M. (1976). *Dilemmas of masculinity.* New York: Norton.

Mellen, J. (1977). *Big bad wolves: Masculinity in the American film.* New York: Pantheon Books.

Messner, M. A. (1993). *Power at play: Sports and the problem of masculinity.* Boston: Beacon Press.

Wilkinson, R. (1986). *American tough: The tough-guy tradition and American character.* New York: Harper & Row.

section three

Some Issues of Concern to Males

The male experience is much more complex than any one discipline can successfully unravel or than the mere enumeration of a set of socially prescribed norms and expectations can encompass. Although we have covered considerable ground thus far with the previous chapters, we will now tackle several issues that transcend easy analysis and, consequently, require the attention of their own chapters.

In chapter 12 we will focus on men's relationships with others. First we will note the important issue of power in men's relations with women. Traditionally, males have had a greater number of power bases in their relations with females. Noteworthy here is that most social scientists contend that when a relationship is structured around an inequality of power some kind of conflict, either overt or covert, usually arises making for an uneasy and oftentimes troubled relationship. Besides male-female relations, we will also examine several aspects of men's relations with other men, especially men's close same-sex friendships.

At some time or another, whether they will admit it or not, most men have questioned their sexual orientation. Although most males find themselves attracted to females, a significant minority find other males desirable as sex partners. In chapter 13 we will explore homosexuality and, in so doing, explode several myths associated with the gay community. Our goal here is to look at gays as people rather than as a caricature or a stereotype.

More often than most scholars in gender studies would care to note, their analyses are infused with the values of the dominant racial-ethnic group. In recent years, some scholars have begun to look at how a minority racial-ethnic status structures one's gender performances. In chapter 14, then, we will focus our attention on four groups of minority males, namely, African Americans, Hispanics, Asian-Americans and Native Americans, and different aspects of their manhood and masculinity.

In chapter 15, we will discuss fatherhood. Over the past decade, fathers, fathering, and fatherhood have been some of the most studied areas within men's studies. For years, mothers were considered the key to child development. However, as of late, several developmental specialists have come forward and recognized the contributions fathers make in their children's growth.

Finally, in chapter 16, we take up the issue of men's health. We will first examine several important physical health problems, namely, preventable diseases associated with life-styles, cancers of the testes and the prostate gland, and AIDS. We then will discuss one of the most serious psychological health issues, stress. Lastly, we will look at an issue not normally associated with men's health but one arguably gaining in popularity among some circles, men's spiritual quest.

Chapter 12

Power and Men's Relationships

Men's and women's roles are currently caught in the vortex of a darkening social storm, which threatens to spark changes in their relationships as individuals and as groups. Occasional lightning flashes allow us only the briefest glimpse of the different shapes toward which these roles are evolving and the underlying power struggle they symbolize.

Jean Lipman-Blumen (1984)

Our culture has traditionally viewed male friendship as embodying the ideals of comradeship and brotherhood. Men have buddies, pals, lifelong ties—bonds of unspoken, unshakable commitment—the kind of friends for whom one would "lay down one's life." Yet surveys find most men today name their wife as their closest friend.

Drury Sherrod (1987)

When we stop to think about it, most of our waking lives are spent in others' company. Although there are times when we would give almost anything to be only in our own company, being alone for more than a few hours is rather disquieting for all save those few who seek a solitary existence. Whether for good or ill then, our interpersonal relationships are the mainstays of our existence providing us with the necessary strands that make up the social tapestry of our lives.

However important one's relationships with others are, though, one's social involvements can and often do bring with them a number of problems (Carr, 1988). Many of today's working men, for example, are not totally comfortable nor adept at dealing with female colleagues in the workplace. (For a discussion on the "new partnership" among men and women in organizations, see Colwill, 1982.) Furthermore, the near-sacredness attributed to men's relations with other men has recently been challenged as lacking in sustaining ingredients. The point here is that men's relationships with women and other men have become "hot topics" for those who want to know more about the male experience.

In this chapter then, we will examine several key relationships men experience with others in their lives, namely, intimate relations between men and women and friendships among men. To set the stage for this discussion though, we need to note a key element in most human relations, that of power.

the name of the game is power

Setting aside Lord Acton's caveat that above all and absolutely, power corrupts. No matter though; some power can be found in all but the most benign of human relationships. To make this point, think about a wife who willingly defers to her husband's choice of a new car or a father who poses no arguments to his wife's insistence that their daughter attend the distant state university rather than the local community college. Such common examples suggest that one person's influence or power over another can most gently be administered and barely detectable to the one being influenced (Brehm, 1985).

To begin, then, we need to note just what power is. Although literature contains almost as many definitions of power as there are citations, the one proposed by sociologist Jean Lipman-Blumen (1984, p. 6) is more than adequate for our purposes. Accordingly, **power** is the "process whereby individuals or groups gain or maintain the capacity to impose their will upon others." Essentially then, whenever someone alone or in a group imposes their will over others, we are dealing with interpersonal power. (For fuller discussions of interpersonal power, see Becker, 1986; Huston, 1983; Kipnis, 1976; Winter, 1988.) Now when someone uses their power over another, we can speak of an individual as having **influence** over another (Cialdini, 1985). To help us keep the players straight in what can be labeled the interpersonal power game, let's designate those who have power over others as *powerholders* and those who are affected or influenced by others' power as the *target person(s)*. When we think about all the different situations where one person exercises power over another, we quickly realize that there is more than one kind of power.

table 12.1   Interpersonal Power

Types of Power	Type of Interaction Between Powerholder and Target Person(s)
Coercive power	Powerholder uses threats and/or punishments to force a target person's compliance.
Reward power	Powerholder controls positive rewards that induce a target person's compliance.
Legitimate power	Powerholder occupies a social position that others defer to.
Referent power	Powerholder is liked thus causing others to comply to their wishes.
Expert power	Powerholder is thought more knowledgeable causing others to comply.
Informational power	Powerholder is able to explain why another should change.

Types of Power

Some years ago, John French and Bertram Raven (French & Raven, 1959; Raven, 1965) enumerated six basic types of interpersonal power commonly found in social relations: coercive, reward, legitimate, referent, expert, and informational (see Table 12.1). Normally a person is not limited to only one type of power. A person is likely to possess several types; this is especially true of males in our society. To gain some insight into these six power types, let's examine each more closely. (For a critique of French and Raven's power typology, see Frost & Stahelski, 1988; Podsakoff & Schriesheim, 1985.)

Coercive power involves the threat of punishment or the withdrawal of something of value. Coercive power can be effective only when a person has control over another or has the means (e.g., physical strength, weapons) to carry out a threat. For example, when a parent threatens a child with punishment or withdrawal of privileges, usually the parent has control over the child's life and/or the strength to carry out the threat of punishment to ensure the child's compliance with the parent's demands. Sadly, coercive power is an all-too-common form of influence in many parent-child and husband-wife relationships. Even though coercive power is relatively easy for those possessing greater strength or control over another to obtain, there are some definite problems in any relationship built primarily on this power base. The relationship between the powerholder and the target person will be filled with distrust and either open or hidden conflict. Furthermore, a victim of coercive power will in most instances come to dislike if not despise the coercive person. Often a person subjected to another's coercive control will leave the relationship when the opportunity presents itself. The fact of the matter is that coercive power does not make for a lasting and caring relationship.

Reward power involves the dispensing of reinforcements to induce another to change. Rewards or reinforcements can be either material (for example, money) or nonmaterial (for example, praise). Although reward power is generally more effective than coercive power, it also has some drawbacks. If, perchance, the powerholder loses his or her source of reinforcement or rewards, the target person may cease to perform the desired behavior. For example, the child who keeps his or her room clean only to get an allowance may let the room become messy if the parents can no longer afford an allowance. Furthermore, rewarding a person for some desired behavior oftentimes does not induce long-term changes in that person's behavior. Granted, reward power is more humane than coercive power, but it often induces a person to change for the wrong reason—only to get a reward, not because the changed behavior is good in and of itself.

Legitimate power derives from a particular position or role a person occupies. For example, the role of father confers certain authority or power to a man over his children. His influence over his children comes not because of rewards, punishments, or other factors but strictly because he occupies a particular role in relationship to his children. When a child balks at taking out the garbage, with the plaintive, "Why do I have to?" the child is influenced with the words, "Because I'm your father and I told you to do it!" A problem with legitimate power, however, is that it tends to put up barriers between the powerholder and the target person.

Referent power is possessed by people who are admired or liked by others. Most people imitate to some degree or another the behaviors of people they admire. Consequently, the admired person either knowingly or unknowingly has some power over his or her admirers. The son who respects and wants to be like his dad when he grows up is showing this kind of influence the father has over his son.

Expert power is found among those people thought by others to have expertise in a particular area or subject. For example, a certified mechanic is considered an expert on car maintenance and is therefore able to influence another person when it comes to the subject of cars. The mechanic-father who goes with his son to purchase the son's first car is better able to dissuade his son from buying a "lemon" than is another father who barely knows where to put the gasoline.

If "knowledge is power," then a person who uses knowledge and can explain in a credible way why another should do something has **informational power.** Noteworthy is the fact that informational power differs from expert power. The one with expert power needs only to tell another to do something and the other complies because of the presumed expertise of the influencer. The informational powerholder causes another to change because he or she is able to explain *why* the change is desirable. For example, a father who explains to his daughter's satisfaction the need for her to take difficult science courses in high school to help her get into an excellent university later on is likely to influence his daughter's choice of classes. On this point, fathers play a larger part than many once thought in directing the successful outcome of their daughters' academic success and personal growth (Marone, 1988).

Thus far, we have described six types of power. Next we will look at how males and females traditionally have had access to different power bases and how this affects their relationships.

The Genders and the Balance of Power

Several factors act as determinants of the amount of power a person holds or can use in his or her relations with others: status, concrete resources, expertise, and self-confidence. Males and females traditionally have had differing amounts of power at their disposal leading most to perceive some basic differences in how each uses power in their relationships (Grauerholz, 1987; Gruber & White, 1986; White, 1988). The consequent imbalance of power between the genders, then, is largely the result of how these determinants relate to each gender.

Status is a socially defined position or rank. A person gains status by possessing certain characteristics (for example, money, titles, beauty) that are prized by his or her group. One can either work for and thus earn status (this is known as **achieved status**) or simply have status arbitrarily bestowed by virtue of something he or she has no control over (this is known as **ascribed status**). For instance, a student who completes college and gets a B.A. degree earns achieved status. A person who is exceptionally attractive automatically has ascribed status in a society that values beauty. Societies vary in the kinds of characteristics they consider valuable, but one characteristic that is prized in nearly every society is being male. Most societies, in fact, place greater value—that is, confer higher status—on their male members than on their female members.

By virtue of the male's greater ascribed status in society, in nearly every situation, males have more legitimate power (power based solely on rank or position) than do women. (An exception to the imbalance in legitimate power is the female's influence over children in the positions of mother and teacher.) When a male and a female are involved in the same activity, however, the male's activity is usually more highly valued. Males, it seems, are the standard or norm by which many people make their judgments of worth or value. Not surprisingly, both males and females are quick to point out that males have more advantages than females in our society (Fabes & Laner, 1986).

Obviously a person who possesses or has control over certain **concrete resources** (such as physical strength, money, sexual favors) can use them to control others. For example, males are usually physically stronger than females, and some males are inclined to use their strength to control females (coercive power). Furthermore, males in our society are more apt to control money and other valuable commodities, and some males use these resources as rewards to gain control over females (reward power). On the other hand, some females use sexual favors to gain leverage over males (again, reward power). However, on the whole, males have traditionally had more resources and consequently a greater number of power bases than females have had.

Recall that expert power belongs to those who are perceived as possessing **expertise** or specialized knowledge and/or skills in a particular field. More often than not, males are seen as experts in nearly every major field in society (medicine, law, government, science, literature, music). Even in those fields where females are generally presumed to have greater experience and knowledge, males are still viewed as experts. To illustrate this, think about the field of cooking. To most people's way of thinking, cooking is traditionally thought of as one of women's special areas of competence and, lest we forget, linked to their prescribed family duties. However, in the vast majority of noteworthy restaurants, we find males running the kitchen and overseeing all food preparations.

A generalized sense of competence and numerous experiences of success give a person an overall sense of **self-confidence.** For the reasons previously outlined, males tend to possess greater self-confidence in themselves and their abilities than do

females (Granleese, Trew & Turner, 1988; Kuhlenschmidt & Conger, 1988). However, some recent research suggests that the differences in self-confidence are narrowing, if not disappearing, between females and males in those situations calling for supervisory skills in dealing with worker problems or in situations where women hold authority positions (Etaugh, Houtler & Ptasnik, 1988; Koberg, 1985). Overall though, males have been favored in the number of their power bases (coercive, reward, legitimate, expert, and informational) and in the determinants that reinforce a male's use of these bases (higher status, resources, expertise, and self-confidence).

intimate male-female relationships

Intimate relationships have long been a favorite subject of poets, playwrights, and novelists; only recently, though, have these special relations captured the attention of social scientists (Rubin, 1984). One can think of several reasons for the social scientific community being so slow in examining intimate relations: Difficulty in objectively defining the elements of an intimate relationship and the belief espoused by many that intimate relations are sacrosanct and thus off-limits for empirical study are two reasons that come to mind. Another problem we find hampering our understanding of such relations is that intimate male-female relationships are presently in a state of flux. Changing gender roles, greater social acceptance of divorce and serial marriages, changing sexual mores, economic pressures, and greater educational and employment opportunities for females are only a few of the recent social forces shaping new patterns of intimate involvements between the sexes. (For a more complete discourse on the many factors influencing intimate relationships, see Brody, Neubaum & Forehand, 1988; Duck & Perlman 1985; Gilmour & Duck, 1986;

Kelley et al., 1983; Kelley, 1987.) Some males—and females—find these changes disquieting and uncomfortable. Rather than try to describe all of the ingredients involved in and the various factors affecting intimate male-female relationships, we will focus on a few specific areas, namely, the balance of power in intimate relationships and the satisfaction and well-being found in intimate relationships.

As noted earlier, power is a key ingredient in all relationships. When it comes to intimate relationships, who holds more power in the relationship, and how do women and men use the power they have? Letitia Anne Peplau provides an analysis of how power is distributed in an intimate relationship and how each gender is apt to use power to influence the other (Peplau, 1984; Peplau & Gordon, 1985).

Power and Intimate Relationships

The ideal versus the reality of the balance of power. Males seem less likely to espouse egalitarianism as an important goal for intimate relationships than do females. Nevertheless, in several studies conducted during the 1960s, researchers concluded that most North American couples favored egalitarian relationships as the basis for marriage (Blood & Wolfe, 1960; Centers, Raven, & Rodriguez, 1971). Granted, in most marriages, husbands make certain decisions, wives others, and both together still others. But what kinds of decisions do husbands customarily make as opposed to those made by their wives? If a wife controls the time at which supper is served or decides what detergent to use for the family's wash and the husband decides to add another bedroom to the house or trade in the three-year-old car for a new model, are these really the same kinds of decision-making powers? In fact, husbands generally have more power and influence in a marriage than wives do (see also Wagner et al., 1990).

Let's examine the following scenario: John and Mary Smith have been married for fifteen years and both have careers. The couple's children, David and Dianne, seem quite happy in the fourth and sixth grades with their many friends. Mary has worked for a stock brokerage firm for the past five years, and John has been a salesperson at a small computer company for the past nine years. The family has a nice home located in a suburb just outside Boston where all of the Smiths are well respected and liked by their neighbors. One day Mary's boss tells her that the company has been watching her for over a year and has decided that she is their candidate to head a new branch office in Denver with a significant increase in her annual salary. Mary goes home that night with the good news, and while at supper, she tells her family they are heading for Denver!

When the author has presented this scenario in several classes, the reactions have usually been the same from both male and female students. What about the contented husband and children, and how can Mary just assume that the others will want to leave the Boston area for Denver? What about John's career, and what can he do in Denver with no prospects for a job? What about the problems of uprooting the children from their school and all of their friends? A majority of students seem to feel that Mary's potential career advancement does not warrant the uprooting of the Smith family.

What if John had come home and announced his computer firm was transferring him to another district several states away where he could expect to do better in sales? Would my students feel as adamant about John's uprooting the family?

Probably not, because husbands are expected to go where the work is and the family is expected to follow. Husbands, it seems, can make more significant decisions that affect the family than can wives.

But what is the basis for the husband's greater power in marriage? Peplau suggests three factors to account for the imbalance of power that decidedly favors husbands over wives. First, as we noted earlier, males by social convention have more power by virtue of their higher status, and this favored male status accrues to the husband in marriage. Second, males generally have more resources within their marriage (for example, greater income, education, age) than their wives do, and this gives males an additional edge in the power equation. Third, females have tended to be more dependent on their husbands for their security than vice versa. Peplau cites Jessie Bernard's analysis of the wife's dependent status as bearing on an egalitarian relation:

> Take a young woman who has been trained for feminine dependencies, who wants to "look up" to the man she marries. Put her at a disadvantage in the labor market. Then marry her to a man who has a slight initial advantage over her in age, income, and education, shored up by an ideology with the male bias. . . . Then expect an egalitarian relationship? (quoted in Peplau & Gordon, 1985, pp. 273–74)

Power Tactics. How do men and women influence each other, especially in those situations where there is a conflict between them (Zietlow & Sillars, 1988)? Researchers have found some evidence that both do in fact use different tactics to influence each other in conflict situations. For example, in studies of dating couples and newlyweds, females reported using more indirect or emotional methods such as pouting or becoming silent and withdrawn in order to influence males. Males noted that they were more likely to rely on logical arguments to persuade the female to change her mind (Falbo & Peplau, 1980; Grauerholz, 1987). Apparently, there is some truth to the common stereotypic view of females and males in their use of different power tactics in conflict situations.

However, we have noted elsewhere that males are socialized to be less emotionally expressive and taught that they should rely on logical arguments to persuade others. Likewise, females are expected to express their feelings openly. What would people think of a husband who softly cries as he pleads with his wife to let him go bowling with the guys? Why, most would think that he is no man at all. But what of the wife who silently throws the burned toast at her husband who disagrees with her decision to buy a new coat? That seems totally in character and probably a good way to get the coat if her husband doesn't want his next meal overcooked. How the sexes are raised and how they are taught to deal with conflict seem to play a large role in the gender differences to conflict resolution. Another feature we should not forget is that pleading, crying, withdrawal, and other emotional displays are more appropriate in conflict situations for the person with less power in the relationship (Kelley et al., 1978). Relying on displays of emotion is basically a tactic used by children and females (powerless people). The common tactical differences in male-female conflict situations seem related, first, to the socialization of gender role differences and, second, to the relative differences in power found between males and females.

When married men get together they often lament about how misunderstood, mistreated, and henpecked they are by their wives. If we were to believe the talk, we would think marriage fraught with problems and restrictions and that a married man's lot must be a rather bleak and an unhappy one. However, the research into marital satisfaction presents an almost entirely different picture. Overall, researchers have found that both husbands and wives agree marriage provides considerable personal happiness and satisfaction (Campbell, Converse & Rodgers, 1976). Despite the fact that many men feel compelled to "bad mouth" marriage, there is some evidence that in certain ways males may benefit from marriage more than females do.

Generally speaking, marriage provides more benefits to an individual than being single, divorced, or widowed; this is especially true for males. When it comes to personal well-being and mental and physical health, husbands tend to accrue more positive benefits from marriage than do wives (Antill & Cotton, 1988; Bernard, 1982; Gove, 1972). Not all of the causes for this gender difference in marital benefits are fully understood, but we can list several of the more obvious ones.

First, in most traditional (male-dominated) marriages, the husband gains the services of someone—the wife—to cook, clean, and do the daily chores around the house. Although the husband is expected to work outside the home, after work he often uses the remainder of the day for hobbies and other leisure-time pursuits. In those marriages where both the husband and wife work outside the home, the wife is still more likely to perform most of the housework (Lawrence et al., 1987; Pleck, 1985). In most cases the wife who holds a full-time job finds herself strapped with double duty, and for many this can cause distress, frustration, and considerable fatigue. Thus in most male-dominant marriages and many egalitarian ones, for that matter, husbands definitely benefit more than wives.

A second benefit many males gain in marriage is the number of situations in which the wife acts as a kind of socioemotional bridge between her husband and others. For example, many husbands feel so inept or uncomfortable in dealing with special emotional relations such as those with children, parents, or close friends that the wife will act as a personal emissary to convey the husband's feelings to these other people. Because so many males come to believe they should not show tenderness, caring, and sensitivity, they leave these expressions to their wives to carry out.

One other area in which males benefit more than females do from marriage is that of physical health care. The role of wife and mother includes the expectation of caring for the health and physical well-being of family members. Consequently, many wives express concern over their husband's physical health, often prompting him to take better care of himself than he would if he were single, divorced, or widowed. For many husbands, the first person they turn to with their aches and pains is the ever-present family nurse, who is expected to make it all better. Not surprisingly, wives do not receive the same concern over their health from their husbands.

Now let's turn our attention to another relationship in men's lives—their relations with other men.

male friendships

In their studies of early human groups, anthropologists have speculated that men and women kept pretty much to themselves in sex-segregated groups (O'Kelly & Carney, 1986). Apparently, in a number of pretechnological societies, for instance, males spent a majority of their time exclusively in the company of other males either in the men's lodge or on extended treks into the bush or across the savannah or out to sea. Not surprisingly then, some investigators consider that such well-established, sex-segregated relationships grow out of a predisposition among males, at least, to bond and that such male bonding underlies most male-dominant social institutions (Tiger, 1969; Wilson, 1978). Whether or not one accepts that male bonding underlies all men's relations, one thing is certain: In recent years, journalists and scholars alike have shown a new interest in examining various aspects of boys' and men's same-sex relations (Bell, 1981; Elkins & Peterson, 1993; Lyman, 1987; McGill, 1985; Pogrebin, 1987, chap. 13; Rose, 1985; Rubin, 1983; Sherrod, 1987).

In this section, however, we will not attempt to answer once and for all whether or not men's relations with each other stem from their biology or their social surroundings. Rather we will simply accept that men are capable of having special, nonerotic relationships with each other; in so doing, we will examine one special class of male-male relationships, notably men's friendships.

Quantity versus Quality

One often hears how common it is for people to have many acquaintances but they must count themselves lucky if they have more than one true friend. If friends are so rare, then one is tempted to ask, who—males or females, in general—is the luckier in having more friends? One way to see who wins what we might facetiously call the "I-have-more-friends-than-you" contest is to poll a group of males and females about the number of friends they have. That's exactly what two researchers did a couple years back to their students—and with some rather interesting results we might add.

Setting out to study male and female friendships, social psychologists Mayta Caldwell and Letitia Anne Peplau (1982) asked their students to simply count up the number of their same-sex friends. Overall, these males and females reported quite similar numbers—males and females reporting between three or four really close friends and between six or seven casual friends. Furthermore, these students reported similar amounts of time spent in same-sex relations, on average; both women and men reported spending about thirteen hours per week with their friends. Other researchers have found comparable data in terms of various quantitative indexes of same-sex friendships (Fischer & Oliker, 1983). Thus it seems both women and men report having about the same number of friends and spending about equal amounts of time with their friends.

If women's and men's same-sex friendships are similar in quantitative ways (i.e., number of friends and hours spent with friends), are their respective friendships similar in qualitative ways as well? In other words, are men's and women's same-sex friendships analogous in terms of certain qualities, or characteristics, such as what goes into making a friendship, what kinds of activities do friends engage in, and what kinds of communications are common among same-sex friends? Generally speaking, the answer is no. Let's be more specific and flesh out some of the qualitative differences found in men's and women's same-sex friendships.

First of all, does friendship, or having a special person one can be with, mean the same to men and women? Although we might be hard pressed to find total agreement on just what constitutes a real friendship, for the most part, males and females think of and value different aspects of what they label as friendship (Banikotes, Neimeyer & Lepkowsky, 1981; Bukowski, Nappi & Hoza, 1987; Burke & Fuqua, 1987). Specifically, females tend to see friendship as an occasion for sharing feelings with another special person or persons (Brehm, 1985). As for males, however, friendship means having another person to share an activity with (e.g., hunting, working on a car's motor, playing cards). If you doubt just how ingrained this distinction is for most people, take a moment and read "What's A Friend For?" Sound rather strange reading about two females out in the garage working on an old 1960 Chevy and two males sitting up all night talking about their love lives? Actually, Sharon Brehm (1985) purposely reversed the names in these two vignettes to show just how embedded men's friendships are in "doing activities," and women's friendships in "sharing confidences." Several years ago, Paul Wright (1982) captured this distinction by noting that men's friendships tend to be side-by-side (i.e., performing some kind of activity), whereas women's are more often face-to-face (i.e., sharing emotions).

Another common difference found in men's and women's same-sex friendships is the kind of communications each of them tend to focus on in their relationships. In a very general way, researchers usually find that males, especially those who act in very traditional masculine ways, are less likely to open up and discuss personal matters with other men, even with those few men identified as their best friends (Dosser, Balswick & Halverson, 1986; Reis, Senchak & Solomon, 1985; Snell, Jr., Miller & Belk, 1988; Winstead, Derlega & Wong, 1984).

To illustrate this aspect of men's and women's same-sex friendships, let's examine Lynne Davidson and Lucile Duberman's (1982) research on the communication patterns found in same-sex relationships. These researchers asked one hundred young, single people to describe the content of their discussions with their same-sex

what's a friend for?

Jim and Henry were good close friends. Often, they would stay up half the night talking about love and life and how they felt about everything and everyone. In times of trouble, each was always there for the other to lean on. When they experienced any conflicts in their romantic relationships with women, they'd immediately be on the phone to each other, asking advice and getting consolation. They felt they knew everything about each other.

Sally and Betty were good close friends. Often, they would stay up half the night playing chess or tinkering with Sally's old car, which was constantly breaking down. In times of trouble, they'd always help each other out. Sally would loan Betty money, or Betty would give Sally a ride home from work whenever their best efforts had failed to revive Sally's beloved 1960 Chevy. They went everywhere together—to the bars, to play basketball, to the latest sci-fi movie. They felt they were the best of buddies. (Brehm, 1985, p. 346)

friends. Next the researchers assigned all the responses mentioned by their sample into one of three content categories: topical (i.e., talking about work, hobbies), relational (i.e., discussing various aspects of the friendship), and personal (i.e., dealing with one's feelings and thoughts). Overall, women's discussions with their same-sex friends tended to fall in all three content areas, whereas men's verbal interactions were limited to topical matters only. These men, it seemed, kept their relationships with their male friends on a somewhat superficial plane. One is tempted to suggest that for many men the only appropriate conversation they allow with other men is limited to one of three topics: shop, sports, and sex.

Interestingly then, when we take a closer look at what men and women share with their same-sex friends, we see a curious pattern of male reserve. Generally speaking, men keep their deeply personal, or private, thoughts and feelings from their male friends. Women, on the other hand, seem more likely to share these kinds of personal matters much more readily with their female friends. Social scientists have labeled the sharing of personal material with another as **self-disclosure.** Generally speaking, males tend to self-disclose less to another man than a woman would to another woman. Finding males as a group less self-disclosing to others, especially other males, has received more than its share of research support over the years (Fox, Gibbs & Auerbach, 1985; Hacker, 1981; Rotenberg, 1986). However, Jeanne Tschann (1988) found married men were much less self-disclosing with a same-sex friend than single men. As for either married or single women though, Tschann's samples showed no difference in the amount of their self-disclosures with a same-sex friend. Apparently then, marital status influences self-disclosure in friendship for men but not for women. Why? Could it be that married men become complacent about "working at" keeping their friendships after marriage? If their intimacy needs are met by a spouse, married men may be tempted to let other supportive close relationships atrophy. Although Tschann's research does not provide the answer, it does raise a perplexing issue: married men work even less at keeping their same-sex relationships intact and growing than single men do. No matter what the reason, maybe we should pay more attention to within-group variability when dealing with the issue of gender differences in friendship rather than placing too great an emphasis or importance on the between-group differences (Wright, 1988).

Why, though, should men—granted, some men more than others—hold back their feelings, create false appearances about how they feel, or withhold their real emotions from the very individuals who they openly call their best male friends, their buddies? One possible answer lies in the proscriptive norm that most males in our society subscribe to—under no circumstances let down your emotional guard in the company of other men (Douvan & Adelson, 1966). To do so would more than likely get one branded as an emotional weakling, a sissy, or the latest in unkind cuts delivered to a man these days, a wimp. Thus we might suspect that males hold back their feelings around other men, even their male friends, because they simply do not want to appear unmanly or weak in other men's eyes (Derlega & Berg, 1987; Lewis, 1978; Sattel, 1976; Williams, 1985).

Thus many see the underlying cause(s) for men's relative inability to be more self-disclosing with their same-sex friends as somehow related to society's norms that poignantly prohibit males from being overly expressive with other men. However, recently two researchers, Elizabeth Mazur and Rose Olver (1987), suggested yet another possible reason males keep up an emotion reserve or defend against disclosing too much about themselves. As these researchers see it, men are inclined to perceive their relations with other men as basically dangerous, threatening, something to be wary of. How these two researchers uncovered this troublesome aspect of men's same-sex relationships is quite interesting.

To study men's feelings about being with other men, Mazur and Olver asked college men to make up stories after reading one of two short sentences. Psychologists often ask a person to make up a story after looking at a picture or reading a short passage as a way to study some aspect about that person that he or she is either totally or only dimly aware of. Such a technique is called a projective or unstructured method of studying personality. The specific passages the males in this study read simply noted that either two men sat on a bench waiting their turns at bat or, in the other case, two men sat on a bench with no mention of what brought them there or what they were doing there. The question here was what kind of story would men make up when they were presented with an unstructured situation (i.e., a situation with no rules—"two men sitting on a bench") as opposed to a structured situation (i.e., a situation with rules governing interaction—"two men sitting on a bench waiting for their turn at bat"). Although this study provided a rich amount of data, suffice it to say that many of those men who wrote stories based on the unstructured situation ("two men sitting on a bench") projected various kinds of danger or threat in the situation. To get the sense of this undercurrent of threat or danger when men come together with no rules governing their interactions, let's quote a rather lengthy passage from one of Mazur and Olver's male participants who made up the following story about two men sitting on a bench.

> These two men are waiting for some type of bus, and hence, they are sitting on this bench. One . . . has a beard and is questioning the other man about his background. The beardless man is reading a newspaper as the bearded man talks to him and is answering his questions very curtly. Nothing particularly unusual had led up to this situation, other than it appears that both men are students and are utilizing the bus service. The fact that the beardless man is being so rude to the bearded man is because he is annoyed at having his privacy interrupted, as he always reads the newspaper before school each day. The beardless man is not only frustrated by the bearded man, but he is also very suspicious of him as the bearded fellow is wearing an earring and tattered clothes. The bearded man thinks it is rather rude of his companion to be reading the

newspaper as he is merely making the effort to be friendly. The beardless man not only wants peace to read his newspaper, but also wants to rid himself of this shady character. The most probable way for this situation to conclude is the arrival of the bus and the subsequent separation of our two friends. However, the bus happens to be late on this specific day and our story concludes with the beardless man robbing the bearded one and then fleeing back to his dormitory at college. (p. 554)

An interesting story, yes? Why, though, should a man make up such a tale with such a twist of violence at the end? Could it be that for unconscious reasons males, at least the one who made up this story, feel threatened in other males' company unless there are some rules or norms governing their interactions or what is expected of them? As already noted, men do tend to be less open, more guarded, and somewhat tentative in the company of other males, even those they consider their friends. Most men seemingly feel comfortable with other men, even their good male friends, only when they are doing something (Farr, 1988). Who knows what would happen if men would just let themselves be with their male friends and do nothing except just enjoy being with each other. Maybe men would come to discover they don't have to be doing something all the time to enjoy being in male company.

---

important terms

Achieved status *213*
Ascribed status *213*
Coercive power *211*
Concrete resources *213*
Expertise *213*
Expert power *212*
Influence *210*
Informational power *212*

Legitimate power *212*
Power *210*
Referent power *212*
Reward power *211*
Self-confidence *213*
Self-disclosure *220*
Status *213*

---

suggested readings

Fitzpatrick, M. (1988). *Between husbands and wives: Communication in marriage*. Newbury Park, CA: Sage.
Kammer, J. (1994). *Good will toward men:* Women talk candidly about the balance of power between the sexes. New York: St. Martin's Press.
Lipman-Blumen, J. (1984). *Gender roles and power*. Englewood Cliffs, NJ: Prentice-Hall.
Nardi, P. (Ed.). (1992). *Men's friendships*. Newbury Park, CA: Sage.

Chapter 13

Homosexuality

We have learned among other things, that the values and experiences of homosexual couples are similar to those of heterosexuals in many ways. Whatever their sexual preferences, most people strongly desire a close and loving relationship with one special person. For both homosexuals and heterosexuals, intimate relationships can—and often do—provide love and satisfaction. But neither group is immune to the perils of relationships—conflict and possible breakup. Whatever their sexual preferences, people in intimate relationships today struggle to reconcile a longing for closeness with a desire for independence and self-realization.

Letitia Anne Peplau (1981)

Despite evidence that homosexuality is, in part, neuroendocrinologically determined; that homosexuals are equivalent to heterosexuals in expressed psychological symptomatology; and that coupled gays and lesbians report levels of relationship qualities indistinguishable from those reported by married heterosexual couples, negative attitudes toward homosexuals still prevail. Such attitudes are of grave concern in light of evidence that violence against homosexuals is a serious national problem aggravated by the current AIDS crisis.

Lawrence A. Kurdek (1988a)

Few topics cause males to become more angry, anxious, irrational, and strident in their views than does the subject of **homosexuality.** Several years ago this disturbing fact became obvious when this author instigated a classroom discussion on homosexuality and the gay community. As the discussion became more heated, one male proclaimed that he would "put the lights out" of any male who approached him with sexual overtures. Another male declared that all homosexuals should be castrated or at least put in prison. Although several other males voiced no condemnation of homosexuality, not one male student offered an opposing view against his more outspoken and vehement classmates. It was as if the male students in that classroom recognized that by taking a more moderate approach to the topic they might themselves be labeled gay. In an article on **homophobia,** a term coined by Smith (1971) meaning the irrational fear and extreme intolerance of homosexuality, Gregory Lehne (1976) pointed out that the threat of being labeled gay is a powerful means whereby males reinforce their own traditional gender stereotype (De Cecco, 1984). What was surprising about this classroom discussion is that so many males *still* feel the necessity to condemn and vilify a minority of people who happen to have a different sexual orientation from the majority. (For a recent review on people's attitudes toward gay men and lesbians, see Abrams, Carter & Hogg, 1989; Kurdek, 1988a; Martin & Hetrick, 1988; Newman, 1989; Whitley, 1987.)

In this chapter we will take a close look at homosexuals and the homosexual community—hereafter referred to as gays and the gay community—in order to understand the problems gays encounter in the heterosexual or straight world. First we will briefly review the history of gay people and attempt to put in perspective the reasons for this group being so systematically condemned and attacked down through the centuries. We also will examine the recent development of the gay liberation movement and its impact on the larger society and on current social attitudes toward homosexuality. Next we will look at several pernicious myths that have grown up around the gay person and the gay community. We will see that these myths have little if any basis in the real world. Finally we will examine gay relationships in order to understand how gay people relate socially and sexually to each other.

By presenting the facts about gays and debunking the many myths associated with them, this chapter attempts to provide a basis for our understanding and acceptance of one another as human beings who all have needs to form close, sharing, and loving relationships with others no matter what our sexual orientation. With a greater understanding of gay relationships, heterosexuals may learn something of value for their own relationships. Specifically, the roles that primarily structure most male-female relationships are often absent in gay relationships. Possibly, heterosexual couples could learn some new ways of living, loving, and sharing if they would only try to understand gay couples better.

from hatred to understanding and back again

If we are to understand the gay person and the gay community, we must first deal with the hostility, discrimination, and violence that have been heaped on this group for most of the last two thousand years. During this time, homosexuality has been labeled a "crime against nature," "an abomination," and "a sin." Gays and those thought to be gay have been executed, jailed, blackmailed, and in various other ways, persecuted by the "righteous" majority. The most heinous and largest scale antihomosexual violence took place in Nazi Germany, where hundreds of thousands of suspected homosexuals were rounded up and sent off to gas chambers along with millions of Jews and other "undesirables" (Haeberle, 1982; Heger, 1980; Lautmann, 1990; Plant, 1986). Closer to home, in North America, gays have borne such dehumanizing abuses as castration, lobotomy, shock treatment, and assault by roving gangs of macho adolescents out for an evening's fun of "queer-baiting" (De Cecco, 1985; Katz, 1976; Licata & Petersen, 1982; Murphy, 1990).

Why gays have warranted such inhuman treatment over the centuries is an issue that needs to be addressed. Part of the reason can be found in an all-too-brief review of the major religious traditions that have influenced Western cultures. The first large-scale attempt to eliminate homosexual practices, a common and accepted sexual variation among many ancient civilizations, occurred within the early Jewish community. For both secular and religious reasons, the Jewish leadership during the fifth century B.C.E. proclaimed homosexuality an abomination and a defilement of Yaweh's injunction for the Jewish people to increase and multiply (Genesis 8:15–17). As so often happens in any newly fashioned religious movement, the early Christian Church adopted the established Jewish views on sex and sexuality and reinforced the view that any sexual activity outside of marriage was grounds for eternal damnation (Ariès & Béjin, 1985). The early Christians went a step further in undermining homosexual activity by prescribing that sexual intercourse be permitted for procreative ends only. Sex as a human expression of love, joy, and pleasure seeking was strictly forbidden even among married couples. A sixth-century pope, Gregory the Great, went so far as to decree that married couples should not befoul "their intercourse with pleasure." Because homosexuality could never serve procreative ends and because it was considered a source of sexual pleasure only, homosexuality was doubly vilified by the early church fathers. Consequently, the antihomosexual sentiment and practices instituted in the Judaic and Christian traditions set the stage for most of the Western world's prohibitions and sanctions against homosexuality (Boswell, 1980; Bullough, 1979; Nugent & Gramick, 1989).

Some argue that another reason for current antihomosexual bias is the purported "dysfunctional" nature inherent in homosexual activity. Their argument goes something like this: If everyone were somehow to become homosexual overnight (a highly unlikely turn of events and yet one that the opponents of homosexuality fear will happen if homosexuality becomes a socially acceptable sexual orientation), the human species would disappear in a few short decades. Granted, in a pretechnological society where a high birth rate would be necessary to offset a high infant mortality rate, the prevalence of homosexual activity could indeed threaten the viability of the group's future existence. An often repeated example of the negative consequences of the absence of heterosexual activity is the recent diminution of the religious sect known as the Shakers, whose religious beliefs prohibit *all* sexual activity. This argument, however, is baseless and the Shaker example irrelevant to the discussion when one recognizes the social and technological realities of contemporary society. In fact, in most postindustrial societies where zero population growth is seen as the only long-term solution to the world's diminishing resources, the number of

The Roots of Antihomosexual Sentiment

Homosexuality

males and females who abstain from procreative sex either as practicing homosexuals or as lifelong celibates may be performing a valuable service. Thus homosexuality in contemporary Western culture can be viewed as a functional alternative sexual orientation rather than as a dysfunctional sexual aberration.

A Short-Lived
About-Face

Prejudicial attitudes and discriminatory practices can only change when their dehumanizing consequences are viewed in the light of public awareness. As in the case of African Americans and women, the social movement to win gays their rights as human beings began when gay people came out of the closet and became visible. The beginning of the gay movement started on the West Coast after World War II with the founding of the **Mattachine Society** in 1950 in Los Angeles. Originally a secret society, the Mattachine came out in the public in 1954 and soon there were Mattachine chapters in most large cities across the United States (see D'Emilio, 1990).

The early gay organizations like the Mattachine served primarily as meeting places where gays could find support and camaraderie. Formal discussion groups became a central fixture of these organizations and provided gays an opportunity to talk about their concerns. Counseling services for "troubled" gays were often provided in many of the organizations that sprang up in most large cities.

In general, the 1950s was a decade of quiet involvement by a minority of gays who began coming out of the closet. The 1960s, with the growing social consciousness of various groups' oppressions, found more gays joining different homophile organizations and lobbying for a relaxation in many of the discriminatory laws that had accumulated over the years (Lauritson & Thorstad, 1974). The public's first real awareness of the gay community came not from the efforts of one of the formal organizations but rather from an incident of police harassment in New York City.

On June 28, 1969, the New York City police raided a popular gay bar located on Christopher Street in Greenwich Village known as the **Stonewall.** Suspected of violating liquor laws, the police arrested the management and employees. After moving the patrons out on the street, the authorities prepared to take their prisoners out but were met by an angry group of patrons and a riot broke out. Sociologists Martin Weinberg and Colin Williams (1975) describe what happened next.

> On emerging from the Stonewall, the police were pelted with pennies, cans, rocks, and other objects and were driven back into the Stonewall, which was locked from the outside and set afire. The Tactical Police Force (riot police) was summoned, and several hours of street fighting ensued, resulting in many arrests and beatings.
>
> The following night, the more militant homosexuals (under the slogan of "Gay Power") decided to "liberate" Christopher Street. Their activities swelled the crowds again, this time including Black Panthers, "yippies," and "crazies." A riot situation developed, and again the Tactical Police Force was called to clear the streets.
>
> June 28, 1969, and the Stonewall incident become one of the major symbols of the gay liberation movement. On its anniversary one year later, Gay Liberation Day was proclaimed with a march that has been repeated every June to the present: the number of participants has ranged from about five thousand to fifteen thousand. Whatever the merits of the Stonewall event, it was a turning point that brought many disaffected young homosexuals into the mainstream of the homophile movement. (pp. 53–54)

After Stonewall, the gay liberation movement began to demand full and equal rights for those people whose only difference from the majority of North Americans was their sexual orientation. Soon, major organizations began rethinking their positions on homosexuality. For instance, in 1973 the American Psychiatric Association and in 1974 the American Psychological Association passed resolutions removing homosexuality from the official list of mental disorders (Bayer, 1981; Ross, Paulsen & Stalström, 1988). In 1975 the Civil Service Commission, moved by a federal court decision, stated its policy that people could not be denied federal employment because of their sexual orientation. For a time, the gay liberation movement looked as if it were at last making real headway in changing the general public's social consciousness and values (Levitt & Klassen, 1974; Morin & Garfinkle, 1978). Around the country, various cities and counties passed ordinances prohibiting discrimination against gays in housing and employment. However, a vicious and openly hostile backlash loomed on the horizon.

In 1977 in Dade County Florida, a movement to repeal the county's antidiscriminatory housing and employment ordinance began to gather momentum. In the forefront of the opposition to the ordinance was Anita Bryant, a beauty-contest winner and popular singer. Bryant warned the Dade County citizenry that if they did not repeal the antidiscriminatory ordinance they would soon be living in a contemporary sodomite land. Unexpectedly, the ordinance was repealed overwhelmingly. Buoyed by this initial success, Bryant went on a national spree, warning all who would listen—and there were plenty—of the dangers of homosexuality.

To add more fuel to the antigay fire, a goodly number of psychiatrists recanted their profession's earlier destigmatization of homosexuality and argued that homosexuality was indeed linked to mental illness (Lief, 1977; Smith, 1988). One survey of nearly two thousand five hundred psychiatrists, in fact, found that 69 percent felt homosexuality was a pathological condition, 73 percent believed that gay men were less happy than heterosexual men, 60 percent indicated that gay men were less likely to have mature, loving relationships, and 70 percent viewed a gay male's problems as stemming from personal conflict rather than from social stigmatization (Martin & Hetrick, 1988). Notwithstanding all of the scientific evidence to the contrary, the psychiatric community appeared to step back into the nineteenth century (Brzek & Hubalek, 1988; Ross, Paulsen & Stalström, 1988; Smith, 1988).

Overall then, the 1970s were a kind of seesaw decade that saw large numbers of gays coming out, marching, protesting, and demanding an end to antigay prejudices, whereas some—mostly fundamentalist religious groups—began anew their campaigns against the gays. In other words, the 1970s found gays experiencing some major gains and every now and then the bite of old prejudices.

However, the early 1980s found the strident tones of just a few years earlier much muted as many gays moved back into the shadows as they began to feel a more vitriolic form of prejudice and discrimination. What happened in the space of just a few short years to account for this turnaround not only in the public's sentiment but among the gay community as well can be summed up with one word: AIDS.

Although the 1970s provided a short respite from the centuries-long hatred for gays, today's gay community is once again a target for people's prejudice and discrimination. Source: © James L. Shaffer.

The social gains made during the 1970s were not swept away because some psychiatrists saw gays as pathological nor because some fervent fundamentalists saw them as abominations. No, the gains were lost because of a virus; a virus that quickly became linked inextricably in most people's minds to gays (Altman, 1987; Witt, 1990). AIDS not only sapped its victims of their lives, but also fueled a whole new round of hysterical antigay sentiment among large segments of the public (Walter, 1986). Just when many were beginning to see gays as individuals, not a faceless group thoughtlessly depersonalized with negative stereotypes, a killing virus came along and pushed the clock backward. We will take a closer look at AIDS later in Chapter 16 (Men's Health). Now we want to focus our discussion on some of the more prevalent myths that surround the gay community.

some common myths about gays

Sexual orientation is an either-or condition (males are either heterosexual or homosexual—and never the twain shall meet).

Gay males have a poorly developed or confused masculine gender role identity.

Gay males hate and/or fear women.

Mothers of gay males are overprotective, domineering, and even seductive toward their sons.

Gay males have an insufficient amount of testosterone.

Gay couples usually mimic heterosexual marital relationships (that is, one partner takes the role of "husband" while the other acts out the role of "wife").

Gay males act effeminate in dress and mannerisms, and lesbians act masculine or "butch."

Gays are generally unhappy and/or neurotic people.

Gay teachers are likely to foist their sexual orientation on their students.

Gays are all alike.

As just noted, gays have been the target of discrimination and persecution in most Western societies during the past two thousand years. A majority of North Americans still espouse prejudicial attitudes toward gay people. For example, a majority of adults questioned in a national sample believe that gays are responsible for a loosening of our nation's moral fiber and that the acceptance of homosexuality will eventually lead to our civilization's downfall (Levitt & Klassen, 1974; Storms, 1978). Many believe the frequently repeated contention that the demise of the Greco-Roman civilizations was based solely on their acceptance of homosexuality. One feature that stands out in any survey of people's attitudes toward gays is how little understanding the general public has about gays as individuals and about the gay community (Paul, Weinrich, Gonsiorek & Hotvedt, 1982). Consequently, gays, like most other minority groups, suffer the negative effects of stereotypes, misconceptions, and myths (see "Some Common Myths About Gays"). We will take a close look at several prominent myths pertaining to gays, especially gay males, and present some of the relevant research findings that for the most part debunk these myths (Norton, 1982).

debunking some myths about gays

One myth that persists about gay and straight males alike is that a man is totally and exclusively either heterosexual or homosexual in his sexual orientation. As so often is the case, reality does not match this illusion that sexual behaviors, interests, and orientation fit neatly into a dichotomous, either-or category. However, the erroneous view of a dichotomous male sexuality has endured and been supported through centuries of hostility and violence against gays—more frequently and with greater vigor against gay males than gay females, or lesbians—especially in those countries espousing a Judeo-Christian value system (Katz, 1976).

The Either-Or Perspective on Sexual Orientation

Just over forty years ago, the extent of the "varieties" of male sexual behaviors was systematically reported for the first time. To be exact, the year was 1948 when Alfred Kinsey and his colleagues at Indiana University published their findings from the first large-scale survey of United States males' sexual activities in the monumental *Sexual Behavior in the Human Male*. This work made Kinsey, a professor of biology, both famous for the myth-shattering findings and despised for what some people considered his impropriety in studying such a taboo subject as human sexuality

Homosexuality

figure 13.1
Kinsey's homosexual
rating scale. Adapted from
Alfred C. Kinsey et al., *Sexual
Behavior in the Human Male*
p. 638, 1948. Reproduced by
permission of The Kinsey
Institute for Research in Sex,
Gender, and Reproduction,
Inc.

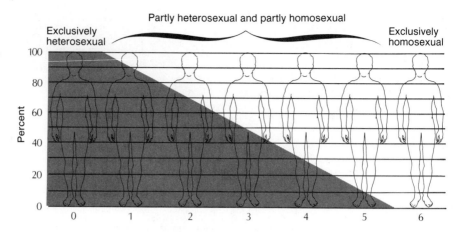

(Minton, 1988). One of the study's more intriguing revelations was that 37 percent of the men interviewed reported having had "some overt homosexual experience to the point of orgasm between adolescence and old age." Thus the commonly accepted belief that only a few men had ever engaged in a homosexual act was shown to be patently false (Chilman, 1983; Kinsey, 1941). Another myth-shattering idea presented in Kinsey's work was that sexual orientation must be defined along a continuum of sexual behaviors and interests rather than in a strict either-or fashion. To this end, Kinsey introduced a seven-point scale, or continuum, ranging from zero, indicating exclusive heterosexual behaviors and interests, to six, indicating exclusive homosexual behaviors and interests (see Figure 13.1). This formulation allowed for a much more precise description of the real varieties of male sexual orientations. For example, a primarily heterosexual male who has had, say, two or three homosexual experiences and now and then fantasizes about a homosexual encounter would rank a one or possibly a two on Kinsey's scale, whereas a primarily gay male who has had intercourse with a female on a few occasions would probably rate a four or five on the scale. Kinsey's pioneering work changed the scientific community's view of sexuality and more importantly of male sexual orientation. However, the average layperson still believes that sexual orientation is an either-or feature of a male's sexual makeup.

To highlight Kinsey's approach toward the continuum of male sexual orientation, let's briefly review the controversial research of sociologist Laud Humphreys (1970). As Kinsey suggested, in the real world people's sexual behaviors and interests do not usually fit into mutually exclusive categories. In order to observe a small minority of men who engage in periodic and impersonal homosexual activity, Humphreys acted as lookout to protect the participants who frequented certain men's rooms (referred to as "tearooms" in the gay community) used for sexual activities. As lookout, Humphreys was able to record the license plates of the participants; much later he visited the car owners in their homes on the pretext of being a survey researcher. Humphreys discovered that a large number of the tearoom trade were in fact married family men who were highly respected in their communities.

Now what are we to make of these men with respect to their sexual orientation? They are certainly not exhibiting what most people assume to be a basic either-or sexual orientation. On Kinsey's scale, these men would rank a two or possibly even a three. Humphrey's research dramatically points out the need for viewing homosexuality as existing along a continuum of varying degrees of sexual behaviors and interests (see Harry, 1990).

A common myth that most people believe is that masculinity and homosexuality are mutually exclusive features of a male's personality. Basically, this myth suggests if a male exhibits a masculine role identity (that is, behaves in appropriate gender-typed ways and expresses appropriate gender-typed attitudes and interests), he certainly cannot be homosexual. Many psychologists and psychiatrists have borrowed this myth and suggested that male homosexuality is the result of a disordered or deficient masculine role identity (Bieber et al., 1962). This view of male homosexuality is based on Sigmund Freud's (1953/1905) inversion model wherein he speculated that male homosexuality stemmed from a boy's "primary feminine identification." Like Freud, others have described male homosexuality as a deficiency in masculine identity, using such phrases to describe the nature of male homosexuality as "a flight from masculinity," "a search for masculinity," "a confession of masculine failure," and "a secret longing to play the female's less demanding role" (Kardiner, 1963; Ovesey, 1969; Ruitenbeek, 1963; Socarides, 1968). What all of these views have in common is the belief that homosexuality results when a boy develops a feminine rather than a masculine role identity (Brown, 1957; Fisher, 1972; Kite & Deaux, 1987).

It's All a Problem of Gender Identity

The idea that male homosexuality is related to a deficient, or inadequately developed, male identity requires we accept certain assumptions about male development. Recall that in Chapter 4 we discussed the persistence of certain assumptions about male gender development, namely, the eleven assumptions that make up what Joseph Pleck called the male gender identity paradigm. Basic to the identity paradigm is the assumption that males have an innate psychological need to develop a masculine gender identity, which according to the male gender identity perspective is a risky and failure-prone undertaking for most males. Recall also that in Pleck's analysis of the identity paradigm, he found little scientific evidence to substantiate the existence for the purported construct of a psychological masculine identity. Furthermore, in a review of the research linking male homosexuality with a deficient male identity, Pleck (1981) found little, if any, actual scientific support for such an assumed relationship (see Troiden, 1989). Thus the belief that gay males possess a deficient psychological masculine identity is just one more myth hampering an understanding of gay males.

Another myth one commonly hears about gay males is that they hate or have an aversion to the opposite gender. According to this myth, all "normal" males are naturally sexually attracted to females and so a male whose sexual orientation is for another man must either hate and/or possibly fear females. Again, theoretical speculation to support the antifemale perspective about gay males abounds. For example, Sandor Ferenczi (1963), a staunch advocate of Freud's views, suggested that gay

Misogyny is the Answer

Homosexuality

males approach women "with pronounced antipathy and not rarely with hatred that is badly, or not at all concealed." Others have followed Ferenczi's lead and suggested that gay males hold a "general contempt . . . for females" (Kardiner, 1963) or that "only men incapacitated for the love of women by their insurmountable fears and resentments become dependent for gratification upon the escape into homogeneous pairs" (Rado, 1963) or that homosexuality stems, at least partially, from "the result of covert but incapacitating fears of the opposite sex" (Meyer, 1975).

The problem with this line of reasoning is that the vast majority of gay males do not exhibit the purported hatred, fear, or aversion toward females many theorists attribute to them. As a matter of fact, the research into the feelings and attitudes gay males have toward females convincingly debunks these notions and shows them to be more akin to myth than to reality. For example, in a series of well-controlled studies, Kurt Freund and his colleagues found gay males as physically attracted (as measured by their penile erections) by pictures of nude females and descriptions of heterosexual intercourse as were heterosexual males (Freund et al., 1973, 1974a, 1974b). As for gay males' attitudes toward women in general, Robert Moore and Gary McDonald (1976) found gay males actually held more positive and egalitarian attitudes toward women and their roles than did heterosexual males.

It's the Mother's Fault Females are often blamed for many if not most of men's problems. Females also seem to be a favorite scapegoat among some social scientists when they explain a male's development and subsequent problems he may suffer (Chodorow, 1974; Dinnerstein, 1976). More to the point of our discussion is a popular notion among some that mothers are somehow responsible for their sons' homosexuality. For example, Meyer (1975) suggests the hatred for women that leads to male homosexuality basically stems from a "mother's overprotective and seductive relationship with her son." Others also have linked a mother's domineering, overprotective, and controlling behaviors as essential ingredients causing male homosexuality (Bieber et al., 1962; Snortum et al., 1969).

However, in studies dealing with normally adjusted (that is, psychologically healthy) gay males, there is no evidence that mothers were seen as cold, rejecting, domineering, or seductive in their relationships with their sons (Robertson, 1972; Siegelman, 1974). Gay males who did perceive their mothers in such negative ways were more likely to exhibit dysfunctional neurotic symptoms. But the same relationship between a male's psychological pathology and his negative views of his mother-son relations were also found in heterosexual males. Therefore, one might conclude that a mother's dominance and control are more likely to be related to a son's psychological health than to his sexual orientation. Again, however, we must be wary of falling into the fault-trap—this time faulting a mother for her sons's psychological adjustment. We could just as well suggest that a male's psychological adjustment is related to his relationship to his father, to his relationships with his peers, or to some other social factors. We should be extremely cautious in labeling any one feature of a man's entire male experience as the root of all his problems—especially when it is so easy and convenient to blame women.

As noted in Chapter 3, many social scientists are looking with interest at the possibility that the male hormone testosterone is an important chemical agent influencing the outcome of the male experience. Thus it should come as no surprise to find some speculating that male homosexuality is the "result of an insufficient proportion of the male sex hormone" (Karlen, 1971; see also Dörner, 1980; Ellis & Ames, 1987; Gladue, Green & Hellman, 1984; Treadwell, 1987). In one of the most frequently cited studies bearing on the possible relationship between testosterone levels and homosexuality, Robert Kolodny (Kolodny, Masters, Hendryx & Toro, 1971) studied the levels of plasma testosterone concentrations in thirty gay males and fifty heterosexual males. Overall, Kolodny found no significant differences in the testosterone levels between these two groups of college males. However, when Kolodny compared the levels of only those gay males who scored a five or six on Kinsey's scale (that is, males with an exclusively homosexual orientation and interests) with the levels of all heterosexual males, he found the gay males' testosterone levels to be significantly lower than heterosexual males' levels.

Kolodny's research spurred a series of studies that tried to replicate his findings. Although some researchers found similar results to Kolodny's most have been unable to confirm Kolodny's data suggesting that exclusive gay males suffered a deficit of testosterone. In fact, in one study the researchers found the plasma testosterone levels significantly *higher* among exclusively gay males than among a comparable group of heterosexual males (Brodie, Gartrell, Doering & Rhue, 1974). Thus the idea that testosterone levels may somehow be linked to homosexuality seems at best a precarious proposition and at worst just another myth, which pretends to explain male homosexuality in terms of a man's chemistry (Doell & Longino, 1988; Gartrell, 1982).

Another persistent myth about gay males is the belief that gay couples who live together play out the traditional roles of "husband" and "wife." The stereotypic view of the gay couple pictures one partner acting out the functions of the traditional husband—the primary breadwinner, the active and dominant partner in sexual activity, and the one responsible for all major decisions. The other partner in the relationship is portrayed as the submissive and passive wife—primarily responsible for the household chores, the passive and submissive partner in sex, and more apt to follow the decisions of the other (Marecek, Finn & Cardell, 1988).

As with the other myths, this one does not stand up to research findings. The idea that one partner is financially responsible for the couple and the other tends to the household chores is just plain nonsense. Actually, most gay couples' live-in relationships find both partners involved in full-time paid employment and sharing the household tasks fairly equally (Bell & Weinberg, 1978). As for sex, gay couples report a fairly equal give-and-take approach to sex. When it comes to who makes the decisions, gay couples generally espouse a fairly egalitarian approach to decision making (Harry, 1988; Spada, 1979). However, the ideal of both partners sharing an equal voice in decisions is not always found in gay relationships—or in most heterosexual relationships for that matter. Researchers have found the gay partner who has the greater resources of money and education is more apt to have the greater say in

It's All in the Hormones

Just Like Husbands and Wives

Homosexuality

the relationship (Harry & De Vall, 1978; Tuller, 1988). One thing seems certain: Most gay couples who live together stress the ideal of equality and role flexibility to a greater degree than do most heterosexual couples (Larson, 1982; Tuller, 1988).

You Can Spot 'Em a Block Away

Many people picture a gay male as decidedly effeminate in dress and mannerisms and a lesbian as decidedly macho or butch in dress and mannerisms. The caricatures of a gay male who talks with an affected lisp, walks with a swishing motion, and gestures exuberantly with a limp wrist and of a lesbian who saunters around in a leather jacket and motorcycle boots are all too common. However, researchers find no evidence whatsoever that most gay males and lesbians exhibit these presumed effeminate behaviors and butch masculinity, respectively (Hotvedt, 1982).

The Miserable Lot

Similarly, many people think of gay males as being unhappy, lacking in self-esteem, and being quite disturbed individuals. It would take several pages to list all of the psychological and psychiatric literature that has detailed the pathology associated with homosexuality. The problem with most of this literature, however, is that it has assumed that heterosexuality is a more "natural" and hence healthier aspect of a male's personality. This "heterosexual bias" in most research on homosexuality has caused researchers and theorists alike to assume that all homosexuals were *de facto* psychological cripples (Morin, 1977). Nevertheless, several studies find little or no evidence that gay males are any more likely to exhibit pathological symptoms than are comparable heterosexual males (Gonsiorek, 1982; Jones & Bates, 1988; Kurdek, 1987; Modrcin & Wyers, 1990).

Protect the Children

During the late 1970s, Anita Bryant and her followers crusaded against gay males and lesbians using as one of their most powerful weapons—the idea that the children of the land were in danger of being coerced into homosexuality. Wherever Bryant spoke, she never failed to charge that gays were always looking for young recruits to snare into their homosexual world. One of the major targets of this vicious slander was gay teachers who were depicted as somehow infusing their classrooms with the sensual lure of homosexuality. Gays were also portrayed as prowling the streets ever watchful for young and impressionable children who could be tempted by the "corrupt and evil" world of homosexuality. Bryant did not seem to care that what she was preaching had little to do with the facts. To the contrary, she seemed more concerned with whipping up the public's sentiment and emotions against all gays. In her attempt to create a strong backlash against gays, she was fairly successful. As a matter of fact, however, gays—as teachers or members of any other profession—do not proselytize their sexual orientation to young children any more than heterosexuals do. For example, when gay teachers speak about their goals in the classroom, they talk of creating an environment in which children can learn and think and grow as intelligent, creative human beings (Trent, 1978). Does that sound like homosexual propaganda? The idea that gays lurk in the shadows or in the hallways or behind desks in our schools, ever watchful for young children whom they can somehow draw into a homosexual life, serves little value except to show just how far some people will go to slander, misrepresent, and mythologize gay people (Norton, 1982).

Every time a person speaks about some group that he or she has little or no contact with or firsthand knowledge of, that person presents a group stereotype, most often an unflattering one. For example, we overhear two males leaning over their beers at a local tavern as one of them pontificates to the other, "You know about those queers, don't you? Hell, those fags are marching in the capital demanding—get that, *demanding*—equal rights! Why, hell, what they need is to be thrown out of the country or maybe into prison. You know what, those sissies are all a bunch of pansies who should be glad guys like you and me don't just up and beat the hell out of 'em!" Even in less vituperative discussions, most people lump all gays into one category as if they had all come out of some assembly-line punch press. It should go without saying, but researchers have found that gays—like all groups that are easy prey for homogeneous labels (for example, African Americans, Chicanos, Asians, and women)—have been found to vary among themselves in every possible way (Paul, 1982; Paul & Weinrich, 1982). Most gay males do not fit the stereotype of effeminate hairdressers who lure children, live miserable and disturbed lives, and psychologically speaking, are more likely to identify with females than with males. Clearly, none of the stereotypes that have grown into cultural myths are true for the vast majority of gay people.

There seem to be two reasons for so many myths growing around gays and the gay community. First, most heterosexuals have never taken the time to examine their own fears of homosexuality. Second, they have never bothered to learn the fact that just because another person has a different sexual orientation does not mean that he or she does not have the same needs, desires, and problems common to *all* human beings. The myths about gays will continue to hold sway in many people's minds as long as gays are seen as "deviants" and "unnatural" rather than as human beings who want to find love and intimacy with another human being who happens to be of the same sex.

We now turn our attention away from the myths about gay males and focus on that special human phenomenon in which two people seek mutual satisfaction, find acceptance and companionship, and experience sexual gratification, namely, the intimate relationship between two people who happen to be gay (De Cecco, 1988). We will focus our discussion in this section on two different and yet interrelated aspects of the intimate gay relationship: the physical (physical aspects of gay sex, frequency of gay sexual contact, and the sexually exclusive versus the sexually open relationship) and the psychological (commitment, satisfaction, and love within a long-term intimate gay relationship). Naturally, we do not mean to imply that any intimate relationship between two people—either gays or heterosexuals—can be so easily reduced into its physical and psychological spheres, but such an admittedly arbitrary division does allow us to understand better the patterns and dynamics of intimate gay relationships.

In 1979 famed sex-researchers William Masters and Virginia Johnson published their eagerly awaited physiological study on gay sexual practices, *Homosexuality in Perspective*. Beginning in 1964 and ending in 1968, 176 gays (94 men and 82 women) and 567 male and female heterosexuals performed various sexual activities under the watchful gaze of scientists and movie cameras. As in their previous studies, Masters and Johnson quickly cautioned the reader not to go too far with their findings because of the possibility that people, no matter their sexual orientation, may act quite differently in front of an audience than they would behind closed doors. However, Masters and Johnson's study reveals some interesting insights into the varieties and various sexual techniques found among gay and heterosexual couples.

Obviously, many kinds of sexual activities between gays are similar to those between heterosexuals. Almost everyone kisses, caresses, and experiences orgasm to a similar degree. However, setting aside the similarities, Masters and Johnson found several striking differences in the ways gays and heterosexuals went about their sexual activities.

Long-standing gay couples, or those who had lived together for at least a year, seemed quite in tune with each other's sexual needs, wants, and pleasures. By and large, gay couples engaged in longer periods of sexual foreplay than did heterosexuals and did not seem eager to reach orgasm quickly. During this extended foreplay, many gay couples talked a great deal to each other, giving subtle cues as to what pleased them sexually. When orgasm was reached, it occurred by means of mutual masturbation, fellatio (oral stimulation of the penis), anal penetration, or some combination thereof. A majority of the gay couples reported enjoying a variety of sexual activities and techniques. Interestingly, some gay men experienced heterosexual fantasies during homosexual activity. So much for the purported hatred and/or fear of women thought to afflict gay males.

What may be even more enlightening than the fact that some gay males have heterosexual fantasies are some of the study's findings about the heterosexuals' lovemaking activities. For the most part, the heterosexual men observed by Masters and Johnson seemed almost obsessed with reaching orgasm. In the minds of most of the heterosexual males, sex seemed to be goal oriented; that is, the final objective—their own orgasm—was the most important element of their sexual activity. Sexual foreplay such as prolonged kissing, caressing, and massaging their partner was nearly absent in many heterosexual couples or little more than a series of prescribed motions that had to be performed before the men got down to the real business at hand—penetration and ejaculation. Many heterosexual men in this study showed little sensitivity or knowledge for that matter of the "little things" that would excite and stimulate their female partner. Communication between heterosexual couples was considerably less than the communication that Masters and Johnson found among their gay couples. Not surprisingly, heterosexual females also showed little awareness of the varieties of male genital stimulation that could be employed during periods of sexual foreplay. Overall, the lack of communication and the resulting ignorance about his or her partner's likes and dislikes appeared to be a major stumbling block in a majority of the heterosexual couples' sexual activities. Another interesting note about the heterosexual men studied was that several reported having homosexual fantasies during their sexual activity.

Without going too far in generalizing from such small samples that were observed under what most would agree were very unusual conditions, two features stand out about the sexual activities of long-term gay and heterosexual couples.

First, gay couples seem more knowledgeable and sensitive when it comes to each other's physical needs and wants than do heterosexual couples. Second, heterosexual men, at least those studied in this research, seem to approach sex with their minds focused primarily on their own orgasm. Little wonder then that many women complain to one another about their husband's callousness when it comes to his wife's sexual needs (see Brannock & Chapman, 1990).

Many people believe gay males are insatiable in their sexual appetites (another myth some people want to perpetuate). The fact of the matter is that gay couples have sexual relations with about the same frequency or maybe a little more than do heterosexual couples (Larson, 1982; Peplau & Amaro, 1982; Peplau & Gordon, 1983). In a sample of gay males studied by researchers Karla Jay and Allen Young, 11 percent of the gays surveyed reported having sex daily with their partners, 38 percent engaged in sexual relations three to four times a week, 40 percent one to two times a week, and 11 percent had sex less than once a week. Bell and Weinberg's sample of 574 white gay males presents a wider range of sexual frequencies, with the following percentages: Three percent reported no sexual activity in the past year, 3 percent only once or a few times in the past year, 3 percent every other month, 17 percent two to three times a month, 32 percent once a week, 30 percent two to three times a week, 13 percent four to six times a week, and 4 percent seven times or more a week. Approximately half of the gay males in both samples reported having sex on an average of one to three times a week. It seems that sex between two people on the average of one to three times per week is not sufficient evidence to suggest that gay males are sexual satyrs.

Does an intimate relationship require the two parties to remain sexually "faithful" to each other? The answer to this question seems to depend on the two parties (Clark, 1992; Long, 1994). Gay males are often portrayed as less committed to the ideal of sexual exclusivity than are heterosexuals, and researchers have found this to be the case. In other words, gay males are less likely to remain monogamous in their relationships than are heterosexuals or lesbians for that matter (Bell & Weinberg, 1978; Harry & Lovely, 1979; Peplau & Cochran, 1988; Plummer, 1978). However, heterosexual husbands are more likely to have more extramarital relations than are their wives (Blumstein & Schwartz, 1983; Hunt, 1974; Pietropinto & Simenauer, 1979). Thus if gay and heterosexual males are more likely to seek sexual relationships outside their "primary" relationships than are lesbians and heterosexual women, one might conclude that the promiscuity found among gay males is more a factor of their maleness than of their sexual orientation. In the words of one gay male,

> Promiscuity is inbred in all boy children, and since most boy children don't find out they're gay until later in life, their promiscuity has nothing to do with their gayness. It has to do with their *male*ness. (Mendola, 1980, p. 55)

In summary, long-term gay couples seem to have an enjoyable and mutually satisfying sex life, with much of the credit going to their ability and/or willingness to communicate with each other about their physical needs and wants and their approach to sexual relations as more than an occasion for an orgasm. Furthermore, the frequency of sexual activity among gay couples appears to fall across a wide spectrum, ranging from daily sexual encounters to over a year's abstinence. Finally, gay males seem less committed to sexual exclusivity in their primary relations, but this is more likely a feature of their being socialized males than of their being gay.

The Psychological Side of Gay Relationships

Most would agree that it is much easier to gather data on the frequency of and techniques used in sexual encounters between people than it is to plumb the psychological components (such as personal joy, satisfaction, happiness, commitment, and love) of an intimate relationship. As we have already noted, gay males are thought by many to be bereft of such psychological intangibles in their lives and in their intimate relationships. The myth of the lonely gay male endlessly cruising for quick and impersonal sex still persists. However, research casts serious doubt on such a generalization. In several studies, the percentages of lesbians and gay males reporting their involvement in long-term and personally satisfying relationships approximates 75 and 50 percent, respectively (Peplau & Gordon, 1983; Peplau, 1988). Even so, some people still insist that what gay couples experience certainly is not real satisfaction and love, at least not like that found among many heterosexual couples.

How then does one measure satisfaction and love in a relationship? One way is to ask each person if he or she finds satisfaction, happiness, and feelings of loving and being loved with his or her partner. Researchers who have asked gay men and lesbians to respond to such questions have been virtually unable to differentiate between gay couples' and heterosexual couples' responses on various measures of satisfaction, liking, and love in their relationships.

But what about the values thought essential to and the priorities involved in intimate relationships? Do gays have different concerns, values, and personal priorities in their relationships than do heterosexuals? Social psychologist Letitia Anne Peplau and several of her associates investigated the values and priorities within gay and heterosexual relationships and found some interesting answers to these questions. During the late 1970s, Peplau studied the responses given by 127 lesbians, 128 gay men, and 65 male and 65 female heterosexuals to a lengthy questionnaire. Peplau asked her samples to rank on a scale from one to nine the importance of certain features associated with personal relationships. Her findings showed some striking similarities and differences between gays and heterosexuals and—what may be more significant to the issue of intimate relationships—between males and females in general, no matter their sexual orientation (Kurdek, 1988b, 1988c; Kurdek & Schmitt, 1986).

The major difference between gays' and heterosexuals' priorities in their relationships revolve around the issue of sexual fidelity or sexual exclusivity. Both heterosexual males and females place significantly greater importance on the value of remaining sexually faithful than do gay men and lesbians. We might explain this difference by noting the not-so-subtle social pressures for sexual faithfulness that are placed on married heterosexual couples by the institutions of marriage and religion. For the most part, gay couples do not "contract" their primary relationships in the same way that most heterosexual couples do. Furthermore, many married heterosexual couples remain faithful—and thus espouse faithfulness as a value—not because of a personal commitment to the relationship but rather, for example, because of the children, joint properties, and the expenses involved in costly divorce settlements. These "barriers" are nearly nonexistent in most gay relationships, and thus gays have fewer pressures to remain sexually faithful other than their own personal inclination to do so (Foa et al., 1987).

What may be more significant about Peplau's research is the degree to which the sexes, no matter their sexual orientation, differed with respect to certain values and priorities they felt important in their intimate relationships. Most striking among these differences was the generally greater importance females—both heterosexuals and lesbians—placed on having egalitarian relationships, having a supportive group of friends, sharing similar political attitudes with their partner, and having their own career. Most of these values appear to have a decidedly feminist overtone. (Recall that Peplau gathered her data in the late 1970s and thus most of her female respondents probably had been exposed to feminist issues, if not by being involved in the feminist movement itself then at least through various media presentations.) Feminists have argued that women must have an equal voice in matters relating to their intimate relationships, have their own group of friends and not rely only on their partner as their major conduit to other friendships, and have their own career interests. It would seem, at least among Peplau's female samples, that the feminist perspective has influenced the ordering of priorities in intimate relations among many females.

The one value that all of the groups ostensibly agreed on as a significant one for a loving relationship was being able to communicate intimate feelings to their partner. The ability and willingness to share feelings, thoughts, and concerns was judged by almost everyone in Peplau's study to be an essential ingredient in a loving and involved partnership. What is somewhat surprising about this almost unanimous valuing of communication skills is the fact that in Masters and Johnson's research on sexual intimacies, heterosexual couples were lacking in respect to communicating their feelings and desires about sexual matters. It would seem that although most people agree that communication is an extremely important element in an intimate relationship, some are more adept at it than others, at least in certain respects (Lee, 1988).

Traditionally, most males have felt extremely uneasy and some downright hostile about the issue of homosexuality. The reasons for homophobia among most males are, of course, debatable (Herek, 1984a, 1984b). Rather than suggest that homophobia springs from some unconscious homosexual urge within males, we tend to think that most males have been taught to hate anything even vaguely feminine as part of the male role. Because gay males are often viewed by heterosexuals as being feminine, they become targets for a "real man's" hatred and derision. Furthermore, the social forces reinforcing hatred toward gay people are plentiful; not the least of these is the Judeo-Christian portrayal of gays as wanton and lustful sinners. In addition, a number of other myths have grown up around gays and the gay community. Myths tend to distort and falsify reality, and thus most people do not have a clear understanding of the gay person.

Recent social psychological research has tended to demystify gays and to show them to be human beings whose psychological needs and wants are for all intents and purposes identical to those of heterosexuals. Possibly because of what we have learned recently about gay relationships and their apparent lack of traditionally restrictive male and female roles, heterosexuals would be wise to take a lesson or two from gays in order to improve relationships between the sexes.

important terms	Homophobia *224*
	Homosexuality *224*
	Mattachine society *226*
	Stonewall *226*

suggested readings	Blumenfeld, W. J. (Ed.). (1992). *Homophobia*. Boston: Beacon Press.
	Clark, J. M. (1992). Men's studies, feminist theology, and gay male sexuality. *The Journal of Men's Studies, 1,* 125-155.
	De Cecco, J. (Ed.). (1988). *Gay relationships*. New York: Harrington Park Press.
	Duberman, M., Vicinus, M., & Chauncey, Jr., G. (Eds.). (1990). *Hidden from history: Reclaiming the gay and lesbian past*. New York: Meridian.
	Mohr, R. D. (1992). *Gay ideas. Outing and other controversies*. Boston: Beacon Press.
	Paul, W., et al. (Eds.). (1982). *Homosexuality: Social, psychological, and biological issues*. Beverly Hills, CA: Sage.
	Plant, R. (1986). *The pink triangle: The Nazi war against homosexuals*. New York: Henry Holt.

Chapter 14

Men of Color

It is difficult to think of a more controversial role in American society than that of the black male. He is a visible figure on the American scene, yet the least understood and studied of all sex-race groups in the United States. His cultural image is usually one of several types: the sexual superstud, the athlete, and the rapacious criminal. That is how he is perceived in the public consciousness, interpreted in the dominant media and ultimately how he comes to see and internalize his own role. Rarely are we exposed to his more prosaic role as worker, husband, father and American citizen.

Robert Staples (1982)

In the United States the word [macho] is meant to be insulting and degrading to men. It has no other meanings, as it does in Latin America, to soften its intent. The word became popular with the feminist movement and their attempt to undo some of the negative characteristics of masculinity and became a serviceable catch-all word. Hispanic men, regrettably, have often been thought of as macho, which places us in a negative light in this country.

Ramiro Valdez (1986)

[W]hile male dominance is only a polite fiction in most Japanese homes, it is an overwhelming reality in professional and public life. As a result, from birth on male children in Japan get favored treatment.

Robert Christopher (1983)

In order for employment to qualify as "real work," it must be "hard" in a physical sense. It must be marginal and not of the line of what is perceived as the "ordinary" work that North American men find themselves engaged in. Finally, for a Mohawk man, work must be dangerous, or pose some challenge to the skills of climbing, balance and steadiness. These qualities have characterized the work of Kahnawake men since the foundation of the settlement in 1667. Today at Kahnawake "real work" is ironwork.

David Blanchard (1983)

The United States as melting pot—an overly used but somewhat descriptive metaphor suggestive of a country where people of every class, creed, and color with their different customs have melded together to create a new culture. However, the United States is not now and never was some kind of homogenized culture where people from around the globe somehow softened their prickly differences into a new kind of supraculture. Since its beginning, one and only one racial-ethnic group has dominated and become the standard for others to emulate, namely, Western Europeans.

Throughout much of the previous discussions, we've enumerated several rather generalized features related to most North American males' gender role—with the exception of the discussion in Chapter 6 on pretechnological societies. However, we should not forget that some North America males experience their masculinity and their male roles somewhat differently from those prescribed by the dominant Euro-American ethos. Not surprisingly then, many social scientists have grown cautious of making generalizations or treating certain social patterns as universals when only the dominant group has been studied. Some men's studies scholars have followed suit and begun to study how minority status, for instance, influences a man's sense of masculinity.

We need to understand how being a member of a minority ethnic-racial group affects men's lives. Such analyses should lead us to yet another consideration, namely, there is no one masculine template for all males to follow. Rather, conceivably, there are as many male templates or masculine types as there are identifiable racial, ethnic, and class identities.

In this chapter we want to rectify the predominately "white-Anglo" bias that permeates much of the research reported in earlier chapters. Consequently, we will highlight four racial-ethnic minority groups. In turn, then, we will focus on various features of the male role found among the African-American, the Hispanic, the Asian-American, and the Native American males.

the african-american man: an endangered species

Since the 1970s, a growing number of African-American scholars and journalists have dealt with the "African-American male" and his experience of masculinity in a white-dominated culture (Evans & Whitfield, 1988; Gary, 1981; Monroe, 1987; Staples, 1978, 1982, 1986a). A chilling theme permeates many of these analyses: African-American men in the United States occupy a significantly higher-risk or more vulnerable status when compared to other male groups (Gary & Leashore, 1982; Hatter & Wright, 1993). Some would even argue that African-American males are fast becoming an "endangered species" (Gibbs, 1987; Jones, 1986; Leavy, 1983). Although calling African-American males "endangered" might sound like so much hyperbole, Lawrence Gary (1987, p. 232), Director of Urban Affairs at Howard University, recently stated the case for such concern over the "plight of the black man" by noting they "have higher rates of morbidity, mortality, incarceration, and criminal victimization than have white men and women and black women." Furthermore, if we listen to African-American men recount their experiences, their words have an ominous ring to them as they recount how others fear, suspect, and remain hostile toward African-American males (Jones, 1988).

warning: being african american and male could be hazardous to one's health

I was born a suspect, came out of my mother's stomach, anything that happened within a three-block radius I was the suspect. White America is so scared of black teenagers, I walk down the streets, and women are like grabbing ahold of their mace, and everybody's tucking in their chains, everybody's getting in their car doors, and big 300-pound white guys start flexing, trying to scare me. First of all, I weigh 120 pounds soaking wet, holding a brick. I asked this white guy for the time and he gave me his watch.

*Young male comic**

I was skating once with a group of my white friends, and I was separated from them a little bit, I was doing something else. And a policeman walked over to me and he pushed me against the wall, and he took out his club and he was like, "What do you think, you're like them? Do you think you have the privileges they do?" He said, "I know them, but I don't know you. I think you'd better get off this property." And he actually kicked me out of the place.

*Jamil Toure** (fifteen-year-old male living in New York City)*

I was on 86th Street, and I was walking around looking for a friend. I decided to go home, because I couldn't find him. So when I went into the train station—and from behind—I guess a plainclothes policeman grabbed me and threw me up against the wall. And all of a sudden I was getting pushed around and a woman policeman was calling me names—I don't know—like scum—I don't know—just some—she thought I was a criminal. And so they handcuffed me and they took me down to the station. [At the police station, several officers accused him of] following old people, [as if] I was going to mug them, and . . . had. And they showed me a picture of some guy who looked nothing like me, but he was black.

*Kamau Patton** (a tenth-grader at one of New York City's most prestigious high schools)*

Beyond a shadow of a doubt, being black and male in the United States is hazardous to one's health because black males in America continue to face disproportionate dangers—both outside and within the black community—well into the 1980s.

Clyde W. Franklin II, sociologist (1987, p. 155)

Black men are six times as likely as white men to be murder victims. We are two and a half times as likely to be unemployed. We finish last in practically every socioeconomic measure from infant mortality to life expectancy. . . . Black men in America seem almost an endangered species.

Sylvester Monroe, journalist (1987, p. 55)

*Source: Quotes taken from a report aired on the *MacNeil/Lehrer NewsHour,* January 18, 1988.

Although being an African-American man in our society today brings with it numerous problems, few can deny the positive social contributions and important consciousness-raising that public figures like David Wilder, Jesse Jackson, Andrew Young, David Dinkins, Spike Lee, Nelson Mandela and Bishop Desmond Tutu have made in the past few years. And what about the many positive television images of African-American men? Throughout the 1980s Bill Cosby gave a whole new meaning to fatherhood with his portrayal of Cliff Huxtable. In the 1990s, Tony Brown continues to chart the frontiers of African-American consciousness on his weekly public television show "Tony Brown's Journal" and both Bryant Gumble and Ed Bradley are widely respected as skilled television interviewers (see Waters & Huck, 1988). However, in a recent analysis of the media, Ronald Hall (1993) takes the television industry and Hollywood to task for what he sees as their overall unflattering portrayal of the African-American man. Thus, although a majority of African-American men daily combat the insidious effects of poverty, unemployment, and racism, a growing number are presenting images that all men can applaud and emulate (see Harris & Majors, 1993).

Let's now focus on several important features related to the African-American male's gender experience.

Men of Color

Stimulated by the civil rights agenda for full equality, the African-American community found itself a focus of considerable social attention during the early 1960s. Researchers, theorists, and social pundits from every social school and political ilk were soon noting that African-American institutions, especially the African-American family, were in serious trouble. (For a discussion on early research into the African-American family, see Allen, 1978.) Soon the African-American family was portrayed as caught in a "tangle of pathology." Casting the African-American family as "pathological," for all intents and purposes, can be laid to a single document, the now-famous Moynihan Report.

In 1965, then head of the United States Department of Labor's Office of Planning and Research, sociologist turned United States senator, Daniel P. Moynihan argued that most of the problems found in African-American families (e.g., welfare dependency, school dropouts, out-of-wedlock children), arose out of an excessive degree of female dominance, a kind of **"African-American matriarchy,"** if you will, found within African-American families. In other words, as Moynihan saw it, a major problem facing most African-American families was that they were dominated by their women and not their men. Not surprisingly, the notion of an "African-American matriarchy" within African-American families has been refuted by African-American scholars (Staples, 1977). Nonetheless, the "Moynihan thesis" on an "African-American matriarchy" soon caused a controversy between those who laid responsibility for much of the African-American communities' problems on their womenfolk and those who fingered racism as the true culprit undercutting the African-American community (Staples, 1986b).

What does a debate over whether African-American women have the upper hand in African-American families have to do with African-American men? The reason for noting this issue here is that a majority of social scientists writing during this period (circa 1960s and 1970s) consciously or unconsciously accepted the tenets of the male gender identity paradigm (see Chapter 4). Recall that the gender identity model of masculine development argued that a male's development was particularly risky and that any number of things could go wrong. Specifically, this perspective contended if a male's gender identity was undermined or disturbed, he would, in all probability, develop in "unmanly" ways.

A concern expressed by many during this time, then, was over the "unnatural" or dominant influence an African-American mother could have over her son. Consequently, when people decried the influence of the "African-American matriarchy," many were suggesting African-American males suffered far more problems in their masculinity than white males. In other words, African-American males were generally thought less secure in their masculine identity, as evidenced by various masculine hang-ups (e.g., hyperaggressivity), than white males. The cause for the African-American males' masculine identity problems was attributed to their being stifled by overly dominant mother figures. Thus a fallout for much of the discussion of the "pathology" associated with African-American families landed squarely on the backs of African-American males who were seen as suffering from all kinds of insecurities in their masculinity. For most of these years then, African-American males have not only suffered from racist ideology but have also been burdened with the notion that their masculine identity was extremely tenuous because of the influence of their "overly dominant" mothers.

Viewing the African-American family as pathological is not only ridiculous but it serves no useful purpose and, many could argue, has only created further complications, especially for African-American men and their relations with African-American women (Asante, 1981; Braithwaite, 1981). Most would agree that relationships with the opposite sex are an important ingredient in experiencing one's gender. Thus it seems a worthwhile venture to view just what kind of relationships exist between African-American men and women in our society.

How do African-American men look upon African-American women? Are African-American men more liberal in their definitions of gender roles than white males? Are African-American male-female relationships plagued with more problems than white male-female relationships? Let's begin at the top of the list by noting how African-American men view women.

African-American Men's and Women's Relations

Are African-American men more chauvinistic—more sexist—toward women and more conventional in how they define men's and women's roles both in the home and at work than comparable white men? Not wishing to muddy up the issue, the available research and discussions are rather equivocal on these topics (Hatchett & Quick, 1983). On the one hand, some argue that African-American men hold more conservative attitudes (sexist?) toward how the genders should behave (Gackenbach, 1978; Scanzoni, 1975; Staples, 1979, 1982; Wallace, 1979; Williams, 1980), whereas others claim African-American men are more egalitarian toward gender roles than white men (Beckett, 1976; Ten Houten, 1970). If such contradictions weren't enough, along come still others who argue that African-American men and white men are really quite similar in how they look at gender role behavior—both groups leaning toward less traditional or more egalitarian attitudes toward how each gender should behave (Gary, 1987; Lyson, 1986; Rao & Rao, 1985). Finding African-American and white men holding similar attitudes toward gender roles shouldn't come as a surprise, however, when we note that many of these latter studies focused on African-American and white college males. The similarity here could then stem from a college education's liberalizing effect on its students' attitudes on a variety of social issues. Interestingly, when we examine contemporary African males (e.g., Zimbabweans), even those in college, we find they hold very conservative attitudes toward how each gender should act (McMaster, 1985). Given the conflicting results of the many studies dealing with African-American men's attitudes toward women and their proper role, can any sense come out of such a jumble?

Recently, Noel Cazenave and George Leon (1987) described that much of the confusion over whether African-American men are more traditional or modern than white men stems from the inherent problem of dichotomizing the expectations of the male role into either/or categories (e.g., instrumental or expressive, traditional

African-American Men and the Provider Role

Men of Color

or modern, achievers or nurturers). Focusing their research primarily on middle-class African Americans and whites, Cazenave and Leon found that, generally speaking, white middle-class men emphasize the more expressive aspects of their male role (e.g., sharing emotions, being more nurturant), whereas African-American middle-class men emphasize a more instrumental approach to their male role (e.g., work hard, be a good provider).

To explain their findings, Cazenave and Leon have postulated two perspectives that describe some of the differences found in what African-American and white men emphasize in their male role enactments. Specifically, white middle-class males approach their male role expectations from what Cazenave and Leon call a *majority-status maintenance* perspective. Because white middle-class males occupy a dominant position in society, much of their effort to prove their masculinity is directed toward maintaining the status quo and their resulting male privileges. In a sense, then, because white middle-class males do not have to overextend themselves in traditional ways to prove their manhood (e.g., become overachievers at work), they can afford to be more expressive, less traditional in their male role behaviors (e.g., sensitive and caring for others).

On the other hand, Cazenave and Leon contend that African-American middle-class males exhibit (what they call) a *minority-status attainment* approach in performing their male role. Being a minority member, with few privileges, forces most middle-class African-American men to work especially hard to attain the highly desired "good life." To accomplish this, African-American men, especially those moving into the middle class, place special importance on the provider role. As Cazenave and Leon see it:

> Black males . . . differ substantially from the white respondents in the degree of their emphasis on the provider role for men because of a history many blacks have shared of difficulty in providing adequately for their families, even when they were fortunate to have regular employment. (p. 251)

One interesting feature coming out of Cazenave and Leon's work is the relatively greater value African-American men and women place on an African-American man being a career success compared to white men and women. That an African-American man should achieve success in a career fits well with the notion that middle-class African-American men are driven to attain an upwardly mobile status, whereas many white men simply want to maintain their already privileged status.

The Young African-American Man and the Manhood Hustle

Recently, sociologist Robert Staples (1982, p. 136), a noted authority on African-American men, posed a troubling question: "How can we account for the fact that black male children consistently perform below grade level at a rate twice as high as black females in the public schools?" Following Staples's lead, why is it so many African-American males graduate from high school unable to read and write well enough to pass a college entrance exam? Or why have more than a few African-American male college athletes been unable to get anything more than menial work after graduation? Does the problem lie with a school system that historically has spent less on educating minority children? Granted, the educational system does bear more than its share for not providing a quality education for all. However, other social forces have conspired to push young African-American males down a path of few opportunities. Let's focus here on just one, but one that has done more than its share of damage to African-American men.

A few years ago sociologist Harry Edwards described a prevalent peer group-reinforced message called the **manhood hustle.** Essentially, the manhood hustle is a dream, a distant achievement many young African-American males talk about—a dream of making it big, of being a success, of having it all. Now wanting to be a success is not to be shunned, most of us do aspire to distant goals. The problem encountered in the manhood hustle is the promise held out to so many African-American male youths to seek their future fame, success, money, others' respect not in the normal ways of pursuing a career in science, business, or some skilled trade. No, success, according to the manhood hustle, is found in being a star athlete, for example, an achievement that few males of any race can reach. Edwards, himself an Olympic star and now a respected teacher-scholar at the University of Southern California, put the athletic aspect of the manhood hustle in perspective when he noted that "perhaps three million black youths between thirteen and twenty-two are dreaming of careers as professional athletes. But, the odds against them are at least 20,000 to 1" (Staples, 1982, p. 137).

For so many young African-American males, to be a success in school brings anything but honor. To be accepted by one's peers, an African-American man often as not must demonstrate "his masculine prowess in terms of sexual conquests, athletic success or fighting" (Staples, 1982, p. 138). A separate but related aspect of the manhood hustle can be seen in a type of enactment put on by many young African-American men known as the cool pose.

The "Cool Pose"

Recently, Richard Majors (1986, 1989; Majors & Billson, 1992) described a prevalent coping or defense mechanism employed by many African-American men who must find an alternative "masculine style" from that one embodied in the dominant, middle-class culture's expressions of masculinity (e.g., achieve a good paying job, be a success in one's work, buy a home, send children to camp, own a station wagon). For many African-American men—especially those in the lower socioeconomic groups—have learned to posture or pose themselves as if to tell everyone who sees them, "Hey, look at me, I'm somebody!" when the whole world seems to conspire to scream in their face "You're a nobody!" Majors (1986, p. 5) has noted that because most African-American men sensed early on "to mistrust the words and actions of dominant white people, black males have learned to make great use of 'poses' and 'postures' which connote control, toughness, and detachment." Speaking about the need to be cool, Majors (1989, p. 85) pointed out that:

> Being cool is a unique response to adverse social, political and economic conditions. Cool provides control, inner strength, stability and confidence. Being cool, illustrated in its various poses and postures, becomes a very powerful and necessary tool in the black men's constant fight for his soul. The poses and postures of cool guard, preserve and

protect his pride, dignity and respect to such an extent that the black male is willing to risk a great deal for it. One black male said it well: 'The white man may control everything about me—that is, except my pride and dignity. That he can't have. That is mine and mine alone.'

Needless to say, the **cool pose** is not without its cost. The "cool" African-American man must always maintain his "manly" posture for fear others may think him less than a manly man. He must never appear vulnerable for fear of being ridiculed or humiliated by others. Also, there may be a cost in the kinds of relations a cool African-American man can have with others, say, with a special woman or a special male friend. Although one's friends and lovers may accept his cool pose as a part of his identity, there may be times when such a contrived and controlled posture is bound to prevent him from letting down his guarded pose, relaxing, and just being himself.

The cool pose doesn't always work, or at least, doesn't always work well. A cool and posturally defiant African-American man is little more than a caricature reinforcing, of all things, the very version of masculinity epitomized by white society for decades (e.g., no emotional expression, avoid nurturant qualities, denigrate and abuse females). Although being cool may provide an African-American man some protection from the onslaughts of racism, being cool reinforces all the negative qualities of the dominant, white man's supermasculine role. Thus being cool may be a way to show contempt for all the racist aspects of white society while providing little, if any, relief from the damaging demands of an outmoded view of what being a man means.

Overall then, what can we say of the African-American man's male experience today? What does being a man mean to most African-American males in a white-dominated society? Are African-American men moving increasingly toward greater problems, or are there signs of positive change? Will African-American male youths turn to education as a means to succeed or to the ever-present hustles found on every corner in the guise of easy money with drugs or the dream of being a superstar?

Recently, Susan Taylor (1985), editor in chief of *Essence* magazine, described the plight of what many African-American men are going through these days. Although not overly optimistic, Taylor's views about the majority of African-American men living in a racist society are essentially a tribute to the courage of all those African-American men who have not given in or been vanquished by a system that has conspired to emasculate them.

Let's be real. There's a war on Black people in America. And the cannons are pointed directly at our men. Pain has been the central theme in our brothers' lives. They've been whipped, shackled, locked up, strung out, castrated physically and mentally. Yet through all their suffering, and without the benefits of quality education or international alliances to shore them up or financial stability passed from prior generations or any positive messages from media that affirm them, our men have waged a courageous battle for the freedom of Black people. They've managed to survive despite the sophistication of the forces arrayed against them.

If Black men seem to be losing ground today, it's that they're weary and wounded from trying to thrive in a society that is determined they won't.

I'm not an apologist for Black men. Like most sisters, I've had my share of blues with the brothers. And in retrospect it was often because they were struggling with their own lives.

Today, as I travel this nation, in every city I see the pain and confusion of our brothers as they huddle in alleys, on corners—out of work—or driving taxis, delivering the mail, doctoring, struggling to stay afloat in corporate America. Struggling to *feel* like men.

the hispanic man: macho personified

Spanish-speaking people living in the United States number about 15 million. Although Spanish-speaking people, or Hispanics, share a number of common characteristics (e.g., most are poor, most live in the Southwest, and most have been raised Roman Catholic), considerable diversity also exists among this multinational ethnic group. Hispanics come from several different countries all with very different histories and traditions. A quick tally of the different national origins of Hispanic-Americans and their numbers will prove this point.

For instance, Chicanos, or Mexican-Americans, make up the largest number of Hispanics (approximately 8.7 million), followed by the Puerto Ricans (near 2 million), then the Cubans (almost 1 million), with the remaining 3 million divided among a number of Spanish-speaking countries in Central and South America. For many reasons (not the least of which are the Catholic ban against birth control, the large number of Hispanic females of childbearing age, and the continual flow of new immigrants, both legal and illegal) Hispanics are expected to become the largest minority group within the United States by the first decade or so of the next century (Bureau of the Census, 1985; Moore & Pachon, 1985; Ramirez, 1988).

In the discussion that follows, we will focus our attention on two aspects of the Hispanic male experience—his role in the family as husband and father and the controversial and often misunderstood issue of machismo.

The Hispanic Husband and Father

Most early Hispanic family studies (circa 1940s and into the early 1970s) presented an unflattering view—some would call it little more than blatant Anglo bias—of the Hispanic male and female (Amaro, Russo & Pares-Avila, 1987; Senour, 1977). For instance, Hispanic husbands were often portrayed as domineering and overbearing in their relations with their wives and children. Several studies cast the husband-father as little more than a "lord and master" within the family where his every wish was law. Wives, for their part, were totally dominated and little more than a husband's childbearer or a convenient mistress to be frequented by an oversexed male (Humphrey, 1944; Jones, 1948; Steward, 1956; Stycos, 1955). Casting Hispanic males only in domineering roles and females as totally submissive creatures simply reinforced a very common and, we would add, a particularly negative stereotype of the Hispanic family. To illustrate such an unflattering portrayal of a Hispanic family, listen to Alvin Rudoff's (1971) description of a "typical" Chicano family.

> The family constellation is an unstable one as the father is seen as withdrawn and the mother as a self-sacrificing and saintly figure. The Mexican-American has little concern for the future, perceives himself as predestined to be poor and subordinate, is still influenced by magic, is gang-minded, distrusts women, sees authority as arbitrary, tends to be passive and dependent, and is alienated from the Anglo culture.

Men of Color

One would be hard pressed to think of a Hispanic family in other than negative ways after reading that description. Along similar lines, some years ago William Madsen (1973) described a Chicano man as likened to, of all things, a "rooster." Madsen portrayed a Chicano man as "one who can drink more, defend himself best, have more sex relations, and have more sons borne by his wife" (p. 22). Overall then, we can say that most of the early research on Hispanic families, especially the men, presented a pejorative or highly unflattering view with few redeeming qualities to be found among Hispanic males and females. (For critiques of these early Hispanic studies, see Staples & Mirandé, 1986; Vazquez-Nuttall, Romero-Garcia & De Leon, 1987.)

Due to a heightened "minority" consciousness that developed in the 1960s, though, Hispanic scholars began to question many of the negative conceptions of Hispanic families that had pervaded much of the earlier research (Mirandé, 1977, 1985; Montiel, 1970; Zinn, 1989). Correcting for the Anglo bias as well as the lack of sensitivity and ethnocentrism that infused much of the earlier work, some contended that "only a person who has never experienced the warmth of the Mexican-American family would tend to see it primarily from a negative perspective" (Alvirez & Bean, 1976, p. 277). The notion of male dominance and female submissiveness and rigid family roles were soon refuted by a growing number of reports and studies that were more sensitive to the nuances of the Hispanic culture (Andrade, 1982; Cromwell & Ruiz, 1979; Hawkes & Taylor, 1975; Romano, 1973).

To illustrate a more "positive" view of the Hispanic family and the relations between husband and wife, compare the following description with the one previously quoted.

> A large number of Chicano husbands helped their wives with household chores and child care. Also, the Chicanos interviewed were not as obsessed with the idea of machismo as has been suggested in the literature. The overwhelming majority of Chicano husbands preferred to participate in social and recreational activities with their wives and children. Overall, the data indicate that the majority of Chicano wives played an important and/or equal part in most facets of conjugal role relationships. (Staples & Mirandé, 1986, p. 485)

Noteworthy here is the mention of machismo as an important feature of Hispanic men's identity. Much of the previous misunderstanding about Hispanic men and the more recent positive views about them centers on just what is meant by machismo. Let's turn our attention, then, to this important concept involving Hispanic male identity.

The Myth and Reality of Machismo

Few concepts are more often associated with Hispanic men than machismo, or being macho. Exactly what do **macho** and **machismo** mean, though? Macho is Spanish for the male sex. Thus in Spanish a *male* dog is macho. Machismo refers to those features related to being a male. Simply, machismo is Spanish meaning one is acting male or displaying masculine characteristics.

However, for reasons unknown, the term machismo as used by most Anglos has taken on the connotation of a self-centered, dominant, and overbearing male who uses women for his own pleasure. Often as not, the caricature of a macho-type male is of a strutting peacock. However, machismo means many things depending on which Spanish-speaking country we focus on (De La Cancela, 1986, 1993).

For instance, Brazilian men view machismo in terms of meaning male dominance over women. To this day, a Brazilian husband can abuse his wife with little concern over social and legal sanctions if his wife threatens his socially sanctioned dominance. Here then, machismo, as defined in Brazil connotes a very chauvinistic meaning.

However, as defined among most Central American countries and most Hispanic-American communities, machismo does not convey a negative sense of male dominance over women. Granted, research finds most Hispanic males more traditional toward women's roles than non-Hispanic males (Fischer, 1987). But as used by most Hispanic-American males nowadays, machismo and macho connote a very positive image of maleness (Mirandé, 1979, 1985; Valdez, 1986). In a recent article on machismo, sociologist and social worker Ramiro Valdez (1986, p. 4) noted that the image of an abusive and domineering male as being a model of machismo does not ring true with his life's experience.

> Experience has taught me that the literature that focuses only on the negative aspects of macho is in error. My uncle used to beat my aunt. He was abusive and insulting, hitting her and degrading her in public. Through all the years of my childhood I do not recall one time when my father or another male figure in my life pointed to my uncle and said to me "That is what you should be like." On the contrary, my uncle was despised for doing what he did. He fit the image depicted in the literature exactly, yet he was the exception in the family. My experience of living most of my life in Mexican neighborhoods and over a decade of therapeutic efforts with Hispanic men has shown me that the male depicted in the social science and feminist literature does exist, but he is not the norm nor is he regarded as an example to young boys.

It seems then that macho, or machismo, as many Anglos use the term would be offensive to most Hispanic males. The notion of a macho man as one who dominates and controls women might be part of what many Anglo men consider being a man is all about, but such is not the case for the majority of Hispanic men (Gutierrez, 1990). Granted, some Hispanic men, more in some Spanish-speaking countries than in others, define their maleness and masculinity as requiring them to dominate women. However, such cases of male dominance can be found among non-Hispanic males as well. The point is that machismo simply refers to the essential features found among males. What is essentially male that is macho? Courage, strength, assertiveness, and whatever else we can think of. The problem is that such qualities are not found only among males but females as well.

The time has come to use macho to mean other things besides the negative characteristics attributed to most brutish men. A macho man could be one who is strong and sensitive, assertive and nurturant, independent and dependent, and all the rest of the seemingly paradoxical features that make a male a man.

the asian-american man: inscrutable only to outsiders

Life in the United States for Asian-Americans has been checkered, to say the least. At times welcomed as tireless workers for jobs others did not want and, at other times, brutalized as easy targets of the white majority's prejudice and discrimination, today's nearly 5 million Americans of Asian descent are the only racial minority to come even close to true economic equality with the dominant white society. However, let's not be blind to the fact that prejudice and discrimination still haunt even the most successfully assimilated Asian-Americans (Nakanishi, 1988; Simpson & Yinger, 1985; Woodrum, 1981). To speak of Asian-Americans as a single group, however, misses an important point: The Asian-American label includes several diverse ethnic and culturally distinct groups. To be sure, we need to recognize that under the Asian-American umbrella, we find large ethnic communities composed of Chinese, Filipinos, and Japanese as well as smaller numbers of Koreans, Asian Indians, and the newly arrived Vietnamese.

During the decades between 1850 and 1880, over 300,000 mostly male Chinese were brought into the western United States primarily to work for the owners of railroads, farms, lumber mills, and fishing canneries. Soon, however, as more eastern whites moved West, Chinese laborers, or "coolies," bore the brunt of prejudice and discrimination. To protect themselves from ill-treatment, the Chinese isolated themselves by moving into ethnic enclaves called Chinatowns. In recent years, the ancestors of the first Chinese have begun to move more into the mainstream of North American society (Chu, 1986; Wong, 1982).

As for the Japanese, they came somewhat later than the Chinese and settled mainly in the Pacific states as well. One of the saddest events in recent United States history occurred shortly after Japan attacked Pearl Harbor on December 7, 1941, causing the United States government to round up over 100,000 Japanese-Americans living on the West Coast and forcibly detain them in "relocation" or "internment" camps (Drinnon, 1987). Ironically, the nearly 150,000 Japanese living in Hawaii close to Pearl Harbor were never swept up in a dragnet like their relatives living in the western states. Since World War II, the Japanese-Americans have become some of the most successful among all minority groups in United States history as measured by their family income and educational attainment (Petersen, 1971; Sowell, 1981).

Since the spring of 1975 when the United States-backed South Vietnamese government fell to the North Vietnamese, nearly 300,000 Vietnamese have relocated to the United States. Many of these immigrants were high-ranking government officials and military personnel making this group somewhat different from other immigrants in terms of education and status. No matter though, the Vietnamese have also experienced their share of prejudice and discrimination especially in those areas where white workers blamed the hardworking Vietnamese for taking away their jobs (Montero, 1979).

Overall, most contemporary Asian-American men have assimilated many traditional Western male role elements (e.g., success in the workplace and in educational attainment). Setting them apart, though, is that Asian-American men generally hold more conservative attitudes about women's roles than their white male counterparts (Braun & Chao, 1978). This should not surprise us given the severe social restrictions historically placed on Asian women and the greater value placed on males over females in most Asian cultures where the social norm supported the male as playing a dominant role in the family (Christopher, 1983; Kingston, 1976). Although some find contemporary Japanese fathers living in Japan spending about as much time with their children as their American counterparts (Bales, 1988), others find Japanese fathers less and less involved in their children's lives (Bankart & Bankart, 1985; Wagatsuma, 1977).

An interesting aspect of many Asian cultures is how men openly express friendship among themselves. For instance, it is not uncommon to see two Vietnamese men holding hands while walking together. Such a common expression of male friendship among Vietnamese men caused many United States servicemen stationed in South Vietnam during the 1960s and early 1970s to think only one thing, the Vietnamese men were homosexual. Needless to say, the common perception among many United States servicemen that large numbers of Vietnamese men were homosexual, especially those that served in the Army of the Republic of (South) Vietnam (ARVNs), did not make cordial relations between many United States and ARVN troops (Levy, 1971).

For the moment, we must note how little attention has been directed to the elements of Asian-American men and their definitions of manhood (Sue, 1990). Do Japanese-American men exhibit as much dominance over their wives in social situations as Japanese men do (Christopher, 1983)? Are there major differences in how Asian-American men define their male role related to their diverse cultures (Chinese, Korean, Japanese)? Although social scientists are beginning to pay more attention to Asian-Americans as a group (Endo, Sue, & Wagner, 1980; Kennedy, 1993; Williams, 1991), more attention is needed to understand better how Asian-American males define their male experience.

the native american man: a proud tradition of manhood

Probably, no other minority group has been so systematically vilified and oppressed as have North America's indigenous peoples, almost since the first days when Europeans landed on the islands off the southern seaboard of what is now Florida (Trimble, 1987). Although blacks were brought to this country in slave ships and sold into bondage, a case can be made that many were at least valued by their masters. The early white settlers, after a very brief period of accommodation toward native peoples, however, initiated various policies of extermination toward the Native American (Trimble, 1988).

Although we might want to assume that Native Americans fare much better in today's society, such an assumption would be erroneous. To illustrate this point, many non-Indians continue to characterize Native Americans in blatantly prejudicial and unflattering ways (Trimble, 1988). For instance, Native Americans are often characterized as "lazy, drunkard, and suspicious." Casting the

Men of Color

Native American in such a negative light not only is incorrect but continues to cast the majority of Native Americans in anything but a positive light (Snipp & Sandefur, 1988).

One problem we encounter in any discussion of Native Americans is the tendency to lump all tribes as if they belonged to one cultural group. The fact is that the label "Native American" does not adequately capture the extreme cultural diversity found among the over 250 separate Native American societies. Joseph Trimble (1987, p. 210) provides a sense of the extreme diversity found among America's Native Indian groups in the following passage:

> America's indigenous people were and are extraordinarily diverse socially, culturally, and in physical appearance. In fact, it's relatively safe to conclude that far more diversity existed among the American Indians than among *all* of the population of Europe, Scandinavia, and countries of the Middle East.

How then shall we deal with the male role of the Native American when, in fact, we have countless native groups to choose from? Obviously, there are as many male roles as there are separate Native American groups. Given our limited space here, we will confine our discussion to one Native American group describing its particular perspective on masculinity and manhood. Let's now examine how the Mohawk Indians living in the southern part of the Canadian province of Quebec define the male gender.

The Mohawk Man: One Who Walks Among High Steel

Few jobs are as dangerous as heavy construction and few heavy construction jobs are as dangerous as "high steel" construction. For over a hundred years now, a single group of men has been associated with high steel construction, the Kahnawake (or Caughnawaga) Mohawks (Blanchard, 1983; Devine, 1922; Freilich, 1958, 1963; Katzer, 1988; Mitchell, 1966). Not only have the Kahnawake people benefited economically from their long-established tradition of working in the high steel trade, but "this trade is viewed by the Mohawks themselves as part of a 'system of symbols and meanings' that fosters a distinct, Mohawk self-consciousness amongst the male members of the settlement" (Blanchard, 1983, p. 41). In our discussion here, we will borrow heavily from anthropologist David Blanchard's work among the Kahnawake and focus on what he considers three important symbolic aspects of high steel work for the Kahnawake man, namely, ironwork as a rite of passage from youth to adulthood, as a link with one's Mohawk traditions and past heritage, and as a ritual defining one's gender role.

Ironwork as a Rite of Passage. Among contemporary Kahnawake Mohawks, nearly 70 percent of the active work force are employed in ironwork (Blanchard, 1983, p. 52). Although other types of work (e.g., various clerical, semiprofessional jobs) are available both on and off the reservation, generally speaking Kahnawake men do not consider these normally sedentary jobs as "real work." Real work, according to the Mohawk tradition, must be physically demanding, hard, and dangerous, and it must require one to exhibit various skills such as climbing and keeping one's balance in a precarious position. What better way to qualify for "real work"

For Mohawk men, "men's work" should have an element of danger associated with it like that found in the high steel or heavy construction trades. Source: © Catherine Ursillo/Photo Researchers.

than working some fifty, sixty, or more stories up, guiding and fastening tons of steel into place, while keeping one's balance on a narrow steel girder?

Although most Kahnawake fathers and mothers do their best to dissuade their young boys from going to work on the high steel for many reasons, not the least of which are its dangerous and seasonal nature, nevertheless, the pressure for a young Kahnawake man to follow in the footsteps of most Iroquois menfolk is extremely strong. In fact, among most Kahnawake, a young boy's first job on high steel is treated much like a type of initiation or rite of passage into manhood. Blanchard recounts a family scene where a young man leaves for his first "real work" and receives a nominal blessing from his father.

> When his friend's car pulled up in front of his house, the horn sounded, and the passengers shouted for him to get moving. The boy's moment had arrived. His mother forced a kiss on her son, and the sisters held back their tears. The father remained seated. Finally, this boy-turned-man picked up his gear and left the house. The car honked its horn once more and pulled away. Unbeknownst to the family, the father had risen from his chair, and stepped to the front window. As his son and his friends pulled away, he raised his hand in a wave, and a faint smile passed over his lips. (pp. 54–55)

Why should there be so much emotional overtone to a young man going off to his first real job? Because to the Kahnawake, this young man is doing more than merely leaving home for his first work. Symbolically, one can argue that this boy leaving home is about to move through a passageway, a passageway entered by a boy and exited by a man. Over the millennia, countless fathers have watched their sons move through an initiation rite, a passage from one's childhood into the adult world of other men. For the Kahnawake, a boy who leaves home for the high steel is a boy no longer but a man who walks with his society's menfolk.

Men of Color

Ironwork as an Expression of Mohawk Tradition. A second feature of working among the high steel for the Kahnawake is its link to Mohawk tradition and past heritage. As previously noted, Kahnawake men have been involved in ironwork since the latter part of the last century. Before that, bands of Iroquois men ventured out away from their homelands as voyageurs, trappers, and fur traders throughout Canada's vast interior. When the fur trade diminished, many rafted timber down the rivers to saw mills. Whatever their work, Iroquois men loved adventure and work that took them to distant places (Katzer, 1988).

A young Kahnawake man who wishes to find adventure and travel much like his ancestors immediately thinks of moving with the high steel trade nowadays. The work may take him away from his family for weeks to distant places such as New York, Boston, Cleveland, Detroit or wherever skyscrapers are rising. Chances are a young Kahnawake steelworker is following in his father's and uncles' footsteps as an itinerant ironworker. This connection with those who preceded him is made even more pronounced when, for example, a young Kahnawake man uses the tools belonging to an elder or retired family member. True to form to the matrilineal nature of the Iroquois nations, a young Kahnawake man takes special pride in using the very same tools owned by the menfolk from his mother's side of the family.

Ironwork as a Way to Define Gender Roles. The Iroquois people have long believed that both men and women possess their own special kinds of power, a power that defines just what makes a male and a female. To mix these powers is not good especially when Iroquois men and women are sexually active and fertile. One way, a way approved for centuries, is for males and females not to spend much time together. In other words, tradition has it that Iroquois men are better off in the company of other men, and the same is true of Iroquois women. Ironwork, as the distant adventure of their forefathers, takes a young Kahnawake man away from his womenfolk for long periods of time.

Furthermore, Iroquois tradition supports the belief that a man is more manly, acquires more manly power, that is, when he is tested physically. Today, a Kahnawake ironworker believes he acquires much of his manly power from all the smells associated with his work: the sweat of his body, the smell of red-hot steel, the aroma of working outside. A Kahnawake ironworker senses his power in many ways.

Because the Iroquois nations have always been matrilineal in nature, many Kahnawake men feel it necessary to take their leave from the reservation in order to reaffirm their manly self-respect. Traveling to distant job sites and staying with other Kahnawake men provide the kind of all-male group that reinforces a sense of manhood distant from the supportive role they provide their womenfolk on the reservation.

In sum then, working in high steel provides the Kahnawake Mohawk man with the means to support several aspects of his manhood. Ironwork provides a passageway to manhood, a way to keep Iroquois traditions and heritage alive, and an important ritual to define manhood in a matrilineal society.

Now that we've discussed various aspects of how several ethnic/racial groups define manhood, what lesson can we draw? Obviously, an important lesson, and only one among many, is how diverse the male experience is among these groups. We found that among many African-American male youths being cool, detached, and in control are not only a way to defend themselves against a racist society but a means of showing others how very masculine they are. For many a Hispanic male to be courageous and unflinching reflects best his macho persona. The Asian-American male is dominant in the family and in his social world as well befitting his honored status as a male in a very male-dominant culture. For the Iroquois man of the Northeast, manhood comes with his walking among the steel girders atop an eighty-story skeletal skyscraper. Basically then, viewing all these masculine personas makes an intriguing and wondrous addition to the field of men's studies.

---

important terms

African-American matriarchy *244*
Cool pose *248*
Machismo *250*

Macho *250*
Manhood hustle *247*

---

suggested readings

Blanchard, D. (1983). High steel! The Kahnawake Mohawk and the high construction trade. *Journal of Ethnic Studies, 11*(2), 41–60.

Cazenave, N., & Leon, G. (1987). Men's work and family roles and characteristics: Race, gender, and class perceptions of college students. In M. Kimmel (Ed.), *Changing men: New directions in research on men and masculinity* (pp. 244–262). Newbury Park, CA: Sage.

De La Cancela, V. (1986). A critical analysis of Puerto Rican machismo: Implications for clinical practice. *Psychotherapy, 23,* 291–296.

Harris, S., & Majors, R. (Eds.). (1993). African-American men [Special issue]. *The Journal of Men's Studies, 1*(3).

Majors, R., & Billson, J. M. (1992). *Cool pose.* Lexington, MA: Lexington Books.

Mirandé, A. (1985). *The Chicano experience.* Notre Dame, IN: University of Notre Dame Press. (Chapter 8)

Valdez, R. (1986, March). The macho in contemporary America. *Nurturing News, 8*(1), 4, 16.

Williams, W. L. (1991). *Javanese lives: Women & men in modern Indonesian society.* New Brunswick, NJ: Rutgers University Press.

Zinn, M. B. (1989). Chicano men and masculinity. In M. Kimmel & M. Messner (Eds.), *Men's lives* (pp. 87–97). New York: Macmillan.

Chapter 15

Fatherhood

Fathers reside near the core of human experience, yet they remain elusive. The father lacks the mother's bodily ties to birth and nursing. His role is more culturally than biologically determined, so it is more difficult to define.
Charles Scull (1992)

I am a thirty-seven-year-old father of a three-year-old. I have master's degrees in social science and in library science. I have been a VISTA volunteer, dorm father (for twenty teenagers), a history teacher, a feed mill laborer, a student and head of maintenance at a Quaker Study Center. I am presently a reference librarian at a college in New England; and I have never done anything more difficult than to parent.
Daniel F. Schnurr (1986)

Despite men's differences, breadwinning has remained the great unifying element in fathers' lives. Its obligations bind men across the boundaries of color and class, and shape their sense of self, manhood, and gender. Supported by law, affirmed by history, sanctioned by every element in society, male breadwinning has been synonymous with maturity, respectability, and masculinity.
Robert L. Griswold (1993)

We need to know more about what becoming a father and being a father means to men. . . . It is important that we hear more from men about this major adult role.
Carolyn Pape Cowan & Phyllis Bronstein (1988)

"Father," a word that conjures up many images in people's minds: a middle-aged man going to work everyday to support his family, a single parent bathing his children while telling them imaginary stories, a divorced man picking his children up for their twice-monthly "dad's weekend," or a man whose kids only infrequently hear from him after his remarriage. No matter the image, for most of us, **fathers** and what we think of as **fatherhood** are essential parts of most men's experience.

In this chapter we begin by examining a key role not only for men in general but especially important in terms of defining fatherhood, the provider role. From there we move our discussion to the many sides of fatherhood today: fatherhood as a time of change and development for men, fathers' participation in family work, and some variants of fathering in keeping with the changing family systems, namely, single fathers and stepfathers.

Let's begin our discussion by examining what many think of as one of fatherhood's defining elements, the provider role.

Throughout most of human history, men and women have worked closely together either in small, nomadic hunter-gatherer kinship groups or, beginning around 8,000 to 10,000 B.C.E. up until the 19th century, in more stable, agricultural-based family groups. During this time, men's worth was judged primarily in terms either of their hunting skills or, with the advent of agriculture, their skills at tilling the land. Men have also provided for their children, especially their male children, by teaching them the abilities and knowledge considered necessary to a male (see Hewlett, 1991). Throughout most of human history then, a primary means of defining the male role has been through the enactment of the **provider role** (see Griswold, 1993; Rotundo, 1993). However, during the 18th century, with the dawn of the industrial revolution's factory system, man-as-provider and his provider role underwent a significant change.

a historical sketch of the provider role

Beginning with the **Industrial Revolution,** men's lives and manhood underwent dramatic changes (see Chapter 2). Among the more dramatic changes were those involving age-old relationship patterns between men and women. In preliterate hunter-gatherer groups and agricultural societies, men and women cooperated to provide for their families' sustenance. The defining feature of the Industrial Revolution though, the factory and its centralized location, drew men away from their homes and the land thus creating a gulf between men and their families. As a result, men's and women's work environs (i.e., public/factory world versus private/family world) diverged and more separate and exclusive worlds became the norm.

Industrialization redefined men as the *sole* provider of their family's material needs. No longer did husbands/fathers work closely with their wives and children in open fields, cottages, or small shops. Industrialization retooled men's provider role causing them to distance themselves from their families and forcing them to spend their days closeted in foul-smelling and dangerous factories. From a hunter-farmer-artisan-based definition of manhood, the industrial revolution reshaped men to fit the needs of a factory system and its voracious appetite for strong, pliant workers. The measure of manhood soon became identified with the **good-provider role.**

Industrialization's Impact on Men's Lives

Although the Industrial Revolution provided people with mass-produced consumer goods, there were definite costs. Sociologist Jessie Bernard (1981) noted as much when she wrote:

> The most serious cost [of the good-provider role] was perhaps the identification of maleness not only with the work site but especially with success in the role. . . . To be a man one had to be not only a provider but a good provider. Success in the good-provider role came in time to define masculinity itself. The good provider had to achieve, to win, to dominate. He was a breadwinner. . . . Men were judged as men by the level of living they provided. . . . The good provider became a player in the male competitive macho game. What one man provided for his family in the way of luxury and display had to be equalled or topped by what another could provide. Families became display cases for the success of the good provider. (p. 2)

Thus the male role heaved to the strains and pressures of the Machine Age as new attributes and new ways of defining manhood became necessary. Men began to place greater emphasis on their wages and the acquired goods purchased as proofs of their worth. For centuries, men had contributed in tangible ways first to the group and then to the family. The industrial system ended all of that and created a new man—the paid laborer—whose major contribution to the family was his wages (Gould, 1974). The more money earned, the better a provider a man was considered to be for his family.

The Twentieth Century and the Provider Role

By the early decades of the twentieth century, the good-provider role was firmly embedded in the nation's psyche and a new image of manhood had emerged. But all was not to remain placid. Beginning in the early decades and extending to the early 1940s, the provider role, fatherhood, and manhood itself went through several crises (Filene, 1986; Griswold, 1993; Mintz & Kellogg, 1988). Although the whole period saw numerous crises, one particular event affected a majority of men in very disquieting ways. That event began one fateful day in October, 1929, when the whole of our market economy collapsed as the stock market crashed. Few events in human history of a non-aggressive nature have had such a catastrophic consequence on people's lives as what followed during the 1930s—the Great Depression (Watkins, 1993). Not only did millions of men lose their jobs but they lost something even more important—a primary means of validating their masculinity (Komarovsky, 1940; Terkel, 1970). Because of the importance attached to the good-provider role, unemployed men suffered a form of psychological emasculation. Furthermore, during these troubling years, challenges occurred not only to father-child relationships but to the "competency" of fathers in general (see LaRossa et al., 1991; LaRossa & Reitzes, 1993).

After more than a decade of unemployment and a battering of husbands'/fathers' identities, World War II reinvigorated a sense of "revitalized" masculinity in countless men. However, this same event split up countless families as husbands and fathers went off to war leaving their wives to shoulder family responsibilities alone. After the war, and with the economy turned around, the returning husbands and fathers again wrapped themselves in the mantle of the good-provider role. Wives, after a liberating stint as "Rosie the Riveter," returned again to their kitchens.

Yet, the good-provider role was never the same after World War II. In numbers alone, men as sole providers for their families began a significant decline. For instance, in 1960, forty-two percent of all families were supported solely by men, a figure that dropped to 15% in 1988 (see Mencher & Okongwv, 1993; Wilke, 1991). Another change affecting men's good-provider role during these years was the growing number of women in the labor force.

During the last fifty years, women have entered the labor force in unprecedented numbers. For instance in 1940, about 25 percent of all women aged 16 and over were employed outside the home; a figure that more than doubled to over 57 percent by 1991. And in 1991, women aged 16 and over made up 45 percent of the *entire* labor force. The reason why millions of women have entered the labor force are as varied as the women themselves, but several reasons stand out.

First, two paychecks provide a significantly higher family income than a single paycheck. In 1990, for instance, the median income for dual-earner families was $42,146 as compared to $25,878 for single-earner families. Second, a paycheck provides more than money alone; it also has symbolic value providing its recipient with a heightened sense of worth and dignity. The fact is that our society values people and their activities in proportion to their earned income. Consequently, women in the labor force have garnered not only their own money but also a greater sense of self-worth and self-esteem in the process.

In this short history of the provider role, we have seen how men's lives and family responsibilities have changed over the centuries. Now, let us turn our attention to what fatherhood means and what becoming a father provides for most men.

People are more cognizant of fatherhood today. Television talk shows feature fathers sharing their experiences dealing with the conflict pressures of jobs versus family responsibilities in raising children; prime time television shows focus on various fatherhood arrangements (e.g., "Home Improvement," "Coach," "Full House," "Who's the Boss"; see Klumas & Marchant, 1994); books and magazine articles examine fathers and fathering practices; credit is given fathers for playing an important role in shaping their children's development—daughters as well as sons (see Marone, 1988; Secunda, 1992); and many of society's institutions are reexamining their views of fathers and fathering (e.g., courts dealing with fathers' claims in child-custody cases).

Glen Palm and Rob Palkovits (1988) argue that our society's greater awareness of fathers during the past several decades grows out of four assumptions most of us make about fathers and fathering. First, nearly everyone sees fatherhood or more accurately the role of fatherhood as being in a state of flux. Open most any parenting book and you'll find stories and reports about how today's fathers are playing a more significant part in their children's development and sharing in child caretaking than did their fathers and grandfathers.

Further, most accept that men and women approach their parenting role differently. For instance, researchers find different interactional patterns between fathers and mothers with their infants and toddlers. Fathers, for their part, tend to engage in more play activities (i.e., vigorous, arousing, state-disruptive activities) while mothers engage in more caregiving activities (see Yogman, Cooley, & Kindlon, 1988).

becoming and being a father: the meaning of fatherhood

Fatherhood

A third assumption is that there is no single way to be a "good father." Rather, becoming or being a "good father" can take any number of paths. Here we do not mean that anything goes and that *all* fathers regardless of what they do are "good" or even "adequate" fathers. However, a majority of today's fathers are constantly negotiating with their spouses, children, and their employers about how to accommodate the paternal role into the mix of other role behaviors expected of them.

And last, being a father—an involved father, that is—means spending time, being motivated, and acquiring the skills and knowledge associated with parenting. This is more difficult than it might appear on the surface as women have numerous models and support systems while men have few models of paternal caretaking and nurturant abilities.

But what does being a father mean to most men? As fathers and fatherhood have captured people's attention, numerous questions have arisen dealing with just what fatherhood is all about. For instance, is fathering an innate activity or something learned? Is there a special bond or attachment that occurs early in the father-child relationship? Does the transition from non-parent to parent bring with it personal stress and crisis, promising instability to the relationship between a man and his mate or spasms of joy and delight portending prolonged happiness, a period that fosters personal and relational growth, or does fatherhood bring both? Let's examine each of these issues in turn.

Fatherhood: Nature or Nurture?

Everything about human behavior or, more precisely, the explanation of human behavior seems at one time or another to come down to the issue of nature or nurture. Is the particular behavior inborn or learned? It is not surprising, then, to question whether or not paternal behaviors are inborn or learned.

For most people, the issue of women and their ability to care for the young and weak has been settled by positing an innate predisposition called the **maternal instinct.** Women, it seems, are viewed as innately gifted with nurturing and caretaking abilities as most everyone includes "nurturing" and "caring" in their list of descriptive traits of women. Granted, females of most nonhuman species show evidence of strong infant caretaking behaviors almost immediately after the birth of their young. But is there such evidence of such inborn tendencies or predispositions among humans—females or males?

In presenting his research on fathers, Philip Cowan (1988) notes:

> We live in a culture that idealizes the mother as someone who intuitively knows what to do for a child, who is inherently calm and patient and responsive to the needs of others, and who takes care without awkwardness or ambivalence. This mythical ideal does a disservice to parents on two counts. It assumes that the ability and desire to nurture the growth of a child are inborn, and it suggests that these qualities are inborn exclusively in women. But nurturance is not a matter only of endowment. *It calls for development—in both sexes.* (p. 41; italics added)

Although it flies in the face of popular wisdom, the evidence for an inborn nurturing or caretaking ability among humans—females or males—is lacking. Such proof though is not called for by those who accept and believe fully in the existence of a maternal instinct. Thus, with Cowan, let us note that fathering is made up of a set of skills and a variety of attitudes that are learned over time and experience. Can any man become a father—a biological father, that is? Yes, if he possesses a functional reproductive system and a mate. Can any man become a caring and nurturing father? The evidence confirms that given the proper mix of experience, positive attitudes, and support, a man can become an affectionate, caring, and indulgent caretaker of infants and children (see Yogman, Cooley, & Kindlon, 1988).

Some years ago, Martin Greenberg and Norman Morris (1974) reported on their observations with fathers and newborns. They described and defined a special state of father-newborn involvement called **engrossment**—a "sense of absorption, preoccupation, and interest in the infant" (p. 521). Furthermore, the authors contended that "the potential for engrossment in one's newborn is considered *an innate potential* [caused] by early contact with the infant" (p. 521; italics added).

No one who has observed an involved father interact with his baby will disagree that fathers can become very attached, even "engrossed" in their child. A problem with Greenberg and Morris's notion of engrossment however, is their suggestion that such "absorption" by a father with his baby has an innate, a biological basis. What's a father to think if he doesn't feel totally absorbed in his new paternal role? Is he lacking in some genetically programmed paternal "right stuff"? Is he deficient in an innate potential for paternal involvement?

In a review of the literature of father-child involvement and interaction, Rob Palkovitz (1985) found no support for a special father-newborn engrossment phenomenon triggered by contact soon after birth among fathers. That is not to say though, that fathers cannot and do not become highly engrossed in their fathering experience. Listen to one father's view of his new son and his prescription that fatherhood may provide a much needed palliative for the world's overworked.

> From the moment he was born, I was smitten with Jake, more, I think, than even my wife dared to hope. I never knew how much you could get by giving. Jake takes a lot of time, but he gives back a dimension to my life that I cherish, and I've come to think the world might be a very different place if its workaholics had more of this dimension in their lives. (Riley, 1992, p. 44)

We are not arguing here that fathers cannot achieve an almost indescribable sense of connectedness with their children but rather that such a "peak experience" is not an innate feature of fatherhood.

Most researchers today contend that fatherhood is both a time of change—bringing with it numerous crises—and a developmental stage—allowing a father to experience opportunities that foster personal growth (Cowan, 1988; Palm, 1993). To understand how fatherhood can be both—an experience providing both crisis and growth—let us first look at the transition to fatherhood from the crisis model.

Fatherhood: A Crisis Model. Although research into fatherhood is still rather new, much of the early work viewed both men's and women's transition to parenthood in rather negative terms focusing on the change in couples' routines and loss of freedom (see Dyer, 1963; LeMasters, 1957). More recent studies have highlighted numerous "negatives" like finding that new fathers run a greater risk for emotional upheaval and stress (Osofsky & Osofsky, 1985), are likely to evidence symptoms of depression (Ventura & Stevenson, 1986), and for those men with previous psychiatric histories, linking fatherhood to the presence of certain emotional disorders (Weiner, 1982).

Others have noted that the transition to parenthood can also provoke marital problems (e.g., Belsky, Spanier, & Rovine, 1983; Grossman, 1988). In a longitudinal study of 72 couples' adjustment to parenthood and its effects on their relationship, Philip Cowan (1988) found that the couples' overall "satisfaction with the[ir] marriage declined for both spouses from pregnancy to 18 months after they became parents" (p. 19). Furthermore, for a significant minority of these couples, conflict and dissatisfaction in their marriages was not inconsequential. "In fact," Cowan reports, "one in eight of the new parents in our study separated or divorced by the time the children were 18 months old" (p. 30). Thus, parenthood can provoke crisis within and between parents. However, as we have heard, for many growth can come out of crisis.

Fatherhood: A Growth Model. In its more idealized version, many people think of fatherhood—like motherhood—in the most positive ways, a means promoting healthy adult development (see Newman & Newman, 1988). Further supporting this idealized version is the number of "fatherhood" books that tend to paint fatherhood in the rosiest of terms (e.g., Kort & Friedland, 1986). Although transition to parenthood brings with it inevitable changes in men's lifestyle, activities, and their relations with others, such changes are not necessarily all bad nor all good but rather an opportunity for growth. In Cowan's study (noted above), he found that many of his fathers found parenthood fostered a fuller sense of their identity and self-esteem as well as a maturing of their relationships with their mates as they came to grips with the polar issues of independence (personal autonomy) and mutuality (interdependence).

Recently, Glen Palm (1993) suggested that fatherhood could provide the opportunity for men to learn often overlooked or poorly developed skills. Specifically, Palm suggests that involved fathers—involvement is key to Palm's prescription—could learn how better to express certain emotions they may have had little practice with before fatherhood like patience, compassion, and self-honesty, for instance. Fatherhood also provides men with numerous opportunities to learn and practice skills associated with nurturance and caregiving. Palm argues that men can be as nurturant as women if they would only take the time and expand the effort to learn such parenting skills. A reason why so many men have not developed these skills is simply that they lack practice. Compared to most women whose early experiences provided opportunities for learning nurturant and caregiving activities (e.g., babysitting), most men find themselves approaching fatherhood needing assistance and support from others (e.g., wives, peers, work colleagues) in order to achieve their full potential as nurturant fathers. Too often, new fathers do not receive such support and consequently continue acting as a distant and uninvolved parent.

Next, we need to look at the involvement most fathers have with their children and their participation in other family chores.

I'm not one to read a story a second time nor see a movie more than once, no matter how good I find them the first go-around. However, I can count at least four readings and more than half a dozen viewings of Arthur Miller's (1949) *Death of a Salesman*. In Miller's play, we meet Willy Loman, an aging traveling salesman, who wants others—wife, sons, colleagues—simply to respect him. A crucial ingredient that never fails to capture my interest is Willy's relationship with his oldest son, Biff—a father-son relationship like so many others filled with pain and misunderstanding (see Osherson, 1986).

In recent years, there's been an "explosive" interest in father-child relationships by family specialists and popular writers alike (see Anderson, 1988; Hanson & Bozett, 1985; Lamb, 1986; Lewis, 1986; Lewis & O'Brien, 1987; Pleck, 1987a). Interestingly, for much of this century, most experts thought fathers played little more than a "peripheral" role in their children's socioemotional development (Biller, 1971; Bowlby, 1969; Rapoport, Rapoport, Strelitz, & Kews, 1977). However, today, most view fathers' involvement in their children's development to be quite significant involving both a child's gender role development and various competencies, for instance (Bronstein, 1988; Lamb, Pleck, Charnov, & Levine, 1985; MacDonald & Parke, 1986; Secunda, 1992). The caricatures of fathers as either mindless buffoons or distant authoritarians are fading fast and being replaced with the view that fathers are important contributors to their children's growth and development (Gilbert, 1985; Giveans & Robinson, 1985; Lamb, Pleck, Levine, 1985; Mackey, 1985).

One of the factors accelerating the need to know more about fathers' influence on children's development is the large numbers of wives/mothers who have entered the labor force, making it essential that husbands and fathers share more child care responsibilities. The issue of just how much fathers participate in child care and household chores has demanded considerable attention of late.

Fathers' Participation in Family Work

In a review of the literature on dual-earner families, sociologist Nijole Benokraitis (1985) remarked that:

> During the last 10 to 15 years, one of the most dramatic changes in the American family has been the precipitous increase of families in which both parents work outside the home. . . . Two out of three readers of this chapter either are or will be members of a dual-earner family by the next decade. Yet, outside of some general demographic data, we know very little about the dual-earner family—especially about the father. (p. 243)

One of the most often asked questions about the growing number of husbands-fathers involved in dual-earner families is, just how much of the "work load" do they carry in dealing with household chores and in child care? For the answer, we need to turn to a number of researchers who have looked into husbands' involvement in family chores.

Joseph Pleck (1985) reanalyzed several national time-diary surveys of dual-earner families and found that in general men's time in family involvement (e.g., child care) is increasing, whereas women's time is decreasing. Although this trend may make one think that husbands' and wives' involvement in family work is moving toward greater parity, Pleck's data does not suggest true parity in family work involvement in either the near or distant future as most other studies have borne out.

In another study, Teresa Jump and Linda Haas (1987) interviewed fifty dual-earner couples living in Indianapolis. Although their sample was not representative of the general population of dual-working couples (i.e., their sample was made up primarily of professional working couples), they did find that these husbands provided just under 40 percent of the total care for the children. Overall, Jump and Haas believe that most fathers in dual-earner families are presently in a state of transition moving away from the more traditional expectation that fathers should be virtual nonparticipants in the daily chores involving the home and child care to one of greater egalitarianism where husbands take on a relatively greater share of the family chores.

Rosalind Barnett and Grace Baruch (1988) interviewed 160 middle-class fathers of kindergarten or fourth-grade children, half of whose wives were employed and half whose wives were unemployed. Although Barnett and Baruch found the fathers' "overall" family work participation was lower than the mothers', fathers with employed wives interacted more with their children relative to their wives than did fathers with unemployed wives—a finding supported by other researchers as well (e.g., Cowan & Cowan, 1988; McKenry, Price, Gordon, & Rudd, 1986).

One other finding in Barnett and Baruch's study is quite interesting. A majority of the fathers reported extremely low levels of "responsibility" for child-care tasks and home chores. Even among fathers who were involved with child-care tasks and home chores, there was a general perception on their part of a lack of responsibility for "remembering, planning, and scheduling" such duties. In other words, even the involved fathers in this study were less likely to be responsible for organizing the various aspects of their children's lives. Such a perception can be seen in the following quote (taken from another study),

> If I come in at night Jane [wife] will say, "She's done this today" or "She's done that today" . . . . Jane tends to come up with ideas on it [child care], and then I'll sort of follow it on. . . . In sort of routine things, Jane will sort of decide, basically . . . there's no way I would sort of say, "I think we ought to stop that and do that." (Quoted in Lewis, 1986, p. 89)

Although fathers in single-earner families were less involved in child care than dual-earner fathers, Barnett and Baruch found that their "feelings about the quality of the fathering they received as youngsters" (p. 74) provided a good predictor of their (single-earner fathers) family involvement. Possibly, these fathers' memories of their own childhood motivated them to interact more with their children.

Although the underlying fact that women assume the major responsibility for home and children, we must emphasize that men have *increased* their participation in family life over the past several decades, a change not only among American fathers but fathers in Canada and Western Europe as well (see Horna & Lupri, 1987; Hossain & Roopnarine, 1993; Sandqvist, 1987). Further, we need to note that some well-intentioned and willing fathers do face barriers restricting their involvements with their children (see, for instance Cowan & Cowan, 1987, 1988; Lein, 1979). For the record then, let's examine some of the more prominent barriers preventing fathers' greater involvement in family chores.

One of the more significant, and surprising, barriers to men's greater involvement with paternal activities is women in their roles as wife and mother. Much of how women define themselves (self-identity) and how they feel about themselves (self-esteem) is derived from their enactment of and perceived competence in their motherhood role. Thus many women, just how large a number is difficult to measure, are reluctant to share parenting responsibilities with their mate. This is not to suggest that a majority of husbands have been prohibited from sharing in family chores because of a conspiracy by their insecure wives. No. However, it is fair to note that some wives/mothers may send subtle signals to their husbands that they don't regard them as competent in performing certain family chores, especially those involving child care. Such bias on some women's part should not surprise us as the common stereotypic perception of fathers is one of incompetence and awkwardness when it comes to fathering skills in general.

Another barrier preventing men from becoming more involved with their children is the workplace itself. For the most part, the business community views women/mothers as the primary and best suited caretaker of children while men/fathers are seen as only secondarily involved and not that wholly competent in terms of parenting skills (Catalyst, 1988). Safe to say, businesses will not change their traditional view of men's and women's family roles until and unless society as a whole begins to value fathers' involvement with their families.

Another barrier and one that is slowly coming down is the availability of suitable materials designed specifically for men/fathers to learn new or enhance their already acquired parenting skills. Books and educational programs are only recently beginning to appear that take fathering and men's need to learn fathering skills seriously by providing expectant and/or new fathers with materials helpful in adjusting to their new responsibilities (e.g., Johnson & Palm, 1992; Levant, 1988; Minirth, Newman, & Warren, 1992; Pruett, 1987).

How then can we increase men's involvement even more with their families? Joseph Pleck, Michael Lamb, and James Levine (1985) have noted at least four factors that play a role in facilitating fathers' greater involvement with their families, especially their involvement in child care, namely, motivation, skills, social supports, and a reduction in social-institutional barriers. In turn, they reason that fathers will only become more involved with their children to the degree that they are motivated to do so. If one uses the growing number of books, journal articles, and other media presentations about increased father involvement with children as a gauge, we could suggest that more and more men are increasingly motivated to become more active fathers.

Further, if men are to feel more comfortable and thus take a more involved and active role in child care, they must become more skillful in those activities needed to care for an infant or young child. All too many young men have never changed a diaper, prepared a bottle, or dressed a squirming infant. Yet, these are

Increasing Fathers'
Family Participation

Fatherhood

the skills required for infant and child care. When we begin to see young boys as perfectly capable and responsible baby-sitters, for example, we will begin to raise young boys with the encouragement to learn the necessary skills to be active and participatory fathers later on.

If we want men to incorporate the role of child-care provider into their repertoire of behaviors, significant others must support them in such behavior. Wives, parents, and friends must encourage the young father to jump right in there and feed, bathe, and clothe, their youngster. A wife who encourages her husband's attempts at caring for their newborn is going a long way in helping him develop the confidence that he can do for his own child rather than waiting for someone else.

And last, social and institutional barriers must be dismantled if we as a society truly want fathers to become more active in their children's upbringing. Career tracks and job schedules must be made more flexible (e.g., flextime) so that more fathers can arrange their work schedules to permit them to be at home while their wives are at work. Another social factor that would encourage more fathers to become more involved in fathering duties would be for more companies to institute paternity leave for fathers of young infants. Granted, in those societies where some kind of paternity leave is available (e.g., Sweden, Norway, Denmark, and Portugal), the numbers of fathers who avail themselves of the time off are not always high. However, the data on paternity leave is both complex and difficult to make generalizations from (Pleck, 1987b). One thing companies could do to encourage greater use of paternity leave, though, is to promote the message that a man's career or job security would not be placed in jeopardy if he were to take time off with his children. It is vitally important for society to stress the importance of a father's involvement in child care and childrearing.

variants on the fatherhood role

Although fatherhood encompasses numerous types of father-child relations, people generally think of fatherhood in terms of a white, middle-class, intact family system comprised of a father, mother, and child(ren). In other words, a stereotypic view of fatherhood. However, as interest in fatherhood has increased, variants of fatherhood types have begun to garner more attention. For instance, researchers have turned their attention to issues involving adolescent fathers (e.g., Barrett & Robinson, 1985; Marsiglio, 1987; Robinson, 1988), role-reversal husbands or what some call "househusbands" (Radin, 1988; Russell, 1987), African-American and Chicano fathers (e.g., McAdoo, 1988; Mirandé, 1988), and gay fathers (Bozett, 1988). All these fatherhood types are worthy of our attention here, however, we will only deal with two fatherhood variants—single fathers with custody and stepfathers. The rationale for this selection is not based on an abundance of data but rather the judgment that these two present us with special insights into the fatherhood experience. Specifically, single fathers as a group break the stereotypic image of the detached and uninvolved father while stepfathers face challenges unlike most non-stepfathers. We can learn much about the peaks and valleys of fatherhood by looking at these two groups more closely.

Single Fathers

Throughout the ages, the question of child custody was a moot point—fathers always got custody. Two reasons account for this age-old, father-preference custody practice. First, until relatively recent improvements in medical practices and facilities, childbirth was one of the most frequent causes of women's mortality. Fathers, consequently, were frequently left widowed and responsible for their child(ren). However, more often than not, a widower turned to the women in either his or his wife's families for help in raising the children.

A second reason for father custody was more social. Simply, a husband/father has traditionally had near total dominance over his wife and children. Thus any dissolution of a marriage guaranteed the father custody of children. Even in these cases, most fathers turned the child care over to women within his extended family.

However, with the Industrial Revolution and its creation of a man's world (i.e., factories) and a woman's world (i.e., the home), women were seen as nature's intended in dealing with the needs of children. Consequently, courts began to favor mothers over fathers in determining custody cases. And so, for well over a hundred years, mothers have been preferred in custody cases and routinely awarded sole custody in a majority of divorce cases. Needless to say, the issue of preferential treatment of mothers in child custody cases has become a *cause celebre* for many men's groups (see Warshak, 1992).

Today, single-parent families are one of the fastest growing family types accounting for over 21 percent of all families (over 14 million). Of these single-parent households, just over 20 percent are headed by men (2.9 million; never married, separated, divorced, widowed). These **single fathers** find themselves in a real quandary—they don't match the social stereotype of what fatherhood is supposed to entail—a shared experience with a mate—and they must deal with the needs of a group of individuals—children—that their previous experiences have provided few "how tos." The life of a single dad then is not easy. (I am not suggesting here that the life of a single mom is any easier. In fact, given that most single fathers would have higher incomes or potential incomes, single fathers may have it relatively easier than single mothers.)

What do we know about single fathers? Although research on single fathers has not been voluminous, a number of researchers have made it a point to focus their interest on single fathers. For instance, Shirley Hanson's (1985, 1988) work has been especially illuminating about the single father experience. Based on her work, we can make a number of fairly reliable generalizations about single fathers.

With respect to the relationship between a single father and his children, Hanson contends that fathers who frequently and effectively interacted with their children beginning in early infancy were better able to adjust to their single-parent status later on. Further, single fathers perceive themselves as able to provide emotional support and nurturant understanding for their children. On this point, Hanson (1988) writes:

> On four separate measures, . . . [single] fathers viewed themselves as being loving and concerned. Furthermore, fathers who sought custody viewed themselves as more supportive and nurturing than men who assented to custody. One of the more interesting findings . . . was that children of single fathers rated their fathers as more nurturing than children from two-parent families rated either parent. (p. 182)

In terms of child care and social support, single fathers not only avail themselves of their communities' child-care facilities but are more apt to turn to others for assistance in dealing with parenting problems. However, on this point, Hanson reported that single fathers are more apt to turn "to single mothers for help and friendship" (p. 183) rather than to other men. Single fathers choosing women over men to confide in and seek counsel from should not surprise us as most men are quite resistant to acknowledge their "need" to other men.

Stability of environment is another important feature noted by Hanson in her work with single fathers. Overall, single fathers tend to provide a highly stable or consistent living environment for their children. Hanson reported that "single fathers were less likely than single mothers to move from their homes and communities following divorce, which . . . may have enhanced the adjustment of single-father families" (p. 183). The single fathers' often better job situation and pay scale compared to their ex-wives' probably played a large part in this difference. Overall, Hanson concluded that "the research on single fathers demonstrates that they are doing well as primary caregivers" (p. 184). Although somewhat understated, the fact that single fathers have been found to be competent and capable as *primary* caregivers is a most noteworthy fact in the growing literature on men's experiences.

Like Hanson, Geoffrey Greif (1986, 1990) has also been a long-term observer of single fathers and author of numerous studies detailing their day-to-day struggles and accomplishments. In a recent book, *The Daddy Track and the Single Father* (1990), Greif describes his research based on surveys and interviews with over 1100 self-identified single fathers. Therein, Greif concludes that single parenting is not an easy role for most men to enact given their lack of preparation in terms of their socialization. However, near the end of his book, Greif provides a testimonial to the single fathers he interviewed.

> Single parenting is not for every father. A few regret having the responsibility and wish it could be shifted to someone else. Most men, though, are happy the children are with them. They believe things are working out for the best for everyone involved. . . .
>
> The commitment demonstrated by these fathers is testimony to the level of commitment men are capable of. Men have often been accused of being passengers on the emotional boat rides life provides. Believed to be incapable of caring as deeply about relationships as women and painted as distant fathers, men are excluded, and exclude themselves, from many opportunities for closeness. Yet the fathers in this book are, for the most part, men who are willing to get close, who want a hands-on approach, and who are capable of giving more than they thought. (p. 222)

This statement sums up why I believe we need to know more about single fathers. Setting aside the uniqueness of their relationships, they provide an excellent example of how men can express some of the finest qualities in human relations—providing not only for another's physical needs but their psychological and emotional ones as well. Single fathers provide a much needed picture of what men are capable of.

Stepfathers

Recently, John Santrock and his colleagues (1988) noted that the study of stepfathers "has remained relatively neglected" (p. 144). However, the tide is turning and researchers are beginning to focus attention on this most interesting and often times exasperating type of fatherhood (see Pasley, 1985; Pasley & Ihinger-Tallman, 1984).

What constitutes a stepfather? In most instances, a **stepfather** is a man who marries a woman with children from a previous marriage. He may—or may not—have been previously married himself and may—or may not—have children from a previous marriage. Thus, more often than not, a stepfather is one who must break into an already established family unit. He is an intruder in the new family and like most intruders, with the exception of his new wife, not everyone in the family may be happy with his arrival. It is precisely because most men are ill-equipped to handle the new roles of husband and father in an already established family unit that makes being a stepfather so difficult.

To get a sense of the more important issues facing stepfathers, let us focus on Santrock's research with stepfamilies. Of interest is that roughly a half of the stepfathers interviewed reported that their stepchildren's feelings played a decisive role in their entrance into the stepfamily. This is noteworthy because these men not only had to deal with their own and their potential bride-to-be's feelings about marriage but they also had to cope with their future stepchildren's feelings as well.

Another issue confronting these stepfathers was the issue of discipline within the new family. A significant number of stepfathers reported that not only did the children's biological father undermine their involvement in the stepfamily but often times the mother also presented reservations with respect to whether or not the stepfather should discipline her children.

Regarding the relationship between stepfathers and their stepchildren Santrock reported:

> The reports of parental involvement from the stepfathers, their wives, and their stepchildren clearly indicated that the stepfather-child relationship was more detached and uninvolved, while the remarried mother-child relationship was closer, warmer, and characterized by more shared activity. Specifically, stepfathers were less likely to take the child along with them when running errands, were less likely to go to watch the child, whether a son or daughter, in outdoor activities such as soccer practice, and were less involved in disciplining the child or attending school-related functions. (p. 156)

We should not conclude given the above findings, that all is bleak with respect to stepfathers and their stepchildren. Santrock contends that even with the pattern of "greater distance" and "less involvement" found between stepfathers and their stepchildren, by and large, most stepchildren in this study expressed "positive feelings about their stepfathers." Further, the overall adjustment of the children in stepfather families appeared comparable to children in never-divorced families. Thus, we could conclude that even with problems most fathers can only imagine, stepfathers, at least those in Santrock's study, are providing a positive and effective father role for their stepchildren.

fatherhood: a future perspective

Given all the interest in the "new" father, what does the future portend for fathers and fatherhood? Here we will only note briefly some of the most general tendencies likely to affect fatherhood in the near future (see Palm, 1993).

First, it seems reasonable that our society's view of fathers will continue to change in the near future. Hopefully, a more positive view of fatherhood will evolve in the process and society will learn to incorporate and value the nurturant and caring aspects of paternal behaviors (Ritner, 1992). Next, fathers need more social services to increase their parenting skills. As fathers become more involved with family responsibilities, new learning strategies need to be developed to assist them toward fuller participation in their families. And last, we need more research on all aspects of fatherhood. Only with increased knowledge of the many varieties of fatherhood and with greater understanding of fathers' successes and failures can some of the mystery and mystique of fatherhood be eliminated.

---

important terms

Engrossment *263*
Fatherhood *259*
Fathers *259*
Good-provider role *259*
Industrial Revolution *259*

Maternal instinct *262*
Provider role *259*
Single fathers *269*
Stepfather *271*

---

suggested readings

Bronstein, P., & Cowan, C. P. (Eds.). (1988). *Fatherhood today: Men's changing role in the family.* New York: Wiley.

Gerson, K. (1993). *No man's land: Men's changing commitments to family and work.* New York: Basic Books.

Greif, G. L. (1990). *The daddy track and the single father.* Lexington, MA: Lexington Books.

Griswold, R. L. (1993). *Fatherhood in America: A history.* New York: Basic Books.

Minirth, F., Newman, B., & Warren, P. (1992). *The father book: An instruction manual.* Nashville, TN: Thomas Nelson Publishers.

Scull, C. (Ed.). (1992). *Fathers, sons, and daughters: Exploring fatherhood, renewing the bond.* Los Angeles: J. P. Tarcher

Chapter 16

Men's Health

We have evidence of a pattern of mortality data in the country that favors females over males. . . . Death rates for men resulting from clear behavioral influences such as homicide, accidents, and suicide also exceed those of women by two to three times. These disparate rates, most likely occur as a function of sex-role expectations that lead men . . . to engage in life-threatening, high-risk, and competitive behaviors.
Bonnie R. Strickland (1988)

The traditional male role is a self-denying and stoic-heroic combination of characteristics, which takes its toll on men's physical and mental health.
Ronald F. Levant (1990)

I suspect that men . . . are, as I am, not only hurting but also deeply yearning. We are yearning for closer, more fulfilling, more life-giving connectedness with others, with our world, and with ourselves. This means we are yearning for closer connectedness with God, the heart of the universe itself.
James Nelson (1988)

One doesn't have to be overly aware to notice that we are living in a health-conscious society. Turn on a television set, sit back, and watch most any of the thirty- or sixty-second commercials. If you watch for a couple of hours, you're bound to be treated to a number of commercials pitching health-promoting products. All those healthy and happy people seemingly owe everything to a product: a caffeine-free diet cola; a high-fiber, low-sodium cereal; a new calcium enriched antacid tablet; or a revolutionary new "tracker" machine that mimics the perfect exercise to eliminate unwanted fat.

If we want more proof we need only look at all the books and articles describing how we should open up, express ourselves, be the person we're meant to be, all promising if we change our behavior and attitudes we'll be happier. And what about all those workshops or weekend gatherings at some secluded lodge where we can sit around campfires singing, dancing, and drumming, if so inclined, again guaranteed to help us find what we've lost—those parts of ourselves we've discarded as we've progressed up life's civilizing path. Men's health—their physical, emotional, and spiritual well-being—has become a major issue among many today.

In this the final chapter then, we're going to take a look at men's health. We begin by looking at some statistics showing that men's prospects for living a long life—long in the sense of equal to women's—are less than optimal. We then explore some of the more serious physical illnesses and/or diseases that affect men—namely, testicular and prostate cancers, coronary heart diseases, and AIDS. Next, we examine the issue of stress, or rather the maladaptive ways that men handle their stress, as being one of the more serious psychological problems facing men today. And last, we look at the issue of men's spirituality, an arguably important aspect of men's health needs. With this chapter then, we hope to show that for all their privilege and power, men as a group do have some significant health problems that need addressing.

Let's begin by looking at men's life expectancies to see that if they are more likely to suffer a significant natural setback sooner than a female of comparable age—death.

the question
of longevity

With all the hype and hoopla over staying fit in order to live a longer life, one might think that people's average length of life, that is their **life expectancy,** has increased over the years. And that's exactly what's happened. We are living longer than our ancestors. For instance, the average person living in ancient Greece was lucky to see their twentieth birthday, while those born in the United States in 1900 didn't quite make it to their fiftieth (actually, just over forty-seven years on average). However, a person born in the United States in 1988 can expect to live for almost seventy-five years—over a quarter century has been added to our life expectancy this century. Staying healthy and fit, it seems, has paid off.

Yet, if we were to take a cursory look at nearly any obituary column, we would discover a disconcerting fact. On average, men don't live as long as women (Nathanson, 1984; Stillion, 1985; Strickland, 1988; Waldron, 1983). Such an observation becomes more unnerving when we realize that throughout most of this century a man's chances of dying have been greater than a woman's at *every* age—from

table 16.1 — Life Expectations at Birth by Race and Sex in Select Years★

Years	White males	All other males	White females	All other females
1981	70.82	65.63	78.22	74.00
1989	72.7	67.1	79.2	75.2

★Source: From the Department of Health and Human Services, National Center for Health Statistics.

table 16.2 — Death Rates by Age, Race, and Sex in 1990★

Age	White males	All other males	White females	All other females
Under 1 year	9.0	15.3	7.1	12.7
1–4	0.4	0.6	0.3	0.5
5–14	0.2	0.3	0.1	0.2
25–34	1.7	3.4	0.6	1.3
35–44	2.6	5.5	1.1	2.3
45–54	5.4	9.5	3.0	4.7
55–64	14.5	18.8	8.2	12.1
65–74	33.1	37.1	19.5	23.5
75–84	79.7	77.0	49.2	51.3

★Provisional. Based on a 10 percent of deaths. Excludes fetal deaths. Rates are per 1,000 population in each group.

Source: From the Department of Health and Human Services, National Center for Health Statistics.

birth to over 80 (see Tables 16.1 & 16.2). More troubling is how non-white men die at an even greater rate than all other groups. As we can see in the tables, being a non-white male from birth onward is tantamount to having a very short lease on life. The obvious question then is why do men die younger and have a higher risk of death at every age than women? Good question. Not everyone, however, agrees on the answer.

One possible explanation for a man's shorter life expectancy is that it is programmed in his genes (Madigan, 1957). As we noted in chapter 3 (The Biological Perspective), the male's Y-bearing sex chromosome is much smaller and contains less genetic material than the X-bearing sex chromosome. When a defective gene is found along one thread of the X chromosome, chances are that the matching gene on the Y chromosome *may* not provide a "healthy" replacement message. Consequently, the number of sex-linked diseases—some of which are fatal—are more

Men's Health

prominent among males (Montagu, 1974; Waldron, 1976). Male fetuses also have a more complicated developmental path to traverse. If a genetic or intrauterine problem arises, a male fetus is more likely to be aborted naturally than a female fetus. Given these biological "strikes" then, a case could be made that men are simply genetically programmed to finish life's race ahead of women!

However, the biological approach has been criticized for disregarding several social-environment factors that play a leading role in a man's relatively early demise (Retherford, 1975). Traditionally, men have engaged in all kinds of activities some of which place their lives in serious jeopardy, such as war, for an extreme example. Besides war, men tend to inhabit other kinds of environments that can shorten their lives such as factories, construction sites, and farms. Frequently we read about a tragic accident where a construction worker fell to his death or was buried alive. Yet, when have we read of a similar accidental death occurring to a secretary working in an office? The fact is that many traditional "men's jobs" are more dangerous than most traditional "women's jobs."

A third way of viewing men's penchant for dying early is labeled a psychosocial approach. Some years ago, Sidney Jourard (1974) penned an article entitled "Some Lethal Aspects of the Male Role" followed a couple years later by a book written by Herb Goldberg (1976) entitled *The Hazards of Being Male*. Both authors argued that men are conditioned to take chances and risk their lives, all for the sake of appearing "tough." When we look at several of the leading causes of death where there is a clear sex differential, unhealthy or unsafe lifestyles seemingly play a role. For instance, compared to women, males are nearly twice as likely to die from heart disease (more on this later in the chapter), nearly three times as likely to die in an auto accident, twice as likely from a homicide, over twice as likely from chronic liver disease and cirrhosis, and over nine times more likely from AIDS. Why are men fated for such diseases, illnesses, and accidents? A number of authors think the answer is simple: a significant proportion of men think being masculine requires them to take chances with their lives—work in unsafe places, drink and drive, get into fights, etc. (see Harrell, 1986; Harrison, 1978; Kristiansen, 1990; Lash, Eisler, & Schulman, 1990; O'Donovan, 1988).

The bottom line then is that large numbers of men put themselves in jeopardy, take risks, flaunt danger all of which leave them open to increased chances of injury and/or death all for the sake of appearing masculine. It may not be comforting to think about but many men seemingly are willing to cut short their lives for the sake of appearing manly to others. With the above noted, let's move on now and take up yet another uncomfortable subject, one that most men avoid thinking about—cancer—specifically the two types of cancer that affect men directly.

the male cancers

Few illnesses create more anxiety and arouse more concern among the public than cancer, and for good reason. In 1990 and 1991, cancer was linked to just over 20 percent of *all* deaths in the United States. Fortunately, we can reduce our chances of cancer by avoiding or ceasing certain behaviors: avoid all tobacco products, reduce the amount of high-fat foods in our diets, limit exposure to ultraviolet radiation (sunlight), and restrict the use of alcohol. While the above lifestyle changes can help reduce your chances of developing many forms of cancer, here we want to focus on two types of cancer that affect men and whose causes are still a puzzle: testicular and prostatic cancers.

Testicular Cancer

For some years now, television commercials, magazine ads, and billboards have urged, even cajoled, women to examine their breasts regularly for any sign of unusual swellings or lumps as an early way to detect possible cancerous tissue. Not that many years ago, breast cancer and breast exams were taboo topics and countless women suffered terribly from not detecting their breast cancer soon enough. However, this veil of secrecy was pushed aside when public figures like Happy Rockefeller, Betty Ford, and Betty Rollins stepped forward and described their battles with and victory over breast cancer. With the publicity, breast cancer came out of the closet and its early detection via routine breast examination has drastically reduced the need for drastic types of treatment.

And yet, when we think of cancer *and* men we think of lung cancer or possibly throat cancer and take some solace that such cancers are chiefly related to smoking. The man who doesn't smoke might feel smug then that cancer is not a problem. However, "the most common cancer in white men between 20 and 34 years of age, the second most common form from 35 to 39, and the third most common form from 15 to 19" is **testicular cancer** (National Cancer Institute, 1987a, p. 2). Tragically, the incidence of testicular cancer is on the rise in the United States reaching nearly 6,000 new cases in 1990 (Silverberg, Boring, & Squires, 1990). I purposely say "tragically" because testicular cancer *is* "one of the most curable of all cancers" (National Cancer Institute, 1987a). When detected early, chemical and radiation treatments have proven very effective and only in the most advanced cases is the most drastic form of treatment used, castration. Not surprisingly then, given the feelings most men have regarding their testes (for many men their testes signify their masculinity much like breasts signify femininity for many women), being treated for testicular cancer can cause numerous psychological problems (Reiker, Edbril, & Garnick, 1985).

Although there are many reasons why men avoid thinking about cancer especially cancer related to their genitals (see Sabo, 1990), it is essential that men, especially young men under the age of 35, know about testicular cancer and the ways to detect possible problems by learning how to perform a regular **testicular self-examination** (TSE; see National Cancer Institute, 1987b). Somewhat surprising, knowledge about testicular cancer and testicular self-examination is especially lacking among the very group that needs the information the most—young men (see Pinch, Nilges, & Schnell, 1988). Apparently though when young men have correct information, information that dispels much of the misinformation about testicular cancer (e.g., the only treatment option is castration), they are more apt to perform TSE on a regular basis (Brubaker & Fowler, 1990).

Although I know of no male personally who has come forward to discuss how he has dealt with his testicular cancer, all men, especially those between 15 to 40 years need to pay special attention to their testes and learn how to examine them for any possible signs that may suggest that further action is needed.

figure 16.1
The testis.
_____

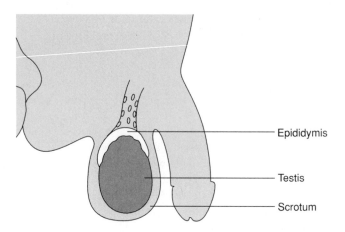

Epididymis

Testis

Scrotum

The most common "symptom" for testicular cancer is the appearance of a small, hard lump—about the size of a pea—on the front or the side of a testicle. Although the presence of a lump is the most telling symptom, other "warning signals" warrant our attention like a feeling of heaviness in the testes, a dull ache in the groin, a change in the consistency of the testes or a sudden accumulation of blood or fluid in the scrotum. Any of these symptoms should be taken seriously and prompt a man to see a physician immediately.

Besides knowing the symptoms that *may* signal testicular cancer, we also need to learn how to perform a testicular self-examination (TSE), the single best method for early detection of testicular cancer. *Remember, performing a TSE is easy and painless and performing it monthly may save your life.*

1. Perform a TSE once a month—preferably after a warm bath or shower. The heat causes the scrotal skin to relax, making it easier to find anything unusual. So after your shower or bath . . .
2. Stand naked in front of a mirror. Look for any swelling on the skin of the scrotum (Figure 16.1).
3. Examine each testicle gently with both hands. The index and middle fingers should be placed underneath the testicle while the thumbs are placed on the top. Roll the testicle gently between the thumbs and fingers. One testicle may be larger than the other (Figure 16.2).
4. Find the epididymis (a cord-like structure on the top and back of the testicle that stores and transports the sperm). Do not confuse the epididymis with an abnormal lump.
5. Feel around for a small lump—again, about the size of a pea—on the front and the side of each testicle. These lumps are usually painless.

Dear Male Reader: Now that you know what to look for and how to examine your testes, please practice this easy and painless examination each and every month. Remember, testicular cancer is easily detected and with early detection, you and your physician can plan the best option to remove the cancer.

Prostatic Cancer

Located just below the bladder and in front of the inner wall of the rectum lies a muscle-gland called the prostate. The **prostate** is an important bundle of tissue involved in ejaculation. Surrounding a part of the urethra (the tube that carries urine

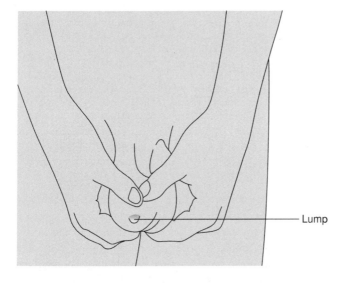

figure 16.2
Testicular self-examination.

Lump

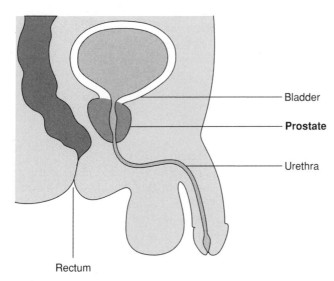

figure 16.3
The prostate.

Bladder

Prostate

Urethra

Rectum

from the bladder), the prostate emits a fluid that combines with the testes' spermatozoa and a fluid produced in the seminal vesicles all of which make up the milky and viscous seminal fluid (Figure 16.3). For most of a man's first 40 to 50 years, the prostate poses few problems. However, beginning in middle age and for reasons not yet entirely clear, a man's prostate oftentimes begins to enlarge causing what the medical profession calls a **benign prostatic hyperplasia** (BPH) or a non-cancerous enlargement of the prostate gland.

The symptoms associated with benign prostatic hyperplasia are rather slow in their onset and as the name would suggest quite mild or benign in their consequences. If you're a middle-aged or older man, you may know first hand one or

**common symptoms
associated with
a prostate problem**

A slowing of urine stream or force.

A frequent urge to urinate, most noticed by needing to get up
two or three times a night.

Slowness in starting to urinate. Hesitancy, stopping and starting.

A spasm that stops urination.

Discomfort or pain during urination.

A sharp pain in pelvic or rectal area.

Incomplete emptying of the bladder.

Inability to stop urinating, a continuing dribble.

Trace or stains of blood in urine.

Nausea, dizziness or unusual sleepiness.

From the book *The Prostate Problem,* by Chet Cunningham and United Research, Inc. Published by Pinnacle Books, an imprint of Windsor Publishing Corp. Reprinted by permission.

more of the following symptoms of BPH: a reduction in the force and stream of urine, a hesitancy to begin urination, and the need to get up two to three times a night to urinate or what doctors call *nocturia.* It's estimated that as many as sixty percent of men over sixty years and more than ninety-five percent of men in their eighties have some of the symptoms associated with BPH (Cunningham, 1990).

If BPH was the only problem, few men would complain because their urine flow was less-than-fire-hose pressure or the slight inconvenience associated with their frequent nightly shuffles to the bathroom. However, according to the American Cancer Society, one out of every eleven men will develop **prostatic cancer** sometime in their lives. And according to a recent report, *prostatic cancer kills about 35,000 American men a year* (Adler, 1993; Cowley, 1993a, 1993b). Again, this fact is disturbing as prostatic cancer is easily detected and treatable. But, you must know its symptoms (see "Common Symptoms Associated With a Prostate Problem"). Remember, just having one or more of the following symptoms does not mean you have prostatic cancer, only that you should see your physician for a prostate examination, more than likely a **digital rectal exam.**

Although it may sound a bit unnerving to most men, the digital rectal exam is simple, quick, and only slightly uncomfortable. The physician will put on a plastic glove and lubricate one finger. You'll need to bend over an examining table so that the physician can gently insert his (her) finger into your rectum. The physician can feel the prostate and readily tell if it is enlarged or not.

Surgery is the most common form of treatment for prostatic cancer. One myth that keeps many men with a prostate problem from seeing their physician is the notion that prostate surgery always causes impotency. Today's surgical techniques avoid disturbing the nerve bundles that run along either side of the prostate and control a man's ability to have an erection and intercourse. Remember, early detection is the key.

Now let's move up from a man's genital area to his chest where we find that most marvelous pump, the heart.

**a man and
his heart**

The average adult man's heart weighs about 10 ounces and beats some 60 to 80 times a minute (about 40 million times a year!). At each beat, the heart takes in and discharges about a quarter of a pint of blood (130cc). Over the course of an average day, a man's heart will pump about 2000 gallons of blood and over an average lifetime nearly 50 million gallons. When you consider the amount of work a heart does in a lifetime, one begins to appreciate just how important it is to keep it working properly.

And yet, **coronary heart disease** (CHD) is the number one killer of men! According to the best estimates, every year some 123,000 men between 29–44 years of age experience a heart attack. The yearly figures skyrocket to nearly 425,000 men between the ages of 45–64 years and 440,000 men 65 years and older. The incidence of CHD alone is one of the major factors behind men's shorter life expectancy as compared to women. Why do men suffer from CHD in such great numbers? Some argue that the female sex hormones provide a positive barrier to cardiovascular reactivity especially among premenopausal women (see Polefrone & Manuck, 1987; Saab, 1989). However, others point to certain non-biological factors as contributing to men's higher CHD incidence over women. It is these nonbiological factors that we will direct our attention to in this section. Specifically, we will look at three contributing factors that have been linked to the high incidence of CHD among men: unhealthy lifestyles, coronary prone personality, and the male gender role itself.

Unhealthy Lifestyles

Sadly, far too many of us live a lifestyle that is truly hazardous to our hearts. Everyone by now has heard about the twin evils of saturated fat and cholesterol. We see "Low Saturated Fat" and "Low Cholesterol" plastered on many of the packaged foods we buy. Everyone it seems is working to get their cholesterol level down to that elusive blood level of 200 (mg/dl). A diet rich in saturated fat and high in cholesterol (the bad LDL type, that is) has been found to increase the chances of CHD. The by-product of such diets is a fatty substance that accumulates along the inner arterial lining causing the passageway to narrow and thus forcing the heart to work harder to circulate blood, a condition called **atherosclerosis.**

Often times, a sensation of pressing and/or squeezing chest pains (angina pectoris) accompanies atherosclerosis. If the passageway becomes more restricted, the artery can become totally blocked. This blockage cuts the blood supply off completely and causes serious damage to the heart itself. Sudden blockage by a clot will cause a person to experience the classic symptoms of a heart attack: intense and persistent chest pain often followed by shooting pains to the shoulders, neck or arms, and symptoms of shock such as cold and sweaty skin, a weak pulse, and fast and labored breathing. *Immediate medical attention is necessary!*

The amount of damage to the heart depends on just how much of the heart is affected by the blockage and how quickly heart action is restored to normal functioning. As the brain also requires blood to survive and function, the time it takes to restore the heart's normal action can be crucial in preventing permanent brain damage.

As just mentioned, our high-fat diets have been indicted in this life-and-death drama. But diet alone is only one factor. Lack of exercise, use of tobacco and excessive alcohol, and maladaptive ways of handling stress all add up to heart problems. A man, for instance, who must have "real" food (e.g., fried foods, highly marbled red meats, eggs and bacon, butter, etc.), watches rather than participates in regular cardiovascular exercise, smokes and consumes excessive amounts of alcohol to ease the toll of daily tension is flirting with a heart attack.

Further, many men behave in ways that jeopardize their heart's health. Many stubbornly ignore some of the early warning signals (e.g., chest pains) and if the symptoms are present they avoid seeking help (e.g., refuse to see a doctor), or simply deny they have a problem at all because they do not want to appear weak (Verbrugge, 1985). Disregarding symptoms or denying them can be lethal. Consider that over fifty percent of those who die from CHD do so before reaching the hospital. Acting upon the early symptoms (within four hours) could reduce the death toll by anywhere between 55–80 percent. Some men it seems are just too stubborn to pay attention to what their bodies tell them and pay a terrible price.

Coronary Prone Personality

Some twenty years ago, two physicians, Meyer Friedman and Ray Rosenman (1974), examined the case histories of heart attack victims and found a common denominator in their behavior pattern. Friedman and Rosenman labeled the pattern **Type A behavior** (see Classical Type A Behaviors) and defined it as "an action-emotion complex that can be observed in any person who is aggressively involved in a chronic, incessant struggle to achieve more and more in less and less time, and if required to do so, against the opposing efforts of other things or other persons" (p. 84). In other words, a Type A person is constantly racing the clock to achieve more and more and feeling terribly frustrated if anything or anyone gets in his (her) way.

To determine if you exhibit Type A behavior, answer the following questions:

1. Do you have a habit of explosively accentuating key words in your ordinary speech and finishing your sentences in a burst of speed?
2. Do you *always* move, walk, and eat rapidly?
3. Do you feel (and openly show) impatience with the rate at which most events take place? Do you find if difficult to restrain yourself from hurrying others' speech?
4. Do you get irritated at delay—when the car in front is going too slow, when you have to wait in line, or wait to be seated in a restaurant?
5. Does it bother you to watch someone else perform a task you know you can do faster?
6. Do you often try to do two things at once such as dictating while driving or reading a paper while eating?
7. Do you *always* find it difficult to refrain from talking about or bringing the conversation around to those subjects that interest you, and when unable to, do you merely pretend to listen?
8. Do you almost always feel vaguely guilty when you relax and do absolutely nothing for several hours to several days?
9. Are you so preoccupied that you fail to observe important or beautiful objects in your environment?
10. Do you leave little or no time to become things worth *being* because you are so busy getting things worth *having*?

Although there is no "official" scoring key for this list, answering "yes" to five or more of them strongly suggests a Type A personality.

Does being a Type A person (man or woman) necessarily mean you are likely to suffer from a coronary disease? Does being a clock-watching, hard-driven, overly ambitious, no-nonsense person predict an eventual heart attack? The answer seems to be NO. After reviewing the literature on Type A behavior and coronary problems, Kenneth Matheny and Richard Riordan (1992) summarized the research this way.

> *It now seems that only part of the Type A pattern may be coronary prone.* . . . . [T]he toxic part appears to be hostility associated with "cynical contempt." Such persons are deeply suspicious and constantly on guard against others whom they believe are dishonest, antisocial, and immoral. . . . [T]his type of hostility predicts death, not only from blockages to the coronary arteries but from other causes as well. . . . [A]mong all the Type A factors, only "potential for hostility" and "anger-in," a tendency to swallow one's anger rather to express it, were predictors of coronary artery disease. In another analysis . . . these factors [were found] to be interactive, that is the potential for hostility was associated with coronary artery disease only for patients who were also high on the anger-in dimension. The lethal combination, then, appears to be: Hostility + Cynical Distrust + Anger-in. (p. 49; italics added)

The Male Gender Role and Coronary Heart Disease

Interestingly, many of the components of Type A behavior (i.e., the "toxic part") are likewise elements of the traditional male role (e.g., aggression or hostility, a basic mistrust of others especially other men as they are seen as competitors, emotional suppression or "anger-in"). In fact, numerous studies have linked many of the characteristic male behaviors (e.g., success-oriented, aggressive, and self-reliant to the point of avoiding others' support) with a Type A pattern (Auten & Hull, 1985; Chusmir & Hood, 1988; Grimm & Yarnold, 1984, 1985; Wright, 1988). Others have further noted that such behaviors can prove harmful and undermine one's health (Barnett, Beiner & Baruch, 1987; Spence, Helmreich & Pred, 1987).

The research of Vicki Helgeson (1990, 1991), a social psychologist at Carnegie Mellon University, is especially relevant to this area. Helgeson studied seventy hospitalized men who were diagnosed with an acute myocardial infarction (MI), damage to the middle layer of heart tissue as a result of arterial blockage. Helgeson wanted to see if there were any connections between traditional male gender role behaviors, certain CHD-related behaviors (i.e., Type A's "lethal combination"), and a prognostic indicator of heart attack severity (i.e., the Peel Index). In this research, Helgeson made a distinction between "positive" and "negative" masculine characteristics where positive masculinity meant the more socially acceptable side of masculine behavior (e.g., competence, self-reliance) and negative masculinity represented the worse side of the male gender role (extremes in aggression, emotional avoidance). Basically, Helgeson's research found a link between "negative masculinity" and the severity of the heart attack. In other words, extreme or "negative male characteristics (e.g., aggression, emotional constriction) were found to predict the severity of a heart attack.

Why do so many men experience heart attacks? A good possibility is that a majority of the nearly one million men who die each year lived an unhealthy lifestyle and exhibited a number of male gender characteristics identical to those noted above as "toxic" or "negative." These men are placing extreme strain or stress on their heart.

In their recent book on the subject, Matheny and Riordan (1992) proclaimed that "Stress is public enemy number 1!" (p. 27). It seems that everyone is talking about stress these days—job stress, family stress, stress in relationships, the never ending stress that comes with living. Stress is the "hot topic" in classrooms, boardrooms, workshops, and the car pool. Stress is a favorite problem to be dealt with in assorted self-help programs (e.g., college courses, seminars, and workshops), its been implicated in numerous job-related problems (e.g., absenteeism, burnout), and identified as a prime factor contributing to numerous health problems (e.g., ulcers, hypertension, heart disease). Yet, for all the attention stress gets these days, most overlook a fundamental truism about it—stress is a part of life—if you're alive you're going to experience stress. **Stress** is the body's reaction to all those situations that we have little or no control over. The key then is not how to avoid all stress (that's impossible) but rather how to adapt to the situations that cause us stress, in other words, learn to cope with it.

As stress is part of everyone's life, what can we say specifically about it in terms of men's lives? For an answer we can turn to the work of a group of Virginia Polytechnic Institute and State University researchers who have made serious inroads in understanding what kinds of situations are more stressful for men and what kinds of coping mechanisms men are more apt to use in dealing with stressful situations.

The Masculine Gender Role Stress Syndrome

During the mid-1980s, psychologist Richard Eisler and his colleagues (Eisler & Skidmore, 1987; Eisler, Skidmore, & Ward, 1988) speculated that not only do men and women differ in the kinds of events or situations they find stressful but that they also differed in the ways they cope with stress-producing events. Consequently, Eisler developed a scale (the *Masculine Gender Role Stress Scale,* MGRS) designed to measure the appraisal and coping abilities found among men. Further, Eisler proposed the concept of *Masculine Gender Role Stress* to refer to the particular kind of stress men experience stemming from the cultural imposition of masculine values and norms, which can lead to unhealthy or dysfunctional coping behaviors.

Based on early studies, Eisler identified a number of general areas that men more so than women find stressful. Specifically, men are more likely to feel greater stress when they find themselves in situations where they feel challenged or threatened—situations, for example, in which their physical abilities, intellectual endeavors, performance expectations (e.g., in the occupational or sexual arenas), and/or their emotional expressions are challenged. Conversely, women experience more stress in situations where their nurturing ability and physical appearance is challenged, in personal relationships calling for assertiveness, or in situations where they may be victimized (Gillespie & Eisler, 1991).

Building on the finding that different situations elicit different levels of stress for men and women, the next area the researchers uncovered involved the different coping styles routinely used by men which allow them to deal more effectively with the stress-producing situations. Further, the researchers found that some coping styles (or mechanisms) used by men were more adaptive than others. For instance, Eisler and Blalock (1991) isolated a number of specific coping strategies that seemed problematic or dysfunctional in men's attempt to deal with stress in their lives. Specifically, men who are faced with challenge or threat and who rely on rigid (extreme) traditional male gender role behaviors, who depend on aggression, power, and control, who place undo value on performance, achievement, and success in relationships, and who exhibit a general pattern of emotional inexpressiveness in their lives, appear to deal with stress much more poorly than men who do not show such a pattern (see Lash, Gillespie, Eisler, & Southard, 1991).

What Eisler and others have found then is a rather fascinating picture of how some men deal with stress. Those who see threat and challenge to their manhood coming from numerous sources and who appraise and approach life in a rigidly controlling fashion are the ones who are more likely to suffer a variety of potentially harmful consequences. Recall in Helgeson's research that men who exhibit "negative" aspects of the male gender role are more likely to suffer the most serious (lethal) heart attacks. Eisler's findings that men who use the most destructive and restrictive aspects of the male role as coping mechanisms for stress in their lives are more likely to suffer serious physical ailments (e.g., heart attacks).

a i d s

In 1980 and 1981, the United States Department of Public Health's Centers for Disease Control (CDC) began charting a disturbing series of puzzling clinical cases. Slowly at first but increasing with each passing month, the CDC's headquarters in Atlanta tallied cases where men, mostly living in metropolitan areas such as New York and San Francisco, were succumbing to a variety of diseases following a failure of their immune system. Deathly ill men were seen in clinics and hospitals suffering from a rare type of skin cancer called *Kaposi's sarcoma* or a particularly threatening type of pneumonia called *pneumocystic carinii*. Month after month, more and more men died; a common thread among many was that they had been openly gay and had well-documented histories of frequent bouts with various sexually transmitted diseases. Slowly, a pattern emerged from the CDC's files: a viral condition that destroyed a person's immune system leaving him susceptible to a variety of opportunistic illnesses. Initially, scientists thought the virus was somehow confined to the gay men's community. Given this pattern then, little wonder that some in the medical community dubbed the new syndrome the **gay-related immune deficiency (GRID).**

Soon, though, and as other groups began showing up in the statistics—intravenous drug users, recent Haitian immigrants, and hemophiliacs—the CDC's files reflected the knowledge that this new virus had no special proclivity for gay men only. By mid-1982, there was no reason to label nor think of this disease as gay related. Workers at CDC's headquarters argued for a more sexually neutral name. Someone, somewhere, came up with just such a label; one that provided a rather catchy acronym as well. From then on everyone has known the disease as **Acquired Immune Deficiency Syndrome,** or more simply **AIDS** (Osborn, 1987).

Most researchers today believe that AIDS is caused by a virus, the **human immunodeficiency virus** (HIV), which attacks the body's immune system thus making the body susceptible to various serious disease organisms. (However, some within the research community like Peter Duesberg, a professor at University of California, Berkeley, who specializes in virology, argue that AIDS is *not* caused by a virus but rather by "high risk" behaviors such as intravenous drug use or frequent sexual contact with many partners [see Duesberg & Ellison, 1994; Kelleher, 1993; Root-Bernstein, 1993].) Once the virus gets into the bloodstream it attacks the immune system by first invading and then destroying a type of white blood cell called the helper T cell. By destroying the helper T cell, the virus disables the very cells that would allow the body to fight it and other disease-causing organisms. In a healthy human, the normal level of helper T cells is about 1,000 per cubic millimeter of blood. After HIV infection and for several years, a person may look and act normal because the level of helper T cells remains near normal. However, after several years, the number of helper T cells may drop. When the helper T cells fall below 200 per cubic millimeter of blood, the infected person becomes susceptible to all kinds of illnesses and begins to show a variety of symptoms like fatigue, night sweats, persistent fever, swollen lymph nodes, diarrhea, and unexplained weight loss. As the syndrome progresses, the AIDS victim may develop any number of *opportunistic* diseases (called opportunistic as none would normally affect a person with an intact and healthy immune system) such as Kaposi's sarcoma (a rare form of cancer), pneumocystic carinii pneumonia, and what is called the "wasting syndrome" wherein a person literally wastes away until succumbing to death.

Since 1981 when fewer than 100 people in the United States had died of AIDS, the number of deaths attributable to AIDS has reached between 285,000 to 340,000 through 1993. On a worldwide scale, the World Health Organization (WHO) estimates that in early 1992 at least 10 to 12 million adults and children have been infected with HIV since the late 1970s. By 2000, WHO estimates a total of 30 to 40 million men, women, and children will have been infected, and 12 to 18 million will have developed AIDS (DeVita, Hellman, & Rosenberg, 1993).

In order to survive, the AIDS virus must get into the bloodstream to do its damage (i.e., destroy helper T cells). Normally, a person's skin acts as a barrier warding off the rather fragile HIV which will die rather quickly when exposed to air. However, a cut in the skin can allow the virus entrance into the bloodstream. The most common activities that allow the virus to enter the bloodstream are the exchange of fluids through vaginal or anal intercourse, sharing hypodermic needles, or being stuck with a contaminated needle.

What does this have to do with men's health though? Isn't AIDS a problem primarily for gay men, intravenous drug users, and prostitutes? No, AIDS is everyone's problem. Yes, the incidence of AIDS is dramatically increasing among women. But still, the majority of AIDS victims continue to be men. All men—no matter if they are gay, straight, or bisexual, IV drug users or those who frequent prostitutes—must wake up to the fact that the way they have been socialized makes them susceptible to being infected with HIV. Men are taught early on that being cautious, careful, safe is not manly. Taking risks is manly. Having unprotected sex is manly. How many times have you heard a young man say that "wearing condoms is like taking a shower with your socks on." "Condoms are more trouble than they're worth." "Come on. I don't need to use a condom, nothing is going to happen to me." And what about having sex with as many partners as possible. Isn't that manly? Take Magic Johnson, for instance. Johnson was at the height of his athletic career and enjoying some of the "perks" that go along with being a superstar—easy access to numerous sex partners (see McKay, 1993). Yet, Johnson contracted HIV and his athletic (and commercial) career suffered as a result. I dare say Johnson never thought much about AIDS nor the possibility that his "high risk" behaviors could change his life so dramatically. The lesson to be learned here: men who like to live life on the edge often fall off.

Over the past decade or so, significant numbers of men have begun to question many of the values they were raised with (e.g., be a success at others' expense, dominate your relationships and your environment, don't show weakness) and their lifestyles (e.g., accumulating possessions, having little regard for others and themselves). Consequently, many have begun searching for something more; they have begun a "spiritual" journey or quest, so to speak, to find something deeper, more meaningful in their lives. Some have turned to traditional or mainline religions for directions (see Murphey, 1991), while others have sought greater meaning in their lives through other, less conventional practices (e.g., fasting, sweat lodges, meditation). No matter the path, the fact is that many men are searching, questing, hungering for something deeper, something more meaningful in their lives causing many to chart a new avenue of spiritual growth, what some are calling a **men's spirituality.** In any discussion of men's health, we need to address what for many is a missing element in men's lives, the spiritual dimension.

men and spirituality

First, let's be clear about what we mean by spirituality. And how does spirituality or, more specifically, men's spirituality differ from women's spirituality? Theologian James Nelson (1988) defines spirituality as "the ways and patterns by which the person—intellectually, emotionally, and physically—relates to that which is ultimately real and worthful for him or her" (p. 21). Thus spirituality can be said to comprise those activities a person uses to relate to what for him or her is perceived as most deeply real or worthful. Said another way, spirituality consists of those ways or patterns (e.g., rituals or practices like prayers, readings, meditation, song, dance) that allow a person to intimately connect with what is "ultimately" important to him or her (e.g., the Absolute, god/dess, spirit). Still, how does such a broad definition of spirituality help us to understand what is unique to "men's spirituality" as compared to "women's spirituality," for instance?

To answer this let us first inquire about what entails women's spirituality or the practices used to achieve the "ultimately real and worthful" growing out of the female experience. We do this here simply because a distinct "women's spirituality" has been evolving for a number of years now, much longer than a comparable men's spirituality movement. What then constitutes women's spirituality?

Recently, Cynthia Eller (1993) analyzed the many forms of women's spirituality (e.g., wicca, Christian women's/feminist spirituality, Jewish women's/feminist spirituality) and found that all, regardless of their differences, share five areas of agreement in greater or lesser degrees. Specifically, women's spirituality seeks to empower women, has an interest in ritual and/or magic, reveres nature, uses the feminine gender as the primary focus of analysis, and espouses a revisionist view of Western history.

Given that women's spirituality embraces some very definite practices that incorporate women's experiences, what then can we say about the experiences which constitute men's spirituality. Although the terrain of men's spirituality is not as well mapped as women's spirituality (men, it seems, are latecomers to dealing with these issues), a number of theologians have recently begun examining men's lives and experiences in an attempt to draw a rudimentary outline of what constitutes men's spirituality. While most have focused primarily on the experiences of white, heterosexual men (see Arnold, 1991; Culbertson, 1992; Owen-Towle, 1991; Rohr & Martos, 1992), a number of gay theologians have provided insightful treatises on spirituality pointing out the inherent problems in traditional "heteropatriarchal" theologies (see Clark, 1989, 1992; McNeill, 1988). While no single author on men's spirituality can speak for all, here we will rely on the works of James Nelson (1989, 1992) to give a sense of some of the broader issues related to a specific male spirituality.

Nelson contends that three "underlying issues" have shaped men's search for intimacy with or relatedness to the ultimately real and worthful over the centuries: sexism, genitalization, and separation. Nelson also argues that these three have *negatively* affected men's overall view of spirituality by restricting or limiting their ability for reaching a fulfilling (i.e., intimate) relationship to that which is ultimately real for them. Let's briefly deal with these issues to see how each has shaped not only men's view of spirituality, but that of most people.

Given our Western civilization's heritage of Greek philosophies and heteropatriarchal (biased toward heterosexual and male dominant) institutions, most of us (Euro-Americans, that is) see the world and define reality from a bifurcated (dualistic) perspective. Thus the majority view reality as dichotomously constructed with most dichotomies arranged and evaluated hierarchically, for instance, male/female, mind/body, sacred/profane, thought/emotion, heterosexual/homosexual, independent/dependent, up/down, etc. Consequently, the major Western religions have constructed their images of ultimate reality in hierarchically dominant male or masculine terms. Thus in the Christian, Jewish, and Islamic religions, we find the divine, the ultimate reality imaged and addressed as a dominant male (God the Father, Yahweh, Allah). To allow the ultimate to be imaged as female or feminine is unthinkable (sacrilegious) for many.

A second issue shaping how most men have viewed spirituality is what Nelson calls genitalization. A man's genitals (penis and testes), his sexual center, so to speak, are external, separate, appendages to his sense of self. Women's genitals, on the other hand, are internal, inclusive of her sense of self. A man's external genital experience then, argues Nelson, helps shape his ability for intimacy or connectedness. A man can use his sexual organs without requiring himself to be intimately involved (take another into his most central self). Thus men's genitalization causes them to separate (split-off, divide) their basic need for intimacy with another—the ultimately real—from their basic (defining) sexual/sensual selves. A man's bodily self (sexual) is separated from his image of the spiritual. As a woman's need for intimacy is merged with her sexual/sensual self, she is able to bring her whole self (including her sexual/sensual self) to a spiritual path.

A sense of basic separation is the third influence shaping men's spiritual awareness. Nelson draws on the developmental literature (primarily psychoanalytic) speculating as to how a young boy's identity grows out of his basic separation from (and renouncing of) his primary relationship (mother) and is complete when he accepts a distant other (father). A collateral separation from mother is not necessary for a girl's identity to develop (see Chodorow, 1978). Nelson suggests that the boy's separation from his mother and identification with his father (distant and removed) sets the stage for his later spiritual life when as a man he seeks a distant and removed (father) figure for approval, all the while rejecting or renouncing any trace of the feminine.

What then do the features of sexism, genitalization, and separation have to do with our discussion on men's spirituality? Recall that Nelson contends that these features form the basis for what most have defined as spirituality. A spirituality based on sexism (a spiritual imaging of the Ultimate as Father), on genitalization (a spirituality that separates the body from the spirit thus requiring one's need for intimacy to evolve asensually or asexually), on separation rather than merging (a spirituality idealizing separation rather than merger or mutuality). Nelson argues then that men must first examine the basis for their views on spirituality. From there, he argues they must restructure and move beyond traditional spirituality (move beyond their dualistic, genitalized, and separate image of the spiritual) and incorporate a new definition of intimacy with the "ultimately real and worthful."

What form(s) will this men's spirituality take? No one is quite sure yet. The authors noted at the beginning of this section are only now beginning to examine new ways for men to be spiritual. One thing is certain though—more and more men will continue to seek ways and patterns (rituals, prayers) that incorporate their male experiences into their relation to what is real and worthful in their lives. As men explore and understand themselves, their whole selves including mental, emotional, and physical features, they will evolve new and more fully integrated spiritual paths that flow out of their complete male experience.

Here with the spiritual, we end our journey of examining the male experience. One last wish I leave you: May your life be filled with love, peace, and joy.

Acquired Immune Deficiency Syndrome (AIDS) *285*

Atherosclerosis *281*

Benign Prostatic Hyperplasia (BPH) *279*

Coronary heart disease (CHD) *281*

Digital rectal exam *280*

Gay-related immune deficiency (GRID) *285*

Human immunodeficiency virus (HIV) *285*

Life expectancy *274*

Masculine gender role stress *284*

Men's spirituality *287*

Prostate *278*

Prostatic cancer *280*

Stress *284*

Testicular cancer *277*

Testicular self-examination *277*

Type A behavior *282*

important terms

Men's Health

suggested readings

Cunningham, C. (1990). *The prostate problem*. New York: Pinnacle.

Matheny, K. B., & Riordan, R. J. (1992). *Stress and strategies for lifestyle management*. Atlanta, GA: Georgia State University Business Press.

Nelson, J. (1989). *The intimate connection: Male sexuality, masculine spirituality*. Philadelphia: Westminster.

Rathus, S. A., & Bough, S. (1993). *AIDS: What every student needs to know*. Fort Worth, TX: Harcourt Brace Jovanovich.

Resources

The following contain information subject to change (e.g., addresses). Every effort has been taken to assure its accuracy as of November, 1993. Further, there are too many local men's councils, men's groups, and regional newsletters to include here. If you are interested in locating a local group contact its parent national organization and request information about local organizations.

national organizations

The **American Men's Studies Association** (AMSA) is a national organization of men and women dedicated to teaching, research, and clinical practice in the field of men's studies whose goal is to provide a forum for teachers, researchers, and therapists to exchange information and gain support for their work with men. The AMSA hosts a men's studies conference each spring that brings together scholars from various perspectives. For more information contact, AMSA, 22 East Street, Northampton, MA 01060.

The **Men's Health Network** seeks to develop specific programs in disease awareness, therapy, veterans' support, youth, and fatherhood that are oriented toward positive, collaborative, life-enhancing steps rather than gender conflict. The Network promotes educational campaigns, data collection, networking, and referral of health care providers, and will serve individuals seeking to join with others in common effort. For more information contact, Men's Health Network, P.O. Box 770, Washington, DC 20044–0770.

The **Men's Studies in Religion Group** is an officially recognized group within the American Academy of Religion (AAR) involved in assisting theology/religious studies scholars interested in men's studies issues. For more information contact, Dr. Stephen Boyd, Department of Religion, Box 7212, Wake Forest University, Winston-Salem, NC 27109.

The **National Coalition of Free Men** is a pro-male (men's rights) organization concerned with dealing with issues where men experience discrimination such as in courts. The Coalition publishes its own journal, *Transitions*. For more information contact, Tom Williamson, c/o National Coalition of Free Men, P.O. Box 129, Manhasset, NY 11030.

The **National Congress for Men and Children** (NCMC) is a national organization dedicated to serving the needs of fathers and working to ensure equal rights for fathers in divorce and child custody cases. For more information write, National Congress for Men and Children, 2020 Pennsylvania Avenue, N.W., Suite 277, Washington, DC 20006–1846.

The **National Council for African-American Men** (NCAAM) is a national organization devoted to serving the interests of African-American men. NCAAM hosts an annual conference focusing on African-American men's issues and concerns as well as publishing a biannual journal, the *Journal of African-American Men's Studies*. For more information contact, Jacob Gordon, c/o NCAAM, 1028 Dole Center, University of Kansas, Lawrence, KS 66045.

The **National Organization for Men Against Sexism** (NOMAS) is a profeminist national organization devoted to ending sexism in all its forms as well as being gay affirmative and male positive. NOMAS also hosts the annual national Men & Masculinity conference at various locations usually in the summer months. For more information contact, NOMAS, 54 Mint Street, San Francisco, CA 94103.

The **Society for the Psychological Study of Men and Masculinity** (SPSMM) promotes advances in both scientific and applied psychology that are focused on (a) advancing psychological understanding of male behavior and experiences, (b) developing intervention strategies for responding to maladaptive behavior patterns in men, (c) fostering empathic dialogue between the genders, (d) advocating for public policy and social change initiatives derived from scientific and professional investigation and practice aimed at expanding the options for male role behavior and improving the quality of men's lives. For more information contact, SPSMM, c/o Gary Brooks, Ph.D., 902 South 31st Street, Temple, TX 76504.

national magazines or newsletters

Changing Men is a biannual publication that presents articles dealing with men's issues from an anti-sexist, gay-affirmative perspective. Book reviews and information about the National Organization for Men Against Sexism are included in each issue. For more information contact, *Changing Men,* 306 N. Brooks Street, Madison, WI 53715.

Fathers' Rights Newsline is a bimonthly newsletter serving divorced and separated fathers, their second families and parents. For more information contact, *Fathers' Rights Newsline,* P.O. Box 713, Havertown, PA 19083.

First Class Male is a small newsletter devoted to issues involving male victims of sexual abuse and their helpers. For more information contact, William L. Sprague, 50 N. Arlington Avenue, Indianapolis, IN 46219.

The Green Man is a magazine devoted to exploring the mysteries and rituals that celebrate men's connections with each other, with women, and with the natural world. *The Green Man* is published to create space and to explore the challenges and joys of being a "pagan" man in today's society. For more information contact, *The Green Man,* P.O. Box 641, Point Arena, CA 95468.

Journeymen is a quarterly that explores the "male-positive" men's movement and issues of interest to men. For more information contact, *Journeymen,* 513 Chester Turnpike, Candia, NH 03034.

The Liberator is the official newsmagazine of Men's Equality Now (M.E.N.) devoted to correcting what the publishers see as an anti-male bias toward males in areas like domestic relations and divorce proceedings. This publication represents a men's rights perspective. For more information contact, *The Liberator,* c/o Men's Rights Association, Rt. #6, Forest Lake, MN 55025.

Man! is a glossy quarterly journal devoted to building better relations between men and women and to disseminate information about the men's movement. *Man!* has a decidedly mythopoetic orientation. For more information contact, *Man!,* 1611 W. Sixth Street, Austin, TX 78703.

Men As We Are is a national quarterly magazine that publishes writing, art and photography from and about men in their "diverse communities." For more information contact, *Men As We Are Publishing,* 581 Tenth Street, Brooklyn, NY 11215–4401.

Men's Council Journal is a mythopoetic-oriented quarterly journal giving coverage through poetry, articles, and personal reflections to this growing segment of the men's movement. For more information contact, *Men's Council Journal,* Box 4795, Boulder, CO 80306.

Men's Health Newsletter is a monthly publication devoted to a wide variety of men's health issues. In one recent issue there was a quiz on "sexual literacy," an informative article on chest pains, and an informative article on male sexuality and the aging process. For more information contact, *Men's Health Newsletter,* 33 E. Minor Street, Emmaus, PA 18098.

Men's Reproductive Health is a quarterly newsletter published by the American Public Health Association's Task Force on Men in Family Planning and Reproductive Health. This journal is published with the needs of health care professionals and educators in mind. Each issue carries the latest news about a variety of topics including men's reproductive health, AIDS, and male sexuality. For more information contact, *Men's Reproductive Health,* P.O. Box 661, Capitola, CA 95010.

National Men's Resource Calendar is published quarterly and contains information of events, services, workshops, cultural programs, listing of book stores with men's studies sections, and men's studies classes and lectures that are involved with a positive change in male roles and relationships. For more information contact, NMRC, P.O. Box 800-CM, San Anselmo, CA 94979.

Network is the publication of the National Congress for Men and Children. The publication contains information about court proceedings, legislative alerts, and articles dealing with issues of interest to divorced and separated fathers. For more information write, National Congress for Men and Children, 2020 Pennsylvania Avenue, N.W., Suite 277, Washington, DC 20006–1846.

Partners magazine for gay and lesbian couples is a quarterly journal supporting same-sex couples with information, interviews, and ideas. For more information contact, *Partners,* Box 9685, Seattle, WA 98109.

Wingspan: Journal of the Male Spirit is an international quarterly devoted to chronically mythopoetic men's activities. Each issue contains material representing men's work through leadership interviews, workshop profiles, discussions of myth and poetry, and reviews of books, films, and tapes. For more information contact, *Wingspan,* Box 23550, Brightmoor Station, Detroit, MI 48223.

academic journals

GLQ: A Journal of Lesbian and Gay Studies is a new journal that provides a forum for the interdisciplinary field of lesbian and gay men's studies. **GLQ** is particularly interested in publishing research dealing with pre-20th century historical periods, non-anglophone cultures, and the experiences of those who have been marginalized by race, ethnicity, social class, or sexual practice. For more information contact, Carolyn Dinshaw, Department of English, University of California, Berkeley, CA 94720, or David M. Halperin, 14N–432, Massachusetts Institute of Technology, 77 Massachusetts Avenue, Cambridge, MA 02139.

The *Journal of African-American Men's Studies* is the official publication of the National Council of African-American Men. Under the editorship of Courtland Lee, the journal appears twice yearly and presents articles and book reviews for those interested in the latest issues affecting African-American men. For more information contact, Jacob Gordon, c/o NCAAM, 1028 Dole Center, University of Kansas, Lawrence, KS 66045.

The Journal of Men's Studies is a quarterly publication presenting the work of scholars from various academic fields, diverse theoretical perspectives, and different cultures. Each issue contains original articles, book reviews, and information of interest to men's studies scholars (call for papers, announcements, etc.). For more information contact, James A. Doyle, P.O. Box 32, Harriman, TN 37748.

Masculinities is a quarterly publication exploring the meanings of manhood in the contemporary world. The journal focuses on feminist research on gender issues. For more information contact Guilford Publications, Journals Department, 72 Spring Street, New York, NY 10012.

specialized resources

August, E. R. (forthcoming). *Men's studies: A selected and annotated interdisciplinary bibliography* (2nd ed.). Littleton, CO: Libraries Unlimited.

Duroche, L. L. (Ed.). (forthcoming). *Men's studies encyclopedia*. Westport, CT: Greenwood Press.

Femiano, S. (1991). *Directory of men's studies courses taught in the United States and Canada*. The listing includes course title, department, university, as well as names, addresses, and telephone numbers of instructors, and other information. For more information contact, Sam Femiano, 22 East Street, Northampton, MA 01060.

Femiano, S. (nd). *Men's studies syllabi*. A collection of syllabi from about 30 different courses representing a variety of disciplines. For more information contact, Sam Femiano, 22 East Street, Northampton, MA 01060.

Gertner, D. M., & Harris, J. E., (1993). *Exploring masculinity: Exercises, activities, and resources for teaching and learning about men* (3rd ed.). Contains dozens of experiential exercises, individual and group activities, sample workshops, syllabi, lesson plans, and bibliographies designed to assist participants in recognizing, exploring, and understanding the social constructed aspects of their gender roles. For more information contact, Douglas M. Gertner, 922 Madison Street, Denver, CO 80206.

References

The numbers in parentheses at the end of each citation refer to the chapters the reference appears in.

Abra, J. (1988). *Assaulting Parnassus: Theoretical views of creativity.* Lanham, MD: University Press of America. (4)

Abrahamsen, D. (1960). *The psychology of crime.* New York: Columbia University Press. (9)

Abrams, D., Carter, J., & Hogg, M. (1989). Perceptions of male homosexuality: An application of social identity theory. *Social Behaviour, 4,* 253–264. (13)

Adelson, J. (1979, January). Adolescence and the generalization gap. *Psychology Today,* 33–37. (4)

Adler, J. (1993, December 27). The killer we don't discuss. *Newsweek,* 40–41. (16)

Ahlgren, A., & Johnson, W. (1979). Sex differences in cooperative and competitive attitudes from the second through the twelfth grades. *Developmental Psychology, 15,* 45–49. (8)

Albin, R. (1977). Psychological studies of rape. *Signs, 3,* 423–435. (9)

Alland, Jr., A. (1988). Phallic symbolism and reproductive expropriation: Sexual politics in cross cultural perspective. In R. Randolph et al. (Eds.), *Dialetics and gender: Anthropological approaches* (pp. 20–37). Boulder, CO: Westview Press. (6)

Allen, L., Hines, M., Shryne, J., & Gorski, R. (1989). Two sexually dimorphic cell groups in the human brain. *Journal of Neuroscience, 9,* 497–506. (3)

Allen, W. (1978). Black family research in the United States: A review, assessment and extension. *Journal of Contemporary Family Studies, 9,* 167–189. (14)

Altman, D. (1987). *AIDS in the mind of America.* Garden City, NY: Anchor Books. (13)

Altorki, S. (1986). *Women in Saudi Arabia.* New York: Columbia University Press. (6)

Alvirez, D., & Bean, F. (1976). The Mexican family. In C. Mindel & R. Habenstein (Eds.), *Ethnic families in America* (pp. 271–292). New York: Elsevier. (14)

Amaro, H., Russo, N., & Pares-Avila, J. (1987). Contemporary research on Hispanic women: A selected bibliography of the social science literature. *Psychology of Women Quarterly, 11,* 523–532. (14)

American Association of University Women. (1992). *How schools shortchange girls: A study of major findings on girls and education.* Washington, DC: AAUW Educational Foundation and the National Education Association. (5)

Andersen, C. (1988, January 31). What their fathers taught them. *Parade Magazine,* 4–5. (15)

Andrade, S. (1982). Family roles of Hispanic women: Stereotypes, empirical findings, and implications for research. In R. Zambrana (Ed.), *Work, family, and health: Latina women in transition* (pp. 95–107). New York: Hispanic Research Center. (14)

Angier, N. (1990, July 19). Scientists say gene on Y chromosome makes a man a man. *The New York Times,* A1, A19. (3)

Anonymous. (1974). Life in the military. In J. Pleck & J. Sawyer (Eds.), *Men and masculinity* (pp. 127–129). Englewood Cliffs, NJ: Prentice-Hall. (11)

Anson, O., Antonovsky, A., Sagy, S., & Adler, I. (1989). Family, gender, and attitudes toward retirement. *Sex Roles, 20,* 355–369. (4)

Antil, J., & Cunningham, J. (1980). The relationship of masculinity, femininity, and androgyny to self-esteem. *Australian Journal of Psychology, 32,* 195–207. (4)

Antill, J., & Cotton, S. (1988). Factors affecting the division of labor in households. *Sex Roles, 18,* 531–553. (12)

Arade, N. (1988). The partner's role in impotence. Paper presented at the American Association of Sex Educators, Counselors, and Therapists Twenty-First Annual Meeting, San Francisco. (10)

Arias, I., Samios, M., & O'Leary, K. (1987). Prevalence and correlates of physical aggression during courtship. *Journal of Interpersonal Violence, 2,* 82–90. (9)

Aries, E., & Olver, R. (1985). Sex differences in the development of a separate sense of self during infancy: Directions for future research. *Psychology of Women Quarterly, 9,* 515–532. (5)

Ariès, P., & Béjin, A. (1985). *Western sexuality.* New York: Blackwell. (13)

Arkin, W., & Dobrofsky, L. (1978). Military socialization and masculinity. *Journal of Social Issues, 34,* 151–168. (11)

Arnold, P. M. (1991). *Wildmen, warriors, and kings: Masculine spirituality and the Bible.* New York: Crossroad. (16)

Asante, M. (1981). Black male and female relationships: An Afrocentric context. In L. Gary (Ed.), *Black men* (pp. 75–82). Beverly Hills, CA: Sage. (14)

Asch, S. (1956). Studies of independence and conformity: A minority of one against a unanimous majority. *Psychological Monographs, 70,* Whole No. 416 (4)

Ashmore, R., Del Boca, F., & Wohlers, A. (1986). Gender stereotypes. In R. Ashmore & F. Del Boca (Eds.), *The social psychology of female-male relations* (pp. 69–119). Orlando, FL: Academic Press. (4)

Attorney General's Commission on Pornography: Final Report. (1986, July). Washington, DC: U.S. Department of Justice. (9)

August, E. R. (1993). Neither backlash nor fad: The new men's studies. *Reference Service Review, Fall,* 15–22. (1)

Ault, D. A. (1992, January). Let's ratify a gender-inclusive Equal Rights Amendment. *Seattle M.E.N,* 3, 11. (1)

Austin, A., Salehi, M., & Leffler, A. (1987). Gender and developmental differences in children's conversations. *Sex Roles, 16,* 497–510. (4)

Auten, P., & Hull, D. (1985). Sex role orientation and type A behavior pattern. *Psychology of Women Quarterly, 9,* 288–290. (16)

Bachman, J., & Jennings, M. (1975). The impact on trust in government. *Journal of Social Issues* 31(4), 141–155. (1)

Baenninger, M., & Newcombe, N. (1989). The role of experience in spatial test performance: A meta-analysis. *Sex Roles, 20,* 327–344. (4)

Bahr, R. (1976). *The virility factor: Masculinity through testosterone, the male sex hormone.* New York: Putnam. (3)

Bain, J. (1987). Hormones and sexual aggression in the male. *Integrative Psychiatry, 5,* 82–89. (3)

Baker, M. (Ed.). (1987). *Sex differences in human performance.* New York: Wiley. (4)

Bales, J. (1988, June). Japanese "derelict dads" just another myth. *The APA Monitor,* 29. (14)

Bales, J. (1988, August). Sex stereotyping data valid, brief says. *The APA Monitor, 19,* 23. (4)

Ballard-Reisch, D., & Elton, M. (1992). Gender orientation and the Bem Sex Role Inventory: A psychological construct revisited. *Sex Roles, 27,* 291, 306. (4)

Bancroft, J. (1982). Erectile impotence: Psyche or soma? *International Journal of Andrology, 5,* 353–355. (10)

Bancroft, J. (1984). Hormones and human sexual behavior. *Journal of Sex and Marital Therapy, 10,* 3–21. (3)

Banikotes, P., Neimeyer, G., & Lepkowsky, C. (1981). Gender and sex role orientation effects on friendship choice. *Personality and Social Psychology Bulletin, 7,* 605–610. (12)

Bankart, C., & Bankart, B. (1985). Japanese children's perceptions of their parents. *Sex Roles, 13,* 679–690. (14)

Bardwick, J. (1973). *Men and work.* Unpublished paper. (8)

Bardwick, J., & Schumann, S. (1967). Portrait of American men and women in TV commercials. *Psychology, 4.* (5)

Baring, A., & Cashford, J. (1993). *The myth of the goddess: Evolution of an image.* New York: Penguin. (2, 6)

Baritz, L. (1985). *Backfire: A history of how American culture led us into Vietnam and made us fight the way we did.* New York: Ballantine Books. (1)

Barker-Benfield, G. (1976). *The horrors of the half-known life: Male attitudes toward women and sexuality in nineteenth-century America.* New York: Harper & Row. (2)

Barlow, D. (1986). Causes of sexual dysfunction: The role of anxiety and cognitive interference. *Journal of Consulting and Clinical Psychology, 54,* 140–148. (10)

Barnett, R., & Baruch, G. (1988). Correlates of fathers' participation in family work. In P. Bronstein & C. P. Cowan (Eds.), *Fatherhood today: Men's changing role in the family* (pp. 66–78). New York: Wiley. (15)

Barnett, R., Biener, L., & Baruch, G. (Eds.). (1987). *Gender and stress.* New York: Free Press. (3, 16)

Barr, H., Streissguth, A., Darby, B., & Sampson, P. (1990). Prenatal exposure to alcohol, caffeine, tobacco, and aspirin: Effects on fine and gross motor performance in 4-year-old children. *Developmental Psychology, 26,* 339–348. (3)

Barret, R., & Robinson, R. (1985). The adolescent father. In S. Hanson & F. Bozett (Eds.), *Dimensions of fatherhood* (pp. 353–368). Beverly Hills, CA: Sage. (15)

Barry, H., Bacon, M., & Child, I. (1957). A cross-cultural survey of some sex differences in socialization. *Journal of Abnormal and Social Psychology, 55,* 327–332. (6)

Basch, N. (1982). *In the eyes of the law: Women, marriage and property in nineteenth-century New York.* Ithaca: Cornell University Press. (2)

Basow, S. (1985). Correlates of sex-typing in Fiji. *Psychology of Women Quarterly, 10,* 429–442. (6)

Baum, A., & Paulus, P. (1987). Crowding. In D. Stokols & I. Altman (Eds.), *Handbook of environmental psychology* (Vol. 1, pp. 533–570). New York: Wiley-Interscience. (6)

Baumli, F. (Ed.). (1985). *Men freeing men.* Jersey City, NJ: New Atlantic Press. (1)

Baumrind, D. (1983). Are androgynous individuals more effective persons and parents? *Child Development, 53,* 44–75. (4)

Bayer, R. (1981). *Homosexuality and American psychiatry: The politics of diagnosis.* New York: Basic Books. (13)

Beall, A., & Sternberg, R. (Eds.). (1993). *The psychology of gender.* New York: Guilford Press. (4)

Becker, B. (1986). Influence again: An examination of reviews and studies of gender differences in social influence. In J. Hyde & M. Linn (Eds.), *The psychology of gender: Advances through meta-analysis* (pp. 178–209). Baltimore: Johns Hopkins University Press. (4, 12)

Beckett, J. (1976). Working wives: A racial comparison. *Social Work, 21,* 463–471. (14)

Belenky, M., Clinchy, B., Goldberger, N., & Tarule, J. (1986). Women's ways of knowing: The development of self, voice, and mind. New York: Basic Books. (4)

Bell, A. (1978, January 23). Asexuality: Everybody's not doing it. The *Village Voice.* (10)

Bell, A., & Weinberg, M. (1978). *Homosexualities: A study of diversity among men and women.* New York: Simon & Schuster. (13)

Bell, D. (1981). Up from patriarchy: The male role in historical perspective. In R. Lewis (Ed.), *Men in difficult times.* Englewood Cliffs, NJ: Prentice-Hall. (2)

Bell, R. (1981). *Worlds of friendship.* Beverly Hills, CA: Sage. (7, 12)

Belsky, J., Spanier, G., & Rovine, M. (1983). Stability and change in marriage across the transition to parenthood. *Journal of Marriage and the Family, 45,* 553–556. (15)

Bem, S. (1974). The measurement of psychological androgyny. *Journal of Consulting and Clinical Psychology, 42,* 155–162. (4)

Ben Tsvi-Mayer, S., Hertz-Lazarowitz, R., & Safir, M. P. (1989). Teachers' selection of boys and girls as prominent pupils. *Sex Roles, 21,* 231–245. (5)

Benderly, B. (1987). *The myth of two minds: What gender means and doesn't mean.* New York: Doubleday. (4)

Bennett, L. (1983). *Dangerous wives and sacred sisters.* New York: Columbia University Press. (6)

Benokraitis, N. (1985). Fathers in dual-earner families. In S. Hanson & F. Bozett (Eds.), *Dimensions of fatherhood* (pp. 243–268). Beverly Hills, CA: Sage. (15)

Berger, K. (1988). *The developing person through the life span* (2nd ed.). New York: Worth. (4)

Berger, P. (1985). *The goddess obscured: Transformation of the grain protectress from goddess to saint.* Boston: Beacon Press. (2)

Berger, T. (1964). *Little big man.* New York: Fawcett Crest Books. (6)

Berglas, S. (1986). *The success syndrome: Hitting bottom when you reach the top.* New York: Plenum. (8)

Bergman, B. (1986). *The economic emergence of women.* New York: Basic Books. (2)

Berk, R., Berk, S., Loseke, D., & Rauma, D. (1983). Mutual combat and other family violence myths. In D. Finklehor et al. (Eds.), *The dark side of families: Current family violence research* (pp. 197–212). Beverly Hills, CA: Sage. (9)

Berlin, I. (1958 February). *Theater Arts.* (8)

Berman, J., et al. (1988). Sex differences in friendship patterns in India and the United States. *Basic and Applied Psychology, 9,* 61–71. (12)

Bernard, J. (1981). *The female world.* New York: Free Press. (4, 7)

Bernard, J. (1981). The good-provider role: Its rise and fall. *American Psychologist, 36,* 1–12. (1, 8, 15)

Bernard, J. (1982). *The future of marriage.* New Haven: Yale University Press. (12)

Bettelheim, B. (1962). *Symbolic wounds.* New York: Collier Books. (6)

Bieber, I., et al. (1962). *Homosexuality: A psychoanalytic study of male homosexuals.* New York: Basic Books. (13)

Biller, H. (1971). *Father, child, and sex role.* Lexington, MA: Lexington Books. (15)

Billigimeier, J., & Turner, J. (1981). The socio-economic roles of women in Mycenean Greece: A brief survey from evidence of linear B. tablets. In H. Foley (Ed.), *Reflections of women in antiquity.* New York: Gordon & Breach. (6)

Billy, J., & Udry, J. (1985). Patterns of adolescent friendship and effects on sexual behavior. *Social Psychology Quarterly, 48,* 27–41. (4, 5)

Binford, S. (1979, May). Myths & matriarchies. *Human nature,* 62–66. (6)

Bingham, D. (1993). *Masculinities, male spectatorship and Hollywood stars.* New Brunswick, NJ: Rutgers University Press. (11)

Blakemore, J. (1990). Children's nurturant interactions with their infant siblings: An exploration of gender differences and maternal socialization. *Sex Roles, 22,* 43–57. (4)

Blakemore, J., Baumgardner, S., & Keniston, A. (1988). Male and female nurturing: Perceptions of style and competence. *Sex Roles, 18,* 449–459. (4)

Blanchard, D. (1983). High steel! The Kahnawake Mohawk and the high construction trade. *Journal of Ethnic Studies, 11*(2), 41–60. (14)

Blanchard, W. (1959). The group process in gang rape. *Journal of Social Psychology, 49,* 259–266. (9)

Blau, F., & Ferber, M. (1985). Women in the labor market: The last twenty years. In L. Larwood et al. (Eds.), *Women and work* (Vol. 1, pp. 19–49). Beverly Hills, CA: Sage. (5)

Bleier, R. (1984). *Science and gender: A critique of biology and its theories on women.* New York: Pergamon Press. (3)

Block, J. (1978). Another look at sex differentiation in the socialization behaviors of mothers and fathers. In J. Sherman & F. Denmark (Eds.), *The psychology of women: Future directions of research.* New York: Psychological Dimensions. (4)

Block, J. (1983). Differential premises arising from differential socialization of the sexes: Some conjectures. *Child Development, 54,* 1335–1354. (5)

Blood, R., & Wolfe, D. (1960). *Husbands and wives: The dynamics of married living.* New York: Free Press. (12)

Blumenfeld, W. J. (Ed.). (1992). *Homophobia: How we all pay the price.* Boston: Beacon Press. (1, 7)

Blumenstein, P., & Schwartz, P. (1983). *American couples.* New York: Morrow. (13)

Blumenthal, M., Kahn, R., Andrews, F., & Head, K. (1972). *Justifying violence: Attitudes of American men.* Ann Arbor: Institute for Social Research, The University of Michigan. (9)

Bly, R. (1987). The Vietnam War and the erosion of male confidence. In R. Williams (Ed.), *Unwinding the Vietnam War: From war into peace* (pp. 161–175). Seattle: The Real Comet Press. (1)

Bly, R. (1990). *Iron John: A book about men.* Reading, MA: Addison-Wesley. (1)

Bohan, J. S. (1990). Contextual history: A framework for re-placing women in the history of psychology. *Psychology of Women Quarterly, 14,* 213–227. (4)

Bose, C. (1987). Dual spheres. In B. Hess & M. Feree (Eds.), *Analyzing gender* (pp. 267–285). Newbury Park, CA: Sage. (7)

Boswell, J. (1980). *Christianity, social tolerance, and homosexuality.* Chicago: University of Chicago Press. (2, 13)

Bowlby, J. (1969). *Attachment and loss* (Vol. 1). New York: Basic Books. (15)

Boyd, S. B. (1990). Domination as punishment: Men's studies and religion. *Men's Studies Review, 7*(2), 1, 4–9. (2)

Boyd, S. B. (1993). On listening and speaking: Men, masculinity, and Christianity. *The Journal of Men's Studies, 1,* 323–345. (2)

Bozett, F. W. (1988). Gay fatherhood. In P. Bronstein & C. P. Cowan (Eds.), *Fatherhood today* (pp. 214–235). New York: Wiley. (15)

Brace, C. (1979). *The stage of human evolution: Human and cultural origins.* Englewood Cliffs, NJ: Prentice-Hall. (6)

Braithwaite, R. (1981). Interpersonal relations between black males and black females. In L. Gary (Ed.), *Black men* (pp. 83–97). Beverly Hills, CA: Sage. (14)

Brannock, J. C., & Chapman, B. E. (1990). Negative sexual experiences with men among heterosexual women and lesbians. *Journal of Homosexuality, 19*(1), 105–110. (13)

Brannon, R. (1976). The male sex role: Our culture's blueprint of manhood, and what it's done for us lately. In D. David & R. Brannon (Eds.), *The forty-nine percent majority* (pp. 1–45). Reading, MA: Addison-Wesley. (S2, 7, 8, 10, 11)

Braun, J., & Chao, H. (1978). Attitudes toward women: A comparison of Asian-born Chinese and American Caucasians. *Psychology of Women Quarterly, 2,* 195–201. (14)

Braybon. G. (1989). *Women workers in the First World War.* New York: Routledge. (2)

Bredemeier, B., & Shields, D. (1985, October). Values and violence in sports today. *Psychology Today,* 22–25, 28–29, 32. (9)

Brehm, S. (1985). *Intimate relationships.* New York: Random House. (12)

Brehm, S. (Ed.). (1988). *Seeing female: Social roles and personal lives.* Westport, CT: Greenwood Press. (4)

Bretl, D., & Cantor, J. (1988). The portrayal of men and women in U.S. commercials: A recent content analysis and trend over 15 years. *Sex Roles, 18,* 595–609. (5)

Brinson, S. L. (1992). The use and opposition of rape myths in prime-time television dramas. *Sex Roles, 27,* 359–375. (9)

Brod, H. (1984). Eros thanatized: Pornography and male sexuality. *Humanities in Society, 7*(1–2). (9)

Brod, H. (1990, March 21). Scholarly studies of men: The new field is an essential complement to women's studies. *The Chronicle of Higher Education,* B2–B3. (1)

Brod, H. (Ed.). (1987). *The making of masculinities.* Boston: Allen & Unwin. (1)

Brodie, H., Gartrell, N., Doering, C., & Rhue, T. (1974). Plasma testosterone levels in heterosexual and homosexual men. *American Journal of Psychiatry, 131,* 82–83. (13)

Brody, G., Neubaum, E., & Forehand, R. (1988). Serial marriage: A heuristic analysis of an emerging family form. *Psychological Bulletin, 103,* 211–222. (12)

Bromley, D. (1974). *The psychology of human ageing* (2nd ed.). New York: Penguin. (4)

Bronstein, P. (1988). Father-child interaction: Implications for gender role socialization. In P. Bronstein & C. P. Cowan (Eds.), *Fatherhood today* (pp. 107–124). New York: Wiley. (15)

Brooks, G. R. (1990). Post-Vietnam gender role strain: A needed concept? *Professional Psychology: Research and Practice, 21,* 18–25. (1)

Brooks, J., & Lewis, M. (1974). Attachment behavior in thirteen-month-old, opposite-sex twins. *Child Development, 45,* 243–247. (5)

Brothers, J. (1987, Sept. 27). Date rape. *Parade Magazine,* 4–6. (9)

Broverman, I., Vogel, S., Broverman, D., Clarkson, F., & Rosenkrantz, P. (1972). Sex-role stereotypes: A current appraisal. *Journal of Social Issues, 28,* 59–78. (4)

Brown, D. (1957). The development of sex-role inversion and homosexuality. *Journal of Pediatrics, 50,* 613–619. (13)

Brown, G. (1978). *The new celibacy.* New York: McGraw-Hill. (10)

Brown, J. (1975). Iroquois women: An ethnohistorical note. In R. Reitner (Ed.), *Toward an anthropology of women* (pp. 235–251). New York: Monthly Review Press. (6)

Brown, J., & Campbell, K. (1986). Race and gender in music videos: The same beat but a different drummer. *Journal of Communication, 36,* 94–106. (5)

Brown, W. (1987). Hormones and sexual aggression in the male: Commentary. *Integrative Psychiatry, 5,* 91–93. (3)

Brubaker, R., & Fowler, C. (1990). Encouraging college males to perform testicular self-examination: Evaluation of a persuasive message based on the revised theory of reasoned action. *Journal of Applied Social Psychology, 20,* 1411–1422. (16)

Brzek, A., & Hubalek, S. (1988). Homosexuals in Eastern Europe: Mental health and psychotherapy issues. *Journal of Homosexuality, 15,* 153–162. (13)

Buckley, J. (1986). *Female fault and fulfillment in gnosticism.* Chapel Hill, NC: University of North Carolina Press. (2)

Buckley, W., Yesalis, C., Friedl, K., Anderson, W., Streit, A., & Wright, J. (1988, December 16). Estimated prevalence of anabolic steroid use among male high school seniors. *Journal of American Medical Association, 260,* 3441–3445. (3)

Bukowski, W., Nappi, B., & Hoza, B. (1987). A test of Aristotle's model of friendship for young adults' same-sex and opposite-sex relationships. *Journal of Social Psychology, 127,* 595–603. (12)

Bullough, V. (1974). *The subordinate sex: A history of attitudes toward women.* New York: Penguin. (2, 7)

Bullough, V. (1979). *Homosexuality: A history.* New York: New American Library. (13)

Burant, C. (1988). Of wild men and warriors. *Changing Men, 19,* 7–9, 46. (1)

Bureau of the Census, U.S. Department of Commerce. (1985). Persons of Spanish Origin in the United States: March 1985 (Advance Report). *Current Population Reports,* Series P-20, No. 403. Washington, DC: U.S. Government Printing Office. (14)

Burke, R., & Fuqua, D. (1987). Sex differences in same- and cross-sex supportive relationships. *Sex Roles, 17,* 339–352. (12)

Busby, L. (1974). Defining the sex-role standards in commercial network television programs directed toward children. *Journalism Quarterly, 51,* 690–696. (5)

Butler, T., Giordano, S., & Neren, S. (1985). Gender and sex-role attributes as predictors of utilization of natural support systems during personal stress events. *Sex Roles, 13,* 515–524. (11)

Butterfield L., Friedlander, M., & Kline, M. (Eds.). (1975). *The book of Abigail and John: Selected letters of the Adams family, 1762–1784.* Cambridge: Harvard University Press. (2)

Bybee, J., Glick, M., & Zigler, E. (1990). Differences across gender, grade level, and academic track in the content of the ideal self-image. *Sex Roles, 22,* 349–358. (5)

Byrne, D., & Kelley, K. (1984). Pornography and sex research. In N. Malamuth & E. Donnerstein (Eds.), *Pornography and sexual aggression* (pp. 1–15). Orlando, FL: Academic Press. (9)

Caesar, P. (1988). Exposure to violence in the family-of-origin among wife-abusers and maritally nonviolent men. *Violence and Victims, 3,* 49–63. (9)

Cahill, S. (1983). From babies into boys and girls: The acquisition of gender identity. Paper presented at the annual meeting of the American Sociological Association, Detroit. (5)

Cahill, S. (1986a). Language practices and self definition: The case of gender identity acquisition. *The Sociological Quarterly, 27,* 295–311. (5)

Cahill, S. (1986b). Childhood socialization as recruitment process: Some lessons from the study of gender development. In P. Adler & P. Adler (Eds.), *Sociological studies of child development* (Vol. 1, pp. 163–186). Greenwich, CT: JAI Press. (5)

Caldera, Y., Huston, A., & O'Brien, M. (1989). Social interaction and play patterns of parents and toddlers with feminine, masculine, and neutral toys. *Child Development, 60,* 70–76. (5)

Calderwood, D. (1987, May). The male rape victim. *Medical Aspects of Human Sexuality,* 53–55. (9)

Caldwell, M., & Peplau, L. (1982). Sex differences in same-sex friendship. *Sex Roles, 8,* 721–732. (12)

Calhoun, K., & Atkeson, B. (1991). *Treatment of rape victims: Facilitating social adjustment.* New York: Pergamon Press. (9)

Campbell, A. (1993). *Men, women, and aggression.* New York: Basic Books. (9)

Campbell, A., Converse, P., & Rodgers, W. (1976). *The quality of American life.* New York: Russell Sage Foundation. (12)

Campbell, J. (1968). *The hero with a thousand faces* (2nd ed.). Princeton, NJ: Princeton University Press. (1)

Campbell, J. (1988). *Myths we live by.* New York: Bantam Books. (1)

Cantarella, E. (1987). *Pandora's daughters: The role and status of women in Greek and Roman antiquity* (trans. M. Fant). Baltimore: Johns Hopkins University Press. (2)

Carmody, D., & Williams, K. (1987). Wife assault and perceptions of sanctions. *Violence and Victims, 2,* 25–38. (9)

Carnes, M. (1989). *Secret ritual and manhood in Victorian America.* New Haven: Yale University Press. (2)

Carnes, M., & Griffen, C. (Eds.). (1990). *Meanings for manhood: Constructions of masculinity in Victorian America.* Chicago: University of Chicago Press. (2)

Carnes, P. (1983). *Out of the shadows: Understanding sexual addiction.* Minneapolis: Compcare Publication. (10)

Carpenter, C. (1983). Activity structure and play: Implications for socialization. In M. B. Liss (Ed.), *Social and cognitive skills: Sex roles and children's play.* New York: Academic Press. (5)

Carr, J. (1988). *Crisis in intimacy.* Pacific Grove, CA: Brooks/Cole. (12)

Carrigan, T., Connell, B., & Lee, J. (1985). Toward a new sociology of masculinity. *Theory and Society, 14,* 551–603. (1)

Carson, R., Butcher, J., & Coleman, J. (1988). *Abnormal psychology and modern life* (8th ed.). Glenview, IL: Scott, Foresman. (10)

Carter, D. (1987). The role of peers in sex role socialization. In D. B. Carter (Ed.), *Current conceptions of sex roles and sex typing: Theory and research* (pp. 101–121). New York: Praeger. (4)

Castleman, M. (1980). *Sexual solutions: An informative guide.* New York: Simon & Schuster. (10)

Catalyst. (1988). Workplace policies: New options for fathers. In P. Bronstein & C. Cowan (Eds.), *Fatherhood today* (pp. 323–340). New York: Wiley. (15)

Cazenave, N., & Leon, G. (1987). Men's work and family roles and characteristics: Race, gender, and class perceptions of college students. In M. Kimmel (Ed.), *Changing men: New directions in research on men and masculinity* (pp. 244–262). Newbury Park, CA: Sage. (14)

CBS "60 Minutes." (1988, August 7). Machismo. (14)

Centers, R., Raven, B., & Rodriguez, A. (1971). Conjugal power structure: A reexamination. *American Sociological Review, 36,* 264–278. (12)

Changeux, J. (1985). *Neuronal man: The biology of mind.* New York: Pantheon. (3)

Chappell, B. (1983, June). How women are portrayed in television commercials. *Admap,* 327–331. (5)

Chaze, W. (1981, June 29). Youth gangs are back—on old turf and new. *U.S. News & World Report,* 46–47. (5, 9)

Cherry, F. (1983). Gender roles and sexual violence. In E. Allgeier & N. McCormick (Eds.), *Changing boundaries* (pp. 245–260). Palo Alto, CA: Mayfield. (9)

Chilman, C. (1983). The development of adolescent sexuality. *Journal of Research and Development in Education, 16,* 16–26. (13)

Chodorow, N. (1974). Family structure and feminine personality. In M. Rosaldo & L. Lamphere (Eds.), *Woman, culture, and society* (pp. 43–66). Stanford: Stanford University Press. (6, 13)

Chodorow, N. (1978). *The reproduction of mothering: Psychoanalysis and the sociology of gender.* Berkeley: University of California Press. (16)

Choti, S., Marston, A., & Holston, S. (1987). Gender and personality variables in film-induced sadness and crying. *Journal of Social and Clinical Psychology, 5,* 535–544. (7)

Christie, R., & Geis, F. (1970). *Studies in Machiavellianism.* New York: Academic Press. (8)

Christopher, R. (1983). *The Japanese mind.* New York: Fawcett Columbine. (14)

Chu, L. (1986). *Eat a bowl of tea.* Secaucus: NJ: Lyle Stuart. (14)

Chusmir, L., & Hood, J. (1988). Predictive characteristics of Type A behavior among men and women. *Journal of Applied Social Psychology, 18,* 688–698. (16)

Cialdini, R. (1985). *Influence: Science and practice.* Glenview, IL: Scott, Foresman. (12)

Cicone, M., & Ruble, D. (1978). Beliefs about males. *Journal of Social Issues, 34,* 5–16. (S2, 10)

Clark, J. (1989). *A place to start: Toward an unapologetic gay liberation theology*. Dallas: Monument. (16)

Clark, J. (1992). Men's studies, femininst theology, and gay male sexuality. *The Journal of Men's Studies, 2,* 125–155. (16)

Clatterbaugh, K. (1990). *Contemporary perspectives on masculinity: Men, women, and politics in modern society*. Boulder, CO: Westview Press. (1)

Clatterbaugh, K. (1993). Mythopoetic foundations of new age patriarchy. *Masculinities, 1*(3&4), 2–12. (1)

Clatterbaugh, K. (in press). "Men and masculinity": A guide to selected journals, magazines, and newsletters from the men's movements. (1)

Clawson, M. (1986). Nineteenth-century women's auxiliaries and fraternal orders. *Signs, 12,* 40–61. (2)

Clawson, M. (1989). *Constructing brotherhood: Class, gender, and fraternalism*. Princeton, NJ: Princeton University Press. (2)

Coakley, J. (1986). *Sport in society*. St. Louis, MO: Times Mirror/Mosby College Publishing. (5)

Cohan, S., & Hark, I. R. (Eds.). (1993). *Screening the male: Exploring masculinities in Hollywood cinema*. New York: Routledge. (11)

Cohen, T. (1992). Men's families, men's friends. In P. M. Nardi (Ed.), *Men's friendships* (pp. 115–131). Newbury Park, CA: Sage. (4)

Coleman, D., & Straus, M. (1986). Marital power, conflict, and violence in a nationally representative sample of American couples. *Violence and Victims, 1,* 141–157. (9)

Coleman, J. (1976). Athletics in high school. In D. David & R. Brannon (Eds.), *The forty-nine percent majority* (pp. 264–269). Reading, MA: Addison-Wesley. (11)

Collins, L., Ingoldsby, B., & Dellman, M. (1984). Sex-role stereotyping in children's literature: A change from the past. *Childhood Education, 60,* 278–285. (5)

Colwill, N. (1982). *The new partnership: Women and men in organizations*. Palo Alto, CA: Mayfield. (12)

Conant, J. (1988, February). The high-priced call of the wild: Today's manly kind of guy is hot on the trail of elegant and expensive outdoor clothing. *Newsweek,* 56–57. (11)

Connell, R. (1987). *Gender and power*. Stanford: Stanford University Press. (1)

Constantinople, A. (1973). Masculinity-femininity: An exception to a famous dictum? *Psychological Bulletin, 80,* 389–407. (4)

Constantinople, A. (1979). Sex-role acquisition: In search of the elephant. *Sex Roles, 5,* 121–133. (5)

Cook, A., Fritz, J., McCornack, B., & Visperas, C. (1985). Early gender differences in the functional usage of language. *Sex Roles, 12,* 909–915. (4)

Cook, B. (1987). Women judges in the opportunity structure. In L. Crites & W. Hepperle (Eds.), *Women, the courts, and equality* (pp. 143–174). Newbury Park, CA: Sage. (4)

Cook, E. (1985). *Psychological androgyny*. New York: Pergamon Press. (4)

Cooper, A. (1986). Progestogens in the treatment of male sex offenders: A review. *Canadian Journal of Psychiatry, 31,* 73–79. (3)

Cooper, H. (1979). Statistically combining independent studies: A meta-analysis of sex differences in conformity research. *Journal of Personality and Social Psychology, 37,* 131–146. (4)

Corballis, M., & Beale, I. (1983). *The ambivalent mind: The neuropsychology of left and right*. Chicago: Nelson-Hall. (4)

Costanzo, P., & Shaw, M. (1966). Conformity as a function of age level. *Child Development, 37,* 967–975. (5)

Costin, F., & Schwarz, N. (1987). Beliefs about rape and women's social roles: A four-nation study. *Journal of Interpersonal Violence, 2,* 46–56. (9)

Cott, N. (1977). *The bonds of womanhood*. New Haven: Yale University Press. (2)

Courtney, A., & Whipple, T. (1974). Women in TV commercials. *Journal of Communication, 24,* 110–118. (5)

Cowan, C., & Bronstein, P. (1988). Fathers' roles in the family: Implications for research, intervention, and change. In P. Bronstein & C. P. Cowan (Eds.), *Fatherhood today: Men's changing role in the family* (pp. 341–347). New York: Wiley. (15)

Cowan, C., & Cowan, P. (1987). Men's involvement in parenthood: Identifying the antecedents and understanding the barriers. In P. Berman & F. A. Pedersen (Eds.), *Men's transitions to parenthood*. Hillsdale, NJ: Erlbaum. (15)

Cowan, C., & Cowan, P. (1988). Who does what when partners become parents: Implications for men, women, and marriage. In R. Palkovitz & M. Sussman (Eds.), *Transitions to parenthood* (pp. 105–131). New York: Haworth Press. (15)

Cowan, P. (1988). Becoming a father: A time of change, an opportunity for development. In P. Bronstein & C. Cowan (Eds.), *Fatherhood today: Men's changing role in the family* (pp. 13–35). New York: Wiley. (15)

Cowley, G. (1993a, October 18). Seeking the cause of a killer. *Newsweek,* 78. (16)

Cowley, G. (1993b, December 27). To test or not to test. *Newsweek,* 42–43. (16)

Crabb, P., & Bielawski, D. (1994). The social representation of material culture and gender in children's books. *Sex Roles, 30,* 69–79. (5)

Craig, S. (Ed.). (1992). *Men, masculinity, and the media*. Newbury Park, CA: Sage. (11)

Craik, K. (1986). Personality research methods: An historical perspective. *Journal of Personality, 54,* 18–51. (4)

Crews, D. (1987). Functional association in behavioral endocrinology. In J. Reinisch et al. (Eds.), *Masculinity/femininity: Basic perspectives* (pp. 83–106). New York: Oxford University Press. (3)

Cromwell, R., & Ruiz, R. (1979). The myth of macho dominance in decision making within Mexican and Chicano families. *Hispanic Journal of Behavior Sciences, 1,* 355–373. (14)

Crooks, R., & Baur, K. (1990). *Our sexuality* (4th ed.). Redwood City, CA: Benjamin/Cummings Publishing. (3)

Cross, S., & Markus, H. (1993). Gender in thought, belief, and action: A cognitive approach. In A. Beall & R. Sternberg (Eds.), *The psychology of gender* (pp. 55–98). New York: Guilford Press. (4)

Crowley, C., & Crowley, C. (1963, December). Rugby-Gem of the Cumberlands. *The Tennessee Conservationist,* 14–16. (2)

Cruikshank, M. (1992). *The gay and lesbian liberation movement.* New York: Routledge. (2)

Culbertson, P. (1992). *New Adam: The future of male spirituality.* Minneapolis: Augsburg Fortress. (16)

Cunningham, C. (1990). *The prostate problem.* New York: Pinnacle. (16)

Curtis, B. (1989, November). The wimp factor. *American Heritage,* 40–50. (11)

D'Emilio, J. (1983). *Sexual politics, sexual communities: The making of a homosexual minority in the United States, 1940–1970.* Chicago: University of Chicago Press. (2)

D'Emilio, J. (1990). Gay politics and community in San Francisco since World War II. In M. Duberman, M. Vicinus, & G. Chauncey, Jr. (Eds.), *Hidden from history: Reclaiming the gay & lesbian past* (pp. 456–473). New York: Meridian. (13)

D'Emilio, J. & Freedman, E. (1988). *Intimate matters: A history of sexuality in America.* New York: Harper & Row. (3)

Dahlberg, F. (1981). Introduction. In F. Dahlberg (Ed.), *Woman the gatherer* (pp. 1–33). New Haven: Yale University Press. (6)

Darling, C., & Davidson, J. (1986). Enhancing relationships: Understanding the feminine mystique of pretending orgasm. *Journal of Sex and Marital Therapy, 12,* 182–196. (10)

Darwin, C. (1859/1967). *On the origin of species.* New York: Atheneum. (6)

Dash, M. (1993). Betwixt and between in the mens [sic] movement. *Masculinities, 1*(3&4), 49–51. (1)

Davidson, L., & Duberman, L. (1982). Friendship: Communication and interactional patterns in same-sex dyads. *Sex Roles, 8,* 809–822. (12)

Davies, M., & Kandel, D. (1981). Parental and peer influences on adolescents' education plans: Some further evidence. *American Journal of Sociology, 87,* 363–387. (5)

Davis, A. (1984). Sex differentiated behaviors in nonsexist picture books. *Sex Roles, 11,* 1–16. (5)

Davis, E. (1972). *The first sex.* New York: Penguin. (2, 6)

Davis, S. (1990). Men as success objects and women as sex objects: A study of personal advertisements. *Sex Roles, 23,* 43–50. (1)

De Cecco, J. (Ed.). (1984). *Homophobia: An overview.* New York: Haworth Press. (13)

De Cecco, J. (Ed.). (1985). *Bashers, baiters, and bigots: Homophobia in American society.* New York: Harrington Park Press. (7, 13)

De Cecco, J. (Ed.). (1988). *Gay relationships.* New York: Harrington Park Press. (13)

De La Cancela, V. (1986). A critical analysis of Puerto Rican machismo: Implications for clinical practice. *Psychotherapy, 23,* 291–296. (14)

De La Cancela, V. (1993). "Coolin": The psychosocial communication of African and Latino men. *The Urban League Review, 16*(2), 33–44. (14)

De Rios, M. (1978). Why women don't hunt: An anthropologist looks at the origin of the sexual division of labor in society. *Women's Studies, 5,* 241–247. (6)

De Vries, G., et al. (Eds.). (1984). *Sex differences in the brain: The relation between structure and function* (Progress in Brain Research, Vol. 61). New York: Elsevier. (3)

Degler, C. (1980). *At odds: Women and the family in America from the Revolution to the present.* New York: Oxford University Press. (2)

Del Boca, F., & Ashmore, R. (1986). Male-female relations: A summing up and notes toward a social-psychological theory. In R. Ashmore & F. Del Boca (Eds.), *The social psychology of female-male relations: A critical analysis of central concepts* (pp. 311–332). Orlando, FL: Academic Press. (4)

Delaney, J., Lupton, M., & Toth, E. (1988). *The curse: A cultural history of menstruation.* Champaign, IL: University of Illinois Press. (3)

Delk, J., Madden, B., Livingston, M., & Ryan, T. (1986). Adult perception of the infant as a function of gender labeling and observer gender. *Sex Roles, 15,* 527–534. (5)

DeLoache, J., Cassidy, P., & Carpenter, C. (1987). The three bears are all boys: Mothers' gender labeling of neutral picture book characters. *Sex Roles, 17,* 163–178. (5)

Denmark, F. (1983). Integrating the psychology of women into introductory psychology. In C. Scheirere & A. Rogers (Eds.), *The G. Stanley Hall Lecture Series* (Vol. 3, pp. 37–71). Washington, DC: American Psychological Association. (5)

Derlega, V., & Berg, J. (Eds.). (1987). *Self-disclosure: Theory, research, and therapy.* New York: Plenum. (12)

Derlega, V., & Winstead, B. (Eds.). (1986). *Friendship and social interaction.* New York: Springer-Verlag. (12)

Desertrain G., & Weiss, M. (1988). Being female and athletic: A cause for conflict? *Sex Roles, 18,* 567–582. (5)

Deutsch, M. (1973). *The resolution of conflict: Constructive and destructive processes.* New Haven: Yale University Press. (8)

Devine, E. (1922). *Historic Caughnawaga.* Montreal: Messenger Press. (14)

DeVita, Jr., V. T., Hellman, S., & Rosenberg, S. A. (Eds.). (1993). *AIDS: Etiology, diagnosis, treatment, and prevention* (3rd ed.). Philadelphia: Lippincott. (16)

Dews, C. L. (1994). Gender tragedies: East Texas cockfighting and *Hamlet. The Journal of Men's Studies, 2,* 253–267. (2)

Diamond, J. (1983). *Inside out: Becoming my own man.* San Raphael, CA: Fifth Wave. (1)

Diamond, M. J. (1992). Creativity needs in becoming a father. *The Journal of Men's Studies, 1,* 41–45. (1)

Dillenberger, J. (1985). The Magdalen: Reflections on the image of the saint and sinner in Christian art. In Y. Haddad & E. Findly (Eds.), *Women, religion, and social change* (pp. 115–145). Albany: State University of New York Press. (2)

Dinnerstein, D. (1976). *The mermaid and the minotaur.* New York: Harper & Row. (13)

Dobbins, G. (1986). Equity vs. equality: Sex differences in leadership. *Sex Roles, 15,* 513–525. (7)

Doell, R. G., & Longino, H. E. (1988). Sex hormones and human behavior: A critique of the linear model. *Journal of Homosexuality, 15*(3/4), 55–78. (13)

Doering, C., Brodie, H., Kraemer, H., Becker, H., & Hamburg, D. (1978). Plasma testosterone levels and psychologic measures in men over a 2-month period. In R. Friedman et al. (Eds.), *Sex differences in behavior* (pp. 413–431). Huntington, NY: Krieger. (3)

Doering, C., Brodie, H., Kraemer, H., Moos, R., Becker, H., & Hamburg, D. (1975). Negative effect and plasma testosterone: A longitudinal human study. *Psychosomatic Medicine, 37*, 484–491. (3)

Donegan, J. (1985). *Women & men midwives: Medicine, morality, and misogyny in early America*. Westport, CT: Greenwood Press. (2)

Donnell, M., & Hall, J. (1980). Men and women as managers: A significant case of no difference. *Organizational Dynamics*, 60–77. (7)

Donnerstein, E., & Linz, D. (1987). Mass-media sexual violence and male viewers: Current theory and research. In M. Kimmel (Ed.), *Changing men: New directions in research on men and masculinity* (pp. 198–215). Newbury Park, CA: Sage. (9)

Donnerstein, E., Linz, D., & Penrod, S. (1987). *The question of pornography: Research findings and policy implications*. New York: Free Press. (9)

Dörner, G. (1980). Neuroendocrine aspects in the etiology of sexual deviation. In R. Forleo & W. Pasini (Eds.), *Medical sexology* (pp. 190–209). Littleton, MA: PSG Publications. (13)

Dorr, A. (1986). *Television and children*. Newbury Park, CA: Sage. (5)

Dosser, D., Balswick, J., & Halverson, C. (1986). Male inexpressiveness and relationships. *Journal of Social and Personal Relationships, 3*, 241–258. (12)

Douglas, A. (1977). *The feminization of American culture*. New York: Knopf. (2)

Douvan, E., & Adelson, J. (1966). *The adolescent experience*. New York: Wiley. (12)

Doyle, J. (1976). Attitudes toward feminism—Forty years later. *Sex Roles, 2*, 399–400. (7)

Doyle, J. (1986). Men's studies and nurturant men. *Nurturing News, 8*(3), 7, 13. (4, 7)

Doyle, J. (1987). Fraternity develops poster on date rape. *Men's Studies Review, 4*(3), 4. (9)

Doyle, J. (1992). Editorial. *The Journal of Men's Studies, 1*, 1–4. (1)

Doyle, J., & Paludi, M. (1991). *Sex and gender* (2nd ed.). Dubuque, IA: Wm. C. Brown. (2, 5)

Doyle, J., & Shahade, R. (1977). College males' academic field and attitudes toward women. *Psychological Reports, 40*, 1089–1090. (7)

Dozier, E. (1966). *Hano: A Tewa Indian community in Arizona*. New York: Holt, Rinehart & Winston. (6)

Drass, K. (1986). The effect of gender identity on conversation. *Social Psychology Quarterly, 49*, 294–301. (4)

Drinnon, R. (1987). *Keeper of concentration camps*. Berkeley: University of California Press. (14)

Drucker, W. D. (1984). Androgen therapy in patients with decreased libido. *Medical Aspects of Human Sexuality, 18*, 223–228. (3)

Dubbert, J. (1979). *A man's place: Masculinity in transition*. Englewood Cliffs, NJ: Prentice-Hall. (2)

Duberman, M., Vicinus, M., & Chauncey, Jr., G. (Eds.). (1990). *Hidden from history: Reclaiming the gay and lesbian past*. New York: Meridian. (13)

Duck, S., & Perlman, D. (Eds.). (1985). *Understanding personal relationships: An interdisciplinary approach*. Beverly Hills, CA: Sage. (12)

Duesberg, P., & Ellison, B. (1994). *Inventing the AIDS virus: The truth behind the world's greatest medical miscalculation*. Reading, MA: Addison-Wesley. (16)

Durkin, K. (1985a). Television and sex-role acquisition. 1: Content. *British Journal of Social Psychology, 24*, 101–113. (7)

Durkin, K. (1985b). Television and sex-role acquisition. 2: Effects. *British Journal of Social Psychology, 24*, 191–210. (7)

Durkin, K. (1985c). Television and sex-role acquisition. 3: Counter-stereotyping. *British Journal of Social Psychology, 24*, 211–222. (7)

Dutton, D. (1988). Profiling of wife assaulters: Preliminary evidence for a trimodal analysis. *Victims & Violence, 3*, 5–29. (9)

Duveen, G., Lloyd, B., & Smith, C. (1988). A note on the effects of age and gender on children's social behaviour. *British Journal of Social Psychology, 27*, 275–278. (5)

Dyer, E. (1963). Parenthood as crisis: A restudy. *Marriage and Family Living, 25*, 196–201. (15)

Eagly, A. (1978). Sex differences in influenceability. *Psychological Bulletin, 85*, 86–116. (4)

Eagly, A. (1987a). *Sex differences in social behavior: A social-role interpretation*. Hillsdale, NJ: Erlbaum. (4)

Eagly, A. (1987b). Reporting sex differences. *American Psychologist, 42*, 756–757. (4)

Eagly, A., & Carli, L. (1981). Sex of researchers and sex-typed communications as determinants of sex differences in influenceability: A meta-analysis of social influence studies. *Psychological Bulletin, 90*, 1–20. (4)

Eagly, A., & Crowley, M. (1986). Gender and helping behavior: A meta-analytic review of the social psychological literature. *Psychological Bulletin, 100*, 283–308. (4)

Eccles, J. (1987). Adolescence: Gateway to gender role transcendence. In D. Carter (Ed.), *Current conceptions of sex roles and sex typing: Theory and research* (pp. 225–241). New York: Praeger. (4)

Eccles, J., Jacobs, J., Harold, R., Yoon, K., Arbreton, A., & Freedman-Doan, C. (1993). Parents and gender-role socialization during the middle childhood and adolescent years. In S. Oskamp & M. Costanzo (Eds.), *Gender issues in contemporary society* (pp. 59–83). Newbury Park: Sage. (5)

Eder, D., & Sanford, S. (1986). The development and maintenance of interactional norms among early adolescents. In P. Adler & P. Adler (Eds.), *Sociological studies of child development* (Vol. 1, pp. 283–300). Greenwich, CT: JAI Press. (5)

Edwards, R., Honeycutt, J., & Zagacki, K. (1989). Sex differences in imagined interactions. *Sex Roles, 21,* 263–272. (4)

Ehrenkranz, J., Bliss, E., & Sheard, M. (1974). Plasma testosterone: Correlation with aggressive behavior and social dominance in man. *Psychosomatic Medicine, 36,* 469–475. (3)

Ehrhardt, A., & Baker, S. (1978). Fetal androgens, human central nervous system differentiation, and behavior sex differences. In R. Friedman et al. (Eds.), *Sex differences in behavior* (pp. 33–51). Huntington, NY: Krieger. (3)

Eisler, R. (1988). *The chalice and the blade.* New York: Harper & Row. (2)

Eisler, R., & Blalock, J. (1991). Masculine gender role stress: Implications for the assessment of men. *Clinical Psychology Review, 11,* 45–60. (16)

Eisler, R., & Skidmore, J. (1987). Masculine gender role stress: Scale development and component factors in the appraisal of stressful situations. *Behavior Modification, 11,* 123–136. (4, 16)

Eisler, R., Skidmore, J., & Ward, C. (1988). Masculine gender role stress: Predictor of anger, anxiety, and health risk behaviors. *Journal of Personality Assessment, 52,* 133–141. (16)

Elkins, L. E., & Peterson, C. (1993). Gender differences in best friendships. *Sex Roles, 29,* 497–508. (12)

Eller, C. (1993). *Living in the lap of the goddess.* New York: Crossroad. (16)

Elliott, M. (1985). The use of "impotence" and "frigidity": Why has "impotence" survived? *Journal of Sex and Marital Therapy, 11,* 51–56. (10)

Ellis, L., & Ames, M. (1987). Neurohormonal functioning and sexual orientation: A theory of homosexuality-heterosexuality. *Psychological Bulletin, 101,* 233–258. (13)

Endo, R., Sue, S., & Wagner, N. (Eds.). (1980). *Asian-Americans: Social and psychological perspectives* (Vol. 2). Palo Alto, CA: Science and Behavior. (14)

England, P., & McCreary, L. (1987). Gender inequality in paid employment. In B. Hess & M. Feree (Eds.), *Analyzing gender* (pp. 286–320). Newbury Park, CA: Sage. (7)

Epstein, J. (1990). Either/or—neither/both: Sexual ambiguity and the ideology of gender. *Genders, 7,* 99–142. (3)

Erikson, E. (1968). *Identity, youth, and crisis.* New York: Norton. (4)

Eron, L., et al. (1987). Aggression and its correlates over 22 years. In D. Crowell (Ed.), *Childhood aggression and violence.* New York: Plenum. (9)

Estioko, A., & Griffin, P. (1981). Woman the hunter: The Agta. In F. Dahlberg (Ed.), *Woman the gatherer* (pp. 121–151). New Haven: Yale University Press. (6)

Estioko, A., & Griffin, P. (1985). Women hunters: The implications for Pleistocene prehistory and contemporary ethnography. In M. Goodman (Ed.), *Women in Asia and the Pacific: Toward an East-West dialogue.* Honolulu: University of Hawaii Press. (6)

Etaugh, C., Grinnell, K., & Etaugh, A. (1989). Development of gender labeling: Effect of age of pictured children. *Sex Roles, 21,* 769–773. (1)

Etaugh, C., Houtler, B., & Ptasnik, P. (1988). Evaluating competence of women and men: Effects of experimenter gender and group gender composition. *Psychology of Women Quarterly, 12,* 191–200. (12)

Etzioni, A. (1968, September). Sex control, science, and society. *Science,* 1107–1112. (5)

Evans, B., & Whitfield, J. (1988). *Black males in the United States: An annotated bibliography from 1967 to 1987.* Washington, DC: American Psychological Association. (14)

Fabes, R., & Laner, M. (1986). How the sexes perceive each other: Advantages and disadvantages. *Sex Roles, 15,* 129–143. (12)

Fagot, B. (1978). The influence of sex on parental reactions to toddler children. *Child Development, 49,* 459–465. (5)

Fagot, B. (1985). A cautionary note: Parents' socialization of boys and girls. *Sex Roles, 12,* 471–476. (5)

Fagot, B., & Patterson, C. (1969). An *in vivo* analysis of reinforcing contingencies for sex role behaviors in the preschool child. *Developmental Psychology, 1,* 563–568. (5)

Falbo, T., & Peplau, L. (1980). Power strategies in intimate relationships. *Journal of Personality and Social Psychology, 38,* 618–628. (12)

Farr, K. (1988). Dominance bonding through the good old boys sociability group. *Sex Roles, 18,* 259–277. (4, 12)

Farrell, W. (1974). *The liberated man.* New York: Random House. (1, 7)

Farrell, W. (1975). Beyond masculinity: Liberating men and their relationships with women. In L. Duberman (Ed.), *Gender and sex in society.* New York: Praeger. (1)

Farrell, W. (1986). *Why men are the way they are.* New York: McGraw-Hill. (1, 9)

Farrell, W. (1993). *The myth of male power: Why men are the disposable sex—fated for war, programmed for work, divorced from emotion.* New York: Simon & Schuster. (1)

Fasteau, M. (1974). *The male machine.* New York: McGraw-Hill. (1, 7)

Fausto-Sterling, A. (1992). *Myths of gender: Biological theories about women and men* (revised edition). New York: Basic Books. (3)

Feder, H. H. (1984). Hormones and sexual behavior. *Annual Review of Psychology, 35,* 165–200. (3)

Fedigan, L. M., & Fedigan, L. (1989). Gender and the study of primates. In S. Morgen (Ed.), *Gender and anthropology: Critical reviews for research and teaching* (pp. 41–64). Washington, DC: American Anthropological Association. (6)

Feingold, A. (1988). Cognitive gender differences are disappearing. *American Psychologist, 43,* 95–103. (4)

Feingold, A. (1994). Gender differences in variability in intellectual abilities: A cross-cultural perspective. *Sex Roles, 30,* 81–92. (4)

Felson, R., & Russo, N. (1988). Parental punishment and sibling aggression. *Social Psychology Quarterly, 51,* 11–18. (5)

Femiano, S. (1990). Developing a contemporary men's studies curriculum. In D. Moore & F. Leafgren (Eds.), *Problem solving strategies and interventions for men in conflict* (pp. 237–248). Alexandria, VA: American Association for Counseling and Development. (1)

Ferenczi, S. (1963). The nosology of male homosexuality. In H. Ruitenbeek (Ed.), *The problem of homosexuality in modern society* (pp. 3–16). New York: Dutton. (13)

Fernberger, S. (1948). Persistence of stereotypes concerning sex differences. *Journal of Abnormal and Social Behavior, 43,* 97–101. (4)

Ferrante, J. (1980). The education of women in the Middle Ages in theory, fact, and fantasy. In P. Labalme (Ed.), *Beyond their sex: Learned women of the European past* (pp. 9–42). New York: New York University Press. (2)

Ficarrotto, T. J. (1990). Racism, sexism, and erotophobia: Attitudes of heterosexuals towards homosexuals. *Journal of Homosexuality, 19,* 111–116. (7)

Fiebert, M. (1987). Some perspectives on the men's movement. *Men's Studies Review, 4*(4), 8–10. (1)

Fields, M., & Kirchner, R. (1978). Battered women are still in need: A reply to Steinmetz. *Victimology, 3,* 216–222. (9)

Filene, P. (1985). Between a rock and a soft place: A century of American manhood. *South Atlantic Quarterly, 84,* 339–355. (2)

Filene, P. (1986). *Him/her/self: Sex roles in modern America* (2nd ed.). Baltimore: Johns Hopkins University Press. (2, 15)

Filene, P. (1987). The secrets of men's history. In H. Brod (Ed.), *The making of masculinities: The new men's studies* (pp. 103–119). Boston: Allen & Unwin. (2, 11)

Findlay, J., Place, V., & Snyder, P. (1989). Treatment of primary hypogonadism in men by the transdermal administration of testosterone. *Journal of Clinical Endocrinology and Metabolism, 68,* 369–373. (3)

Fine, G. (1979). Small groups and culture creation: The idioculture of Little League baseball teams. *American Sociological Review, 44,* 733–745. (5)

Fine, G. (1987). *With the boys: Little League baseball and preadolescent culture.* Chicago: University of Chicago Press. (5, 8, 11)

Fine, G. (1988). Friends, impression management, and preadolescent behavior. In G. Handel (Ed.), *Childhood socialization.* Hawthorne, NY: Aldine de Gruyter. (5)

Finkelhor, D., & Yllo, K. (1985). *License to rape: Sexual abuse of wives.* New York: Holt, Rinehart & Winston. (9)

Finn, J. (1986). The relationship between sex role attitudes and attitudes supporting marital violence. *Sex Roles, 14,* 235–244. (9)

Finn, J. (1987). Men's domestic violence treatment: The court referral component. *Journal of Interpersonal Violence, 2,* 154–165. (9)

Fischer, C., & Oliker, S. (1983). A research note on friendship, gender, and the life cycle. *Social Forces, 62,* 124–133. (12)

Fischer, G. (1987). Hispanic and majority student attitudes toward forcible date rape as a function of differences in attitudes toward women. *Sex Roles, 17,* 93–101. (14)

Fisher, P. (1972). *The gay mystique: The myth and reality of male homosexuality.* New York: Stein & Day. (13)

Fjermedal, G. (1986). *The tomorrow makers: A brave new world of living brain machines.* New York: Macmillan. (1)

Flanagan, S. (1989). *Hildegard of Bingen, 1098–1179.* New York: Routledge. (2)

Flexner, E. (1959). *Century of struggle.* Cambridge: Harvard University Press. (2)

Foa, U., et al. (1987). Gender-related sexual attitudes: Some cross-cultural similarities and differences. *Sex Roles, 16,* 511–519. (13)

Fogel, G., Lane, F., & Liebert, R. (Eds.). (1986). *The psychology of men: New psychoanalytic perspectives.* New York: Basic Books. (4)

Foote, N. (1951). Identification as the basis for a theory of motivation. *American Sociological Review, 16,* 14–21. (5)

Ford, C., & Beach, F. (1951). *Patterns of sexual behavior.* New York: Harper & Row. (3)

Forisha, B. (1978). *Sex roles and personal awareness.* Morristown, NJ: General Learning Press. (5)

Forman, B. (1982). Reported male rape. *Victimology, 7,* 235–236. (9)

Fox, C., et al. (1972). Studies in the relationship between plasma testosterone levels and human sexual activity. *Journal of Endocrinology, 52,* 51–58. (3)

Fox, M., Gibbs, M., & Auerbach, D. (1985). Age and gender dimensions of friendship. *Psychology of Women Quarterly, 9,* 489–501. (12)

Fracher, J., & Kimmel, M. (1987). Hard issues and soft spots: Counseling men about sexuality. In M. Scher et al. (Eds.), *Handbook of counseling and psychotherapy with men* (pp. 83–96). Newbury Park, CA: Sage. (10)

Franck, K., & Rosen, E. (1949). A projective test of masculinity/femininity. *Journal of Consulting Psychology, 13,* 247–256. (4)

Franklin II, C. (1984). *The changing definition of masculinity.* New York: Plenum. (1)

Franklin II, C. (1987). Surviving the institutional decimation of black males: Causes, consequences, and intervention. In H. Brod (Ed.), *The making of masculinities: The new men's studies* (pp. 155–169). Boston: Allen & Unwin. (14)

Franklin II, C. (1988). *Men & society.* Chicago: Nelson-Hall. (1)

Freeman, H. (1987). Structure and content of gender stereotypes: Effects of somatic appearance and trait information. *Psychology of Women Quarterly, 11,* 59–67. (4)

Freilich, M. (1958). Cultural persistence among the modern Iroquois. *Anthropos, 53,* 473–483. (14)

Freilich, M. (1963). Scientific possibilities in Iroquois studies: An example of Mohawks past and present. *Anthropologica, 5,* 171–186. (14)

French, J., & Raven, B. (1959). The bases of social power. In D. Cartwright (Ed.), *Studies in social power* (pp. 150–167). Ann Arbor: Institute for Social Research, University of Michigan. (12)

Freud, S. (1925/1953). Some psychical consequences of the anatomical distinction between the sexes. In J. Strachey (Ed.), *Standard edition of the complete works of Sigmund Freud* (Vol. 19). London: Hogarth. (6)

Freud, S. (1935/1960). *A general introduction to psychoanalysis* (trans. J. Riviare). New York: Washington Square Press. (4)

Freud, S. (1953/1905). Three essays on the theory of sexuality. In J. Strachey (Ed.), *The standard edition of the complete psychological works of Sigmund Freud*. New York: Macmillan. (13)

Freudenberger, H. (1987, December). Today's troubled men. *Psychology Today, 46–47.* (10)

Freund, K., et al. (1973). Heterosexual aversion in homosexual males. *British Journal of Psychiatry, 122,* 163–169. (13)

Freund, K., et al. (1974a). The phobia theory of male homosexuality. *Archives of General Psychiatry, 31,* 495–499. (13)

Freund, K., et al. (1974b). Heterosexual aversion in homosexual males: A second experiment. *British Journal of Psychiatry, 125,* 177–180. (13)

Frey S., & Morton, M. (Eds.). (1986). *New world, new roles: A documentary history of women in preindustrial America.* Westport, CT: Greenwood Press. (2)

Friday, N. (1981). *Men in love, male sexual fantasies.* New York: Dell. (10)

Friedan, B. (1963). *The feminine mystique.* New York: Dell. (1)

Friedl, E. (1978, April). Society and sex roles. *Human Nature, 1,* 68–75. (6)

Friedman, M., & Rosenman, R. (1974). *Type A behavior and your heart.* New York: Knopf. (16)

Frost, D., & Stahelski, A. (1988). The systematic measurement of French and Raven's bases of social power in workgroups. *Journal of Applied Social Psychology, 18,* 375–389. (12)

Fry, D., & Gabriel, A. (Eds.). (1994). On aggression in women and girls: Cross-cultural perspectives [Special issue]. *Sex Roles, 30,* 3–4. (9)

Gackenbach, J. (1978). The effect of race, sex, and career goal differences on sex role attitudes at home and at work. *Journal of Vocational Behavior, 12,* 93–101. (14)

Gagnon, J. (1976). Physical strength, once of significance. In D. David & R. Brannon (Eds.), *The forty-nine percent majority* (pp. 169–178). Reading, MA: Addison-Wesley. (11)

Garbarino, M. (1976). *Native American heritage.* Boston: Little, Brown. (6)

Gardner, J. (1986). *Women in Roman law and society.* Bloomington: Indiana University Press. (2)

Garrison, D. (1974). The tender technicians: The feminization of public librarianship, 1876–1905. In M. Hartman & L. Banner (Eds.), *Clio's consciousness raised: New perspectives on the history of women* (pp. 158–178). New York: Harper & Row. (2)

Gartrell, N. (1982). Hormones and homosexuality. In W. Paul et al. (Eds.), *Homosexuality: Social, psychological, and biological issues* (pp. 169–182). Beverly Hills, CA: Sage. (13)

Gary, L. (1987). Predicting interpersonal conflict between men and women: The case of black men. In M. Kimmel (Ed.), *Changing men: New directions in research on men and masculinity* (pp. 232–243). Newbury Park, CA: Sage. (14)

Gary, L. (Ed.). (1981). *Black men.* Beverly Hills, CA: Sage. (14)

Gary, L., & Leashore, B. (1982). The high risk status of black men. *Social Work, 27,* 54–58. (14)

Gelles, R. (1974). *The violent home: A study of physical aggression between husbands and wives.* Beverly Hills, CA: Sage. (9)

Gelles, R. (1987). *Family violence* (2nd ed.). Newbury Park, CA: Sage. (9)

Gelles, R., & Cornell, C. (1985). *Intimate violence in families.* Newbury Park, CA: Sage. (9)

Gelles, R., & Straus, M. (1988). *Intimate violence.* New York: Simon & Schuster. (9)

Gelman, D. (1993, August 2). The violence in our heads. *Newsweek,* 48. (9)

Gerrol, R., & Resick, P. (1988, November). *Sex differences in social support and recovery from victimization.* Paper presented at the meeting of the Association for Advancement of Behavior Therapy, New York. (9)

Gerson, K. (1993). *No man's land: Men's changing commitments to family and work.* New York: Basic Books. (15)

Gerzon, M. (1992). *A choice of heroes: The changing faces of American manhood.* New York: Houghton Mifflin. (1)

Giacomini, M., Rozee-Koker, P., & Pepitone-Arreola-Rockwell, F. (1986). Gender bias in human anatomy textbook illustrations. *Psychology of Women Quarterly, 10,* 413–420. (5)

Gibbs, J. (Ed.). (1987). *Young, black and male in America: An endangered species.* Boston: Auburn House. (14)

Gibbs, N. (1991, June 3). When is it rape? *Time,* 48–54. (9)

Gibson, J. W. (1994). *Warrior dreams: Paramilitary culture in post-Vietnam America.* New York: Hill and Wang. (1)

Gies, F., & Gies, J. (1980). *Women in the Middle Ages.* New York: Harper & Row. (2)

Gilbert, L. (1985). *Men in dual-career families: Current realities and future prospects.* Hillsdale, NJ: Erlbaum. (15)

Gill, D. (1986). Competitiveness among females and males in physical activity classes. *Sex Roles, 15,* 233–247. (8)

Gill, S., Stockard, J., Johnson, M., & Williams, S. (1987). Measuring gender differences: The expressive dimension and critique of androgyny scales. *Sex Roles, 17,* 375–400. (4)

Gillespie, B., & Eisler, R. (1991). Female gender role stress: Preliminary validation and factor analysis. (16)

Gilmartin, B. (1987). Peer group antecedents of severe love-shyness in males. *Journal of Personality, 55,* 467–489. (S2)

Gilmore, D. (1990). *Manhood in the making: Cultural concepts of masculinity.* New Haven: Yale University Press. (1, 6)

Gilmour, R., & Duck, S. (Eds.). (1986). *The emerging field of personal relationships.* Hillsdale, NJ: Erlbaum. (12)

Giveans, D., & Robinson, M. (1985). Fathers and the preschool-age child. In S. Hanson & F. Bozett (Eds.), *Dimensions of fatherhood* (pp. 115–140). Beverly Hills, CA: Sage. (15)

Gladue, B., Green, R., & Hellman, R. (1984). Neuroendocrine response to estrogen and sexual orientation. *Science, 225,* 1496–1499. (13)

Glass, G., McGaw, B., & Smith, M. (1981). *Meta-analysis in social research.* Beverly Hills, CA: Sage. (4)

Godelier, M. (1985). *The making of great men: Male dominance and power among the New Guinea Baruya.* Cambridge: Cambridge University Press. (6)

Gold, D., Crombie, G., & Noble, S. (1987). Relations between teachers' judgments of girls' and boys' compliance and intellectual competence. *Sex Roles, 16,* 351–358. (5)

Gold, P. (1985). *The lady and the virgin: Image, attitude, and experience in twelfth-century France.* Chicago: University of Chicago Press. (2)

Goldberg, H. (1976). *The hazards of being male: Surviving the myth of male privilege.* New York: Signet. (1, 10, 16)

Goldberg, H. (1979). *The new male.* New York: Signet. (1)

Goldberg, S. (1974). *The inevitability of patriarchy.* New York: Morrow. (1)

Goldberg, S., & Lewis, M. (1969). Play behavior in the year-old infant: Early sex differences. *Child Development, 40,* 21–31. (4, 5)

Goldstein, J. (1983). *Sports violence.* New York: Springer-Verlag. (9)

Gonsiorek, J. (1982). Results of psychological testing on homosexual populations. In W. Paul et al. (Eds.), *Homosexuality: Social, psychological, and biological issues* (pp. 71–80). Beverly Hills, CA: Sage. (13)

Goodman, M., Griffin, P., Estioko-Griffin, A., & Grove, J. (1985). The compatibility of hunting and mothering among the Agta hunter-gatherers of the Philippines. *Sex Roles, 12,* 1199–1209. (6)

Gordon, M. (1980). The ideal husband as depicted in the nineteenth-century marriage manual. In E. Pleck & J. Pleck (Eds.), *The American man* (pp. 145–157). Englewood Cliffs, NJ: Prentice-Hall. (2)

Gordon S., & Snyder, C. (1989). *Personal issues in human sexuality* (2nd ed.). Boston: Allyn and Bacon. (10)

Gorn, E. (1986). *The manly art: Bare-knuckle prize fighting in America.* Ithaca: Cornell University Press. (2)

Gough, H. (1952). Identifying psychological femininity. *Educational and Psychological Measurement, 12,* 427–439. (4)

Gough, K. (1986). The origin of the family. In A. Skolnick & J. Skolnick (Eds.), *Family in transition* (5th ed., pp. 22–39). Boston: Little, Brown. (6)

Gould, R. (1974). Measuring masculinity by the size of a paycheck. In J. Pleck & J. Sawyer (Eds.), *Men and masculinity* (pp. 96–100). Englewood Cliffs, NJ: Prentice-Hall. (15)

Gould, R. (1978). *Transformations: Growth and changes in adult life.* New York: Simon & Schuster. (4)

Gould, R. (1982). Sexual functioning in relation to the changing roles of men. In K. Solomon & N. Levy (Eds.), *Men in transition: Theory and therapy* (pp. 165–173). New York: Plenum. (10)

Gould, S. (1981). *The mismeasure of man.* New York: Norton. (3)

Gove, W. (1972). The relationship between sex roles, mental illness and marital status. *Social Forces, 51,* 34–44. (12)

Granleese, J., Trew, K., & Turner, I. (1988). Sex differences in perceived competence. *British Journal of Social Psychology, 27,* 181–184. (12)

Grant, B. (1980). Five liturgical songs by Hildegard von Bingen (1098–1179). *Signs, 5,* 557–567. (2)

Grauerholz, E. (1987). Balancing the power in dating relationships. *Sex Roles, 17,* 563–571. (12)

Greenberg, B. (1982). Television and role socialization: An overview. In National Institute of Mental Health, *Television and behavior: Ten years of scientific progress and implications for the eighties* (pp. 179–190). Washington, DC: U.S. Government Printing Office. (5)

Greenberg, M., & Morris, N. (1974). Engrossment: The newborn's impact upon the father. *American Journal of Orthopsychiatry, 44,* 520–531. (15)

Greenblatt, C. (1983). A hit is a hit is a hit . . . Or is it? Approval and tolerance of the use of physical force by spouses. In D. Finklehor et al. (Eds.), *The dark side of families: Current family violence research* (pp. 235–260). Beverly Hills, CA: Sage. (9)

Greif, G. (1985). *Single fathers.* Lexington, MA: Lexington Books. (15)

Greif, G. (1990). *The daddy track and the single father.* Lexington, MA: Lexington Books. (15)

Griffen, C., & Carnes, M. (1988). Men's history: Whither and whether? *Men's Studies Review, 5*(4), 3–5. (2)

Griffin, E., & Sparks, G. (1990). Friends forever: A longitudinal exploration of intimacy in same-sex friends and platonic pairs. *Journal of Social and Personal Relationships, 7,* 29–46. (7)

Grimm, L., & Yarnold, P. (1984). Performance standards and the Type A behavior pattern. *Cognitive Therapy and Research, 8,* 59–66. (16)

Grimm, L., & Yarnold, P. (1985). Sex typing and the coronary-prone behavior pattern. *Sex Roles, 12,* 171–178. (16)

Griswold, R. (1993). *Fatherhood in America: A history.* New York: Basic Books. (15)

Gross, A. (1978). The male role and heterosexual behavior. *Journal of Social Issues, 34,* 87–107. (10)

Gross, A., Smith, R., & Wallston, B. (1983). The men's movement: Personal vs. political. In J. Freeman (Ed.), *Social movements of the sixties and seventies.* New York: Longman. (1)

Gross, H., et al. (1979). Considering "a biosocial perspective on parenting." *Signs, 4,* 695–717. (3)

Grossman, F. K. (1988). Strain in the transition to parenthood. In R. Palkovitz & M. B. Sussman (Eds.), *Transitions to parenthood* (pp. 85–104). New York: Haworth Press. (15)

Groth, A., & Birnbaum, J. (1979). *Men who rape: The psychology of the offender.* New York: Plenum. (9)

Groth, A., Burgess, A., & Holmstrom, L. (1977). Rape: Power, anger and sexuality. *American Journal of Psychiatry, 134,* 1239–1243. (9)

Gruber, K., & White, J. (1986). Gender differences in the perception of self's and others' use of power strategies. *Sex Roles, 15,* 109–118. (12)

Gundersheimer, W. (1980). Women, learning, and power: Eleonora of Aragon and the court of Ferrara. In P. Labalme (Ed.), *Beyond their sex: Learned women of the European past* (pp. 43–65). New York: New York University Press. (2)

Gurian, M. (1992). *The prince and the king.* Los Angeles: Tarcher/Putnam. (1)

Gutierrez, F. (1990). Exploring the macho mystique: Counseling Latino men. In D. Moore & F. Leafgren (Eds.), *Problem solving strategies and interventions for men in conflict* (pp. 139–151). Alexandria, VA: American Association for Counseling and Development. (14)

Hacker, H. (1981). Blabbermouths and clams: Sex differences in self-disclosure in same-sex and cross-sex friendship dyads. *Psychology of Women Quarterly, 5,* 385–401. (12)

Haeberle, E. (1982). Swastika, pink triangle, and yellow star: The destruction of sexology and the persecution of homosexuals in Nazi Germany. *Journal of Sex Research, 18,* 270–287. (13)

Hall, E. (1959). *The silent language.* Garden City, NY: Doubleday. (5)

Hall, E. (1966). *The hidden dimension.* Garden City, NY: Doubleday. (5)

Hall, E., Howard, J., & Boezio, S. (1986). Tolerance of rape: A sexist or antisocial attitude? *Psychology of Women Quarterly, 10,* 101–118. (9)

Hall, G. (1904). *Adolescence.* New York: Appleton. (4)

Hall, N., & Dawson, W. R. (1989). *Broodmales.* Dallas: Spring Publications. (6)

Hall, R. E. (1993). Clowns, buffoons, and gladiators: Media portrayals of the African-American man. *The Journal of Men's Studies, 1,* 239–251. (14)

Hallberg, E. (1978). *The grey itch: The male metapause syndrome.* New York: Stein & Day. (4)

Halpern, D. (1986). *Sex differences in cognitive abilities.* Hillsdale, NJ: Erlbaum. (4)

Hamberger, L., & Hastings, J. (1986). Characteristics of spouse abusers: Predictors of treatment acceptance. *Journal of Interpersonal Violence, 1,* 363–373. (9)

Hampton, R., Gullotta, T., Adams, G., Potter, E., & Weissberg, R. (Eds.). (1993). *Family violence: Prevention and treatment.* Thousand Oaks, CA: Sage. (9)

Handel, G. (1988). *Childhood socialization.* Hawthorne, NY: Aldine de Gruyter. (5)

Hanneke, C., Shields, N., & McCall, G. (1986). Assessing the prevalence of marital rape. *Journal of Interpersonal Violence, 1,* 350–362. (9)

Hanson, S. (1985). Single custodial fathers. In S. Hanson & F. Bozett (Eds.), *Dimensions of fatherhood* (pp. 369–392). Beverly Hills, CA: Sage. (15)

Hanson, S. (1988). Divorced fathers with custody. In P. Bronstein & C. P. Cowan (Eds.), *Fatherhood today: Men's changing role in the family* (pp. 166–194). New York: Wiley. (15)

Hanson, S., & Bozett, F. (Eds.). (1985). *Dimensions of fatherhood.* Beverly Hills, CA: Sage. (15)

Hantover, J. (1980). The Boy Scouts and the validation of masculinity. In E. Pleck & J. Pleck (Eds.), *The American man* (pp. 285–301). Englewood Cliffs, NJ: Prentice-Hall. (2)

Harlow, H. (1958). The nature of love. *American Psychologist, 13,* 673–685. (10)

Harlow, H., & Harlow, M. (1962). Social deprivation in monkeys. *Scientific American, 207*(5), 136–146. (10)

Harrell, W. (1986). Masculinity and farming-related accidents. *Sex Roles, 15,* 467–478. (16)

Harris, M. (1977a, November 13). Why men dominate women. *New York Times Magazine, 46,* 115–123. (6)

Harris, M. (1977b). *Cannibals and kings.* New York: Random House. (6)

Harris, P., & Stobart, J. (1986). Sex-role stereotyping in British television advertisements at different times of day: An extension and refinement of Manstead & McCulloch (1981). *British Journal of Social Psychology, 25,* 155–164. (5)

Harris, S., & Majors, R. (Eds.). (1993). African-American men [Special issue]. *The Journal of Men's Studies, 1*(3). (14)

Harrison, J. (1978). Warning: The male sex role may be hazardous to your health. *Journal of Social Issues, 34,* 65–86. (16)

Harry, J. (1988). Decision making and age differences among gay male couples. In J. De Cecco (Ed.), *Gay relationships* (pp. 117–132). New York: Harrington Park Press. (13)

Harry, J. (1990). A probability sample of gay males. *Journal of Homosexuality, 19*(1), 89–104. (13)

Harry, J., & DeVall, W. (1978). *The social organization of gay males.* New York: Praeger. (13)

Harry, J., & Lovely, R. (1979). Gay marriages and communities of sexual orientation. *Alternative Life Styles, 2,* 177–200. (13)

Hartley, R. (1974). Sex-role pressures and the socialization of the male child. In J. Pleck & J. Sawyer (Eds.), *Men and masculinity* (pp. 7–13). Englewood Cliffs, NJ: Prentice-Hall. (5)

Hartley, R., & Hardesty, F. (1964). Children's perceptions of sex roles in childhood. *Journal of Genetic Psychology, 105,* 43–51. (5)

Harvey, J., Heath, J., Spencer, M., Temple, W., & Wood, H. (1917). *Competition: A study in human motive.* London: Macmillan. (8)

Hatchett, S., & Quick, A. (1983). Correlates of sex-role attitudes among black men and women: Data from a national survey of black Americans. *Urban Research Review, 9*(2), 1–3, 11. (14)

Hatter, D., & Wright, J. (1993). Health and the African-American man: A selective review of the literature. *The Journal of Men's Studies, 1,* 267-276. (14)

Havighurst, R. (1972). *Developmental tasks and education* (3rd ed.). New York: McKay. (4)

Hawkes, G., Taylor, M. (1975). Power structure in Mexican-American farm labor families. *Journal of Marriage and the Family, 37,* 807–811. (14)

Hayden, B. (1981). Subsistence and ecological adaptations of modern hunter/gatherers. In R. Harding & G. Teleki (Eds.), *Omnivorous primates: Gathering and hunting in human evolution.* New York: Columbia University Press. (6)

Hays, H. (1966). *The dangerous sex: The myth of feminine evil*. New York: Pocket Books. (6, 7)

Hearn, J. (1987). *The gender of oppression: Men, masculinity and the critique of Marxism*. New York: St. Martin's Press. (1, 7)

Hearn, J., & Morgan, D. (1990). *Men, masculinities & social theory*. London: Unwin Hyman. (5)

Heger, H. (1980). *The men with the pink triangle*. Boston: Alyson Publications. (13)

Heilbrun, A. (1984). Sex-based models of androgyny: A further cognitive elaboration of competence differences. *Journal of Personality and Social Psychology, 46*, 216–229. (4)

Heilbrun, A., & Bailey, B. (1986). Independence of masculine and feminine traits: Empirical exploration of a prevailing assumption. *Sex Roles, 14*, 105–122. (4)

Heilbrun, A., & Mulqueen, C. (1987). The second androgyny: A proposed revision in adaptive priorities for college women. *Sex Roles, 17*, 187–207. (4)

Heilbrun, C. (1973). *Toward a recognition of androgyny*. New York: Knopf. (4)

Heilman, M., Block, C., Martell, R., & Simon, M. (1989). Has anything changed? Current characterizations of men, women, and managers. *Journal of Applied Psychology, 74*, 935–942. (7)

Heim, N. (1981). Sexual behavior of castrated sex offenders. *Archives of Sexual Behavior, 10*, 11–19. (3)

Helgeson, V. (1990). The role of masculinity in a prognostic predictor of heart attack severity. *Sex Roles, 22*, 755–774. (16)

Helgeson, V. (1991). The effects of masculinity and social support on recovery from myocardial infarction. *Psychosomatic Medicine, 53*, 621–633. (16)

Heller, J., & Gleich, P. (1988). Erectile impotence: Evaluation and management. *Journal of Family Practice, 26*, 321–324. (10)

Heller, S. (1993, February 3). Scholars debunk the Marlboro man: Examining stereotypes of masculinity. *The Chronicle of Higher Education*, A6–A8, A15. (1)

Helmreich, R., & Spence, J. (1977). The secret of success. *Discovery, Research and Scholarship at the University of Texas at Austin, 2*(2), 4–7. (8)

Helmreich, R., Spence, J., & Gibson, R. (1982). Sex-role attitudes: 1972–1980. *Personality and Social Psychology Bulletin, 8*, 656–663. (7)

Helson, R., & Moane, G. (1987). Personality change in women from college to midlife. *Journal of Personality and Social Personality, 53*, 176–186. (4)

Henderson, S., & Cunningham, J. (1993). Women's emotional dependence on men: Scale construction and test of Russianoff's hypothesis. *Sex Roles, 28*, 317–334. (4)

Henley, N. (1977). *Body politics: Power, sex, and nonverbal communication*. Englewood Cliffs, NJ: Prentice-Hall. (7)

Herdt, G. (1981). *Guardians of the flute: Idioms of masculinity*. New York: McGraw-Hill. (6)

Herdt, G. (1987). *The Sambia: Ritual and gender in New Guinea*. New York: Holt, Rinehart & Winston. (4, 6)

Herek, G. (1984a). Beyond "homophobia": A social psychological perspective on attitudes toward lesbians and gay men. *Journal of Homosexuality, 10*, 1–22. (13)

Herek, G. (1984b). Attitudes toward lesbians and gay men: A factor-analytic study. *Journal of Homosexuality, 10*, 39–52. (13)

Hersh, B. (1980). "A partnership of equals": Feminist marriages in 19th-century America. In E. Pleck & J. Pleck (Eds.), *The American man* (pp. 183–215). Englewood Cliffs, NJ: Prentice-Hall. (2)

Herzberger, S., & Tennen, H. (1985). "Snips and snails and puppy dog tails": Gender of agent, recipient, and observer as determinants of perceptions of discipline. *Sex Roles, 12*, 853–865. (5)

Hewlett, B. (1991). *Intimate fathers: The nature and context of Aka pygmy paternal infant care*. Ann Arbor: University of Michigan Press. (15)

Hines, M. (1982). Prenatal gonadal hormones and sex differences in human behavior. *Psychological Bulletin, 92*, 56–80. (3)

Hoffman, L. (1972). Changes in family roles, socialization, and sex differences. *American Psychologist, 32*, 644–657. (6)

Hoffman, L. (1975). Early childhood experiences and women's achievement motives. In M. Mednick, S. Tangri, & L. Hoffman (Eds.), *Women and achievement: Social and motivational analysis* (pp. 129–136). Washington, DC: Hemisphere Publishing. (5)

Hofman, M., & Swaab, D. (1989). The sexually dimorphic nucleus of the preoptic area in the human brain: A comparative morphometric study. *Journal of Anatomy, 164*, 55–72. (3)

Hogrebe, M. (1987). Gender differences in mathematics. *American Psychologist, 42*, 265. (4)

Hole, J., & Levine, E. (1984). The first feminists. In J. Freeman (Ed.), *Women: A feminist perspective* (pp. 533–542). Palo Alto, CA: Mayfield. (2)

Holmes, R. (1986). *Acts of war: The behavior of men in battle*. New York: Free Press. (2)

Honey, M. (1984). *Creating Rosie the Riveter: Class, gender, and propaganda during World War II*. Amherst: University of Massachusetts Press. (2)

Horn, J. (1985, October). Fan violence: Fighting the injustice of it all. *Psychology Today*, 30–31. (9)

Horna, J., & Lupri, E. (1987). Fathers' participation in work, family life and leisure: A Canadian experience. In C. Lewis & M. O'Brien (Eds.), *Reassessing fatherhood: New observations on fathers and the modern family* (pp. 54–73). London: Sage. (15)

Horney, K. (1967). *Feminine psychology*. New York: Norton. (6)

Hossain, Z., & Rooprnarine, J. (1993). Division of household labor and child care in dual-earner African-American families with infants. *Sex Roles, 29*, 571–583. (15)

Hotaling, G., & Sugarman, D. (1986). An analysis of risk markers in husband to wife violence: The current state of knowledge. *Violence and Victims, 1*, 101–124. (9)

Hotvedt, M. (1982). Introduction. In W. Paul et al. (Eds.), *Homosexuality: Social, psychological, and biological issues* (pp. 215–217). Beverly Hills, CA: Sage. (13)

Houseworth, S., Peplow, K., & Thirer, J. (1989). Influence of sport participation upon sex role orientation of Caucasian males and their attitudes toward women. *Sex Roles, 20,* 317–325. (5)

Hovland, C., Janis, I., & Kelley, H. (1953). *Communication and persuasion.* New Haven: Yale University Press. (4)

Howell, M. (1986). *Women, production, and patriarchy in late medieval cities.* Chicago: University of Chicago Press. (7)

Hoyenga, K., & Hoyenga, K. (1979). *The question of sex differences.* Boston: Little, Brown. (3)

Hughes, T. (1881/1973). *Rugby, Tennessee.* Rugby, TN: The Rugbian Press/Big Sink Books. (2)

Humphrey, H. (1944). The changing structure of the Detroit Mexican family: An index of acculturation. *American Sociological Review, 9,* 622–626. (14)

Humphreys, L. (1970). *Tearoom trade.* Chicago: Aldine. (13)

Hunt, M. (1974). *Sexual behavior in the 1970s.* Chicago: Playboy Press. (10, 13)

Huston, A. & Carpenter, C. (1984). Gender differences in preschool classrooms: The effects of sex-typed activity choices. In L. Wilkinson & C. Marett (Eds.), *Gender-related differences in the classrooms.* New York: Academic Press. (5)

Huston, A., Wright, J., Rice, M., Kerkman, D., & St. Peters, M. (1990). Development of television viewing patterns in early childhood: A longitudinal investigation. *Developmental Psychology, 26,* 409–420. (5)

Huston, T. (1983). Power. In H. Kelley et al. (Eds.), *Close relationships* (pp. 169–219). New York: W. H. Freeman. (12)

Hyde, J. (1981). How large are cognitive gender differences? A meta-analysis using *w2* and *d. American Psychologist, 36,* 892–901. (4)

Hyde, J. (1984). How large are gender differences in aggression? A developmental analysis. *Developmental Psychology, 20,* 722–736. (4)

Hyde, J. (1986a). Introduction: Meta-analysis and the psychology of gender. In J. Hyde & M. Linn (Eds.), *The psychology of gender: Advances through meta-analysis* (pp. 1–13). Baltimore: Johns Hopkins University Press. (4)

Hyde, J. (1986b). Gender differences in aggression. In J. Hyde & M. Linn (Eds.), *The psychology of gender: Advances through meta-analysis* (pp. 51–66). Baltimore: Johns Hopkins University Press. (4)

Hyde, J., & Linn, M. (1988). Gender differences in verbal ability: A meta-analysis. *Psychological Bulletin, 104,* 53–69. (4)

Hyde, J., & Linn, M. (Eds.). (1986). *The psychology of gender.* Baltimore: Johns Hopkins University Press. (4)

Iacocca, L., & Novak, W. (1986). *Iacocca: An autobiography.* New York: Bantam Books. (8)

Ide, A. (1985). *Gomorrah & the rise of homophobia.* Las Colinas, TX: The Liberal Press. (2)

Idle, T., Wood, E., & Desmarais, S. (1993). Gender role socialization in toy play situations: Mothers and fathers with their sons and daughters. *Sex Roles, 28,* 679–691. (5)

Jacklin, C. (1979). Epilogue. In M. Wittig & A. Peterson (Eds.), *Sex related differences in cognitive functioning: Developmental issues.* New York: Academic Press. (4)

Jacklin, C., & Baker, L. (1993). Early gender development. In S. Oskamp & M. Costanzo (Eds.), *Gender issues in contemporary society* (pp. 41–57). Newbury Park: Sage. (5)

Jacklin, C., Macccoby, E., & Dick, A. (1973). Barrier behavior and toy preference: Sex differences (and their absence) in the year-old child. *Child Development, 44,* 196–200. (5)

Jacklin, C., & Reynolds, C. (1993). Gender and childhood socialization. In A. Beall & R. Sternberg (Eds.), *The psychology of gender* (pp. 197–214). New York: Guildford Press. (5)

Jacobs, J. (1985). Sex segregation in American higher education. In L. Larwood et al. (Eds.), *Women and work* (Vol. 1, pp. 191–214). Beverly Hills, CA: Sage. (5)

Jacobs, J., & Eccles, J. (1985). Gender differences in math ability: The impact of media reports on parents. *Educational Researcher, 14,* 20–25. (4)

Janis, I., & Field, P. (1959). Sex differences and personality factors related to persuasibility. In C. Hovland & I. Janis (Eds.), *Personality and persuasibility.* New Haven: Yale University Press. (4)

Jay, K., & Young, A. (1977). *The gay report.* New York: Summit. (13)

Jeffery L., & Durkin, K. (1989). Children's reactions to televised counter-stereotyped male sex role behaviour as a function of age, sex and perceived power. *Social Behaviour, 4,* 285–310. (7)

Jensen, J. (1986). *Loosening the bonds: Mid-Atlantic farm women, 1750-1850.* New Haven: Yale University Press. (2)

Johanson, D., & Edey, M. (1981). *Lucy: The beginnings of humankind.* New York: Simon & Schuster. (6)

Johnson, D., & Johnson, R. (1983). The socialization and achievement crisis: Are cooperative learning experiences the solution? In L. Bickman (Ed.), *Applied social psychology annual* (Vol. 4, pp. 119–164). Beverly Hills, CA: Sage. (8)

Johnson, D., Maruyama, G., Johnson, R., Nelson, D., & Skon, L. (1981). Effects of cooperative, competitive, and individualistic goal structures on achievement: A meta-analysis. *Psychological Bulletin, 89,* 47–62. (8)

Johnson, L., & Palm, G. (Eds.). (1992). *Working with fathers: Methods and perspectives.* Stillwater, MN: nu ink unlimited. (15)

Jones, H., et al. (1979). The role of the H-Y antigen in human sexual development. *The Johns Hopkins Medical Journal, 145,* 33–43. (3)

Jones, J. (1988). Racism in black and white: A bicultural model of reaction and evolution. In P. Katz & D. Taylor (Eds.), *Eliminating racism: Profiles in controversy* (pp. 117–135). New York: Plenum. (14)

Jones, K. (1986, March). The black male in jeopardy. *The Crisis, 93,* 17–21, 44–45. (14)

Jones, R. (1948). Ethnic family patterns: The Mexican family in the United States. *American Journal of Sociology, 53,* 450–452. (14)

Jones, R., & Bates, J. (1988). Satisfaction in male homosexual couples. In J. De Cecco (Ed.), *Gay relationships* (pp. 237–245). New York: Harrington Park Press. (13)

Jourard, S. (1964). *The transparent self*. New York: Van Nostrand. (4)

Jourard, S. (1974). Some lethal aspects of the male role. In J. H. Pleck & J. Sawyer (Eds.), *Men and masculinity* (pp. 21–29). Englewood Cliffs, NJ: Prentice-Hall. (1, 7, 16)

Jump, T., & Haas, L. (1987). Dual-career fathers participating in child care. In M. Kimmel (Ed.), *Changing men: New directions in research on men and masculinity* (pp. 98–114). Newbury Park, CA: Sage. (15)

Jung, C. (1933). *Modern man in search of a soul*. New York: Harcourt Brace Jovanovich. (1)

Kammer, J. (1994). *Goodwill toward men: Women talk candidly about the balance of power between the sexes*. New York: St. Martin's Press. (12)

Kanter, R. (1984). *Men and women of the corporation* (2nd ed.). New York: Basic Books. (7)

Kantrowitz, B. (1993, August 2). Wild in the streets. *Newsweek*, 40–46. (9)

Kaplan, A., & Sedney, M. (1980). *Psychology and sex roles: An androgynous perspective*. Boston: Little, Brown. (4)

Kardiner, A. (1963). The flight from masculinity. In H. Ruitenbeek (Ed.), *The problem of homosexuality in modern society* (pp. 17–39). New York: Dutton. (13)

Karlen, A. (1971). *Sexuality and homosexuality: A new view*. New York: Norton. (13)

Katchadourian, H. (1977). *The biology of adolescence*. San Franscisco: Freeman. (4)

Katchadourian, H. (1987). *Biological aspects of human sexuality* (3rd ed.). New York: Holt, Rinehart and Winston. (3)

Katz, J. (1976). *Gay American history*. New York: Crowell. (13)

Katz, J. (1983). *Gay/lesbian almanac: A new documentary*. New York: Harper & Row. (2)

Katz, J. (Ed.). (1985). *Gay American history: Lesbians and gay men in the U.S.A.* New York: Harper & Row. (2, 3)

Katz, P. (1979). The development of female identity. *Sex Roles, 5*, 155–178. (4)

Katz, P. (1986). Gender identity: Development and consequences. In R. Ashmore & F. Del Boca (Eds.), *The social psychology of female-male relations* (pp. 21–67). Orlando, FL: Academic Press. (1, 4, 5)

Katzer, B. (1988). The Caughnawaga Mohawks: The other side of ironwork. *Journal of Ethnic Studies, 15*(4), 39–55. (14)

Kaufman, A., et al. (1980). Male rape victims: Noninstitutional assault. *American Journal of Psychiatry, 137*, 221–223. (9)

Kaufman, M. (1990). A framework for the study of men and masculinity. *Men's Studies Review, 7*(3), 14–19. (5)

Kaylor, J., King, D., & King, L. (1987). Psychological effects of military service in Vietnam: A meta-analysis. *Psychological Bulletin, 102*, 257–271. (1)

Kedar-Voivodas, G. (1983). The impact of elementary children's school roles and sex roles on teacher attitudes: An interactional analysis. *Review of Educational Research, 53*, 415–437. (5)

Keen, S. (1991). *Fire in the belly*. New York: Bantam Books. (1)

Kelleher, C. (1993, June). Beyond HIV: Assembling the AIDS puzzle. *Omni*, 53–56, 88–90. (16)

Kellerman, A., & Reay, D. (1986). Protection or peril? An analysis of firearm-related deaths in the home. *New England Journal of Medicine, 314*, 1557–1560. (9)

Kelley, H, et al. (1978). Sex differences in comments made during conflict with close heterosexual pairs. *Sex Roles, 4*, 473–492. (12)

Kelley, H. et al. (Eds.). (1983). *Close relationships*. New York: W. H. Freeman. (12)

Kelley, J., & Worrell, J. (1977). New formulations of sex roles and androgyny: A critical review. *Journal of Consulting and Clinical Psychology, 45*, 1101–1115. (4)

Kelley, K. (Ed.). (1987). *Females, males, and sexuality: Theories and research*. Albany: State University of New York Press. (12)

Kelly, M. (1981). Development and the sexual division of labor: An introduction. *Signs, 7*, 268–278. (2)

Kennedy, E. (1987, October). Points to ponder. *Reader's Digest*, 53. (12)

Kennedy, J. (1962, June 11). Commencement address. New Haven, CT: Yale University. (4)

Kennedy, M. (1993). Clothing, gender, and ritual transvestism: The Bissu of Sulawesi. *The Journal of Men's Studies, 2*, 1–13. (1, 6)

Kerber, L. (1974). Daughters of Columbia: Educating women for the Republic. In S. Elkin & E. McKitrich (Eds.), *The Hofstadter Aegis: A memorial* (pp. 36–59). New York: Knopf. (2)

Kesselman, A. (1990). *Fleeting opportunities: Women shipyard workers in Portland and Vancouver during World War II and reconversion*. Ithaca, NY: State University of New York Press. (2)

Kessler, S., & McKenna, W. (1978). *Gender: An ethnomethodological approach*. New York: Wiley. (6)

Keuls, E. (1985). *The reign of the phallus: Sexual politics in ancient Athens*. New York: Harper & Row. (2)

Kihlstrom, J. (1971). A male sexual cycle. In A. Ingelman-Sundberg & N. Lunell (Eds.), *Current problems in fertility*. New York: Plenum. (3)

Kimmel, M. (1987). The contemporary "crisis" of masculinity in historical perspective. In H. Brod (Ed.), *The making of masculinities: The new men's studies* (pp. 121–153). Boston: Allen & Unwin. (2)

Kimmel, M. (Ed.). (1987). *Changing men: New directions in research on men and masculinity*. Newbury Park, CA: Sage. (5)

Kimmel, M. (1990). Baseball and the reconstruction of American masculinity, 1880–1920. In M. Messner & D. Sabo (Eds.), *Sport, men, and the gender order: Critical feminist perspectives*. Champaign, IL: Human Kinetics. (2)

Kimmel, M. (1993). The politics of accountability. *Changing Men, 26*, 3–4. (1)

Kimmel, M., & Messner, M. (Ed.). (1989). *Men's lives*. New York: Macmillan. (1)

Kimmel, M., & Mosmiller, T. (Eds.). (1992). *Against the tide: Pro-feminist men in the United States, 1776–1990*. Boston: Beacon Press. (2)

King, L., & Emmons, R. (1990). Conflict over emotional expression: Psychological and physical correlates. *Journal of Personality and Social Psychology, 58,* 864–877. (7)

Kingsdale, J. (1980). The "poor man's club": Social function of the urban working-class saloon. In E. Pleck & J. Pleck (Eds.), *The American man* (pp. 255–283). Englewood Cliffs, NJ: Prentice-Hall. (2)

Kingston, M. (1976). *The woman warrior.* New York: Vintage Books. (14)

Kinsey, A. (1941). Homosexuality. *Clinical Endocrinology, 1,* 424–428. (13)

Kinsey, A., Pomeroy, W., & Martin, C. (1948). *Sexual behavior in the human male.* Philadelphia: W. B. Saunders. (10, 13)

Kipling, R. (1976). If. In D. David & R. Brannon (Eds.), *The forty-nine percent majority* (pp. 163–166). Reading, MA: Addison-Wesley. (11)

Kipnis, A. (1991). *Knights without armor.* Los Angeles: Tarcher/Perigee. (1)

Kipnis, D. (1976). *The powerholders.* Chicago: University of Chicago Press. (12)

Kirshner, A. (1977). *Masculinity in a historical perspective.* Washington, DC: University Press of America. (2)

Kite, M., & Deaux, K. (1987). Gender belief systems: Homosexuality and the implicit inversion theory. *Psychology of Women Quarterly, 11,* 83–96. (13)

Klumas, A. L., & Marchant, T. (1994). Images of men in popular sitcoms. *The Journal of Men's Studies, 2,* 269–285. (5, 15)

Knight, G., & Dubro, A. (1984). Cooperative, competitive, and individualistic social values: An individualized regression and clustering approach. *Journal of Personality and Social Psychology, 46,* 98–105. (8)

Knight, G., & Kagan, S. (1981). Apparent sex differences in cooperative-competition: A function of individualism. *Developmental Psychology, 17,* 783–790. (8)

Koberg, C. (1985). Sex and situational influences on the use of power: A follow-up study. *Sex Roles, 13,* 625–639. (12)

Kohlberg, L. (1966). A cognitive-developmental analysis of children's sex-role concepts and attitudes. In E. Maccoby (Ed.), *The development of sex differences* (pp. 82–173). Stanford: Stanford University Press. (5)

Kohn, A. (1986). *No contest: The case against competition.* Boston: Houghton Mifflin. (8)

Kohn, A. (1987, October). It's hard to get left out of a pair. *Psychology Today,* 52–57. (8)

Kohn, M. (1977). *Class and conformity* (2nd ed.). Homewood, IL: Dorsey. (5)

Kolbe, R., & Langefeld, C. (1993). Appraising gender role portrayals in TV commercials. *Sex Roles, 28,* 393–417. (5)

Kolbe, R., & LaVoie, J. (1981). Sex-role stereotyping in preschool children's picture books. *Social Psychology Quarterly, 44,* 369–374. (5)

Kolodny, R., Masters, W., Hendryx, J., & Toro, G. (1971). Plasma testosterone and semen analysis in male homosexuals. *New England Journal of Medicine, 285*(21), 1170–1174. (13)

Komarovsky, M. (1940). *The unemployed man and his family.* New York: Dryden Press. (2, 15)

Komarovsky, M. (1967). *Blue-collar marriage.* New York: Random House. (4)

Komarovsky, M. (1976). *Dilemma of masculinity.* New York: Norton. (4, 7, 10, 11)

Komisar, L. (1976). Violence and the masculine mystique. In D. David & R. Brannon (Eds.), *The forty-nine percent majority* (pp. 201–215). Reading, MA: Addison-Wesley. (9)

Koop, C. (1987). Report of the Surgeon General's workshop on pornography and public health. *American Psychologist, 42,* 944–945. (9)

Korda, M. (1978). *Success!* New York: Ballantine. (8)

Kort, C., & Friedland, R. (Eds.). (1986). *The fathers' book.* Boston: G.K. Hall. (15)

Kortenhaus, C. M., & Demarest, J. (1993). Gender role stereotyping in children's literature: An update. *Sex Roles, 28,* 219–232. (5)

Koss, M. (1983). The scope of rape: Implications for the clinical treatment of victims. *The Clinical Psychologist, 36,* 88–91. (9)

Koss, M. (1985). The hidden rape victim: Personality, attitudinal, and situational characteristics. *Psychology of Women Quarterly, 9,* 193–212. (9)

Koss, M., & Oros, C. (1982). The sexual experiences survey: A research instrument investigating sexual aggression and victimization. *Journal of Consulting and Clinical Psychology, 50,* 455–457. (9)

Koss, M., Leonard, K., Beezley, D., & Oros, C. (1985). Nonstranger sexual aggression: A discriminant analysis of the psychological characteristics of undetected offenders. *Sex Roles, 12,* 981–992. (9)

Kossen, S. (1987). *The human side of organizations* (4th ed.). New York: Harper & Row. (7)

Krafft-Ebing, R. (1965/1866). *Psychopathia sexualis.* New York: Putnam. (9)

Krebs, D., & Miller, D. (1985). Altruism and aggression. In G. Lindzey & E. Aronson (Eds.), *The handbook of social psychology* (3rd ed., Vol. II, pp. 1–17). New York: Random House. (9)

Kreuz, L., & Rose, R. (1972). Assessment of aggressive behavior and plasma testosterone in a young criminal population. *Psychosomatic Medicine, 34,* 321–332. (3)

Kristiansen, C. (1990). The role of values in the relation between gender and health behaviour. *Social Behaviour, 5,* 127–133. (16)

Kronsberg, S., Schmaling, K., & Fagot, B. (1985). Risk in a parent's eyes: Effects of gender and parenting experience. *Sex Roles, 13,* 329–341. (5)

Kruk, E. (1991). The grief reaction of noncustodial fathers subsequent to divorce. *Men's Studies Review, 8*(2), 17–21. (1)

Kuhlenschmidt, S., & Conger, J. (1988). Behavioral components of social competence in females. *Sex Roles, 18,* 107–112. (12)

Kurdek, L. (1987). Sex role self schema and psychological adjustment in coupled homosexual and heterosexual men and women. *Sex Roles, 17,* 549–562. (13)

Kurdek, L. (1988a). Correlates of negative attitudes toward homosexuals in heterosexual college students. *Sex Roles, 18,* 727–738. (13)

Kurdek, L. (1988b). Perceived social support in gays and lesbians in cohabitating relationships. *Journal of Personality and Social Psychology, 54,* 504–509. (13)

Kurdek, L. (1988c). Relationship quality of gay and lesbian cohabitating couples. *Journal of Homosexuality, 15*(3/4), 93–118. (13)

Kurdek, L., & Schmitt, J. (1986). Interaction of sex role self-concept with relationship quality and relationship beliefs in married, heterosexual cohabitating, gay, and lesbian couples. *Journal of Personality and Social Psychology, 51,* 365–370. (13)

Labalme, P. (1980). Introduction. In P. Labalme (Ed.), *Beyond their sex: Learned women of the European past* (pp. 1–8). New York: New York University Press. (2)

Laeuchli, S. (1972). *Power and sexuality: The emergence of canon law at the Synod of Elvira.* Philadelphia: Temple University Press. (2)

Lamb, M. (1986). *The father's role: Applied perspectives.* New York: Wiley. (3, 15)

Lamb, M., Pleck, J., & Levine, J. (1985). The role of the father in child development: The effects of increased paternal involvement. In B. Lahey & A. Kazdin (Eds.), *Advances in clinical child psychology* (Vol. 8, pp. 229–266). New York: Plenum. (15)

Lamb, M., Pleck, J., Charnov, E., & Levine, J. (1985). Paternal behavior in humans. *American Zoologist, 25,* 883–894. (15)

Lambert, W., Yackley, A., & Hein, R. (1971). Child training values of English Canadian and French Canadian parents. *Canadian Journal of Behavioral Sciences, 3,* 217–236. (5)

Lang, R., Holden, R., Langevin, R., Pugh, G., & Wu, R. (1987). Personality and criminality in violent offenders. *Journal of Interpersonal Violence, 2,* 179–195. (9)

LaRossa, R., & Reitzes, D. C. (1993). Continuity and change in middle class fatherhood, 1925–1939: The culture-conduct connection. *Journal of Marriage and the Family, 55,* 455–468. (15)

LaRossa, R., Gordon, B., Wilson, R., Bairan, A., & Jaret, C. (1991). The fluctuating image of the 20th century American father. *Journal of Marriage and the Family, 53,* 987–997. (15)

Larson, P. (1982). Gay male relationships. In W. Paul et al. (Eds.), *Homosexuality: Social, psychological, and biological issues* (pp. 219–232). Beverly Hills, CA: Sage. (13)

Lash, S., Eisler, R., & Schulman, R. (1990). Cardiovascular reactivity to stress in men: Effects of masculine gender role stress appraisal and masculine performance challenge. *Behavior Modification, 14,* 3–20. (16)

Lash, S., Gillespie, B., Eisler, R., & Southard, D. (1991). Sex differences in cardiovascular reactivity: Effects of the gender relevance of the stressor. *Health Psychology, 10,* 392–398. (16)

Lau, S. (1989). Sex role orientation and domains of self-esteem. *Sex Roles, 21,* 415–422. (4)

Lauritson, J., & Thorstad, D. (1974). *The early homosexual rights movement.* New York: Times Change Press. (13)

Lautmann, R. (1990). Categorization in concentration camps as a collective fate: A comparison of homosexuals, Jehovah's witnesses and political prisoners. *Journal of Homosexuality, 19*(1), 67–88. (13)

Lawrence, F., Draughn, P., Tasker, G., & Wozniak, P. (1987). Sex differences in household labor time: A comparison of rural and urban couples. *Sex Roles, 17,* 489–502. (12)

Leafgren, F. (1990). Men on a journey. In D. Moore & F. Leafgren (Eds.), *Problem solving strategies and interventions for men in conflict* (pp. 3–10). Alexandria, VA: American Association for Counseling and Development. (8)

Leavy, W. (1983, August). Is the black male an endangered species? *Ebony,* 41–46. (14)

Lederer, W., & Botwin, A. (1982). Where have all the heroes gone? Another view of changing masculine role. In K. Solomon & N. Levy (Eds.), *Men in transition: Theory and therapy* (pp. 241–246). New York: Plenum. (11)

Lee, J. (1988). Forbidden colors of love: Patterns of gay love and gay liberation. In J. De Cecco (Ed.), *Gay relationships* (pp. 11–32). New York: Harrington Park Press. (13)

Lee, J. (1991). *At my father's wedding: Reclaiming our true masculinity.* New York: Bantam Books. (1)

Lee, R., & Daly, R. (1987). Man's domination and woman's oppression: The question of origins. In M. Kaufman (Ed.), *Beyond patriarchy: Essays by men on pleasure, power, and change* (pp. 30–44). Toronto: Oxford University Press. (6)

Lefkowitz, B. (1979). *Breaktime: Living without work in a nine to five world.* New York: Hawthorne Books. (8)

LeGuin, U. (1969). *The left hand of God.* New York: Fawcett. (4)

Lehne, G. (1976). Homophobia among men. In D. David & R. Brannon (Eds.), *The forty-nine percent majority* (pp. 66–88). Reading, MA: Addison-Wesley. (7, 13)

Leiblum, S., & Rosen, R. (Eds.). (1988). *Sexual desire disorders.* New York: Guilford. (10)

Lein, L. (1979). Male participation in the home: Impact of social supports and breadwinners' responsibility on the allocation of tasks. *Family Coordinator, 28,* 489–496. (15)

LeMasters, E. (1957). Parenthood as crisis. *Marriage and Family Living, 19,* 352–355. (15)

Lenney, E. (1991). Sex roles: The measurement of masculinity, femininity, and androgyny. In J. Robinson, P. Shaver & L.Wright (Eds.), *Measures of personality and social psychological attitudes* (pp. 573–660). New York: Academic Press. (4)

Leo, J. (1989, January 9). Baby boys, to order. *U.S. News & World Report,* 59. (5)

Lerner, G. (1979). *The majority finds its past: Placing women in history.* New York: Oxford University Press. (2)

Lerner, G. (1986). *The creation of patriarchy.* New York: Oxford University Press. (2)

Lerner, H. (1986). *A mote in Freud's eye: From psychoanalysis to the psychology of women*. New York: Springer. (5)

Lerner, R., & Foch, T. (Eds.). (1987). *Biological-psychological interactions in early adolescence*. Hillsdale, NJ: Erlbaum. (4)

Levant, R. (1988). Education for fatherhood. In P. Bronstein & C. P. Cowan (Eds.), *Fatherhood today* (pp. 253–275). New York: Wiley. (15)

Levant, R. (1990). Psychological services designed for men: A psychoeducational approach. *Psychotherapy, 27*, 309–315. (16)

Lever, J. (1978). Sex differences in the complexity of children's play and games. *American Sociological Review, 43*, 471–483. (5)

Lever, J. (1988). Sex differences in the complexity of children's play. In G. Handel (Ed.), *Childhood socialization*. Hawthorne, NY: Aldine de Gruyter. (5)

Levine, S. (1966, April). Sex differences in the brain. *Scientific American*, 84–90. (3)

Levine-MacCombie, J., & Koss, M. (1986). Acquaintance rape: Effective avoidance strategies. *Psychology of Women Quarterly, 10*, 311–320. (9)

Levinson, D., Darrow, C., Klein, E., Levinson, M., & McKee, B. (1978). *The seasons of a man's life*. New York: Knopf. (4)

Levitt, E., & Klassen, A. (1974). Public attitudes toward homosexuality: Part of the 1970 National Survey by the Institute for Sex Research. *Journal of Homosexuality, 1*, 29–43. (13)

Levy, C. (1971, October). ARVN as faggots: Inverted warfare in Vietnam. *Transaction*, 18–27. (14)

Lewin, M. (1984a). "Rather worse than folly?" Psychology measures femininity and masculinity, 1: From Terman and Miles to the Guilfords. In M. Lewin (Ed.), *In the shadow of the past: Psychology portrays the sexes* (pp. 155–178). New York: Columbia University Press. (4)

Lewin, M. (1984b). Psychology measures femininity and masculinity, 2: From "13 gay men" to the instrumental-expressive distinction. In M. Lewin (Ed.), *In the shadow of the past: Psychology portrays the sexes* (pp. 179–204). New York: Columbia University Press. (4)

Lewin, R. (1984). *Human evolution: An illustrated introduction*. New York: W. H. Freeman. (6)

Lewin, R. (1987). *Bones of contention: Controversies in the search for human origins*. New York: Simon & Schuster. (6)

Lewis, C. (1986). *Becoming a father*. Philadelphia: Open University Press. (15)

Lewis, C., & O'Brien, M. (Eds.). (1987). *Reassessing fatherhood: New observations on fathers and the modern family*. London: Sage. (15)

Lewis, R. (1987). Emotional intimacy among men. *Journal of Social Issues, 34*, 109–121. (12)

Lewontin, R., Rose, S., & Kamin, L. (1984). *Not in our genes*. New York: Pantheon. (3)

Licata, S., & Petersen, R. (1982). *Historical perspectives on homosexuality*. New York: Haworth Press. (13)

Liddy, G. (1980). *Will*. New York: Morrow. (7)

Liebert, R., & Sprafkin, J. (1988). *The early window: Effects of television on children and youth* (3rd ed.). Elmsford, NY: Pergamon Press. (5)

Lief, H. (1977, November). Sexual survey 4: Current thinking on homosexuality. *Medical Aspects of Human Sexuality*, 110–111. (13)

Linn, M., & Petersen, A. (1986). A meta-analysis of gender differences in spatial ability: Implications for mathematics and science achievement. In J. Hyde & M. Linn (Eds.), *The psychology of gender: Advances through meta-analysis* (pp. 67–101). Baltimore: Johns Hopkins University Press. (4)

Linz, D., Donnerstein, E., & Penrod, S. (1987). The findings and recommendations of the Attorney General's commission on pornography. *American Psychologist, 42*, 946–953. (9)

Lipman-Blumen, J. (1980). Dilemmas of sex. In E. Douvan, H. Weingarten, & J. Scheiber (Eds.), *American families*. Dubuque, IA: Kendall/Hunt. (10)

Lipman-Blumen, J. (1984). *Gender roles and power*. Englewood Cliffs, NJ: Prentice-Hall. (12)

Livingston, S., & Green, G. (1986). Television advertisements and the portrayal of gender. *British Journal of Social Psychology, 25*, 149–154. (5)

Lochman, J. (1987). Self- and peer perception and attributional biases of aggressive and nonaggressive boys in dyadic interactions. *Journal of Consulting and Clinical Psychology, 55*, 404–410. (9)

Long, M., & Simon, R. (1974). The roles and status of women on children and family TV programs. *Journalism Quarterly, 51*, 107–110. (5)

Long, R. (1994). An affair of men: Masculinity and the dynamics of gay sex. *The Journal of Men's Studies, 3*. (13)

Longwood, M. (1988, April 13). Male sexuality: Moving beyond the myths. *The Christian Century*, 363–365. (10)

LoPiccolo, J. (1978). Direct treatment of sexual dysfunction. In J. LoPiccolo & L. LoPiccolo (Eds.), *Handbook of sex therapy* (pp. 1–17). New York: Plenum. (10)

LoPiccolo, J. (1985). Diagnosis and treatment of male sexual dysfunction. *Journal of Sex and Marital Therapy, 11*, 215–232. (10)

LoPiccolo, J., & Stock, W. (1986). Treatment of sexual dysfunction. *Journal of Consulting and Clinical Psychology, 54*, 158–167. (10)

Lott, B., & Maluso, D. (1993). The social learning of gender. In A. Beall & R. Sternberg (Eds.), *The psychology of gender* (pp. 99–123). New York: Guilford Press. (5)

Lovdal, L. (1989). Sex role messages in television commercials: An update. *Sex Roles, 21*, 715–724. (5)

Luebke, B. (1989). Out of focus: Images of women and men in newspaper photographs. *Sex Roles, 20*, 121–133. (5)

Lueptow, L. (1984). *Adolescent sex roles and social change*. New York: Columbia University Press. (4, 5)

Lyman, P. (1987). The fraternal bond as a joking relationship: A case study of the role of sexist jokes in male group bonding. In M. Kimmel (Ed.), *Changing men: New directions in research in men and masculinity* (pp. 148–163). Newbury Park, CA: Sage. (12)

Lyson, T. (1986). Race and sex differences in sex role attitudes of Southern college students. *Psychology of Women Quarterly, 10*, 421–428. (14)

Lytton, H., & Romney, D. (1991). Parents' differential socialization of boys and girls: A meta-analysis. *Psychological Bulletin, 109,* 267–296. (5)

Macaulay, J. (1985). Adding gender to aggression research: Incremental or revolutionary change? In V. O'Leary et al. (Eds.), *Women, gender, and social psychology* (pp. 191–224). Hillsdale, NJ: Erlbaum. (4)

Maccoby, E. (1980). *Social development: Psychological growth and the parent-child relationship.* New York: Harcourt Brace Jovanovich. (10)

Maccoby, E. (1990). Gender and relationships: A developmental account. *American Psychologist, 45,* 513–520. (4)

Maccoby, E., & Jacklin, C. (1974). *The psychology of sex differences.* Stanford: Stanford University Press. (3, 4)

Maccoby, E., & Jacklin, C. (1980). Sex differences in aggression: A rejoinder and reprise. *Child Development, 51,* 964–980. (4)

MacDonald, K., & Parke, R. (1986). Parent-child physical play: The effects of sex and age of children and parents. *Sex Roles, 15,* 367–378. (15)

Mackey, W. (1985). A cross-cultural perspective on perceptions of paternalistic deficiencies in the United States: The myth of the derelict dad. *Sex Roles, 12,* 509–533. (15)

Maclean, I. (1980). *The Renaissance notion of woman.* Cambridge: Cambridge University Press. (2)

Macleod, D. (1983). *The Boy Scouts, YMCA, and their forerunners, 1870–1920.* Madison: University of Wisconsin Press. (2)

Madigan, F. (1957). Are sex mortality differential biologically caused? *Millbank Memorial Fund Quarterly, 35,* 202–213. (16)

Madsen, W. (1973). *The Mexican-Americans of South Texas* (2nd ed.). New York: Holt, Rinehart & Winston. (14)

Maier, M. (1993). Revisiting (and resolving?) the androgyny/masculinity debate in management. *The Journal of Men's Studies, 2,* 157–171. (7)

Maiuro, R., Cahn, T., & Vitaliano, P. (1986). Assertiveness deficits and hostility in domestically violent men. *Violence and Victims, 1,* 279–289. (9)

Major, B., & Konar, E. (1984). An investigation of sex differences in pay expectations and their possible causes. *Academy of Management Journal, 27,* 777–792. (7)

Majors, R. (1986). Cool pose: The proud signature of black survival. *Changing Men, 17,* 5–6. (14)

Majors, R., & Billson, J. M. (1992). *Cool pose: The dilemmas of black manhood in America.* Lexington, MA: Lexington Books. (14)

Malamuth, N., & Donnerstein, E. (1984). *Pornography and sexual aggression.* Orlando, FL: Academic Press. (9)

Malamuth, N., Sockloskie, R., Koss, M., & Tanaka, J. (1991). Characteristics of aggressors against women: Testing a model using a national sample of college students. *Journal of Consulting and Clinical Psychology, 59,* 670–681. (9)

Mandelbaum, D. G. (1988). *Women's seclusion and men's honor: Sex roles in North India, Bangladesh, and Pakistan.* Tucson: University of Arizona Press. (6)

Mandell, N. (1986). Peer interaction in day care settings: Implications for social cognition. In P. Adler & P. Adler (Eds.), *Sociological studies of child development* (Vol. 1, pp. 55–79). Greenwich, CT: JAI Press. (5)

Mangan, J., & Walvin, J. (Eds.). (1987). *Manliness and morality: Middle-class masculinity in Britain and America, 1800–1940.* New York: St. Martin's Press. (2)

Mansbridge, J. (1986). *Why we lost the ERA.* Chicago: University of Chicago Press. (7)

Maracek, J., Finn, S., & Cardell, M. (1988). Gender roles in the relationships of lesbians and gay men. In J. De Cecco (Ed.), *Gay relationships* (pp. 169–175). New York: Harrington Park Press. (13)

Maracek, J., Piliavin, J., Fitzsimmons, E., Krogh, E., Leader, E., & Trudell, B. (1978). Women as TV experts: The voices of authority? *Journal of Communication, 28,* 159–168. (5)

Marhoefer-Dvorak, S., Resick, P., Hutter, C., & Girelli, S. (1988). Single- versus multiple-incident rape victims: A comparison of psychological reactions to rape. *Journal of Interpersonal Violence, 3,* 145–160. (9)

Marini, M. (1989). Sex differences in earnings in the United States. *Annual Review of Sociology, 15,* 343–380. (7)

Mark, M., & Miller, M. (1986). The effects of sexual permissiveness, target gender, and attitudes toward women on social perception: In search of the double standard. *Sex Roles, 15,* 311–322. (10)

Marone, N. (1988). *How to father a successful daughter.* New York: McGraw-Hill. (12, 15)

Marsh, H., & Myers, M. (1986). Masculinity, femininity, and androgyny: A methodological and theoretical critique. *Sex Roles, 14,* 397–430. (4)

Marsiglio, W. (1987). Adolescent fathers in the United States: Their initial living arrangements, marital experience and education outcomes. *Family Planning Perspective, 19*(6), 240–251. (15)

Martin, A., & Hetrick, E. (1988). The stigmatization of the gay and lesbian adolescent. *Journal of Homosexuality, 15,* 163–183. (13)

Martin, M., & Voorhies, B. (1975). *Female of the species.* New York: Columbia University Press. (6)

Marwick, A. (1970). *The nature of history.* New York: Macmillan. (2)

Masters, W., & Johnson, V. (1979). *Homosexuality in perspective.* Boston: Little, Brown. (13)

Matheny, K. B., & Riordan, R. J. (1992). *Stress and strategies for lifestyle management.* Atlanta, GA: Georgia State University Business Press. (16)

May, M., & Doob, L. (1937). *Cooperation and competition.* New York: Social Science Research Council. (8)

May, R. (1990). Finding ourselves: Self-esteem, self-disclosure, and self-acceptance. In D. Moore & F. Leafgren (Eds.), *Problem solving strategies and intervention for men in conflict* (pp. 11–21). Alexandria, VA: American Association for Counseling and Development. (7)

Mazur, E., & Oliver, R. (1987). Intimacy and structure: Sex differences in imagery of same-sex relationships. *Sex Roles, 16,* 539–558. (12)

McAdoo, J. L. (1988). Changing perspectives on the role of the black father. In P. Bronstein & C. P. Cowan (Eds.), *Fatherhood today: Men's changing role in the family* (pp. 79–92). New York: Wiley. (15)

McCahill, T., Meyer, L., & Fischman, A. (1979). *The aftermath of rape.* Lexington, MA: Lexington Books. (9)

McCary, J. (1979). *Human sexuality* (2nd ed.). New York: Van Nostrand. (10)

McCauley, C., Thangavelu, K., & Rozin, P. (1988). Sex stereotyping of occupations in relation to television representations and census facts. *Basic and Applied Social Psychology, 9,* 197–212. (5)

McFarlane, J., Martin, C., & Williams, T. (1988). Mood fluctuations: Women versus men and menstrual versus other cycles. *Psychology of Women Quarterly, 12,* 201–223. (3)

McGee, M. (1979). Human spatial abilities: Psychometric studies and environmental, genetic, hormonal, and neurological influences. *Psychological Bulletin, 86,* 889–918. (4)

McGill, M. (1985). *The McGill report on male intimacy.* New York: Holt, Rinehart & Winston. (12)

McKay, J. (1993). "Marked men" and "wanton women": The politics of naming sexual "deviance" in sport. *The Journal of Men's Studies, 2,* 69–87. (16)

McKenry, P. C., Price, S. J., Gordon, P. B., & Rudd, N. M. (1986). Characteristics of husbands' family work and wives' labor force involvement. In R. A. Lewis & R. E. Salt (Eds.), *Men in families* (pp. 73–83). Beverly Hills, CA: Sage. (15)

McKenzie-Mohr, D., & Zanna, M. P. (1990). Treating women as sexual objects: Look to the (gender schematic) male who has viewed pornography. *Personality and Social Psychology Bulletin, 16,* 296–308. (9)

McKinney, K. (1987). Age and gender differences in college students' attitudes toward women: A replication and extension. *Sex Roles, 17,* 353–358. (7)

McLoughlin, M. (1988, August 8). Men vs. women. *U.S. News & World Report,* 50–56. (4)

McMaster, J. (1985). Reasons black African adults use to explain their acceptance of sex-role reversals. *Sex Roles, 13,* 393–403. (14)

McNeely, R., & Robinson-Simpson, G. (1987, November-December). The truth about domestic violence: A falsely framed issue. *Social Work,* 485–490. (9)

McNeill, J. (1988). *The church and the homosexual* (3rd ed.). Boston: Beacon Press. (16)

Mead, G. (1934). *Mind, self, and society.* Chicago: University of Chicago Press. (5)

Mead, M. (1935/1963). *Sex and temperament in three primitive societies.* New York: Norton. (6)

Meade, M. (1993). *Men and the water of life: Initiation and the tempering of men.* San Francisco: Harper SanFrancisco. (1)

Media & Values. (1989, Fall). Special issue on "Men, myth and media." (5)

Meggitt, M. (1964). Male-female relationships in the highlands of Australian New Guinea. *American Anthropologist, 66,* 204–224. (6)

Mehren, E. (1991). Books on men, masculinity quickly turning into best-sellers. *The Los Angeles Times.* (1)

Mellen, J. (1977). *Big bad wolves: Masculinity in the American film.* New York: Pantheon. (11)

Mencher, J., & Okongwu, A. (Eds.). (1993). *Where did all the men go? Female-headed/female-supported households in cross-cultural perspective.* Boulder, CO: Westview Press. (15)

Mendola, M. (1980). *The Mendola report: A new look at gay couples.* New York: Crown. (13)

Messerschmidt, J. (1993). *Masculinities and crime: Critique and reconceptualization of theory.* Lanham, MD: Rowman & Littlefield Publishers. (9)

Messner, M. (1987). The meaning of success: The athletic experience and the development of male identity. In H. Brod (Ed.), *The making of masculinities: The new men's studies* (pp. 193–209). Boston: Allen & Unwin. (8, 11)

Messner, M. (1993). *Power at play: Sports and the problem of masculinity.* Boston: Beacon. (11)

Messner, M., & Sabo, D. (Eds.). (1990). *Sport, men, and the gender order: Critical feminist perspectives.* Champaign, IL: Human Kinetics Press. (5, 11)

Meyer, J. (1975). Individual psychotherapy of sexual disorders. In A. Freedman et al. (Eds.), *Comprehensive textbook of psychiatry-II.* Baltimore: Williams & Wilkins. (13)

Meyer-Bahlburg, H., Boon, D., Sharma, M., & Edwards, J. (1974). Aggressiveness and testosterone measures in man. *Psychosomatic Medicine, 36,* 269–274. (3)

Mezey, G., & King, M. (1989). The effects of sexual assault on men: A survey of 22 victims. *Psychological Medicine, 19,* 205–209. (9)

Michaels, L. (1981). *The men's club.* New York: Farrar, Strauss & Giroux. (7)

Michener, J. (1971). *Kent State: What happened and why.* New York: Random House. (9)

Mihalik, G. (1989). More than two: Anthropological perspectives on gender. *Journal of Gay & Lesbian Psychotherapy, 1,* 105–118. (6)

Miles, R. (1990). *The women's history of the world.* New York: Harper & Row. (2)

Milkman, R. (1987). *Gender at work: The dynamics of job segregation by sex during World War II.* Champaign, IL: University of Illinois Press. (2)

Millen, J., & Hinds, B. (1976). *If I quit baseball, will you still love me?* New York: Sheed & Ward. (8)

Miller, A. (1949). *Death of a salesman.* New York: Viking Press. (15)

Miller, C. (1987). Qualitative differences among gender-stereotyped toys: Implications for cognitive and social development in girls and boys. *Sex Roles, 16,* 473–487. (5)

Miller, D. (1987). The limits of schooling by imposition: The Hopi Indians of Arizona. Unpublished doctoral dissertation, University of Tennessee, Knoxville. (6)

Miller, S. (1974). The making of a confused, middle-aged husband. In J. Pleck & J. Sawyer (Eds.), *Men and masculinity* (pp. 44–52). Englewood Cliffs, NJ: Prentice-Hall. (8)

Miller, S. (1983). *Men and friendship.* Los Angeles: Tarcher. (7)

Miller, S. (1985). Men and friendship. In A. Sargent (Ed.), *Beyond sex roles* (pp. 326–339). St. Paul, MN: West Publishing. (7)

Miller, S. (1987, October). Men and child care: The plot thickens. *Ms.,* 54–56. (1)

Miner, M. (1991). Manhood on the make: Owen Wister's *The Virginian. Men's Studies Review, 8*(4), 14–19. (1)

Miner, M. (1992). Documenting the demise of manly love: *The Virginian. The Journal of Men's Studies, 1,* 33–39. (1, 2)

Minirth, F., Newman, B., & Warren, P. (1992). *The father book: An instruction manual.* Nashville, TN: Thomas Nelson Publishers. (15)

Minton, H. (1988). American psychology and the study of human sexuality. *Journal of Psychology & Human Sexuality, 1,* 17–34. (13)

Mintz, S., & Kellogg, S. (1988). *Domestic revolutions: A social history of American family life.* New York: Free Press. (15)

Mirandé, A. (1977). The Chicano family: A reanalysis of conflicting views. *Journal of Marriage and the Family, 39,* 747–756. (14)

Mirandé, A. (1979). Machismo: A reinterpretation of male dominance in the Chicano family. *The Family Coordinator, 28,* 473–479. (14)

Mirandé, A. (1985). *The Chicano experience.* Notre Dame, IN: University of Notre Dame Press. (14)

Mirandé, A. (1988). Chicano fathers: Traditional perceptions and current realities. In P. Bronstein & C. P. Cowan (Eds.), *Fatherhood today: Men's changing role in the family* (pp. 93–106). New York: Wiley. (15)

Mischel, W. (1966). A social-learning view of sex differences in behavior. In E. Maccoby (Ed.), *The development of sex differences* (pp. 56–81). Stanford: Stanford University Press. (5)

Mitchell, G. (1969). Paternalistic behavior in primates. *Psychological Bulletin, 71,* 339–417. (3)

Mitchell, J. (1966). The Mohawks in high steel. In E. Wilson (Ed.), *Apologies to the Iroquois.* New York: Vintage Books. (14)

Modrcin, M. J., & Wyers, N. L. (1990). Lesbian and gay couples: Where they turn when help is needed. *Journal of Gay & Lesbian Psychotherapy, 1*(3), 89–104. (13)

Mohr, R. (1992). *Gay ideas: Outing and other controversies.* Boston: Beacon Press. (13)

Moltmann-Wendel, E. (1990). *The women around Jesus.* New York: Crossroad. (2)

Money, J. (1974). Prenatal hormones and postnatal socialization in gender identity differentiation. *Nebraska symposium on motivation* (Vol. 21, pp. 221–295). Lincoln: University of Nebraska Press. (3)

Money, J. (1987). Propaedeutics of diecious G-I/R: Theoretical foundations for understanding dimorphic gender-identity/role. In J. Reinisch et al. (Eds.), *Masculinity/femininity: Basic perspectives* (pp. 13–28). New York: Oxford University Press. (1)

Money, J. (1987). Sin, sickness, or status?: Homosexual gender identity and psychoneuroendocrinology. *American Psychologist, 42,* 384–399. (3)

Money, J., & Bennett, R. (1981). Postadolescent paraphilic sex offenders: Antiandrogenic and counseling therapy follow-up. *International Journal of Mental Health, 10,* 122–133. (3)

Money, J., & Ehrhardt, A. (1972). *Man & woman, boy & girl.* Baltimore: Johns Hopkins University Press. (1, 3)

Money, J., & Tucker, P. (1975). *Sexual signatures.* Boston: Little, Brown. (3)

Monroe, S. (1987, March 23). Brothers. *Newsweek,* 54–57. (14)

Montagu, A. (1974). *The natural superiority of women.* New York: Collier Books. (3, 16)

Montero, D. (1979). *Vietnamese Americans: Patterns of resettlement and socioeconomic adaptation in the United States.* Boulder, CO: Westview Press. (14)

Montiel, M. (1970). The social science myth of the Mexican American family. *El Grito: A Journal of Contemporary Mexican American Thought, 3,* 56–63. (14)

Moore, D. (1990). Helping men become more emotionally expressive: A ten-week program. In D. Moore & F. Leafgren (Eds.), *Problem solving strategies and intervention for men in conflict* (pp. 183–200). Alexandria, VA: American Association for Counseling and Development. (7)

Moore, J., & Pachon, H. (1985). *Hispanics in the United States.* Englewood Cliffs, NJ: Prentice-Hall. (14)

Moore, R., & Gillette, D. (1991). *King, warrior, magician, lover: Rediscovering the archetypes of the mature masculine.* San Francisco: Harper Collins. (1)

Moore, R., & McDonald, G. (1976). The relationship between sex-role stereotypes, attitudes toward women and male homosexuality in a nonclinical sample of homosexual men. Paper presented at the Canadian Psychological Association, Toronto. (13)

Moore, T. (1967). Language and intelligence: A longitudinal study of the first eight years. *Human Development, 10,* 88–106. (4)

Moore, T., Griffiths, K., & Payne, B. (1987). Gender, attitudes toward women, and the appreciation of sexist humor. *Sex Roles, 16,* 521–531. (4)

Morawski, J. (1985). The measurement of masculinity and femininity: Engendering categorical realities. *Journal of Personality, 53,* 196–223. (4)

Morawski, J. (1987). The troubled quest for masculinity, femininity, and androgyny. In P. Shaver & C. Hendrick (Eds.), *Sex and gender* (Vol. 7, pp. 44–69). Newbury Park, CA: Sage. (4)

Morgan, R. (1970). Know your enemy: A sampling of sexist quotes. In R. Morgan (Ed.), *Sisterhood is powerful* (pp. 33–38). New York: Vintage Books. (4, 7)

Morin, S. (1977). Heterosexual bias in psychological research on lesbianism and male homosexuality. *American Psychologist, 32,* 629–637. (13)

Morin, S., & Garfinkle, E. (1978). Male homophobia. *Journal of Social Issues, 34,* 29–47. (13)

Morse, N., & Weiss, R. (1955). The function and meaning of work and the job. *American Sociological Review, 20,* 191–198. (8)

Mortley, R. (1981). *Womanhood: The feminine in ancient Hellenism, Gnosticism, Christianity, and Islam.* Atlantic Highlands, NJ: Humanities Press. (2)

Mosmiller, T. (1987). The progress of movement history. *Men's Studies Review, 4*(2), 8.

Moye, A. (1985). Pornography. In A. Metcalf & M. Humphries (Eds.), *The sexuality of men* (pp. 44–69). London: Pluto Press. (9)

Moyer, K. (1978). Sex differences in aggression. In R. Friedman et al. (Eds.), *Sex differences in behavior* (pp. 335–372). Huntington, NY: Krieger. (3)

Moynihan, D. (1965). *The Negro family: The case for national action.* Washington, DC: U.S. Government Printing Office. (14)

Mrozek, D. (1987). The habit of victory: The American military and the cult of manliness. In J. Mangan & J. Walvin (Eds.), *Manliness and morality: Middle-class masculinity in Britain and America, 1800–1940* (pp. 220–241). New York: St. Martin's Press. (2)

Muehlenhard, C., Friedman, D., & Thomas, C. (1985). Is date rape justifiable? The effects of dating activity, who initiated, who paid, and men's attitudes toward women. *Psychology of Women, 9,* 297–310. (9)

Mueller, E., & Cooper, C. (Eds.). (1985). *Process and outcome in peer relationships.* Orlando, FL: Academic Press. (5)

Murdock, G. (1937). Comparative data on the division of labor by sex. *Social Forces, May,* 551–553. (6)

Murphey, C. (1991). *Mantalk: Resources for exploring male issues.* Louisville, KY: Presbyterian Publishing House. (16)

Murphy, L. R. (1990). Defining the crime against nature: Sodomy in the United States Appeals Courts, 1810–1940. *Journal of Homosexuality, 19*(1), 49–66. (13)

Murphy, Y., & Murphy, R. (1985). *Women of the forest* (2nd ed.). New York: Columbia University Press. (6)

Myers, M. (1989). Men sexually assaulted as adults and sexually abused as boys. *Archives of Sexual Behavior, 18,* 203–215. (9)

Nakanishi, D. (1988). Seeking convergence in race relations research: Japanese-Americans and the resurrection of the interment. In P. Katz & D. Taylor (Eds.), *Eliminating racism: Profiles in controversy* (pp. 159–180). New York: Plenum. (14)

Nanda, S. (1987). *Cultural anthropology* (3rd ed.). Belmont, CA: Wadsworth. (6)

Nathanson, C. (1984). Sex differences in mortality. *Annual Review of Sociology, 10,* 191–213. (16)

National Cancer Institute. (1987a). *Testicular cancer. Research report.* (16)

National Cancer Institute. (1987b). *Testicular self-examination.* (16)

Neisen, J. H. (1990). Heterosexism: Redefining homophobia for the 1990s. *Journal of Gay & Lesbian Psychotherapy, 1,* 21–35. (7)

Nelson, J. (1988). *The intimate connection: Male sexuality, masculine spirituality.* Philadelphia: Westminster Press. (16)

Nelson, J. (1992). *Body theology.* Louisville, KY: Westminster/John Knox Press. (16)

Newman, B. S. (1989). The relative importance of gender role attitudes to male and female attitudes toward lesbians. *Sex Roles, 21,* 451–465. (13)

Newman, P., & Newman, B.. (1988). Parenthood and adult development. In R. Palkovitz & M. B. Sussman (Eds.), *Transitions to parenthood* (pp. 313–337). New York: Haworth Press. (15)

Newsweek. (1990, July 16). The victims of violence. 23. (9)

Nichols, J. (1975). *Men's liberation: A new definition of masculinity.* New York: Penguin. (8)

Norton, J. (1982). The effects of changing sex roles on male homosexuals. In K. Solomon & N. Levy (Eds.), *Men in transition: Theory and therapy* (pp. 151–164). New York: Plenum. (13)

Nugent, R., & Gramick, J. (1989). Homosexuality: Protestant, Catholic, and Jewish issues; a fishbone tale. *Journal of Homosexuality, 18*(3/4), 7–46. (13)

O'Donovan, D. (1988a). Health and femiphobia. *Men's Studies Review, 5*(2), 14–16. (7, 16)

O'Donovan, D. (1988b). Femiphobia: Unseen enemy of intellectual freedom. *Men's Studies Review, 5*(3), 5–8. (7)

O'Kelly C., & Carney, L. (1986). *Women & men in society: Cross-cultural perspectives on gender stratification.* Belmont, CA: Wadsworth. (6, 12)

O'Neil, J. (1981). Patterns of gender role conflict and strain: The fear of femininity in men's lives. *The Personal and Guidance Journal, 60,* 203–210. (7)

O'Neil, J. (1982). Gender and sex role conflict and strain in men's lives: Implications for psychiatrists, psychologists, and other human service providers. In K. Solomon & N. Levy (Eds.), *Men in transition: Theory and therapy* (pp. 5–44). New York: Plenum. (7)

O'Neil, J. (1993). *The paradox of success.* New York: J. P. Tarcher. (8)

O'Neil, J., Egan, J., Owen, S. V., & Murry, V. M. (1993). The gender role journey measure: Scale development and psychometric evaluation. *Sex Roles, 28,* 167–185. (4)

O'Neil, J., Helms, B., Gable, R., David, L., & Wrightman, L. (1986). Gender-role conflict scale: College men's fear of femininity. *Sex Roles, 14,* 335–350. (4, 7)

Ochberg, R. (1987). *Middle-aged sons and the meaning of work.* Ann Arbor, MI: UMI Research Press. (4)

Ochberg, R. (1988). Life stories and the psychosocial construction of careers. *Journal of Personality, 56,* 173–204. (4)

Olien, M. (1978). *The human myth.* New York: Harper & Row. (6)

Oliver, L. (1987). Research integration for psychologists: An overview of approaches. *Journal of Applied Social Psychology, 17,* 860–874. (4)

Osborn, J. (1987). The AIDS epidemic: Discovery of a new disease. In H. Dalton et al. (Eds.), *AIDS and the law* (pp. 17–27). New Haven: Yale University Press. (16)

Osherson, S. (1986). *Finding our fathers: The unfinished business of manhood.* New York: Free Press. (4, 15)

Osherson, S. (1992). *Wrestling with love: How men struggle with women, children, parents, and each other.* New York: Fawcett Columbine. (4)

Oskamp, S. (Ed.). (1987). *Television as a social issue.* Newbury Park, CA: Sage. (7)

Oskamp, S., & Costanzo, M. (Eds.). (1993). *Gender issues in contemporary society.* Newbury Park, CA: Sage. (5)

Osofsky, J., & Osofsky, H. (1985). Psychological and developmental perspectives on expectant and new parenthood. In R. Parke (Ed.), *Review of child development research: The family* (Vol. 7). Chicago: University of Chicago Press. (15)

Ovesey, L. (1969). *Homosexuality and pseudohomosexuality.* New York: Science House. (13)

Owen-Towle, T. (1991). *Brother-spirit: Men joining together in the quest for intimacy and ultimacy.* San Diego: Bald Eagle Mountain Press. (16)

Page, D., Mosher, R., Simpson, E., Fisher, E., Mardon, G., Pollack, J., McGillivray, B., de la Chapelle, A., & Brown, L. (1987). The sex-determining region of the human Y chromosome encodes a finger protein. *Cell, 51,* 1091–1104. (3)

Pagelow, M. (1985). The "battered husband syndrome": Social problem or much ado about little? In N. Johnson (Ed.), *Marital violence* (pp. 172–195). London: Routledge. (9)

Pagels, E. (1976). What became of god the mother. *Signs, 2,* 293–303. (2)

Pagels, E. (1986). *Adam, Eve, and the serpent.* New York: Random House. (2, 6)

Paley, V. G. (1984). *Boys and girls: Superheroes in the doll corner.* Chicago: University of Chicago Press. (5)

Palkovitz, R. (1985). Fathers' birth attendance, early contact, and extended contact with their newborns: A critical review. *Child Development, 56,* 392–406. (15)

Palm, G. (1993). Involved fatherhood: A second chance. *The Journal of Men's Studies, 2,* 139–155. (15)

Palm, G., & Palkovitz, R. (1988). The challenge of working with new fathers: Implications for support providers. In R. Palkovitz & M. Sussman (Eds.), *Transitions to parenthood* (pp. 357–376). New York: Haworth Press. (15)

Paludi, M., & Gullo, D. (1987). The effect of sex labels on adults' knowledge of infant development. *Sex Roles, 16,* 19–30. (5)

Parent, G. (1977). *David Meyer is a mother.* New York: Bantam. (10)

Parlee, M. (1978, April). The rhythms in men's lives. *Psychology Today, 82,* 85–86, 91. (3)

Parnes, H. (Ed.). (1981). *Work and retirement: A longitudinal study of men.* Cambridge: MIT Press. (4)

Pasley, K. (1985). Stepfathers. In S. Hanson & F. Bozett (Eds.), *Dimensions of fatherhood* (pp. 288–306). Beverly Hills, CA: Sage. (15)

Pasley, K., & Ihinger-Tallman, M. (Eds.). (1984). *Family Relations: Remarriage and Step-parenting* [Special issue], *33*(3). (15)

Paul, W. (1982). Social issues and homosexual behavior: A taxonomy of categories and themes in anti-gay argument. In W. Paul et al. (Eds.), *Homosexuality: Social, psychological, and biological issues* (pp. 29–54). Beverly Hills, CA: Sage. (13)

Paul, W., & Weinrich, J. (1982). Whom and what we study: Definition and scope of sexual orientation. In W. Paul et al. (Eds.), *Homosexuality: Social, psychological, and biological issues* (pp. 23–28). Beverly Hills, CA: Sage. (13)

Paul, W., Weinrich, J., Gonsiorek, J., & Hotvedt, M. (Eds.). (1982). *Homosexuality: Social, psychological, and biological issues.* Beverly Hills, CA: Sage. (13)

Payne, F. (1987). "Masculinity," "femininity," and the complex construct of adjustment. *Sex Roles, 17,* 359–374. (4)

Pearson, J., Turner, L., & Todd-Mancillas, W. (1991). *Gender & communication* (2d ed.). Dubuque, IA: Brown & Benchmark. (4)

Peiss, K. (1986). *Cheap amusement: Working women and leisure in turn-of-the-century New York.* Philadelphia: Temple University Press. (2)

Peplau, L. (1981, March). What homosexuals want. *Psychology Today.* (13)

Peplau, L. (1984). Power in dating relationships. In J. Freeman (Ed.), *Women: A feminist perspective* (3rd ed., pp. 100–112). Palo Alto, CA: Mayfield. (12)

Peplau, L. (1988). Research on homosexual couples: An overview. In J. De Cecco (Ed.), *Gay relationships* (pp. 33–40). New York: Harrington Park Press. (13)

Peplau, L., & Amaro, H. (1982). Understanding lesbian relationships. In W. Paul et al. (Eds.), *Homosexuality: Social, psychological, and biological issues* (pp. 233–247). Beverly Hills, CA: Sage. (13)

Peplau, L., & Cockran, S. (1988). Value orientations in the intimate relationships of gay men. In J. De Cecco (Ed.), *Gay relationships* (pp. 195–216). New York: Harrington Park Press. (13)

Peplau, L., & Gordon, S. (1983). The intimate relationships of lesbians and gay men. In E. Allgeier & N. McCormick (Eds.), *Changing boundaries: Gender roles and sexual behavior* (pp. 226–244). Palo Alto, CA: Mayfield. (13)

Peplau, L., & Gordon, S. (1985). Women and men in love: Gender differences in close heterosexual relationships. In V. O'Leary et al. (Eds.), *Women, gender, and social psychology* (pp. 257–291). Hillsdale, NJ: Erlbaum. (12)

Perdue, W., & Lester, D. (1972). Personality characteristics of rapists. *Perceptual and Motor Skills, 35,* 514. (9)

Perelman, M. (1984). Rehabilitative sex therapy for organic impotence. In R. Segraves & E. Haeberle (Eds.), *Emerging dimensions of sexology*. New York: Praeger. (10)

Persky, H. (1978). Reproductive hormones, moods, and the menstrual cycle. In R. Friedman et al. (Eds.), *Sex differences in behavior* (pp. 455–466). Huntington, NY: Krieger. (3)

Persky, H., Smith, K., & Basu, G. (1971). Relation of psychologic measures of aggression and hostility to testosterone production in man. *Psychosomatic Medicine, 33,* 265–277. (3)

Person, E. (1980). Sexuality as the mainstay of identity: Psychoanalytic perspectives. *Signs, 5,* 605–630. (10)

Peters, L., O'Connor, E., Weekly, J., Pooyan, A., Frank, B., & Erenkrantz, B. (1984). Sex bias and managerial evaluations: A replication and extension. *Journal of Applied Psychology, 69,* 349–352. (7)

Petersen, A. (1987, September). Those gangly years. *Psychology Today,* 28–34. (4)

Petersen, W. (1971). *Japanese-Americans: Oppression and success.* New York: Random House. (14)

Pettegrew, J. (1993). The return to primal man: The psychology of primitivism in turn-of-the-century naturalist fiction and college football. *The Journal of Men's Studies, 2,* 29–52. (1, 2)

Piercy, M. (1976). *Woman on the edge of time.* New York: Fawcett. (4)

Pietropinto, A., & Simenauer, J. (1979). *Husbands and wives.* New York: Berkeley. (13)

Pinch, W., Nilges, A., & Schnell, A. (1988). Testicular self-examination: Reaching the college male. *Journal of American College Health, 37*(3), 131–132. (16)

Plant, R. (1986). *The pink triangle: The Nazi war against homosexuals.* New York: Henry Holt. (2, 13)

Pleck, E. (1987). *Domestic tyranny: The making of American social policy against family violence from colonial times to the present.* New York: Oxford University Press. (9)

Pleck, E., & Pleck, J. (1980). Introduction. In E. Pleck & J. Pleck (Eds.), *The American man* (pp. 1–49). Englewood Cliffs, NJ: Prentice-Hall. (2)

Pleck, E., & Pleck, J. (Eds.). (1980). *The American male.* Englewood Cliffs, NJ: Prentice-Hall. (1)

Pleck, E., Pleck, J., Grossman, M., & Bart, P. (1978). The battered data syndrome: A comment on Steinmetz's article. *Victimology, 2,* 680–683. (9)

Pleck, J. (1980). Men's power with women, other men, and society: A men's movement analysis. In E. Pleck & J. Pleck (Eds.), *The American man* (pp. 417–433). Englewood Cliffs, NJ: Prentice-Hall. (4)

Pleck, J. (1981). *The myth of masculinity.* Cambridge: MIT Press. (3, 4, 9, 13)

Pleck, J. (1984). The theory of male sex role identity: Its rise and fall, 1936 to the present. In M. Lewin (Ed.), *In the shadow of the past: Psychology portrays the sexes* (pp. 205–225). New York: Columbia University Press. (4)

Pleck, J. (1985). *Working wives/working husbands.* Beverly Hills, CA: Sage. (12, 15)

Pleck, J. (1987a). American fathering in historical perspective. In M. Kimmel (Ed.), *Changing men: New directions in research on men and masculinity* (pp. 83–97). Newbury Park, CA: Sage. (15)

Pleck, J. (1987b). Fathers and infant care leave. In E. Zigler & M. Frank (Eds.), *Infant care leave.* New Haven: Yale University Press. (15)

Pleck, J., & Sawyer, J. (Ed.). (1974). *Men and masculinity.* Englewood Cliffs, NJ: Prentice Hall. (1)

Pleck, J., Lamb, M., & Levine, J. (1985). Epilog: Facilitating future change in men's family roles. In R. Lewis & M. Sussman (Eds.), *Men's changing roles in the family* (pp. 11–16). New York: Haworth. (15)

Pleck, J., Sonenstein, F., & Ku, L. (1993). Masculinity ideology and its correlates. In S. Oskamp & M. Costanzo (Ed.), *Gender issues in contemporary society* (pp. 85–110). Newbury Park, CA: Sage. (4)

Pleck, J., Sonenstein, F., & Ku, L. (in press). Problem behaviors and masculinity ideology in adolescent males. In R. Ketterlinus & M. Lamb (Eds.), *Adolescent problem behaviors.* Hillsdale, NJ: Erlbaum. (4)

Plummer, K. (1978). Men in love: Observations on male homosexual couples. In M. Corbin (Ed.), *The couple* (pp. 173–200). New York: Penguin. (13)

Podsakoff, P., & Schriesheim, C. (1985). Field studies of French and Raven's bases of power: Critique, reanalysis, and suggestions for future research. *Psychological Bulletin, 97,* 387–411. (12)

Pogrebin, L. (1987). *Among friends: Who we like, why we like them, and what we do with them.* New York: McGraw-Hill. (12)

Polefrone, J., & Manuck, S. (1987). Gender differences in cardiovascular and neuroendocrine response to stressors. In R. Barnett et al. (Eds.), *Gender and stress* (pp. 13–38). New York: Free Press. (16)

Pomerleau, A., Bloduc, D., Malcuit, G., & Cossette, L. (1990). Pink or blue: Environmental gender stereotypes in the first two years of life. *Sex Roles, 22,* 359–367. (5)

Postman, N., Nystrom, C., Strate, L., & Weingartner, C. (1987). *Myths, men & beer: An analysis of beer commercials on broadcast television, 1987.* Washington, DC: AAA Foundation for Traffic Safety. (5)

Pruett, K. (1987). *The nurturant father.* New York: Warner. (4, 15)

Prusak, B. (1974). Woman: Seductive siren and source of sin? In R. Ruether (Ed.), *Religion and sexism* (pp. 89–116). New York: Simon & Schuster. (2)

Pugh, D. (1983). *Sons of liberty: The masculine mind in nineteenth-century America.* Westport, CT: Greenwood Press. (2)

Purcell, P., & Stewart, L. (1990). Dick and Jane in 1989. *Sex Roles, 22,* 177–185. (5)

Rabinowitz, F., & Cochran, S. (1994). *Man alive: A primer of men's issues.* Pacific Grove, CA: Brooks/Cole Publishing Company. (1)

Radcliffe-Brown, A. (1965). *Structure and function in primitive society.* New York: Free Press. (6)

Radin, N. (1988). Primary caregiving fathers of long duration. In P. Bronstein & C. P. Cowan (Eds.), *Fatherhood today: Men's changing role in the family* (pp. 127–143). New York: Wiley. (15)

Rado, S. (1963). An adaptational view of sexual behavior. In H. Ruitenbeek (Ed.), *The problem of homosexuality in modern society* (pp.94–125). New York: Dutton. (13)

Rajecki, D., De Graaf-Kaser, R., & Rasmussen, J. (1992). New impressions and more discrimination: Effects of individuation on gender-label stereotypes. *Sex Roles, 27,* 171–185. (4)

Ramey, E. (1972, January). Men's cycles. *Ms., 8,* 11–12, 14–15. (3)

Ramirez, A. (1988). Racism toward Hispanics: The culturally monolithic society. In P. Katz & D. Taylor (Eds.), *Eliminating racism: Profiles in controversy* (pp. 137–157). New York: Plenum. (14)

Randolph, R., Schneider, D., & Diaz, M. (Eds.). (1988). *Dialectics and gender: Anthropological approaches.* Boulder, CO: Westview Press. (6)

Rao, V., & Rao, V. (1985). Sex-role attitudes across two cultures: United States and India. *Sex Roles, 13,* 607–624. (6)

Rao, V., & Rao, V. (1985). Sex-role attitudes: A comparison of sex-race groups. *Sex Roles, 12,* 939–953. (14)

Rapoport, R., Rapoport, R., Strelitz, Z., & Kews, S. (1977). *Fathers, mothers, and society.* New York: Basic Books. (15)

Rapoport, T., Lomski-Feder, E., & Masalha, M. (1989). Female subordination in the Arab-Israeli community: The adolescent perspective of "social veil." *Sex Roles, 20,* 255–269. (6)

Raven, B. (1965). Social influence and power. In I. Steiner & M. Fishbein (Eds.), *Current studies in social psychology.* New York: Holt, Rinehart & Winston. (12)

Ravinder, S. (1987). An empirical investigation of Garnet's and Pleck's sex role strain analysis. *Sex Roles, 16,* 165–179. (4)

Rawlins, W. (1983). Openness as problematic in ongoing friendships: Two conversational dilemmas. *Communication Monographs, 50,* 1–13. (7)

Reid, H., & Fine, G. (1992). Self-disclosure in men's friendships. In P. M. Nardi (Ed.), *Men's friendships* (pp. 132–152). Newbury Park, CA: Sage. (4)

Reiker, P., Edbril, S., & Garnick, M. (1985). Curative testis cancer therapy: Psychosocial sequelae. *Journal of Clinical Oncology, 3,* 1117–1126. (3, 16)

Reis, H., Senchak, M., & Solomon, B. (1985). Sex differences in the intimacy of social interaction: Further examination of potential explanations. *Journal of Personality and Social Psychology, 48,* 1204–1217. (12)

Reiss, I. (1967). *The social context of premarital sexual permissiveness.* New York: Holt, Rinehart & Winston. (10)

Remafedi, G. (1990). Study group report on the impact of television portrayals of gender roles on youth. *Journal of Adolescent Health Care, 11*(1), 59–61. (5)

Remick, H. (1984). *Comparable worth and wage discrimination.* Philadelphia: Temple University Press. (7)

Retherford, R. (1975). *The changing sex differential in mortality.* Westport, CT: Greenwood Press. (16)

Rheingold, H., & Cook, K. (1975). The contents of boys' and girls' rooms as an index of parents' behavior. *Child Development, 46,* 459–463. (5)

Richman, R., & Kirsch, L. (1988, December 15). Testosterone treatment in adolescent boys with constitutional delay in growth and development. *New England Journal of Medicine, 319,* 1563–1567. (3)

Rideau, W., & Sinclair, B. (1982). Prison: The sexual jungle. In A. Scacco, Jr. (Ed.), *Male rape* (pp. 3–29). New York: AMS Press. (9)

Riley, D. (1992). The joys of fatherhood. In C. S. Scull (Ed.), *Fathers, sons, and daughters: Exploring fatherhood, renewing the bond* (pp. 44–47). Los Angeles: Jeremy P. Tarcher. (15)

Ritner, G. (1992). *Father's liberation ethics.* Lanham, MA: University Press of America. (15)

Roberts, M. (1988, February). School yard menace. *Psychology Today,* 52–56. (9)

Robertson, G. (1972). Parent-child relationships and homosexuality. *British Journal of Psychiatry, 121,* 525–528. (13)

Robertson, I. (1987). *Sociology* (3rd ed.). New York: Worth. (5)

Robinson, B. (1988). *Teenage fathers.* Lexington, MA: Lexington Books. (15)

Robinson, J. (1988, December). Who's doing the housework? *American Demographics, 63,* 24–48. (15)

Rohr, R., & Martos, J. (1992). *The wildman's journey: Reflections on male spirituality.* Cincinnati: St. Anthony Messenger Press. (16)

Rohrlich-Leavitt, R. (1977). Women in transition: Crete and Sumer. In R. Bridenthal & C. Koonz (Eds.), *Becoming visible: Women in European history* (pp. 36–59). Boston: Houghton Mifflin. (6)

Romano, O. (1973). The anthropology and sociology of the Mexican Americans: The distortion of Mexican American history. In O. Romano (Ed.), *Voices: Readings from El Grito* (pp. 43–56). Berkeley, CA: Quinto Sol Publications. (14)

Root-Bernstein, R. (1993). *Rethinking AIDS: The tragic cost of premature consensus.* New York: Free Press. (16)

Rosaldo, M., & Lamphere, L. (Eds.). (1974). *Women, culture, and society.* Stanford: Stanford University Press. (6)

Roscoe, W. (1987). Bibliography of berdache and alternative gender roles among native American Indians. *Journal of Homosexuality, 14*(3/4), 81–171. (6)

Rose, D. (1987, December). Personal communication. (1)

Rose, R. (1975). Testosterone, aggression, and homosexuality: A review of the literature and implications for future research. In E. Sachar (Ed.), *Topics in psychoendocrinology.* New York: Grune & Stratton. (3)

Rose, S. (1985). Same- and cross-sex friendships and the psychology of homosociality. *Sex Roles, 12,* 63–74. (12)

Rosenbaum, M. (1980). Cooperation and competition. In P. Paulus (Ed.), *Psychology of group influence.* Hillsdale, NJ: Erlbaum. (8)

Rosenberg, C. (1980). Sexuality, class and role in 19th-century America. In E. Pleck & J. Pleck (Eds.), *The American man* (pp. 219–254). Englewood Cliffs, NJ: Prentice-Hall. (2)

Rosenthal, K., Gesten, E., & Shiffman, S. (1986). Gender and sex role differences in the perception of social support. *Sex Roles, 14,* 481–499. (11)

Rosenthal, R. (1984). *Meta-analytic procedures for social research.* Beverly Hills, CA: Sage. (4)

Ross, L., & Mirowski, J. (1984). Men who cry. *Social Psychology Quarterly, 47,* 138–146. (7)

Ross, M., Paulsen, J., & Stalström O. (1988). Homosexuality and mental health: A cross-cultural review. *Journal of Homosexuality, 15*(1/2), 131–152. (13)

Rossi, A. (1977). A biosocial perspective on parenting. *Daedalus, Spring,* 1–31. (3)

Rossi, A. (1984). Gender and parenthood. *American Sociological Review, 49,* 1–19. (3)

Rotenberg, K. (1986). Same-sex patterns and sex differences in the trust-value basis of children's friendship. *Sex Roles, 15,* 613–626. (12)

Rotundo, E. (1993). *American manhood: Transformations in masculinity from the Revolution to the modern era.* New York: Basic Books. (1, 2, 15)

Roznowski, M. (1987). Use of tests manifesting sex differences as measures of intelligence: Implications for measurement bias. *Journal of Applied Psychology, 72,* 480–483. (4)

Ruben, H. (1981). *Competing.* New York: Pinnacle Books. (8)

Rubin, J., Provenzano, F., & Luria, Z. (1974). The eye of the beholder: Parents' views on sex of newborns. *American Journal of Orthopsychiatry, 44,* 512–519. (4, 5)

Rubin, L. (1983). *Intimate strangers.* New York: Harper & Row. (12)

Rubin, L. (1985). *Just friends: The role of friendship in our lives.* New York: Harper & Row. (7)

Rubin, Z. (1984). Toward a science of relationships. *Contemporary Psychology, 29,* 856–858. (12)

Rudoff, A. (1971). The incarcerated Mexican-American delinquent. *Journal of Criminal Law, Criminology and Police Science, 62,* 224–238. (14)

Ruether, R. (1974). Misogynism and virginal feminism in the fathers of the church. In R. Ruether (Ed.), *Religion and sexism* (pp. 150–183). New York: Simon & Schuster. (2)

Ruether, R. (1987). Christianity. In A. Sharma (Ed.), *Women in world religions* (pp. 207–233). Albany: State University of New York Press. (2)

Ruitenbeek, H. (Ed.). (1963). *The problem of homosexuality in modern society.* New York: Dutton. (13)

Russell, D. (1982). *Rape in marriage.* New York: Macmillan. (9)

Russell, D., & Howell, N. (1983). The prevalence of rape in the United States revised. *Signs, 8,* 688–695. (9)

Russell, G. (1987). Problems in role-reversed families. In C. Lewis & M. O'Brien (Eds.), *Reassessing fatherhood* (pp. 161–179). London: Sage. (15)

Rutherford, J. (1992). *Men's silences: Predicaments in masculinity.* New York: Routledge. (1)

Ryan, T. (1986). Problems, errors, and opportunities in the treatment of father-daughter incest. *Journal of Interpersonal Violence, 1,* 113–124. (9)

Saab, P. (1989). Cardiovascular and neuroendocrine response to challenge in males and females. In N. Schneiderman et al. (Eds.), *Handbook of research methods in cardiovascular behavioral medicine* (pp. 453–481). New York: Plenum. (16)

Sabo, D. (1985). Sport patriarchy and male identity: New questions about men and sport. *Arena Review, 9*(2). (11)

Sabo, D. (1986). Pigskin, patriarchy and pain. *Changing Men, 16,* 24–25. (11)

Sabo, D. (1987). Feminist analysis of men in sports. *Changing Men, 18,* 31–32. (11)

Sabo, D. (1990). Denial and men's responses to illness and death: Critical feminist perspectives. *Men's Studies Review, 7*(4), 23–27. (16)

Sabo, D., & Runfola, R. (1980). *Jock: Sports and male identity.* Englewood Cliffs, NJ: Prentice-Hall. (11)

Saegert, S. (1978). High-density environments: Their personal and social consequences. In A. Baum & Y. Epstein (Eds.), *Human response to crowding.* Hillsdale, NJ: Erlbaum. (6)

Salholz, E. (1987, May 11). In Detroit, kids kill kids. *Newsweek,* 74. (9)

Salmon, M. (1986). *Women and the law of property in early America.* Chapel Hill, NC: University of North Carolina Press. (2)

Samuelson, P. (1976). *Economics* (10th ed.). New York: McGraw-Hill. (7)

Sanday, P. (1981). *Female power and male dominance: On the origins of sexual inequality.* Cambridge: Cambridge University Press. (6)

Sanders, B., Soares, M., & D'Aquila, J. (1982). The sex difference on one test of spatial visualization: A nontrivial difference. *Child Development, 53,* 1106–1110. (4)

Sanders, G., & Schmidt, T. (1980). Behavioral discrimination against women. *Personality and Social Psychology Bulletin, 6,* 484–488. (7)

Sandqvist, K. (1987). Swedish family policy and the attempt to change paternal roles. In C. Lewis & M. O'Brien (Eds.), *Reassessing fatherhood: New observations on fathers and the modern family* (pp. 144–160). London: Sage. (15)

Sands, D. (1954). Further studies on endocrine treatment in adolescence and early adult life. *Journal of Mental Science, 100,* 211–219. (3)

Santrock, J., Sitterle, K., & Warshak, R. (1988). Parent-child relationships in stepfather families. In P. Bronstein & C. P. Cowan (Eds.), *Fatherhood today: Men's changing role in the family* (pp. 144–165). New York: Wiley. (15)

Sapiro, V. (Ed.). (1985). *Women, biology, and public policy.* Beverly Hills, CA: Sage. (3)

Sarrel, L., & Sarrel, P. (1981, February). Sex problems we don't talk about—and should. *Redbook.* (10)

Sarrel, P., & Masters, W. (1982). Sexual molestation of men by women. *Archives of Sexual Behavior, 11,* 117–131. (9)

Sattel, J. (1976). The inexpressive male: Tragedy or sexual politics? *Social Problems, 23,* 469–477. (12)

Sawin, D., & Parke, R. (1979). Fathers' affectionate stimulation and caregiving behaviors with newborn infants. *The Family Coordinator, 28,* 509–513. (4)

Sayers, J. (1982). *Biological politics.* New York: Tavistock. (3)

Scacco, Jr., A. (Ed.). (1982). *Male rape: A casebook of sexual aggression.* New York: AMS Press. (9)

Scanzoni, J. (1975). Sex roles, economic factors, and marital solidarity in black and white marriages. *Journal of Marriage and the Family, 37,* 130–144. (14)

Schein, V. (1973). The relationship between sex role stereotypes and requisite management characteristics. *Journal of Applied Psychology, 57,* 95–100. (7)

Schein, V. (1975). Relationship between sex role stereotypes and requisite management characteristics among female managers. *Journal of Applied Psychology, 60,* 340–344. (7)

Schein, V., Mueller, R., & Jacobson, C. (1989). The relationship between sex role stereotypes and requisite management characteristics among college students. *Sex Roles, 20,* 103–110. (7)

Schifellite, C. (1987). Beyond Tarzan and Jane genes: Toward a critique of biological determinism. In M. Kaufman (Ed.), *Beyond patriarchy: Essays by men on pleasure, power, and change* (pp. 45–63). New York: Oxford University Press. (3, 6)

Schnurr, D. (1986). Feet to the fire. In C. Kort & R. Friedland (Eds.), *The fathers' book: Shared experiences* (pp. 30–33). Boston: G. K. Hall. (15)

Schreiner-Engel, P. (1981). Therapy of psychogenic erectile disorders. *Sexuality and Disability, 4,* 115–122. (10)

Schulz, D. (1988). *Human sexuality* (3rd ed.). Englewood Cliffs, NJ: Prentice-Hall. (10)

Scott, R., & Tetreault, L. (1987). Attitudes of rapists and other violent offenders toward women. *Journal of Social Psychology, 124,* 375–380. (9)

Scull, C. (1992). Prologue. In C. Scull (Ed.), *Fathers, sons, and daughters: Exploring fatherhood, renewing the bond* (pp. xii-xvii). Los Angeles: Jeremy Tarcher. (15)

Scully, D. (1988). Convicted rapists' perceptions of self and victim: Role taking and emotions. *Gender & Society, 2,* 200–213. (9)

Secunda, V. (1992). *Women and their fathers.* New York: Delta Books. (15)

Segel-Evans, K. (1987). Rape prevention and masculinity. In F. Abbott (Ed.), *New men, new minds: Breaking male tradition* (pp. 117–121). Freedom, CA: The Crossing Press. (9)

Senour, M. (1977). Psychology of the Chicana. In J. Martinez, Jr. (Ed), *Chicano psychology,* (pp. 329–342). New York: Academic Press. (14)

Serbin, L., et al. (1973). A comparison of teacher responses to the preacademic and problem behavior of boys and girls. *Child Development, 44,* 796–804. (5)

Shabsigh, R., Fishman, I., & Scott, F. (1988). Evaluation of erectile impotence. *Urology, 32,* 83–90. (10)

Shahar, S. (1983). *Fourth estate: A history of women in the Middle Ages.* New York: Methuen. (2)

Shakeshaft, C. (1987). *Women in educational administration.* Newbury Park, CA: Sage. (5)

Shapiro, J. (1988). Gender totemism. In R. Randolph, D. Schneider, & M. Diaz (Eds.), *Dialectics and gender: Anthropological approaches* (pp. 1–19). Boulder, CO: Westview Press. (6)

Shaver, P., & Hendrick, C. (Eds.). (1987). *Sex and gender* (Vol. 7, Review of Personality and Social Psychology). Newbury Park, CA: Sage. (4, 5)

Sherif, M., Harvey, O., White, B., Hood, W., & Sherif, C. (1961). *Intergroup conflict and cooperation: The robbers' cave experiment.* Norman, OK: University Book Exchange. (8)

Sherrod, D. (1987). The bonds of men: Problems and possibilities in close male relationships. In H. Brod (Ed.), *The making of masculinities: The new men's studies* (pp. 213–239). Boston: Allen & Unwin. (7, 12)

Sherwin, B., Gelfand, M., & Brender, W. (1985). Androgen enhances sexual motivation in females: A prospective crossover study of sex steroid administration in the surgical menopause. *Psychosomatic Medicine, 47,* 339–351. (3)

Shields, S. (1982). The variability hypothesis: The history of a biological model of sex differences in intelligence. *Signs, 7,* 769–797. (4)

Shields, S. (1987). Women, men, and the dilemma of emotion. In P. Shaver & C. Hendrick (Eds.), *Review of personality and social psychology* (Vol. 7, pp. 229–250). Beverly Hills, CA: Sage. (7)

Shor, F. (1993). Contrasting images of reconstructing manhood: Bly's Wild Man versus Spielberg's Inner Child. *The Journal of Men's Studies, 2,* 109–128 (1).

Shotland, R., & Craig, J. (1988). Can men and women differentiate between friendly and sexually interested behavior? *Social Psychology Quarterly, 51,* 66–73. (10)

Sidorowicz, L., & Lunney, G. (1980). Baby X revisited. *Sex Roles, 6,* 67–73. (5)

Siegelman, M. (1974). Parental backgrounds of male homosexuals and heterosexuals. *Archives of Sexual Behavior, 3,* 3–18. (13)

Signorielli, N. (1989). Television and conceptions about sex roles: Maintaining conventionality and the status quo. *Sex Roles, 21,* 341–360. (5)

Signorielli, N. (1990). Children, television, and gender roles: Messages and impact. *Journal of Adolescent Health Care, 11*(1), 50–58. (5)

Signorielli, N., & Gerbner, G. (Eds.). (1988). *Violence and terror in the mass media: An annotated bibliography.* Westport, CT: Greenwood Press. (9)

Signorielli, N., & Lears, M. (1992). Children, television, and conceptions about chores: Attitudes and behaviors. *Sex Roles, 27,* 157–170. (5)

Silverberg, B., Boring, C., & Squires, T. (1990). Cancer statistics, 1990. *Cancer Journal for Clinicians, 40*(1), 9–26. (16)

Simone, A. (1987). *Academic women: Working toward equality.* South Hadley, MA: Bergin & Garvey. (7)

Simpson, G., & Yinger, M. (1985). *Racial and cultural minorities: An analysis of prejudice and discrimination* (5th ed.). New York: Plenum. (14)

Sinclair, A., et al. (1990). A gene from the human sex-determining region encodes a protein with homology to a conserved DNA-binding motif. *Nature, 346,* 240–245. (3)

Sistrunk, F., & McDavid, J. (1971). Sex variable in conforming behavior. *Journal of Personality and Social Psychology, 17,* 200–207. (4)

Sitterly, C., & Drake, C. (1988). *A woman's place: Management.* Englewood Cliffs, NJ: Prentice Hall. (8)

Smith, H. (1980). The mountain man as Western hero: Kit Carson. In E. Pleck & J. Pleck (Eds.), *The American man* (pp. 159–172). Englewood Cliffs, NJ: Prentice-Hall. (2)

Smith, J. (1988). Psychopathology, homosexuality, and homophobia. *Journal of Homosexuality, 15*(1/2), 59–73. (13)

Smith, K. (1971). Homophobia: A tentative personality profile. *Psychological Reports, 29,* 1091–1094. (13)

Smith, P., & Midlarsky, E. (1985). Empirically derived conceptions of femaleness and maleness: A current view. *Sex Roles, 12,* 313–328. (4)

Smoll, F., & Schutz, R. (1990). Quantifying gender differences in physical performance: A developmental perspective. *Developmental Psychology, 26,* 360–369. (3)

Snell, Jr., W., Belk, S., & Hawkins II, R. (1986). The masculine role as a moderator of stress-distress relationships. *Sex Roles, 15,* 359–366. (4)

Snell, Jr., W., Miller, R., & Belk, S. (1988). Development of the emotional self-disclosure scale. *Sex Roles, 18,* 59–73. (12)

Snell, Jr., W., Miller, R., Belk, S., Garcia-Falconi, R., & Hernandez-Sanchez, J. (1989). Men's and women's emotional disclosures: The impact of disclosure recipient, culture and the masculine role. *Sex Roles, 21,* 467–486. (4)

Snipp, C., & Sandefur, G. (1988). Earnings of American Indians and Alaskan natives: The effects of residence and migration. *Social Forces, 66,* 994–1008. (14)

Snortum, J., et al. (1969). Family dynamics and homosexuality. *Psychological Reports, 24,* 763–770. (13)

Snyder, S. (1985, October). The molecular basis of communication between cells. *Scientific American, 253,* 132–141. (3)

Socarides, C. (1968). *The overt homosexual.* New York: Grune & Stratton. (13)

Soeken, K., & Damrosch, S. (1986). Randomized response technique: Application to research on rape. *Psychology of Women Quarterly, 10,* 119–126. (9)

Sommers-Flanagan, R., Sommers-Flanagan, J., & Davis, B. (1993). What's happening on music television? A gender role content analysis. *Sex Roles, 28,* 745–753. (5)

Sonenstein, F., Pleck, J., & Ku, L. (1991). Levels of sexual activity among adolescent males in the United States. *Family Planning Perspectives, 23*(4), 162–167. (10)

Sonkin, D. (1988). The male batterer: Clinical and research issues. *Violence and Victims, 3,* 65–79. (9)

Sonkin, D., & Dutton, D. (1988). Editorial. *Violence and Victims, 3,* 3–4. (9)

Sonkin, D., Martin, D., & Walker, L. (1985). *The male batterer: A treatment approach.* New York: Springer. (9)

Sowell, T. (1981). *Ethnic America: A history.* New York: Basic Books. (14)

Spada, J. (1979). *The Spada report: The newest survey of gay male sexuality.* New York: New American Library. (13)

Spence, J. (1984). Masculinity, femininity and gender-related traits: A conceptual analysis and critique. *Progress in Experimental Personality Research, 13,* 2–97. (4)

Spence, J. (1993). Women, men, and society: Plus ça change, plus c'est la même chose. In S. Oskamp & M. Costanzo (Eds.), *Gender issues in contemporary society* (pp. 3–17). Newbury Park, CA: Sage. (4)

Spence, J., & Helmreich, R. (1978). *Masculinity and femininity: Their psychological dimensions, correlates and antecedents.* Austin: University of Texas Press. (7)

Spence, J., & Helmreich, R. (1983). Achievement-related motives and behavior. In J. Spence (Ed.), *Achievement and achievement motives: Psychological and sociological approaches.* San Francisco: W. H. Freeman. (8)

Spence, J., Helmreich, R., & Pred, R. (1987). Impatience versus achievement strivings in the Type A pattern: Differential effects on students' health and academic achievement. *Journal of Applied Psychology, 72,* 522–528. (16)

Spence, J., Helmreich, R., & Stapp, J. (1974). The personal attributes questionnaire: A measure of sex-role stereotypes and masculinity-femininity. *JSAS Catalog of Selected Documents in Psychology, 4,* 127. (4)

Spender, D. (Ed.). (1981). *Men's studies modified.* New York: Pergamon Press. (1)

Spielberg, W. (1993). Why men must be heroic. *The Journal of Men's Studies, 2,* 173–188. (1).

Spiess, W., Geer, J., & O'Donohue, W. (1984). Premature ejaculation: Investigation of factors in ejaculatory latency. *Journal of Abnormal Psychology, 93,* 242–245. (10)

Sprecher, S., McKinney, K., & Orbuch, T. (1987). Has the double standard disappeared?: An experimental test. *Social Psychology Quarterly, 50,* 24–31. (10)

Sprecher, S., & Sedikides, C. (1993). Gender differences in perceptions of emotionality: The case of close heterosexual relationships. *Sex Roles, 28,* 511–530. (7)

Springer, S., & Deutsch, G. (1985). *Left brain, right brain* (revised ed.). New York: Freeman. (4)

Stanworth, M. (1983). *Gender and schooling: A study of sexual divisions in the classroom.* London: Hutchinson. (5)

Staples, R. (1977). The myth of the black matriarchy. In D. Wilkinson & R. Taylor (Eds.), *The black male in America: Perspectives on his status in contemporary society* (pp. 174–187). Chicago: Nelson-Hall. (14)

Staples, R. (1978). Masculinity and race: The dual dilemma of black men. *Journal of Social Issues, 34*(1), 169–183. (14)

Staples, R. (1979). A rejoinder: Black feminism and the cult of masculinity, the danger within. *The Black Scholar, 10,* 63–67. (14)

Staples, R. (1982). *Black masculinity: The black male's role in American society.* San Francisco: The Black Scholar Press. (14)

Staples, R. (1986a). Black masculinity, hypersexuality, and sexual aggression. In R. Staples (Ed.), *The black family* (3rd ed., pp. 57–63). Belmont, CA: Wadsworth. (14)

Staples, R. (1986b). Changes in black family structure: The conflict between family ideology and structural conditions. In R. Staples (Ed.), *The black family* (3rd ed., pp. 20–28). Belmont, CA: Wadsworth. (14)

Staples, R., & Mirandé, A. (1986). Racial and cultural variations among American families: A decennial review of the literature on minority families. In A. Sholnick & J. Sholnick (Eds.), *Family in transition* (5th ed., pp. 474–497). Glenview, IL: Scott, Foresman. (14)

Statement of Principles. (1987, December). *Brother, 6*(1), 11. (1)

Statham, A. (1987). The gender model revisited: Differences in the management styles of men and women. *Sex Roles, 16,* 409–429. (7)

Stearns, P. (1979). *Be a man! Males in modern society.* New York: Holmes & Meier. (2)

Steele, A. (1978). *Upward mobility.* New York: Times Books. (8)

Stein, H. (1993, November 6). Old-fashion gender roles are back—in a commercial. *TV Guide, 41*(45), 39. (5)

Stein, P., & Hoffman, S. (1978). Sports and male role strain. *Journal of Social Issues, 34,* 136–150. (11)

Steinberg, R., & Shapiro, S. (1982). Sex differences in personality traits of female and male master of business administration students. *Journal of Applied Psychology, 67,* 306–310. (7)

Steinem, G. (1974). Introduction. In M. F. Fasteau, *The male machine* (pp. xi–xv). New York: McGraw-Hill. (1)

Steinhart, J. (1982). The most erotic part of your body. In O. Pocs (Ed.), *Human sexuality* (pp. 50–52). Guilford, CT: Dushkin. (10)

Steinmetz, S. (1977–78). The battered husband syndrome. *Victimology, 2,* 499–509. (9)

Steinmetz, S. (1980). Women and violence: Victims and perpetrators. *American Journal of Psychotherapy, 34,* 334–350. (9)

Stern, M., & Karraker, K. (1989). Sex stereotyping of infants: A review of gender labeling studies. *Sex Roles, 20,* 501–522. (5)

Sternglanz, S., & Serbin, L. (1974). Sex role stereotyping in children's television programs. *Developmental Psychology, 10,* 710–715. (5)

Stets, J., & Pirog-Good, M. (1987). Violence in dating relationships. *Social Psychology Quarterly, 50,* 237–246. (9)

Stevens, G., & DeNisi, A. (1980). Attitudes and attributions for performances by men and women. *Academy of Management Journal, 23,* 355–361. (7)

Steward, J. (Ed.). (1956). *The people of Puerto Rico.* Urbana: University of Illinois Press. (14)

Stewart, A., & Lykes, M. (Eds.). (1985). Conceptualizing gender in personality theory and research. *Journal of Personality, 53*(2), Special Issue. (4)

Stewart, A., Winter, D., Jones, A. (1975). Coding categories for the study of childrearing from historical sources. *Journal of Interdisciplinary History, Spring,* 687–701. (2)

Stillion, J. (1985). *Death and the sexes: An examination of differential longevity, attitudes, behaviors, and coping skills.* New York: Hemisphere Publishing. (16)

Stockard, J., Schmuck, P. A., Kempner, K., Williams, P., Edson, S. K., & Smith, M. A. (1985). *Sex equity in education.* New York: Academic Press. (5)

Stoll, C. (1979). *Female and male* (2nd ed.). Dubuque, IA: Wm. C. Brown Publishers. (5)

Stoltenberg, J. (1989). *Refusing to be a man: Essays on sex and justice.* Portland, OR: Breitenbush Books. (1)

Stone, M. (1976). *When god was a woman.* New York: Harcourt Brace Jovanovich. (6)

Stopes-Roe, M., & Cochrane, R. (1990). The child-rearing values of Asia and British parents and young people: An inter-ethnic and inter-generational comparison in the evaluation of Kohn's 13 qualities. *British Journal of Social Psychology, 29,* 149–160. (5)

Storms, M. (1978). Attitudes toward homosexuality and femininity in men. *Journal of Homosexuality, 3,* 257–263. (13)

Stouffer, S., et al. (1976). Masculinity and the role of the combat soldier. In D. David & R. Brannon (Eds.), *The forty-nine percent majority* (pp. 179–183). Reading, MA: Addison-Wesley. (11)

Stouffer, S., Suchman, E., DeVinney, L., Starr, S., & Williams, R. (1949). *The American soldier: Adjustment during army life.* Princeton: Princeton University Press. (2)

Strathern, M. (Ed.). (1987). *Dealing with inequality.* Cambridge: Cambridge University Press. (6)

Straus, M. (1975). The marriage license as a hitting license: Social instigation of physical aggression in the family. Paper presented at the meeting of the American Psychological Association, Chicago. (9)

Straus, M. (1977). Normative and behavioral aspects of violence between spouses: Preliminary data on a nationally representative USA sample. Paper presented at the Conference on Violence in Canadian Society, Ottawa. (9)

Straus, M. (1977–78). Wife beating: How common and why? *Victimology, 2,* 443–458. (9)

Straus, M. (1993). Husband abuse and the woman offender are important problems. In R. J. Gelles & D. Loseke (Eds.), *Current controversies on family violence.* Thousand Oaks, CA: Sage. (9)

Straus, M., & Gelles, R. (1986). Societal change in family violence from 1975 to 1985 as revealed by two national surveys. *Journal of Marriage and the Family, 48,* 465–479. (9)

Straus, M., Gelles, R., & Steinmetz, S. (1980). *Behind closed doors: Violence in the American family.* Garden City, NY: Doubleday. (9)

Strauss, S. (1982). *Traitors to the masculine cause: The men's campaign for women's rights.* Westport, CT: Greenwood Press. (2)

Strickland, B. (1988). Sex-related differences in health and illness. *Psychology of Women Quarterly, 12,* 381–399. (16)

Strong, B., Wilson, S., Robbins, M., & Johns, T. (1981). *Human sexuality* (2nd ed.). St. Paul: West. (10)

Struckman-Johnson, C. (1988). Forced sex on dates: It happens to men, too. *The Journal of Sex Research, 24,* 234–241. (9)

Struckman-Johnson, C., & Struckman-Johnson, D. (1992). Acceptance of male rape myths among college men and women. *Sex Roles, 27,* 85–100. (9)

Stuart, J. (1990). Unmarried fathers and gendered justice. *Men's Studies Review, 7*(1), 1, 3–8. (1)

Stycos, J. (1955). *Family and fertility in Puerto Rico: A study of the lower income group.* New York: Columbia University Press. (14)

Sue, D. (1990). Culture in transition: Counseling Asian-American men. In D. Moore & F. Leafgren (Eds.), *Problem solving strategies and interventions for men in conflict* (pp. 153–165). Alexandria, VA: American Association for Counseling and Development. (14)

Summerfield, P. (1989). *Women workers in the Second World War.* New York: Routledge. (2)

Svare, B., & Kinsley, C. (1987). Hormones and sex-related behavior: A comparative analysis. In K. Kelley (Ed.), *Females, males, and sexuality* (pp. 13–58). Albany: State University of New York Press. (3)

Swanson, J., & Forrest, K. (Eds.). (1984). *Men's reprodcutive health.* New York: Springer. (10)

Symons, D. (1979). *The evolution of human sexuality.* New York: Oxford University Press. (3)

Talese, G. (1980). *Thy neighbor's wife.* New York: Dell. (10)

Tannahill, R. (1982). *Sex in history.* New York: Stein & Day. (2, 3)

Tavris, C. (1977, August). Men and women report their views on masculinity. *Psychology Today,* 35–37. (1)

Taylor, B. (1983). *Eve and the new Jerusalem: Socialism and feminism in the nineteenth century.* New York: Pantheon Books. (2)

Taylor, M., & Hall, J. (1982). Psychological androgyny: Theories, methods, and conclusions. *Psychological Bulletin, 92,* 347–366. (4)

Taylor, S. (1985, November). Give the man a hand. *Essence.* (14)

Taylor, W. (1985a, May). Super athletes made to order. *Psychology Today,* 62–66. (3)

Taylor, W. (1985b). *Hormonal manipulation: A new era of monstrous athletes.* Jefferson, NC: McFarland. (3)

Tedesco, N. (1974). Patterns in prime time. *Journal of Communication, 24,* 119–124. (5)

Ten Houten, W. (1970). The black family: Myth and reality. *Psychiatry, 33,* 145–173. (14)

Terkel, S. (1970). *Hard times: An oral history of the Great Depression.* New York: Avon. (2, 15)

Terman, L., & Tyler, L. (1954). Psychological sex differences. In L. Carmichael (Eds.), *Manual of child psychology* (2nd ed.). New York: Wiley. (4)

The Pentagon Papers. (1971). New York: Times Books. (1)

Thompson, Jr., E. (1990). Courtship violence and the male role. *Men's Studies Review, 7*(3), 1, 4–13. (4)

Thompson, Jr., E., Grisanti, C., & Pleck, J. (1985). Attitudes toward the male role and their correlates. *Sex Roles, 13,* 314–427. (7)

Thompson, Jr., E., Pleck, J., & Ferrera, D. (1992). Men and masculinities: Scales for masculinity ideology and masculinity-related constructs. *Sex Roles, 27,* 573–607. (4)

Thorne, B. (1993). *Gender play: Girls and boys in school.* New Brunswick, NJ: Rutgers University Press. (5)

Tiefer, L. (1987). In pursuit of the perfect penis: The medicalization of male sexuality. In M. Kimmel (Ed.), *Changing men: New directions in research on men and masculinity* (pp. 165–184). Newbury Park, CA: Sage. (10)

Tieger, T. (1980). On the biological basis of sex differences in aggression. *Child Development, 51,* 943–963. (3, 4)

Tiger, L. (1969). *Men in groups.* New York: Random House. (6, 7, 12)

Tolson, A. (1977). *The limits of masculinity.* New York: Harper & Row. (1)

Torjesen, K. (1993). *When women were priests.* San Francisco: Harper SanFrancisco. (2)

Treadwell, P. (1987). Biologic influences on masculinity. In H. Brod (Ed.), *The making of masculinities: The new men's studies* (pp. 259–285). Boston: Allen & Unwin. (3, 13)

Trent, M. (1978, April). On being a gay teacher: My problems—and yours. *Psychology Today,* 136. (13)

Trepanier, M., & Romatowski, J. (1985). Atttributes and roles assigned to characters in children's writing: Sex differences and sex-role perceptions. *Sex Roles, 13,* 263–272. (5)

Trimble, J. (1987). American Indians and interethnic conflict. In J. Boucher et al. (Eds.), *Ethnic conflict* (pp. 208–229). Newbury Park, CA: Sage. (14)

Trimble, J. (1988). Stereotypic images, American Indians, and prejudice. In P. Katz & D. Taylor (Eds.), *Eliminating racism: Profiles in controversy* (pp. 181–202). New York: Plenum. (14)

Troiden, R. (1989). The formation of homosexual identities. *Journal of Homosexuality, 17*(1/2), 43–73. (13)

Trump, D., & Schwartz, T. (1988). *Trump: The art of the deal.* New York: Random House. (8)

Tschann, J. (1988). Self-disclosure in adult friendship: Gender and marital status differences. *Journal of Social and Personal Relationships, 5,* 65–81. (12)

Tuddenham, R. (1958). The influence of a distorted group norm upon individual judgment. *Journal of Psychology, 46,* 227–241. (4)

Tuller, N. (1988). Couples: The hidden segment of the gay world. In J. De Cecco (Ed.), *Gay relationships* (pp. 45–60). New York: Harrington Park Press. (13)

Turnbull, C. (1982). The ritualization of potential conflict among the Mbuti. In E. Leacock & R. Lee (Eds.), *Politics and history in band societies* (pp. 133–155). Cambridge: Cambridge University Press. (6)

U'Ren, M. (1971). The image of women in textbooks. In V. Gornick & B. Moran (Eds.), *Women in sexist society* (pp. 318–328). New York: Mentor Books. (5)

U.S. Department of Health, Education and Welfare. (1978). *Project on equal rights, stalled at the start: Government action on sex bias in the schools.* Washington, DC: U.S. Printing Office. (5)

U.S. Department of Justice. (1992). *Uniform crime reports: Crime in the United States.* Washington, DC: U.S. Government Printing Office. (9)

U.S. News & World Report. (1981, January 19). TV's "disastrous" impact on children. 43. (5)

Vaillant, G. (1977). *Adaptation to life.* Boston: Little, Brown. (4)

Valdez, R. (1986, March). The macho in contemporary America. *Nurturing News, 8*(1), 4, 16. (14)

Vazquez-Nuttall, E., Romero-Garcia, I., De Leon, B. (1987). Sex roles and perceptions of femininity and masculinity of Hispanic women: A review of the literature. *Psychology of Women Quarterly, 11,* 409–425. (14)

Ventura, J., & Stevenson, M. (1986). Relations of mothers' and fathers' reports of infant temperament, parents' psychological functioning, and family characteristics. *Merrill-Palmer Quarterly, 32,* 275–289. (15)

Verbrugge, L. (1985). Gender and health: An update on hypotheses and evidence. *Journal of Health and Social Behavior, 26,* 156–182. (16)

Villimez, C., Eisenberg, N., & Carroll, J. (1986). Sex differences in the relation of children's height and weight to academic performance and others' attributions of competence. *Sex Roles, 15,* 667–681. (5)

Wagatsuma, H. (1977). Some aspects of the contemporary Japanese family: Once Confucian, now fatherless? In A. Rossi et al. (Eds.), *The family.* New York: Norton. (14)

Wagenvoord, J., & Bailey, P. (1978). *Men: A book for women.* New York: Avon. (7, 10, 11)

Wagner, S. (1984). William Lloyd Garrison. *Changing Men, 13,* 20–21. (2)

Wagner, S. (1986). Martin R. Delany: Black nationalist and woman's rights activitist. *Changing Men, 17,* 24–26. (2)

Wagner, S. (1988). The Iroquois confederacy: A native American model for non-sexist men. *Changing Men, 19,* 32–34. (6)

Wagner, W., Kirchler, E., Clack, F., Tekarslan, E., & Verma, J. (1990). Male dominance, role segregation, and spouses' interdependence in conflict: A cross-cultural study. *Journal of Cross-Cultural Psychology, 21,* 48–70. (12)

Walczak, Y. (1988). *He and she: Men in the eighties.* Boston: Routledge. (4)

Waldron, I. (1976). Why do women live longer than men? *Social Science and Medicine, 10,* 349–362. (16)

Waldron, I. (1983). Sex differences in human mortality: The role of genetic factors. *Social Science and Medicine, 17,* 321–333. (16)

Wallace, M. (1979). *Black macho and the myth of the superwoman.* New York: Warner Books. (14)

Walter, D. (1986, November). Gays testify on homophobic violence. *The Advocate, 13.* (13)

Walvin, J. (1987). Symbols of moral superiority: Slavery, sport and the changing world order, 1800–1950. In J. A. Mangan & James Walvin (Eds.), *Manliness and morality: Middle-class masculinity in Britain and America, 1800–1940* (pp. 242–260). New York: St. Martin's Press. (2)

Warbasse, E. (1987). *The changing legal rights of married women, 1800–1861.* New York: Garland. (2)

Ward, C. (1985). Sex trait stereotypes in Malaysian children. *Sex Roles, 12,* 35–45. (6)

Ward, D., Seccombe, K., Bendel, R., & Carter, L. (1985). Cross-sex context as a factor in persuasibility sex differences. *Social Psychology Quarterly, 48,* 269–276. (4)

Warren, A. (1987). Popular manliness: Baden-Powell, scouting, and the development of manly character. In J. A. Mangan & James Walvin (Eds.), *Manliness and morality: Middle-class masculinity in Britain and America, 1800–1940* (pp. 199–219). New York: St. Martin's Press. (2)

Warren, M. (1985). *Gendercide: The implications of sex selection.* Totowa, NJ: Rowman & Littlefield. (5)

Warshak, R. (1992). *The custody revolution: The father factor and the motherhood mystique.* New York: Poseidon. (15)

Warshaw, R. (1988). *I never called it rape.* New York: Harper & Row. (9)

Wasserman, G., & Lewis, M. (1985). Infant sex differences: Ecological effects. *Sex Roles, 12,* 665–675. (5)

Waters, H., & Huck, J. (1988, January 25). TV's new racial hue. *Newsweek,* 52–54. (14)

Watkins, T. (1993). *The Great Depression: America in the 1930s.* Boston: Little, Brown. (2, 15)

Weinberg, M., & Williams, C. (1975). *Male homosexuals.* New York: Penguin. (13)

Weiner, A. (1982). Childbirth-related psychiatric illness. *Comprehensive Psychiatry, 23,* 143–154. (15)

Weisberg, R. (1986). *Creativity: Genius and other myths.* New York: Freeman. (4)

Weitzman, L. (1979). *Sex role socialization.* Palo Alto, CA: Mayfield Publishing. (5)

Weitzman, L. (1984). Sex-role socialization: A focus on women. In J. Freeman (Ed.), *Women: A feminist perspective* (pp. 157–237). Palo Alto, CA: Mayfield Publishing. (5)

Weitzman, L., Eifler, E., & Ross, C. (1972). Sex-role socialization in picture books for preschool children. *American Journal of Sociology, 77,* 1125–1150. (5)

Welter, B. (1966). The cult of true womanhood: 1820–1860. *American Quarterly, Summer,* 151–174. (2)

Welter, B. (1974). The feminization of American religion, 1800–1860. In M. Hartman & L. Banner (Eds.), *Clio's consciousness raised: New perspectives on the history of women* (pp. 137–157). New York: Harper & Row. (2)

Werner, P., & LaRussa, G. (1985). Persistence and change in sex-role stereotypes. *Sex Roles, 12,* 1089–1100. (4)

White, J. (1988). Influence tactics as a function of gender, insult, and goal. *Sex Roles, 18,* 433–448. (12)

Whiting, B., & Edwards, C. (1973). A cross-cultural analysis of sex differences in the behavior of children aged three through eleven. *Journal of Social Psychology, 91,* 171–188. (5)

Whiting, J., Kluckhohn, R., & Albert, A. (1967). The function of male initiation ceremonies at puberty. In R. Endelman (Ed.), *Personality and social life* (pp. 294–308). New York: Random House. (6)

Whitley, B. (1987). The relationship of sex role orientation to heterosexuals' attitudes toward homosexuals. *Sex Roles, 17,* 103–113. (13)

Whitley, B. (1990). The relationship of heterosexuals' attributions for the causes of homosexuality to attitudes toward lesbians and gay men. *Personality and Social Psychology Bulletin, 16,* 369–377. (13)

Whyte, Jr., W. (1957). *The organization man.* Garden City, NY: Doubleday/Anchor Books. (2)

Widdowson, F. (1984). *Going up into the next class: Women and elementary teacher training 1840–1914.* Dover, NH: Longwood Publishing. (2)

Wilcox, B. (1987). Pornography, social science, and politics. *American Psychologist, 42,* 941–943. (9)

Wilke, J. (1991). The decline in men's labor force participation and income and the changing structure of family economic support. *Journal of Marriage and the Family, 53,* 111–122. (15)

Wilkinson, R. (1986). *American tough: The tough-guy tradition and American character.* New York: Harper & Row. (11)

Will, J., Self, P., & Datan, N. (1976). Maternal behavior and perceived sex of infant. *American Journal of Orthopsychiatry, 46,* 135–139. (5)

Will, R., & Lydenberg, S. (1987, November). 20 corporations that listen to women: A *Ms.*/Council on Economic Priorities survey. *Ms.,* 45–52. (7)

Williams, D. (1982). Weeping by adults: Personality correlates and sex differences. *Journal of Psychology, 110,* 217–226. (7)

Williams, D. (1985). Gender, masculinity-femininity, and emotional intimacy in same-sex friendship. *Sex Roles, 12,* 587–600. (12)

Williams, J. (1980). Sex role stereotypes, women's liberation and rape: A cross-cultural analysis of attitudes. *Sociological Symposium, 25,* 61–97. (14)

Williams, J., & Bennett, S. (1975). The definition of sex stereotypes via the adjective checklist. *Sex Roles, 1,* 327–337. (4)

Williams, J., & Best, D. (1982). *Measuring sex-stereotypes: A thirty-nation study.* Beverly Hills, CA: Sage. (6)

Williams, J., & Best, D. (Eds.). (1990). *Sex and psyche: Gender and self viewed cross-culturally.* Newbury Park, CA: Sage. (6)

Williams, R., De La Cruz, X., & Hintze, W. (1989). The stereotypical nature of stereotyping. *Journal of Social Psychology, 129*(3), 397–411. (4)

Williams, W. (1986). *The spirit and the flesh: Sexual diversity in American Indian culture.* Boston: Beacon Press. (6)

Williams, W. (1991). *Javanese lives: Women and men in modern Indonesian society.* New Brunswick, NJ: Rutgers University Press. (14)

Wilson, A. (1992). *Jesus: A life.* New York: Fawcett Columbine. (2)

Wilson, E. (1978). *On human nature.* Cambridge: Harvard University Press. (3, 6, 12)

Wilson, G. (1982). *The Coolidge effect: An evolutionary account of human sexuality.* New York: Morrow. (3)

Windle, M. (1987). Measurement issues in sex roles and sex typing. In D. Carter (Ed.), *Current conceptions of sex roles and sex typing: Theory and research* (pp. 33–45). New York: Praeger. (4)

Winstead, B., Derlega, V., & Wong, P. (1984). Effects of sex-role orientation on behavioral self-disclosure. *Journal of Research in Personality, 18,* 541–553. (12)

Winston, S. (1932). Birth control and the sex ratio at birth. *American Journal of Sociology, 38,* 225–231. (5)

Winter, D. (1988). The power motive in women—and men. *Journal of Personality and Social Psychology, 54,* 510–519. (12)

Winther, D., & Green, S. (1987). Another look at gender-related differences in leadership behavior. *Sex Roles, 16,* 41–56. (7)

Witherington III, B. (1984). *Women in the ministry of Jesus.* Cambridge: Cambridge University Press. (2)

Witkin, H., Dyk, R., Faterson, H., Goodenough, D., & Karp, S. (1962). *Psychological differentiation.* New York: Wiley. (4)

Witkin, H., Lewis, H., Hertzman, M., Machover, K., Meissner, P., & Wapner, S. (1954). *Personality through perception.* New York: Harper & Row. (4)

Witt, L. (1990). Factors affecting attitudes toward persons with AIDS. *Journal of Social Psychology, 130,* 127–129. (13)

Wittig, M. (1985). Sex-role norms and gender-related attainment values: Their role in attribution of success and failure. *Sex Roles, 12,* 1–13. (7)

Wolfe, T. (1980). *The right stuff.* New York: Bantam Books. (1)

Wong, B. (1982). *Chinatown: Economic adaptation and ethnic identity of the Chinese.* New York: Holt, Rinehart & Winston. (14)

Wooden, W., & Parker, J. (1982). *Men behind bars: Sexual exploitation in prison.* New York: Plenum. (9)

Woodrum, E. (1981). An assessment of Japanese American assimilation, pluralism, and subordination. *American Journal of Sociology, 87,* 157–169. (14)

Wright, L. (1988). The type A behavior pattern and coronary artery disease. *American Psychologist, 43,* 2–14. (16)

Wright, P. (1982). Men's friendships, women's friendships and the alleged inferiority of the latter. *Sex Roles, 8,* 1–20. (12)

Wright, P. (1988). Interpreting research on gender differences in friendship: A case for moderation and a plea for caution. *Journal of Social and Personal Relationships, 5,* 367–373. (12)

Wundram, I. (1984). Sex differences in the brain: Implications for curriculum change. In D. Fowlkes & C. McClure (Eds.), *Feminist visions: Toward a transformation of the liberal arts curriculum* (pp. 158–169). University, AL: University of Alabama Press. (3)

Wynn, R., & Fletcher, C. (1987). Sex role development and early educational experiences. In D. Carter (Ed.), *Current conceptions of sex roles and sex typing: Theory and research* (pp. 79–88). New York: Praeger. (4)

Yoder, J., & Sinnett, L. (1985). Is it all in the numbers: A case study of tokenism. *Psychology of Women Quarterly, 9,* 413–418. (7)

Yogman, M., Cooley, J., & Kindlon, D. (1988). Fathers, infants, and toddlers: A developing relationship. In P. Bronstein & C. P. Cowan (Eds.), *Fatherhood today: Men's changing role in the family* (pp. 53–78). New York: Wiley. (15)

Yorburg, B. (1974). *Sexual identity.* New York: Wiley. (6)

Your pursuit of happiness. (1976, August). *Psychology Today.* (10)

Zammuner, V. (1987). Children's sex role stereotypes: A cross-cultural analysis. In P. Shaver & C. Hendrick (Eds.), *Sex and gender* (Vol. 7, pp. 272–293). Newbury Park, CA: Sage. (4)

Zietlow, P., & Sillars, A. (1988). Life-stage differences in communication during marital conflicts. *Journal of Social and Personal Relationships, 5,* 223–245. (12)

Zihlman, A. (1989). Woman the gatherer: The role of women in early hominid evolution. In S. Morgen (Ed.), *Gender and anthropology: Critical reviews for research and teaching* (pp. 21–40). Washington, DC: American Anthropological Association. (6)

Zilbergeld, B. (1978). *Male sexuality.* Boston: Little, Brown. (10)

Zilbergeld, B. (1992). *The new male sexuality.* New York: Bantam Books. (10)

Zillman, D., & Bryant, J. (1988). Pornography's impact on sexual satisfaction. *Journal of Applied Social Psychology, 18,* 438–453. (9)

Zinn, M. (1989). Chicano men and masculinity. In M. Kimmel & M. Messner (Eds.), *Men's lives* (pp. 87–97). New York: Macmillan. (14)

Name Index

Kreux, L., 58
Kristiansen, C., 276
Kronsberg, S., 95
Kruk, E., 9
Ku, L., 182
Kuhlenschmidt, S., 214
Kurdek, L., 223, 224, 234, 238

Labalme, P., 123
Laeuchli, S., 29
Lamb, M., 58, 265, 267
Lambert, W., 95
Lamphere, L., 118
Lane, F., 84
Laner, M., 213
Lang, R., 168
Langefeld, C., 98
Langevin, R., 168
Larossa, R., 260
Larson, P., 234, 237
LaRussa, G., 62
Lash, S., 276, 285
Lau, S., 86
Lauritson, J., 226
Lautmann, R., 225
LaVoie, J., 99
Lawrence, F., 217
Leafgren, F., 148
Lears, M., 97
Leavy, W., 242
Lederer, W., 206
Lee, C., 19
Lee, J., 6, 10, 15, 239
Lee, R., 117
Leffler, A., 67
Lefkowitz, B., 156, 157
LeGuin, U., 86
Lehne, G., 145, 224
Leiblum, S., 186
Lein, L., 267
LeMasters, E., 263
Lenney, E., 85
Leo, J., 93
Leon, G., 245–46
Leonard, K., 170
Lepkowsky, C., 219
Lerner, G., 26, 27
Lerner, H., 105
Lerner, R., 77
Lester, D., 168
Levant, R., 267, 273
Lever, J., 108
Levine, E., 36
Levine, J., 265, 267

Levine, S., 52, 53
Levine-MacCombie, J., 170
Levinson, D., 79–81, 82
Levinson, M., 79–81
Levitt, E., 227, 229
Lewin, M., 61, 63, 84
Lewin, R., 111
Lewis, C., 265, 266
Lewis, M., 71, 94, 95, 106
Lewis, R., 221
Lewontin, R., 44
Licata, S., 225
Liddy, G., 141
Liebert, R., 84, 96
Lief, H., 227
Linn, M., 64, 67, 68
Linz, D., 175, 177
Lipman-Blumen, J., 178, 209, 210
Livingston, M., 94, 106
Livingston, S., 98
Lloyd, B., 103
Lockman, J., 160
Lombardi, V., 149
Lomski-Feder, E., 120
Long, M., 97
Longino, H., 233
Longwood, M., 183
LoPiccolo, J., 184, 185, 188
Lorenz, K., 120
Loseke, D., 174
Lovdal, L., 98
Lovely, R., 237
Luebke, B., 99
Lueptow, L., 71, 103
Lunney, G., 94
Lupri, E., 266
Lupton, M., 56
Luria, Z., 76
Luther, M., 135
Lykes, M., 75
Lyman, P., 218
Lyndenberg, S., 140
Lyson, T., 245
Lytton, H., 96

McAdoo, J., 268
Macaulay, J., 74
McCauley, C., 97
McCornack, B., 67
McCreary, L., 137
McGillivray, B., 46
Mangan, J., 26
Marwick, A., 26

McCahill, T., 170
McCall, G., 169
McCary, J., 181
Maccoby, E., 57, 64, 66, 68, 69–70, 71, 72, 74, 76, 94, 106, 181
McDavid, J., 72
McDonald, G., 232
MacDonald, K., 265
McFarlane, J., 56
McGaw, B., 64
McGee, M., 68
McGill, M., 218
McKay, J., 287
McKee, B., 79–81
McKenna, W., 127
McKenry, C., 266
McKenzie-Mohr, D., 169
Mackey, W., 265
McKinney, K., 137, 190
Maclean, I., 32
Macleod, D., 37
McLoughlin, M., 69
McMaster, J., 245
McNeely, R., 174
MacNeil/Lehrer News Hour, 243
McNeill, J., 288
Madden, B., 94, 106
Madigan, F., 275
Madsen, W., 250
Maier, M., 139
Maiuro, R., 174
Major, B., 140
Majors, R., 247–48
Malamuth, N., 175, 177
Malcuit, G., 94
Mandelbaum, D., 120
Mandell, N., 103
Mansbridge, J., 136
Manuck, S., 281
Marchant, T., 99, 261
Mardon, G., 46
Marecek, J., 233
Marhoefer-Dvorak, S., 167
Marini, M., 137
Mark, M., 190
Markus, H., 62
Marone, N., 212, 261
Marsh, H., 85
Marston, A., 142
Martell, R., 139
Martin, A., 224, 227
Martin, C., 56, 185, 230
Martin, D., 174
Martin, M., 113

Martos, J., 288
Maruyama, G., 153
Masalha, M., 120
Masters, W., 233, 235–36, 239
Matheny, K., 283, 284
May, M., 150
May, R., 143
Mazur, E., 221–22
Mead, G., 106
Mead, M., 113–16
Meade, M., 10
Media & Values, 97
Meggitt, M., 116
Mehren, E., 14
Mellen, J., 196–98
Mencher, J., 261
Mendola, M., 237
Messerschmidt, J., 162
Messner, M., 1, 101, 150, 199
Meyer, J., 232
Meyer, L., 170
Meyer-Bahlburg, H., 58
Michaels, L., 144
Midlarsky, E., 62
Mihalik, G., 127
Miles, C., 26, 63
Milkman, R., 40
Millen, J., 150
Miller, A., 265
Miller, C., 94–95
Miller, D., 118, 161
Miller, M., 190
Miller, R., 70, 219
Miller, S., 9, 144, 158
Miner, M., 15, 37
Minirth, F., 267
Minton, H., 230
Mintz, S., 260
Mirandé, A., 250, 251, 268
Mirowsky, J., 142
Mischel, W., 104
Mitchell, G., 58
Mitchell, J., 254
Moane, G., 79
Modrcin, M., 234
Moltmann-Wendel, E., 29
Money, J., 3, 43, 46, 49, 50, 51, 55
Monroe, S., 242, 243
Montagu, A., 43, 48, 276
Montero, D., 252
Montiel, M., 250
Moore, D., 143
Moore, J., 249

Subject Index

Brain, testosterone and, 52
BSRI. *See Bem Sex Role Inventory* (BSRI)
Buss-Durkee Hostility Inventory, 57–58

California Personality Inventory (CPI), 84
Cancer, 176–77
prostatic, 278–80
testicular, 277–78
Cannibalism, 115
Career choice
gender and, 79–81, 100–101
See also Success
Castration, 54–55, 277
Caughnawaga Mohawks, 254–56
Celibacy, 189–91
Cell growth, prenatal, 45–46
Centers for Disease Control (CDC), U.S. Department of Public Health's, 285
Chador garment, 120
CHD. *See* Coronary heart disease (CHD)
Chicanos, 250
Children
custody of by fathers, 13–14, 268–70
dependency of, 112
homosexuality and, 234
Children's books, as socializing agents, 99
Chinese, 252
Chivalric male gender ideal, 30–31
Christianity, 29–30
homosexuality and, 225
muscular Christianity and, 38
Chromosomes, 45–46
X and Y, 46–49
Civil Service Commission, 227
Clitoris, development of, 51–52
Coercive power, 211
of males, 213
Cognitive approach, to gender identity development, 105
Common man gender ideal, 35–37
Communal manhood, 33

Companionship. *See* Male friendship
Comparable worth, 137–38
Competition
male role of, 148, 149–54
See also Athletics; Success
Concrete resources, 213
Condoms, AIDS and, 287
Conformity, gender differences in, 71–72
Consciousness-raising group (C-R)
men's movement and, 7–8
women's movement and, 7
Cool pose, of African-American men, 247–49
Cooperation, between women, 149, 152
Coronary heart disease (CHD), 281
male gender role and, 283
Couvade, 124
CPI. *See* California Personality Inventory (CPI)
C-R groups. *See* Consciousness-raising group (C-R)
Creativity, gender differences in, 69–70
Crow Indians, berdache of, 127
Culture gender behaviors, 111–12
aggression anomaly and, 160–63
of early nonindustrial human groups, 112–17
gender categories and, 126–28
learning behaviors, values and, 91
male dominance and, 117–26

Date rape, 170
Dependency
gender differences in, 71–72, 95–96
punishment and, 95–96
See also Independence
Depo-Provera, 55
Depression, testosterone and, 57

Developmental male gender identity perspective, 76–82
Digital rectal exam, 280
Discipline. *See* Punishment
Division of labor
gender behavior and, 65, 108
in hunter-gatherer societies, 112–13, 123, 259
in Israeli kibbutz, 122
Doctrine of separate spheres, 35, 39
Domestic violence, 172–74
Don Juan complex, 186
Double standard of sexual behavior, 189–90

Early adult transition years, 79–81
Education Amendment of 1972, Title IX of, 101
Educational system, as socializing agents, 100–102
Egalitarianism
in male-female relationships, 215, 239
in societies, 118–19
Emotions
emotional avoidance and, 140–41
emotional constipation and, 142–43
emotional incompetency and, 141–42
homophobia and, 145–47
menstrual cycle and, 56
self-disclosure avoidance and, 143–45, 220–22
spirituality search and, 287–89
testosterone and, 56–57
Engrossment, fathers of newborns, 263
Epic male gender ideal, 28
Equal Rights Amendment (ERA), 136
Erectile insufficiency, 184–85
Expert power, 212–14
male expertise and, 213
Exploratory participation stage, of gender identity development, 107

Fallacy of the average, 63–64
Fallopian tubes, 50
Family, of African-American men, 244–45
Fatherhood
barriers to, 267
child custody and, 13–14, 268–70
children and, 258, 265–68
crisis model of, 263–64
fatherhood meaning, 261–62
fatherhood role variants, 268–71
future perspective of, 271–72
growth model of, 264
nature vs. nurture, 258, 262–63
special bond of, 263
See also Fathers; Patriarchy; Provider role
Father(s)
African-Americans as, 244–45
antifeminism and, 131, 134, 142
Hispanic males as, 249–50
National Congress for Men and Children (NCMC) and, 13–14
power types and, 211–12
self-reliance and, 193
See also Fatherhood
Fear
excessive need to please and, 188–89
of femininity, 194, 195–96
of homosexuals, 14, 30, 145–46, 224–26, 239
men of men, 221–22
performance anxiety and, 187–88
of physical violence, 195
sexual anxiety and, 187
of sexual inadequacy, 195
of success, 155–56
withholding of, 141, 143, 195
of women, 116, 124–25, 135
Female gender identity, male gender identity interdependence and, 6

Textbooks, as socializing
    agents, 102
Thorndike principle of
    behavior consequences,
    106
Type A behavior, 282–83

Uniform Crime Reports (U.S.
    Department of
    Justice), 161
Unwitting participation stage,
    of gender identity
    development, 106
Urethral fold, 51–52
Uterus, 50

Vagina, 50
Validation dependency, of
    masculinity, 72
Variability hypothesis, 66
Vas deferens, 49
Verbal ability, gender
    differences in, 67

Vietnam conflict, 5–7, 253
Vietnamese, 252–53
Violence. *See* Aggression
Virgins (male), 190
Visual-spatial ability, gender
    differences in, 67–68

Wasting syndrome, 286
Westmoreland, William,
    General, 6
Wet dreams, 54
WHO. *See* World Health
    Organization (WHO)
Why Men Are the Way they Are
    (Farrell), 12
Wife beating. *See* Domestic
    violence
Will Wimbles, 38–39
Wolffian duct, 49–50
Women
    African-American, 244–45
    battered husband and,
        174–75

birth control and, 190
bourgeois view of, 32
chivalric view of, 30–31
Christianity view of, 29
colonial view of, 35
common man and, 35–36
cooperation among,
    149, 152
double standard for, 189–90
epic view of, 28
fear of, 116, 124–25, 135
gender stereotypes of, 62–65
gynecocracy and, 27
of the Iroquois nation,
    118–19
male biased historical
    accounts and, 25, 26
maternal instinct of, 262
matriarchal rule by, 27,
    117–19
in the military, 205–206
Renaissance view of, 32
sexual arousal in, 55
spirituality of, 287–88
violence against, 167–77

in the work force, 39,
    40–41, 100–101, 261
See also Antifeminism;
    Culture; Gender
    differences; Gender
    identity; Male dominance;
    Women's movement
Women's movement
    birth of, 36
    male gender identity affected
        by, 6–7
    men in, 39
    voting rights and, 39
    women's studies and, 15
Work force
    sexism in, 137–40
    women in, 39, 40–41,
        100–101, 261
World Health Organization
    (WHO), 286

X and Y chromosomes, 46–49